The World in Time and Space

Talisman: A Journal of
Contemporary Poetry and Poetics
Issues #23-#26

TALISMAN: A JOURNAL OF
CONTEMPORARY POETRY AND POETICS
ISSUES #23-#26

THE WORLD IN TIME AND SPACE

TOWARDS A HISTORY OF INNOVATIVE
AMERICAN POETRY IN OUR TIME

REVIEWS/ESSAYS/INTERVIEWS:
THE REVOLUTION
IN AMERICAN POETRY AND POETICS
AT THE END OF THE TWENTIETH CENTURY
AND THE BEGINNING OF THE TWENTY-FIRST

EDITED BY EDWARD FOSTER
AND JOSEPH DONAHUE

Talisman House, Publishers, Inc. • Jersey City, New Jersey

Copyright © 2001, 2002 by Talisman House, Publishers, Inc.
All rights reserved

Published in the United States of America by
Talisman House, Publishers, Inc.
P.O. Box 3157
Jersey City, New Jersey 07303-3157

Manufactured in the United Sates of America
Printed on acid-free paper

The World in Time and Space constitutes issues #23-#26 (2001-2002) of
Talisman: A Journal of Contemporary Poetry and Poetics, ISSN 0898-8684.
Editor: Edward Foster; Associate editors: Joseph Donahue,
Zoë English, Theodore Kharpertian, David Landrey, Joel Lewis

Editors for these issues: Edward Foster and Joseph Donahue

Acknowledgments

William Bronk's "The World in Time and Space" from *Life Supports* (Talisman), copyright © 1997 by William Bronk, is reprinted by permission of the author. • Selections from Lee Ann Brown, *Polyverse* (Sun & Moon), copyright © 1999 by Lee Ann Brown, are reprinted by permission of Sun & Moon Press. • Archival Materials in the Boggs Collection at Wayne State University's Reuther Library, appear with the permission of Grace Boggs and the Archives of Labor and Urban Affairs, Reuther Library, Wayne State University. • Material from the front page [1] of Correspondence 7:8 (October 1963) is reprinted by permission of Grace Boggs. • Dudley Randall's "Battle of Birmingham" is reprinted by permission of the literary estate of Dudley Randall. • Emails to Loss Pequeño Glazier from mIEKAL aND and Bob Drake are reprinted by permission of their respective authors. • The passage from Bruce Andrews, *Wobbling* (Roof), copyright © 1981 by Bruce Andrews, quoted in Loss Pequeño Glazier, "Poets | Digital | Poetics," is reprinted by permission of the author. • The visual text from Spencer Selby's *Malleable Cast* (Generator), copyright © 1995 by Spencer Selby, is reprinted by permission of the author. • The following refer to passages quoted in Susan Vanderborg's "'If This Were the Place to Begin'": excerpts from John Yau's poem published in *o.blék* II are reprinted by permission of John Yau; excerpts from *ACTS* are reprinted by permission of David Levi Strauss; passages from works by Abigail Child are reprinted by permission of the

Continued on pp. 718-719, which constitute an extension of the copyright page.

IN MEMORY OF
WILLIAM BRONK
(1918-1999)

PREFACE

The four issues of *Talisman* collected here under the title *The World in Time and Space* are, for the most part, book reviews that together suggest the directions followed by avant-garde or innovative American poetry during the past two or three generations.

Initially these reviews were to center on a hundred or so "representative" books, but this soon proved to be an unwieldy and all but impossible undertaking. Reviewing one or two books by, say, William Bronk out of the nearly two dozen he published was to present a very distorted view of his achievement. Each of the books exists in a continuum, and none by itself indicates the range he covered.

We decided to center some of the reviews on the books of various major early poets — to provide comprehensive reviews, that is, of the works of Robert Duncan, William Bronk, Robert Creeley and other major figures at the beginning of the period — and then focus on the books of later poets in terms of shared poetics, communities, and so forth. Thus Standard Schaeffer deals with works of Los Angeles poets, Peter O'Leary reviews works by poets rooted in gnostic poetics, Brian Kim Stefans reviews the work of Asian-American poets, and Michel Delville writes about prose poetry. John Olson decided to review the work of John Ashbery through an intensively close reading of a single poem. We did not insist that the reviews follow any particular formula, and some of the writers, especially when they had to deal with a great expanse of work, chose unconventional and fresh ways to pursue their subject; the review essays by Mary Margaret Sloan and Steve Evans are cases in point.

It was clear as we went along that there was much that was going to be left out if we kept to our original plan. We decided, therefore, to include a few essays which would cover subjects — such as performance poetry and E-poetries — that did not lend themselves to reviews, and we added a series of pieces — Bruce Andrews' essay, the interviews with Alice Notley and Gustaf Sobin — that could further expand the historical picture we wished to present. Together these reviews, essays, and interviews may at least begin to indicate the history of innovative American poetry in recent decades. There has never been a period when American poetry has accomplished so much.

Edward Foster
4 July 2002

CONTENTS

Edward Foster	Preface • vii	
William Bronk	The World in Time and Space • xi	
Edward Foster	Introduction • xiii	
Bruce Andrews	Making Social Sense: Poetics & the Political Imaginary • 1	
Edward Foster	An Interview with Gustaf Sobin • 18	
Michael Boughn	Olson's Buffalo • 34	
David Landrey	Robert Creeley's and Joel Oppenheimer's Changing Visions • 49	
Leonard Schwartz	Robert Duncan and His Inheritors • 64	
Norman Finkelstein	cc: Jack Spicer • 82	
John Olson	The Haunted Stanzas of John Ashbery • 98	
David Clippinger	Poetry and Philosophy at Once: Encounters between William Bronk and Postmodern Poetry • 107	
W. Scott Howard	'The Brevities': Formal Mourning, Transgression, & Postmodern American Elegies • 122	
Mark Scroggins	Z-Sited Path: Late Zukofsky and His Tradition • 147	
Burt Kimmelman	Objectivist Poetics since 1970 • 161	
Jeanne Heuving	The Violence of Negation or 'Love's Infolding' • 185	
Peter Bushyeager	Staying Up All Night: The New York School of Poetry, 1970-1983 • 201	
Stephen Paul Miller	Ted Berrigan's Legacy: Sparrow, Eileen Myles, and Bob Holman • 217	
Thomas Fink	Between/After Language Poetry and the New York School • 224	
David Clippinger	Between Silence and the Margins: Poetry and its Presses • 231	
Linda Russo	'F' Word in the Age of Mechanical Reproduction: An Account of Women-Edited Small Presses and Journals • 243	
	Illustrations • 285	
Standard Schaefer	Impossible City: A History of Literary Publishing in L.A. • 289	
Susan Vanderborg	"If This Were the Place to Begin": Little Magazines and the Early Language Poetry Scene • 298	
Susan M. Schultz	Language Writing • 321	
Marjorie Perloff	After Language Poetry: Innovation and Its Theoretical Discontents • 333	

Daniel Barbiero	Reflections on Lyric Before, During, and After Language • 355	
Christopher Beach	"Events Were Not Lacking": David Antin's Talk Poems, Lyn Hejinian's *My Life*, and the Poetics of Cultural Memory • 367	
Andrew Joron	Neo-Surrealism; or, The Sun at Night • 379	
Dan Featherston	On Visionary Poetics, Robert Kelly, and Clayton Eshleman • 407	
Peter O'Leary	American Poetry & Gnosticism • 431	
Michel Delville	The Marginal Arts: Experimental Poetry and the Possibilities of Prose • 452	
Stephen-Paul Martin	Media / Countermedia: Visual Writing & Networks of Resistance • 469	
Mary Margaret Sloan	Of Experience To Experiment: Women's Innovative Writing, 1965 - 1995 • 498	
Edward Foster	An Interview with Alice Notley • 526	
Aldon Lynn Nielsen	"This Ain't No Disco" • 536	
Kathryne V. Lindberg	Cleaver, Newton and Davis, re: Reading of Panther Lyrics • 547	
Brian Kim Stefans	"Remote Parsee": An Alternative Grammar of Asian North-American Poetry • 576	
Brent Hayes Edwards	The Race for Space: Sun Ra's Poetry • 609	
Julie Schmid	Spreading the Word: A History of the Poetry Slam • 636	
Steve Evans	The American Avant-Garde after 1989: Notes Toward a History • 646	
Loss Pequeño Glazier	Poets	Digital	Poetics • 674	
Alan Golding	New, Newer, and Newest American Poetries • 684	
	Appendices • 695	
	Biographical Notes • 711	
	Index • 718	

William Bronk

THE WORLD IN TIME AND SPACE

If there is a shape to the world in terms of time
and space — our own or, by concessions to shapes
of others, received — if there is such a shape
— in part there is — note that the words we use
referring to time, as *temporary* for one
or *temporal*, admit our diffidence
toward any shape we give the world by time.

The shapes of space share less of this distrust.
We acknowledge chaotic recalcitrance
in space, its endlessness both ways, the great,
and small, and yet respect the finite shape
of bounded places, as much as to say they are true.
Some absolute of shape is stated there
which satisfies the need that makes this shape.

How strange that after all it is rarely space
but time we cling to, unwilling to let it go.

Edward Foster

INTRODUCTION

THE WORKS THAT DONALD ALLEN BROUGHT TOGETHER in *The New American Poetry* (1960) were not, in terms of their poetics, invariably "new." Allen anthologized poets working in traditions outside the American mainstream, but many shared with established or "academic" writers poetics rooted in European and Eastern traditions. Jack Spicer and Robert Duncan, for example, were as indebted to Symbolist poetics as were Allen Tate and the early Robert Lowell. Nonetheless, the poets in Allen's book — to whom one should add Theodore Enslin and William Bronk, among others whom the anthology overlooked — were "new" in the sense that if they were not altogether free of traditions, they were largely free of academic communities and conventions. Unsympathetic to the discussions about poetry — rooted for the most part in the New Criticism — that dominated university classes and literary journals during the 1950s, these poets were for the most part determined individuals, clearly less concerned with community than with their individual work.

The "New American Poets" were, in Anne Waldman's term, "outriders." Whatever they owed to each other or to earlier poetries and poets, they were too independent to be comfortably grouped together in "schools" or traditions (although Allen himself among various critics, myself included, tried to do just that). Allen's book may be important primarily not because it proposed new schools or aesthetics but because it drew attention to poetry that operated on its own terms, regardless of critical authority. In turn, the notion of a "New American Poetry," insisting on the primacy of the individual poet rather than on convention and authority, informs the best work done by American writers in the period covered by the material in these issues of *Talisman*.

The course of American poetry affected, directly or indirectly, by Allen's anthology is immensely complicated. When Joseph Donahue and I decided to compile the present collection of reviews and essays for *Talisman*, we knew that we could not, in a reasonable number of pages, bring together enough to map the full terrain in any comprehensive way. Future critics will undoubtedly argue that certain poets were more "significant" or "greater" than others. But anyone who took part in the American poetry world over the last few decades should recognize such judgments as false. Already, accomplished poets are being forgotten; some died young, others stopped writing. A few discussed in this book have managed to break into the mainstream, with all the advantages that corporate publishing, national awards and prizes, and established literary reviews, can provide. It would be a mistake, however, to assume that these writers represent the range of achievement among outriders.

Recognition in the mainstream, after all, may owe as much to luck and connections as it does to achievement. If occasionally an outrider from an earlier generation, such as Allen Ginsberg, received the kind of attention generally reserved for mainstream poets, we should not forget that others, like Jack Spicer and William Bronk, were never published by the larger firms and rarely received the public recognition and accolades given to those who were.

Editing an anthology of late nineteenth- and early twentieth-century American poets, I discovered that most "major" poets in that period — the poets, that is, who got the best reviews and the prizes and were most commonly anthologized — had been all but erased from history. Who today, for example, reads George Sylvester Viereck, a poet once thought to be outrageously avant-garde, the very cutting edge of American poetry? And who reads Richard Hovey, from whose books young men once took their cue and who became the Jack Kerouac of his day? If the past is any indication, few poets commonly admired today are likely to be lauded by future generations.

The rational behind the mainstream, we should recall, is the belief that there is a hierarchy of "great" poets whose work is of substantial and enduring cultural value. One thing that the current generation learned from the social upheavals of the 1960s and 1970s, however, is that all such pronouncements are likely to be suspect.

Donahue and I did not want this collection of reviews and essays to prescribe a canon or to imagine an authoritative history. Instead we solicited materials from a wide range of poets and critics in the hope that the book that resulted might suggest the complexity of a poetic world where no one has been, or should be, allowed the last word. This has been the editorial approach throughout *Talisman*'s history. Most literary journals begin with a notion about what poems should do; in turn, the works published there are supposed to exemplify that position. *Talisman* has often been called "eclectic," which is descriptively true, but the editorial policy has been "pragmatic," in the way William James used the word. The journal, that is, has tried to represent the range of work in American poetry outside the mainstream while avoiding any close alignment with any particular group or aesthetic. If there is a defining order or affinity that characterizes poetry outside the mainstream in our time, it is not to be found in a single aesthetic or ideology. It is perhaps the variousness of the work that especially matters in a culture in which hierarchies and authorities exist to be challenged and overthrown.

If the poetry considered in this book is for the most part the work of outriders, much of it has also been marked or encouraged by collaborative efforts. Institutions from the Poetry Project at St. Mark's Church in New York, to the Jack Kerouac School at the Naropa Institute in Boulder, Colorado, to New College in San Francisco have offered poets communities within which to pursue their writing. Through these institutions, notions about poetics that are grouped as "Black Mountain," "Beat," and "New York School," among many others, have found incentives and support. Yet there are also radical differences among poets who have been closely associated with any of these institutions and designations, and the poetry itself often transcends institutional and ideological affiliations.

The World in Time and Space takes its name from a poem by William Bronk, in which he considers time and space as constructions peculiar to a given culture or "world." In his work generally, Bronk was fascinated by the fact that other cultures, such as the Mayas, held concepts of time and space radically different from our own, yet they all had "time," and they all had "space." The playing field, so to speak, remained the same from one culture to another, but the ways in which it was measured and understood did not. Perhaps one could say in turn that language is preeminently the game a culture plays. Poetry, however, has the capacity to see beyond its means, to see the field as such or at least to record the struggle to do so. And that in turn may be one of the fundamental differences between poetry and discussions of it. This at least is what we would like to suggest by taking Bronk's words as the title for this collection.

The reviews and essays collected in these issues of *Talisman* embody certain ways through which poetry in our time is interpreted and discussed by readers, critics, and poets themselves. *The World in Time and Space* offers a representative series of discussions that have involved readers, poets, and critics — often strongly at odds with each other — in recent years. The discussions center on such topics as language writing, poetry slams, feminist literary journals, Asian-American poets, neo-Objectivists, gnostic poets, visual poets, E-poetries, African-American poets, New York School poets, neo-Surrealists, prose poetry, poetry anthologies, and much more.

The inclusion or exclusion of a review, or an account, of a given poet is not by itself necessarily a reflection on his or her achievement as a writer. Since it has been common, although clearly misleading, to argue that New York and San Francisco have produced the most interesting work of the past few decades, we chose to focus as well on a poetry community from another city. The city we chose was Los Angeles. Had the choice been Seattle, however, we would have had much deserved discussions of Laynie Browne, Jeanne Heuving, Robert Mittenthal, and John Olson, among others. A chapter on Boston would have included commentary on Gerrit Lansing, William Corbett, Joseph Torra, Michael Franco, Ange Mlinko, Patricia Pruitt, Gian Lombardo, Christopher Sawyer-Lauçanno, Lisa Bourbeau, and Lori Lubeski, to name a few.

Still other communities, as well as ways in which poetry has been shaped and discussed in the past several decades, have been necessarily though regretfully omitted. We might have included essays, for example, on poets from other countries who have settled here. An important essay could have been written, for example, on British poets such as Douglas Oliver and Simon Pettet, who made their homes in New York City. No fully comprehensive history, were such a thing possible, could responsibly overlook such well regarded poets. Some poets such as Murat Nemet-Nejat, John High, Jack Kimball, Timothy Liu, Sean Killian, and Stephen Ellis are as important and admired as others discussed here, but their work did not fit as readily as others into the discussions collected here.

The World in Time and Space is necessarily incomplete and biased, as all of its successors must be. There has never been a period in American poetry when so many have accomplished so much. If mainstream poets have been as productive as they always are, outriders may have exceeded them in every good way. But one must never simply select a handful and say that these are "major," the ones whose work we must preserve. The challenge for those who follow will be to write the history of these generations without nominating yet another slate of "great writers" or canon of essential figures. Poetry, in our time, transcends its place in any institutionally imagined end.

The World in Time and Space constitutes issues #23-#26 of *Talisman: A Journal of Contemporary Poetry and Poetics* and concludes the first series of that journal.

—*Edward Foster*
21 *June* 2002

The World in Time and Space

Bruce Andrews

MAKING SOCIAL SENSE: POETICS & THE POLITICAL IMAGINARY

Poetics tracks the way that writing makes sense (by producing meaning) & makes noise (by risking meaninglessness). This gives it an explanatory trajectory — helping us make sense of the social world we live in by means of writing, as well as a prescriptive trajectory — helping us chart the social troubles & imaginable alternatives we face. When we bring the social dimensions of language to the forefront, we start negotiations of implicit social stance & value. Politics is unavoidable. We can ask of writing: what political identifications & projections does it set up? What conception of power & authority does it sustain or jeopardize? By way of explanation, talk about poetics helps us track the way that certain types of innovative literary practice offer, *as reading*, a grasp of the social & political order — of both its modes of working & our hopes for change. Writing explains the social by implicating it — with an eye toward prescription, by implicating the features of it which are the most problematic, the ones we most need to get beyond. This is explanation by problematicizing — by translation. And prescriptions can be teased out of explanations. We can start to suggest how adventurous writing might imagine the project of social change & how it might fit (or clash with) that effort. Together, these stabs at explanation & prescription give us writing's political imaginary.

Authority, to begin with, rests with choices of patternings of words — distance from, or reliance on: traditional form & genre & persona, rhyme & meter, 'regulated' syntax, stylistic doxa. By now, after a century of avant-garde activity, we're familiar with writing that builds its own authority on the rejection of standardized choices, on abstraction, on the dizzying of convention. An extreme 'structuralist' version of radical modernist work pares away completely the traditional hulls & protocols, along with their compulsive legality (& legibility) — leaving the words no longer so strapped down to possessible & packageable intentions. It tends to bring the arbitrary into relief as something pure: words as purified atoms, released from being conditioned (by etymology, discursive use, or conventional trappings), pulverized. But a radical politics of writing in the postmodern age will need to go beyond this anti-social posture, this near-phobic avoidance of social material. We need to get our hands dirty. A more critical approach to the social dimension of language will chart its inflections, what is *not* neutral about it; what makes formal & contructivist choices so fraught with *bias* & *tilt*. Not as a compensatory move — avoiding social matters to seek a niche in which power & authority could be disappeared — but as an activist one, using authority to refashion power.

Typically — in reviews or talks or conversation — we focus on particular texts, on examples. But we also need to theorize more generally, to make broader remarks about the recovery of the social in contemporary writing. We need to theorize about how the compositional processes of innovative writing can conceivably contribute to a new, political *emphasis*. For poetics, what had been centered around writing — as a preparation for, or orchestration of, reading — gives way to a focus on reading as a means of rewriting. What gives ground is the autonomy (or anti-social separatism) on which literature prided itself. The spotlight is now trained on the entanglements in which an individual's writing finds itself. Reading, as an opportunity for reframing, takes place within those entanglements — within the adventures of the sign & the subject, once both are understood to be social constructions. The task is to probe the political implications & imaginary of different theoretical perspectives on contemporary literary work.

What follows here are notes on several of these vantages, or emphases, in radical or formally adventurous writing: the effort to create an intimate, absorbing dialog with language; to socially reframe language by gaining distance on it; to restore its place within a social context; to reconsider the social processes by which identity is shaped & confirmed; to unsettle the machinery of socialization; to reimagine utopian alternatives. The topic headings follow the sequence presented in the essay, "Revolution Only Fact Confected," in my essay collection, *Paradise & Method: Poetics & Praxis* (Northwestern UP, 1996.] How to create sparks.

DIALOG & ABSORPTION

WITH RADICAL MODERNIST WORK, writing often seems to take on language as a whole — but only from its formalist inside. The reading subject acquires a more spacious arena & a new Other to relate to. For this would be a literature that cuts past the conventional focus on writerly persona or experience or theme. Instead, it offers the chance for playing with the fullest variety of meaningful (signifying & discursive) materials: everything from the tiniest abstract bits to the bigger secondhand connectives. Readerly identity is made from identification — but not with authors or cut-to-size subjects. It gets cast in the shape of a repeatable deduction (from *within* language). It offers an intimacy which is no longer external; the dialog gets pulled inside. It suggests an absorption by the language system, a dialog architected ahead of time to fit the limits of words.

The familiar 'politics' of personal experience & expression at least gets challenged here. But the problem is that our absorption in a 'total' formal field may make language a blur, the white noise of the windowless monad. It threatens a lack of finiteness, an impressionism of presence. It is as if, caught in its aura, readers could experience an immediate face-to-face relationship with the patterning of words — & have it serve as a confirmation, or even a ventriloquism of formalizable language as a whole. Absorption creates the feeling of unity as fixity but with the dangers of suffocation — a permanent 'insider-ism'

Writing can invoke the empathy of face-to-face revelation, the details of 'facework' as the mutual re-creation of 'face' (with 'face' understood as an individual's self-image as it gets reflected off of another). But, here, what seems to be intimately & empathetically calibrated no longer takes shape in the old familiar way: between the subjectified consciousness of two individuals. Instead, more grandly, it solicits a dialog between Reading & Language. Writing can attempt to stage this face-to-face absorption into language, as if through the 'fourth wall' of traditional stage craft. Erstaz presence unifies & unity helps imply presence — as possessive grabbag. A choreography of signs designed to make the reader *at home* — even if less personally.

The politics of absorption might point toward a totalizing formal self-consciousness — a 'mere' politics of the text. Such writing could encourage the type of reception which sparks intimations of *access* to this full, near-total array of formalizable language (something that can overwhelm either the conventional soundings of the reader or the idiosyncratic speech-thrusts of the author). It could valorize the opening up of ever more expansive choices & interpretive options. But only on the formal inside, because no social outside is allowed to show itself.

Such absorption stops short, threatening to make readership commensurate 'fitting,' & confirming the standards of use in literature. Prescriptively, it cannot get beyond the limits of the inside, the adherence to *autonomous form*. And this is also the plight of a distributive (or abstractly libertarian) politics: the sense of available possibility for individual units can be stretched to its formal limit, but that is all. Disablingly, nothing points toward any way to frame or interpret or denaturalize the whole, a seemingly uncontainable materiality & carnality. The translation of the overall is not at issue. The need to transform the whole is ignored.

DISTANCE: QUESTIONING ABSORPTION

Beyond the recuperative dangers of absorption, we need to put forward a thoroughgoing constructivist model of textual performance. To discombobulate, with fiercely negative energies directed toward the apparent, toward language's semblance. We want to be backstage at the carnivalesque.

The 'meaning' of formal (signifying & discursive) language is not enough. The bounds and bonds of *Sense* go beyond those of meaning & help to defamiliarize it. This will be easier to notice if writing can spotlight its contextual *social* entanglements. Context offers up a strategy of Distance with respect to Meaning, just as Discourse does with respect to the Sign and Signification. Reading's self-presence can be cantilevered into distance, unhinging & pluralizing what we take for granted. A plural intertranslatability becomes an option — as strangeness applied to meaning by our restaging of the materials of language, by showily theatricalizing gestures toward an Outside: toward the social.

We start out working self-consciously with a total language: combining what signs can do (& undo) with what discourse can do. Yet the totalizable unity of language — *that aftereffect* — starts to come apart at the hands of distance & its corrosions. The outer shell of apparent autonomy lacks sticking power; the insides — as they interact with each other in writing — leak out if the perimeter gets breached. With perspectival divergence, reading ceases to prop up the purely internal regularities of words. Instead, we work out the details of an osmotic relation to the outside: a reciprocal impingement of internal form & social embodiment. Banners, Intertitles, Collage, Subtitles, Footnotes, Cross-references. A decoagulant for the total grasp: to disunify, to make fluid.

Intelligibility goes beyond all that we take to be formal. If we reverse it — & imagine Language as Defeat — we set the limits of the sign (in a given language or dialect) inside the hegemonic 'common sense' & syntax of the day. Conventions are there to be disassembled, pulling apart the 'lips' of absorption. To deconstruct the spectacle would involve a general defamiliarizing of almost everything that neutral/formal language can do. To confront dialog with opacity — as parasitic backlash, a clouding or darkness (as distance) posed against the transparency of (absorption into & of) language. Give us a hint: scramble is order; excess meaning can be social excess.

Distance transforms the object-like feel for language as a whole into a performative process. Inference moves from the outside in. Part/whole now looks more like Inside/Outside. Far enough away to incite framing possibilities, the distance afforded by radical stylistic moves can offer a lever — to redispossess, to activate flurries of social framing. Coherence is something to restage at every opportunity, jumpstarting a continuous process of *translation* — of seeming everything into other everythings.

Beyond (now well-worn) radical modernist strategies, we stage the critique of the anti-social, the demise of the asocial. We stop worshipping immanence. To be made aware of a social outside helps to defamiliarize the inside — to inspire us to read *through* each & every text, to catch sight of the prior social figuration & computation of meaning. And of consequence, significance, value — all of which play themselves out beyond the formal limits of language. The Outside serves as Meaning's solvent (& insolvency), showing off an incomensurability beyond the perimeter of its forms. We start to look at the social as supralexical, as surplus framing.

In the end, isn't the fixed whole of language starting to look pretty grid-like, closed off, monadic, unilaterally determining? Distance is needed to restore its movement inside. But to create distance in writing sets it *in motion*. It can counteract the endlessness, the static duration, with a dizzying flurry of variation. Seemingly unrepeatable creative acts — what poetry is usually celebrated for — are relocated within a repeatability, or they get broken open to reveal a repeatability inside their contours. Here we find another settled social architecture, where prior choices have set the interior stage, where the conditions by which language can be lived or habitated are already established. Language is always socially produced. Matter can't escape the scars of its assembly line. However multidimensional, it is still *situated*. Its supplemental, prosthetic quality needs to be unveiled.

Writing can show the body of language to be divided, scarred, jostled, worn. It shouldn't just be skirted (by heroic unsigning) or ignored (by frontal embrace). It is the endlessness of this seemingly total embrace that we'll want to get beyond: distance *punctuates*. After all, much of the movement potential inside Meaning has already (always?) been mortgaged to Social Sense, hitched to an Outside. The enlivening shadow of autonomous language play will shrink. And decoding will begin. Distance disparages.

And distance makes language timely. Duration is restored by a feeling on the part of readers that time is something both produced & productive. No timeless moments of readerly engagement are truly self-conjuring. To find a historicity *outside* of the minutiae of 'close reading,' is to pull the text inside out. Any lexicon is circumstantial; writing needs to make it clear that it (or everything) could have been different.

Now, dialogic embrace may tempt us with its weightless abstraction of freedom. The old privileging of the voice (as something free, expressive, or transcendent) can stubbornly reappear within reading, within the polyvocality of language in proximity. But duration carries social weight (due to sizable barriers against social change, the irresistible pull of reterritorialization). To rapturously embrace language in dialog just gives us another version of anarchism: in both cases, we ignore the particularizing social dimension; an excessive abstractness results from the denial of any & all outside. In writing, what is called for is instead to reinject the bindings of time or duration as well as space (the specifics of words' social or institutional placement) — into an otherwise idealized circuit of significance. To take *social* exception.

If the readily available language seems unlimited, we' re looking at it too much up close. We fail to see what its active (external) sources of bonding & choice & constraint consist of. We fail to see its governing capacity. (All of which lends itself to writing prone to merely repeat the superficial anarchism of revolt & unsigning.) With distance, we can make meaning finite, less amorphous — reframing the 'auratic generic'. Writing which works best by helping dethrone the fixed & dehistoricized position of the reader. To combat the stare. To counteract containment — by *stance*, by a particularizing grasp of the constructed connnections, watching from the cheap seats. To make reception homeless.

The embrace of language as some rich & free pluralism still ends up covering up its tracks, hiding its government, its mechanisms of authority & reinforcement. We'd be better off in radical writing that conducts a tour of the factory & its *noise* — its primary materials, the noise particulars underneath the spectacle or the smooth surface. To make the semantic rigging reveal itself, rather than take the easier route of trying to make it disappear. For beyond complicity & complacency, we want a physical connection with the text & its specifics to override any absorption into 'language as a whole.' An anti-absorptive reading *made readily available* by means of socially drastic & obstreperous writing practice. A theatricalizing & tropicalizing of limits, supercharging semantic possibilities. Extremity & exaggeration or hypersubtlety & seditious exposé as direct address.

To recompose language in writing may now require a push to reconstruct an overall social lexicon. The social as readymade. Even the whole is a quote, unsourced — something which comes into focus if we take the extremest lexicon on adventures so that we make the overallness of meaning seem object-like, monad-like. By framing the familiarities of the reader's micro-frames, we spotlight the limits of possible framing. The *between* is now a *within*. Praxis: to restore potential fluidity & waywardness & more concave complexity to the social text (to the text which has built-in mechanisms of social saturation, of self-recognition or self-branding). To polysignify. To generate a plasticity beyond reception. Make yourself a counter-containment, putting language (back) on its polydifferential(izable) social plane. Gifts.

CONTEXT: QUESTIONING AUTONOMY

WHAT IS TO BE DONE. Meaning = Signification + Discourse. Sense = Meaning + Social Deployment (or Ideology). *Context: What are we up against* — & how to deal with it in writing.

With Sense, something even more contained & more directed from Meaning, another concentric circle of understanding shows up outside the pumped-up generalities of meaning we've been trying to get some distance on. Discursive norms are tilted, socialized; they offer new ways to anchor (& new vantages *on*) the overall play of (formal) meaning. We don't want to let our claims on language prefabricate the image of the reader as a positionless sovereign. Instead, we need to implicate the social logic that adds itself on top of any formal logic or system. It makes for a division of labor we are *inside* of.

The Social materializes inside & through the adventures of Form. We're not talking about old-fashioned notions of a return to Content (as if it were something unformalized or something we could transparently represent or tell the story of). It is more like social structure has insinuated difference back inside language. Social context as palimpsest, as staining or inflection of meaning, as another layer — or (progressive) concentric circle — that shapes & collectivizes our efforts to make sense. Impurity starts at the beginning: any inside is caught up within swallowed outside webs, within prior indelible codings.

Everything that had been given apparent autonomy from coding, or that had resisted recuperation, must now be open to perpetual *recoding*. Autonomy needs to be socialized & historicized, so that we can chart the codes which 'operate a social order.' The key is for writing to restore *choice* as an outside dimension: not the choices we spin off from our personal preferences, but the prior choices (or *strata*) that let specific matters carry their current of significance. To do this, we make a multilayer confection of fillings & toppings & swirls.

Context is readymade code, a social leverage or transport. Openness is rigged, not guaranteed. The roving freedom of the subject in dialog butts up against preexisting barriers & contextual determinations. Action theory fails, intentions crash into the grid-like codes of conduct outside of words. In fact, context serves to motivate — or *translate* — our acts of language. Getting absorbed in language we often forget this, reassuring ourselves with an image of equalized atomic bits (a distribution of speaking parts & listening headsets). But context offers a rebuke: any seeming logic of equivalence or neutrality is a trick with mirrors.

Context creates additional containment, with seepage: a compensatory staging to call the bluff of any purported autonomy (or octopus-like expansion) of language use as a whole. Underneath discourse is a stubbornly shaping skeleton, the secondhand as socialized —

maybe even bureaucratized — flesh The contexts aren't so scrambled or waywardly overlapping that they simply cancel each other out. Usually we can notice the marks of a settled social grid or provisional suturing. They add up. Classic recuperation instances: global positioning, gender, class, race, ethnicity, age, sexual orientation. And so: we're up against context as normative, yet open to unconventional 'showings' (as 'showing up').

Auratic proximity licenses possession. Context, if we can recognize it will stimulate dispossession: shaking up the markers of circumstance, the secondhand, so that we don't take them so much for granted. Praxis: to take *social exception*, reframing & reembodying sense in reception. To defamiliarize language by defamiliarizing its containers — not to put a lid on contextual 'work' just to sustain an illusion of disinterestedness or formalist autonomy. To show normativity as a puzzle — or a curse. To make context strange, to liquefy its obviousness. To bring up for questioning, *by words*, as much as we can: especially all the scaffolding & apparently contractual obligation leaned on by the subject as a socialized — & perhaps actively self-socializing strategic unit.

If social frames interrogate the insides, we want to encourage this exterior decoding, this figuring & disfiguring. We do so by the way we wield these socially intelligible bits & connections, by showing off the contextual markings inside the words & phrases & patterns, by incitements as well as demolitions of the framing that, if left invisible, would otherwise produce a social *promotion*. Beyond such lush personalizing of reading (& readability), playing with outside social materials can open up interpretation to the transpersonal & the everychanging. To historicize the context, to give a feeling for how it gets reproduced, shows up consensus as fraudulent.

But there are risks. Writing may make possible a social reading, but often one that is too mechanical, too doggedly polemical — not mutually relativizing & estranging. The social building blocks & cues we rely upon as footholds can seem just as prepackaged as any ornamentally firmed up personal expression — a Potemkin village. We risk the bad habit of valorizing fixed group identifications, creating the myth of a kind of social transparency — but, as ever, at the price of a certain blindness about the mixed & fluid nature of its containers. Often this brand of 'socially relevant' writing leaves us with a politics of demographic categories — where 'contextual fit' reigns over the dizzy & extravagant voicings of those who do not (completely) 'fit.' The social elements are offered up, but without the active work that can mutually transform them. Still too possessive, such writing appeals complacently to social background or family heritage, 'owning up' to what it still claims to own. Instead of being intercontextual, the politics remains at the one person/one context level.

Authority, as cachet, may attach itself to displays of context. But politically, this *niche strategy* may limit us. Once trotted out for display, these backstage cues or demographic layerings threaten to become fixed items in the liberal agenda of 'interest group pluralism,' sticking with the equivalent of the 'organic intellectual,' trapped within her 'heritage,' fighting for recognition but without having to change. A feel for multivocality might result, yet the subject evoked (either speaking or listening *sotto voce*) still looks to be playing from a fixed script — as well as sporting identifiable 'gang colors.' That is the danger. To bring these contextually characteristic materials to the forefront can create complicity, upping the chances for fixating on signposted familiars & taken-for-granted social markers. Of course these contextual identifications — 'show us your colors' — may just seem compensatory, the payback for an essential homelessness. The boomerang returns.

For a more drastic political writing, we can chart an alternative trajectory: circling around a radical (delirious) experimentalism with meaning (in formal language) as a whole, we help make visible an outer layer of social constructedness. But dependency cuts both ways: we have a language system dependent on context, as well as a dominant social context dependent on the norms of language. Either can be a means by which to destabilize the other. If the prescription leads us toward a shaking up (or loosening) of the social frame, disruptions of language will serve as a fitting method. But one danger remains: the need for radicalism *within each concentric circle* may not register. Operating *with* Context in standardized ways may make it harder for language practices to revel in their *insides*. The external glare may be internally homogenizing.

With a contextually attuned writing, we would need to reinstate a sense of *otherness* (rather than ownership) in the face of imaginable (& contextually marked-off) difference. Here is one key positive element of its political imaginary: exposing a social dictionary which is both definite, polylingual, & personally unsettling. For why be possessive or prideful about the remote-controlled? — "My Roots No Thanks". We'll need an exploded social (body/embodiment) to highlight the *between*, to get us beyond the usual comparisons & equivalencies, the punching bag of identity politics, the addictive stories of social belonging & family background, the certainties of putting things 'in their place'. What may work better is an ironizing lack of fit, a flamboyant potlatch of identification. To re-denominate; to hyperventilate the dominant context; to imagine & track its alternatives — all the way to the extremes of intercontextuality, of hetero*deg*lossia.

INTERPELLATION; QUESTIONING SOCIALIZATION

WHAT ABOUT *the person* in writing? Has Context put it out of business? Can it be rehabilitated?

Contrast sets any 'me' in motion, spinning around to respond to the "Hey, you!" of hailing. This is interpellation. It confirms, or freezes in place, the individualizing pressure of ideology. NAME IDEAL: heterology persists, but cut to fit the size of the individual massege. We confront a social differentiation, not unlike the equivalencies of the sign.

It's naive to imagine that identity could float free (& relaxedly) inside given circumstances. It's more like a byproduct of those circumstances: the phony voluntarism of the ventriloquist's dummy. Magnified & Puffed up, its aptitude inflated, self-authorship serves as the standard, the be-all-end-all. Personal control & possession: these are what the ideologies of everyday life tend to celebrate. But what's usually going on instead is the promotion of particular brands of *social subjects*. And literary style (in the way that texts treat social materials) often does little more than decorate this 'life style' or social (often subcultural) self-styling. Duplicity loves company.

Interpellation fosters a *perspectival*, almost pictorial quality within the social discourse with which writing operates. Overdetermination skinnied down to publish subjectivity as an ideological imprint: self as flare, as lexical lens. A near-Panopticon of individual regard, interpellation works to make a personalized social transparency, a dematerializing of identity — almost as if Ideology can 'see through' it.

It's hard to valorize the particulars when they're this heavily mortgaged — with text as the dummy of semblance. Doesn't holding high the banner of the 'self-made possessive individual' distract us? Doesn't it make it harder to recognize how much conflict & vulnerability & lack of consensus marks the raw materials of social sense? Still, we don't just want to *reduce* the subject to its contextual 'fit,' to embody it in a mechanical — even if 'politically correct' — form. Instead: how to make the false seem false. How to scramble the tableau.

As long as today's status quo depends on this ideological fashioning of subjects, a conservative (or counter-revolutionary) poetics will be quick to salute it. It valorizes writing as the honor guard for the expressive (or is that: intimately declamatory?) subject. Now, to imagine a poetics in opposition — a counter-counter-revolutionary poetics — this subjectifying process would need to be contested. A different determinate shape for the reader would need to be solicited, to do battle with what is offered up so pervasively (& tantalizingly) by the status quo.

Some types of experimental writing do propose a more abstract sedition. Flamboyantly, they bypass the determinacy of shape (& momentary personal fixedness) altogether. But is it enough of a challenge to this social subjectification (upholding the status quo) to simply erase it from writing, to shortcircuit it from the start — to make art which is indifferent or even phobic about the self . . . the subject . . . the human . . . ? We might begin to wonder about such an extreme form of modernism. For don't we touch off a crisis in the reader's participation if s/he is made nomadic — & surrounded by an atmosphere of pervasive strangeness? Wouldn't this (classical) alienation lead to a breakdown in reading altogether? As if readership, entirely resistant to the subject-form, would only be allowed to cavort in a prediscursive sublime, limited to a condition of meaninglessness & nonsense, of personal & social illegibility. Given what we're up against, to blur is not enough.

Writing needs a politics of personal transformability — to nudge us toward a reception which is socially creative, looser than anything deductive. To disunify by throwing a monkeywrench into the interpellative machinery; to combat the mythic transparency of an invisible control mechanism with a social opacity. Not just to ironize these subject positions (& the grid that pins them down), but to make them ambiguous by reading — that is, by writing designed for innovative reading practices. An anti-recuperative strategy. If writing builds in enough of a complexity of personal materials — a frenzy of overlapping or mutually distortive perspectives which words make present — we can prefigure a much less constrained style of readership. Subjects can embody duration (in time) — in praxis: highlighted by a move away from the atomism of single words, by greater use of longer (ownable, socially loaded) phrases & sentence units. And subjects can embody cultural difference (in space) — in praxis: paralleled by more use of materials with a popular cultural slant & by greater dailiness in styles of contact, format, & intermediation. This can be *social noise*.

Unity is fake. The centered & 'in charge' lyric subject has become tiresome. A drastic postmodernism would try to solicit something quite different: a thicker, wider (socially out-of-place) structuring of identity. A heterological explosiveness, a way to desovereignize, to spotlight the maze of overdetermination.

Reception might become reperformance, a polyframing that shows up in choices of materials & style, a social reversal as the de-positing of the reader. Political authority returns to the text, but as an oppositional force: now on behalf of the maximum potential for (social space & time of) reading.

If writing helps us be more conscious of this social internalizing, it holds out the promise of self-reflection on *prosthesis*. This is the opposite of what a retro 'humanist' literature inclines toward. By encouraging identification with standardized personae, such a literature tends to reinforce the socialization process, freezing the trajectory of self-development. A more radical praxis would stoke up these self-actualizing dynamics — to *make impossible* any such reinforcing or massaging. Writing would work against identification; it would make an anti-compensatory move, to solicit a multiplicity of subjecthood by resocializing & rehistoricizing it. The desired result: more than just a comforting ambivalence or ambiguity; instead, a complicated layercake of readership to match the complexities of the social context.

This is politics as dethroning, or impeachment. What makes it interesting springs from something we notice when we try to explain the lack of social change: how much the settled social order depends for its stability on the promise of individual sovereignty. This is a taken-for-granted ideology ripe for challenge. A praxis which fits it: to activate a more resistant & performative style of reception. A counter-ventriloquism. To construct an experimental model of future self-fashioning out of bricolage. To socially reconstruct identity, moment by moment, to contest the usual perspectival fixing — but only *after* we use the details that make it noticeable. So we're playing with the building blocks of personal motivation — the granular matter of cultural soliciting & cultural reinforcement — with an eye toward remotivating, with hints of the polymorphous. Can we make the standardizing social materials indigestible, or at least can we help them resist a smooth & blind assimilation? To offer up rough drafts & raw materials of this social calling may foster a better chance for imagining large-scale reconstruction, for shattering the illusion of the writer's (& reader's) expressive command. But how?

Do we really believe that literary texts themselves have some big direct impact on the socializing of reception? Do they spur (or reinforce) an ongoing critical stance? Or do they map out an allegory of attractive, conceivable readership — even if it is one beyond our current reach? Most likely, with radical postmodernist writing, the reader cohabits an allegory or a map of the process by which the reader's singular position gets socially constructed: out of seductions, admonitions, cheap rhetoric, flattery, recruitment, threats, reassurances, scares & the like. On the far horizon, in our experience as readers, some new intersubjectivity (with a collective/societal referent) starts to spin itself off from the wild possibility of an *intercontext* & new forms of *intercontextuality*.

APPARATUS: QUESTIONING THE MACHINERY

A POLITICALLY-POINTED WRITING cannot just refer to some external *content*; it's as if nothing is external. Writing's overall Other is more like a social machinery which *includes* language use. Sense, that expansive body of connections, makes up a machinic assemblage, grounded in the articulated patterning of language. The process of interpellation or hailing is part & parcel of it; subjects serve as its points or nodes of articulation.

So what has this machinery done to the space allowed for the agency of the reader? After all, not only are writing's discursive materials 'second hand' — so is reception. Any subject faces a body of norms & protocols, customary habits, standardized procedures, objects for cathexis — all machine-tooled: an everyone-ism. Presence, for the individual, becomes a synthetic civil pleasure or expectation, as the self-made reader is recruited.

How can there be an uncontainable language — especially if it produces its own containers (people) right along with the messages & energies it propels? More & more, the social machinery of making sense depends upon on a subject-forming (& speech-encouraging) 'positive power.' It works to stage an identification with a specific self — neutralizing the neutral, offering up instead a prefab particularity. After all, the social machine depends upon individuals with a personally felt need for acquisitiveness, for prosthesis & supplementation (as well as blindness, distraction, other-directedness, etc.). Perhaps we have hit an extreme here, in the postmodernity with which writing dances. Perhaps the particles have gotten so efficiently socialized that they operate almost entirely functionally, or deductively, as cogs, as parts swallowed up by the whole. It makes no sense to talk about *alienation* if we're really faced by dispossession engineered by machinic possession. There may not have been anything 'original' to lose or be dispossessed of in the first place. So: how much of the reader or spectator's self-fashioning has been culturally preempted, hijacked? How much is it a blinded ventriloquism 'voicing' the social apparatus? How much does the dummy salute its sovereignty? — a kind of social auratic, a body coding — with accessories, an intimacy which has become overinternalized & yet irresistible.

To varying degrees, the individual is culturally sewn up — & helping the overall social body sew itself up. And suture — *writing's adversary* — doesn't just involve stitching up units which stay the same. It points up something else: machinic processes that not only stitch things together, but at the same time block the tranformation (or reduce the risk of change) of the units that get stitched together. (And this spectacular blocking of change — or at least its 'risk-reduction — involves intricate processes of private media-tion: publicity/

advertising/public relations/propaganda/counter-intelligence — in socialization, consumerism, gender damage, sexual heat.) Processes we can *implicate* in writing.

Resistance. A truly oppositional writing would need to resist the finishedness & repeatability of the sutured subject. And here we face the limits of a personal writing politics of the social. It may not be enough to expand available possibility to the limit — for *me*, singled out &, very likely, privileged — rather than questioning the whole or implicating a different future for it in writing: its transformation. In order to try to guarantee more expansive interpretive options, writing's horizon would intersect the *mode of production* (for individuals). How? — by foregrounding words & phrases that capture some of the feel & mood & gears of the process of personal construction (or, more often, of personal *reinforcement*).

Writing can help us imagine what the full array of socializing language looks like — even given its usual imperialist, racialist, sexist, bossist, & capital accumulationist embodiments & blockages. Certainly the social machine doesn't help us out by theatrically & rhetorically calling attention to its workings. For a brace, it leans up against an imaginary fourth wall. But we can wonder whether that will work: whether it can hold together, avoid major change, or even stay the same. Writing can always raise the corrective line: these social arrangements could have been different!

Political writing offers a probe opposed to standardized reinforcement — on behalf of an acknowledgeably or revealably less-than-neutral subject. And also a less-than-absent subject: these days, who *doesn't* speak? But how freely? We certainly may doubt whether the social wires can be pulled out enough to create niches or zones of autonomy, or a bracketing of discipline. One more reason why writing to empower existing subjectivities is not enough. To let the 'silenced' tell their stories or audition for speaking parts still assumes a model of repression, the overcoming of 'negative power.' Rather than promote *naming* in a more egalitarian way, the project really ought to be to challenge its hidden construction. Gradually, tentatively, to make it impossible to empathize with the very subject that the machinery seems determined to crank out & empower. To resist social closure, to make the future unsuturable.

The abnormal threatens the norms. And so a politicizing writing will want to take on these very normative social materials (tokens of attitude, perception, experience, action) that can't be comfortably identified with — arranging & playing with them to secure a glimmer of the incommensurate. Such a project — of opposing absorption — can highlight how fragile & vulnerable these mechanisms can be. Specifics are unleashed as *clues* — not as deductive confirmations or as parts of the cover-up. They become socially disconfirming details: a counter-metonymy. To crack the mirror. To tear the roof off. To defamiliarize comfort. To make the reader homeless — but *ready*.

We do not belong. And we want to intimate this in writing — by soliciting a resistant readership. But resistant to what? Perhaps sense itself (or sense altogether). Or perhaps only those aspects of making sense & making meaning which are thoroughly disciplined & socially way too well-behaved. The key is to work with the raw materials of sense in order to preserve their difference or their otherness, to keep them from being homogenized. Writing would need to take the itch to empathize with the apparatus & outfit it with a gag reflex. Imagine writing serving up the wildest smorgasbord of possible items & connections & commensurabilities: first, as a staging of Otherness, & second, as a possible dream or scenario of potential personal habitation. A counter-choreography of persons. The untitled is majoritarian.

Again, we might attribute to writing the ability, inside itself & all by itself, to reshape this outside social machinery. Or we could grant it just enough oomph — & Authority — to help ongoing efforts (by readers) to get out from under the machine. Or, finally, we might give it the looser, more ambiguous task of proposing — as the basis for its Authority — an *allegory* of reconstitution. Is the machine rebuildable? Gertainly if texts elicit greater self-consciousness, it can create greater mutuality — as well as a sharing of the text's authority. The task is to allegorize the release from determination & control, to let a little light temporarily slant through closed circumstance in a way that 'makes strange' any of the closures we would otherwise take for granted.

How do we arrange the material or the physique of a potentially free community? If we think about the acoustics of writing, for instance, it points to sounds that are not deductively derived from any imposed grid, ones that do not smoothly & lyrically flow from some characteristically well-behaved persona. An informalism — like *une musique informelle* — could work like the process, within a hegemonic struggle, by which *identities* get transformed as they realign & relate & recombine. Whereas just to wield discursive materials in a spirit of intertextual play tends to be much more limited; it gives us an interweaving or 'free arrangement' of *fixed* (as if: already culturally approved & consensual) materials. An informalist writing, instead, would forge the conditions for reciprocal mutual adventure And it would do so by means of another celebration of the plasticity of — this time, social — raw materials. To foster a mutualizable multiplicity, a social carnalized carnivalesque. To run a curved, jagged line through both Meaning (the combination of signifying & discourse) as well as Social Sense as a (conceivable & heuristic) whole.

IMAGINING UTOPIA

Politics: coming to terms with as much of making sense as possible. A collectivizing writing: to expose the work of social construction(and of production *as* reception). To participate in hostessing a public readabilityship — as encyclopedia, as uncontainable plenitude.

Any incessant 'becoming' we want for our lives & our world gets boxed in socially: contained by consensus, by context, by personal coding. Writing, as counter, can act to activate refusals of containment. Just Say Yes — a solvent for all recuperations. Wanted: a fullest imaginable defamiliarizing of everything fixed. Smear the boundaries. Free the cages.

We're taking language — as the insides (the combination: signifying & discursive) — & we're bringing it into proximity with the social outside. New forms of social address — beyond simplistic notions of 'content' or 'representation' or 'narrative'. The resurrection of the object (& the other) as multifaceted subject — which we can start to gravitate toward, without possessiveness. Scramble the overall. As if: distance as transparency!

To distantiate more encompassingly. Preferred position: deep inside the outside: a moebius strip, or a space which is simultaneously convex *and* concave. A more active & demystifying contact — not with the formal autonomy of language as a whole, but with Sense as a social landscape. An 'overall,' more encompassing subjectivity, with readership vamping out toward the maximal limits. And limits get reflexive: a translation of deepening.

Politics: writing emboldening the possibilities of language — & its Authority (given how threaded together our governance & our opportunities for making sense have become). To make writing an impresario of the future as *open*. Horizoning: to put the everything within reach. Here we get hints of a real totality — well beyond the limits of language — but as the stubbornly untotalizable. A maximalism.

We uncode rather than decode: to find quicksand where the grid once was — (or to gain 'overstanding,' to 'outterpret'). The details of such a writing are socially wayward; you can't extrapolate out from them deductively. Language vagabondage. Familiar constellations gone on strike.

Results: a relationism of language — unimposed, sometimes pointed, sometimes slurry. Motive: to unsettle by making plural, to give in to fabulous full connectivity, all criss-crossings & cross-hatchings & cohabitings. *As politics*, the imaginary is encompassing & pluralist. And while it would embody a future social possibility, pluralism — except in textual terms or within a narrow niche strategy — has yet to become fact.

Closure is way too pushy. We want to get beyond any totalistic erasure of Otherness or any possessive domestication by it. Beyond the same & beyond the merely personal . . . into a forcefield of internal mutuality.

The model (for the future, implicit in such free-spirited 'informalism') is a participatory, carnal democracy. Getting there, however, demands more critique, more disrespect, more disruption — (as in: 'back when verse was rebellion & not classroom instruction'). To imagine a postindividual world — anonymity as collective constellation, individually stylized & embodied: the horizon of the reciprocal. Togetherness as fit — an embrace without nametags. Not to accessorize but to excessorize.

Edward Foster

AN INTERVIEW WITH GUSTAF SOBIN

This interview was conducted at Gustaf Sobin's home in southern France. Originally published in *Talisman #10*, it was reprinted in *Postmodern Poetry: Interviews with Contemporary Poets*.

GS: I was thinking, in light of this interview, that ideally it's the poem itself that should be interviewed, not the poet. It's the poem itself, after all, that has something to say. Something substantially *more* to say, at least, than the poet. And that's probably why we write them, the poems: to hear what they alone might disclose, tell us about ourselves and the world around us. What the poems, the words of the poems, once awakened, might reveal.

EF: And yet I think if one is looking at the circumstances out of which the poem comes, there are conditions and suppositions shaping it which are particular to that poet and which are very different from what other poets might give it.

GS: Of course, and particularly in regard to process. To the making of the poem itself: the ritual, one might say, of its elaboration. In my own work, for instance, I find myself moving, in nearly every poem I write, and usually somewhere toward its conclusion, from a place, a locus, a set of material circumstances, to a proposition. A postulate. And, in so doing, going — in terms of verbal time — from the present to the conditional. From an "is" to a "would," a "could," to the ever-present possibility of a "might." This movement doesn't aim so much at the utopic as at the potential. At what, linguistically speaking, still remains possible. Pronounceable. Can still at least be postulated within the yet untapped combinations of speech. In this sense, all my poems basically trace a thirst, a desire, trace a potential line of expansion from, say, a set of circumstances to — or rather towards — the fulfillment of what, at the outset, was merely dormant, incipient, undeclared. It's a narrow line of approach, but it's very much mine, and the one in which I seem to function — that my words seem to function — most naturally.

EF: That isn't what I would have assumed. Your work does not seem to me as much a poetry of place and objects as a poetry that finds its sense of location and objects along the way. It has seemed to me much more a poetry that begins in movement, music, time.

GS: It begins in movement, certainly, but I must have, *a priori*, a highly concrete sense of place, circumstance, before starting. I need some palpable "somewhere" out of which the poem can spring, if it springs at all. It's the palpables, for me, that motivate, instigate the poem, not the concepts, the preconceptions. "No ideas," I'd paraphrase, "but in cherry pips. Acorns. In those germinal images out of which the whole living organism of the poem, indeed, can develop." In fact, the more anchored my imagery and the more carefully perceived my verbal landscape, the freer I feel to expand, extrapolate, and — in so doing — create a movement, a momentum which — curiously enough — will release the poem, finally, from that very landscape. The very points of its inception. Will, in a sense, allow the poem to travel past itself.

EF: You use the word "release." The effect is to release from . . .

GS: From those points. From those images, if you like. I think of a poem as a trajectory going from image to image, point to point, in an increasingly ineluctable pattern. The points aren't significant in themselves, but only in regard to the manner in which they relate, and relating, guide the poem forward. Only a few days ago, I was talking with my doctor in Avignon who treats by acupuncture about, in fact, this very same subject. She was explaining to me how the needle (call it the "point," for our purposes) only acquires a curative force in its relationship to other points. These constitute what is called, in acupuncture, a meridian. In poetry, too, by a well-placed sequence of images, we touch upon meridians. And, in so doing, liberate — yes, release — an energy of sorts from the poem itself.

EF: This liberation of energy from objects, from matter, sounds perhaps like Mallarmé's desire for "an Orphic explanation of the earth." Does that make sense in the context you are describing?

GS: Absolutely. But only out of an immediate perception of particulars. Out of, that is, earth itself. Only then does a proper expansion of sense — an extrapolation — become, I feel, possible.

EF: Where did this sense of the poem as releasing the energy of particulars occur to you?

GS: Here, certainly, in Provence. Here, I learnt how to read the landscape as one might read a text, a *textus*, a woven fabric. As something drawn between the tension of its lines (the strict lineations, say, of orchards, vineyards, melon fields) and the sensuous roll, undulation, of its contours. How the lines — be they agrarian or verbal — insinuate themselves in the pitch and heave of the earth: become yang to the earth's yin. How, in turn, they constitute together the necessary counterpoint for their own transcendence. Yes, here, very much here. In Provence.

EF: It was nothing that you could have found, for example, in the landscapes in New England when you were growing up?

GS: No, not in the least. I'd seen it, however, in certain Mediterranean landscapes I'd traveled through as a student, but I'd never inhabited — been immersed in — a landscape so lyrical. So immanently textual. No, I'd never felt that in New England. In the Southwest, perhaps — in New Mexico and Arizona — with its stratifications, its tabletop "mesas" and, of course, its overwhelming luminosity, but no, in the Northeast, never.

EF: It interests me that you don't see New England in that way, yet you're from New England, and there's a deep tradition of reading the landscape in a lyrical fashion there whether it is Bryant or Thoreau or even, in some ways, Olson. But you put yourself outside that tradition.

GS: Perhaps it's the hills there. Their self-enclosure. I never felt any inner sense of breadth, respiration, expansiveness. The lines of one hill would bring the lines of the next too quickly to closure. And this closure, for me, only underscored a prevailing sense of the private: the mystification of private property, and, along with it, the turning of the spirit inward. Yes, a deliberate sense of self-enclosure. Inner constriction. Property, rather than the soil itself, considered sacred.

EF: Whatever the specific geography or the object or image, the result in the poem is the release of energy from it.

GS: Exactly. And I think those points we spoke of, those specific images, are also the germinal instances from which the poem takes its movement, its motion forward. Moves in the direction of its own particular *dis*-closure. By touching upon an interrelated sequence of images (we might even, for the sake of context, call them "properties"), energy is released. How so? It would seem to me that the images, in their distribution, relate to a field. They charge that field with their own specific instances. If the image, as conveyor of energy, releases, the field receives. The former is active; the latter, passive. A poem without a recipient surface, without a field, that is, would be nothing more than an exercise in literality. For it's upon the field that the poem diffuses, distributes its sound particles, its properties. And it's there, just there, that the poem can move from statement to implication. From the present to the conditional. From the experiential to the potential.

EF: That potential or conditional, is it something which exists only in the language, or is it something that is reached through the language?

GS: For me it would have to be postulated by language before it could become actual — actualized — by experience. It's something, it seems to me, that precedes experience.

Precedes what it postulates. So, no, in answer to your question, it wouldn't end in language; it would end in life. But it would have to be spoken before it could come into existence.

EF: Spoken before it could come into existence.

GS: Yes, speech, that is, as prelude. As precedent. As, in a sense, instigating agent.

EF: So would you say then that the poem is literally creation, not recognition or identification or naming or, for that matter, revelation?

GS: No, not exactly. Call it, rather, the necessary precondition. For a poem in itself doesn't create; rather, it establishes the circumstances, provides the materials, out of which creation might then become possible. This is why I feel that a poem must lead, elaborate, allow its materials — its subject matter, if you like — to reach what I'd call a level of availability. You spoke, earlier on, of the momentum inherent in my work. Each syllable, I feel, should add to those that preceded it, not simply in a cumulative sense but in a directive one. The poem leading, cajoling, urging its way forth toward a "might be," a "would be," a "could." And it does so through a continuous set of oscillations, running forth between a "this" and a "that," a *yin* and a *yang*, in so many paired images in the direction — the elucidation — of its own desire.

EF: Could you elaborate on that: the poem moving "in the direction — the elucidation — of its own desire"?

GS: I don't think I've ever written a poem that doesn't implicitly express some form of wish, of latent desire. In a recent poem called "Tracing a Thirst," I speak of language as something made up of so many dry utterances and moving in the direction of a source. The source may be read literally or figuratively. Towards it, its dampness, towards that lip out of which — over which — the source springs, the poem is driven. Language, in a sense, driven toward language. The words, towards their source. Our utterances, toward origin.

EF: There seems to be two things here — that the language is its own act, yet the language moves toward its source, desire, which is already there, is a given, to be apprehended and named.

GS: Apprehended, at least, if not named. Approached, let's say. Intuited. Even, in the archaic sense, divined. The mouth, moving toward the lips: speech, our speech, toward its inception. And this inception, this origin, can only be apprehended — as I see it — in the eventual. In the about-to-be. Very much in that verbal time Benjamin Lee Whorf discovered in his study of Hopi linguistics. For the Hopis have no past tense whatsoever; origins can only be expressed — because they can only be experienced — in time incipient. Impending.

EF: There seem to be certain parallels, here, with George Oppen as well.

GS: Very definitely. With both George Oppen and Robert Duncan. They are the two poets, the two predecessors in American poetry, at least, I feel closest to.

EF: What is Duncan's contribution to your work?

GS: The sense of the Orphic. Of language as the generator, the mother, the source of all being. And the poem itself as a virtual act of reverence, offered up to its very own origins. Yes, Duncan for the mystery, the magic, the immensity of it all.

EF: And Oppen?

GS: Oppen for that focused intensity. For investing the particular with its all-too-lost significance. For threading the needle with fire. There's an urgency, a necessity to every syllable Oppen writes. It's as if life itself were being wagered with each of those syllables. And who's to say that it isn't.

EF: What about Spicer, who seems to me a strong source of the Orphic in American poetics?

GS: I need to reread Spicer, I feel. So much of anyone's reading depends on their own disposition at any particular period.

EF: You dedicate a major poem to Duncan, "A Portrait of the Self as Instrument of Its Syllables," in which you name a number of figures central to the development of your poetry. In the context of what we are discussing now, the one that seems particularly pertinent is Mallarmé — your reference there to his "rush of crushed shadow,"

GS: Yes, there seems to be a certain nothing — such as Eckhart's *nicht* or de la Cruz's *nada* — running throughout Mallarmé's work. That single drop he spoke of that the whole ocean's missing. Yes, an implication, running throughout, that there's something that *isn't*. A certain, irreducible *not*. The famous *blancheur de la page* upon which the heavy black characters of language never quite settle. Yes, Mallarmé. Sometimes I think of him, curiously enough, as the last poet of the T'ang dynasty. Those shadows, those gusts of darkness, that impalpable world he gives breath to. Because, certainly, it's there, that *not*. And underlies virtually everything we'd say. Everything we'd wish to say.

EF: Another whom you mention is Traherne. Yet he is the opposite, isn't he — certainly a poet of the immaterial, but a poet of light, presence, luminosity.

GS: I love Traherne's poems of Thanksgiving, and most especially their spirit of celebration. I find him the most luminous — the most weightless — of the metaphysical poets, all of whom I read and admired and whose work I hopefully assimilated quite a number of years ago. He had, of course, an established liturgy to draw from, as Mallarmé hadn't. He didn't have to generate, single-handedly, the kind of spaces Mallarmé, or any other modern poet for that matter, must today.

EF: What do you read with particular concern now?

GS: Most of the reading I do nowadays is research reading for my fiction. In the case of *Venus Blue*, I felt obliged to read an immense amount of memoir touching on cinema, the 1930s, on early aviation. Quite aside from that, however — from sporadic, research reading, that is — I haven't read in a serious, consistent manner for over twenty years, now. In "A Portrait of the Self as Instrument of Its Syllables," I speak of a period immediately preceding those years. It was a time when exactly the opposite was true: when I read, but didn't — couldn't — write. Those were my first years here. Here, in Provence. I'd come, of course, to write but had probably set up standards for myself that were well beyond my reach. So I read. For ten years, I read poetry, philosophy, anthropology. I'd read the collected works of one novelist after another. I'd read a play of Shakespeare every month, two, three, four times over, underlining, annotating as I went. That was the period between 1963 and 1972. It wasn't until December 1972, in fact, that I wrote what I could call my "first poem." It was quite short, five, six lines, as I remember, but I immediately recognized — there and then — that I'd begun. I'd managed, in that poem, to include a term of omission. Yes, a kind of crushed shadow of my own. The word itself was "crystal." "Crystal," for me, is something both palpable and impalpable, solid and yet transparent. Neutral in itself, it nonetheless shatters light. The word alone, at that time, possessed for me an essential ambivalence. It shimmered, it seemed, between the *was* and the *wasn't*. And doing so gave me the kind of license I needed. This one word, curiously enough, was the beginning of my first book of poems, *Wind Chrysalid's Rattle*. The book, in fact, is filled with "crystals." They run throughout the entire text. Concurrently, I was reading a lot of anthropology and, in the late afternoons, in whatever spare time I had, wandering across these very fields, locating, as I went, one neolithic site after another. And, along with the flint blades and scrapers, and, occasionally, an arrowhead or diorite axehead, I'd find — sure enough — crystals themselves. It felt, somehow, as if I'd conjured them! Similar artifacts, you know, found in America, might not be more than a few hundred years old. Here, they couldn't date from any less than four, five thousand years. I'd look for them as I'd look for words. In a curious way, they — the artifacts — came to substantiate the words. No ideas but in arrowheads! It was a very exciting time: 1972, 1973, the period of *Wind Chrysalid's Rattle*. A highly generative moment in which everything I wrote could well come under the title: "becoming." A person who helped immensely at that particular time, I remember, was Michael McClure.

EF: When you say that, I assume you are referring to his work — clearly there is a parallel sensibility. But I believe you once said or wrote that you did not actually meet him until much later.

GS: Oh, much, much later. Nearly fifteen years later. No, I mean his work, his poetry. It held a kind of conviction, a thrust, a kind of gutsiness, rising as it did out of the germinal, the seminal. A Blakean sort of precipitation. A sense of the poem as conjuring, creating as it went, whole, unexplored areas — worlds — of potential experience. Tapping, in a sense, the divine. I'd picked up *Star* between two airplanes, as I remember, at the Harvard Coop, and read it at the perfect moment. Maybe if I'd read it a year or two earlier, or later . . .

EF: And this was in 1972 or thereabouts?

GS: Yes, exactly. In September 1972. And, in December, I began *Wind Chrysalid's Rattle*.

EF: Who, after McClure, proved important?

GS: Of the American poets, none, certainly, more than Robert Creeley, but for very opposite reasons. His quietness, his gentleness, his profound exploration — in often nothing more than monosyllables — of the human heart. From Creeley, I learnt enjambment, how and exactly where to break my lines, yes, line lengths, breath lengths. What could be called the cadence of disclosure. The one time we met — it was in Buffalo, in 1988 — Creeley expressed a certain admiration for the way I handled prosody, and most especially how I measured out my lines, breaking them where I did. It was one of those rare moments — at least in a literary life — where a deep sense of gratitude could be directly expressed. For I'd learnt all that, of course, from Creeley himself. Creeley, a perfectly wonderful person, laughed, and said that he, in turn, had learnt it all from Doctor Williams! We had a delightful exchange and went on to talk of the poem as — potentially — a vertical gesture. Rather than allowing the line to run out, left to right, to a momentary point of exhaustion, letting it, instead, fall, drop, oscillating as it goes, the lines themselves like so many ledges and the poem, the thrust of the poem, like a waterfall, falling down over those ledges, splashing, plummeting as it does. That vertical tracking originated, no doubt, at least in English, in those first marvelous translations from the Chinese that began appearing in English and American reviews around the turn of the century.

EF: How would you characterize the change it brought about?

GS: For me, at least, it helped me to break with linear thought as conveyed by linear prosody: that each line has to contain so many feet, more or less, and run, more or less, a certain length. And, somewhat like the carriage of a typewriter, terminate at one extremity to recommence at another. With vertical tracking, language takes on a kind of natural dynamic, a gravitational pull, a proclivity downward. It's an innate movement, rather than an intellectually acquired one. And it allows, of course, for endless variations. If one wants a long line because the materials being expressed are expansive, meditative, or simply hesitating, then one can employ — just there — a long line. If, however, motion or a sudden acceleration of sense is required, the line, in turn, can be tightened, shortened, so that it retains our attention that much less. The eye as if falls through. There's a kind of release, an ease to it all. Yes, very much like a waterfall falling over its own ledges.

EF: You mention Duncan, Oppen, McClure, and Creeley, but there is a dimension to your poetry which is perceptibly not American, but perhaps returns to or reinvokes a symbolist sensibility.

GS: Perhaps. But you were kind enough, at one point, to call me Emersonian and very American, particularly in my way of treating language as something vehicular.

EF: And I certainly continue to believe that, but there is the other aspect. Perhaps I am wrong in calling it symbolist, but that's what it feels to me, and I was wondering if you read René Char in that context.

GS: He was certainly very much influenced by the Symbolists.

EF: And would you see your work there as well?

GS: Yes and no. I don't think I've ever consciously used a symbol without endowing that symbol with material, palpable, perceptual qualities. Without, that is, investing the symbol with a certain non-symbolic autonomy. Giving it, one might say, a literal life of its own. In answer to your question regarding René Char, he is, of course, of all the French poets, the one who influenced me most. I first came upon his work in America, in a Random House edition edited by Jackson Mathews. On the dust jacket, there was a blurb by William Carlos Williams that read, as I remember: "I don't know of a poet in my own language to equal him or that I more enjoy reading." On opening the book, I found this to be equally true for myself. It was a luminous experience, and one, in fact, that would determine the rest of my life. For it was that very volume that brought me to France, to Provence, and — by a happy set of circumstances — to encountering Char himself. More than anything else, his work moved me by the sheer, irreducible necessity of every line he wrote. Its urgency. And by a language that was never more nor less than the violent imprint — the impact — of experience itself. Yes, Char's work, Char's presence, certainly, was central. But beyond that, it's difficult, you know, for a poet to draw up a kind of literary geography, tracing those — those voices — whose work influenced his. There are so many forces at play, not only in literature and the arts, but in whole areas of interrelated studies that any geography today, I fear, is likely to be reductive. There's such a wealth, don't you find, of cross-cultural, cross-disciplinary influences at work that we might be the last, the very last to know where — linguistically speaking — our own words, today, originated.

EF: I would agree that a geography like that is always reductive, but I have always felt there is a value in it for the person who is entering the work for the first time. Eventually, the work may reveal itself in its own coherence, but particularly now when, as you say, the range of voices one hears is so vast, a new reader is perhaps better able to find a way through the work initially if there are some guideposts.

GS: I find, in terms of my own work, that a new reader either "gets it" or doesn't. It's a real hit-or-miss affair. And this seems to happen — or not happen — out of an immediate and natural affinity with the materials expressed. Out of an intuitive, rather than a cultural, or intellectual understanding of the poem itself. Someone once said to me that I write about things most people don't even know exist. I don't think that's true. To the contrary, I feel that I write about the basic intimacies of life itself. Only, I'm locating those intimacies upon a field in which the signature of personal identity — of so much individual attitude and posturing — is held to a strict minimum, if not eliminated altogether. There's little room in my poetry, I find, for myself. I'm there to structure the poem. To get it to fly. In this sense, I feel closer to the artisan than the artist. To the mechanic who, tightening a syllable here, releasing a line there, manages to get language to lift. To defy — for an instant or two — the weights of the explicit. And, in so doing, turns the poem into what might be called a kind of flying machine. Over and over, it's the poem that "takes wing," I'd insist, not the poet. It's the poem that soars. The mechanic, whoever he be, remains very much here, on the ground, and, if he's lucky, already at work on the rudder, the ailerons of yet some other flying machine.

EF: There are obvious cultural differences that distinguish one poetry from another. In distinguishing, say, between the French and American traditions, at least as they emerge from the last century, it seems to me that the American seeks a transcendence while the French seeks a transformation. It's a difference that, for me, sets Rimbaud opposite Whitman.

GS: All of which I feel is totally true. At the same time, however, I don't feel altogether happy making *post facto* comments on poetry. My own, or anybody else's. It's undoubtedly a shortcoming on my part. I'm thoroughly incapable of discussing a completed poem, or poetry in general, for that matter. A poem — poetry — should discuss itself, I feel. I'm a good deal happier, in fact, discussing process. How the poem "happens," comes about. You know, the nitty-gritty, the technical aspects. How the parts finally fit.

EF: Perhaps one could say that the commentary merely reproduces what should be found in the experience of the poem itself.

GS: One might even say that the commentary, by its very nature, can only give us something less than the poem at hand. Poetry, after all, exists on one level of rhetoric; commentary, on another. Commentary, at least for me, always ends up as something reductive, or — even worse — recuperative. I don't think of the poem as a sacred object, but I do feel that the poem, at its completion, deserves a certain measure of silence. Enough, at least, for the poem to say itself. To be heard on its own terms.

EF: In terms of the actual construction of the poem, could we go back to the poem as growing from images to abstractions? Could you give an example of how that occurs in the practice of writing the poem?

GS: Here, in this little *cabanon*, which is no more than eight feet by eleven, and where I've written all of my books and most of my letters, I begin — I always begin — with a palpable. For me, it's a point of departure. One spring, for instance, it was the spring of 1981 if I remember correctly, I wrote a series of little poems called "Irises." First of all, I virtually covered whatever free space I have here — this writing table, the tiled floor — with vases, jugs, bottles of irises. In Provence, it's the purple ones that blossom first, then the white, then Van Gogh's favorites: pale, ephemeral, sky-blue. I wrote, as I sometimes will, directly from nature. Wrote, you might say, a kind of "easel poetry." From the petals, from staring at those floppy, overlapping blossoms for hours at a time, I drew, extracted, extrapolated what could be called, for lack of a better word, meanings. I moved, that is, from, image to abstraction. From a sensuous appreciation of the palpable to whatever those palpables — at any particular moment — might suggest, infer, denote. Yes, the words as if emanating from the petals, from their rich, androgynous structures. Letting, as I went, the particulars speak.

EF: Speak, that is, as the poem itself.

GS: Exactly, as the poem itself. As the poet, letting the poem speak itself forth. And finding, as I did, that I'd be writing things down I could never have thought of otherwise. Not writing so much as translating, transforming so much substance into sound. It's a process, I find, particular to poetry, at least to the kind of poetry that concerns me. The poem itself as revelatory. I might add, at this point, that I find the process involved in writing prose, prose fiction, totally opposite. I always know what I'm after in fiction, and it's always me, as novelist, who's determining the novel, not the contrary. If poetry could be called the realm of the unexpected, prose, at least as I see it, is that of the planned, the foreseen, the predetermined. What Degas called "the perfect crime" in regard to laying out a painting — calculating its every element — well in advance. No, for me, poetry is totally unforeseeable. If anything, poetry foresees us! The poem, at least in my case, begins, each time, with two or three words, a nexus of sounds, a buzz line. Something seminal, germinal. Something that wants to be said, extended, elaborated. Within this nexus, this buzz line, I'm totally convinced, the entire poem lies hidden. Writing a poem, for me, implies drawing — with each line — the hidden, incipient meaning out of the line that preceded it. Letting the poem, that is, grow out of the poem, the branches out of the boughs, the boughs out of the roots, the roots out of that single, incipient cluster, that nexus, that burst acorn. It's just here, of course, that I feel very close to Duncan. To his vision, that is, of the poet as medium.

EF: In Duncan's sense that the relation of the poet to the poem is like the relation of the priest to the rite. Both allow the event to occur, calling it into being.

GS: Yes, the poem as something spoken *through* the poet as opposed to something spoken by the poet. One's responsibility to the words themselves, getting the words to accord, one with another. And, in according, allowing them to grow. There's something wonderfully organic, I find, in the way words push, thrust, creating as they do their own dynamic. Over and over I'm reminded of Fenollosa's magnificent line: "there are no nouns in nature." Perhaps, in its very origins, there were no nouns in poetry either. Only verbs, adverbs, verbal derivatives: the instruments of process. Of growth, abundance, decay. A singular discourse of continuous becoming, unobstructed by the nounal, the nominal. By anything whatsoever that might have inhibited that first, germinal insistence.

EF: Nouns are in some functions like verbs, I think. Their usual intent may be to obstruct motion, or so it may seem, but under the right circumstances, they have verbal qualities that can be released.

GS: For me, a noun, left to its own devices, will block the free circulation of the line. Will create stasis. Accumulate — stockpile — verbal energy. In my own work, I'm very mindful of this: the noun as a kind of solid; the verb, a kind of fluid. I try to wrap my nouns, as much as possible, in the flow, current, the irresistible rush of the verbs themselves. This, for me, is how the poem happens. Goes on happening.

EF: In Emersonian poetics, the poem follows or is driven by some compulsion in time as opposed to Pound's construction of the poem out of bits and pieces — the poem not emerging in exact sequence but discrete illuminations that later find their sequence. Given those extremes, where would you locate your own work, one of your own poems?

GS: Totally in the Emersonian sense. In the organic construct. There, lines not only follow lines, they emerge, germinate, evolve one out of the other until the poem itself reaches a natural conclusion. Exhausts itself like a wave. Touches upon its own promise. I should add, however, that there's one exception to this particular practice. Each year, at the end of the year or the beginning of the next, I go through the scraps, the fragments of the preceding year, and try to draw — from so many disparate passages — a sense. A sequence. What I call an itinerary, a transparent itinerary. Here, certainly, I come very close to those "bits and pieces" you spoke of in regard to Pound's concept of a poem's construction. Here, indeed,

I create a mosaic out of so many given pieces, a collage of sorts. I type up whatever passages might be potentially useful, then, cutting each into a separate strip of paper, lay them out over the bedspread. There, keeping an eye on the *ensemble*, I begin making a sequential arrangement, adding passages as I need them, while eliminating others as I go. Bit by bit, they begin describing a direction, a thematic itinerary, taking me somewhere that I've never been before. Here, the process, as you can see, is quite different: composing a poem out of so many given elements. But the result is identical: extending sense past oneself, and reaching into the revelatory. Revelatory, at least, for oneself. The poet, that is, stunned in those moments not so much by what he has just written, but just *read*.

EF: In all this, does the poem ever arise from or express anything of personality? Is there any . . .

GS: No, of personality, nothing whatsoever, I can assure you. Of the individual as some separate entity, no, nothing at all. Of the person, however — of what constitutes presence within the presence of the person — of this, most definitely, yes. And, in my case, this almost invariably occurs when the person within the context of the poem is coupled. Doubled. Is a figure that exists — can only exist — in its relation to some posited other. This other is often situated in the conditional. Often, indeed, *represents* the conditional. Is what the voice of the poem is directed toward. Is, in a sense, the poem's ambition. Its aim. But the voice *per se*, that of the poet, that is, has no identity of its own except to the extent it can conjure reflection, create reference, bathe in the mirrors of some potential other. Buber's "thou," no doubt. The self, substantiated by its other, and taking its stance at one extremity of that primal word — that primeval equation — "I-Thou."

EF: In the light of what you've just said, would you consider Buber one of the major influences on your work?

GS: Most definitely. And more and more so with the years, thanks especially to that one, long, poetic meditation.

EF: And Heidegger?

GS: Strangely enough, they're not to be disassociated, Buber and Heidegger. In a small circle of poets and philosophers, I once heard Heidegger, asked whom he considered essential in twentieth-century philosophy, answer without an instant's equivocation, "Buber." And most particularly, for that same text, that meditative poem on that primal relationship: "I-Thou." It must have come very close, I suspect, to Heidegger's own reading of the relationship between "being" and "Being" — "*seiendes*" and "*Sein* ."

EF: How did you happen to meet Heidegger? Was it here in Provence?

GS: Yes, in the mid-1960s. He'd come down, for several summers running, to visit René Char. He had immense respect for Char, his poetry, his *pensée*, and together, of course, they shared a great affinity for the pre-Socratic philosophers. Along with the major French Heideggerians, Beaufret and Fédier, and a few poets, such as myself, they'd sit in the deep shade of René Char's plane tree and discuss — for several hours running — a single, lapidary fragment of Heraclitus, say, or Empedocles. It was heady stuff. And one could only feel privileged to witness their exchange, two giants discussing a handful of words from the dawn of civilization, there, on a hillside, in the shade of a spreading plane tree, in what both of them — in regard to our own civilization — could only consider its dusk. That must have been in 1965, 1966, I believe. Heidegger was also drawn to Provence, of course, for its Mediterranean culture. His own work was so rooted in the Greek and in that of those Germans — Hölderlin and Nietzsche — who'd drunk from exactly the same sources, he could only feel amazed, strolling at last among the olive groves, or down some long, black corridor of cypresses. I should add, in parentheses, that the cultural, historical proximities between Provence and Greece are not at all fortuitous. Only about a hundred yards from this *cabanon*, for instance, and after a good rain, one can find, oozing up out of the soil, fat little green coins with the faces of Artemis, Demeter. They're stamped in profile and have the long, straight noses and immense eyes of all archaic Greek effigies. In fact, according to the local archaeologists, the coins are Gallo-Greek.

EF: Speaking of Provence, I wonder if living here rather than in a place where one is always in the midst of one's language encourages the kind of poetry, and investigation into poetry, that you are doing. I think that for many who are more immersed in the language day-to-day, it would be more difficult to separate the personal completely from the language.

GS: I agree. It's an advantage, I find, living at a distance in which one's own language is used — almost exclusively — for writing. The words take on a kind of buoyancy, a kind of freshness. They're free of so much exhausted usage. You know, from media, publicity. From laundry lists, too, and one's own idle chatter. All that day-to-day attrition. There's a risk, though, of becoming too removed. Of losing one's sense of the colloquial, the spoken, the pure vitality of living speech. Happily, though, I teach American students at a local art school, and this helps to keep my ears tuned. Keeps me — at least I hope it does — from falling too easily into gallicisms and the like.

EF: What language do you use in your family?

GS: English for the most part.

EF: But the business of living is . . .

GS: . . . mostly French. Almost exclusively French. This means that English, a better part of the time, is kept in reserve. Exempt, that is, from the usual banalizations. You know, it's such a beautiful thing to hear a perfectly common word in one's own language being turned, weighed, rolled as if across one's palm, blown across the room like a fresh thing: like the fresh, vibrant thing it really is! It becomes an event, a celebration. But it needs . . . at least for me . . . the strangeness of an alien culture in which to resonate. In March 1986, to give you an example, I travelled across New Mexico with the express idea of writing what I call a "road poem." I took endless notes as I went, filling one notebook after another with all kinds of observations, reflections, direct quotes from overheard conversations. But at the end — the end of this road trip — I realized that I didn't have a poem, not even the outlines of a poem, but a whole junkpile of notes. Of so much scrap. So I carried it all back to France, to Provence, to this little *cabanon* we're sitting in now. Yes, my own records of a huge hunk of New Mexico compressed into these very walls, and here, just here, got to work. Sorting, selecting, but most especially listening to what I'd written — listening to my own words, written in my own country but in the midst of this alien silence — I began, at last, composing my poem. Bit by bit, the junkpile turned into so much organized language, and the language, eventually, into poetry. The poem, incidentally, is called "Road, Roadsides, and the Disparate Frames of Sequence."

EF: Do you have a community of other Americans living nearby?

GS: No, not really. There's a smattering of rich, retired Americans living in the area, but they don't form a community except perhaps unto themselves. But as to artists, writers, an artistic community of any sort, no, none at all. The economy swept all that away, years ago, forced most everyone into some kind of dependency on an institution, or academy, or whatever. And that meant cities. Living in the cities.

EF: So there is no poetic community, locally at least?

GS: Not unless you want to include ourselves, this afternoon. For the duration, that is, of this interview we're according one another.

EF: Do you identify yourself at all with the tradition of expatriation among American writers?

GS: Well, I certainly did. Growing up in America in the 1950s, in a culture that was far more critical than it was creative, when the professors seemed to be holding most of the strings, I took refuge, you might call it, in the twenties. In the American expatriate twenties. It began, significantly enough, with Hemingway. No one, in those culturally paranoiac 1950s, could be considered more American than Hemingway, and, at the same time, more consummately expatriate. For me, he was the bridge. The gateway out. From there, I can trace my literary itinerary just like on a roadmap. It led to Pound, of course, and immediately after, Eliot. Eliot sent me reeling back to the English Metaphysicals and — through his translation of *Anabase* — forward, or at least sideways, to the French Symbolists. Pound, in the meanwhile, had opened my eyes onto the Chinese, onto Dante and the Troubadours. More or less at the same time (I was an avid reader then), one of the roads on the roadmap led, inevitably, to Joyce, and soon after that, to Djuna Barnes. Her novel, *Nightwood*, has had — continues to have — a considerable effect on my work. Along with all this reading, and before I'd turned nineteen, I had standing permission, every Thursday afternoon, to visit the Stein Collection at the Yale University Library. I could literally touch the twenties, and, believe me, in the mid-1950s, this had an immensely influencing effect on the young man — the young writer — I was.

EF: When did you permanently move to this side of the Atlantic?

GS: In 1962. The climate in America was already changing by then, but I had little sense of it. Anyway, for me, the die had already been cast a full decade earlier. Leafing, no doubt, through Miss Stein's correspondence.

EF: And you already spoke fluent French?

GS: More or less.

EF: Had you studied it at Brown?

GS: I studied it at Brown and previously, at Choate.

EF: But that still suggests a special attraction to the language, given the usual quality of language instruction in America, particularly at that time. I studied French, and it is one thing to read and listen, quite another to order dinner in a restaurant.

GS: Sometimes, quite often, actually, I dream in French. A few nights ago, for instance, I had a rather funny dream about this *cabanon* we're sitting in. I call it a *cabanon* rather than a cabin because cabin, to me, suggests a log cabin, and this, of course, is made of brick and stucco. Anyway, in my dream, I heard myself cry out: "That's not a *cabanon*; it's a *maison de correction*."

EF: A house of correction?

GS: Exactly, a house of correction. Because basically I don't write; I rewrite. I correct. And it's my sentence (no play on words intended) to live incarcerated within these walls so many hours a day!

EF: You came here, as you said earlier, because of René Char.

GS: Yes, we met, first, in Paris. And Char, an immensely warm man of unpredictable humor, urged me to visit Provence. If I admired his poetry so much, he told me, I should, at least, see where the poems themselves came from. He, his work, this earth immediately around us, formed, you see, an inseparable mass. And so, two weeks later, I arrived at L'Isle-sur-la-Sorgue and had René Char himself as guide — guide in every sense of the word — to this powerful landscape.

EF: And so the decision to move here followed immediately from that initial visit. And it was Char's presence that provided the stimulus.

GS: Yes, very much so. Char and Provence itself, a Provence that I'd need many years to make — at least partially — my own. But on that first visit, I remember, I had what the French call a *coup de foudre*. I was simply thunderstruck by the beauty of the place. That was in March 1962. A year later, I came back with a "bag and a briefcase," very much the way I describe it in "A Portrait of the Self as Instrument of Its Syllables." I'd come back, in fact, to stay. Those were years when one could live on very little. Two thousand dollars a year was all one needed to pay for the groceries and as much local wine as one could drink. For three hundred dollars, I remember, I bought a battered but running 2CV, and for eight hundred dollars, a handsome stone cottage. It's something young people today can't even conceive of. It meant time. It meant time to grow, develop in. It meant one could read for ten years! It's something, certainly, I could never afford to give my own children. But those were the 1960s. Life was cheap, and I was very, very lucky.

Michael Boughn

OLSON'S BUFFALO[*]

> "When wallflowerism becomes sufficiently established to control history then we have a hell of time believing what is said (of what is said) — the Herodotean Way — over what we suspect (& we are suspicious, no?) & therefore speculate as to, what went on, like REALLY. It's the urge toward the MONO — ...."
>
> —John Clarke to Tom Clark, 1/20/87

WHEN CHARLES OLSON FIRST CAME TO BUFFALO IN 1963, it had been some 18 years since he'd turned from politics to writing as the work which would center and drive his life (although, in another sense, as the Berkeley reading demonstrated, he never left politics).[†] He came to Buffalo with a significant body of work already accomplished. *Call Me Ishmael, Y & X, The Mayan Letters, In Cold Hell, In Thicket, The Maximus Poems,* and *The Distances* had all been published, as well as "As the Dead Prey Upon Us," "The Kingfishers," "The Lordly and Isolate Satyrs," not to mention the important philosophical essay, "Projective Verse." *Maximus* IV, V, VI, though unpublished, was already written. He'd been to Yucatan and led the wild, intellectual free for all at Black Mountain. Crucially important for many of those who came to Buffalo to work with Olson was the tremendous push he had made to rethink the epic as a way around the lyric impasse much contemporary poetry was locked in. How, that is, to rethink this crucial mode of discourse and move it past the limits it had been taken to by Pound and Williams. He was thus what Albert Glover recalls as "a living connection to an 'old' tradition rather than simply an isolated lyrical voice which was pretty much all there was otherwise." Though Donald Allen's groundbreaking anthology, *The New*

---

[*]Special thanks to Albert Glover, Ron Caplan, and Fred Wah for their invaluable assistance in putting this history together. All errors and inaccuracies are my own. Also, thanks to B. Cass Clarke for generously allowing me access to John Clarke's papers.

[†]Daniel Belgrad, in *The Culture of Spontaneity* (Chicago: U of Chicago P, 1998) usefully locates Olson in this regard within a community of writers, artists and musicians, arguing that Olson's poetics are inherently political, having largely been formulated in response to his experience of the liberal/corporate takeover of the Office of War Information and the Office of Facts and Figures (which had been led by Archibald MacLeish) in 1942 and 1943. As a result of the takeover advertising techniques and content replaced reasoned argument for democratic principles.

American Poetry, had opened people's eyes to a wider range of writing than Glover's comment might suggest, his point about the dominance of the lyric mode still largely holds true, even today.

All this work was implicated in a move away from what we think of as the "literary," finally claiming for poetry an altogether other range of importance. What Olson founded in Buffalo, what followed from his arrival there, begins with that. "Literary" in this context, that is both Olson's work and the work he engendered in Buffalo, has to do with two different but related issues. It refers both to the conventions, modes and procedures of writing that mark, however broadly and ambiguously, what is proposed at any given moment as "literature," and also with the "life worlds" such practices are implicated with, something loosely called, say, the "literary life," complete with all its competitions, prizes, career paths, disciplinary bodies, canonical aspirations, and so on — the literary, then, as an institution, as institutionalized practices. Crucial to Olson's sense of a move beyond or around the literary is his notion that it's possible to reconnect with or recover energies that pre-exist their historical institutionalization into a specific, fixed grammar of social practices. And even more importantly, that to do that, to push one's self toward that connection, is to disrupt or alter that grammar, a profoundly political act.

Such a move involves two crucial linked concepts — the ordinary and the archaic — and depends on an understanding of how they might be seen — or revealed — as converging in a new world. The ordinary is just that — where we are, what we do, here, today, this laundry, those dirty dishes, that which is arrayed around us. Olson's crucial move here is to understand that the ordinary, as such, is archaic, has always been, so that what we are in fact estranged from, as Heraclitus and Wittgenstein had it, is so familiar because it has always been there. In this sense, Olson's proposal is not so much anti-literary (a move which paradoxically is locked in an economy with the literary — the fate of the oppositional and the non-ordering) as pre-literary, an antithetical decentering in whose prolific and devouring wake the unprecedented is recovered.

What Olson called the projective accompanies this convergence. Like form and content in the famous proposal that emerged from the Olson/Creeley correspondence, they are really a Janus-faced energy. To take up the archaic/ordinary invokes the projective that is its method, the way forward. And to take up the projective invokes the archaic/ordinary, which is its ground.

Let me bring in one more term that is crucial to the antithetical practice here proposed — *community*, which Olson famously had as *polis*. Of all the terms so far raised, this is in some ways, given our current condition, the most difficult to come to terms with, if only because of the ubiquitous nostalgia for it. Following Jean-Luc Nancy here, I'm proposing to come at this term along the lines of what he says "happens to us — question, waiting, even imperative — in the wake of society" (Nancy 11), what appears to us as "neither a work to be produced, nor a lost communion, but rather as space itself, and the spacing of the experience of the outside, of the outside-of-self" (Nancy 19). I don't think I need to dwell here on the way Olson's sense of America as space foreshadows Nancy's proposal. One of the ways Olson's poetics as enacted in the Berkeley reading are antithetical to the literary (in both the senses given here) is in their insistence that such a discharge of energies arises from the circulation and generation of those energies within just such a space as Nancy identifies, and that that process is the act in which community reveals itself to itself.

Such a proposal undermines not so much the concept of genius (there's still room for the extraordinary within the space of the ordinary) as the promotion of individual production and the specific product, even in its current generic, non-author specific forms. It holds that work to the responsibility of an ordering intervention. Genius, as the Romantics experienced it, is really just an especially intense receptivity to those circulating energies mentioned before. But the community orders (as in ordinary) itself out of the exchange — the call and response — that arises in the projective practice of the ordinary. Whatever else such a community may be, it's a "place" where hierarchical/anti-hierarchical orderings are dissolved in a synergistic circulation of authorities (*authoritative finitudes*, Nancy might say) that egg each other on toward their further possibilities — which are the further possibilities of the self-revelation of the community as well.

The critics of the community Olson engendered in Buffalo have from the beginning proposed its defining relation as one of dominance and submission, with Olson positioned as what's been called the "High Priest." Typically, those around him then become identified as "disciples," "acolytes," or some other usually religious term meant to signify a loss of "autonomy" or "individual authority." Within such a community as I'm attempting to define here, however, such traditional vocabularies (mostly directly derived from Enlightenment polemics against the *ançien régime*) having to do with static hierarchical relations of power — equality, autonomy, derivative, original, subservient — as well as the accompanying package of anti-religious/pro-Reason pejorative labels like cult, church, disciple, etc., are drained of meaning and become inoperative, along with the cosmology that generates them. This is not to say specific persons who still passively identified themselves in that old cosmology didn't enter into such relations. But they weren't part of what I'm calling here "the community," which actively proposed itself as further. In any case, as we've known for some time now, that old cosmology (the cosmology of critical modernity)* is in acute, probably terminal crisis. One of Olson's great contributions here was, as Ralph Maud has pointed out, to link the resolution of that crisis to the emergence of the archaic/ordinary, to propose that what he called after Toynbee the post-modern is identical with the archaic/ordinary.

Don't mistake me. This exercise in clarifying vocabularies is not intended as an encompassing picture, some theory that can include Olson's work and what it engendered in Buffalo in a neat package. I only want to make clear at the outset what I see as the provocation and the challenge before turning to what followed from that, the response to that call, what Olson furthered. It equally moved the other way. Each call elicits a response, but each response in turn becomes a call. That is the circulation of authoritative finitudes. How else understand what happens with Frontier Press or in the *Magazine of Further Studies*, for instance, unless you simply want to give up the game and resort to literary judgments, which in the final case can only say what isn't ("this isn't literature"), not what is. Given that, each instance in this circulation remains its own splendid and irreducible finitude.

The earliest appearance of community in this sense was around Harvey Brown's Frontier Press. Harvey Brown came to Buffalo in the fall of 1964. Like many of the others then flocking to the city, he came from Cleveland, Ohio, via the Al Cook connection. Cook, who had been teaching at Case Western, was hired as Chair of the English Department at the new State University of New York and was given tremendous resources to build the Department. Many of those he had worked with and taught at Case Western were hired to teach at Buffalo, or followed others there as students. Unlike most others, however, Brown was a millionaire, a designation that still meant something of consequence in 1964. His grandfather had invented a mechanism that facilitated the off-loading of materials from river barges, and the money he accumulated from his invention propelled his family into the upper echelons of Ohio society.

By the time Harvey Brown got to Buffalo, he had rejected both his social position, preferring the company of jazz musicians to debutantes, and his financial position. His relation to the money he inherited was based on the understanding that it embodied two contradictory energies or powers: accumulation and circulation. Call them angels. Brown felt that to capitulate to the angel of accumulation was to give power over your life to money, to allow it to rule your spirit. To give that power over to the angel of circulation, on the

---

*Writing of the modern critical passion, Octavio Paz says: "In love with itself and at war with itself, it cannot affirm anything permanent or take any principle as base, it's sole principle being the negation of all principles, perpetual change" (5).

other hand, was to subjugate money to spirit. That was the path he chose, and Olson became one of the main instruments he used to realize it.

Harvey Brown's connection with Charles Olson was immediate and intense. In so far as they shared a sense of political priorities, Olson fit into Brown's plans to use his money to further certain specific ends. Brown, through his connections with jazz musicians in New York and Cleveland, had started a recording company to further the work of struggling artists such as Don Cherry, Ornette Coleman, Clifford Brown, and Clifford Jordan. Brown understood the work of these artists to constitute the ground of a new American republic, the visionary incarnation of Winthrop's "City on a Hill." It was an eccentric community whose importance was both in its antithetical message, and in the method it had pioneered: improvisation based on the call and response of traditional African-American music (see Brown's fascicle "Jazz Playing" in *A Curriculum of the Soul*). That method for Brown resonated precisely with Olson's sense of the projective, and that correspondence provided the basis for Brown's ongoing support for both the recording project, and for Frontier Press.

His first act was to fund the *Niagara Frontier Review*. After he arrived in Buffalo during the fall semester of 1964, he took over active editorship of the magazine. The *Niagara Frontier Review* eventually ran to three issues between 1964 and 1966, and became one of the centers for the diverse writers represented in Allen's anthology. In addition to Charles Olson, Edward Dorn, John Weiners, Ray Bremser, Robert Duncan, Gary Snyder, and LeRoi Jone (Amiri Baraka), the magazine also carried work by John Temple, Diana DiPrima, Albert Glover, Fred Wah, the jazz musician Don Cherry, Stephen Rodefer, Herbert Huncke, Charles Boer, and Andrew Crozier. The third issue also carried Cantos CX and 116 by Ezra Pound.

Olson's interest, however, extended beyond the magazine, and largely through his instigation, Harvey Brown expanded Frontier Press into book publishing. The initial idea was to publish books central to Olson's current thinking but otherwise out of print. The project soon expanded far beyond that, however, with the "editorial" participation of Ed and Jenny Dorn, and Ron Caplan, so that the list eventually emerged out of a kind of uncentered collectivity. Deeply interested in the new poetries then emerging, Caplan had first met Olson in 1963 when he'd gone to visit the poet in Gloucester. As the book-publishing venture took shape, Olson suggested to Brown that Caplan, who had a small design business in his native Pittsburgh, be involved in designing the books. Given their shared interest, Caplan's involvement soon extended beyond design, to participation in the selection of books for the press's list. The Dorn's had been in Buffalo that summer when Ed Dorn taught in the first Buffalo Summer Program in Modern Literature. The process was so open, that it's almost impossible at this point to know who was responsible for which books. Ron Caplan writes, it was "eccentric but with a strange unity."

> I know there were books I loved that I wished were in print — the Haniel Long stuff in particular, and *Spring and All*. I think *Mid-American Chants* was something we both had in waiting. Lenz is Harvey. I THINK I remember it being something Dorn wanted. . . . I think Olson was the main person to please in choosing the books. Then Dorn. Then? Perhaps me . . . .[*]

Between 1967 and 1971, Frontier Press published twenty-five books and pamphlets. There is no other list quite like it (see Appendix A for a checklist of the publications). For all of its eclectic mix, however, it is possible to discern certain unifying features.

It is above all else a political list, though the definition of politics here needs to be pushed beyond its institutional sense toward a kind of visionary activism (see Charles Olson's 1968 Berkeley lecture). During the time the press was active, the U.S. war against Viet Nam was in full swing, and the social discord it bred in the U.S. was reaching crisis proportions. More and more Americans actively opposed a government that, in turn, was trying desperately to repress them, using increasingly violent tactics that culminated in the slaughter of unarmed students at Jackson State University and Kent State University in May of 1970. All those involved in Frontier Press shared a sense of the extremity of the Constitutional crisis and an understanding that it was first and foremost a visionary crisis. To move ahead (to finally discover America) necessitated the nurturing of an eccentric, antithetical community that might provide the ground of an American conversion, as Emerson would have it. Call it a recovery of what had been lost to the usurpation of America by the Angel of Accumulation.

The politics of the Frontier Press list proliferate in unpredictable and often surprising directions. The core books suggested by Charles Olson — Brooks Adams' *The New Empire*, W. E. Woodward's *Years of Madness* — characteristically propose a reading of American history that is antithetical to the authoritative history that founds the current regime of power. Adams proposes a history that explains the advent of an American Empire whose origins he locates in European pre-history. Woodward radically rereads the U.S. Civil War in terms that call into question the assumption that it was waged to end slavery.

---

[*]Caplan to Boughn, 15 July 1998.

Other books supplement that reopening of American history. The Haniel Long books are two of the most beautiful productions on the list. *Interlinear to Cabeza de Vaca* presents us with an extraordinary figure from the days of the Conquest, a Spaniard who, rather than colonising America, was possessed and transformed by what he became lost in. It leaves us in an other America, one yet to be discovered. *The Paths of the Mound-Building Indians* by Archer Butler Hulbert also moves through that range of experience. Tracking the archaic paths over which the America of today is built, the book re-opens this world to its archaic realities, the hidden realities that found and shape such mundane experiences as a trip to the store. *The Book of Daniel Drew*, with its marvellous introduction by Ed Dorn, gives us an utterly lucid and unabashed revelation of primitive accumulation in America, one most historians and free marketeers have since rushed to hide. Those politics become explicit in Alexander Berkman's *Memoirs of a Prison Anarchist*, as well as in the pamphlet *The Decline and Fall of the 'Spectacular' Commodity Economy*, reprinted from the *Situationist International* of December, 1965.

The poetry equally reflects a visionary, antithetical politics. One of the great contriubtions of Frontier Press was to reprint William Carlos Williams' *Spring and All*, which had been out of print for almost fifty years. H.D.'s *Hermetic Definition* had never been in print. It had been copied by hand by poets visiting the Beinecke Library, and circulated around the United States. Norman Holmes Pearson, H.D.'s literary executor, claimed that he was unable to place it with a publisher of sufficient standing and proposed that Brown was trying to make a profit off the pirated edition. Both Brown and Caplan felt that Pearson was holding back the book for reasons of his own, and that the only way to force his hand was to go ahead and get it in print. In any case, there was a great clamour among poets to have the poems made available so that they could work with them. From the point of view of many poets, the prestige of the publisher was less important than having the poems to work with, and that was the position that Brown took. He illegally published the text, beautifully designed by Ron Caplan, in 1971, and continued to distribute it free until he died. Within a year of the Frontier publications of *Spring and All* and *Hermetic Definition*, both books had been copyrighted and published by New Directions in trade editions and have been in print ever since.

Frontier Press was also well known for publishing contemporary poetry and fiction in beautiful editions designed by Graham Macintosh, Ron Caplan, and Philip Trussell. The writing was extremely diverse, including work by Edward Dorn, Edward Sanders, Michael McClure, Stan Brakhage, Albert Glover, and Robert Kelly. As different as all of those writers are, most of them had been in Buffalo during this period, and had participated in the energetic exchanges that took place there. Not that they constituted in that sense a unity, or held some common "theory." Only that the energies unleashed arose out of a common provocation, and are, in that very general sense, part of a community, both the more general community that the Allen anthology registers, as well as the community specific to Buffalo at that moment.

Some of the work — Sanders' *Peace Eye*, for instance — is specifically political in its address. But even the work that isn't — Dorn's love poems, McClure's mammalian cosmological body poem, Kelly's visionary investigations — are radical departures from the then (and largely still) dominant notion of the well-made poem as literary construct. That departure for parts unknown to the "literary" imagination constitutes, even more than any explicit content otherwise would, the nature of the "political" as it in turn constituted this antithetical community.

One of the criticisms of Frontier Press that eventually arose from within that community was that, however valuable the work being done, the high quality of the production standards themselves were interfering with, or slowing down, the circulation of the work. Not that Brown's work wasn't deeply admired. But some people wanted to be able to get things in print faster. "Some of us wanted to move more quickly than Harvey," Fred Wah writes.[*] Wah had come to Buffalo from Vancouver via New Mexico, drawn by Al Cook's active solicitation of poets to join the new program at Buffalo. He had become involved on the editorial board of Niagara Frontier Review at Olson's suggestion. At the time he was a graduate student in linguistics taking Olson's seminars. Sharing Wah's desire for more speed were John Clarke, a new Assistant Professor in the English Department, and Albert Glover, a graduate student in Olson's seminars.

Clarke had met Olson in the spring of 1964. Al Cook had directed Clarke's dissertation on William Blake and was trying to hire him away from the University of Illinois, Champagne-Urbana. Clarke came to the interview knowing nothing of Olson, and with several reservations about the possible move to Buffalo. After the interview, there was a party at Cook's house. Clarke recalled:

> Later that night Charles came down to the party. I was sitting on a straight chair by the fireplace and he sat down on the couch, like so ——*— and the connection was instaneous — maybe that's a new word, I meant instantaneous, but like that one better, it accents the *sta* etymon . . . . Olson's report of the meeting, as someone later told me, was that he dug my pants, the material they were made of, and the

---
[*]Wah to Boughn, 7 August 1998.

way I was sitting with my legs crossed. Upshot of course was that all other considerations were blown away: I was coming to Buffalo.[*]

Al Glover had come to Buffalo in the fall of 1964 from McGill University. He was following his teacher, Irving Massey, whom Cook had also hired. Knowing nothing of Olson, but being deeply interested in contemporary poetry (he had won a poetry prize at McGill the year after Leonard Cohen had won the same prize) Glover enrolled in Olson's two graduate seminars ("Poetry and Myth" and "Contemporary Poetry"). The fourth person involved in the move toward more speed was George Butterick, later to be Olson's editor and literary executor.

The issue these four were addressing with their collective desire for more speed was the "projective" and the community founded on it. The projective method relies on speed — speed of production and speed of circulation — in order to reach a kind of escape velocity needed to break free from the inertial pull of the "literary." Before Olson left Buffalo in the fall of 1965, he had proposed founding an Institute along the lines of the Princeton Institute of Advanced Studies, with which he'd been connected through Black Mountain College. When he left, and Al Cook was unsuccessful in getting the new University at Buffalo to support the project, Clarke, Wah, Glover, and Butterick decided to go ahead on their own.

They immediately began publishing *The Magazine of Further Studies*, the first issue of which appeared in the fall of 1965. "I think it was Glover's IBM Selectric we used," Fred Wah writes. "And we got a big roll of corrugated stuff for covers . . . and us and our wives wld set up in one of our basements and cut covers and paint chicken blood (George wanted the thing to decay in the readers' hands) and glue fur." Butterick's desire for decay emphasized the projective nature of the magazine, the fact that as you held it, it disintegrated, leaving you with nothing to hold on to but what was further. Butterick was successful in that the various objects and substances applied to the covers of the magazine have by and large either faded over time or fallen off.

Between 1965 and 1969 IFS published six issues (see Appendix B, item 8). Al Glover describes the first issue as "awkward" beside the professionalism of the Niagara Frontier Review: "this homemade thing that did put most people off. The lucky part was that Charles (and then Robert Duncan shortly) were interested in finding a means of production

---

[*]Clarke to Clark, 23 October 1986.

outside the establishment, even the 'small press' one."[†] Olson joined the conversation in the second issue, Duncan in the sixth.

The magazine was unique for its time for a couple of reasons, both of which had to do with the rejection of the showcase model of the poetry magazine, already prevalent even then among small press magazines. The showcase magazine typically presents poems completely isolated and decontextualized. They appear as beautiful (or ugly) objects on the page. This mode of presentation reinforces the culture of the literary by stripping the poem from the intellectual matrix it is part of, and then emphasizing its object status as a pure literary event.

The Magazine of Further Studies refused, first of all, to isolate the poem. It included, in the body of the magazine, letters, prose exchanges, and bibliographies (most from the Poetry/Myth class John Clarke took over when Olson left), so that the poems that were also presented there were clearly proposed as simply one kind of event in a larger discourse that included many different kinds of events. They were not proposed as products with implicit value in and of themselves. On the contrary, the larger discourse was emphasized.

As the magazine developed, it increasingly embodied an active conversation, further undermining the product-status of the "poetry" it included. Rather than including poems intended as finished and self-sufficient literary products, the magazine increasingly published fragments, challenges, responses, broken utterances that provoked other broken, incomplete utterances, so that by the final issue, the magazine had become a kind of clamor, a convocation of a conversation, in action. The result is that even within a single issue, there is nothing to hold on to, not even a poem, which can be proposed as "literature." There is rather an event that is constantly pushing beyond itself.

The Institute of Further Studies went on to publish a number of items that reinforce this sense of an antithetical dynamic. In 1968, there was a burst of small publications, designed as "letters." The goal, according to Al Glover, "was to be fastest, and Charles did, in fact, love the speed."[†] Olson would send poems he'd just written from Gloucester and they'd be printed and distributed within a week (see Appendix B, items 3,4,5,7). Again, the push here was to move the poem into the realm of discourse, communication, provocation, and conversation, and away from the object-status that turned it into a commodity and founded the culture of the "literary."

---

[*]Glover to Boughn, 28 August 1998.

[†]Glover to Boughn, 22 May 1998.

Other publications pushed toward the same goal. John Clarke pushed the Institute to publish plate twenty-five from William Blake's *Milton*. His plan, though it wasn't finally realized, was to mail the "letter" to the delegates to the Democratic Party convention in Chicago. The Olson note, item 4, was another provocation printed as a postcard for immediate dissemination.

Perhaps the most lasting accomplishment of the Institute of Further Studies has been the ongoing publication of A Curriculum of the Soul. Olson's "poem," "A Plan for a Curriculum of the Soul," first appeared in *The Magazine of Further Studies* 5. After Olson's death, the Institute decided to break up the curriculum into discrete topics and get different writers to take them on. Twenty-nine fascicles (including one numbered 0 — Charles Olson's "Pleistocene Man"), initially imagined as akin to the Cambridge Ancient History Project, were assigned to various poets with relationships to Olson's work. Al Glover has called it both "a collaborative epic," (Glover, Review) and "a bouquet on the grave"[*]:

> Original "vision" was of a large book written by "Olson" — and I would still, someday, hope to publish it as such. It is that sense of "Homer" and would make only the second one (this one, of course, somewhat different in its concept of "history" and "narrative") in "the tradition." You see it in "The Mushroom" ("as if we were all one voice / of various sounds" — since revised: "we are all one voice / of various sounds."[†]

The reference to "Homer" here is to Milman Perry's famous proposal that in fact, rather then being an individual, Homer was the name given to a collective of bards who had invented and assembled the *Iliad* and the *Odyssey* over hundreds of years. The notion of "epic" as it's deployed here, and as it always was used by Olson, is not what is now proposed as a monomaniacal drive toward a singular representation of the world. Olson always saw epic in that sense as a late, literary derivation, something he hated.[‡] The pre-literary "epic," as he proposed it, was a communal invention of culturally shared narrative meanings, the invention of a cohesion of diversities within the otherness of language. The problem for

---

[*] Glover to Boughn, 28 August 1998.

[†] Glover to Boughn, 2 September 1998.

[‡] "WHY I HATE / Greeks & Italians / [The Vatican since / Dante / [Grecian since / the earliest Renaissance / —including in fact Thomas Aquinas at least] / is / the Classical — Representational, either one / THE STATE———COLORED TELEVISION" (Olson 17).

Olson was how get to a procedure, a method that would make possible a similar mode of knowing/speaking as/for community.

A Curriculum of the Soul certainly addresses that issue in its own way. Whether it is truly an epic is in a sense beside the point. Perhaps more important is its conscious invocation of a specific notion of community. The community revealed here in relation to Olson's provocation and the call and response of the participants is anything but uniform, anything then but a communion with and within, say, a "theory," the unobstructed visibility of what John Clarke called the MONO. It is rather a register of the immensity and incommensurability of the relations of authoritative finitudes circulating within and beyond the space of the thought Olson's work provokes.

Both this sense of community and of epic are central to understanding the work of John Clarke which always moved, as he proposed in his seminal work on poetics, *From Feathers to Iron*, "to [constellate] the epiphany in a communal place" (Clarke 152).* Perhaps more than anyone else to emerge from "Olson's Buffalo," Clarke worked with unwavering dedication to further the understanding of the complex implications of the notions that haunt this essay, and to realize them in his life and work. Never given to the kinds of self-promotion required for literary success, he was largely unknown outside a small group of dedicated readers when he died in 1992. "I personally enjoy the ultimate freedom of being unknown," he wrote to his friend, Albert Glover (Glover, Review)

Clarke's work culminated in three interrelated efforts: the editing of *intent.: letter of talk thinking & document*, *From Feathers to Iron: A Concourse of World Poetics*, and *In the Analogy*, which is made up of six books, each consisting of a sequence of forty sonnets, and a seventh incomplete book. In many ways, the newsletter, *intent.*, was a furthering of the work begun in the *Magazine of Further Studies*. By the time of its publication (11 issues between 1989-91) small press magazines had generally opted for the showcase model, though some exceptions existed. *Exquisite Corpse*, *Sulfur*, and *Rolling Stock*, for instance, embedded poetry in a context of reviews, polemical articles, and letters. By and large, though, even those magazines that thus contextualized poetry, still presented the poems themselves as literary productions.

Clarke's goal in *intent.* was to provide an alternative to that state of affairs. In a letter to Tom Clark, for instance, he discussed using the poems Clark sent as reviews, situating them in discussions of films that themselves were embedded in the thematic discourse of each specific issue of the newsletter. Clarke's insistence that all submissions, including poems,

---

*Octavio Paz, Clarke points out, calls this the "convocation and gravitation of the world in a magnetic here."

adhere to the particular theme of a given issue was a way of establishing each issue, not as a showcase, but as a space within which a community was revealed at work in language.*

Each issue embodied that community in conversation by including a wide range of work that was transgenerational and trans-genre-ational. The lead article was always from the ancestors, establishing the continuity of the conversation. Charles Olson, Robert Duncan, Eric Gill, Dora Marsden, Robert McAlmon, Simone Weil, and H.D. were featured in various issues. Art work, poems, reviews, essays, and letters were collected from sources as diverse as the Fugger Newsletter, contemporary writers, both known and relatively unknown, musicians, and children of various ages, some as young as seven or eight. The operative center of each issue was "The Mail," an encapsulation of the enormous correspondence Clarke carried out with myriad writers around the world, as well as what he came to call "The Editor's Quotron." The Quotron was a collection of quotes from diverse sources relevant to the particular theme at hand. It extended the conversation taking place in the newsletter beyond the bounds of the particular moment, or perhaps more accurately, situated that moment in its further complexity. This use of quotation as a way of locating the work in a world of thinking and talk became crucial to the practice of the epic that Clarke developed in his own poetry.

The two places where, in his final years, he worked that out were *From Feathers to Iron* and *In the Analogy*. These two books can be seen as embodying the theory and practice of Clarke's projective art — though such a distinction finally won't hold up. *Feathers*, the book of "poetics," is not only a "poetic" text — a text where language is constantly pushed toward what Roman Jackobson called the "poetic function" — it literally incorporates poetry in its body. Clarke's earlier book of poems, *The End of This Side*, is reprinted within the text as part of an elaborate complicating counterstructure of footnotes that amplify, develop, and sometimes overtake the thinking of the text. In the same way, *In the Analogy* develops a complex argument within the structure of the sonnet sequences, while also incorporating chunks of "theoretical" thinking in the numerous quotations which precede each of the sonnets. In this way Clarke confronts and demolishes the still dominant Platonic notion that poetry and thought are distinct, even at odds with one another. He creates an interdependence of texts that enacts a complex passionate thinking.

This work was not meant to demolish or escape genre. Rather it's meant to call our attention to the inadequacies of our thinking of it, and comes out of Clarke's reading of Romanticism as an unfinished project. Blake, Friedrich Schlegel, Novalis, and Coleridge

---

*Themes included Plants & Animals, For the Sexes, Alphabetics, UFOs, Heaven, Trust, and Embryons.

were all active in his thinking here. The title of *From Feathers to Iron* is taken from a letter by John Keats. At the heart of the writing is Clarke's ongoing struggle to further Olson's work with the epic. As Clarke thinks the issue through in *Feathers*, it becomes evident that the issue is not a literary problem. If anything, it might be called a political problem, as long as politics is kept located within the visionary. His push is always toward the reconstitution, or re-cognition, of the elsewhere here, something he argues we lost with the collapse of Minoan civilization. This is one of the ways in which he continued to address Olson's proposal about the archaic/ordinary. *From Feathers to Iron*, a complex and difficult book that defies summary, proposes the problem as a loss of order and sees the epic as the form of what it calls "the strengthening method of world completion." Within this framework, poetry plays a role that has nothing to do with the literary.

By the late 1980s, Clarke had been writing sonnets for a number of years. More than 1,000 of them remain unpublished in his notebooks. For someone so thoroughly focussed on the importance of the epic, it was always curious to him that he had been given to write so extensively in what was the quintessential lyric form. During the last five years of his life he came to see how he could push that form beyond its limits toward the scope necessary for the epic. The result was an enormous outpouring of work that he called *In the Analogy*. It consists of six completed books and a fragmentary seventh. Clarke's plan, as Cass Clarke has transcribed it in the opening pages of *In the Analogy*, was to write twelve books, pushing it toward the classic epic form. The fact that it remains fragmentary itself is significant.

Of all the recent criticism that has been leveled against the epic, the most serious has focussed on the inherent totalitarianism of the form as handed down in the literary tradition from Virgil to Pound. As John Thorpe has pointed out in the introduction of *From Feathers to Iron*, however, "Clarke doesn't envision the epic as a literary genre so much as an inherent human narrative comprehension, wherever there's an interplay of story with its telling." In *In the Analogy*, Clarke made that archaic comprehension a continuing projective event of community, the voice not of a single person (or even mythic persona), but of a world, itself revealed in a clamor of relations.

One of the ways he accomplished this was to embed each sonnet, as well as each sequence of sonnets, deeply within a world of thought. He did this by preceding each poem and each sequence of poems with a number of quotations. The quotes are myriad and diverse, and they provide a universe within which the poems are actively located in conversation. Some quotes mirror the poem, others contradict it, some seem to be its inspiration, while others raise questions about the issues it addresses, and still others develop thinking tangential to it. The overall result is to push the reader into the world of thought out of which the poems arise. The very notion, "Clarke's poems," is called actively into question at every moment, even as the poems proceed to address the questions crucial to the epic impulse as it asserts itself here, now. This is what Clarke calls a non-central position, as opposed to a non-ordering intervention. That this epic finally is fragmentary is a fact itself as rich and full of complexity as every other aspect of this truly extraordinary work.

The influence of Olson's Buffalo — and finally it must be seen, I think, in those collective terms rather than singularly — is not easy to measure, precisely because of the resistance to the literary that is central to its thought of itself. Movements come and go. Theories are hot one day and cold the next, mirroring the dynamics of the consumer culture that gives rise to them and the controlling conceit of "modernization" that has seized hold of "reality" in this century. But the sense of "work" that this community of circulating, authoritative finitudes has consistently embodied continues to percolate quietly and invisibly in diverse corners of the world. What it will give rise to, what it has already given rise to, remains to be seen. Donald Byrd has proposed that the works "of Olson and Clarke demand our attention as few others because they occasionally find means to make and to think at once. That is, they bring evidence that there are means of preoccupation with life that is sufficient to life."* This is perhaps as accurate and concise a sense of the various threads winding through this all too brief history of Olson's Buffalo as anything I've managed to say so far. To make and to think at once. What's at stake in such a gesture will always exceed itself as it pushes to shake off the stupor of the literary and realize poetry's possible vocation.

WORKS CITED

Charke, John. *From Feathers to Iron: A Concourse of World Poetics*. Bolinas, CA: Timbouctou, 1987.

———. *In the Analogy*. Buffalo/Toronto: shuffaloff press, 1997.

Glover, Albert. Review of *In the Analogy*. *Poetry Project Newsletter* (1998).

Nancy, Jean-Luc Nancy. *The Inoperative Community*. Minneapolis: U of Minnesota P, 1991.

Olson, Charles. *Pleistocene Man*. Canton, NY: IFS, 1968.

Paz, Octavio. *Children of the Mire*. Cambridge: Harvard UP, 1974.

---

*Byrd to an informal internet discussion group, 14 August 1997.

David Landrey

ROBERT CREELEY'S AND JOEL OPPENHEIMER'S CHANGING VISIONS

Fielding Dawson had known both Robert Creeley and Joel Oppenheimer at Black Mountain when all three were in the early stages of their writing lives. Over twenty years later, Dawson wrote, in a short but prophetic piece, "On Creeley's Third Change" (which may be said to apply as well to Oppenheimer as to Creeley),

> There are, it seems to me — talk about brevity — three major changes in an artist's life and art (maybe four). The first is the approach to and a crystallizing of commitment (as in highschool and shortly after) to one's art. The second is the formation of a prototypal use of paint or language which carries us through most of our lives, and, chances are, in our forties approaches a third change no fool would desire, though we must follow and become that process of change, and in our anxiety of our present, the future changes shape, becomes, actually an odd limbo, and the past looms huge and deadly. (*Athanor* 57)

He contended that Creeley was approaching his third change and asserted that he would make it, although he acknowledged that "hardly anyone makes the third change," for, after all, the huge deadliness scares most artists away. But Dawson saw forthcoming, "anxiety *and* diminished ego, and — *and* note — the discovery of the whole or at least more complete art through constant responsiveness to all persons, places, things and feelings and all action in view of relativity." Finally: "Creeley will make death an actual future fact of his body in the awareness of his living spirit, . . . " (*Athanor* 57-58).

That was 1973. One might argue that Creeley had already begun the process with the 1969 publication of *Pieces* and had continued in *A Day Book* in 1972; and perhaps the 1970 death of their friend and mentor, Charles Olson, had done much to catalyze change in both Creeley and Oppenheimer, the latter of whom defeated alcoholism in that same year. But the first stages of change may be primarily disintegrative, not yet integrative. Change of this sort is rarely instantaneous (and perhaps never finished; or perhaps the hinted fourth change always hovers), and full engagement with their futures' "odd limbo" probably occurred later in the post-Vietnam decade with the publication by Creeley of *Later* (1979) and by Oppenheimer of *The Woman Poems* (1975). One might also note the breakup of second marriages for both men in this decade. The question for present purposes is: what have their third changes offered to the rapidly changing world of late-millennium poetry? Let us consider each separately.

CREELEY

The work of Creeley's early years was characterized especially by his famous use of linebreak and by a unique sense of person as locus of activity, not ego but the essence of the Olson figure who "stays inside himself" and "as he is participant in the larger force ... [is] able to listen, and his hearing through himself will give him secrets objects share" (*Selected Writings* 25). He would ring changes on these — never to this day abandoning either — but fragmenting both sentence and self in *Pieces* and in *A Day Book*. One might wonder why he would tamper with success. Creeley himself offers an explanation in his 1972 "Introduction to the Penguin *Selected Whitman*," saying that Whitman's vision is of use for contemporary American poets, "who can no longer assume either their world or themselves in it as discrete occasion," that Whitman "emphasizes that it is space and process which are unremittingly our condition" (*Collected Essays* 10). No doubt contributing to this less secure sense was the social upheaval of the 1960s, the various aspects of which Creeley typically internalized and increasingly responded to, often indirectly, in his poetry.

In a 1969 interview, although speaking against the Vietnam War, he noted that, "this hasn't entered my poetry. It's almost as if I've given so damn much to that idiot war I'm damned if I'm going to give it my experience of words" (*Contexts of Poetry* 194). Yet more and more the world would enter his poems, much in the way Paul Auster's narrator puts it in his novel, *Moon Palace*, as he speaks of 1968 and thereafter:

> Everyone is familiar with the story of that time, and there would be no point in going over it again. That does not mean I want it to be forgotten, however. My own story stands in the rubble of those days, and unless this fact is understood, none of it will make sense. (25)

Creeley's story since *A Day Book* (and Oppenheimer's, too, as we shall see) most eloquently stands in the rubble of those and later days, and sense (though perhaps not order) has been his quest. What had to happen for Creeley was a location in that space and process mentioned in the Whitman introduction.

At a forum in Buffalo in November 1995, Creeley said that he had come around to the necessity to be somewhere, "that you don't have to worry, that the minute you draw breath, you're on your way." He added of this placement, "You are where you are at all points" (Unpublished talk). A simple list of his titles since *Later* will begin to carry us to his evolving sense of place: *Mirrors* (1983), *Memory Gardens* (1986), *Windows* (1990), *Echoes* (1993), and *Life & Death* (1998). He has blended memory and the present, time and place; and within the volumes he locates himself at the cusps between these.

Tom Clark, in his marvelous collaboration with Creeley, *Robert Creeley and the Genius of the American Common Place* (1993), includes Creeley's long 1991 rumination, "Some Senses of the Commonplace," wherein *commonplace* refers both to language (e.g., "a passage of general application" or "trite, trivial, hackneyed") and to location. For Creeley those have never been separate, but in his "third change" he interweaves them with increasing seamlessness. In addition, Clark shows how each common place now embraces Creeley's *company*[*]: "across the bulkheads of the still isolated yet now much less rigid 'I' of Creeley's writing there flooded a new awareness of the human commonalty of all experience" (70).

So we see the unfolding of what Dawson intuited: "the discovery of the whole or at least more complete art through constant responsiveness to all persons, places, things and feelings . . . ." Friends and family permeate the poetry; the world impinges everywhere: "What/matters as one/in this world?" (*Later* 5). Furthermore, Creeley turns more often to longer poems, culminating most recently in the two almost epic pieces from *Life & Death*: "Histoire de Florida" and "The Dogs of Auckland." Oppenheimer commented favorably on this growth in a late interview:

> he's come back to a more solid base, that the poems are much more their own thing, and not just him writing what he knows how to write — that in a funny way although they're quieter he's taking chances again. He's dealing with narrative in his poems like he never did before. (Beach 97)

---

[*] One of Creeley's recurrent words, whether used to refer to "present company" or to the men and women he has been blessed to know in the world of the arts. At every forum one may hear him revel in his blessing as he says the word *company* with reverence. See the important poem "The Company" in *Windows*.

Later opens with a poem revealing the new voice. Significantly entitled, in a way typical of the old Creeley, "Myself," it cries out to a world that, in his "Autobiography," he noted, "has hardly been a nice place to live in." He begins,

> What, younger, felt
> was possible, now knows
> is not—but still
> not changed enough—

but says later,

> I want, if older,
> still to know
> why, human, men
> and women are
>
> so torn, so lost,
> why hopes cannot
> find better world
> than this. (3)

The book ends with the long "Prayer to Hermes," which concludes,

> All who know me
> say, *why* this man's
> persistent pain, the scarifying
> openness he makes do with?
>
> Agh! Brother spirit,
> what do they know
> of whatever *is* the instant
> cannot wait a minute—
>
> *will* find heaven in hell,
> *will* be there again even now,

and *will* tell of itself
all, *all* the world. (121)

So the reach is now powerfully outward, but he simultaneously builds and rebuilds his base, his standpoint — commonly within a dwelling, a scene of domesticity.[*]

Excerpting from Creeley's books has always been difficult, for each volume has a total coherence. Perhaps because there are more long poems from 1979 on, one may lose less by doing so, yet recent volumes have spoken even more as total entities, as patterns governed by their titles.[†] Nevertheless, *Later* and the thrust of his recent work may be well illustrated by three of the longest poems (as well as by what we've seen above): "Later" (the one in ten sections[‡]), "Desultory Days," and "If I Had My Way."

The first and third find him at his base, his domestic setting. In "Later" he is looking inward to the mementos of his attic and to his past as well as out the window at milieu: neighbors, political signs, etc.. Skating across the "sticky sentimental," he molds the commonplace into "a willingness/to live," to feeling his place among others, and to locating — beyond his small space but ever within it — "a home/on earth" (79).

"If I Had My Way," playing off the popular song of that name and weaving lines from it throughout the poem (a long-time Creeley technique for incorporating the commonplace), is addressed to the woman he had recently married. He achieves a crucial recognition as he meditates on what she can never know of his past; his life "learns to let go" and "lets the presence/of you be" (115). Paradoxically, letting go becomes the only way to strengthen his hold on "where you are at all points."

"Desultory Days" focuses Creeley's new admission of the political. It is a visionary work of ecological sensibility without resort to easy solutions. Quoting all of Emily Dickinson's "The Brain, within its Groove," he acknowledges sharing her "existential terror," laments the human tendency to "take everything with us," and achieves a stubborn tragic vision — a true purification (*catharsis*) of pity and terror, so that we may look them courageously in the eye (97).

Later establishes his new ground; the volumes since explore it, often presenting mortality both in unsentimental elegies, e.g. "Oh Max" in *Mirrors*, and in reflections on his own aging

---

[*] Recall that Olson had dedicated *Maximus* (1960) to Creeley as "the Figure of Outward."

[†] Past long works such as "The Door" (for Robert Duncan) or "The Finger" stand well alone. Typically, though, Creeley's work is ill-represented by anthology. Even *Selected Poems* leaves one bothered by what is missing.

[‡] Creeley uses the same titles again and again — often several times in the same volume — as if to emphasize that no single take can represent the complex vision.

(again we see Dawson's intuition realized: "Creeley will make death an actual future fact of his body in the awareness of his living spirit"). His viewpoint (and the book covers so beautifully illustrate it) is composed of windows, doorways, mirrors, passageways, photos, etc. — all set at curious angles to what may be seen in, through, and beyond them. He is now freer to find the locale for such angles of vision in diverse places, e.g., Finland, New Zealand (Creeley has been a constant world traveller in recent years), as if to prove that his home is indeed "on earth."

Full examination of the volumes since 1979 will not be necessary, nor does space permit. A brief selection of lines expressive of his new sense of place will suffice.

A two-stanza poem in *Mirrors*, "Some Echo," finds Creeley thinking on his own thought of nature:

and thought is a patient security then,
a thing in mind at best or else
some echo of physical world
it is but can know nothing of. (58)

Thought *is* part of the world, is comforting and essential and inevitable, but ultimately it cannot know the world — a veritable presentation of existential absurdity.[*]

In "Help," from *Windows*, recalling the "curious stumble" life has been to get where he is, he concludes,

Now you're inside entirely,
he whispers in mock self-assurance,
because he recognizes at last, by god,
he's not all there is. (120)

Again we see his dual vision of self and other, but he manifests some sense of satisfaction about the long journey.

A final example is from *Echoes* and may be seen as a summation of Creeley's coming to place. The poem is "This House." It begins, as so many of these later poems, with Creeley

---

[*]Creeley established, at SUNY Buffalo, and sponsored for over ten years, the annual "Charles Olson Memorial Lectures." The first, in 1979, was given by Robert Duncan, during which he said: "We will always be at a place where we face what we cannot know. . . . How to have a world that is so illustrated that we don't confront what we confront all the time, and that is that some vast part of it isn't even anything we can possibly experience; and we, of course, are exactly of that vast part."

inside looking out: "Such familiar space/out there, the window/frame's locating . . . ." He then balances present and past, confusion and sense, invoking the house to hold on, and concludes,

> You are my mind
> made particular,
> my heart in its place. (74)

Person and place have found their necessary fusion.

Impossible here to address the achievment of *Life & Death*. Let it simply be said that "Histoire de Florida" and "The Dogs of Auckland" show Creeley at home wherever he is, still tensely poised in relation to locale and past, still troubled, but able utterly to render the circumstances of life in a torn world and to demonstrate the person's capacity to carry on. Asked by Andrei Codrescu and Laura Rosenthal for a poem to be included in their anthology, *American Poets Say Goodbye to the Twentieth Century*, Creeley replied with "Goodbye" and then included it in *Life & Death*. In it he wonders why the century had to kill everything in sight and ponders his own role in it as a camera "set to expose"; but he comes around to a simple resolution: "I want no sentimentality./I want no more than home" (36)

OPPENHEIMER

1970 WAS A WATERSHED YEAR for Joel Oppenheimer. Not only, as mentioned above, did his mentor, Charles Olson, die and his alcohol habit end, but he wrote a memoir of Olson for *The Village Voice*, his fourth piece for that journal in two years. By 1971 he was writing a regular column for the *Voice* and was to do so through late 1984. Largely because of this, he was able eventually to stabilize his academic career — to hold the Caroline Werner Gannett Distinguished Visiting Professor of the Humanities chair at Rochester Institute of Technology in 1984-85 and to find a new and final place as professor of poetry and journalism at New England College in New Hampshire.

More important than jobs, though, was the change wrought in his poetry. Like Creeley, he had established a unique style in the 1950s and 1960s, one which he formed under the influence of Olson, one characterized by short lines, use of lower case, and cryptic twists; and he became known as a writer of occasional verse. All of this was achieved in what he called a discursive voice.

An inveterate story-teller, Oppenheimer often told of the development of that voice. Writing for a class with Olson at Black Mountain, he submitted a manuscript done with various Olson techniques (open parentheses, mythic overtones, various line indentations). It came back with a single comment by Olson: "Dear Joel, I have enough trouble writing these damn things myself. Find your own voice" (Beach 90). A few years later, probably 1961, when Olson visited New York City, Oppenheimer shyly asked his mentor to read the long "The Fourth Ark Royal." Olson did so and commented, "Great. This is what I've been waiting for. You've always had this discursive quality, like you tell great jokes, and you've made it happen in the poems" (Beach 94).

Oppenheimer had thus achieved his second change at age 31, but he recalls that, as he worked his discursive voice into longer poems, "I got awfully pretentious and sententious" (Beach 99). Then came the *Voice* columns, wherein he was confined by editor Ross Wetzsteon to an approximately 700 word space, which became known as the "Oppenheimer Box."[*] In his SUNY Buffalo "Charles Olson Memorial" lectures of 1982 (the fourth in the series after Robert Duncan, Michael McClure, and Edward Sanders), he says, "I had to get out of [discursiveness] through the *Voice* columns and get back to the sparseness. Retain the voice but stop throwing so much stuff in" (SUNY tape).

Sparseness and the discursive became curiously blended in his "third change" and were a perfect analogue for his new creative life and vision. That is, he hunkered down in search of a proper place to raise his two youngest sons, Nat and Lem, a place increasingly steeped in tradition, even as his poems — no doubt cued by the permission, granted by writing the *Voice* columns, to speculate and comment — moved out into the world of social issues and politics. Thus, though vastly different in tone and style from Creeley's, his work adopts a similar stance, that of the figure inside, looking out, "An acute chronicler of the decline of his civilization" (*Drawing From Life* xii). And, as Creeley had, he located new standpoints. The volume *New Spaces* (1983), perhaps the best of his late work, is a direct recognition of his expansion, a fact he further recognizes in the dedication to *Why Not* two years later:

> for the friends who have
> taken me in and
> sheltered me and
> fed me so well
> in laurinburg

---

[*]For more on this, see *Drawing From Life*, eds. Robert J. Bertholf and David Landrey (Wakefield, RI: Asphodel Press,1997), a collection of Oppenheimer *Voice* columns.

>
> and bar harbor
> and oneonta
> and buffalo
> and henniker
> and rochester
>
> "seeing them i still open
> still enclose myself in them" (*Collected Later* 331)

The Woman Poems (1975) was Oppenheimer's breakthrough. He frequently testified that the poems of this volume were a rare instance of his having been "given" the material, "that the muse had come in and was sitting there" (*Ecology* 30). In 1971 he had heard Robert Bly lecture about the Great Mother; two years later he read Bly's "I Came Out of the Mother Naked," and "these poems started bubbling out" (*Ecology* 30). Significantly, his second marriage was deteriorating and was to end in 1975.*

The Woman Poems is a fiercely direct confrontation of all aspects of The Great Mother — as mother, lover, destroyer, muse, etc.. But it's more. In a class at Buffalo State College in 1978, because of the flagrant content and language of the work, one student returned the book for a refund, and the males in the class seemed puzzled and embarrassed. Quickly, though, the women saw and admired his purpose. They saw that Oppenheimer was addressing, in himself and in history, the presumptions and obsessions of men, that he was admitting his own worst impulses, but that he was also discovering how to change:

>   i
> want to fuck you, and
> if poems still come
> then that will be alright,
> but that is secondary.
> i have discovered what
> is secondary, what is first. (*Collected Later* 47)

Furthermore, in "Screaming Poem," he finds something new inside:

---

*For a thorough and insightful analysis of this, see Lyman Gilmore, *Don't Touch the Poet: The Life and Times of Joel Oppenheimer* (Jersey City, NJ: Talisman House,1998). Gilmore deals also with the mixed reception of *The Woman Poems*.

> the woman inside me
> does not murmur she
> screams. it has
> been so ever since
> i gave up breast for
> bottle, the geometry
> of shapes for the
> algebra of numbers.
> this woman claws at
> my innards, sits
> patiently waiting, beats
> in my head, wakes up
> when i sleep, occasionally
> relents, opening herself
> before me. i don't
> know what to do when
> that happens, draw back,
> look for the solace of
> straight lines, draw
> plans all night on my
> checkered graph paper,
> plan out the rational life
> of a man, and make no
> room for magics. i am
> torn by the ravening
> screams echoing over
> and over. love. love. love. (*Collected Later* 33)

Ross Wetzsteon spoke of Oppenheimer as "A hard-drinking Bohemian, a wencher" (*Drawing From Life* xvii), and so he had been, but, as he studied the ambivalences within himself and within society, he moved on, and so did the poetry.

Oppenheimer never lost his essential lustiness — not in life nor in poetry — but from *The Woman Poems* until his death in 1988, the work was grounded in a sense of community and in a keen sense of location in his places. As Robert J. Bertholf says in his introduction to the *Collected Later Poems*, Oppenheimer saw "how to live one's life in an authentic way in the middle of New York City" and "made up the streets and passages of urban space as accurately as he made up the rural forms of behavior in the poems written in New Hampshire late in his life" (xviii). Among his recurring themes to this end were baseball, the household, and holidays such as the neglected Ground Hog Day (especially important to him as honoring Persephone's return from the underworld).

"First Poem For My Last Son," in *Names, Dates & Places* (1978), admits that for all his efforts at fathering, "i have lost it again/as with all my sons," but the poet opens himself to learn from the child:

> but i will try to learn to walk
> at least while you can teach me
> but you must bear with me
> since it is hard even though
> i try my damnedest. (*Collected Later* 103)

"Poem For the New Year" questions to what his new vision may lead:

> having been
> a dirty young man shall
> i now start being clean? (*Collected Later* 112)

The answer appears to be "yes," but the cleansing requires tenacity:

> we walk on, and sleep each night.
> he said: hold on, hold on,
> until the new vision comes.
> it comes, it opens up,
> it always comes. but some years
> are long waits in which we
> sleep and dream of basilisks
> and mother medusa waiting
> waiting to stop us. (*Collected Later* 113)[*]

---

[*] "He," elsewhere in the poem called "the old poet," is Charles Olson, still the mentor, even in dreams.

Names, Dates & Places then works through a variety of domestic settings until the end.* Two of the last four poems are fine examples of political verse. In "If There Were Sense," Oppenheimer wonders, in the face of "the country/lost," "where I should be," and dreams of being part of brigades forming to march towards Wounded Knee and finally to shout, "give it back":

> give them
> their land. they can do
> no worse. give them their
> hostages against fate, their
> lives against death, give them
> give them give them give them. (*Collected Later* 129)

In "Celebrating the Peace," looking out at the people of his Greenwich Village, he provides a chilling antidote to the euphoria prompted by the end of the Vietnam War, and concludes,

> there is never any peace
> there will never be peace
> the war goes on
> the marines are landing
> we don't take shit from anyone
> we'll show them
> peace is not a victory but a natural state
> do not celebrate the end of war
> nobody wins. (*Collected Later* 135)

A few poems may serve as representations of the rich diversity of *New Spaces* (1985). In "A Village Poem," wherein he recounts taking his son to the Cedar Tavern, long one of his hangouts, Oppenheimer recalls events involving such figures as Franz Kline and Jackson Pollock, sees that his son sees, and that:

---

*Oppenheimer often told the story of Gregory Corso at a party making advances to Joel's wife. When she rebuffed him, saying, "Gregory, you know I'm Joel Oppenheimer's wife," he allegedly replied, "Joel Oppenheimer? The Domestic Poet?"

> it is history whether we
> want it or not
> it is what we learn from
> it where the paintings
> come from and the poems. (*Collected Later* 237)

"Lessons I" and "Lessons II" cast his personal history in the light of Menelaus's returning to Sparta with Helen (the name of Oppenheimer's wife at the time as well) after the Trojan War. "Acts" is a poignant parallelling of a walk with his son and his own father's taking him to Madison Square Garden to see Hugo Zacchini, the "human cannonball." The volume concludes with two long poems, "Cacti" and "Houses," two works his audiences invariably asked him to read. Both make the personal and domestic universal and leave us with a rich sense of how, like the cacti, to survive in a more-and-more hostile environment.

Oppenheimer's final environment was anything but hostile. Henniker, New Hampshire, home of New England College, took him in and gave him a final permission for his enlarged spirit. *New Hampshire Journal* (1994) finds him facing death with unsentimental courage. The series begins with "Chaos," which recognizes that,

> FORM we reach
> occasionally
> then fall back
> into chaos
> to start again
> renewed. (*Collected Later* 390)

It ends with "Animals," wherein he locates his failing body alongside neighbors' goat and dog and renders final loss with dignity. Along the way he tells of hearing of a friend's loss of his son and speculates about what he might offer:

> there are no answers
> but we are more able
> to bear that each time
>
> I cannot tell you more
> though you ask

>   you ask and asking
>   make me feel wise
>
>   we do our work
>   we believe it matters
>
>   if we cannot do this
>   we will stop working
>
>   we will stop
>
>   we will stop all. (*Collected Later* 409)

This final affirmation of the power of the poetic act is his great legacy.

ROBERT CREELEY AND JOEL OPPENHEIMER had achieved their best known verse innovations before 1970. They would continue to experiment, gravitating to longer poems especially, but their basic sense of the line, developed as "dutiful sons" of William Carlos Williams, has remained essentially the same.* Oppenheimer, in the *Sagetrieb* interview, did argue that Black Mountain poets did not write like one another, saying,

> If you read the poems carefully, you'll see that Creeley's poems, that early stuff, is far more complex than mine, far more involuted, turned in on itself, dramatically both more complicated and more "interesting" than mine — that I'm aiming, almost consciously then and more consciously as I went along, to get close to a flatness of syntax, a flatness of speech, a non-interference in order to let the words come through, and that Creeley's almost going at the problem from the opposite direction by turning the language inside-outside, by forcing the syntax in awkward situations to make you then concentrate on the words and the images. (Beach 95)

---

*Oppenheimer's first book, published by Jonathan Williams, was *The Dutiful Son* (1956), a title honoring Williams. Creeley's and Williams's relationship has been documented often.

He added, "Bob's poetry is always very introspective. I mean, he's, certainly in the early stuff, trying to figure out where *he* is in this crazy universe. I'm trying to figure out the universe" (Beach 96). Furthermore, Oppenheimer was proud of having eliminated punctuation in his late work, thus enhancing the flat voice, which was evident in his oral presentations (Creeley's are tense, dramatic). Still, stylistic innovation precedes our period.

What Creeley and Oppenheimer offer is a new sense of place in a fluxional time (a "crazy universe"), or, perhaps, guidance in how to locate a place. They are both willing to risk their spirits in moves to new spaces, acting as suffering servants for their readers; and we may say of them, as their mentor Olson said of that great risk-taker Herman Melville, "He lived intensely his people's wrong, their guilt. But he remembered the first dream" (*Call Me Ishmael* 15).

WORKS CITED

Auster, Paul. *Moon Palace*. New York: Penguin Books, 1989.
Beach, Christopher. "Interview with Joel Oppenheimer." *Sagetrieb* 7:2, Fall 1988.
Clark, Tom. *Robert Creeley and the Genius of the American Common Place*. New York: New Directions, 1993.
Creeley, Robert. *Collected Essays*. Berkeley & Los Angeles: U of California P, 1989.
-------. *Contexts of Poetry: Interviews 1961-1971*. Ed. Donald Allen. Bolinas, CA: Four Seasons Foundation, 1973.
-------. *Echoes*. New York: New Directions, 1993.
-------. *Later*. New York: New Directions, 1979.
-------. *Life & Death*. New York: New Directions, 1998.
-------. *Memory Gardens*. New York: New Directions, 1986.
-------. *Mirrors*. New York: New Directions, 1983.
-------. *Windows*. New York: New Directions, 1990.
Dawson, Fielding. "On Creeley's Third Change." *Athanor* 4, Spring 1973.
Gilmore, Lyman. *Don't Touch the Poet: The Life and Times of Joel Oppenheimer*. Jersey City, NJ: Talisman House, 1998.
Olson, Charles. *Selected Writings*. New York: New Directions, 1966.
-------. *Call Me Ishmael*. New York: Grove Press, 1947.
Oppenheimer, Joel. *Collected Later Poems*. Buffalo, NY: The Poetry/Rare Books Collection, SUNY Buffalo, 1997.
-------. *Drawing From Life*. Wakefield, RI: Asphodel Press, 1997.
-------. *Poetry: The Ecology of the Soul*. Buffalo, NY: White Pine P, 1983.

Leonard Schwartz

ROBERT DUNCAN AND HIS INHERITORS

In the poetry and rhetoric of Robert Duncan (1919 -1988) there is a self-conscious contradiction, a contradiction which does not limit the work but rather serves as its inexhaustible source. This contradiction might be conceived of as one between poetry as an act of original perception that grants to words their meanings, and the poem as an object derived from a tradition of language: a unique act of composition versus a history of poems that makes the one currently being composed possible. These two postures — the first associated with either theories of genius or the intentions of the avant-garde, the second associated with traditionalism, even conservatism — are both embraced by Duncan, and the result is that the normal associations one makes with "innovative" and "traditional" are turned on their head in his work.

Indeed, for the line of poets one might aptly describe as Duncanian (as opposed to Duncanesque, which would consist of those drawn to his highly attractive lyric style, as well as other of his affects), this desire to be prior to language and this knowledge that one all the same stands within a being already constituted by language, may be said to comprise its most consistent feature. Placed within such a framework, some of the poetry of established poets like Michael Palmer and Nathaniel Mackey, and some of the poetry of promising newer poets like Eleni Sikelianos and Joseph Donahue, might be understood. Above all, it is a matter of a certain attitude towards the possibilities of poetry. As Duncan put it in a 1976 interview with Robert Peters and Paul Trachtenberg: "Unless you see what I experience as 'language mysticism,' I don't want to be seen as a mystic" (104). For the real work of living in the contradiction is poetry's, not religion's, and language is the field. Yet mystery does pertain to the act of writing.

The essays included in Duncan's *Fictive Certainties*, spanning the mid-1950s to 1979, are the most revealing statements of Duncan's poetics. In "Poetry Before Language," Duncan writes, "I want to describe Poetry as it was before words, or signs, before beauty, or eternity, or meaning" (61). In a famous passage in "The Truth and Life of Myth" this desire is amplified, this time formulated as an actual experience afforded by the act of poetic composition itself:

> In the world of saying and telling in which I first came into words, there is a primary trouble, a panic that can still come upon me where the word no longer protects, transforming the threat of an overwhelming knowledge into the power of an imagined reality, or abstracting from a shaking experience terms for rationalization, but exposes me the more. (7)

This passage might mean many things — but amongst those meanings is clearly an account of an experience of words as "primary," that is, as free floating signifiers unpinned to their prior meanings. This is the sense in which a book of poetry is the dialectical opposite of a dictionary: in a dictionary the words are all pinned to their meanings, held to their past associations, fixed in their contour and life, like mounted butterflies. The yield is communicative, but the price is an absolute conservatism, since all definitions must come from the past. But part of the experience of poetry is that these past senses, these pat definitions, "protections" and "terms for rationalization," suddenly are irradiated in the rays of poetic thought, on the basis of which the word fills with new meaning, liminal meaning, or a meaning not yet defined except by itself in the act of the poem. Sense, then, is an act established in a radically present tense, active and self-constituting. Indeed, throughout Duncan's poetry and prose there is a romance for the figure of the child — the child's fresh way of seeing, the child's unmediated relation to the world, the original discoveries of self and world that only the child-like provides for. The romantic trope of child-like discovery serves throughout Duncan's work as a figural illustration for "primary trouble."

Yet in an equally famous quote Duncan asserts the following:

> I am not an experimentalist or an inventor, but a derivative poet, drawing my art from the resources given by a generation of masters — Stein, Williams, Pound; back of that by the generation of poets that have likewise been dreamers of the Cosmos as Creation and Man as Creative Spirit; and by the work of contemporaries: Zukofsky, Olson, Creeley and Denise Levertov. (*Roots* back jacket)

In this respect Duncan sees his work as indissolubly bound up with the works of certain immediate peers (in effect, some of the major poets of *The New American Poetry* as anthologized by Donald Allen in the 1960s), founded upon certain formal possibilities brought into the field by Pound, Williams, and Stein, and most importantly of all drawn in spirit from the words of the past masters — Baudelaire, Blake, Dante, Homer, Virgil, and Hesiod, as well as other more heterodox sources, like the Gnostics. These poets and myth sources are all active tropes, as oppposed to mere allusions, returned to over and over again from early books like *A Book of Resemblences* (1952) and the seminal *The Opening of the Field* (1960) through *Roots and Branches* (1964) *Bending The Bow* (1968) to *Groundwork : Before The War* (1984) and *Ground Work II: In The Dark* (1987). This means that the poem is a social act — Creeley, Olson, Levertov are all people Duncan interacts with directly: a learned act — Pound and the generation of masters are teachers, if not in person than by example: and a triumphant act over the crushing effects of time — Duncan can commune with the work of Dante in the same way that Ginsberg could commune with the ghost of Blake, except that Duncan's mysticism works at the level of the language, not of ghosts, and Dante's word is therefore alive in the fullest sense.

How does the contradiction between primary meaning as it is generated in the poet's child-like gaze and the poem drawn from the well of an ancient tradition work itself out in particular pieces? In the proclamation of "The Structure of Rime I" from *The Opening of The Field*, Duncan writes:

> I ask the unyielding Sentence that shows Itself forth in the language
> as I make it,
>
> Speak!   For I name myself your master, who come to serve.
> Writing is first a search in obediance. (*Opening* 12)

Here then the contradiction is squarely addressed. Writing is an act of obedience to a particular Sentence that predates the poem. At the same time the Sentence only "shows forth" to the extent the poet makes it. Indeed, the poet names himself the master of the Sentence he has come to serve: the Sentence only speaks at all through his own making of it. Master and servant are confused, though the two roles remain paramount.

The most famous poem from *The Opening of The Field*, "Often I am Permitted To Return To A Meadow," begins this way:

> as if it were a scene made up by the mind,
> that is not mine, but is a made place,

>   that is mine, it is so near to the heart,
>   an eternal pasture folded in all thought
>   so that there is a hall therein
>
>   that is a made place, created by light
>   wherefrom the shadows that are forms fall. (*Opening 7*)

The meadow named in the title corresponds to a beloved site of childhood perception, a place of primary apprehension. The site is figured as "made by the mind" but not made up by the mind of the poet ("not mine") : then it is a made place that belongs to the personal pronoun "I" even though "I" did not make it: then it is an eternal pasture: then it is a made place, created by light: finally it is all of these things at once, casting forms and shadows into the visible world. This place, to which the poet returns again and again, becomes constitutive of perceptions in the present so much so that past tense and present tense are powerfully intertwined; the poem becomes a way of violating the laws of temporality, of cupping past and present contiguously in the hand. The poem concludes with . . ."that is a place of first permission,/everlasting omen of what is," evoking, finally, the future, as well as the eternal ("everlasting"), the past (the memory of the original site), and the site of the trouble itself("first permission"). Thus the contradiction of "original" versus "derivative" is only surmounted by a procedure which vanquishes time, for which the ideas of "eternity" and "everlasting" are the signs.

Near the very end of Duncan's body of work, in his final book *Ground Work II*, these concerns are articulated as strongly as at the start. In "The Quotidian":

>   I do not speak here of that river
>   you read to be an allusion
>   to ancient myth and poetry,
>   though it too belongs to a story,
>   but of a rushing underground in the very life-flow,
>   a sinking-back,
>   a loss of the essential in the
>   shadows and undertow —
>
>   from which I come up into the day time.

> The bedside radio I turned on just as I woke
>   announces the minute of the hour.
>
>   In the realm of the mind I return to,
> the steps in the sun have already
>   set into motion and number
>   the rememberd measures. (*Ground Work* II)

Here the present tense, the time in which the birth of meaning can be achieved, and the past tense, which lends the genetic material that will allow that meaning to be realized later on, are almost seamlessly one, at least in the first stanza, in which the ancient world, the objects and bodies named in myth, rush underground in the daily flow of the quotidian. As the passage proceeds the two seem to slightly separate: "the sinking-back," the "undertow" and some of the other language used prefigure the notion that the ancient world is to become the world of dream, while the bedside radio wakes us into the present. The fusion of dream and reality — of ancient and contemporaneous — breaks apart at this point, to be fused again further on in later moments of indistinguishable unity between perception and source, domesticity and grandeur. Duncan produces a flow of composition that, like the Norns themselves, would bind together all of time. "Every day that I am here   I recall/early notes in the sounding of the late."

This passage from "The Quotidian" echoes Duncan's "Towards an Open Universe," one of the statements on poetics with which Duncan is represented in *The Poetics of The New American Poetry*, the text dated to 1966:

> In the very beginnings of life, in the source of our cadences, with the first pulse of the blood in the egg then, the changes of night and day must have been there. So that in the configuration of the living, hidden in the exchanging orders of the chromosome sequences from which we have our nature, the first nature, child of deep waters and of night and day, sleeping and waking, remains (Allen 213).

And more directly, after quoting Hesiod ("Night and Day address each other in their swift course, crossing the great brazen threshold"):

> As consciousness is intensified, all the exciting weave of sensory impression, the illustrations of time and space are "lost" as the personality is lost; in focus we see

only the dancer.... This presentation, our immediate consciousness, the threshold that is called both here-and-now and eternity, is an exposure in which, perilously, identity is shared in resonance between the person and the cosmos. (Allen 220)

Duncan's poetry consistently seeks out this "threshold that is called both here-and-now and eternity." His ability to realize this threshold so consistently in the writing is what has singled him out as one of the major poets of the second half of the twentieth century. Much writing and research remains to be done into this amazing body of work.

If scholars and critics have only just begun to fully explore the wealth of Duncan's writing, this is not true of the poets, who have known of it for quite some time. One contemporary poet to have inherited some of Duncan's concerns is Michael Palmer (b. 1943). Author of 8 books, including *Blake's Newton* (1972), *The Circular Gates* (1974), *Notes For Echo Lake* (1981) and *Sun* (1988), Palmer has long been associated with San Francisco and Robert Duncan. In his "Robert Duncan and Romantic Synthesis: A Few Notes," Palmer reflects on Duncan's work: "Duncan interprets (the) Romantic impulse as an eternal one, alive in the perverse, resistant voices of poets, but equally so in the syncretic impulse of Hellinistic philosophy, the songs of the Cathars, gnostic texts, OZ, Alice, Freud, George MacDonald, George Herriman, and others." At the same time Palmer notes: "As an engaged, twenty-year old student of modernist principles, however, I was disturbed by Duncan's free use of ornament, of archaic diction and grandiose rhetoric, and by the neoplatonic aura surrounding much of the work" ("Robert Duncan" 8). Yet Palmer concludes:

My own friendship with Duncan, and with his companion, the painter Jess, dates from the early 70's. By then the days of the Berkeley Renaissance, with its youthful community around Duncan, Jack Spicer and Robin Blaser, and the latter days of the much more public San Francisco Renaissance, were over. Jack Spicer had died in 1965. Robin Blaser had moved to Vancouver, where his work in poetry and poetics continued to thrive and deepen. Robert became the central figure in a new, activist poetic community that would emerge in part from the New College of California Poetics Program, of which he was the head. ("Robert Duncan" 9)

Clearly, Palmer's claim is that a kind of poetics associated with Duncan, one closer to his own proclivities, stems from this later period. To be sure, Palmer's poetry shares none of the surface features of Duncan's work; indeed, critics often mistake the orientation of Palmer's work for the very Language poetry aesthetic that Duncan himself went to such lengths to oppose. Instead of lush embankments of words and phrases through which the river of myth brazenly runs, Palmer's texts are cliffs and crevices, the distant sound of rushing water somewhere far below, and it isn't always clear how to step from one cliff to the next without falling into the crevice. The dislocation of meaning, in a Palmer poem more at the level of one phrase from the next than one word from the next, calls into question the reader's prior notions of meaningful arrangement. Indeed, one is always just on the edge of meaningful arrangement, sensing its presence without yet being obliged to commit to the literal, the limited, or the parochial that any explicit formulation of meaning would bind one to. It is also true that in his most recent book, *At Passages*, Palmer can be seen in many ways opening up to embrace a certain kind of "dense lyricism," as John Ashbery puts it in a back cover blurb, a lyricism which conjures up the song of Duncan and which is perhaps already prefigured in Palmer's own writing by its sometime relation to Surrealism. But even if one goes back and reads his earlier, more systematically dislocated work one sees a shared project: to simultaneously thrust the reader into a primary experience of words and to make present what, strictly speaking, are the voices of the absent.

At Passages, a title which surely accesses Duncan's own ongoing series of poems, "Passages," houses among other works a series of poems simply titled "Untitled." "Untitled (September 92): begins this way:

Or maybe this
is the sacred, the vaulted and arched, the
nameless, many gated
zero where children

where invisible children
where the cries
of invisible children rise
between the Cimetiere M

and the Peep Show Sex Paradise... (*At Passages* 73)

First, one notes that the word that conditions all the other words in the text is "sacred," however tenuous its assertion. Of course what is meant by "sacred" is clearly an open question. And it is this opening that is the central figure of the poem — "the many-gated zero" which poetics enters and exits, poetry in search of its subject as Duncan once put it. The many gates of this Zero are enumerated in the course of "Untitled": "Gate of Sound," "Gate of Sand," "Gate of the Body and Gate of the Law," "Gate of Public Words, or Passages," and so on. And yet for all these gates and the castle-like facade such a baroque structure must present, the entrances and exits are still into "zero." At the center of all this coming and going is an absolute Nothingness, the blank space in the circle of the sign, the empty egg, the zone the cemetery memorializes. Is there any doubt that this void is language, that grand edifice of meaning, apparently so busy and yet at its heart Nothing except to the degree the word is defamiliarized and realized again, or the idea of entering into language through some gate is finally renounced altogether? Yet the poem also hypothesizes:

Is it that a fire
once thought long extinguished
continues to burn

deep within the ground,
a fire finally acknowledged
as impossible to put out,
and that plumes of flame and smoke

will surface at random
enlacing the perfect symmetries
of the Museum of the People
and the Palace of the Book... (*At Passages* 74)

In its lyric density such a passage holds up as part of the collage of the possible the Duncanesque notion of an eternal ground from which poetic thought arises, a spark on the basis of which language can catch fire. The "many-gated zero" then, periodically lights up, since its opening is also a receptive space, and its airs are filled with invisible tinder whose pages burn every time a new page is written.

But even in Palmer's earlier work the difficult stance between conserving the ground of language and insisting that meaning in language can only be generated by my particular usage of it in the act of writing is very much at work. Here the dictionary senses of words are not so much rendered obsolete as tilted, because the surface on which they have been placed is so entirely defamiliarized.

The title poem of *Without Music* (1977), which offers an epigraph from Reverdy ("Les lettres qui formaient des mots artificiels"), begins this way:

> Small sun against the lower edge licking us
> She showed me her tongue coated with thorns
>
> A careful life of stars in a redwood box
>
> times labor's loss not mine
> based upon the loss itself, 'not mine'
>
> ... formed such words imperfectly bodied (....)

It ends:

> luminous city   sounds that pour
> from the center of a courtyard
>
> where we watch ourselves talk
> This poem is called Rebuilding the House (*Lion* 56)

The poem begins with a series of jarring juxtapositions of image, each interesting in and of itself, each resistant to any kind of narrative ordering. Clarity follows not from order per se but the locution of each line, the text's sure trajectory towards "sun" and "thorns" and "stars," so named as part of a canvas or world in these utterances. Thus particularity of word and thing are gained by an absolutely unpredictable array of phrases. Yet the poem ends by centering us in a courtyard and a source of light, the luminous city, where language is self-reflexive since we can see ourselves using it there. It ends, interestingly, with an architectural image: a poem called "Rebuilding the House," the illusion of an interior space in which Duncan's prized domesticity (as for example in "The Quotidian") might one day be achieved.

Interestingly, Palmer chooses to conclude the selection from *Without Music* for his selected poems, *The Lion Bridge*, with this final piece, dedicated to Robert Duncan and

Leonard Schwartz

evocative of both "Often I Am Permitted To Return To A Meadow" and the problematized take on Duncan gathered up in Palmer's pages.

> Resembling a meadow
> 'folded in all thought'
> a lamp is lit only vaguely remembered
> for its form, an elephant
> of pale blue porcelain
> with trunk curved upward
> lighting a room   a gift
> towards a featureless room
> whose walls are lined with children's books
> whose readers are unable to read   (*Lion* 58)

In my view Eleni Sikelianos is perhaps the most interesting younger poet working in the Duncan-to-Palmer line. Her recent books *Poetics of the Exclamation Point* and *The Book of Tendons* have garnered wide attention. As in Palmer, each concisely rendered phrase is dislocated from the next, a dislocation which is not unnavigable or absolute but rather, tricky. The connections are there to be made, but only through a series of imaginative leaps, with the distance between stepping stones widening and growing closer, allowing for difficult passages and pleasurable dalliances. As in Duncan there is water running through this landscape, a river of mythic possibility, physical light, and sub-atomic matter, articulated as such. Here is a passage from *"The Book of Tendons"*:

> In the River's cream
> as if milky then
> could mean anything
>
>   Via Lactica, the road we tore out of summer
>
> foot-split on eden's damp edge, limbs ghastly
> & a glass of something's water
>
> at June's door   we could not drink it, the atmosphere

> 's wall of glass we could not open, asteroids glanced
>
> off the eye-corners, there was grass
> for a shrapnel-bed
>
> in the magnum amnesia
>
> Lay me down, L(ord), my little
> boat-gun gone dim   (*Book of Tendons* 4)

Sikelianos' work is most striking in terms of its ability to broach the contradiction between the particular and the universal — and since the particular is always a specified thing, often enough couched in the present tense, while the universal lays claim to a kind of atemporality or lasting status, it is tempting to see Duncan's synthesis between "primary trouble" and "ancient survivals," creation of meaning and derivation of meaning, realized here again in other form. The reach is indeed planetary at times in Sikelianos' verse, as in "The Decameron":

> and a blue square applied to the body of the EARTH:
> and if they said; here; live here; six billion of you; and
> we did; ready
>
> to smile in the morning and shed tears at night; and tomorrow and in
>   the evening and
> the next day again;
>
> (caesura)
>
> To the fireball that started off
> the universe some
> 15 billion years ago: Hello
>
> to us with origins in dust (Jarnot 265)

As behooves any effort to grasp the improbable ball, this passage is both playful and ambitious. It is noteworthy for several reasons. For one, it evidences the way in which Sikelianos uses typographic elements (often more radically than in this passage) to particularize and materialize her word, even at its most expansive moment of planetary reach. (One thinks of Duncan's *Ground Work*, in which the author insisted on handsetting himself and publishing as such, so central to his vision was its spacing and typography.) The block lettering, as of EARTH, is a technique found throughout her writing; so are interruptive parenthesis — "J(OY)'S THE AIM," etc. — italicizations, sliding margins, open spaces, announced punctuation ("caesura"), armies of dashes, and so on. The effect is one of a pleasurable but difficult materiality, the language very much present as stuff, as opposed to being disposed of via transparency. If language is not passed off as transparent, all the same the universe *is* addressed, in all its complexity and wonder; knee jerk self-referentiality is never enough for Sikelianos. If this is not quite "romantic synthesis," it is certainly a strategy for working in the contradiction between the transparent and the opaque. Moreover, in a statement on poetics entitled "Eternals," Sikelianos quotes approvingly from Mandelstam: "Poetry is the plow that turns up time so deep that the layers of time, the black soil, appear on top." She goes on to conclude: "The idea of art as a field in which progress is made is inherently conservative. Make it new. But out of the disintegrated decay of the old" (*Tripwire*). The connection to Duncan is strong.

Perhaps the clearest route between Robert Duncan and his currents inheritors is the one that leads from Duncan to Nathaniel Mackey (b. 1947). Indeed, as the editor of the California literary journal *Hambone*, Mackey has fostered a number of poets whose work shares affinities with his own and with Duncan's, most notably, the poetry of Joseph Donahue. Mackey is the author of several fine collections of poetry including *Eroding Witness* (1985) and *School of Uhdra* (1993), as well as of works of criticism and two novels. In an interview with Edward Foster in 1992, Mackey offered the following:

> Robert Duncan is someone whose work is very important to me. One aspect of that importance is the fact that Robert was so insistent upon the heterodox tradition in the West, that marginalized tradition within the West which was in significant ways victimized by the very will to order that we've been talking about being imposed on other parts of the world. You know, the supression of witchcraft, the supression of the occult, the supression of the irrational. . . ." (Foster 70)

Indeed, the project of *Eroding Witness* and *School of Udhra*, as well as of Mackey's continuing poetic sequence "Song of the Andamboulou" (which runs through all the books) draws its impetus from Duncan's call for a poetry that reaches back into a despised past for its inspiration even as it invents for itself a future in which it is possible to read, live, and make ready. Mackey draws much of his material, textual and otherwise, from African ceremonial rituals, ancestral names, oral wisdom, the gods and demi-gods Osiris, Isis, Ghede, and Ogotemmeli — only all of this isn't just material, its substance, a soul making, in which the language is changed and words take on new meaning. I've written on Mackey's *Eroding Witness* elsewhere (see my *A Flicker At The Edge of Things: Essays Towards A Poetics*), so I'd here like to briefly touch on a few of the other works.

One of the most interesting sections in the more recent *School of Uhdra* is the section entitled "Outlantish." It begins with a quote from Jane Harrison, the classicist whose account of Greek myth was so important to Duncan: "a myth is not merely a word spoken; it is a reutterance or pre-utterance, it is a focus of emotion. . . . Possibly the first *muthos* was simply the interjectional utterance *mu*." The second epigraph is from Duncan himself: "a continent of feeling beyond our feeling." Given its placement in the arena of the self-conscious myth of Africa constructed in Mackey's work, it is tempting to read Duncan's phrase literally, that is, as referring to a continent, in Mackey's case Africa but perhaps paradigmatically for the American poet, any continent, the continent from which one comes, that always other place of origin. In "Melin," the stutter of closely related syllables, that muttered *mu* from which myth comes, the babble of sound from which meaning is readying itself to emerge, become intermingled with the sound of a flute:

> Serenaded
> by words they'd erase the
>   sense of, hearing its
>   whisper,
> wind-afflicted hymn.
>
>   Adamant
> flute amid muted brass,
>   baited
> light. Dailiness, weight of a
>   life preserved in salt.
>   Lost as

> they began to reminisce,
> fleeting foothold...
>
>   Heard it again.
>   Cupped.
> Hollow.
>   Hummed. (*Uhdra* 24)

Mackey here succeeds in evoking an experience of language very close to music, language as sound which speaks to us emotively and metaphysically without necessarily committing to a denotative meaning which would force the words to freeze in their definitions. These are "words they'd erased the sense of": not so as to be satisfied with mere erasure, but in order to allow something new to begin to fill in. Myth, then, means not only to go back to ancient sources, it is also to stand at the moment of original "mu" or meaning. "Derivation" and "inspiration" are thus demonstrably one, as in the synthesis of opposites sought in Duncan's work. Moreover, Mackey's references to an "Adamant flute," "wind-afflicted hymn" and earlier, an "ungraspable it," serve to conflate nature's whispers with music itself as that rhythm beyond our ability to conceptualize — thankfully, because it is only that rhythm that lets us elude our own habits.

Mackey's sequence "Songs of the Andoumboulou" is perhaps his most ambitious plunge into "language mysticism." Paul Naylor, in his introduction to a CD recording of "Strick: Song of the Andoumboulou 16-25," in which Mackey reads the poems to the musical accompaniement of a drum set, Chinese opera percussion instruments, West African string tension, Turkish frame drums, tenor saxophone, and so on, states that "it is a commonplace that poetry and music both originate in the pre-articulate soundings of human beings." Naylor continues:

> The Andoumboulou are mythological beings encountered in the cosmology of the Dogon of West Africa. The Andoumboulou are, as Mackey puts it, 'the spirits of an earlier, flawed, or failed form of human being — what, given the Dogon emphasis on signs, traces, drawings, graphicity I tend to think of as a rough draft of a human being.' But Mackey's treatment of the Andoumboulou offers much more than an antiquarian interest in cultural mythology since 'the Andoumboulou are in fact us; we're the rough draft'. For Mackey, then, the 'Song of the Andoum-

boulou" is also potentially our song — the song of a form of humanity not quite complete, still in the process of becoming more than it presently is. ("Notes")

Mackey's poetry, made up of taut and intricately organized musical spindles, is almost impossible to quote without cutting some telling link. Nevertheless Song 22 begins this way:

>   Took me aside with more talk of
>   Sophia.   Hot summer stillness.
>   Hieratic stir.   Press of her
>   hips beneath a loose cotton
>   dress,
>   bright sun behind her. Graspable
>   waist, sinewy limbs, see-thru
>   cloth. . .

It ends:

>   Played flute in the shade of a
>   tree she called her woodshed.
>   Book of anabatic limbs,
>   bruited win-stir. Fell
>   for the
>   look of the child in him,
>   he for the same in her.
>   Gnostic remains
>   of what, come into the world, she
>   relinquished,   wed short of
>   wood becoming water, wrought wood out
>   of water,
>   would they were
>   there again.   ("Song 22" 101-3)

Passages like this employ an explicitly gnostic rhetoric. The gnostic is of course a major piece of the "heterodox" tradition Duncan championed in his own writing.* "Sophia," for example, for whom the first person pronoun is taken aside, is often seen in Gnostic texts as the female divinity or semi-divinity who offers wisdom. In "Song 22," the female figure reveals her inner and outer form to the observer, who then sorts through his imaginings of what has just been seen, in an effort to leave himself behind. Interestingly, Mackey's account of the Andoumboulou as rough drafts of a human being, as failed attempts to achieve full-fledged *anthropos*, in other words as "us," is an almost perfect rendering of the Gnostic view of creation, in which the demiurge badly botched his work — that is to say, "us." Thus the phrase "gnostic remains" refers perhaps to what is left of the idea of form that was lost in the flawed act of creation, "remains" that can be reenergized as material is turned into extra-material song in creation's latest act.

The most basic element of gnostic ideology is, of course, the existence of a point of origin idealized out from its later historical degradations, a point of origin to be achieved once more through an intense spiritual practice realized in the present — the continent behind the continent, the original image, the words undefined, the child in the meadow. In this way what appeared to be archaic and lost is revealed to the language mystic as radically immanent. Perhaps Joseph Donahue (b. 1954), in his "Christ Enters Manhattan" from *World Well Broken*, best realizes these ideas in poetic thought, this time by use of figures from Western myth:

Dawn, the fallen
world's red and fiery edge —
terror of that first sunrise

Adam and Eve, reconciled, suicidal.
They consider dashing themselves down in their despair.
Sea's green as astonishing as Eden: light on stone & grass & water. . .

& what new music
floats through the forest

---

*There are references to the Gnostic throughout Duncan's *Fictive Certainties*. He tends to emphasize the dream of a grand wisdom in Gnosticism, as opposed to its subversive and caustic tone — although this is present in Duncan too, especially in the explicitly political poems.

of a spliced Bible... (*World* 40)

The passage asks us to see the world through the eyes of the freshly dumped Adam and Eve. Their mood is set between despair at the fallen world and astonishment at the greeness of the sea, a melancholy zone perched upon the wreck of the past and the wonder of the present. Donahue, the author of several collections of poetry including *Before Creation*, *Monitions of the Approach*, *World Well Broken*, and *Terra Lucida*, poses an extraordinary thought: what new music can be discovered floating through the forest of a spliced Bible, once those splices are noticed? In a way Donahue here anticipates the wonderfully gnostic readings Harold Bloom and David Rosenberg managed to come up with of the Hebrew Bible by insisting on undoing the splices and reading *The Book of J* on its own terms, without any of the latter strands of the Bible edited in. Duncan's insistence that the stuff of myth remain molten, not hard, compositional, not canon-fodder, is revealed as efficacious in terms of breaking apart the West's most basic myths, not in order to debunk them but in order to invigorate them. In this respect Donahue, a poet in mid- career, is certainly participating in Duncan's legacy. What new musics *do* float through the forests of the Bible? Donahue's is one of them.

Donahue's "Monitions of the Approach" was first published in Mackey's journal *Hambone*. The version of the poem that appears in *Hambone* begins:

All's intimation, some
future intoxicant, & yes even in exile Ovid
held his crown in the regency of erotic tumult.

Your turn. You believe all must be written out again:
the totality upholding & consuming all things —
& that your secret & useless hours

already flare & glimmer in a great book. ("Monitions" 113)

In "The Theory of The Flower" in *First Figure* Michael Palmer offers the line, "This is Paradise, an unpunctuated book" (*Lion* 111), as if punctuation, hence artificial order, were hell. In "Monitions of the Approach" Joseph Donahue offers the thought "all must be written out again," in which no flicker of conscious life is ever wasted as the task stretches before us. Donahue's "all must be written out again" and Palmer's "this is Paradise, an unpunctuated book": these, then, are the twin boundaries within which the inheritors of Robert Duncan currently work. The book Duncan's poetry calls our attention to even as he made his own entry into it is still being written.

WORKS CITED

Allen, Donald, and Warren Tallman, eds. *The Poetics of The New American Poetry* New York: Grove Press, 1973.

Donahue, Joseph. "Monitions of the Approach." *Hambone* 9, (Winter 1991).

-------. *World Well Broken*. Hoboken, NJ: Talisman House, Publishers, 1995.

Duncan, Robert. *Ground: Work II: In The Dark*. New York: New Directions, 1987.

-------. *The Opening of The Field* New York: New Directions, 1960.

-------. "Poetry Before Language," *Fictive Certainties*, New Directions, New York,: New Directions, 1985

-------. *Roots and Branches*. New York: New Directions, 1964

-------. "The Truth and Life of Myth," *Fictive Certainties*

Foster, Edward., ed. *Postmodern Poetry: The Talisman Interviews*, Hoboken, NJ: Talisman House, Publishers, 1994.

Mackey, Nathaniel. *School of Udhra* San Francisco: City Lights, 1993.

-------. "Song 22." *apex of The M* 1 (Spring 1994).

Naylor, Paul. "Notes to *Strick, Song of the Andoumboulou,*" CD. Tmemphis, TN: Spoken Engine, 1995

Palmer, Michael. *At Passages* New York: New Directions, 1995.

-------. *The Lion Bridge*. New York: New Directions, 1998.

-------. "Robert Duncan and Romantic Synthesis: A Few Notes." *American Poet: The Journal of the Academy of American Poets* (Spring 1997).

Peters, Robert, and Paul Trachtenberg. "A Conversation With Robert Duncan (1976)." *The Chicago Review* (Fall 1997).

Sikelianos, Eleni. *The Book of Tendons*. New York: The Post-Apollo Press, 1997.

-------. "The Decameron." *An Anthology of New (American) Poets*, ed. Lisa Jarnot, Leonard Schwartz, and Christopher Stroffolino. Jersey City, NJ: Talisman House, Publishers, 1998.

-------. *Earliest Worlds*. Minneapolis: Coffee House P, 2001.

-------. *Tripwire*, Spring 98, San Francisco

Norman Finkelstein

CC: JACK SPICER

I

CAN ONE SPEAK OF A SPICER TRADITION in recent American poetry? Much of Spicer's own work indicates that he himself would regard such a discourse as impossible. Even when he is willing to entertain the notion of poetic tradition, in the sense of one generation influencing the next through the passing down of knowledge, style or attitude, he is scathing toward the academic study of tradition and highly idiosyncratic in his presentation of the concept itself. Consider these remarks from *After Lorca:*

> The fools that read these letters will think by this we mean what tradition seems to have meant lately — an historical patchwork (whether made up of Elizabethan quotations, guide books to the poet's home town, or obscure hints of obscure bits of magic published by Pantheon) which is used to cover up the nakedness of the bare word. Tradition means much more than that. It means generations of different poets in different countries patiently telling the same story, writing the same poem, gaining and losing something with each transformation — but, of course, never really losing anything. (15)

Spicer claims the high ground here, but to what end? In his view, tradition is neither the exoteric sources of a poem nor the esoteric wisdom that it may have received. If tradition instead means generations of poets writing the same poem with nothing ever really getting lost, then the sense of history usually implied in the notion of tradition is irrelevant to him. Influence is beside the point: either a given poet is writing that same poem, or not. All poems exist in a state of eternal contemporaneity, and all poets are always already dead. All their poems, to use Spicer's pun, *correspond* to each other: "That is how we dead men write to each other" (34). This is one of the ways in which poetry resists "the big lie of the personal" (48), against which Spicer aims all of his considerable rhetorical resources. The placing of a proper name before the word "tradition," as in "the Spicer tradition," is simply a category mistake, and for Spicer, a rather embarrassing one at that.

"Poet, / Be like God" (336) urges the young Spicer in the *Imaginary Elegies*. Only God creates *ex nihilo*. He exists in an eternal present; "He is the photograph of everything at once" (337). With no care for what came before or what will come after, God need not concern Himself with tradition, that most human of concepts. If the poet could be like God, his creativity would ceaselessly renew itself; as free from his personal history as from the history of his art. But over the course of his career, Spicer learns that God is the least appropriate model for the poet. Rather than a boundless source of creativity, the poet is merely a receiver of messages, a radio tuned in to "Mars," to the "outside." Ostensibly released from the onus of self-expression, he is instead victimized by these indifferent voices, which overcome him with overwhelming force, yet, as in the great poem "Sporting Life," "do not even know they are champions" (218). Under these circumstances, "God is a big white baseball that has nothing to do but go in a curve or a straight line," and His incursions into human existence become the most devastating messages of all. As Spicer says a few lines further in this last of the *Four Poems for the St. Louis Sporting News*, "Off seasons / I often thought of praying to him but could not stand the thought of that big, white, round, omnipotent bastard. / Yet he's there. As the game follows rules he makes them" (258). Totally abject, the poet is alone with God and must play by His rules. In Spicer's gnostic view, the poet must be prepared for whatever pitch (that is, message) God chooses to throw; anything less is a sellout:

> I can't stand to see them shimmering in the impossible music of the Star
>   Spangled Banner. No
> One accepts this system better than poets. Their hurts healed for a few
>   dollars.
> Hunt
> The right animals. I can't. The poetry
> Of the absurd comes through San Francisco television. Directly connected
>   with moon-rockets.
> If this is dictation, it is driving
> Me wild. (265)

Television; pop music ("The Beatles, devoid of color and form. . . ." [261]); the scientific conquest of the unknown and its commercialization through bogus patriotism, as represented by the first moon landing: the slim chance that a poetry of dictation had for conveying the evanescent voice of truth is destroyed in the cacophony of postmodern culture. (As surely as the work of the modernists is a critique of modernity, so Spicer's work, if it is read as an example of postmodernism, is likewise a critique, and not an endorsement, of postmodernity.) Robin Blaser calls Spicer's last work, the *Book of Magazine Verse*, "an unfair interrogation of the public place of poetry" (284). But Spicer had already been interrogating not only the public, but the private place of poetry for some time. "No one listens to poetry" (217), the notorious declaration that begins the book *Language*, is Spicer's guarantee against tradition: even if the terrible isolation and self-sufficiency through which the poem comes into being could ever permit the give-and-take (or agon) of poetic influence, the social conditions of postmodernity have eroded the literary community to so great an extent that even the select audience that Spicer required had ceased to exist. In short, poetic tradition is a myth, sustained neither by the internal dynamics of poetic creativity nor the external dynamics of our contemporary social formations. The despair that we associate with Spicer's last books and with his untimely death overshadows the lingering hope of continuity that remains in lines such as these:

> What is important is what we don't kill each other with
> And a loving hand reaches a loving hand.
> The rest of it is
> Power, guns, and bullets. (267)

II

Spicer's Beckett-like despair over the impossible continuity of poetry — impossible that it cannot go on, impossible that it does — has been diagnosed by Ross Feld as follows: "Spicer in the end was no more able than anyone else to maintain his balance upon the 'taught' wire that stretched across his two chief desires: his wanting an essentially non-personal art, his need for human contact. That we try to write poetry for the first time, he could appreciate as a cosmic joke. That we write it a second and third time, that we *persist* in doing so, was in the end too bitter a jest even for him. He bore the persistence, the repeatability of poetry, a great resentment" (194). Yet Spicer also *believed* in poetry, this "inescapably sentimental illness — but one with roots in salvation" (Feld 194). He understood that just as human beings would continue to seek for salvation, poetry would continue to be written, and that in some way, his testimony as the anti-Orpheus of our time would influence that writing. If poetry could be designed to prevent the idealism upon which it is premised, so that it interrogated the conditions of its making and, in effect, self-destruct, then the despair of the poet, the other condition upon which poetry is premised, would at last be revealed. Idealism and despair are to Spicer what the Prolific and the Devourer are to Blake: the dialectical engine of poetry. As evidence, here is "The Territory Is Not The Map" and its "explanatory note" from "Homage to Creeley," the first part of *The Heads of the Town Up to the Aether*:

What is a half-truth the lobster declared
You have sugared my groin and have sugared my hair
What correspondence except my despair?
What is my crime but my youth?

Truth is the map of it, oily eyes said
Half-truth is half of a map instead
Which you will squint at until you are dead
Putting to sea with the truth.

    This is a poem to prevent idealism — i.e. the study of images.
It did not succeed.

    Edward Lear was allowed to say this some time ago in his books for children. Actually The Poet thought of himself as "oily eyes." That is why The Poem could never prevent idealism (Idealism).

    Orpheus and Eurydice are in their last nuptial embrace during this poem. (122)

I will resist the exegetical pleasures of this text and note only that one of Spicer's most enduring lessons is to be found here. Any poet who takes that lesson to heart will become part of the "Spicer tradition" (a term which could just as well be printed and crossed out, held under erasure in proper Derridean fashion): like those who have come before you, you will write poetry out of idealism and despair, for poetry is the embodiment both of idealism and of the despair which comes with the failure of idealism. The truth of your poetry will mislead you into thinking that *you* know the truth, that *you* have written true poetry. Do not believe it — the territory is not the map. As Spicer says in a neighboring poem, "What I mean is words / Turn mysteriously against those who use them" (124). Yet all we have is the map, the words, from which we draw hope and despair in equal measure.

And so:

I failed to draw a map and you followed it perfectly
because the word for 'cannot' inscribes itself here
to define an atmosphere of absolute trust
which both fastens and unfastens us. (*First Figure* 9)

Michael Palmer's "Lens," like nearly all of his poetry, does not sound like Spicer's work. Its tone is almost never as jokey or caustic; its surfaces are more painstakingly stylized; it has none of the apparent offhandedness and U-turns into urgency that we associate with the progressions in Spicer's books. Yet Palmer's poetry is more deeply imbued with Spicer's sense of language than perhaps any other body of work to develop since his death. For if there is a "Spicer tradition," it has little to do with style and everything to do with stance. The verbal play of absence and presence, the ratio of voice to noise, the production of linguistic zones where may be found "an atmosphere of absolute trust / which both fastens and unfastens us" — these are some of the salient characteristics of Palmer's poetry. Spicer offers a theory to Palmer's practice, for Spicer writes a poetics that slides into poetry (as in the letters to Lorca or "A Textbook of Poetry"), even as Palmer writes a poetry that flaunts itself as poetics:

Because I'm writing about the snow not the sentence
Because there is a card — a visitor's card — and on that card
    there are words of ours arranged in a row

and on those words we have written house, we have written
    leave this house, we
have written be this house, the spiral of a house, channels
    through this house

and we have written The Provinces and The Reversal and
    something called the Human Poems
though we live in a valley on the Hill of Ghosts (*Sun* 5)

"Where we are is in a sentence" (175), writes Spicer in his "Textbook." For Spicer, this is a revelation; for Palmer it is simply a given. The house of language, Spicer's house on a "Hill of Ghosts," is a house which the poet can never leave. Palmer has settled there more easily and has decorated the place with more flair than any other "language poet" (I use the term in its broadest sense) because Palmer most fully perceives the agon behind Spicer's frequently misread statement. Most poets working this territory stop at that statement; Palmer reads on: "Where we are this is idiocy. Where we are a block of solid glass blocks us from all we have dreamed of. But this place is not where we are we are to meet them" (175). Language, presumably, is that block of glass, the transparent but impenetrable barrier through which logos turns to lowghost. The mad imperatives of naming and writing that come to such a painful climax in Palmer's two poems called "Sun" prove that he knows all too well that "this is idiocy": "Write this. We have burned all their villages / Write this. We have burned all the villages and the people in them / Write this. We have adopted their customs and their manner of dress" (*Sun* 83). This is the voice of the "headless man" who "devours himself" (*Sun* 59), the poet's terrible mimicry of a "real world" in which we can say — and do — anything.

But Spicer also tells us in the "Textbook" that "The poet thinks continually of strategies, of how he can win out against the poem. . . . And in the gradual lack of the beautiful, the lock of the door before him, a new Eurydice, stepping up to him, punning her way through his hell" (171). Spicer never finds that new Eurydice, and most poets since then have given up on her entirely. As for Palmer?

> She says, Into the dark —
> almost a question —
> She says, Don't see things —
> this bridge — don't listen

Palmer's reworking of Rilke's "Orpheus. Eurydike. Hermes" indicates that for him, like Spicer, a new Eurydice remains to be found. But Palmer's Eurydice, like Spicer's, like any poet's, is always on the verge of disappearing:

> I'm not here where I walk
> followed by a messenger confused
> (He's forgotten his name)
> I'm not here as I walk

> not anyone on this path
> but a figure of walking
> a figure projected exactly this far
> followed by the messenger confused (*Sun* 24)

Palmer and Spicer always return to that point in the myth when Eurydice disappears, when Hermes (who usually brings the soul into death) is most confused, and when Orpheus learns that poetry must now be a song not of fulfillment but of loss. "Or maybe this / is the sacred" (*At Passages* 73) begins one of the most important of Palmer's recent poems. After the loss of Eurydice, it is the only path the poet may follow.

III

The single most dramatic instance of Spicer's influence upon a younger writer, an almost palpable descent of spirit upon spirit, occurs in Nathaniel Mackey's "Song of the Andoumboulou: 6," from *Eroding Witness*, Mackey's first volume of poetry. Like Duncan's "Passages," "Song of the Andoumboulou" is an open-ended serial poem, shot through with mythic references from various African and Middle Eastern cultures, and concerned with matters of possession and inspiration as they are manifested in both religious rituals and erotic relationships. Most of its text consists of loosely woven, extravagantly syncopated verse, but "Song of Andoumboulou: 6" comes to us as a letter, addressed to an entity called "Angel of Dust" and signed by "N." It is, of course, the first appearance of the form and characters that Mackey will use in his multivolume epistolary novel *From a Broken Bottle Traces of Perfume Still Emanate*. "Song of the Andoumboulou: 1" begins "The song says the / dead will not / ascend without song" (33). "Song of Andoumboulou: 6" takes this Spicerian concern into an explicitly Spicerian underworld:

> Well, what I wanted to say then was this: We not only can but should speak of "loss" or, to avoid, quotation marks notwithstanding, any such inkling of self-pity, speak of *absence* as unavoidably an inherence in the texture of things (dreamseed, habitual cloth).... I see the things of your world as *solid* in a way the world my "myriad words" uncoil can't even hope to be. *Not* "ethereal," mind you. Not insubstantial, unreal or whatever else. Only an other (possibly Other) sort of solidarity, as if its very underseams — or, to be more exact, those of its advent —

sprouted hoofs. (Or as if the Sun, which had come to boat us both away, might've extended horns.) What was wanted least but now comes to be missed *is* that very absence, an unlikely Other whose inconceivable occupancy glimpses of ocean beg access to.

    Not "re-source" so much for me as re: Source.

Yours,
N.

cc:Jack Spicer
    García Lorca
    H-mu (50)

What makes this passage so oddly moving is the way in which the older poet's original ingredients from *After Lorca*, those qualities, as I have tried to show, designed to work *against* the conventional notion of tradition, are recuperated by the younger poet in his inauguration *into* a tradition which Spicer would have regarded with the utmost skepticism. The rhetorical flourish with which Mackey ends the piece, "copying" Spicer and his correspondent García Lorca, is fully merited. Mackey's discovery of *"absence* as unavoidably an inherence in the texture of things" had been previously made by Spicer, who came upon it in the hope of freeing himself from the past, thereby making it a cornerstone of his art. But Mackey's attitude toward the past, and toward tradition in general, is much less combative than Spicer's. Tempered by Robert Duncan's influence, what Duncan calls, in the title of his famous essay, *The Truth & Life of Myth*, Mackey's goal is "an other (possibly Other) sort of solidarity," in which absence becomes, paradoxically, the sign of our connection with the past in the sense of the entire history of human culture. Not only does the poet correspond in gnostic isolation with a single daimonic other (Spicer to Lorca, N. to the Angel of Dust), but in the open weave of the poetic fabric, all poetic configurations become possible. What Michael André Bernstein says of Duncan's *grand collage* is equally applicable to Mackey: "it enacts the different paths a search for knowledge may follow, and so, just as there is no one master tradition, so there is no single collage that stands in a privileged relationship to other possible efforts" (189).

This is why Mackey also "copies" "H-mu," for from *mu* comes our word "myth." Another of Mackey's serial poems is called *"mu,"* and one of its epigraphs comes from Jane Harrison's *Themis:* "a myth is not merely a word spoken; it is a re-uttteance or pre-utterance, it is a focus of emotion. . . . Possibly the first *muthos* was simply the interjectional utterance *mu*" (*Udhra* 21). Spicer's attitude toward myth, toward origin, toward tradition, is never as respectful: one has only to think of his career-long deconstruction of the Orpheus myth and compare it to Mackey's elaborate verbal rituals to see that through Mackey, Orpheus enacts his lyric revenge upon Spicer, his most severe modern critic. Mackey's erudite lyricism, like Duncan's before him, would appear to set him apart from Spicer's caustic vision. But not quite: *absence*, if I may quote the phrase from Mackey's letter one last time, is "an inherence in the texture of things." Compared to Duncan's poetry, there is an uncanny emptiness to Mackey's work, which, though perhaps not as obviously as in Palmer, is due to Spicer's gnosis.

The term from Mackey's lexicon that best sums this sense of emptiness is "bedouin," referring not only to the nomadic tribes of North Africa, but to the more general sense of wandering discourse one finds in his work. Language wanders in Mackey's poetry; narratives are glimpsed at the edge of the horizon; erotic revelations take on the quality of mirage; sounds transform themselves into polyvalent phonemes or musical tones; pronouns shift continually. But again, *"Not* 'ethereal', mind you. Not insubstantial, unreal or whatever else." Mackey's bedouin emptiness is a site, in the way that Palmer's poems are sites, for what is understood to be the ineluctably haunted exchange of words and things. Behind so much of this poetry is the utopian dream of what Spicer calls "Thing Language," the nominalist fantasy, as in the early "Duet For A Chair And A Table," that "Words make things name / themselves" (76). It may originate with Williams, but rather than follow the Objectivist trajectory of a direct engagement with "the materials" (to use Oppen's phrase), poets in the "Spicer tradition," as Spicer himself says in the first Vancouver lecture, "prefer the unknown" (qtd in Blaser 292). For Mackey, this means a "New utopic / thought no sooner / there than discarded," the "City of spirit we / lost our way toward. Utopia / lost in the mind" (*Udhra* 80, 59). Or in a more intimate register,

> Wandering stone, something whispered
> in my ear, lost . . .
>   Bent voice, an
> evaporative kiss, wet quivering
> lip. Quick bit of emptiness, bedouin
>   window I peeped in thru,
>
>   rope

>   unraveling turned me, torn,
>
>   unstrung. . . (*Udhra* 12)

Poetry is that "evaporative kiss," that "bedouin window" that we may peep through, leaving us, like some musical instrument, "unstrung."

IV

Spicer teaches us how difficult it is to propitiate the spirits. "You are dead and the dead are very patient" (15) he writes to Lorca, but soon (perhaps as soon as *Billy the Kid*) he learns just how demanding and insatiable they can be. The noisy, hectoring spooks of *The Heads of the Town*, the mocking voices of *The Holy Grail*, the verbal static of *Language*, the confessionalism in spite of itself of *Book of Magazine Verse* — perhaps the real lesson that begins with *After Lorca*, the most difficult lesson, the lesson that Spicer himself could not learn, is that "A poet is a time mechanic not an embalmer," that "Objects, words must be led across time not preserved against it" (25). For Spicer, after all, conceived of poetry as a haunted house, and poets' houses, as we know all too well, are often turned into museums, monuments in which words are preserved against time, even when the poet in question wishes to prevent such "idealism." But if words could be led across time, then the ghosts who come to inhabit language in time's passage might be more on our side. The struggle (for it is always a struggle) could be entered in a way that would not turn the poet into the "counterpunching radio" (218) of "Sporting Life," desperate to elude the personal and yet stuck, as in *Book of Magazine Verse*, when "The identity of the poet gets more obvious" (265). Rather, "the encysted emotion will itself become an object," as Spicer writes to Lorca, "to be transferred at last into poetry like the waves and the birds." Only then "I will again become your special comrade" (48).

What Spicer intuits here is less a matter of tradition or influence or even of dictation than of affinity, a natural attraction dependent upon similarly inclined sensibilities. As Susan Howe remarks, it is a way "to meet the work with writing — you know, to meet in time, not just from place to place but from writer to writer, mind to mind, friend to friend, from words to words" (Foster 158). Howe is speaking here of *After Lorca*, as well as such works as Williams' *In the American Grain*, Olson's *Call Me Ishmael*, and her own *My Emily Dickinson* — all books which carry the work of an earlier figure across time, melding the work of two or more literary sensibilities. For Howe, writing of this sort both is and isn't a matter of possession or dictation. As she says of her engagement with Dickinson, "I really was concerned to show that she didn't write in rapturous frenzy, that she read to write. So there is an irony here. Because although on one level I firmly believe that messages come from Mars — in Spicer's sense — on another level I don't believe it" (Foster 157).

Howe further revises Spicer when she notes that "the outside is also a space-time phenomenon. I think the outside, or East Mars, partly consists of other people's struggles and their voices. Sounds and spirits (ghosts if you like) leave traces in a geography.... So history and fiction have always been united in my mind. It would be hard to think of poetry apart from history" (156, 158). Spicer's ghosts, insofar as they bring poems, connect the poet to that state of eternal contemporaneity I discussed above; that is, Poetry writ large. Just as Spicer has less respect for myth than Mackey, he has less respect for history than Howe: "Pieces of the past arising out of the rubble. Which evokes Eliot and then evokes Suspicion. Ghosts all of them. Doers of no good" (247). Howe's preoccupation with history in the form of archives, antique texts, "voices that are anonymous, slighted — inarticutate" (*Europe of Trusts* 14), is derived from her own early fascination with the subject, as well as her engagement with figures such as Olson, on the one hand, and with the tradition of feminist writers and thinkers, on the other. But Howe's affinity with Spicer is most clearly seen in the way her work becomes a theater for ghosts. The techniques that she develops, including strategic citation, fragmentation, collage, and echolalia, undermine the authority or full presence of her poems, reinscribing them as palpable absences, phantoms that hover over literature and history, as the figure of James Clarence Mangan hovers over Melville's *Bartleby* in "Melville's Marginalia." A true "time mechanic," Howe, like Palmer, conveys the sense that poetry is both an elaborate artifice and a spontaneous dictation from outside. But Howe's outside, as she points out, has more to do with the specifics of geography and history. Consider the following passage from *Thorow:*

> at Fort Stanwix the Charrokey
> paice
>
> only from that Alarm
> all those Guards
>
> Constant parties of guards
> up & down

Agreseror

Bearer law my fathers

Revealing traces
Regulating traces (*Singulanties* 46)

In *Thorow*, Howe evokes the historical events in the area of Lake George, New York, particularly those events during the French and Indian Wars, through what she calls "Narrative in Non-Narrative" (41). Her poetic techniques produce a warp in the space-time continuum, opening a linguistic space into which come the ghosts that shaped American history in that region. As a discursive practice, history both reveals and regulates traces of the past. Howe says of Lake George that "Pathfinding believers in God and grammar spelled the lake into *place*. They have renamed it several times since. In paternal colonial systems a positivist efficiency appropriates primal indeterminacy" (41). Language changes as borders shift, wars are won and lost, whole peoples and cultures are destroyed or assimilated. These changes usually go unnoticed from our perspective in the seemingly stable present; it takes a poet as much as a scholar to stir our consciousness of the past. "I heard poems inhabited by voices," Howe tells us; ". . . . I went down to unknown regions of indifferentiation. The Adirondacks *occupied* me." The pun is of the utmost seriousness: only by being occupied or possessed by the historical spirit of place can we be fully occupied or involved with our life there in the present. Spicer learned how much of the personal was to be discovered by heeding the impersonal: "The poem begins to mirror itself. The identity of the poet gets more obvious. / Why can't we sing like nightingales? Because we're not nightingales and can never become them" (265). Howe, having "Walked on Mount Vision," discovers "So many true things // which are not truth itself" (*Singulanties* 49). History is a matter of "Mortal particulars / whose shatter we are"; we live "A sort of border life" (50) between the past and the present, the living and the dead. The identity of the poet gets less obvious: "You are of me & I of you, I cannot tell / Where you leave off and I begin" (58).

V

Here is the beginning of Bob Perelman's poem-essay "The Marginalization of Poetry":

"The Marginalization of Poetry" — it almost
goes without saying. Jack Spicer wrote,

"No one listens to poetry," but
the question then becomes, who is

Jack Spicer? Poets for whom he
matters would know, and their poems

would be written in a world
in which that line was heard,

though they'd scarcely refer to it.
Quoting or imitating another poet's line

is not benign, though at times
the practice can look like flattery. (3)

By now, Spicer has become the tutelary spirit for at least one generation of avant-garde poets and critics seeking to bemoan, celebrate, and above all theorize the social circumstances of their practice. In an ironic turn that Spicer himself would have appreciated, the proper name "Jack Spicer," the complex ensemble of literary relations which that figure now represents, has taken on a certain currency, a certain cachet. On one level, Spicer has become to the contemparay avant-garde what Chatterton became to the Romantics. His "legacy," summed up in that one famous line, expresses the double-bind of today's obsessively (but perhaps unavoidably) self-conscious experimentalists: a centripetal "community" of writers known mainly to themselves (and their grad students) engages in a set of practices meant to both "defamiliarize" literary conventions and broaden its social base.

Who is Jack Spicer indeed? Those who know the answer to that question refer constantly to that one line. Their intentions are no more benign than were those of its author, and the results in both cases remain dubious, caught up in contradiction. It is hard to imagine, as Perelman does, that "a self-critical poetry . . . might / dissolve the antinomies of marginality that / broke Jack Spicer into broken lines" (10). Spicer took the notion of a "self-critical poetry" about as far as it could go; he certainly exposed those antinomies, but could not dissolve them. As Paul Mann explains, "The avant-garde has in fact served, in most cases quite unwittingly, as an instrument for the incorporation of its own marginality. The avant-garde is the outside of the inside, the leading edge of the mainstream, and thus marginal in both senses: excluded and salient. The doubleness of this site, the existence of so curious and yet typical a phenomenon as a centralized margin, an internalized exterior, is another reason for the difficulty of discerning in the avant-garde a coherent ideological figure" (13). Thus, those who invoke Spicer in an attempt to determine the fate of poetry in our time may well be implicated in, to use Mann's terms, "the most fully articulated discourse of the technology of recuperation" (15).

Could it have been otherwise? Ron Silliman observes that

> There remains around Spicer's work an aura of mystery which serves to buffer a reader from further (or, at least, other) use of the work.
> The reasons for this are many. While Spicer's insistence that he did not "like his life written down" is integral to his entire project as a poet, the effect of this is less one of focusing attention on the writing-as-such, than of inserting into the place of the writer's biography a narcissistic absence. (147)

This is harsh; and to be fair, Silliman goes on to demonstrate just how Spicer's "writing-as-such" may be put to some other significant and practical uses. But there's a note of truth in that phrase "narcissistic absence"; perhaps it is what results when one is caught, as Ross Feld says of Spicer, between the conflicting desires for non-personal art and human contact. Literary historians of the San Francisco Renaissance, in which Spicer played so important a role, are quick to point out the imporance of the concept of community to this movement. For Michael Davidson, it serves as one of the most important myths or "enabling fictions" motivating San Francisco poets during the period when Spicer was active. Davidson sees Spicer among those poets possessed of the "desire to reach a community by means of an operative or heightened language that can be experienced in nondiscursive ways" (19); indeed, Davidson proposes that even Spicer's notion of "the 'outside' has its base in human intercourse within a community and that its reception takes the form of a conversation" (155). Likewise, Edward Foster writes in his study of Spicer about the importance of the *kreis* or inner circle of initiates which Spicer, Duncan, and Blaser formed early in their friendship, probably in imitation of the *kreis* formed by Stefan George (10). But Spicer was also predisposed to believe in our inability to sustain a shared artistic vision and unifying effort, leading inevitably to the demise of a community, the breaking of a *kreis:* "How can you love that mortal creature" he asks in *The Heads of the Town;* "Everytime he speaks / He makes / Mistakes" (148).

Spicer's utopian concept of tradition as generations of poets writing the same poem is his defense against this much darker belief, a belief shared by another gnostic writer of a rather different sort, Harold Bloom. "All 'tradition' is indistinguishable from making mistakes about anteriority," Bloom declares. "The more 'tradition' is exalted, the more egregious the mistakes become" (103). Spicer, I think, would agree. I have tried not to exalt, that is, idealize tradition in this essay, knowing, as I said at the beginning, that for a gnostic like Spicer, tradition is the most egregious mistake at all. Yet at the same time, I cannot escape the feeling that our boldest poets must meet and contend with Spicer along their way, and will continue to do so for a long time to come. "Tradition is a daemonic term" (98), says Bloom, and Spicer has become a daemon, visiting these poets as Lorca visited him. "A poet is never just a woman or a man. Every poet is salted with fire. A poet is a mirror, a transcriber" (*My Emily Dickinson* 7). This is Howe, *occupied* with the daemonic Emily Dickinson. First one is possessed by the daemon; then, perhaps, one becomes a daemon oneself. Poetry is a *track*, the mark left of a passage from one state to another. In hope of life, poets die into their poems; if they succeed, they will return to live again and again. The alternative, as Spicer knew, is almost too bitter to imagine:

> Dare he
> Write poetry
> Who has no taste of acid on his tongue
> Who carrys his dreams on his back like a packet?
> Ghosts of other poets send him shame
> He will be alive (as they are dead)
> At the final picking. (231)

WORKS CITED

Bernstein, Michael André. "Robert Duncan: Talent and the Individual Tradition." *Sagetrieb* 4.2&3 (Fall & Winter 1985): 177-190.

Blaser, Robin. "The Practice of Outside." *The Collected Books of Jack Spicer*. Santa Barbara: Black Sparrow, 1980. 271-329.

Bloom, Harold. *Kabbalah and Criticism*. New York: Continuum, 1975.

Davidson, Michael. The *San Francisco Renaissance: Poetics and Community at Mid-Century*. Cambridge: Cambridge UP, 1989.

Feld, Ross. "The Apostle's Grudge at the Persistence of Poetry." *Ironwood* 28 (1986): 188-194.

Foster, Edward Halsey. *Jack Spicer*. Western Writers Series 97. Boise, Idaho: Boise State U, 1991.

-------. "An Interview with Susan Howe." *The Birthmark: Unsettling the Wilderness in American Literary History*. By Susan Howe. Hanover, New Hampshire: Wesleyan UP/UP of New England, 1993. 155-181.

Howe, Susan. *The Europe of Trusts*. Los Angeles: Sun & Moon, 1990.

-------. *My Emily Dickinson*. Berkeley: North Atlantic Books, 1985.

-------. *Singularities*. Hanover, New Hampshire: Wesleyan UP, UP of New England, 1990.

Mackey, Nathaniel. *Eroding Witness*. Urbana: U of Illinois P, 1985.

-------. *School of Udhra*. San Francisco: City Lights Books, 1993.

Mann, Paul. *The Theory-Death of the Avant-Garde*. Bloomington, IN: Indiana UP, 1991.

Palmer, Michael. *At Passages*. New York: New Directions, 1995.

-------. *First Figure*. San Francisco: North Point, 1984.

-------. *Sun*. San Francisco: North Point, 1988.

Perelman, Bob. *The Marginalizaion of Poetry: Language Writing and Literary History*. Princeton: Princeton UP, 1996.

Silliman, Ron. *The New Sentence*. New York: Roof Books, 1989.

Spicer, Jack. *The Collected Books of Jack Spicer*. Ed. Robin Blaser. Santa Barbara: Black Sparrow, 1980.

John Olson

THE HAUNTED STANZAS OF JOHN ASHBERY

I HAVE ON OCCASION DREAMED POETRY. I have dreamed words floating through my head like clouds. What delighted me about these word-sequences is that they only made apparent sense. They did not make sense in any conventional way. They made sense strictly according to the logic and syntax of a dream. When I say they floated like clouds I mean that they possessed the fluidity of clouds, the changeableness of clouds, and the buoyancy of clouds. It is this buoyancy that has most fascinated me in these states, that sense of freedom, that sense of imminent change and ongoing possibility. The term psychologists have coined for this partially conscious state prior to full awakening is 'hypnopompic.' It is from the Greek: 'hypno' meaning sleep and 'pompe' meaning to send away. I deeply enjoy this state of being and have often longed for a way to reproduce it during my waking hours, to write a sequence of words in the same manner I have dreamed them, words unencumbered with the weight of a single message but imbued with the light and buoyancy of a thousand different opportunities for wild and playful suggestion. I know it is within the realm of possibility to do so because I have seen at least one poet perform this kind of writing repeatedly: John Ashbery. Ashbery's poetry comes closer than any other poet to presenting, on paper, a writing that has the same fluidity of syntax, the same quality of repose and flow, the same enchantment and thrill of the ineffable as the words that have floated through my mind like clouds, like waves, like majestic April galleons.

The closest analogue I can think of to this hypnopompic pump of poetry is music. Music because it is abstract yet charged with feeling, full of fluidity and movement yet complexly patterned, easy to experience yet hard to define. Words convey specific ideas; music suggests elusive states of mind. Ashbery himself is pretty outspoken about this affinity. "I feel I could express myself best in music," he says in Robert Wallace's book *Writing Poems*. "What I like about music is its ability of being convincing, of carrying an argument through successfully to the finish, though the terms of this argument remain unknown quantities. What remains is the structure, the architecture of the argument, scene or story. I would like to do this in poetry." (Wallace 254)

One of the most characteristic things said about John Ashbery's work is that it approaches and recedes from meaning, that it never really comes to fruition. This has sometimes been a source of embarrassment. I remember on one occasion saying to a friend, "Wow, I just read this terrific poem by John Ashbery." And the friend, of course, asks the inevitable question, "Oh, what was it about?" To which I haltingly reply, "Why . . . it was about . . . you know . . . I'm not really sure . . . but it was a great poem, really!" The difficulty here is one of habit; we are in the habit of saying something is about a particular theme, a particular subject, as if everything in life were packaged in a neatly configured lineal pattern of mathematical certitude. But it's not. Life is messy, often incoherent. If John Ashbery's poetry is about anything, it is about consciousness, the way we experience life at the moment it is being experienced.

This break from strictly mimetic values to an exploration of consciousness itself serves to underscore an especially pivotal drive in contemporary writing. Like Cornell's boxes, and like dreams and daydreams in general, the moment we enter into a John Ashbery poem we enter a theater of enchantment. A theater of the macabre, the droll, the comic, and the sublime. A theater of the mind. To the extent that it is consciousness itself that is being enacted and dramatized, and to the extent that Ashbery's work brings attention to the ways in which language constructions model our understanding of the world, Ashbery's work embodies all the key elements of contemporary American poetry: its facility for making and unmaking meaning, its sense of ironic detachment, its mesh of incongruous emotions, its exhilarating autonomy and puckish delirium.

Ashbery's deferring of completion, distortions and substititions, flux and interplay of meanings, ruminative tone, the quirky glissades, the abrupt shifts in perception, the blithe uncertainty of often extravagant yet fleeting representations, the sense of personal vagueness created by the use of ambiguous, indeterminate pronouns, all help induce a rich state of reverie. It is the work of a Prospero producing banquets and storms and music out of the air.

It is rather erotic, this coquettish insouciance, this now-you-see-it-now-you-don't magic act. Roland Barthes remarks that the most erotic part of a body is where the clothing allows us a peek ("L'endroit le plue érotique d'un corps n'est-il pas là où le vêtement bâille?"). (Barthes 19). This is not to be confused with the strip-tease act of suspense narrative. It is not a progressive unveiling. It opposes to what is functional that which is superfluous. To the stripper, fully revealed and figured—the contracted denouement—it opposes a continually deferred consummation, a prodigal, unceasing diversion.

This quality of dishabille dreaminess, of being in a state of insouciant repose and reflecting on the world with a provocative blend of keen fascination and buoyant detachment runs throughout all John Ashbery's poetry. But the best way to examine it in detail is to take a sample and to put it on a microscope slide. It is not necessary to conjure an entire ocean to see a living system; there is a microcosm in a single drop of water, and a morphology in a single cell. For this reason I have chosen a single poem, "Haunted Stanzas," to bring into the lab for close analysis.

Ashbery is a prolific writer and there is a dizzying array of work to choose from. But the poem "Haunted Stanzas," included in the collection *Hotel Lautréamont*, has an especial appeal. For one thing, it's a good deal smaller than *Flow Chart*. Secondly, it begins with rain, and as everyone knows, rain and reverie go together like rhythm and blues. And thirdly, there was something especially insouciant in its oneiric tilt and acoustic translucence, its supple non sequiturs and infrared semitones. The allusion to both Joseph Cornell and the Comte de Lautreamont on the cover is significant. Cornell's love of the opera and its dreamlike settings is a perfect match for Ashbery's sensibility, as is Lautreamont's penchant for unbridled phantasmagoria.

"Haunted Stanzas:" I'm captivated by this title. It's so suggestive. First, the implication of a poem being a structure, a built thing, like a house, with rooms and plumbing, etc. Second, the suggestion that there is a phantom, a ghost, a spirit somehow involved with this structure. Perhaps this could be read as the meanings generated in the work that never quite congeal into anything definite, but always remain fugitive and unstable, volatile. Also, a ghost is the presence of an absence, which is the very thing language is. Consequently, anything built out of language is haunted.

> It's been raining off and on for a week now:
> drip, drip. (Ashbery 120)

I love the way this sudden 'drip, drip' comes in. It slows the reading up. Forces you to halt. It is a vivid image: water dripping from an eave. It is an image–a gestalt, if you will–powerfully redolent of the atmosphere right after a rainstorm, when everything is quiet, and dripping, and there is the smell of electricity in the air. Those two little words capture the charged atmospheric density ensuing a storm, the thrilling freshness when the residue of all that turbulence is still informing the life of everything and tatters of cloud scud past the moon. There is a wonderful feeling of repose here, the serenity that always follows a storm, which is the perfect ingredient for reverie.

> Already we are beginning to feel the effects of this,
> As life slides insensibly onward. In one corner
> a harpsichord is shelling peas. Watch out for rowboats! (Ashbery 120)

This is wonderful nonsense. The tone is at first portentous, then abruptly cartoonish. Nonsense is a prime ingredient of Ashbery's poetry. Not merely for the sake of making us laugh (though this is an effect he clearly intends), but to insist on the poem's autonomy from the burdensome weight of the empirical world. The language has come unhinged here. We are in a domain where anything can happen. Gaston Bachelard writes: "Yes, we truly dream while reading. The reverie which works poetically maintains us in an intimate space which does not stop at any frontier—a space uniting the intimacy of our being which dreams with the intimacy of the beings which we dream." (Bachelard 162).

Ashbery loves to exploit the conflict between the need inherent in language to make sense and the need to make music. Waves of meaning with no concrete reference. Something heard, but invisible. A present absence. An absent presence.

> When the new series of etudes was published it
> caused quite a stir in the musical world. (Ashbery 120)

Once again, an abrupt shift in narrative and tone. In a mere six lines, we have gone from the aftermath of a storm, to a harpsichord shelling peas, to a sudden command to watch out for rowboats, to the sober, pedagogical tone of these last two lines. The abrupt allusion to etudes, so reminiscent of European salons and Chopin, is another Ashberian lozenge to promote a state of reverie, of dreamy detachment. In the very same way thoughts flow through our minds, these lines flow from statement to statement provoking, invoking, and joking, but without getting weighed down with a specific message. Nothing resolves. As soon as something borders on resolution it dissolves, and turns into something else, something it echoes, or contrasts.

But this is not merely a literary device, either. Life itself is like this. This is the very nature of consciousness.

> Darkness was more perfect. Happiness no longer
> was a thing to hold on to, but became a great curve,
> listening instead. We don't know what pressures
> you to behave as we do. We only do it out

> of fear and love, meddling like
> guardian angels with what does in fact concern us
> a little. (Ashbery 120)

I love the way "a little" comes in here at the end. Like a sudden note at the end of a musical passage one has felt to be sufficiently resolved. ". . . a little" plunk, plunk.

In reading this, the plural first person subject pronoun "we," which is utterly arbitrary (we, the audience, do not have a clue as to whom it refers, and it is too personal to function as a referent for people in general), feels, nevertheless, completely appropriate. Nobody sprinkles pronouns on a page with such blithe dexterity as Ashbery.

The same puzzlement applies to the pronoun 'you,' "We don't know what pressures/ you to behave as we do." Who is you? The reader? The author? A musical composer? A harpsichord shelling peas?

Ashbery's use of pronouns is casual and arbitrary. He shifts point of view with giddy alacrity. The effect of this is twofold: it undermines any sense of a deeply rooted, permanent identity and offers a mutiplicity of perspective throught the entire poem. There is always a discrepancy between a word and an idea and this is especially, and wonderfully, the case with pronouns.

The arbitrariness of Ashbery's pronouns is a subtly performed uprooting of our mundane selves. In the domain of Ashbery's poems we are disburdened of our tiresome, everyday roles. The poem becomes an intermediary between trance and the trivial life, the social life that freezes us in our specific roles of utility and the production of value. We discover, in the poem, an existence that is spontaneous and indefinite. We discover a mystical insouciance that forbids the social organization from intruding on us. Gaston Bachelard writes:

> Active life, the life given animation by the reality function is a fragmented life, fragmenting outside us and within us. It rejects us to the exterior of all things. Then we are always outside. Always opposite things, opposite the world, opposite men with their mottled humanity. Except in the great days of true loves, except in the times of Novalis' Umarmung, a man is a surface for man. Man hides depths. (Bachelard 162).

Ashbery resumes with a fullblown storm:

> Unbattered the storm plays, like a lion cub,
> the bolts tremendous, and the basement is still coming apart.
> I am less than enthused though a cautious display of differentiated
> levels would be the appropriate note here. The thing done
> and the apron that came after. (Ashbery 120)

The pensive drip, drip of the second line has now become a turbulence bordering on total chaos. The language has suddenly acquired a somewhat antique cast. The line "like a lion cub" sounds faintly Elizabethan, like something out of Christopher Marlowe. The anastrophic inversion of the normal adjective-to-noun word order ("the bolts tremendous") further accents this antique quality. Then, in typical Ashbery fashion, we leap from this Elizabethan mise-en-scène to a scene of domestic turbulence ("and the basement is still coming apart") to a note of pomposity, which the paralepsic breeziness ("I am less than enthused") sharpens with a slightly mocking undertone (these are kind of lines Kevin Spacey is so good at uttering, the master of the verbal sneer) and the stanza ends with the quintessential icon of humdrum domesticity, "The thing done/ and the apron that came after." The entire stanza is a collage of disparate tones and voices, the swirl of tones and voices that festoon the masts of a dream, a phantasmal flying Dutchman bulging with polysemic breadfruit. The image of the storm is appropriate to the chaos of voices. This is a salient feature of much of Ashbery's work: the uncertainty of representation. Again, it is this feature, this constant volatility, this teasing uncertainty of the poem's representations, that so completely absorbs our attention and lifts us out of the world of predictability into the dreamworld of ceaseless vicissitude.

> I am not prepared to give up my life for a few drawings.
> Nevertheless I want reassurance, as if this were the Mesozoic era and
> people saw themselves differently as so much meat and whiskers.
> I'm not sure I wouldn't have been enchanted
> to have those advantages and see how women live when they're away
> from men and don't have to think about it.
>
> So the carpenter makes a list of
> whatever might be needed and the ritual
> gains in transparency from that. (Ashbery 120)

When Ashbery (or whoever the identity here happens to be) utters the line "I am not prepared to give up my life for a few drawings" the tone is manifestly ironic. The declamation sounds a little ridiculous. Why would it be necessary to surrender one's life for something as seemingly innocuous as a drawing? What sort of drawing would necessitate such sacrifice? Although the droll melodrama of the line has a comic surface, on another level it provokes speculation. Here again Ashbery subverts the narrative momentum he has just set up and introduces elements that—through irony or nonsense—avoids the deadening grip of control. His deft sense of irony and humor continues to float us through our reverie of chimerical carpentry and Mesozoic whiskers.

> Even the little piles of dust in the schoolyard had their say
> and thought differently about it only they came to be in the end
> what navigators had never asked for: the whole planisphere
> pressed into one's hand like currants. (Ashbery 121)

The word 'planisphere' is intensely interesting here. First, there is the physical sense of the word pressed into the hand like currants, a wad of tart red berries. Secondly, it's an amusing pun: navigators are generally at sea, which is a myriad of currents. These alone are captivating. But the connotation of this word carrries a much larger sense. A planisphere is a polar projection of the celestial sphere and the stars on a plane with adjustable circles or other appendages for showing celestial phenomena. The word excites ideas of distortion, a bending of normal configurations in order to get a broader view of things. It excites feelings of wholeness, of quantum apprehension. Also, its navigational aspect provokes associations of travel and adventure. This feeling of wholeness, joined with its sense of exploit and exotic ports, further induce a fanciful, immaterial domain of quixotic adventure and a sense of being coaxed out of one's habitual way of experiencing things. The world of normal, everyday order is a world of routine in which we feel a dulling confinement, a separation from the things around us. The planisphere serves as a metonymic vehicle, a cartographic device by which we can zestfully embrace everything around us.

> Who praises rigor?
> The ones who have less to lose. Who live
> in harm's way and poetry is as a vice to them. Never
> mind, it is more meaningful that the settlers were unwearied,
> as, given our best days, we all are. So I feel connected,

the car slithers forward, meanwhile

let me lick your shirt. (Ashbery 121)

I love that line, "let me lick your shirt." It's just so ridiculously silly. Who, other than a mad lover, or demented sycophant, would ask to lick your shirt in a slithering car?

> I have an honest proposition to make
> to you, one that I hope you'll find rewarding: turn
> your back so as not to see the parade of prisoners escaping.
> It'll do them good and it'll do you good. You have it in your power
> to offer proof of the equations amid the alembics of the tower
> where the gas flares and your nerves buzz. Well?
>
> Shouldn't you be off and running? Until another day, then.
> And he saddles his horse, which he called "Old Paint" (never
> knew why, except that its rough exterior was somewhat suggestive of old paint)
> and that was it. But I want to pray for you, whole
> afternoons-worth, I do. But sometimes the sledge is honest. It bears us away.
>
> (Ashbery 121)

Can it be that the prisoners are our multiple selves imprisoned in a self of sober responsibilities, a dutiful self locked in a prison of routine?

The hodgepodge of events here is dizzying. Nerves buzz, prisoners escape, gas flares, dust talks, and somebody rides off on a horse with the rough exterior of old, peeling paint. And when somebody—the author?—using the first person 'I' tells us they want to pray for us, "whole afternoons-worth, I do," do we believe them? Can this be the transcendental self mocking the comical limitations of the mundane self? Why, after all, would anyone want to pray for "us." Who is "us?" Are "we" in spiritual turmoil or sinking in a moral quagmire? The jumble of disparate events and multiple voices echoing and caroming and ricocheting off one another is a collage, a theater, like one of Joseph Cornell's boxes, in which everything is charmed with an illimitable and indefinable play of association.

The last line, "But sometimes the sledge is honest. It bears us away," comes as something of a relief. We are literally tugged out of the end of the poem and its jumble of things into a nineteenth century world of abundant snow suggested by the word 'sledge,' a

Dr. Zhivago Russia or twinkling Courrier and Ives Vermont hills. It also serves as a comment on the fundamentally uncontrollable power of language; despite the intentions of the author, the author's sly asides and mock heroics and occasional verbal sneering, a la Kevin Spacey—perhaps a blend of the snide, detached Kevin Spacey of Hurly Burly with the quixotic Kevin Spacey of American Beauty—and despite the interpretive vagaries of the reader, the private associations we bring to a reading of such abstract and evocative poetry, the language has a life of its own. Here again is its hypnotic power, its ability to transport us. The very process of putting one word next to another word generates a moving belt of objects and unexpected associations. But once you remove a specific target and create, as in the life of a poem, a wilder energy, energy delighting in energy, words delighting in words, the free play of ideas and associations induce a trance: transport us, literally, over the hill and into the void, the forever elusive horizon before us.

WORKS CITED

Ashbery, John. *Hotel Lautréamont*. Alfred A. Knopf. New York. 1994.
Bachelard, Gaston. *The Poetics Of Reverie*. Beacon Press. 1960 by Presses Universitaire de France. Translation 1969 by Grossman Publishers, Inc.
Barthes, Roland. *Le Plaisir du Texte*.
Wallace, Robert. *Writing Poems*. HarperCollins. 1991.

David Clippinger

POETRY AND PHILOSOPHY AT ONCE: ENCOUNTERS BETWEEN WILLIAM BRONK AND POSTMODERN POETRY

A work of art's an encounter somebody had.
You'll know it when you meet it. Watch for it.
    —William Bronk, "How it Works (or Doesn't)"

WITHIN THE PERPETUAL EBB AND FLOW OF TWENTIETH-CENTURY AMERICAN POETRY, William Bronk has been an anomaly. Bronk himself has remarked in response to a particular critic's effort to place him within a "tradition" of contemporary poetry that he felt "as though I were a previously unknown fish whose fossil had been discovered" (Ernest 168). Despite such an attempt to place Bronk within "established" poetry, he has lingered on the periphery of mainstream poetry for three reasons: first, his poetry resists the categorization that allows a poet to claim or be named part of a "literary tradition"; second, he has never been a career, academic poet and, therefore, has remained outside of the networking of "reputations" that occurs within university settings, which also facilitates literary labeling; and third, he has lived nearly all of his life in upstate New York in Hudson Falls, which is remote from established poetry centers such as New York City or San Francisco, to name the two of the most obvious sites. This is not to say that Bronk has lived a life of self-exile. His encyclopedic correspondence to fellow poets, writers, thinkers, and artists is far reaching, but this remoteness may help explain his "marginal" position. Consequently, it remains somewhat difficult to fix Bronk within the easy categories that serious poetry readers and critics often rely so heavily upon such as Imagist, Objectivist, High Modernist, Beat, Confessional, New York School, Black Mountain School, Language Poetry, and the like. Bronk cannot be contained by any of these literary tags, and yet he shares certain affinities with the poetry and poetics of many of these movements. Via the exploration of those affinities, this essay will create a space for Bronk's poetry so that it can be seen in all of its vitality and vibrancy. In turn, I will demonstrate the degree to which Bronk contributes to not only the scene of contemporary poetry but how he has cleared the way for what has come to be known as "postmodernity."

In the most basic terms, Bronk's fundamental argument might be stated as the position that human reason and intelligence cannot render truth; consequently, the human conception of the world is, in Bronk's words, always "a world and not the world." Moreover, language and the concomitant desire to name are manifestations of reason and, therefore, contribute to and perpetuate the division that separates a world from the world. His poem "Gnomon of the Pro-Nouns" drives at the heart of this matter:

> Loving you in love but is not you.
> Knowledge of you is knowing but not you.
> He is not, nor she, nor it; you are.
> I am not I. My despair is your despair. (*Life* 185)

The act of naming does not fully manifest its object; rather, the act of naming perpetually retreats from its intended referent in what the structuralist linguist Ferdinand de Saussure refers to as the trace of meaning within the signifying chain. The despair with which the poem concludes addresses this insurmountable distance that inhibits naming and, subsequently, knowing and loving. The limitations of language and naming unveils the inherent partiality of human knowledge, and Bronk's ongoing investigation into language is also, simultaneously, a sustained reflection upon the boundaries of human thought. In a similar vein, the poem "Names Like Barney Cain's" reads,

> Two locks on the Feeder are named for him.
> I have asked and nobody knows who he is.
> Alexander, Alfred, Quetzalcoatl,
> Nobody, nowhere, never, nothing. (*Life* 185)

The name and knowledge of an individual is beyond the grasp of the question of who? What such questioning ultimately unveils is the "nobody, nowhere, never, nothing" of language.

While such ideas many strike some as nihilistic, Bronk isn't proposing that there is no meaning; rather, Truth and the Real remain beyond the ken of language and, therefore, outside of the grasp of the human. "There isn't an I / or a world to know. There is something not known" (*Life* 185). This conception of the Real is directly linked to a self-reflective consciousness that ultimately directs the individual towards the fissures in language — or what is unspeakable — and into the realm of the "not-known." As Bronk writes in "Speech Making,"

> In a world where nothing is known or can be known
> beyond the known-to-be unspeakable,
> only metaphor speaks literally
> and literal speech, itself, is metaphor. (*All* 97)

The poem turns in upon itself at its close and offers up the seemingly paradoxical assertion that "only metaphor speaks literally / and literal speech, itself, is metaphor." In one sense, the poem suggests an infinite loop that circles from the metaphoric to the literal back to metaphoric again (ad infinitum). But on another level, the lines argue that only that which does not attempt to name directly touches upon the heart of the name. Or, to put it into slightly different terminology, to not name directly is to indirectly name.

Ultimately, such attention reinforces the image of the poem as a word construct and the poet as a person laboring over and with language. The poem, though, is not merely a transcription of something perceived and/or experienced. During an extended conversation with Bronk, Paul Auster commented that "the difference between seeing the thing and making it into a word — that's where the poem happens." Bronk responded emphatically that "No, the poem happens in words" (Weinfield 40). Language is the material and the vehicle for the poem, and given such centrality, it requires continual examination. Unlike many who perceive language as an expression of unmediated meaning — a one-to-one correspondence of word and referent — Bronk's comprehension of the inherent limitations of knowledge and language leads him beyond the surface of words and deeper into the chasm of the unspeakable and the unknown.

Bronk's heightened-linguistic consciousness, which has sustained his poetry for well over the last fifty years, can be seen as a prototype for many of the poetic movements that have emerged over the last twenty years and especially poets associated with Objectivism and Language poetry. In order to further explore these connections, this essay examines Bronk's influence in regards to a collection of poets who may seem at first far removed from Bronk's mode of poetry — namely, Susan Howe, Rosmarie Waldrop, Michael Palmer, Robert Creeley, and Keith Waldrop. Bronk shares with each of these poets an understanding of language as an inadequate medium to definitively capture and render its subject as well as the sense of the poem as a vehicle for philosophical inquiry, where the propositional phrase constitutes a foundational base for their poetics.

In his home in Hudson Falls, New York, personally inscribed copies of Rosmarie Waldrop's remarkable *A Key into the Language of America* and Susan Howe's *My Emily Dickinson*, which has reshaped Emily Dickinson scholarship, can be found amongst Bronk's books.[*] The gift of these personally inscribed books speak to the affinity between Bronk, Waldrop, and Howe. And while the issue of gender and cultural marginalization dominate both *A Key into the Language of America* and *My Emily Dickinson*, which may seem far afield of Bronk's poetic focus, his conception of language can be seen as a foundation for such cultural forms of critique. That is, in an attempt to name, language makes certain concessions that efface Truth, and therefore the only way by which meaning can be determined remains outside of language itself — what linguists refer to as a transcendental signifier or a belief that imbues a knowledge system with meaning. Bronk writes in "Spades, Kettles and Anonymity,"

> Each separate entity anywhere had its own
> proper name I needed only to find
> or learn from other's finding.
>   Now I know
> their names are pin-ons we give to them and give
> ourselves, that separation is not the truth
> and much won't be named even with made-up names. (*Mild* 32)

To extend this structure of the separation of word and truth is to call into question how culture, history, and ideology attempt to mediate this linguistic gap and render "meaning" out of absence and silence, which is the step that both Waldrop and Howe take in order to examine the wider social and historical context of language. For Howe and Waldrop, an investigation into the indeterminacy of language uncovers socio-historical tensions and the residue of victors and effaced victims.

While Howe's *My Emily Dickinson* is suggestive in relation to Bronk, her poem "Thorow" is even more compelling as a point of comparison especially since it was com-

---

[*]There are numerous other inscribed books on Bronk's shelves including novels by Paul Auster, Gilbert Sorrentino, Richard Elman, as well as countless poets and critics. To trace the linkage of all of these writers with Bronk would be an interesting and valuable study, but, unfortunately, it is not within the scope of this essay. Nevertheless, these various points of affinity speak to the far-reaching influence of Bronk's writing that often moves across generations and genres.

posed while she was the writer-in-residence at the Lake George Arts Project, a town slightly north of Hudson Falls. (Coincidentally, during her stay in Lake George, Howe visited Bronk for the first and only time. Such a visit is deeply suggestive, to say the least.) Nevertheless, to turn to "Thorow," the prose introduction concludes with lines that echo the gist of Bronk's conception of naming as separate from the universal or the Real: "Every name driven will be as another rivet in the machine of universe flux" (*Singularities* 42). This idea is further amplified by quotations from Deleuze and Guattari — "The proper name is the instantaneous apprehension of a multiplicity" — and Thoreau — "am glad to see that you studied out the ponds, got the Indian names straightened out — which means made more crooked" (*Singularities* 42). These three passages parallel Bronk's stance that language is partial and bound by human temporality and, therefore, cannot embody the universe, the Real, and Truth. But Howe extends this partiality into the arena of the historical in order to demonstrate the degree to which the slippage of language is the product of the cycle of human history — what "Thorow" refers to as the "Original of the Otherside / understory of another word" (50). Certainly one of the driving forces of Howe's poetry is how language and textuality are the manifestations of ideological tensions; and within such a structure, a word is the trace of the underhistory, the history that has been partially effaced. In this light, Howe's poetry reinforces Bronk's sense of naming as ineffectual in relation to Truth since language unveils its own indeterminacy and inability to resolve the questions that it articulates. As the final page of "Thorow" emphasizes, language contributes to the perpetual quest for an elusive definitiveness. As this passage clearly illustrates, the word is in fact the "thief" that disallows any sense of closure.

anthen   uplispth enend

adamap   blue wov   thefthe

folled   floted   keen

                Themis

thouscullingme
Thiefth (59)

The conjoining of words as well as their resultant transformation by blending archaic and modern spelling circles back to Howe's sense of the word as an attempt to rivet certainty into a fluid medium, which reveals the instability of naming: instead of establishing a stable point of reference or an anchor of certainty, the poem continues to be swept away — sculled along — in the current of "universe flux." The desire to strive for an immovable point of certainty evokes the following lines from Bronk's "The World": "I thought that you were an anchor in the drift of the world; / but no: there isn't an anchor anywhere. / There isn't an anchor in the drift of the world. Oh no." (*Life* 189). "Thorow" arrives at this comprehension of perpetual linguistic drift through the interrogation of the inter-relation of language, textuality, and history.

Rosmarie Waldrop's *A Key into the Language of America* shares a similar poetic focus with Susan Howe's *Singularities*, especially since both poets investigate the friction between European language and culture and that of the various Native Indian tribes, but Waldrop's writing also offers a slightly different connection with and perspective upon Bronk. As Waldrop explains in her introduction, "A Key into the Key,"

> In parallel with Roger Williams's anthropological passages, the initial prose section of each of my chapters tries to get at the clash of Indian and European cultures by a violent collage of phrases from Williams with elements from anywhere in my Western heritage. I try to enact the confrontation of the two cultures by juxtapositions, often within a single sentence. Roger Williams's voice will be recognized by its archaic syntax and vocabulary printed in boldface. There is also an additional tension between the values of the seventeenth-century settlers, "Saints," "Pilgrims," and my own, which are not only secular but also informed by twentieth-century hindsight as to the long-range destruction inherent in the settlers' struggle to survive. (xxii-xxiii)

The poem brings into play a number of voices, values, and languages that reveals the unstable foundation upon which language and, concomitantly, cultural meaning are based. The source text for the poem, Roger Williams's *A Key into the Language of America*, an extensive primer for the study of Native languages (and specifically Narragensett) in English, further foregrounds the issues of naming and meaning as the product of culturally-based translations. While the crux of the issue for *A Key into the Language of America* is cultural, it is precisely the language — the archaic "syntax and vocabulary" coupled with the residue of the otherwise dead Narragensett language — and Waldrop's awareness that naming is seeped in absences, violence, and cultural conflicts that permeates the poem as a whole.

> **What paths their swift foot** have cut in history and philosophy,
> with distinct genital extensions toward the Great Plains. A feeling
> of wings in the air will move understanding. So vast, distressed,
> undone, in search of company to **take tobacco and discourse**.
> Whirl of environs, exaggerations and limping, lamenting lingua
> franca.
>
> **Mayuo?**
> **Is There a Way?**
> there is no way
> unscathed
>
> ogue
> agent
> er [bold in the original] (*Key* 23)

By juxtaposing the two languages, the poem accentuates the inherent violence in the clash of languages — "cut," "distressed," "limping," and "lamenting," — and in response to the question, "Is There a Way?" the poem concludes that "there is no way / unscathed." As a path valorizes one form of knowledge, it simultaneously contributes to the erosion of knowledge in another form: any "progress" is therefore balanced by an equal cultural loss, which reveals an inescapable zero-sum equation. Waldrop's poem powerfully illustrates how the act of naming is fraught with historical, cultural, and linguistic difficulties, and which suggest the disturbing relation between language — as mere "pin-ons" — and the dialectic of history. The poem demonstrates how the American language is in fact a palimpsest of cultures and histories — a fact that could be extended to all cultures and peoples.

In this light, consider Waldrop's argument in relation to Bronk's "Casualties":

> It would be good if we could think of the Flood
> as though it had mattered, so that in dry times
> like this with low water in places still

> flooded and never occupied again
> you might catch sight along the shore
> or underneath, of house foundations, old
> stone walls, bits of roads, and think
> of those who lived there once and were, as we
> in those times, all inconsequent. (*Cage* 7)

The resurrection of artifacts and remnants of former cultures prompts Bronk to comment upon both the despair inherent in the mortal limitations of individuals and cultures as well as the ineffectual forms to which people so desperately cling. Such forms are manifestations of the desire for permanence (an "anchor") in an otherwise fluid universe. The issue of how history and culture are manifestations of form — and much the same as language are impositions that are destined to fail — is further developed in Bronk's essays on various Mayan archeological sites collected under the title of *The New World*. He writes in "The Occupation of Space — Palenque,"

> If it is true of space that it is featureless and empty except as we limit its vastness and shape it by our occupation, the form of the cities we impose on it, the direction and location of the boundaries and roads, it is true also that our occupation is never quite successful. It is part of the same truth that the limits we set to space are always in some degree arbitrary, and the names we give it are given names not absolute ones. We are always in some degree still nowhere in an empty vastness. Our passionately occupied Palenques are always abandoned. We tire of the forms we impose upon space and the restricted identities we secure from them. We tire finally even of the act itself of imposition. (*Vectors* 29).

Even though Bronk's essays are subtle in their exploration of language, history, and culture, it is not difficult to recognize that Howe and Waldrop are working within similar boundaries. That is, both Howe and Waldrop explicate how culture and textual history attempt to limit and contain an uncontainable, ever transforming cultural and historical space, and each draws upon language as a means to demonstrate the elusiveness of definitive form, names, and meaning. In this light, Howe and Waldrop transform Bronk's ideas into the postmodern present by extending his conception of language, history, and form into the realm of the socio-historical.

Whereas the linkage between Bronk, Howe, and Waldrop gestures to the extension and expansion of a conception of language into its cultural and historical manifestations, the connection between Bronk and Michael Palmer seems more direct especially since Palmer's focus remains firmly within the purview of language and how it operates. Moreover, Palmer argues that language unveils a primal split that separates the speaker from the object and unveils an impenetrable surface that the speaker cannot penetrate, which is in keeping with Bronk's sense of the webbing of language and knowledge. Within this context, Palmer ruminates upon the "hum of the possible-to-say" (*Passages* 4), which implies a division that parallels Bronk's assertion that everyday things are "not what we call them though but something else / and not such that we can ever know" (*Mild* 34). Palmer's poetry can be seen as engaging in a similar dialogue that investigates the chasm between Truth and Reality (on one hand) and language and knowledge (on the other), but for Palmer the crux of the matter is not only language and form but the dimension of the individual as the messenger and vehicle of language. Consider this stanza from Palmer's "Wheel" within the light of Bronk's lines quoted above.

> You can say the broken word but cannot speak
> for it, can name a precise and particular shade
> of blue if you can remember its name
> (Woman of the South, new Lilac, Second Sky?) (*Passages* 23)

The linkage between individual and object is not only ruptured by the "broken word," but the individual can only "say" the word and not "speak for it." The speaker, bound by such limitations, cannot transcend the impenetrable state of the "broken word," and language, contingent upon the limited consciousness and memory of the speaker and/or writer, is destined to become broken and, eventually, irretrievably lost. As the individual attempts to render and speak things, the inherent limitations of the human intervene and disperse and diffuse the Truth. Language, therefore, is either already broken or is broken in the act of speaking/writing. Subsequently, all that an individual can speak is a reproduction of a particular object, person, action, or subjective position — "what follows is a picture of how things are for me now" (*Passages* 57). Language and the speaker/writer remain firmly within the bind of appearance and surfaces, and the individual is unable to penetrate past the surface (the name) and enter the depths of the Real.

Palmer conceives this schism as the tension between thinking and language: "We think to say in some language" (*Passages* 59). That is, thinking and language are contiguous realms, but the movement from thought to language is filtered and diffused through the body, memory, and knowledge. Immediacy and accuracy are muted. Subsequently, the image of the voice takes on a special resonance especially since it invokes the fleeting presence, temporality, and absence of speaking and the constraints of language. As such, the opening of Palmer's powerful poem "Recursus" reads,

> The voice, because of its austerity, will often cause dust to rise
> The voice, because of its austerity, will sometimes attempt the representation of dust. (*Passages* 57)

Through the breath, voice possesses a physicality that affects the dust, but such physicality is troubled by the notion that the voice "sometimes attempt[s] the representation of dust." Note that it is an *attempt* to render, which gestures toward the inherent partiality of language and the individual. Consequently, many of the ideas that dominate Bronk's poetry — language, representation, knowledge, and how each of those items are the extension of inherent, intractable, and all too human limitations — are re-presented in Palmer's writing, which suggests that Palmer has inherited Bronk's skeptical stance toward language and knowledge, but also that his conception of language is filtered through the lens of memory and subjective identity. Whereas Howe and Waldrop consider how language is engaged and shaped by culture, Palmer focuses upon how the indeterminacy of language is the direct extension of the partiality of human subjectivity.

Given these discussions of the poetry of Bronk, Howe, Waldrop, and Palmer, it should be obvious that linguistic consciousness cannot be divorced from the philosophical: to think about language is to be aware of the inextricable webbing of language, knowledge, and thought. Bronk's unwavering attention to language and the precise thinking manifest in and by his poetry reveals another important facet of his place within contemporary poetry. As Susan Howe remarks, "I love much of [Bronk's] poetry for the same reason I love Wallace Stevens'[s] — it is spare, plain, yet infinitely suggestive; philosophy and poetry at once" (Letter to the author, 18 November 1995). All of the poets mentioned in this essay could be included under this category of poetry/philosophy, but, more importantly, Howe's statement suggests how his writing has affected poetry as a medium and vehicle for thought.

Being philosophically engaged with the world and the sustained meditation upon the place of the human within the world dominates all of Bronk's poetry, but perhaps no poem is more poignant in this regard than "Metonymy as an Approach to a Real World."

> Whether what we sense of this world
> is the what of this world only, or the what
> of which of several possible worlds
> — which what? — something of what we sense
> may be true, may be the world, what it is, what we sense.
> For the rest, a truce is possible, the tolerance
> of travelers, eating foreign foods, trying words
> that twist the tongue, to feel that time and place,
> not thinking that this is the real world.
>
> Conceded, that all the clocks tell local time;
> conceded, that "here" is anywhere we bound
> and fill a space; conceded, we make a world:
> is something caught there, contained there,
> something real, something which we can sense?
> Once in a city blocked and filled, I saw
> the light lie in the deep chasm of a street,
> palpable and blue, as though it had drifted in
> from say, the sea, a purity of space. (*Life* 43)

The overarching flow of the poem effortlessly glides from proposition to proposition as it shifts from an interrogation of the abstract conceptions of space and time to specific observations concerning the human dimensions of "local" time and place; it pivots back and forth between propositions, questions, explications, and examples in a measured balance of ideas. The poem is remarkable in that it offers deeply poignant questions and reflections concerning perception and knowledge, experience and infinity, while employing the striking image of light, "palpable and blue," as a site of condensation for the multi-faceted dimensions that the poem explores. The light, in other words, is a metaphor par excellance, which simultaneously supports the philosophical rigor of the flow of ideas while also reinforcing that the work is "poetic." Consequently, the poem engages in its careful explication of the status of the spatio-temporal without resorting to the abstract quality of philosophical discourse; consequently, the language retains its concision without sacrificing the musicality of such words as "conceded," "palpable," and "chasm" — poetry and philosophy at once. Moreover, "Metonymy as an Approach to a Real World" demonstrates that the poem is the site where the boundaries of knowledge and self are engaged, challenged, measured, affirmed, and/or disputed. The poem is a living form that catalyzes and sustains the thinking process — a point that the title of his collected poems, *Life Supports*, reinforces. Bronk further confirms the immediacy of the poem as an agent of living when he remarks that "the instrument [poetry] is keeping me alive so that I'm available for it" (Weinfield 36). The poem is where thinking *and* living take place, and the poems themselves are the gauge of that life.

Subsequently, when poetic tributes are paid to Bronk (as in the special issue that *Sagetrieb* devoted to Bronk in 1988 or the Bronk issues of *Talisman* in 1989 and 1995), poets tend to focus upon (and imitate) his philosophical mode of poetic inquiry and the relation of thinking and living. For example, Robert Creeley's "Echoes," which was first published in the special issue of *Sagetrieb* and later appeared in the collection *Windows* (1990), is dedicated to Bronk and "echoes" the propositional quality of his poetry. Consider Creeley's poem within the context of "Metonymy as an Approach to a Real World":

The stars stay up there where they first were.
We have changed but they seem as ever.

What was their company first to be, their curious proposal,
that we might get there, which, of course, we did.

How dead now the proposal of life simply, how echoing it is,
how everything we did, we did and thought we did!

Was it always you as one, and them as one,
and one another was us, we thought, a Protestant, a complex

determination of this loneliness of human spaces,
what could status be but something else no longer there,

some echoing light too late to be for us specific.

But there they were and there we thought we saw them. (*Windows* 110)

The poem foregrounds the image of the stars as a prompt for the sustained rumination upon how the self, in order to create a sense of identity, constructs an image of the world: that identity, as the juxtaposing of the first and second lines suggests, is fictive; therefore, one's subjectivity as well as the concomitant view of the world is only an echo or a shadow of some dimly perceived thing. Through the poem's juxtaposing of the lines and overarching exploration of the sense of critical reality, Creeley's poem captures the propositional essence of Bronk's writing, the sense of the poem as the rigorous interrogation into the limits of human existence, as well as the recurring skepticism towards certainty as both the body of knowledge and naming. In this regard, "Echoes" possesses a Bronk-like flare for the indeterminate quality of language and the inadequacy of thought to fix and contain the Real. The tribute paid is both one of imitation as well as the recognition of the pervasive aura of Bronk's ideas.

Keith Waldrop also notes the significance of Bronk's philosophical and linguistic precision when he remarks that

> I have wanted for a long time to address some paragraphs to William Bronk, remembering how some of his poems back in *Origin* — I found out only later that he had already published a volume — helped me unravel snarls in my own expression. Since we last met, an age has gone by. (*Silhouette* 57)

As Waldrop suggests, the dual nature of Bronk's poetry is an achieved balance between precise language, sustained reflection, and carefully phrased ideas. In a further tribute to Bronk, Keith and Rosmarie Waldrop dedicate a section of their book, *WellWellReality*, to him. As evident from the opening poem of that section, their tribute acknowledges the sharpness of Bronk's ideas, the absolute precision of his sense of language, and the mastery of phrasing. The Waldrops' poem reads,

> periodically
> glum
> and the sun
> dials the time
> since after all
> our

pleasant stories a starting
point (28)

Despite the abstract quality of the language, which may be the result of the collaborative nature of the poem, Rosmarie and Keith Waldrop not only invoke issues central to Bronk's poetry — the ebb and flow of human time in relation to infinity, and the sense of fictions constructed as "starting points" or site for exploration—but their language with its plain diction and breathlessly phrased syntax parallels the verbal intensity of Bronk's poetry and its ability to leap off the page with its amazing poignancy as in "No Big Bang":

No big bang.
We begin
with no beginning,
endlessly
end (*All* 162)

Bronk's poetry might best be characterized by this intense precision and intellectual complexity, which suggests a poetic register that within the body of established twentieth-century poetry is unique and exhilarating.

As the discussions surrounding Howe, the Waldrops, Palmer, and Creeley suggest, Bronk has been slowly permeating the fabric of contemporary poetry: his writing has been gaining wider readership, and as a result, Bronk-like motifs and refrains can be heard within the texture of more and more contemporary poetry. Perhaps it is only in retrospect that one can finally realize *and* admire what Bronk has been doing since the 1950s and truly recognize the degree to which his language-intensive, highly reflective poetry anticipates what has been flourishing since the late 1970s in poetry. Whether it is a direct and immediate influence or, rather, that Bronk has simply anticipated the issues and poetics that has risen over the last twenty years or so, Bronk has been emerging as a dominant poetic presence. In this regard, Bronk is both a contemporary and a precursor. He has cleared the way for readers and writers, and his writing has blazed the path that contemporary poetry often finds itself tracing and retracing.

In the Cyclotron

Tiny particles of energy

sometimes collide and make a track we can see.
In ways, a work of art is like that. (*All* 75)

WORKS CITED

Bronk, William. *All of What We Loved*. Jersey City, NJ: Talisman House, Publishers, 1998.

-------. *The Cage of Age*. Jersey City, NJ: Talisman House, Publishers, 1996.

-------. *Life Supports: New and Collected Poems*. Jersey City, NJ: Talisman House, Publishers 1997.

-------. *The Mild Day*. Hoboken, NJ: Talisman House, Publishers, 1993.

-------. *Vectors and Smoothable Curves: Collected Essays*. Jersey City NJ: Talisman House, Publishers, 1997.

Creeley, Robert. *Windows*. New York: New Directions, 1990.

Ernest, John. "Fossilized Fish and the World of Unknowing: John Ashbery and William Bronk" in *The Tribe of John: Ashbery and Contemporary Poetry*. Susan M. Schultz, ed. Tuscaloosa: U of Alabama P, 1995.

Howe, Susan. *My Emily Dickinson*. Berkeley: North Atlantic Books, 1985.

-------. *Singularities*. Hanover: Wesleyan UP, 1990.

Palmer, Michael. *At Passages*. New York: New Directions, 1995.

Waldrop, Keith. *The Silhouette of the Bridge (Memory Stand-Ins)*. Penngrove: Avec, 1997.

Waldrop, Rosmarie. *A Key into the Language of America*. New York: New Directions, 1994.

Waldrop, Rosmarie and Keith. *WellWellReality [collaborations]*. Sausalito: The Post-Apollo Press, 1998.

Weinfield, Henry. "A Conversation with William Bronk." *Sagetrieb* 7 (3):17-44.

W. Scott Howard

'THE BREVITIES': FORMAL MOURNING, TRANSGRESSION, & POSTMODERN AMERICAN ELEGIES[*]

I

Yet each to keep and all, retrievements out of the night . . .
   —Walt Whitman, "When Lilacs Last in the Dooryard Bloom'd"

The art of losing isn't hard to master.
   —Elizabeth Bishop, "One Art"

MAJOR THEORISTS AND CRITICS OF THE 'MODERN' AMERICAN ELEGY (such as Jahan Ramazani, Peter Sacks, Celeste Schenck, W. David Shaw, and Melissa Zeiger) differentiate the pre-modern from the modern poem on the grounds of generic resistance and transgression.[†] The pre-modern elegy, in the tradition of such pastoral elegies as Milton's "Lycidas" and Whitman's "When Lilacs Last in the Dooryard Bloom'd," offers a work of mourning and an art of saving that involves three rhetorical movements (lamentation, praise, and consolation), which culminate in visions of spiritual transcendence, apotheosis, and poetic inheritance. The modern elegy, following such works as Swinburne's "Ave Atque Vale" and Bishop's elegiac villanelle "One Art," constructs a work of melancholic mourning and an art of losing that critiques the genre's pre-modern formal and rhetorical conventions,

---

[*] I would like to thank my graduate students Amy England, Terence Huber, Greg Kinzer, and Bryan Walpert for their spirited and insightful contributions to the 1998 "Theory and History of the Elegy" course that helped shape some aspects of my argument in this essay. I also wish to acknowledge the participation of my colleagues Jerry Chapman and Cole Swensen, who offered constructive suggestions for this chapter's revision.

[†] See Ramazani, "The Wound of History," 405-406, *Poetry of Mourning*, 1-31, and *Yeats and the Poetry of Death*, 7-13; Sacks 312-328; Schenck, "When the Moderns Write Elegy," 97-98, 108; Shaw, *Elegy and Paradox*, 79-102; and Zeiger 1-25.

especially those of spiritual transcendence and consolation.[*] Such a paradigm, however, proves to be somewhat reductive given the diverse history of the poetic elegy in the Classical, English, and American literary traditions.[†]

From the earliest Classical works in the genre by Moschus ("The Lament for Bion"), Theokritos ("The First Idyll"), and Virgil ("Eclogue X") to modern and contemporary American exemplars by Benveniste ("A Measure for LZ"), Levis ("Elegy With a Petty Thief in the Rigging"), Olson ("There was a Youth whose Name was Thomas Granger"), Oppen ("The Book of Job and a Draft of a Poem to Praise the Paths of the Living"), and Tate ("The Lost Pilot") two double-gestures shape the elegy's most prevalent and perplexing generic and modal themes: the simultaneous appropriation of and transgression against generic conventions; and a resistance to both spiritual transcendence and elegiac consolation.[‡] How can generic resistance and transgression be an index of elegy's modernity, as Ramazani argues with frequent qualification, if those same rhetorical gestures condition the poetic genre's possibility?[§] Or, to pose the same question from a more vexing point of view:

---

[*] I am relying mainly upon Ramazani's argument in *Poetry of Mourning* for my presentation here of this paradigm that applies in general to the works of the five critics mentioned in the above note. Sacks grounds the modern American elegy's generic resistance and transgression upon two levels of cultural alienation: intellectual displacement from European literary traditions; and existential angst due to tensions between individual and communal ethics in a capitalist society (312-313). Schenck theorizes a duality: modern American elegies either appropriate spiritual transcendence for literary gain, or resist consolation due to the lack of a sacred vision (98). Shaw holds that the metaphysical trope of paradox — so fundamental to the pre-modern elegy's poetics — "breaks down into an open war of opposites" (5) in the modern elegy. And Zeiger, via Swinburne's "Ave Atque Vale," redefines the elegy's modernity in terms of: anti-consolation; resistance to the "English neoclassical elegy's triumphant relegation of death and the mortal to a feminized, distanced, and disembodied realm of nonbeing" (26); and revisions of the Orpheus myth that foreground the politics of gender.

[†] On the Classical elegy, see: Aiken; Alexiou; Berg; Lambert; Race; Rosenmeyer; and Schenck, "The Funeral Elegy as Pastoral Initiation." On the Renaissance and Early Modern elegy, see: Draper; Fradenburg; Kay; Lange; Lilley; Mell; Pigman; Potts; Scodel; Smith; Williams; and Weinfield. On the modern American elegy, see: Bedetti; Bethea; Blasing; Bradford; Kingsley; Meyer; Minock; Muske; Schenck, *Mourning and Panegyric*, and "Feminism and Deconstruction;" Stanford; and Stone.

[‡] Lilley argues this point for elegies by Renaissance and early modern English women writers (87). The claim holds across the genre's history, especially for elegies by women. Consider, for example, the following poets and poems: Queen Elizabeth I, "Self and Otherself;" Katherine Philips, "*Orinda* upon little *Hector Philips*;" Charlotte Smith, "Sonnet V: To the South Downs;" Emily Dickinson, "#280: I felt a Funeral, in my Brain;" Christina Rossetti, "After Death" and "Dead Before Death;" Sylvia Plath, "Daddy;" Marianne Moore, "A Grave;" Anne Sexton, "The Truth the Dead Know;" Gwendolyn Brooks, "the funeral;" Adrienne Rich, "Not Like That;" Audre Lorde, "The Same Death Over and Over or Lullabies Are For Children;" Lucille Clifton, "move;" Kay Boyle, "To a Proud Old Woman Watching the Tearing Down of the Hurricane Shed;" and Sapphire, "Autopsy Report 86-13504." Such a logic of "renunciation and cancellation," to borrow Lilley's phrase (87), is not, however, limited to elegies written by women, as Schenck asserts in "Feminism and Deconstruction" (22-24).

[§] Ramazani qualifies his central thesis many times in *Poetry of Mourning*, noting precedents for generic resistance and

if generic appropriation, resistance, and transgression inform elegy's rhetorical ground, then are we dealing with a poetic genre that has always been modern or perhaps even postmodern?* Some critics have argued that point.†

This essay addresses a topic no less problematic than the difference between the pre-modern and modern elegy: a poetics of the postmodern American elegy. Is such a thing not impossible? "There is, for instance, the problem of the elegy" ("Origen" 38), writes Bin Ramke, suggesting both the futility and inescapability of elegy for contemporary poets concerned with challenging a poetics of loss dominated largely in America, since 1960, by various cults of personality and "the Confessional mode" (Perkins 588-590). On the one hand, this essay offers an historical scope. Working outward from paradigmatic modern American elegies by Elizabeth Bishop and George Oppen, I will differentiate the characteristics of postmodern works in the genre, focusing primarily upon the poetry of William Bronk. On the other hand, however, this essay does not — nor should it — present a unified theory of the postmodern American elegy. That would be an impossible gesture, given the elegy's current diversity of forms, themes, occasions, and styles. My point of departure, in keeping with this collection's theme, will be a study of innovative American elegies that define poetic tradition as both a working context of artistic change — rather than an unchanging transcendent pattern within and against which all poems should be measured — and "a trust in radical form, however [scrupulously] achieved" (Foster, "Preface," vii-viii).

Given those parameters, I will argue that the postmodern American elegy introduces a new linguistic turn and a concomitant attention to poetic form conceptualized as a discursive field of indeterminate linguistic signification within and against which poetry constructs its subjects and objects of study in so far as they are devisable. This trope of a turning toward poetic form as field distinguishes many innovative American elegies (by poets as diverse as Charles Bernstein, William Bronk, Lyn Hejinian, Susan Howe, W.S. Merwin, and Bin Ramke) from pre-modernist and modernist texts.‡ When the post

---

transgression in pre-modern elegies by both American and English poets. These modifications enrich his book's historical scope and interpretive depth at the same time that they weaken his principal distinction between the pre-modern and the modern elegy.

*In this essay I will attempt to articulate a quasi-periodizing notion of the postmodern American elegy and will not argue for such anachronistic classifications as, for example, a 'postmodernist Classical' elegy.

†See Fradenburg 177-180 and Zeiger 26-42.

‡This trope of elegy's postmodern linguistic turning modifies Sacks' theory of elegy's psychological turning toward a substitute love-object (1-12). On the distinction between modern and postmodern American elegies that I

modernists rewrite elegy, they often not only resist and transgress generic conventions, but also articulate the linguistic and cultural construction of loss and consolation, thereby engaging in meta-critiques of both poetic theory and practice.

One consequence of this heightened ironic self-reflexivity is the aporia of an anti-consolatory consolation, which yet retains traces of pre-modernist and modernist poetics. Another consequence, I believe, that signals the singularity of many postmodern elegies, is the emergence of new ideas of poetic form as field of discursive consolation. For innovative elegists writing today the poetics of loss involves *formal* mourning, as ironic and seemingly implausible propositions of anti-consolatory consolation complement appropriations and critiques of generic conventions, or forms, that turn upon the possibility of indeterminate fields, or forms, of discourse. Form thus refigured becomes a site and sign in many postmodern American elegies of generic resistance and the sure brevities of artistic transgression.

II

Who would I show it to
—W. S. Merwin, "Elegy"

Is a postmodern elegy possible? Upon first reflection, this laconic text by W. S. Merwin would seem to suggest an implausible situation facing the contemporary elegist. On the one hand, the existential absence of the one person to whom this elegy would be written occludes the poem's reason for being. Given this metaphysical and linguistic negation, "Elegy," from Merwin's *The Carrier of Ladders* (1970), can be read strongly as "an anti-elegy, a refusal not simply to mourn, but to write a sonorous, eloquent, mournful, but finally acquiescent, accepting — in a word, 'elegiac' — poem at all" (Scholes 38). Yet the poem's title alone provokes further reflection; for this so-called anti-elegy ironically appropriates and transgresses generic distinction as an elegy, giving us an elegy about elegies and thereby implying a postmodern poetics of loss. (I will return to Merwin's "Elegy" in my essay's

---

formulate here, for example, compare respectively the following modern works (James Tate's "The Lost Pilot," Lorine Niedecker's "Bonpland," Charles Olson's "There Was a Youth Whose Name Was Thomas Granger," and Larry Levis' "Elegy With a Petty Thief in the Rigging") with these postmodern texts (Charles Bernstein's "Internal Loss Control," Lynn Hejinian's "Elegy, for K. B.," Susan Howe's "a bibliography of the king's book; or, eikon basilike," and Bin Ramke's "Elegy as Origin").

conclusion). This double-gesture of generic appropriation and transgression constitutes one of elegy's oldest and most persistent rhetorical components. While all artistic genres variously partake of this two-fold enabling condition — working both within and against aesthetic and cultural traditions — the elegy, perhaps more than any other type or mode of literary production, employs this rhetorical double-gesture as a signature of the genre's most central formal and thematic concern: the dialectical (and/or non-dialectical) tensions between absence and presence.

In what ways do generic and modal literary distinctions apply (if at all) to innovative writings at the close of the twentieth-century? By definition, aren't innovative (i.e. avant-garde) texts concerned primarily, as Poggioli argues (67), with the agonistic, sacrificial struggle of transgressing literary conventions?[*] After an era (since 1950?)[†] in which many poets, theorists, and critics have undertaken an unprecedented critique of traditional components of literary works — in particular: essence, voice, subjectivity, linguistic signification, and transcendence (to name a few) — what poetic remains remain for elegy, the second oldest literary genre (after the epic) with a continuous history? *The New Princeton Encyclopedia of Poetry and Poetics* (1993) tells us that the elegy is usually a short, ceremonious poem written in response to the death of a person, but may also concern more general meditations upon love, death, and philosophical principles (Preminger 322-324).

If the preservation of essence, voice, and subjectivity are central to the elegist's work of mourning that involves a three-fold rhetorical movement from lamentation to praise to consolation wagered on an incarnative poetics of positive signification and spiritual transcendence, then, it would seem, the elegy should cease to exist (as either a definable or devisable genre or mode) for postmodern, innovative, avant-garde poets. Is a 'postmodern' elegy therefore impossible? Is the contemporary American elegy post*mortem*?

The poetic elegy continues to thrive in a remarkable diversity of forms and themes as the twenty-first-century emerges. Some critics have recently remarked that the elegy may be the most popular and vital of poetic genres still being written.[‡] Despite such a proliferation

---

[*] See Barbiero. In response to recent statements on contemporary American poetics by Mark Wallace, Jefferson Hansen, and John Notto, Barbiero modifies Poggioli's central claim that avant-garde artists perforce sacrifice their indebtedness to their predecessors for the sake of achieving the really new work. Barbiero discerns instead a conservative trend emerging within American literary communities, or what he calls "an avant-garde without agonism" (151-153). Barbiero sensitively differentiates this new ethos from the poetics and politics of language writing, thereby articulating a new generation's growing sense of identity within (and perhaps not necessarily against) tradition.

[†] See Perkins 331-334.

[‡] See Muske and Ramazani, *Poetry of Mourning*, 1-31.

in recent years of poetry concerned with so many different kinds of loss, there are no anthologies dedicated specifically to the modern and postmodern elegy. In fact, there is only one collection of the poetic elegy currently in print at the time of this essay's composition: Peter Washington's *Poems of Mourning* (Everyman 1998). Washington's selections range far and wide from Horace to Farid Ud-Din Attar to Elizabeth Bishop and Joseph Brodsky, offering perhaps two dozen works that could be considered modernist, but no elegies to represent postmodern achievements in the genre. Four topically organized anthologies published since 1969 include elegies and elegiac poems within larger contexts both occasional and cultural: Randall Dudley's and Margaret G. Burroughs' *For Malcolm: Poems on the Life and Death of Malcolm X* (1969 and now out of print); Harry Gilonis' *Louis Zukofsky, Or Whoever Someone Else Thought He Was* (1988 and now out of print); Michael Klein's *Poet's For Life: Seventy-Six Poets Respond to AIDS* (1989); and Carolyn Forche's *Against Forgetting: Twentieth-Century Poetry of Witness* (1993). Of these four collections Forche's provides the most comprehensive gathering; but the elegies and elegiac poems included therein comprise a minor portion of the volume's international scope and political focus.

Scholars have neglected the genre's modern and postmodern avatars. At the time of this essay's composition, less than one dozen journal articles follow pioneering studies of the pre-modern and modern elegy by Peter Sacks, *The English Elegy* (1985), Celeste Schenck, *Mourning and Panegyric* (1988), Jahan Ramazani, *Poetry of Mourning* (1994), W. David Shaw, *Elegy and Paradox* (1994), and Melissa F. Zieger, *Beyond Consolation* (1997).[*] Compared to other poetic genres such as epic, or lyric, or prose poem, for example, the modern elegy remains suspiciously unthought (and the postmodern elegy virtually invisible) within critical discourse. In fact only one book, David Rigsbee's *Styles of Ruin: Joseph Brodsky & the Postmodernist Elegy* (1999), promises an investigation of the latter subject. Rigsbee's argument, however, recapitulates much of Ramazani's post-Freudian theory that modern elegies exhibit melancholic mourning and thereby perform oppositional cultural work through their resistance to (and trangsressions against) the genre's conventions, especially those of spiritual transcendence and consolation (Rigsbee, DAI, 210).[†] Yet, as Ramazani reluctantly concedes more than once, even these claims for the elegy's modernity, or postmodernity in Rigsbee's

---

[*] See note on p. 115 above.

[†] At least this is Rigsbee's argument in his dissertation. Although I could not see Rigsbee's book, forthcoming at the time of this essay's composition, he tells me in a recent correspondence that, for his revisions of the dissertation, he has been working outward from "not so much ... Sacks and Ramazani (who cover the psychological terrain well), but from Grossman and Rorty ... [and] from Joseph himself ... whose own views surprisingly, I think, look to Wittgenstein ... and beyond to Derrida" ("Styles of Ruin: Revisions").

case, fail to distinguish the pre-modern from the modern elegy and/or elegiac work because one can readily find evidence of such resistance and transgression throughout the genre's history.

In opposition to those critics who would anachronistically extend the categories of 'modern' and/or 'postmodern' to poems such as "The Book of the Dutchess" by Chaucer, or "Ave Atque Vale" by Swinburne, I wish to reserve the designation postmodern for elegies that are (in terms of practicality) more recent than and (in terms of poetics) truly different from either pre-modernist or modernist works. By employing the term "postmodern" I wish to invoke merely a quasi-periodizing concept; for not all elegies written today are postmodern — nor should they be — according to the generic and modal distinctions I have thus far submitted. To be sure, postmodernism connotes the style of a period, but does not denote the period of a style. In addition to my estimation above of the elegy's two persistent double-gestures, I would also like to offer the following refiguration of the genre's formal and thematic characteristics in order to articulate a working definition of the modern elegy that will inform my central argument concerning the postmodern American elegy. *The New Princeton Encyclopedia* notes that "[t]raditionally the functions of the elegy were three, to lament, praise, and console" (Preminger 324). This construction implies a linear rhetorical progression that does not hold for all modernist elegies, nor does it apply to postmodernist texts. Such a thematic definition, however, can still be useful if slightly modified. First of all, modern and postmodern elegies frequently employ these three rhetorical components, but often in the manner of a collage rather than in a strict linear fashion. Secondly, modernist and postmodernist elegies frequently invoke gestures of lamentation, praise, and consolation only to overturn them through both expressions of ambivalence, anger, and angst, and techniques of erasure, irony, and satire. These strategies of resistance and transgression, it should be noted, extend and exaggerate pre-modern generic conventions, thereby achieving such aporetic propositions as an anti-consolatory consolation.

The modern elegy thus works within and against pre-modern traditions, but often heightens the genre's simultaneous appropriation of and transgression against generic conventions as well as the poetic form's resistance to both spiritual transcendence and consolation. The modern elegy also frequently employs and/or critiques three rhetorical components central to the genre's pre-modern conventions (lament, praise, and consolation), though not necessarily in that order of presentation. The postmodern elegy, I contend, exhibits these traits as well, but often introduces a new linguistic turn and a concomitant concern with poetic form — not form as defined by verse, meter, and rhyme — and not mythopoetic form as construed by modernists, such as T. S. Eliot and Wallace Stevens — but form imagined as a discursive field of indeterminate linguistic signification.[*] This sense of poetic form as field differs as well from Olson's theory of "FIELD COMPOSITION" (387) in which a depersonalized yet kinesthetic and organic artistic intention manages relations between objects (391). The postmodern linguistic turn toward poetic form as a field of indeterminate signification marks the departure of many innovative American elegies today from either pre-modernist or modernist texts. Postmodern elegists often not only resist and transgress generic conventions, but also thematize the linguistic and social construction of loss and consolation. Two consequences, as I have argued above, derive from such meta-critiques of both poetic theory and practice: the aporia of an anti-consolatory consolation (which, I should note, appeals greatly to a generation of readers steeped in a hermeneutics of irony); and new ideas of poetic form as an unstable field of linguistic signification that notwithstanding constitute — albeit in the manner of rhetorical negation — a post-transcendental locus of elegiac consolation.

III

> Not long, but it isn't anyway
> determined by the interval: we mourn,
> maybe, the brevities, as much as to say
> form were the enemy — the length of form —
> to hide from ourselves, of course from ourselves, — who else? —
> that emptiness of content length couldn't fill
> no matter how long it might be — forever if it were.
>   —William Bronk, "The Emptiness of Human Being"

A COMPARISON BETWEEN ELIZABETH BISHOP'S "ONE ART" (1970) and William Bronk's "The Emptiness of Human Being" (1976) yields many of the distinctions between the modern and postmodern American elegy that I have outlined in the above sections of this essay. Bishop's elegiac vilanelle articulates an art of losing; offers an aporetic anti-consolatory consolation; and approaches, yet turns away from, a postmodern concern with poetic form as an unstable discursive field. Bronk's text, on the other hand, engages in a playfully skeptical critique of essence, voice, subjectivity, linguistic signification, and spiri-

---

[*]See Bernstein, Conte, and Holden for further examinations of postmodern notions of poetic form.

tual transcendence to articulate an anti-consolatory consolation of poetic form construed as a contentless field of discursive instability. "One Art" thematically resists elegiac transcendence and consolation, yet recuperates those generic components through the poem's negotiation of the villanelle's variable verse form, metrical pattern, and rhyme scheme. "The Emptiness of Human Being" enacts a postmodernized formal mourning, offering a critique of both the generic conventions of elegy and the field of discourse that informs such losing art.

The first two stanzas of Bishop's elegiac villanelle (which laments, in part, the loss of her companion in Brazil, Lota de Macedo Soares) propose an ironic art of gaining mastery over disaster as a qualified consolation for the small daily losses that gradually accrue with time. The stakes increase in the third, fourth, and fifth stanzas: places, names, intentions, a mother's watch, houses, two cities, two rivers, and a continent are all swept synecdochically into the poem's tragic joy with the ubi sunt motif. As the poem progresses, Bishop achieves a paradoxical sense of both dizzy melancholy and restrained mourning through the villanelle's variable couplet. We are assured that the art of losing is possible to master because no loss ensures complete disaster.

The final stanza, however, complicates this hyperbolic yet balanced equation. In lines 16-19 Bishop imbricates the art of mastering loss with the art of writing disaster. The poem's variable couplet at last emerges intact from this context of existential crisis and discursive play, presenting an ironic anti-consolatory consolation: the art of losing is not impossible to master "though it may look like (*Write it!*) like disaster" (19). Bishop's insistence here upon the act of writing "(*Write it!*)" forces a qualified closure that unsettles more than it consoles. The repetition of the final simile ("like . . . like disaster") heightens our awareness of both the poet's self-reproach and the poem's artifice. What may, at first glance, merely resemble a tragedy (i.e. something like disaster) thus begins to read as a literal disaster (i.e. something like like) that exceeds this poem's figurative capacity to achieve consolation — no matter how ironically qualified.

Jahan Ramazani reads "One Art" as a paradigm for the modern elegy that achieves neither spiritual transcendence nor consolation, but remains immersed in loss beyond recovery (4). Despite Ramazani's attention to verse, meter, and rhyme in his commanding interpretations of many poems in *Poetry of Mourning*, he offers no reflection upon the importance of the villanelle's verse form for Bishop's achievement of an anti-consolatory consolation in this poem. On a thematic level, Bishop's elegiac villanelle does resist elegy's modal conventions of attaining spiritual transcendence and consolation, and also seems to challenge even elegy's more problematic (though no less conventional) double-gesture of generic appropriation and transgression — that is: the articulation of what Celeste Schenck calls "the impossibility of filling the void by means of a compensatory vision" (*Mourning and Panegyric* 11). However, on a formal level — that is, concerning the poem's verse form, metrics, and rhyme scheme — "One Art" recuperates these rhetorical elements central to the elegy's pre-modern and modern traditions. Ronald McFarland reminds us that many twentieth-century villanelles, like "One Art," employ great variation in their use of enjambment and couplet lines and that such modulations in meter and rhyme complement the genre's earliest traditions (97-109). Bishop's villanelle ultimately achieves consolation through a particular form of verse that allows her to lose, revise, then recover the poem's central couplet even as those elusive lines formulate the thematic impossibility of such recuperation. The couplet returns — albeit in a different version — despite (and due to) the poem's art of losing.

In her elegy for Robert Lowell, "North Haven" (1978), Bishop invokes, through a refiguration of the sympathetic nature motif, a similar idea of poetic recovery within and against existential transience. One of the pastoral elegy's most central conventions turns upon a sympathetic understanding of the relationship between the human and natural worlds. While the mortal condition is finite, nature's cycles return from year to year, thus affording a consolation for loss: as the seasons return, so will the departed spirit once installed within the poem's representation of the natural landscape. Bishop's twist on that theme, however, introduces a separation between Lowell and nature. In lines 19-20 Bishop associates nature's sympathetic consolation not with returning cycles, but with modalities of transience akin to poetic principles of revision and metrical variation. Lowell's death signifies his departure from those regenerative forces, as Bishop suggests in lines 26-30. Poetic language may be unstable for Bishop, but not indeterminate nor without content, as it often is for Bronk. In "North Haven," as in "One Art" and other elegies and elegiac poems such as "The Weed," "At the Fishhouses," "Song for the Rainy Season," and "First Death in Nova Scotia," poetry provides an anti-consolatory consolation of linguistic creation within and against existential mutability. Lowell's death remains beyond nature's recuperative powers; yet Bishop's poem enacts a revision of Lowell's words (through modified quotations in the fifth stanza) that ironically performs the work of derangement/re-arrangement he may no longer carry forward. This poetic revision, as in "One Art," suggests a postmodern construction of loss and a critique of consolation, but withdraws from that aporia to secure elegiac consolation within linguistic principles of variable invariability — the one art toward which Bishop's elegies aspire.

In reply to the many questions I posed in the above two sections of this essay, I would now like to turn to William Bronk's "The Emptiness of Human Being," the first stanza of which includes a phrase, "the brevities," that shapes my essay's title and informs my central argument about poetic form, generic transgression, and postmodern American elegies. Bronk's writing has often been compared to the work of Wallace Stevens, W. H. Auden, and Herman Melville among others,[*] but not to that of Bishop despite great affinities between both poets. The work of each excels in a precise economy of intimate and often confrontational statement; expresses desires for friendship, community, and connection to the real; and strives to articulate a mysticism at the heart of both human consciousness and poetic language. Bronk, however, does not embrace Bishop's optimism (however qualified), nor does his poetry delight in the wondrous imagery we find so often in Bishop's work. In fact, Bronk has been described as "a master of the short, imageless poem" (Stefanile 231-232). Bishop's "One Art" and Bronk's "The Emptiness of Human Being" offer valuable points of comparison and contrast in this discussion of modern and postmodern American elegies concerning emerging ideas of poetic form as an indeterminate field of linguistic signification. In "One Art" poetic form serves as a site for both celebrating and recovering loss while in "The Emptiness of Human Being" poetic form turns against such possibilities and toward a more desperate field of language and cultural discourse.

Many of Bronk's readers have argued for the centrality of a desire-for-the-real in his work, but a more apt phrase might be: a desire-and-despair-for-the real.[†] Death plays a significant role in Bronk's poetry — not only physical death, but death construed as the limit of both consciousness and poetic expression. Indeed the distinction between existence and language for Bronk is extremely tenuous because, for this poet, both phenomena are nearly one-in-the-same and equally conditioned by loss and absence. If there is a difference, language only brings us to the realization that we can't know what that difference might be or mean. As John Ernest observes: "Bronk leaves the inexpressible unexpressed and works instead to indicate the limits of expression and thereby to suggest what he cannot hope to say" (71). Bronk's consequent concerns with irony, self-reflexivity, and linguistic subjectivity yield, in his elegies and elegiac poems, meditations upon the limits of poetic genre.

"The Emptiness of Human Being" offers a reflection upon death that turns upon a critique of conventional elegiac transcendence and consolation. Bronk's witty and humorous challenge to the genre's rhetorical characteristics nonetheless articulates a positive,

---

[*] See Bryfonski and Ernest for overviews of criticism of Bronk's poetry.

[†] See Ernest 70, Finkelstein, Foster "Conversations with William Bronk" 13, and Kimmelman 141.

although admittedly partial, gain: an ironic, intellectualized consolation framed as a critique of consolation. But how can that be: an anti-consolatory consolation? As I have argued above, this paradox informs one of the genre's oldest rhetorical conventions. Bronk's poem, however, introduces a heightened concern with poetic form, as the first stanza so succinctly reveals:

> Not long, but it isn't anyway
> determined by the interval: we mourn,
> maybe, the brevities, as much as to say
> form were the enemy — the length of form —
> to hide from ourselves, of course from ourselves, — who else? —
> that emptiness of content length couldn't fill
> no matter how long it might be — forever if it were. (1-7)

What we mourn today in the poetics and poetry of loss, Bronk suggests here, is not the absence of essence, or voice, or subjectivity in language; those are givens — the enabling conditions of self-reflexive, autonomous art. We mourn instead "the brevities" — that is: "the length of form — / . . . that emptiness of content length couldn't fill / no matter how long it might be — forever if it were." In these lines Bronk celebrates the ambivalence and indeterminacy of linguistic signification and thereby indicates his work's affinity with and difference from the poetics of Bishop and other modernist poets, such as George Oppen. "The Emptiness of Human Being" articulates a world fully comprehended by and confounded in language, a world of contentless representational forms within and against which we "hide from ourselves, of course from ourselves, — who else? — / that emptiness of content length couldn't fill." No matter how long a poem might be, the text's contentless form will always appear too brief because no length of linguistic representation can return our presence, voice, intentionality, or subjectivity to us since language signifies merely our disappearance, or, at best, our partial appearance/disappearance within and against a field of indeterminate signification. Bronk's first stanza thus concludes by undercutting the possibility of spiritual transcendence with the somewhat nihilistic prospect that, "no matter how long [form] might be — forever if it were," a poem can neither incarnate human essence, nor announce an interval between vanishings whence presence might emerge. "[T]he brevities" are formal just as the mourning in this poem is purely formal. Bronk's text offers both an elegy upon the formal (i.e. generic) conventions of elegy as well as a consolingly ironic, anti-consolatory reflection upon that formal (i.e. discursive) critique of poetic tradition. This second rhetorical movement — this linguistic turn toward poetic form as a contentless field of signification — distinguishes Bronk's elegy from either pre-modernist or modernist texts because here we discover a singular concern informed by (yet truly new to) the tradition.

The poem's second stanza also articulates such a linguistic turn, extending the first stanza's reflections upon poetic form and an attendant ironic undercutting of elegiac consolation. Here though Bronk underscores the discursive indeterminacy involved in that skeptical understanding:

> No excuses: evasions are what we try:
> form as adversary or, failing form,
> other divisions, assertions by negatives.
> We are the not this, not that.
> The determined self makes be by partialness,
> Sets out his space, says here is truth,
> is his, says less is all, defends, fades. (8-14)

Linguistic form haunts and torments, invites and cajoles, but remains aloof, discontented and contentless, signifying a hollow linguistic subjectivity, as if Bronk were proposing a negative dialectic grounded entirely upon deixis: "We are the not this, not that." The only consolation, it would seem, is the brevity of form, that insufficient poetic space within and against the indeterminate field of signification where "The determined self makes be by partialness, / sets out his space, says here is truth, / is his, says less is all, defends, fades." Bronk's elegy offers an anti-consolation that consoles only in so far as it is partial — that is: a transgression against generic and social codes of mourning that remains both brief and deceptively formal.

One way to articulate the other side of this skeptical view, which some might describe as nihilistic, would be to turn to Derrida's idea of tragic joy: "the Nietzschean affirmation, that is the joyous affirmation of the play of the world and of the innocence of becoming, the affirmation of a world of signs without fault, without truth, and without origin which is offered to an active interpretation" (292). Bronk's elegy, I believe, embraces such a philosophy, especially when one considers the poem's placement within the composition of *The Meantine*. On the facing page we find this poem titled "The Conclusion":

> I thought
> we stood at the door
> of another world
> and it might open
> and we go in.
>
> Well,
> there is that door
> and such a world.

Much like Derrida, Bronk invites his readers to take up the work of an active interpretation that confronts the worldliness of a wordless world. Poetry may be a door to "such a world," but for Bronk, like Derrida, that reality remains aloof, aporetic, irreducibly and irremediably Other, conditioning the possible impossibilities of language and culture.[*]

David Clippinger also argues for the importance of this other side to Bronk's poetry — "a sense of transcendence [that] may seem antithetical to the basic philosophical tenets espoused in his writings, which clearly denounce the possibility of knowing any aspect of what Bronk calls the 'real world'" (9). Although Clippinger's latter claims (26-30) for Bronk's transcription of a purely transcendental "flow of the infinite eternal" (28) contradict his more salient observations concerning what remains irreducibly undecidable in Bronk's use of language and silence, his essay nonetheless offers a necessary corrective to John Taggart's gloomy proclamation of hubris in Bronk's work: "a poetry [that has] begun to choke and feed upon itself" (42). Taggart does argue convincingly for the influence of Stevens' poetry on Bronk's early work (25-28), but his devotion to Stevens dominates in such a way that he can't help but read Bronk as derivative, as a poet who chose to forsake the mythic positivism of Steven's circle (40) and dwell instead within the regions of a disembodied voice "splendid in the solipsistic silence that surrounds it" (46). Taggart's chapter on Bronk in *Songs of Degrees* consequently misses much in the poetry, especially Bronk's playful (if often bitter) humor.

Bronk's elegies included in the seven volumes of his poetry published during the 1970s by The Elizabeth Press signal an important turning in his poetics.[†] Here I agree with John

---

[*] See Derrida, *Aporias*, 20.

[†] These books of poetry are *That Tantalus* (1971), *To Praise the Music* (1972), *Silence and Metaphor* (1975), *The Meantime* (1976), *Finding Losses* (1976), and *The Force of Desire* (1979).

Ernest that Bronk's poetic identity achieves a definitive signature in these books that focus specifically upon his attempts and failures to "meet the demands of the reality beyond the 'truths' of human claim" (74). Bronk's earliest elegies from *My Father Photographed With Friends and Other Pictures* (written in the 1940's, published in 1976) and *Light and Dark* (1956) are not yet postmodern in the sense I have proposed in this essay concerning form as field. "The Remains of a Farm," for example, sifts through the wreck of human hopes for and work toward prosperity in order to "reconstruct the intent" and thereby consolingly "see the things disaster failed to see / and know that a weaker force would have let them be" (19). "Soldiers in Death" and "My Father Photographed With Friends" are indeed poems that resist the elegy's generic conventions, but, in keeping with modernist poetics, nonetheless offer such critiques as anti-consolatory consolations. Through elegiac resistance these poems respect the particularity of loss and, as Ramazani argues, thus oppose "a social 'order' that would pathologize and expel the bereaved" (13). However, Bronk's war elegy, "Memorial," approaches a postmodern idea of linguistic form as a site of impossible compensation for loss:

> The war came as a water rising, leaving us homeless.
> The easy company of the dispossessed was a grave joy.
>
> On the crest of waters we invaded the distance.
> Recession will find our shells far: high up in mountains.
> It will be explained how they came there.
> It will not be understood. (24)

Bronk's concern with the inscrutable linguistic condition of human experience becomes even more pronounced in his longest elegy, "The Arts and Death: A Fugue for Sidney Cox." Joseph Conte argues that this poem, "in keeping with the generic rules [of elegy] offers something other than despair at the close — not redemption, but not oblivion either. Our lives are part of the real, and as such persist; only our language closes, *only forms have an end*" (231) [my emphasis]. Conte's reading of this elegy, however, veers away from the formal aporia Bronk intimates, stressing instead an optimistic recuperation of a quasi-transcendental ground. Here I would echo Ernest's claim that Bronk's poetry discloses the "closure upon which his own reliance on language depends" (79), giving us, I believe, merely a partial glimpse of the real — not as it appears, but as it cannot appear as such — within and against the endless and indeterminate forms of linguistic signification. The difference between Conte's interpretation and mine turns upon the following lines:

> World, world, I am scared
> and waver in awe before the wilderness
> of raw consciousness, because it is all
> dark and formlessness: and it is real
> this passion that we feel for forms. But the forms
> are never real. Are not really there. Are not.
>
> I think always how we always miss the real.
>
> There still are wars though all the soldiers fall.
>
> We live in a world we never understand.
>
> Our lives end nothing. Oh there is never an end. (35)

What is real here? "[T]his passion that we feel for forms." But what are forms? Bronk tempts us to make a clean separation between, on the one hand, "the wilderness / of raw consciousness [which is] dark and formlessness" and forms, on the other hand, which "are never real. Are not really there, Are not." Our passion for forms is the nexus of both concerns: the fear and awe Bronk articulates when confronted by this impossible relationship between consciousness and linguistic structures, which are at once mutually inclusive and exclusive; finite and infinite; sensible and senseless.

From this point Bronk's elegies turn even more resolutely toward the aporia that "The Arts and Death: A Fugue For Sidney Cox" brings to the foreground of his poetics. The Elizabeth Press books in particular offer perhaps the best place to study Bronk's emerging concern with a postmodern notion of what I have here posited as form as field. Unlike Bishop's elegies, which turn to poetic form as a means of recuperating loss, Bronk's elegies and elegiac poems turn poetic form against itself, seeking the formless, yet finding only losses beyond recovery situated within and against an indeterminate field of linguistic signification. Taggart reflects upon "The Increasing Abstraction of Language," also from *The Meantime*, and argues that Bronk hypnotizes us into such nihilism (49). Michael Heller (28) counters that Bronk warns us that Language is the hypnotist:

>   Amazement is not too strong a word
>   so I am amazed at the way the language survives
>   other structures: we go on talking as if
>   we had never lost all we come at last
>   to lose, the time and place the language described,
>   was part of, itself, the hypnotist who set
>   his subjects in trance and movement and walked off stage,
>   left them doing whatever it was they did
>   and walked away to where, wherever it is
>   where there are no subjects any longer, where
>   there is nothing to do, nothing for them to do,
>   nothing doing, where its own sound
>   is all the language hears or listens to
>   and talks and keeps on talking to the end. (10)

An unstable field of language construed as representational form conditions the impossibility of consolation for our existential losses. "[W]e go on talking as if / we had never lost all we come at last / to lose;" yet language does not mediate either subjectivity or voice, but projects merely the form of "its own sound" that exceeds all losses "and talks and keeps on talking to the end." Despite this insistence on linguistic instability, Bronk is not a Language poet; for his work, like the writing of Susan Howe and even Samuel Beckett, pursues irremediable existential phenomena at the limits of language. Unlike Bruce Andrews, for example, who proclaims the need for Language writing to critique linguistic meaning and philosophical depth by achieving a poetics and a politics of syntactic fragmentation and surface non-signification (31-38), Bronk achieves precise meaning, philosophical reflection, and a lyrical direct address while also underscoring the possible impossibility of such linguistic registers.

George Oppen's elegies from *Seascape: Needle's Eye* (1972) and *Myth of the Blaze* (1975) provide a further point of contrast between a modernist and a postmodernist poetics of loss. Critics often draw parallels between Oppen and Bronk, though the tenor of their works differs considerably. Oppen, as is well known, promoted Bronk's poems to New Directions Press, which, in 1964, published *The World, the Worldless* (Ernest 73). However, in a letter written within months of the book's publication, Oppen expresses concerns for "the solipsist position" in Bronk's poetry (Ernest 73). Oppen also felt ambivalent about the quality of Bronk's poetry printed during the early 1970s by The Elizabeth Press. In a letter (dated 18 June 1974) to James Laughlin, New Directions publisher, Oppen worries that those volumes (i.e. *That Tantalus* and *To Praise the Music*) offer "a somewhat damaging amount of [Bronk's] lesser work" (Ernest 73). This last detail is perhaps the most telling for my purposes here, as Bronk's elegies published during the 1970s turn increasingly toward the indeterminacy of linguistic reference and the consequent impossibility of elegiac consolation. Oppen's elegies, in contrast, strive for the recuperation of linguistic signification, transcendence, and consolation within a context of existential loss and artistic fragmentation.

In "Song, The Winds of Downhill," for example, Oppen moves from a lament upon existential impoverishment to a consolatory return to the most radical components of meaning and life: verbs, prepositions, and conjunctions — those elements of grammar and syntax too often taken for granted and thereby dissociated from the objects they inhabit. Rachel Blau DuPlessis cites this poem in her estimation of Oppen's "situational poetics" — that is: his ability to reconfigure both the poem's personae and the reader's perspective in light of "a scrutiny (a reading?) of the 'substantial' meaning of some words: 'would with and' so common as to be unread" (118). Oppen's elegies, I believe, reveal the poet's modernist imperative to re-connect syntax to the world through a disjunctive reading/writing of poetic language that foregrounds both silence and deixis.

In "Of Hours" Oppen recuperates life and language out of "fragments of metal" and the "[d]isgrace of dying" (211). "The Impossible Poem" proposes an antithetical relinquishment of 'sanity' in order to "redeem / Fragments and fragmentary / Histories in the towns and the temperate streets" (226). Oppen's "Myth of the Blaze" initiates a critique of the sympathetic nature theme — that is, the desire to locate consolation within the natural landscape — but then turns toward the sheltering image of an "impossible . . . shack / on the coast" (243). The difficulty of this image and the image of the Tyger, however, signifies the possible resurrection of experience and language: only within a fragmentary structure may the transience and resilience of life be grasped. Existence and language are "bread each side of the knife" (244), the possibilities of each equally conditioned by a harrowing reflection.

Some readers may object to my formal reading of Bronk's elegies on the grounds that "The Emptiness of Human Being" and "The Increasing Abstraction of Language" are, all concessions made, variations upon the sonnet; hence, like Bishop, Bronk situates his anti-consolatory consolations within a traditional verse form. In a 1989 interview with Edward Foster, Bronk discusses his interest in closely reading Shakespeare's sonnets during the early 1970s:

And I went through a period of many months, maybe a year, with Shakespearian sonnets. Almost every night before I went to sleep I would read one or two and read them very carefully: what's he saying here? How's he doing this? What's he mean by this word? Very close reading, so I suppose it probably formed my mind into thinking in that span, and I also occasionally before and after that period wrote in fourteen lines, but it wasn't a decision on my part — except that it was an interesting form and what could be done with it, and I didn't have to force it. (17)

All of the poems in *To Praise the Music* are fourteeners; in *The Meantime*, which contains a mere fifteen poems, all four of the fourteeners are elegies. Many of Shakespeare's sonnets are elegiac in mood and theme. How does Bronk's use of that verse form as a vehicle for elegy differ from Shakespeare's?

Sonnet 74 offers a poignant contrast with "The Emptiness of Human Being," for both elegiac poems confront and construct the difficulty of existential loss at the level of deixis — that is: within and against the linguistic mechanisms that condition all possible articulations of any distinctions between "the here and the there, the now and the then, the we and the you" (Godzich 166). Shakespeare's sonnet, as Helen Vendler convincingly reasons (337-339), sublimes body and language to spirit "by a sleight-of-hand in the couplet, turning on the relative pronoun *that which*" (338): "The worth of that is that which it contains" (13). Thus Shakespeare's elegiac sonnet asserts: after death the worth of the body and language is that which they contain; and [that (spirit) which] is [this (sonnet) which] that with thee, dear reader, remains. Poetic form, in this case, assures the preservation of essence, elegiac transcendence and consolation. In Bronk's case, however, poetic form turns against such metaphysical and linguistic certainty, indicating at best "evasions . . . other divisions, [and] assertions by negatives" (15). Whereas deixis serves Shakespeare as a hub for the sublimation of body and language into spirit, deixis serves Bronk as a spoke toward the indeterminate peripheries of identity and signification: "We are the not this, not that" (15). Bronk turns the sonnet's form against itself in his elegies composed of fourteen lines; articulates a postmodern anti-consolatory consolation of poetic form discovered as an indeterminate field of signification; and thereby denotes the aporetic brevities of such desire and despair for elegiac transcendence and consolation. In this regard Bronk's elegies have much in common with those of many innovative poets writing today.

IV

Ubi sunt in terza rima, o love in translation.
—Bin Ramke, "Elegy as Algorithm: Seasonal Lamentation"

IN *Poetry as Epitaph*, KAREN MILLS-COURTS formulates a theory of representation and poetic language (strongly influenced by the works of Heidegger and Derrida) that pertains to any study of the poetics of loss. One of her central claims concerns two rhetorical motives, the presentational and the representational, that constantly liberate and limit a poet's work with language. Caught between both motives, Mills-Courts argues, poetic discourse creates a work of indirect yet intended revelation (i.e. presentation) within a discursive context of inevitable erasure (i.e. representation); "[f]or the very words that seem to give life simultaneously announce the death of the speaker" (2). This preliminary thesis offers a useful point of departure for discussions of the poetic elegy in any time period.

Mills-Courts' larger argument concerning the emergence of modern subjectivity, however, leads her to problematic inferences. Perhaps the most vexing of these addresses an epistemic shift, which begins somewhere in the seventeenth and eighteenth centuries, from predominantly presentational to representational logics in western literature and, in particular, poetic language (140-150). The devotional writings of George Herbert, for example, reveal such an incarnative, or presentational, poetics; those of Coleridge and Wordsworth a representational poetics conditioned by the disruption of a subjectivity that can only attain presence, in the wake of the Cartesian moment, through a structure of language predicated upon the self's prior absence from and indeterminacy within systems of signification (150-152). To her credit, Mills-Courts cautions that such a paradigm shift can not be located "in a single 'catastrophic' moment" (150). Nonetheless, her theory of Cartesian subjectivity holds that modern poets (since Coleridge and Wordsworth) no longer have unfettered access to an Augustinian incarnative understanding of existence and language as distinct but interpenetrating phenomena (140-150). I wish to disagree with this view.

Many American poets writing elegies — earlier in this century as well as very recently — freely employ what could be called an incarnative poetics of presentation and presence. For that reason I have deliberately avoided in this esssay a total theory of the postmodern American elegy. My central thesis that many innovative elegies turn upon new ideas of poetic form construed as an indeterminate field of linguistic signification complements Mills-Courts' claims for poetic discourse since the emergence of a Cartesian moment somewhere in the seventeenth and eighteenth centuries. However, I would not anachronistically project my articulation of the elegy's 'postmodernity' into those earlier contexts without first undertaking a more thorough analysis of shifting philosophical and cultural relationships between early modern and modern poetics. That topic lies beyond the means of this present work, which situates a point of departure within a limited scope of modern American elegies.

How do we explain the persistence of elegy at a time when so many innovative poets have grounded their work in an epistemological break from literary tradition? Should we be surprised to find poetic elegies in a book such as Lyn Hejinian's *The Cell* (1992)? The first untitled entry (7) in this diaristic sequence, written over roughly a two year period, engages with a deconstructive assessment of spiritual transcendence framed within a meditation upon death that, in the last line, offers an ironic resistance to conventional elegiac consolation. The object of writing, we are reminded, does not concern the representation of a centrally located human essence, voice, subjectivity, or philosophical depth of reflection, but a confrontation with the contentless surfaces of language and the material world (lines 1-10). The poem's concluding irony implies that experiential and physical absences attributable to death, like "concavities" (18) on the surface of language and natural objects, offer a singular perfection. The poem presents this point of view without regret; but how do we understand the implications of such a negative affirmation, especially if our goal is to read this poem/entry as an anti-elegy or anti-elegiac work? How are such antithetical prospects different from the rhetoric of either the pre-modern or modern elegy? If the experience of death no longer offers a cause for lamentation in poetic discourse, then are elegies no longer possible? At what point does such an ironic undercutting of elegiac consolation become a new kind of consolation, albeit in an intellectualized, anti-consolatory way?

Hejinian's *The Cell* consists of one hundred-and-fifty entries, only one of which carries a title, "Elegy, for K. B." (92-93). The persistence of elegy here provides at least one answer to these questions; for Hejinian's ostensible critique of elegiac themes in this book works both within and against the genre's conventions. On the one hand, as in the opening entry, Hejinian recapitulates an anti-consolatory gesture that emerges in such pre-modern elegies as Moschus's "Lament for Bion" and "The Wanderer" as well as in modern elegies such as Swinburne's "Ave Atque Vale," Hardy's "At Castle Boterel," and Bishop's "North Haven." Each of these poems grapples with the idea that the irremediable experience of death is tantamount to a perfection of absence, rather than of presence or of the soul's transcendence from the world of human suffering into an eternal world of spiritual wholeness. On the other hand, Hejinian's elegies emphasize something that these pre-modern and modern poems do not address: the linguistic and cultural construction of both loss and resistance to elegiac consolation, the indeterminate forms of which speak for themselves and have "no further explanation" ("Elegy, for K. B." 93).

Merwin's "Elegy" offers one last clue to the astonishing persistence (and under-theorization) of postmodern elegies: "Who would I show it to" (137). This sardonic anti-poem suggests at once that the ground for a postmodern poetics of loss not only resides within and against the limits of genre, but turns upon the reader's active interpretation of the cultural work of mourning. Following Ramazani's ground-breaking text, we can expect to see further refigurations of modernist poetics, as in the recent studies by Rigsbee and Zeiger, and we can also hope to see a new praxis of reading the elegy as a vehicle for the writing of cultural histories.

WORKS CITED

Aiken, Pauline. "The Influence of the Latin Elegists on English Lyric Poetry, 1600-1650." *University of Maine Studies* 22 (1932): 5-115.

Alexiou, Margaret. *The Ritual Lament in Greek Tradition*. London: Cambridge UP, 1974.

Andrews, Bruce. "Text and Context." *The L=A=N=G=U=A=G=E Book*. Ed. Bruce Andrews and Charles Bernstein. Carbondale: Southern Illinois UP, 1984. 31-38.

Barbiero, Daniel. "Avant-Garde Without Agonism?" *Talisman* 14 (1995): 151-160.

Bedetti, Gabriella. "Prosody and 'The Emperor of Ice-Cream': The Elegiac in the Modern Lyric." *The Wallace Stevens Journal* 8.2 (1984): 96-102.

Berg, William. *Early Virgil*. London: The Athlone P, 1974.

Bernstein, Charles, ed. *The Politics of Poetic Form: Poetry and Public Policy*. New York: ROOF, 1990.

Bethea, David M. "Exile, Elegy, and Auden in Brodsky's 'Verses on the Death of T. S. Eliot'." *PMLA* 107.2 (1992): 232-245.

Bishop, Elizabeth. *The Complete Poems 1927-1979*. New York: Farrar, Straus, and Giroux, 1983.

Blasing, Randy. "Whitman's 'Lilacs' and the Grammars of Time." *PMLA* 97.1 (1982): 31-39.

Bradford, M. E. "A Modern Elegy: Ransom's 'Bells for John Whiteside's Daughter'." *Mississippi Quarterly* 21 (1968): 43-47.

Bronk, William. *Life Supports*. San Francisco: North Point Press, 1982.

-------. *The Meantime*. New Rochelle: The Elizabeth Press, 1976.

Bryfonski, Dedria, ed. *Contemporary Literary Criticism*. Vol. 10/ Detroit: Gale Research, 1979. 73-76.

Clippinger, David. "Luminosity, Transcendence, and the Certainty of Not Knowing." *Talisman* 14 (1995): 9-30.

Conte, Joseph M. *Unending Design: The Forms of Postmodern Poetry*. Ithaca: Cornell UP, 1991.

Derrida, Jacques. *Aporias*. Trans. Thomas Dutoit. Stanford: Stanford UP, 1993.

-------. "Structure, Sign, and Play." *Writing and Difference*. Trans. Alan Bass. Chicago: U of Chicago P, 1978. 278-93.

Draper, John W. *The Funeral Elegy and the Rise of English Romanticism.* New York: Octagon Books, Inc., 1967.
DuPlesses, Rachel Blau. *The Pink Guitar: Writing as Feminist Practice.* New York: Routledge, 1990.
Ernest, John. "William Bronk." *Dictionary of Literary Biography.* Vol. 165. Ed. Joseph Conte. Detroit: Gale Research, 1996. 69-80.
Finkelstein, Norman M. "William Bronk: The World as Desire." *Contemporary Literature* 23 (1982): 480-92.
Foster, Edward. "Conversations with William Bronk." *Postmodern Poetry: The Talisman Interviews.* Hoboken: Talisman House, 1994. 1-19.
-------. "Preface." *Postmodern Poetry: The Talisman Interviews.* Hoboken, NJ: Talisman House, Publishers, 1994. vii-viii.
Fradenburg, Louise O. "'Voice Memorial': Loss and Reparation in Chaucer's Poetry." *Exemplaria* 2 (1990): 169-202.
Godzich, Wlad. *The Culture of Literacy.* Cambridge: Harvard UP, 1994.
Hejinian, Lyn. *The Cell.* Los Angeles: Sun & Moon, 1992.
Heller, Michael. Rev., William Bronk. *The New York Times Book Review* (1977): 28-30.
Holden, Jonathan. "Postmodern Poetic Form: A Theory." *Poetics: Essays on the Art of Poetry.* Ed. Paul Mariani and George Murphy. Ocean Bluff: Tendril, 1984. 13-34.
Kay, Dennis. *Melodious Tears: The English Funeral Elegy from Spenser to Milton.* Oxford: Oxford UP, 1990.
Kimmelman, Burt. *The "Winter Mind" of William Bronk.* Madison, NJ: Fairleigh Dickinson UP, 1998.
Kingsley, Lawrence W. "The Modern Elegy: The Epistemology of Loss." *DAI* 34 (1973): 779A-780A.
Lambert, Ellen Zetzel. *Placing Sorrow: A Study of the Pastoral Elegy Convention from Theocritus to Milton.* Chapel Hill: U of North Carolina P, 1976.
Lange, Marjory E. *Telling Tears in the English Renaissance.* New York: E. J. Brill, 1996.
Lilley, Kate. "True State Within: Women's Elegy 1640-1700." *Women, Writing, History.* Ed. Isobel Grundy and Susan Wiseman. Athens: U of Georgia P, 1992. 72-92.
McFarland, Ronald E. *The Villanelle: The Evolution of a Poetic Form.* Moscow: U of Idaho P, 1987.
Mell, Donand C. *A Poetics of Augustan Elegy.* Amsterdam: Rodopi, 1974.
Merwin, W. S. *The Carrier of Ladders.* New York: Atheneum, 1970.
Meyer, Kinereth. "The Mythology of Modern Death." *Genre* 19.1 (1986): 21-35.
Mills-Courts, Karen. *Poetry as Epitaph: Representation and Poetic Language.* Baton Rouge: Louisiana State UP, 1990.
Minock, Daniel William. "Conceptions of Death in the Modern Elegy and Related Poems." *DAI* 36 (1975): 1496A-1497A.
Muske, Carol. "Rewriting the Elegy." *Poets for Life.* Ed. Michael Klein. New York: Crown Publishers, 1989.
Olson, Charles. "Projective Verse." *The New American Poetry.* Ed. Donald M. Allen. New York: Grove P, Inc., 1960. 386-397.
Oppen, George. *Collected Poems.* New York: New Directions, 1975.
Perkins, David. *A History of Modern Poetry: Modernism and After.* Cambridge: Harvard UP, 1987.
Pigman, G. W. *Grief and English Renaissance Elegy.* Cambridge: Cambridge UP, 1985.
Poggioli, Renato. *The Theory of the Avant-Garde.* Cambridge: Harvard UP, 1968.
Potts, Abbie Findlay. *The Elegiac Mode: Poetic Form in Wordsworth and Other Elegists.* Ithaca: Cornell UP, 1967.

Preminger, Alex, and T. V. F. Brogan, eds. *The New Princeton Encyclopedia of Poetry and Poetics*. Princeton: Princeton UP, 1993.

Race, William H. *Classical Genres and English Poetry*. London: Croom Helm, 1988.

Ramazani, Jahan. "The Wound of History: Walcott's *Omeros* and the Postcolonial Poetics of Affliction." *PMLA* 112.3 (1997): 405-417.

-------. *Poetry of Mourning: The Modern Elegy From Hardy to Heaney*. Chicago: U of Chicago P, 1994.

-------. *Yeats and the Poetry of Death: Elegy, Self-Elegy, and the Sublime*. New Haven: Yale UP, 1990.

Ramke, Bin. "Elegy as Algorithm: Seasonal Lamentation." *Massacre of the Innocents*. Iowa City: U of Iowa P, 1995. 39-41.

-------. "Elegy As Origin." *Denver Quarterly* 23.3-4 (1989): 33-39.

Rigsbee, David. *Styles of Ruin: Joseph Brodsky and the Postmodernist Elegy*. Westport: Greenwood Publishing Group, 1999.

-------. "Styles of Ruin: Revisions." E-mail to the author. 12 Nov. 1998.

-------. "Styles of Ruin: Joseph Brodsky and the Postmodernist Elegy." *DAI* 57.1 (1996): 210A.

Rosenmeyer, Thomas G. *The Green Cabinet: Theocritus and the European Pastoral Lyric*. Berkeley: U of California P, 1969.

Sacks, Peter. *The English Elegy: Studies in the Genre from Spenser to Yeats*. Baltimore: Johns Hopkins UP, 1985.

Schenck, Celeste M. "The Funeral Elegy as Pastoral Initiation: Plato, Theocritus, Virgil." *Mosaic: A Journal for the Interdisciplinary Study of Literature* 21.1 (1988): 93-113.

-------. *Mourning and Panegyric: The Poetics of Pastoral Ceremony*. University Park: Pennsylvania State UP, 1988.

-------. "When the Moderns Write Elegy: Crane, Kinsella, Nemerov." *Classical and Modern Literature* 6.2 (1986): 97-108.

-------. "Feminism and Deconstruction: Re-Constructing the Elegy." *Tulsa Studies in Women's Literature* 5.1 (1986): 13-27.

Scholes, Robert. *Semiotics and Interpretation*. New Haven: Yale UP, 1982.

Scodel, Joshua. *The English Poetic Epitaph: Commemoration and Conflict from Johnson to Wordsworth*. Ithaca: Cornell UP, 1991.

Shakespeare, William. "Sonnet 74" *The Art of Shakespeare's Sonnets*. Helen Vendler. Cambridge: Harvard UP, 1997. 337.

Shaw, David W. *Elegy and Paradox: Testing the Conventions*. Baltimore: Johns Hopkins UP, 1994.

Smith, Eric. *By Mourning Tongues: Studies in English Elegy*. Totowa: Boydell P, 1977.

Stanford, Ann. "The Elegy of Mourning in Modern American and English Poetry." *The Southern Review* 11 (1975): 357-372.

Stefanile, Felix. "Praising the Music." *Parnassus* (1977): 222-33.

Stone, Carole. "Elegy as Political Expression in Women's Poetry: Akhmatova, Levertov, Forche." *College Literature* 18.1 (1991): 84-91.

Taggart, John. *Songs of Degrees: Essays on Contemporary Poetry and Poetics*. Tuscaloosa: U of Alabama P, 1994.

Vendler, Helen. *The Art of Shakespeare's Sonnets*. Cambridge: Harvard UP, 1997.

Weinfield, Henry. *The Poet Without a Name: Gray's "Elegy" and the Problem of History*. Carbondale: Southern Illinois UP, 1991.

Whitman, Walt. "When Lilacs Last in the Dooryard Bloom'd." *The Norton Anthology of Poetry*. Third Edition. New York: W. W. Norton & Co., 1983. 775-780.

Williams, Anne. *Prophetic Strain: The Greater Lyric in the Eighteenth Century*. Chicago: U of Chicago P, 1984.

Zeiger, Melissa F. *Beyond Consolation: Death, Sexuality, and the Changing Shapes of Elegy*. Ithaca: Cornell UP, 1997.

Mark Scroggins

Z-SITED PATH: LATE ZUKOFSKY AND HIS TRADITION

Born in 1904, not half a decade into the new century, Louis Zukofsky was still reinventing himself at the beginning of the 1970s. He had begun his writing career with a savage and funny parody of Eliot's *Waste Land* ("Poem beginning 'The'") and with the opening movements of a *Cantos*-like long poem, *"A."* In the first half of the 1930s he had been the leader and primary theorist of the short-lived "Objectivist" movement, which in its few heady days of public prominence had counted among its members and fellow-travellers Williams Carlos Williams, Kenneth Rexroth, Carl Rakosi, Charles Reznikoff, and George Oppen. But the Objectivists had proved a mere blip on the radar screen of passing poetic trends, and for some thirty-odd years Zukofsky had worked on in the face of seemingly universal public indifference. He was sustained in part by his friendships and correspondences — with Williams, Basil Bunting, Lorine Niedecker — and in part by the sporatic interest of small presses and little magazines.

By the 1970s, however, Zukofsky had begun to achieve somewhat broader public recognition. Although James Laughlin did not publish Zukofsky, Laughlin's New Directions Press revived interest in the Objectivists by publishing volumes of Oppen, Reznikoff, and Rakosi through the 1960s. In 1968, L.S. Dembo consolidated the critical rediscovery of the Objectivist "movement" by inviting Zukofsky and the other three to the University of Wisconsin; the following year he published his interviews with them in *Contemporary Literature* as "The 'Objectivist' Poet: Four Interviews." And Zukofsky's own work was becoming more widely available. *"A" 1-12*, a limited edition of which had been published in Kyoto by Cid Corman's Origin Press in 1959, was reprinted by Doubleday in its Paris Review Editions Series in 1966, and that publisher would also print *"A" 13-21* in 1969. W. W. Norton collected his shorter poems, hitherto available only in periodicals and small press editions, in the volumes *ALL: The Collected Shorter Poems 1923-1958* and *ALL: The Collected Shorter Poems 1956-1964*. In contrast to his earlier small press collections, these books were being reviewed in venues as prestigious as the *New York Times* and *The Nation*.

The Zukofsky of the 1970s, however, was a far different poet from the author of "'The'," the quasi-Imagistic short poems of the 1920s, and the early Poundian movements of "*A.*" "*A*"-21, for instance, written in 1967, was an impacted translation of Plautus's play *Rudens* (*The Rope*), in which Zukofsky compressed each Latin hexameter line into five words of English, striving at the same time to preserve something of the original sound. The result, while one could certainly imagine it on stage — the movement is after all dedicated to Zukofsky's friend, theater critic John Gassner, and to Zukofsky's elder brother Morris, who had taken the future poet to see Yiddish theater of the 1910s — is fast-moving, oblique, and oddly "hip": "My! while that sea operates / only tempest's in his nets. / Today's catch's cooked, slipped these / fingers, fluke vehement sea mar" ("*A*" 475). "*A*"-22 and -23, written between 1970 and 1974, compressed thousands of years of history — linguistic, literary, geological — into two thousand five-word lines of densely concatenated quotation, translation, and transliteration, and somehow at the same time managed to bring to remarkable closure the twenty-one formally various movements that had come before them. "*A*"-24, of course, is the "L .Z. Masque," an arrangement for four voices and harpsichord of a plethora of Zukofsky texts; it was his wife Celia's present to him, and he appropriated it to end "*A*" on both a musical and familial note.

80 Flowers, in press when Zukofsky died in 1978, was a collection of eighty-one poems, each one eight lines long with, again, five words to the line, each named after a flower (plus an epigraph). As in "*A*"-22 and -23, syntax is radically open in these poems; in essence, they are deeply considered collages of quotation and translation, opening seemingly infinite regresses of suggestion and implication to the careful reader, while enforcing no single level of meaning. Late Zukofsky is continuous with early and mid-period Zukofsky in his concern with poetic form and with the musical value of verse, but Zukofsky's 1970s-era poetics effect a quantum leap from his earlier work in syntactic openness, multiplicity of meaning, and sheer readerly difficulty. It is a poetry of deep, angular beauty, and of obdurate but tantalizing resistance. The last lines of "*A*"-23 seem fittingly emblematic. The movement ends by naming both the four voices of the "L.Z. Masque" and by pointing out the "path" of a "z-sited" — a Zukofsky-sited? — tradition: "music, thought, drama, story, poem / parks' sunburst — animals, grace notes — / z-sited path are but us" ("*A*" 563).

The phrase "z-sited path" is temptingly vague to use in describing how younger poets have received Zukofsky's work, for one hesitates to invoke the word "influence" when speaking of his relationship to younger poets — though surely one of the measures of Zukofsky's importance is the wide-ranging and polymorphic nature of his influence. Influence studies, of course, are one of the hoariest of academic pursuits, and the academy has erred greatly by assessing Zukofsky's work in terms of influence: academics, that is, have too often read him as a case study of the influence of Ezra Pound, rather than paying attention to how radically Zukofsky's work differs from his friend's. Zukofsky himself, in a 1930 note on "Influence," argues intelligently enough that direct influence of the sort beloved by academics is really no more important than a writer's absorption of a tendency "in the air," or a writer's sense of kinship with another writer of a far different era — like, for instance, his own obsession with Shakespeare (*Prepositions* 135). Zukofsky's own attitude towards poetic influence is a complex matter, to say the least, and his various statements work to undermine any clear-cut schema (Bloomian or otherwise) of how one poet's work makes a difference in the works of those who follow. To write about Zukofsky's "tradition," then, propels one into a minefield; one has a sense of flying in the face both of Zukofsky's own sense of poetic tradition, and of the actual, highly complex workings of literary history. In the compass of a single essay, as well, it is impossible to treat — or even mention — all of the poets who owe a significant debt to Zukofsky's work. I wish to offer here a representative sampling of the writers who have made use of his work, and to show some of the different and important manners in which they have built upon his achievements. For the most part, I have confined myself to writers who knew Zukofsky or who have explicitly acknowledged the importance of his work to their own. To describe *implicit* Zukofskyan debts and traces, it goes without saying, would take a far longer essay.

Zukofsky's own statements, and his own increasing reclusiveness, did little to mitigate the impression that by the 1960s he was a "forgotten" poet. It is clear, however, that poets were reading Zukofsky even when his books could find no publishers. Robert Duncan had been reading Zukofsky since 1937, and by 1954 considered him among his "masters," though one of a foregoing generation. Through Duncan's and Edward Dahlberg's promptings, Robert Creeley would publish Zukofsky in 1955 in the *Black Mountain Review*, and would later visit the Zukofskys at their Brooklyn Heights home. For Creeley and others, Zukofsky represented an important living link with the modernism of Pound and Williams, a counter-establishment modernism that many of the poets of the "New American Poetry" saw as a crucial alternative to the academically sanctioned modernism of T. S. Eliot, W. H. Auden, and the New Critics. Throughout the late 1950s and the 1960s, then, a procession of poets committed to non-academic verse would visit Zukofsky, among them Allen Ginsberg, Denise Levertov, Joel Oppenheimer, Jerome Rothenberg, and Paul Blackburn. Two of them, Robert Kelly and George Economou, would publish Zukofsky's *I's (pronounced eyes)* under the aegis of their Trobar Press in 1963. They found in Zukofsky far more than a relic of high modernism, but an active and exploratory sensibility that was still inventing, pushing beyond what Pound and Williams had done.

Some of the poets who read, corresponded, and spoke to Zukofsky would assimilate his work as a relatively minor influence, or would take it as an affirmation or explanation of poetics that they had already largely adumbrated. Such is the case with Robert Duncan, who was continually adding new ingredients to the multiply-"staind [coffee] / pot" of his own poetics (*Selected Poems* 37), and Allen Ginsberg, who had early in his writing career established an intense correspondence with Zukofsky's friend Williams. Other poets fell into more absolute, all-compassing relationships with Zukofsky's work. Perhaps the two most overtly "Zukofskyan" of such poets are Cid Corman and the late Frank Samperi. Corman had met Zukofsky in Florence in 1957. The editor of *Origin* (which published Zukofsky on a regular basis) and a close correspondent of Zukofsky's for the last two decades of the latter's life, Corman has over the course of some eighty-odd collections pursued a poetics of the formally compact. His (mostly) short-lined poems are deeply indebted to various Japanese and Chinese models, but his methods of deploying syntax and modulating line length owe more — at times, it seems everything — to Zukofsky. Frank Samperi, another writer associated with *Origin*, left as his major life work the trilogy made up of *The Prefiguration* (1971), *Quadrifarium* (1973), and *Lumen Gloriae* (1973), a sequence of eighteen shorter poem which strive to reinvent in American English the ecstatic-religious poem on a Dantescan scale. In its word-count prosodies and visually-based mysticism, the verse of Samperi's trilogy seems a continual allusion to Zukofsky. Samperi's work, however, whatever the interest of its dense scholastic philosophy and mystical vision, lacks the knotted and difficult lyricism that makes Zukofsky's work ultimately rewarding.

In contrast to those of his contemporaries who taught in poetry writing programs, Zukofsky's teaching position at the Polytechnic Institute of Brooklyn — an intensely pragmatic school, to say the least — was not conducive to the acquisition of poetic disciples. One of his students, however, Hugh Seidman, went on to appear in the Yale Younger Poets Series with *Collecting Evidence* (1970). In that volume, as well as in *Blood Lord* (1974) and *Throne/Falcon/Eye* (1982), Seidman shows himself deeply attentive to the sound values of Zukofsky's verse, marrying the sometimes harsh music and tentative syntax of mature Zukofsky to the surrealism of Cesar Vallejo in poems that with a frightening intensity explore brutal and scarifying personal relationships. In *Throne/Falcon/Eye*, perhaps his finest book, Seidman lays out a quintessentially urban — New York — vision, superimposing personal and social realities upon a framework of Greek and Egyptian mythology. Seidman's work has little in common with the various avant-gardes writing today: he has, most notably, no interest in purging the personal voice from his poetry. But the lessons he learned from Zukofsky — conciseness, music, and precise image — set his poetry apart from that of the workshop poets ubiquitous in the American academy.

Michael Heller, who also began as an engineering student, and who first encountered Zukofsky's work through Seidman's recommendation, is also a New York poet, but of a far less sombre cast. Heller has written an important monograph on the five Objectivist poets (he includes Zukofsky's friend Lorine Niedecker), *Conviction's Net of Branches: Essays on the Objectivist Poets and Poetry*, and the texture and tone of his later work owe as much to Rakosi, Reznikoff, and Oppen as they do to Zukofsky. Nonetheless, Heller's work is obsessed with questions of perception and epistemology — as evidenced in the title of his 1979 collection *Knowledge* — that have a definite family resemblance to those which lie at the heart of Zukofsky's work and thought, and the fine precision of observation in his poetry is deeply akin to Zukofsky's.

Like Heller, Theodore Enslin is a poet who finds in George Oppen's work modes of thought and emotion more congenial than Zukofsky's rigors; nonetheless, Enslin's writing is fundamentally indebted to Zukofsky's musical sensibility. A trained composer who studied with Nadia Boulanger, Enslin has spent much of his life in rural Maine, far from the urban and academic centers of American poetry. Since the 1960s he has published scores of volumes of poetry, many of them installments of such multi-volume long poems as *Ranger* and *Forms*. Following the lead of Zukofsky's work, which often models its forms upon those of classical music, Enslin has systematically explored the ways in which one can write poetry that approaches the formal "condition of music." It is difficult to take in Enslin's whole achievement — his works run to several thousand pages — but his shorter lyrics often strike an extraordinarily Zukofskyan note:

> The tide
>   is dust
> seeped in
>   dry wells
> are dark in
>   deed. (*Carmina* no. XVI, n.p.)

What most struck many of the younger poets reading Zukofsky in the last decades of his life — and what inevitably strikes readers encountering him now — is his sense of compressed form, of the overwhelmingly careful and intelligently weighed placements of his words within the lines of his poems, and the precise, almost fastidious, crafting of the movements from line to line, stanza to stanza. Often this craft is evident in short-lined poems; in his later works, it takes place within a prosody of word-counts, where each line has precisely two, or three, or five words, regardless of the number of syllables or stresses within those words. Traditional poetry in English is most often written in accentual-syllabic forms: in each line, a relatively fixed number of stresses occur within a relatively fixed number of syllables — as in the classic iambic pentameter line, which theoretically has five stresses placed at certain points within ten syllables. By making word-counts rather than syllable- or accent-counts the basis of his later prosody, Zukofsky can radically redefine that balance between fixed order and individual variation that constitutes poetic form.

Zukofsky's sense of poetic form in general has had a profound impact on the work of Robert Creeley, the poet who was closest personally to Zukofsky for the last two decades of Zukofsky's life. Creeley's short-lined poems everywhere evidence the same precision of movement that Zukofsky's do, perhaps most clearly in the poems of *Pieces* (1969), a collection dedicated to Zukofsky: "Late, the words, late / the form of them, al- / / ready past what they were / fit for, one and two and three" (43). Creeley's impressive (and continuing) body of work stands as a thorough working-through of the implications of the Zukofskyan short lyric and lyric sequence. Robert Kelly, whose poetic corpus stretches (like Enslin's) over thousands and pages and encompasses numerous forms, would find the word-counted lines of Zukofsky's "A"-15 (1963) a vital model for his own volume *Axon Dendron Tree* (1967), which employs similar one- and two-word lines. And Lyn Hejinian's *The Cell* (1992), a series of dated, densely philosophical journal poems, while not nearly as formally rigid as Zukofsky's late works, tends to gravitate towards a five-word line that bears a family resemblance to Zukofsky's.

Among the most controversial of Zukofsky's mature poetic techniques was his method of phonetic translation, in which he sought to bring a foreign text into English first and foremost by reproducing its *sound*. Zukofsky's translations bear little resemblance to translation as we usually know it, but they represent an important innovation in poetics. While every formal decision a poet makes imposes a certain limitation upon the words of the poem, phonetic translation does so to an unprecedented degree: the *sound* of the foreign text, that is, becomes the more-or-less rigid template over which the poet must plot his language. As in so much of Zukofsky's work, which constantly deploys the rhetoric of aurality, of music in particular, his method of translation forces meaning — the traditional aim of the translator — into a position of belatedness. If the new text's "meaning" approximates that of the original, well and good, but more often the sounds of the foreign poem generate new and unsuspected significations in its English translation. Zukofsky's 1969 *Catullus* (in collaboration with his wife Celia) is the most notable example of this process at work, but there are passages of such transliteration throughout the later movements of *"A"* and *80 Flowers*. Few poets have taken up this gauntlet: Charles Bernstein has transliterated a poem of Domenique Fourcade's in *The Sophist* (1987), but the method is more expansively exemplified in David Melnick's *Men in Aida, Book One* (1983), a phonetic translation of the *Iliad* which gives Melnick ample space to pursue his own ludic directions — this *Iliad*, that is, seems to take place by turns on a Trojan plain, in a barroom, and in a San Francisco bathhouse.

Bernstein and Melnick are both of course associated with the Language movement, a loosely-organized coalition of East and West Coast poets who came to maturity in the 1970s and public and academic prominence in the 1980s. Language poetry is an extraordinarily diverse phenomenon: it is easier and probably more accurate to describe it as a tendency within (and against) American literary institutions than to summarize any single set of poetic practices its adherents hold in common. I think it safe, however, to describe Language poetics as a generalized reaction to the speech-based poetics practiced (in far divergent forms) by both the workshop-trained poets of the academy and the mavericks of the "New American Poetry," as collected in Donald Allen's 1960 anthology of the same title. One of Language poetry's inaugural moments, for instance, is Robert Grenier's 1971 essay "On Speech," in which Grenier (himself a dedicated student of Zukofsky's work) proclaims — in no uncertain terms — "I HATE SPEECH" (Silliman, *American Tree* 496). For the Language poets, poetry finds its significance as both an exploratory mode of knowledge and a social critique in a renewed emphasis on the text *as* text, rather than as transcript of speaking or singing voice.

As every revolutionary poetic movement does, the Language poets (most of them products of the post-second world war baby boom) looked beyond their immediate predecessors for useful models of poetic technique, turning to an earlier generation of avant-garde writers which included Gertrude Stein and Louis Zukofsky. Ron Silliman, in the introduction to his influential anthology *In the American Tree*, cites Zukofsky and Stein as representatives of "[a] latent tradition of a poetics not centered on speech" (xvi-xvii), and Charles Bernstein and Bruce Andrews' *The L=A=N=G=U=A=G=E Book*, an anthology of selections from their crucial 1970s journal *L=A=N=G=U=A=G=E*, includes numerous poets' responses to Stein and Zukofsky. While the Language poets' borrowings and adaptations of Zukofsky's techniques are as varied and idiosyncratic as their own poetics, it is clear that Language poetry represents the first generation of avant-garde American poets who have taken Zukofsky's work as a central inheritance of the modernist movement.

A few examples of Language poetry's debts to Zukofsky will have to suffice here, though one could write a substantial essay merely tracing their explicit citations of and borrowings from his work. Charles Bernstein, a poet who has experimented with a bewildering variety of forms, tones, and techniques in his work, is intimately familiar with Zukofsky's work, and often echoes him in his disjunctive syntax and almost reckless montage. Most interestingly, Bernstein seems to have internalized the *tone* of mid-period Zukofsky, a dry, wry, Jewish wit that veers from Catskills-level humor to surprising pathos and profundity.

Michael Palmer arranged for Zukofsky to read at Harvard University in 1963, an event commemorated in Zukofsky's poem "After Reading" (*Complete Short Poetry* 233), and Palmer's own work is sprinkled with references to Zukofsky, perhaps most notably in the beautiful elegy, "Notes for Echo Lake 3" (*The Lion Gate* 70-72). Palmer's early verse is clearly influenced by Zukofsky's sense of poetic form in its sharply chiseled, imagistic lines, heavily relying on the torque of enjambement, but his later work — both dreamlike and densely philosophical, rather like a marriage of Wittgenstein and surrealism — seemed profoundly imbued with the senses of space and time manifested in Zukofsky's later poetry.

On a more concrete level, one can note how the structure of Zukofsky's "A" — the only modernist poem of its magnitude actually *completed* during the lifetime of the Language poets — has influenced Ron Silliman's work. Silliman has noted with approval how Zukofsky, in the process of composing "A", arrived at "a new conceptualization as to the function of part-to-whole relations in the formation of a longpoem [sic]" (*New Sentence* 128). Each movement of "A" "is a totalization, complete in itself, capable of entering into larger structures as an autonomous fact," according to Silliman, and Zukofsky's "recognition that the section of a large work must operate as a group, not as a series" is what enables him, in contrast to the authors of *The Cantos*, *Paterson*, and *The Maximus Poems*, to bring his long poem to completion. Just as Zukofsky decided early on that there would be twenty-four movements to "A" — no matter what material those movements would contain or what forms they would take — Silliman has organized his own ongoing long poem, *The Alphabet*, around a similarly arbitrary (and similarly overdetermined) framework, that of the twenty-six letters of the alphabet. "A", of course, is written in an astonishing variety of forms, from the paratactic free verse of its early movements, to the sonnets of "A"-7, the double canzone of "A"-9, the isolated *four words* of "A"-16, the recycled collage of "A"-17, and the word-counted lines of other later movements. The sections of Silliman's *Alphabet*, published in multiple, scattered venues and written — chronologically speaking — out of alphabetical order, manifest a similar formal and topical variety. *Paradise* (1985) is in what looks like prose, its levels of organization the single sentence and the paragraph, as Silliman theorizes in his essay "The New Sentence." *What* (1988) is a left-justified free verse internal monologue, reminiscent of parts of Zukofsky's "A"-13. *Hidden* (1992, in *Demo to Ink*) is in two-line stanzas; *Xing* (1996) in three-line stanzas. To date Silliman has published (by my count) twenty-one sections of *The Alphabet*'s projected twenty-six. While it would probably be premature to attempt to assess this long poem before its actual completion, it is undeniable that *The Alphabet* has all the makings of a major achievement in American poetry — at the very least, it is an unmatched record of the political, social, sensual, and informational *texture* of late-twentieth-century American life. Silliman, by clear-sightedly seizing upon and extending the implications of part-to-whole relationships within Zukofsky's *"A"*, has forged for his own poem a flexible and capacious formal armature within which he has explored a dazzling variety of experiences and issues.

Silliman (who has worked as an organizer for prisoners' and tenants' groups) has argued that poetic experimentation is best conducted within a closely-knit movement of like-minded poets, a group in which, ideally, there can be mechanisms of "articulate self-discipline within the community" (*American Tree* xix). He is inclined to scoff at the (admittedly tired) Romantic notion of the poet as individualistic outsider or solitary innovator. For Silliman, late Zukofsky's isolation is a consequence of the public and personal failure of the Objectivist movement, its failure to provide Zukofsky and his contemporaries with a durable experimental community. What Zukofsky achieved was remarkable, and against tremendous odds: later poets pursuing individual extensions of Zukofsky's techniques without the support and constant critical exchange of a community such as the Bay Area Language poets — such poets, Silliman specifies, as Frank Samperi, John Taggart, and Ronald Johnson — run the risk of simply amplifying and repeating, sterilely, Zukofsky's innovations. Without gainsaying either Silliman's own achievement in post-Zukofsky poetics, or the astonishingly varied and fruitful work produced over the last quarter century by his colleagues in the Language camp, I would argue on the contrary that individualistic — idiosyncratic, fundamentally personal — reconceptions of Zukofskyan poetics have led to some of the highest achievements of American poetry's latest fin-de-siècle — most notably in the cases precisely of Taggart and Johnson.

For his Ph.D. at Syracuse University, John Taggart wrote the first dissertation extensively addressing Zukofsky's work, and in 1973 he devoted an issue of his periodical *MAPS* to commentary on Zukofsky's writings. Taggart's own poetry, more so than that of any of the poets in the Language movement (from which he has studiously distanced himself) is in large part a strikingly original development of elements explicit and implicit in Zukofsky's. His early work is very much in a chiselled, short-lined "objectivist" vein. Later, in the book-length poems *The Pyramid is a Pure Crystal* (1974) and *Dodeka* (1979), Taggart generates poems out of building blocks of strictly circumscribed verbal material, manipulating them through various "fugal" and canonic systems. It is indeed a poetics of "process," but it results in strikingly lively and energetic poetry, and is a direct descendent of the poetry Zukofsky composed through such strict systems as the canzone of "A"-9 and the more recondite prosodies of later movements of "A". In his more recent work, Taggart has meditated long and deeply on the implications of the connections, fundamental to Zukofsky, between poetry and music. But where Zukofsky looked to the fugal forms of Johann Sebastian Bach and other baroque composers for formal analogies in making his poems, Taggart has turned to the systems of repetition and variation in the compositions of contemporary "minimalist" composers — Steven Reich, Philip Glass, LaMonte Young — and in the playing of the great jazz instrumentalists — John Coltrane, Thelonious Monk, Eric Dolphy. By using such musics as a formal model, Taggart has created — in an ongoing series of volumes that includes *Peace on Earth* (1981), *Loop* (1991), *Standing Wave* (1993), and *Crosses* (1998) — poems both short and long that manipulate verbal and cadential repetition in a subtle, shifting movement of great intellectual and emotional power: "Deepened by black red made deep by black / deepened and dark darker at the top / doorway without a door's always darker / deep red dark red always darker at the top" ("The Game With Red," *Loop* 232).

It is a poetry that demands reading aloud, but when the reader renders it the patience and attention it demands, it reveals moving aesthetic and spiritual depths. Taggart has gone on record rejecting much of Language poetics as a dehumanizing technologizing of poetry; his goal, repeated in work after work, is to construct a poetics that is capable of encompassing the spiritual aspect of human experience. Unlike Frank Samperi, however, who simply asserts the spiritual function of poetry, Taggart attempts actively to capture the experience of the numinous in his repetitive, hypnotic lines. While the "music" of his poetry has a far different sound from Zukofsky's, and is directed at a far different end, it nonetheless owes a profound debt to Zukofsky's conception of the interrelatedness of poetry and musical form.

Ronald Johnson died in March 1998, only months after the long-awaited publication of his long poem *ARK* in its single-volume form. In the 1950s and 1960s Johnson, at that time the companion of Jonathan Williams, the polymathic publisher of Jargon Books and — like Creeley — a student of Olson's at Black Mountain, was reading and digesting both the centrifugal concatenations of Olson's "projectivist" verse and the angular austerities of Zukofsky's work. Johnson and Williams were among the poets visiting the Zukofskys in the late 1950s and early 1960s. In his early work, collected in *A Line of Poetry, A Row of Trees* (1964) and *Valley of the Many-Colored Grasses* (1969), Johnson's reading is wide and everywhere evident. The work is collagistic, and Johnson cites as forebears William Carlos Williams, Olson, Charles Ives, and Zukofsky. But where Olson's "projective" poetics advocates a poetry of headlong rush, of fragmented and revised syntax and thought, Johnson's careful, almost fastidious placement of language is deeply reminiscent of Zukofsky. Johnson's book-length poem, *The Book of the Green Man* (1967), based on a walking tour of England he took with Jonathan Williams in 1962-1963, fuses the Romantic nature-worship of Wordworth and Thoreau with the collagistic poetics of Williams and Zukofsky. This volume, published by W. W. Norton and widely reviewed and praised, seemed poised to catapult Johnson into mainstream prominence. Instead, he turned towards more esoteric, individualistic pursuits — among them concrete poetry — and in 1970 began work on a long poem, *ARK*, in the tradition of *The Cantos, Paterson, Maximus*, and Zukofsky's *"A"*.

ARK, which was completed around 1990, is an extraordinary achievement, a 99-section poem that evokes by turns Dante's *Commedia*, Merrill's *Changing Light at Sandover*, Johnson's immediate modernist forebears Pound, Williams, and Olson, and the gnarled later sections of *"A"*. In some sense it is all a hymn to light, to the unbelievably complex and inexhaustible physical and chemical processes by which the energies of the stars are transmuted into the human eyes that behold them, the human language that praises them, and the human cultures that strive to emulate their beauty. It is as well a massive patchwork of found and invented bits of language, all woven together in a homegrown American aesthetic that Johnson compares to those of such visionary eccentrics as Simon Rodia (of the Watts Towers) or Harry Partch. And it is also a rewriting of *The Wizard of Oz*, beginning in Johnson's own childhood home, Kansas, and ending in the Oz of San Francisco — an Oz blighted, in the poem's later sections, by the shadow of the AIDS epidemic.

Johnson is quick to acknowledge, as he does in the afterword to *ARK*, that his chief poles of influence are Zukofsky and Olson — "the Minimalist and the Maximus" (*ARK*, n.p.) But the compositional procedures, the collagistic aesthetic, and above all the musical *ear* of the poem — all these are Zukofsky's: in a passage elegizing Zukofsky himself, Johnson writes of a poetic "music"

> in cherubim cliffed hayseed, rayed
> clouds in plaster
> forever
> or near it
> as consonance gets without
> clef
>
> —ARK 34, *Spire on the death of L.Z.*, n.p.

Like Zukofsky, Johnson has freely borrowed, adapted, and above all *condensed* other texts for his poem: a section of BEAMS 21-23, the "Palms," consists of words abstracted from the Psalms, much as sections of "A"-14 and "A"-15 distill the words of *Paradise Lost* and Gibbon's *Decline and Fall*. As in *"A"*, the various sections of *ARK* have radically different forms, from prose paragraphs to actual musical notation to the center-justified unrhymed triplets of the poem's later sections. And most strikingly, the *texture* of *ARK* — words and phrases set free from prescribed syntax, interacting one with another in multiple and shifting combinations, continually playing with and seriously weighing the implications of their own sounds — brings to mind that of Zukofsky's 70s-era poetry, verse in which the poet seems to be continually striving towards the upper reaches of his own integral: "upper limit music / lower limit speech." It seems to me that Johnson, of all the poets who have read and listened to Zukofsky's work, has come closest to capturing the intricate music of his elder.

Unlike Pound's *Cantos*, Silliman's *Alphabet*, or many of the movements of *"A"*, *ARK* is a long poem that emphatically resists Pound's definition of the epic as a "poem including history." In Johnson's own words, it is a "poem *without* history" ("Planting" 2), a poem that, while including great masses of quotation and found materials, explicitly disclaims the utility of the source-hunting activities so beloved of Pound and Joyce scholars, and disclaims any immediate political, social, or didactic use-value. The "histories" Zukofsky traces in "A"-22 and -23 are assemblages of words set free from originary names, dates, and social relations — "History's best emptied of names' / impertinence met on the ways" (*"A"* 511) — and Zukofsky would have us read the words of these movements, not referentially, as pointers to texts and ideas outside his poem, but as elements *within* the poem itself — "read, not into, it: / desire until all be bright" (*"A"* 528). Johnson's *ARK* presses this poetics to a further point — a long, obsessively formal, collagistic poem whose burden is neither personal, historical, nor didactic, but *aesthetic*. The essential tone of *ARK*, that is, despite its passages of self-doubt, of hushed awe, and of quiet mourning, is one of joyful play, of delight in the beauties of the sensible universe and of the language through which we apprehend and describe it. As much as the knotty, punning music of his lines, this rejoicing in cosmic order is Johnson's inheritance from Zukofsky. As I hope I have made clear, Johnson's is far from the only use to which contemporary writers have put the arsenal of techniques, forms, and intellectual stances Zukofsky has left them; but it is perhaps the most attractive.

WORKS CITED

Bernstein, Charles. *The Sophist*. Los Angeles: Sun & Moon, 1987.
Bernstein, Charles, and Andrews, Bruce, eds. *The L=A=N=G=U=A=G=E BOOK*. Carbondale, IL: Southern Illinois UP, 1984.
Creeley, Robert. *Pieces*. New York: Scribner's, 1969.
Duncan, Robert. *Selected Poems*. Ed. Robert J. Bertholf. New York: New Directions, 1993.
Enslin, Theodore. *Carmina*. Dennis, MA: salt-works p, 1976.
Hejinian, Lyn. *The Cell*. Los Angeles: Sun & Moon P, 1992.
Heller, Michael. *Conviction's Net of Branches: Essays on the Objectivist Poets and Poetry*. Carbondale, IL: Southern Illinois UP, 1985.
-------. *Knowledge*. New York: Sun, 1979.
Johnson, Ronald. *ARK*. Albuquerque, NM: Living Batch P, 1996.
-------. *The Book of the Green Man*. New York: Norton, 1967.
-------. *A Line of Poetry, a Row of Trees*. Highlands, NC: Jargon, 1964.
-------. "Planting the Rod of Aaron." *Northern Lights: Studies in Creativity* 2 (1985-1986): 1-13.
-------. *Valley of the Many-Colored Grasses*. New York: Norton, 1969.
Kelly, Robert. *Axon Dendron Tree*. Annandale-on-Hudson, NY: Matter, 1967.
Melnick, David. *Men in Aida, Book One*. Berkeley, CA: Tuumba, 1983.
Palmer, Michael. *The Lion Gate: Selected Poems 1972-1995*. New York: New Directions, 1998.
Samperi, Frank. *Lumen Gloriae*. New York: Grossman, 1973.
-------. *The Prefiguration*. New York: Grossman, 1971.
-------. *Quadrifarium*. New York: Grossman, 1973.
Seidman, Hugh. *Blood Lord*. New York: Doubleday, 1974.
-------. *Collectioning Evidence*. New Haven, CT: Yale UP, 1970.
-------. *Throne/Falcon/Eye*. New York: Random House, 1982.
Silliman, Ron. *Demo to Ink*. Tucson: Chax P, 1992.
-------. *The New Sentence*. New York: Roof, 1987.
-------. *Paradise*. Providence, RI: Burning Deck, 1985.
-------. *What*. Great Barrington, MA: The Figures, 1988.
-------. *Xing*. Buffalo: Meow P, 1996.

-------, ed. *In the American Tree: Language, Realism, Poetry.* Orono, ME: National Poetry Foundation, 1986.

Taggart, John. *Crosses.* Los Angeles: Sun & Moon P, 1998.

-------. *Dodeka.* Milwaukee: Membrane P, 1979.

-------. *Loop.* Sun & Moon P, 1991.

-------. *Peace on Earth.* Berkeley: Turtle Island Foundation, 1981.

-------. *The Pyramid is a Pure Crystal.* New Rochelle, NY: Elizabeth P, 1974.

-------. *Standing Wave.* Providence: Lost Roads, 1993.

Zukofsky, Louis. *"A".* 1978. Baltimore: Johns Hopkins UP, 1993.

-------. *Complete Short Poetry.* Baltimore: Johns Hopkins UP, 1991.

-------. *Prepositions: The Collected Critical Essays.* Expanded ed. Berkeley: U of California P, 1981.

Burt Kimmelman

OBJECTIVIST POETICS SINCE 1970

THE TWENTIETH CENTURY WILL ALWAYS BE KNOWN for its widespread innovations in all of the arts. Its commitment to the "new" — as Ezra Pound chartered it with this overly simple and now famous coinage ("Make It New" 1934) — has empowered the formation of a vibrant and multifaceted avant-garde poetry. In this century's early years, poetic Modernism evolved as a number of "schools" that — while each was distinct — embraced a world vision Pound and others had articulated. After the second world war, there were more schools. The Modernist enterprise is perhaps most often thought of for its absolute repudiation of Georgian and Victorian aesthetics and philosophy. In terms of style, ideology, and tradition, Modernism reimagined what poetry could be. It was hugely and radically ambitious, and so influential that the poetic projects it gave rise to remained beholden to its fundamentally original principles. Since 1970, however, the core intention of Modernism has become diffused; once clearly defined "schools" have disintegrated. Even so, what is remarkable is that this essential impulse has lost none of its vigor. New gatherings of poets sharing, if not full-blown ideologies then at least identifiable tendencies, have created an astonishing range of literature. If a *school* can be defined as a group of writers who personally know and publish each other, share a tradition, and observe a manifesto (as Ron Silliman has stipulated in his essay "Third Phase Objectivism," 86, n. 1), then it is safe to say that this century's avant-garde "schools" have disappeared from poetry's landscape. The one exception to this development has been the Language poets, who came together in the late 1970s. As might be expected, they have held sway over a great many younger writers, to a variety of ends, and so in its own right Language poetry must be viewed as having been a major force in recent experimental writing. Yet, not surprisingly, the Language school's internal differences have become as salient as its commonalities, that is, when they are being viewed with the helpful hindsight provided by even newer work.

Any school of poetry will have a natural life span — since newer writing, in taking what is groundbreaking, will always explore it to a point at which the original impulse will seem incoherent. Be that as it may, it is possible to look back upon this century and note that one particular school, the Objectivists — a constellation of poets occasioned by the 1931 "Objectivist" issue of *Poetry* magazine and then the 1932 *Objectivists Anthology* — has outlived its own time. How, then, can this one particular school have evolved in this quite unexpected way? What is it about poetic "objectivism" that allows for such longevity? To be sure, the Objectivist school's presence, which permeates Language poetry and much other later writing, while still remarkably palpable, may at first glance be unrecognizable. In fact, to speak of present-day Objectivist poetry is perhaps futile — in great measure because the Objectivists' principles of writing have been appropriated by very many, and frequently very different, poets for their own peculiar uses. Nonetheless, five of these later poets — Norman Finkelstein, Michael Heller, Rachel Blau DuPlessis, John Taggart, and Lyn Hejinian — comprise what can be understood as a third Objectivist generation. While they reveal the lessons they have learned from the second-generation, post-war "objectivists," these younger poets particularly stand out as having inherited certain basic attitudes from their grandparents — as having, in fact, claimed these later Modernists as primary influences. These five, though, represent unique proclivities that are extant throughout late-century experimental writing. In any case, all five have embraced the fundamental program of the original Objectivist movement — which was to create a profoundly fertile, and difficult, world in which the process of its discovery became paramount to all other endeavors. This process is portrayed by these five, both aesthetically and philosophically, as it was by the Objectivists; and, as was the case for their Elders, the process recognizes a necessary interrelationship among language, truth, and tradition.

In all of the first generation's work, there is one prominent feature that is key to understanding how these later poets have taken on and further developed the original Objectivist venture. Their later work, in its multiple styles, has revealed how crucial this feature was. Objectivist poetry pays unusual attention to the textuality of language, not least of all written language. One product of this attention is the poetry's extraordinary textures. Sensitivity to the text itself arises out of an understanding that this text is, first and foremost, an objectification. Moreover, in what at first appears to be an intriguing paradox, the most important consequence of the Objectivist comprehension of language is the possibility that subjective experience can be heightened. In contradistinction to its name, Objectivist poetry does not preclude the subjective but, rather, attests it. This conundrum is captured within Louis Zukofsky's discussion of sincerity, in his essay "An Objective" that introduced the 1931 special issue of *Poetry* he edited. He writes there that

> [i]n sincerity shapes appear concomitants of word combinations, precursors of [. . .] completed sound or structure, melody or form. Writing occurs which is the detail, not the mirage, of seeing, of thinking with the things as they exist [. . .].

> Shapes suggest themselves, and the mind senses and receives awareness [. . . .] Presented with sincerity, the mind tends to supply, in further suggestion, [. . .] complete appreciation. (*Prepositions* 12-13)

With a singular intensity, poetic Objectivism manifests the human encounter of the world. Furthermore, this encounter is defined within, and by, a fleeting moment. Thus time — not just the individual's spatial or otherwise "objective" map of a life's journey — suffuses the Objectivist poem. Time is suspended within its text, a text that demonstrates an awareness of temporal existence. Later Objectivist poetry especially strives to depict this existential condition, in which a life is caught in time, as the process of discovery; the poetry's aim is to find out the moment a world is realized. This processual way of making — perhaps better to say of living — poetry is the one common connection these five contemporary poets have with their ancestors. Consider, for instance, the following two passages. Both are grounded in what may at first seem to be, in comparison, quite different suppositions about the nature of language and knowledge. Both are also quite different formalistically. The first passage is by Finkelstein:

> There are words
> that bind meanings to themselves
> as if they were the strands of a great braid
> forever being wound.
> "Turn it and turn it again,
> for everything is in it":
> the words are infinitely interpretable,
> the commentaries too numerous to count.
> But all of them provide sustenance
> as do these braided loaves of bread,
> glazed and crowned with poppy seeds,
> the patterns almost legible,
> scattered as the bread is sliced.
> —from "Braids," *Restless* 74

Now, here is passage typical of Hejinian:

> The cold of poetry

gobs — continents
My slowness
is increasing
The lake protrudes
convex and anxious
the eye details
the rocks
stand on their heads
with so much violence!
of accuracy
Yes, it is
a poetry
of certainty!

. . . .

Realism is an unimaginable ballad: direct speech
across the trajectory of nature in its trees
Which word is an object of imitation?
And in returning differs

I have achieved the ability to be pathological
Here I refer to beauty when it forms
and every belief which is a move —
I am a contractor
in hunchbacked grammar to a bridge of the elegy

Into an elegy discontinuity implodes
Taken in. . .
My thoughts take a twist, they are always logical
    in this direction
The ear opens onto a setting: audience life
The drone, the wrong word, and the relief
    —from "The Person," *The Cold of Poetry*, 170-71, 179

What these two poems basically share is their concern for language. Each understands language as lying at the heart of experience. In each of these passages, in fact, language not only becomes real in itself but becomes reality itself. For Finkelstein, language contains all — "everything is in it"; for Hejinian (one of the originary Language poets), it can be a "poetry / of certainty."

Yet while each passage might embrace language as reality, only Finkelstein's presumes that reality possesses a coherence — that there is, despite the realness of language per se, a world beyond language even if apart from it, a world tangential to language, one that language cannot signify directly yet can disclose by its very failure to denote it reliably. This questionable relationship between language and world is what each poem imagines — or, more precisely, what each enacts — and, in doing so, the relationship is portrayed as indeterminate and therefore as residing both within and apart from a temporal existence. Finkelstein's situation is one inflected by a deep uncertainty. For him the world lies somewhere, somehow, beyond language; hence, only language's existence can be relied upon, not so much because of language's own substance, but because language is that phenomenon which mediates the world. The uncertainty of his circumstance is yet more pervasive, since the speaker in his poem dwells *within* the realm of language. What he can say with sureness is that the "patterns" of the language are "almost legible." They tantalize to the degree that the real world is almost reachable through linguistic expression. The speaker's world is one of plenitude — even if, finally, only a linguistic plenitude; it is a world of "commentaries too numerous to count." As asserted in the Talmudic *Ethics of the Fathers*, which Finkelstein quotes, the language must be reimagined — "Turn it and turn it again" — and, more than this, reinhabited, "'for everything is in it'," for in the end, mystically or otherwise, it is the world, that place of vitality and genius, that place of the authentic.

Similarly, Hejinian's lines see "speech" as, at best, being able to cross "the trajectory of nature." Still, her universe is absolutely discrete. "Realism is an unimaginable ballad." In her verse, too, there is a heightened sensitivity to the uncertainty of the poet's prosaic understanding of things. In contrast to Finkelstein's, Hejinian's poetry is not so much an expression — perhaps the better word here is "*non*expression" — of a radical nihilism; instead, it is a glorying in the fact of a world entropy. Appropriate to this point of view, Hejinian's is a discourse of starts and stops, of syntactic crosscurrents and eddies. One purpose of her writing strategy is to mimic and often to deconstruct one or another trope or rhetorical gesture grounded in the Western poetic tradition. Therefore, in her work, a reader will come across a line like, "Into an elegy discontinuity implodes." In this regard, her poetry also differs markedly from Finkelstein's. When the speaker in her poem brazenly announces a "poetry / of certainty," nothing could be further from the truth — but then, for Hejinian, what truth can there be other than that which resides in the moment of reading, that site where we encounter her text, in the play that comes from parsing failed statements or fractured sentences?

Finkelstein, just the opposite, is conscientiously recalling and championing that tradition — his syntax is cogent, and, furthermore, the tradition is being self-consciously invoked by him through the metaphor of the "braided loaves" of challah, which plays a central role in his poem when its speaker is arguing, nonetheless, in favor of language's primacy. Finkelstein not only opts for the metaphor; he allows it to be the center of his discourse. The "braid[s]" have a meaning, and by extension so do the "seeds" as they fall off the "loaves" when sliced. Inevitably, the meaning of the poem is "scattered" like the seeds, thereby spread everywhere, even as it is diffused. Hejinian would never allow any trope so much attention, so much importance — so much centrality. In keeping with the original Objectivist poetics, Finkelstein is intent, most of all, on presenting focused objects (e.g., the loaves, their poppy-seed toppings) in his speaker's purview, which draw and hold our attention and fix a locus for reading. He also favors terse, focused expressions. Hejinian, however, consciously works against the consistency necessary to sustain such a focus; her constant swerves and abrupt stops, and then new starts, reflect an awareness of a tradition she means to disavow. All the same, Finkelstein's disposition toward metaphor is not, finally, "Objectivist." For her part, Hejinian avoids metaphor and instead favors metonymy — in keeping with her grandparents. Yet her verse, in its repudiation of direct statement and its obvious intent to luxuriate in language pure and simple — in its proffering of multiple readings — does not appear to be akin to their work. Her poetry, in short, does not *feel* like theirs, while in many respects — his central use of metaphor aside — Finkelstein's work does.

Finkelstein fashions one economy, Hejinian fully another. Hejinian undermines the objects presented in her poem; she prevents their receiving sustained observance, while she makes numerous verbal passes at them. She says the same thing several times although each iteration contains some mutation of an original assertion that dissolves, and so she vitiates any possible ground of any statement. She also posits a speaker whose status within her poem is equal to that of its imagery. For instance, there is a "lake," yet the presence of the speaker insistently comes between the reader's contemplation of that lake for its own sake, and the speaker's perception of it. Likewise, what is emphasized next in the poem is the fact of her visual perception of some rocks instead of the rocks themselves — we are told that "the eye details / the rocks"; the metonymic eye, signifying the speaker's consciousness, occupies the foreground of the poem.

All in all, to compare Finkelstein and Hejinian is to demonstrate the original Objectivists' potential not only for a range of style but, ultimately, of ideology. After its inception in the 1930s Objectivism was to unfold eventually in the hands of the generation prior to Finkelstein and Hejinian. This middle generation — poets such as Paul Blackburn, William Bronk, Theodore Enslin, Armand Schwerner, Robert Creeley, Cid Corman, Denise Levertov, and Charles Tomlinson — worked in tandem with their older counterparts for several decades beginning after the World War Two. To gain a full appreciation of the five poets of the third generation, then, a brief overview of both early and mid-Objectivist poetics is now in order.

The nuclear members of the early Objectivist movement were Zukofsky, Charles Reznikoff, Carl Rakosi, George Oppen, Lorine Niedecker, and, as a sort of father figure, William Carlos Williams; the English poet Basil Bunting is also widely viewed as having been in sympathy with them. Two other writers need inclusion here, however, inasmuch as their work helped to shape the basis for the movement: Ezra Pound and Gertrude Stein. The identifying name *objectivist* comes into being with Zukofsky's essay title, "An Objective." The impetus for the movement, shaped by him and the others, was Imagism, an earlier "school" whose best-known members were Pound, T. E. Hulme, Richard Aldington, and H.D. A 1912 letter from Pound to Harriet Monroe, the editor of *Poetry*, typifies what Imagism was about. Speaking of H. D., he remarks that she employs a "laconic speech," one that is "Objective," without "slither — direct," and containing *"No metaphors that won't permit examination. —* It's straight talk" (*Selected Letters* 11). In rejecting their immediate predecessors, Tennyson conspicuous among them, the Imagists established, instead, a poetry they saw as being devoid of sentiment and even of the subjective. Imagist poetry presented an essentially visualized field, and did so without comment extraneous to its images. This poetics had the greatest effect on Zukofsky and the other Objectivists. His essay recalls both Pound's diction and attitude; moreover, with a typically Poundian flair, it sets out a basic ground rule:

> An Objective: (Optics) — The lens bringing the rays from an object to a focus. That which is aimed at. (Use extended to poetry) — Desire for what is objectively perfect [. . .]. (*Prepositions* 12)

In an interview years later, Reznikoff remembers that he and the others "agreed completely with all that Pound was saying [. . .]. I think we agreed that the term 'objectivism,' as we understood Pound's use of it, corresponded to the way we felt poetry should be written" ("A Talk with L. S. Dembo" 101).

The Objectivists were not merely later Imagists, however. They perceived Imagism's limitations. Therefore, principally Zukofsky's verse contains a strong sense of measure, a musicality Imagist verse was viewed as lacking. Oppen, chiefly, saw in Imagism a slavish obedience to a narrowly objectified poetic landscape he would abandon. Accordingly, he proclaims, in a letter to Serge Fachereau,

> [t]he image for the sake of the poet, not for [. . .] the delectation of the reader who may be imagined to admire the quaintness and ingenuity of the poet, but can scarcely have been a part of the poet's attempt to find himself in the world — unless perhaps to find himself as a charming conversationalist. ("Three Oppen Letters," 83)

The renovation of the Imagist design not only concerned the image. If the image must be demoted, as is attested in Oppen's letter for the reason he gives, then so must metaphor and symbol. What role could either play for the poet who exists, within his text, through the act of discovery? Perhaps images, metaphors and symbols denied language's fundamental instrumentality. These figures might embellish expression for the reader, but they were unwieldy and distracting for the poet. Pound had suggested as much when he praised what he called "the principle move in imaginative writing today" for heading "away from the word as a symbol toward the word as reality" (quoted by Williams in his *Selected Essays* 105). "Words are real, in the Objectivist formulation," Heller has written (in *Conviction's Net of Branches: Essays on the Objectivist Poets and Poetry*, 4), "because they instate an existence beyond the word. They are an expression of a "faith" — as Oppen speaks of it in describing his own poetics — "that the nouns do refer to something; that it's there, that it's true, the whole implication of these nouns; that appearances represent reality, whether or not they misrepresent it" ("The Objectivist Poet: Four Interviews" 163).

Pound had preached a poetry of condensation, simplicity, and directness. Ironically, the Objectivists deepened the possibilities of such expression by restoring the legitimacy of the subjective. They turned away from symbol and metaphor; if there was to be any figuration in their poetry, it would be, for the most part, metonymy, a figure that allowed more accurate recordings of a poet's experience. This was experience as portrayed in direct relation to an objective world. In what sense, though, was this *the* world? How can a poem *be* the world? The "Objectivist poem does not enact a mimesis," Heller explains, "but mediates between representational systems" (Heller 99). Zukofsky, Oppen and the others were true to Pound's objectivist disposition; on the other hand, they were also available for a deep interiority, even as the surfaces of their poems proclaimed something quite to the contrary, an apparently valueless landscape but one that, like language itself, signified a further reality (even if such signification was a necessary *mis*representation of it).

Invested with a full-fledged philosophy of language, Objectivist poetry could not have occurred without Pound most of all. However, neither the original Objectivists nor their descendants can be fully comprehended without acknowledging the work of Stein. An early meeting with Zukofsky, Oppen and Reznikoff, is recalled by Williams who came away from it with the understanding that, as he later wrote,

> the poem, like every other form of art, is an object, an object that in itself formally presents its case and its meaning by the very form it assumes. [. . . .] I for one believe that it was Gertrude Stein, for her formal insistence on words in their literal, structural quality of being words, who had strongly influenced us. (*The Autobiography of William Carlos Williams* 264-65)

Typical of Stein is her essay "Poetry and Grammar" where she asks, if "[a] noun is a name of anything, [then] why after a thing is named write about it. A name is adequate or it is not. If it is adequate then why go on calling it, if is not then calling it by its name does no good" (313). Never to go beyond a language's signifiers, to their signifieds, is to remain with the text itself as the realm of all vitality and meaning. "For Stein," Peter Nicholls notes, "the domain of writing is precisely that of 'sensations which are not objects': once released from the instrumental duties of 'naming', language begins to take on a polymorphous life of its own, generating 'excitement' as it becomes a thing to be enjoyed for itself" (119).

Stein pays special attention to the usually least significant parts of speech, conjunctions, prepositions, and articles that are "delicate," "varied and alive" (Stein, 315). Overall, Stein concludes, "real narrative must of necessity be told by any one having come to the realization that the noun must be replaced not by inner balance but by the thing in itself and that will eventually lead to everything" (336). In an essay on Stein, Williams admires how in her writing a reader senses that "[t]he feeling is of words themselves, a curious immediate quality quite apart from their meaning, much as in music different notes are dropped, so to speak, into repeated chords one at a time, one after another — for themselves alone" ("The Work of Gertrude Stein" 20).

Williams came to regard the poem as a machine of words. Indeed, this view of poetry informs his review of Oppen's first book, *Discrete Series*, in which he observes that a poem's "existence as a poem is of first importance a technical matter, as with all facts, compelling the recognition of a mechanical structure. [. . .] It is the acceptable fact of a poem as a mechanism that is the proof of its meaning and this is a technical matter as in the case of any other machine" ("The New Poetical Economy" in Silliman 86). To know a poem as a machine was to be attuned to, as the Objectivists were, poetry's textual nature. This awareness of *text* was part of a larger cognizance of the world as intensely material (hence the title of one of Oppen's books, *The Materials*). Materialism could translate as desiring to create verse that was true to the speaking voice, a realism that was lacking in Imagism. Materialism also came to mean an emphasis on the tangibility of text as it sat on the page. Especially Oppen's use of ellipses, dashes and other punctuation, and later of gaps and white space generally, reveals an appreciation of a purely textual aesthetics, as it invigorates syntax, often by way of disruption. As Taggart has observed, furthermore, the gaps were "Oppen's signs for the space of the mind, the space made by the mind, the space made by the mind for itself" ("To Go Down Into" 279). More than this, Oppen wished to include silences in his poems — not simply voice, not simply discourse — in an attempt to enlarge a poem's domain. Thus his own "objectivist" poetics demanded that he "leave the world as it is. This is one of the consistent preoccupations running throughout his work. And it is out of this preoccupation that he comes to silence [. . . .] in which there can be moments of vision" (Taggart 281).

Oppen's outlook and practice are uniquely his own. Nevertheless, they can be seen to be rooted in tendencies to be found in both Pound and Stein, which were encouraged by the activities of the other Objectivists, and subsequently were furthered by a new generation of poets. For example, here is a part of Robert Creeley's well-known poem "For WCW":

The rhyme is after
all the repeated
insistence.

There, you say, and

>   there, and there,
>   and *and* becomes
>
>   just so.
>   —*Collected Poems*, 273

Creeley's evident pleasure in his reading of Williams is grounded in a specific literary history some of whose landmarks include: the establishment of "To" Press in 1931; Zukofsky's "Poem beginning 'The'" and his epic poem entitled *"A"*; the titling of Oppen's later book *This in Which*; and recently, Corman's multi-volume book of poems entitled, simply, *Of*. Other second-generation poets have perpetuated this attitude toward language in similar fashion. Schwerner's epic poem *The Tablets* — twenty-four poems made up of words, pictographs and other markings — is quite "material" in its visual and semantic texts. Schwerner means to echo and critique the enterprises of translation (supposedly translations of ancient stone glyphs), paleography and archeology. His twenty-four "translations," accompanied by ancillary and ostensibly scholarly notations, are an "edition" of consummate fiction. Many of them are abundantly rich and ornate, while one is their absolute opposite, made up of only one word, the definite article, repeated twice, set in brackets, and surrounded by ellipses: "[the the]" ("Tablet 10" 80). A poem that epitomizes Bronk's poetics, "The Winter Light," might seem utterly unrelated to Schwerner's or even to Creeley's — unless, of course, the Objectivists are understood as their common denominator:

>   We see light but we live in the cold and the dark
>   — winters anyway. We are aware
>   that that isn't all that there is.

Bronk is playing with the particle "that," first using it as a conjunction, then as a demonstrative pronoun, and then as a relative pronoun, all in the same breath. The machinery of the statement itself is what is being emphasized here, through syntax and rhythm. Whatever else "The Winter Light" may intend, it stands as an object unto itself, to the degree that, in an "object-poem," as Shimon Sandbank writes, "[t]he signifier, not only the signified, is now foregrounded and becomes as much an object as the thing referred to" ("The Object-Poem: In Defence of Referentiality" 469). Thus it is the objectified, textualized matrix, which allows the entrance in of the subject, of a subjectivity that is fostered, not precluded. To be sure, in Oppen's hands poetry becomes the record of his encounter with the real. The very text of that record is what has been objectified. As in Stein, the textuality of the record, its texture, is all-important.

Both aesthetically and philosophically, this alertness to texture is shared by all of the third generation "objectivists." Heller — who is often viewed as the cardinal Objectivist of this group — is closest to Finkelstein in temperament, theme, and style, among the five being discussed here. Still, the voice in Heller's poems is consciously speaking across the flow of a rhetorical tradition Finkelstein wishes to sustain. Like Finkelstein's, Heller's poetry will record the world of the senses, assumes there is such a thing as a fact, and speaks with astonishing directness. But there is in it a striving for a transcendence of the merely factual. The same might be said about Finkelstein's, but in Heller's work the presence of uncertainty is not simply more pronounced; it is ultimately his central concern, and so the move toward transcendence is all the more urgent. Every poet internalizes particular poems, tropes or phrases from the works of others — those usually encountered when the poet is still young and developing his own craft and vision of the world. One such poem for Heller is Oppen's "The Little Hole," and Heller means to preserve, albeit to rewrite, a gesture central to that poem. Oppen, too, has done his own rewriting, of a passage from Williams:

> The little hole in the eye
> Williams called it, the little hole
>
> Has exposed us naked
> To the world
>
> And will not close.
>   —Oppen *Collected Poems* 81

In "4:21 P.M. on St. George's Clock: Film," published in the early 1970s, Heller quotes this poem when he writes,

> solitary park
> solitary benchers
>
> still air, still branches

the green footage stopped
— matter, call it matter
perceived as light, corpuscles of light
in the "little hole of the eye . . ." (Heller *Accidental Center* 43).

Heller concentrates on the fact of perception itself; there is an extraordinary world of both comely and terrifying images rushing toward him as he sits on a park bench. Some twenty-five years later, the remainder of Oppen's poem appears, which ends as follows.

Blankly the world
Looks in

And we compose
Colors

And the sense

Of home
And there are those

In it so violent
And so alone

They cannot rest.
        —from "The Little Hole," *Collected Poems*, 81

Now in full maturity, Heller answers Oppen again, thinking more about text in and of itself and its possible relationship to the world at large:

What sets one free
within the sign and blesses the wordflow

without barrier?
Not literature, which is only for those

> *at home in the world*
> while air is trapped in the sealed vessel,
>
> contained in our
> containment, our relation to earth.
>
> Omnivore language,
> syntax of the real, riddling over matter,
>
> more difficult to ken
> than the talmudic angelus. [. . .]
>   —"Lecture with Celan" *Wordflow* 107

In Finkelstein's work, text is imagined as bread, the eating of which will mean self-connection with a past preserved in Talmudic commentary. In Heller's work, the world is not so symmetrical; rather, it is wonderfully unsettled (Oppen's "they cannot rest," Heller's "syntax of the real, riddling over matter"). The world is infused by language and writing, is overwhelmingly, breathtakingly difficult. Like Oppen, and Hejinian, and less like Finkelstein in this regard, Heller must journey outside of language to state a truth that is provisional, although he realizes he is "trapped in [a] sealed vessel," and yet he continues to fashion a syntax that radically tests that restriction as it reflects a radical undecidability.

Another poet especially close to Oppen of all the Objectivists is DuPlessis. Like both Finkelstein and Heller (and in contrast to the early Modernists), she does not turn her back on her predecessors and instead rewrites—reenvisions them. More in keeping with Hejinian, DuPlessis' style reveals how pronounced such rewriting can be. Her philosophical approach to the issue of language, however, is closer to that of Heller, particularly since her poetry talks directly about the limits of language and thereby perception. For her to address this issue, though, she must strive for a syntax that, by highlighting its limitation, discloses the inherent richness of both language and perception itself.

Unlike Hejinian, DuPlessis explicitly establishes an Objectivist lineage in her poetry — and, again like Finkelstein and Heller, she associates that lineage with a Judaic, textual tradition. She openly avows her lineage in her poem "Midrush" (a pun on *Midrash*):

> Wraithes of poets, Oppen and oddly
> Zukofsky

> renew their open engagement with me
> wreathing smoke-veils
> my eyescreen tearing their insistent
> opaque, startled
> writing was speaking here was
> saying words but,
> befit a shady station,
> sere swallowed up within the
> mouths speaking
> and all the words
> dizzy with tears
> passed again away.
> —"Midrush," *Drafts: 3-14*, 18

Here words become evanescent, vulnerable to being dissolved, much in the way that speech disappears from hearing once it is uttered. The original Objectivists created a text that, in objectifying writing, also monumentalized it. For DuPlessis, on the other hand, this is a text that will not convey the depth of her own experience of the world. In her mature years, she has constructed her own sub-genre she has named the "Draft," which signifies her concept of all utterance as always being unfinished. This poetic form came about, as recently noted in her essay "Haibun: Draw Your/ Draft," through a praxis in which there is

> [n]o plan, no design, no schemata. Just a few procedures: placing works on the big stage of the page, making each be itself intact and autonomous, but connected to themselves as they emerged. No continuous narrative. No myth as explanation. Here *Drafts* are [. . .] quite related to Objectivist ethos and poetics. The works are influenced by objectivist argument and propositions about reality. That the image is encountered not found, as Oppen proposed. That *the* and *a* (said Zukofsky testily) are words worth investigating, as suggestive and staggering in their implications as any epic or myth. (105-06)

As in Heller and Finkelstein, DuPlessis' imagery carries a great deal of semantic weight, because her statements are fundamentally intact. Conversely, as in Hejinian, DuPlessis' work contains an exceptional commitment to openness. Hejinian, in her poetry, wishes to dissolve even the crosscurrents she constructs in order to create an "open" text. DuPlessis creates them to test, and by so doing to amplify, a statement's coherence. Speaking of the "draft," Burton Hatlen has noted that it

> becomes, for DuPlessis, a remarkably flexible and commodious form, incorporating into itself the random one-thing-after-anotherness of daily life, and the eruption into that life of History, and the writer's experience of facing again the blank page and strewing it with words, and, always, the moment by moment rediscovery of a world that is insistently THERE, beyond our will and intentionality. All the drafts are dated, and the poems are arranged in chronological order. In this respect all of the drafts also have titles which point to a unifying principle, often grammatical or typographical. Drafts three and four, for example, revolve respectively around the prepositions "of" and "in." Draft eight reflects on the article "the." Draft ten consists of brief epigrammatic spins on each letter of the alphabet. And Draft fourteen explores a range of conjunctions. The flavor of DuPlessis's writing comes from the way it infuses the dailyness of life with unifying motifs of this sort. (16)

A portion of DuPlessis' recent poem, "Draft 23: Findings," dramatizes the problems a blank page presents for constructing an identity, for engaging the world genuinely yet without eliminating its ambiguities:

>   Delivered
> came a ghost letter, typed, but not with ribbon,
> so only the pressure of letters
> was left, white incised, take a look, it's in
> long paragraphs, but the sheet solid blankness;
> and beyond "hard to read," erasing its palpability,
> and beyond the fact
> it is impossible to read at such length
> inside a dream is
> seeing a glimpse of what forever
> could be of
> words, but was in fact words never.
> Yet even losing it as I skimmed

> and the insult of loss shadowing
> my ebbing tries, still I looked forward then
> now to decipher this token of care, wanted
> badly
> to read it, meaning to me
> so much that it had come thru the mail,
> a corresponding letter, but without black letters on it,
> so black to blank it went unrolling back,
> with the
> "in" from invisible,
> the deeper double "in" and "in" from finding
> and made a dissolve.
> —Section 3 of "Draft 23: Findings," *Drafts 15-XXX, The Fold* 43

DuPlessis' fantasy is itself a tangible sign, an entrance into a viable comprehension of what it means to be a cognizant being. It is precisely in a passage such as this one, where the basic givens of this existential position are laid out, that we are asked to consider the way in which experience, in the poet's act of knowing the world, manifests as constant appearance and transmutation. And, in a nod to the literary tradition whose project has been to observe and also to appropriate a life outside itself, the manifest experience in this fantasy takes the form of language and even more so of writing if only of a phantom sort.

There is a sense in DuPlessis' work that life is miraculous and that writing, as well as the spoken voice, which may or may or may not be represented by writing, must occur out of an openness and spontaneity. This posture is central to Taggart's work especially, and there, as in DuPlessis', we see an even more dramatic tension between "open" text and coherent syntax. Taggart's style is quite his own, nevertheless. He tests the limits of language as much as either DuPlessis or Hejinian, but to much a different effect. One particular aspect of his work places him alongside Hejinian most of all. As true for her, Taggart makes great use of metonymy. Remarkably, her theoretical comments about this figure apply even more to his work than to hers. For instance, Hejinian has said that

> [m]etonymy moves attention from thing to thing; its principle is combination rather than selection. Compared to metaphor, which depends on code, metonymy preserves context, foregrounds interrelationship. (in Armantrout 11)

She might seem to be suggesting here that metonymy restricts the possibilities of utterance. Nothing could be further from the truth, though. She also argues that, "[w]hile metonymy maintains the intactness and discreteness of particulars, its paratactic perspective gives it multiple vanishing points" (in Armantrout 11); hence, metonymy can provide a radically endless text comprised of "an associative network, in which associations are compressed" ("Strangeness" 38 in Quartermain 27), and so the poem, built according to metonyms, emphasizes "structure, distinction, the integrity and separateness of things" (in Jarraway 321)—for the basis of this associative text is "naming [that] provides [. . .] structure, not individual words" (in Jarraway 321).

Taggart's poetry, if it is nothing else, is structure writ large. The same idea might be advanced for Hejinian. What makes the case of Taggart especially interesting is that he does not undermine the syntax of his statements, as do DuPlessis and Hejinian, and instead layers them one into the next, usually by repeating a sentence or a part of it, and by adding a new bit of information to it, which slightly alters the statement's shape and balance. Just the reverse, Taggart overly justifies the syntax. Also, much more like Finkelstein and Heller, Taggart is a precisionist. He isolates images in order to linger with them, to savor them as he repeats them. Imagery of this sort becomes hard to achieve in DuPlessis and Hejinian because of the new directions, the sudden new vectors of statement their poetics invite.

The basis of Taggart's poetry is the *cantus firmus* form, a self-contained framework, with each fixed song slowly merging into a larger configuration made up of other songs like it; it is, overall, what Craig Watson has called "a delicately balanced, almost microscopic linguistic ecosystem" (30):

> The vibration there is the vibration the vibration of a fan
> there is the vibration there is the continuous vibration
> there is the continuous the continuous dull vibration
> continuous vibration of a fan small fan on the wooden floor
> the vibration the continuous the dull vibration
> the vibration of a fan the vibration there is the vibration
> there is the vibration the vibration on the wooden floor
> vibration on the floor in the midst in the midst of stifling heat
> there is the continuous vibration in the heat [etc.]
> —"In the Sense of," *Standing Wave* 26

One at a time, one element after another is added within the syntax; then another is dropped, then another added. A new syntax will eventually coalesce.

In this particular poem, one result of this strategy is to create the very vibration the poem speaks of, which hovers within the reading, nondescript as a kind of white noise. Taggart stresses a minimalism, not simply in his restriction of vocabulary, but also in his penchant for constantly repeating patterns that are syntactic, rhythmic and imagistic, and that are enclosed within marvelous concatenations of sentence-statements fostering an aesthetics of the speaking voice as much as of the silently visual. To be sure, Taggart returns in a most unexpected fashion to the poem as song — much more in keeping with a poet like Zukofsky than any of the other original Objectivists or for that matter those of the second generation. Yet his minimalism has other effects, which are to objectify the written text, and, secondly, to lead the reader beyond it to something essential that underlies it: a fecund silence. The reader Taggart posits is, as he has said about his poetry, like a dancer who "is encouraged to move by the gaps between the notes of music" ("Woven Scarf" 28). Taggart's language is simple, direct, clear, demarcated — it has to be, for what he strives to achieve are the gaps between words and sentences. In one of his early poems he describes writing as "a kind of listening" in which he may "hear / others, voices of others" ("Contrafact," *Prism and the Pine Twig* 18); in another, he asserts that words "say nothing" for they are "Interiors / exteriorizing // themselves," and so not words but "*we / try //* to say / something [. . .]" (*Prism* 10). The fact that Taggart appreciates the crucial importance of these spaces to poetic meaning is itself conveyed by his pacing of change wherein a sentence slowly, through constant repetition, is transformed. The transformative element is, fundamentally, these gaps. If not silence, then these are the glimpses of the poem's immanence, and it is the awareness of the immanent, the primal, which Taggart wishes to communicate, as it manifests variously in one or another form, in this or that formal statement. "Thus," he has commented,

> I am drawn to the poem as a woven scarf with many openings through which light enters. It could be spread out, enlarged to a scarf of migrating birds in the sky. But however dense the weave and however enlarged the area, the poem must contain a perceptible pattern of openings, composed silences, within itself. ("The Poem as Woven Scarf" 28).

While his poems may seem to operate in a manner more akin to the music of a composer like Philip Glass, they are actually founded upon a different assumption from that of minimalism, and yet to consider the work of Glass and other minimalists is helpful in seeing how Taggart operates within the Objectivist tradition.

> The poet, who is first a reader, makes no original discovery in reading; instead, he becomes only more aware of the spider-web connectedness of his sources and of the innumerable ghostly speakers still beyond them. At best, our displacements might operate as clever enough variations on previously laid down themes. But what is finally repeated is an absence. ("Of the Power of the Word" 62)

The belief that underlies this strategy of composition is that "language holds all things in a state of potentiality" ("Interview with Gil Ott" 30).

All five poets of the third generation recognize the value of silence in its relationship to utterance. Finkelstein and Heller treat it directly through overt discussions of it, in their poems, while DuPlessis and Hejinian, and Heller up to a point, wish to invoke it through their respective styles. Heller's statement may trail off or overlap with another. DuPlessis, and Hejinian most of all, radicalize the statement for the ultimate purpose of achieving its erasure, as a way of arriving at silence that plays an equal role with utterance in the creation of poetic meaning. As for Taggart, his invocation of silence is achieved through what he has termed an "enacted speech" ("Woven Scarf" 26). The graphical precision of his imagery, and the syntactic cogency of his statements, would seem to argue that Taggart's poetics is closer to Finkelstein's than to Hejinian's, and that among the five he represents, along that continuum they embody, its dead center. However, what ultimately places him next to Hejinian, at one extreme, is not simply his relinquishing of symbol, metaphor and simile, but his often explicit attempt to show their falsity, such as is evident in this passage where the simile "like a sparrow" is, primarily through repetition, drained of its semantic power, of its occasion, and is employed, not to liken solitude to the life of that bird, but rather to disclose how perception can be sui generis, how we may see ourselves in the act of seeing:

Reflexive

> Consider whether you can be solitary and alone
> whether you can sit alone like a sparrow
> like a sparrow in an indentation in the ground
> an indentation in the deep red ground
> consider whether you can be like this in a valley

> valley of vision where there are no roses
> where there is not even a secret rose
> consider whether you can remain in such a valley
> in a valley of vision which is always the same
> where the ground is always deep red ground
> where there is not even a secret rose
> consider whether you can remain like a sparrow
> whether you can sit alone like a sparrow
> like a sparrow in an indentation in the ground
> in a valley of vision which is always the same.
> —"Reflexive" *Loop* 228

What comes to the fore in reading this poem, finally, is its textuality, its own objectivist "reflexivity." Closer to Stein in this respect than, say, Zukofsky, Taggart is creating a text that, in its spaces, might invite the reader to participate more actively than usual in the construal of meaning. In any case, he is like both Hejinian and Stein to the extent that, as Lisa Ruddick has said of Stein's work, "words-as-things [jut] out from their sentences, are mischievous assaults on the coherence of ordinary speech" (144). Taggart would agree with Finkelstein that

> A handful of stories is all one has to offer
>   Even in seeking to remake the world.
>   —Finkelstein, "A Poem for Storytellers," *Restless Messenger* 27

So would both Heller and DuPlessis subscribe to the underlying conception of how text and tradition intertwine anew in the poetry of the present. Perhaps Taggart wishes to create a presence out of that tradition through a depletion of its language, through its ultimate objectification; then he might agree with Hejinian when she writes of that tradition, that

>   the classics bend around novels because
> anyone likes a story
>   work them up
>   item terminated bit
>   which is useful then replaced

>   a hole of thickness
>   lay it to the side of the greatest distance
>   which I vidual in this passage
>   back vitality the fun of the excitement of it
>   such motion
>   grip this concrete spirit
>   husk at the words
>   sink it
> [etc.]
>   —from *Writing Is an Aid to Memory* 29

That not only syntax in this passage but a single word is being deconstructed — the ghost of *individual* hovers behind "I vidual" — testifies to the legacy of the experimentalism that marked the original Objectivist impulse. Text, words, language, fugitive in their roles as elements of experience, are also its very essence. Yet the problem the Objectivists faced, and which poets today still struggle with, is how to express themselves genuinely, how to invoke the realm of the subjective to its fullest, how not to delimit it and by doing so the world's possibilities.

Subjectivity is enlarged by the objective, most of all when it is registered in the language that mediates the world. It flowers in the Objectivism that emerged out of early Modernism, and then, finally, as it has prospered more than a half-century later. One "problem" that haunts "neo-objectivism" is that the range of its expression threatens to disintegrate the world altogether. Oppen had said, the importance of experience was predicated on the understanding that there was ultimately a ground "to stand on" — that is, "The self is no mystery, the mystery is / That there is something for us to stand on" ("World, World," *Collected Poems* 143). This presumption is being tested today, not only by a poet like Hejinian, but by Heller and even Finkelstein. Their excursions into the textual — into the real — world finally only redound to the original Objectivists, even as those forays open up a very new, if as yet far from comprehensible, universe.

WORKS CITED

Armantrout, Rae. "Feminist Poetics and the Meaning of Clarity." *Sagetrieb* 11.3 (Winter 1992).
Bradbury, Richard. "Objectivism." *American Poetry: The Modernist Ideal.* Ed. Clive Bloom and Brian Docherty. Ed. New York: St. Martin's P, 1995.
Bronk, William. "The Winter Light." *Manifest; and Furthermore.* San Francisco: North Point, 1987.
Corman, Cid. *Of.* Venice, CA: Lapis P, 1990.
Creeley, Robert. *The Collected Poems of Robert Creeley.* Berkeley: U of California P, 1982.
Dembo, Louis. "A Talk with L. S. Dembo [Interview with Charles Reznikoff]." *Charles Reznikoff: Man and Poet.* Orono, ME: National Poetry Foundation, 1984.
-------. "The Objectivist Poet: Four Interviews [with George Oppen]." *Contemporary Literature* 10.
DuPlessis, Rachel Blau. *Drafts: 3-14.* Elmwood, CT.: Potes & Poets P, 1991.
-------. "Haibun: Draw Your/ Draft." *Sulfur* 42 (Spring 1998).
-------. *Drafts 15-XXX, The Fold.* Elmwood, CT.: Potes & Poets P, 1997.
Finkelstein, Norman. "Braids," and "A Poem for Storytellers." *Restless Messenger.* Athens, GA, and London: U of Georgia P, 1992.
Hatlen, Burton. "Neo-Objectivism: A Preliminary Definition." "Poetry and the Public Sphere." Lecture at Rutgers University, New Brunswick, NJ, Spring 1997; transcript sent to the author.
Hejinian, Lyn. *The Cold of Poetry.* Los Angeles: Sun and Moon P, 1994.
-------. "Strangeness." in Quartermain, Peter. "Syllable as Music: Lyn Hejinian's Writing Is an Aid to Memory." *Sagetrieb* 11.3 (Winter 1992): 17-31.
-------. *Writing Is an Aid to Memory.* Los Angeles: Sun and Moon P, 1996.
Heller, Michael. *Accidental Center.* Freemont, MI: Sumac, 1972.
-------. *Conviction's Net of Branches: Essays on the Objectivist Poets and Poetry.* Carbondale and Edwardsville: Southern Illinois UP, 1985.
-------. *Wordflow: New and Selected Poems.* Jersey City, NJ: Talisman House, Publishers, 1997.
Jarraway, David R. "My Life through the 1980s: The Exemplary LANGUAGE of Lyn Hejinian." *Contemporary Literature* 33.2 (1992): 319-36.
Nicholls, Peter "From Gertrude Stein to L=A=N=G=U=A=G=E Poetry." *Contemporary Poetry Meets Modern Theory.* Ed. Antony Easthope and John O. Thompson. Toronto: U of Toronto P, 1991.
Oppen, George. *Collected Poems.* New York: New Directions, 1975.
-------. "The Objectivist Poet: Four Interviews," *Contemporary Literature* 10.
-------. "Three Oppen Letters with a Note." *Ironwood* 5 (1975).
Ott, Gill. "Interview with John Taggart." *Paper Air* 2.1
Pound, Ezra. *Make It New.* London: Faber and Faber, 1934.
-------. *Selected Essays.* New York: New Directions, 1954.
-------. *Selected Letters 1907-1941.* Ed. D. D. Paige. New York: New Directions, 1971.
Quartermain, Peter. "Syllable as Music: Lyn Hejinian's Writing Is an Aid to Memory." *Sagetrieb* 11.3 (Winter 1992): 17-31.
[Reznikoff, Charles. See Dembo above.]

Ruddick, Lisa. *Reading Gertrude Stein: Body, Text, Gnosis*. Ithaca: Cornell UP, 1990.

Sandbank, Shimon. "The Object-Poem: In Defence of Referentiality." *Poetics Today* 6.3 (1985): 461-473.

Schwerner, Armand. *The Tablets I-XXVI*. London: Atlas P, 1989.

Silliman, Ron. "Third Phase Objectivism." *Paideuma* 10.1 (Spring 1981): 85-89.

Stein, Gertrude. "Poetry and Grammar." *Gertrude Stein: Writings 1932-46*. New York: Library of America / Penguin Putnam, 1998.

Taggart, John. "Interview with Gil Ott." *Paper Air* 2.1

-------. "Of the Power of the Word." *Conversant Essays*. Ed. James McCorkle. Detroit: Wayne State UP, 1990.

-------. *Loop*. Los Angeles: Sun and Moon, 1991.

-------. "The Poem as Woven Scarf." *Northwest Review* 19.3 (1981): 26-28.

-------. *Prism and the Pine Twig*. New Rochelle, N.Y.: Elizabeth P, c1977.

-------. *Standing Wave*. Providence: Lost Roads, 1993.

-------. "To Go Down Into." *Ironwood* 16.1-2(31-32) (Spring/Fall 1988): 270-285

Watson, Craig. "The Poetics of Community." *Northwest Review* 19.3 (1981): 29-39.

Williams, William Carlos. *The Autobiography of William Carlos Williams*. London: MacGibbon & Kee, 1968.

-------. "The Work of Gertrude Stein." *Selected Essays of William Carlos Williams*. New York: New Directions, 1954. Repr. *Gertrude Stein*. Ed. Harold Bloom. New York: Chaelsea House, 1986.

-------. "The New Poetical Economy" (Review of Oppen's *Discrete Series*). *Poetry* 44.4 (July 1934): 220-25.

Zukofsky, Louis. Ed. *An "Objectivists" Anthology*. New York and Var, France: Le Beausset, 1932.

-------. "An Objective." *Poetry* (1931). Repr. in *Prepositions: The Collected Critical Essays of Louis Zukofsky*. Expanded Edition. Berkeley: U of California P, 1981.

Jeanne Heuving

THE VIOLENCE OF NEGATION OR 'LOVE'S INFOLDING'

I

SINCE THE GET GO OF MY LIFE AS A POETRY CRITIC AND POETRY WRITER, I have been skeptical of criticism that would upend poetic tradition, that nascent beast of uninterrupted solitude. Born into the middle class in a cold and bleak 1950s Seattle with virtually no poetic horizon whatsoever, I instead spent my aesthetic inclinations rearranging the acoustical tiles on my bedroom ceiling into diverse outcomes. Then, after this childhood of pre-pubescent love, pubescent love, and still no softening of the raw industrial area that formed at the foot of the hill where my family lived in a house above an arterial meanly slashed into the side of the hill, the flayed passage way of our demolished garage left to gape in the clayey hillside. In the far corner of our basement, I would discover this same passage way from the other end of concrete blocks erected to stop the entrance into the house, three steps leading into a blind well of spiders and beetles crawling over dirt. Lifting the planks of wood that covered this hole, I stared alongside my mother with her white eyes into this stopped source. Segmented tears. Cement laughter.

II

IN AESTHETIC AND PHILOSOPHICAL THEORIES OF NEGATION, a distinction is sometimes made between an art of negation as opposition and an art of negativity as différance. In an art of negation, artistic acts negate signifying practices and psychic economies through oppositional strategies. In an art of negativity, the negation is incremental, as the opposition takes the form of reading against existing texts, opening them up. Adorno is contrasted unfavorably to Derrida who "freed himself of the metaphysical or romantic pathos of negation, . . . finally arriving at a programmatic designation of 'deconstruction' as 'affirmation'" (Birus 150). Yet, this very valuation is problematic, since negations through large-scale oppositions similarly open into the affirmative, as the refused signifying practices and psychic economies ask for something else. And the preference for negativity over negation within Western philosophical traditions that value a display of spirit over a display of body augurs something else.

Missing from most discussions of negation and negativity is the violence that attends these acts, either as an originating slash, or as slow seepage from the cut, perhaps even absent mindedly begun. Some writing speaks violence (vehemence, force) louder than other writing, especially when the writer is a woman, since as passive body within Western discourses her protestations are doubly propulsive, a refusal of this passivity and a new formulation.

Freud insisted on the material reality of the body, producing a writing as ideationally complex as any philosophy. For Freud, an unviolent intellectual judgment was an oxymoron in terms. In his essay "Negation," he links intellectual judgment to primary psychic economies of introjection and ejection:

> Expressed in the language of the oldest — the oral — instinctual impulses, the judgment is: 'I should like to eat this', or 'I should like to spit it out'; and, put more generally, 'I should like to take this into myself and to keep that out.' That is to say: 'It shall be inside me' or 'it shall be outside me.' (Freud 668)

Freud was particularly compelled by intellectual judgments of negation since through them the subject could allow repressed contents to surface, removed as they are through their negation from affective significance:

> Negation is a way of taking cognizance of what is repressed; indeed, it is already a lifting of this repression, though not, of course, an acceptance of what is repressed .... one consequence of the process of repression is undone — the fact, namely of the ideational content of what is repressed not reaching consciousness. (Freud 667)

And, it is the removal from affective disturbance that endows thinking with a "measure of freedom." For Freud, "Judging is the intellectual action which decides the choice of motor action, which puts an end to the postponement due to thought and which leads over from thinking to acting." Far from being an activity that exists apart from the body, judgment "is to be regarded as an experimental action, a motor palpating . . . ." (Freud 669)   Freud's theoretically wild landscape is more poetic than most twentieth-century poetry, changing forever poetry's domain.

III

Some of the most exciting (intellectual) women poets of the twentieth century write their poetry through acts of negation and negativity. Laura (Riding) Jackson, Kathy Acker, Susan Howe, and Teresa Cha all imperfectly negate sexist, racist, and elitist signifying practices and psychic economies in search of love, "the most insane idea that any woman can think of" — refusing "the wretched positivism" of the promotion of meaninglessness for its own sake (Acker 9; Birus 146). At a dead end with languages that mispeak them, they compose pastiche, eclectic assemblages of incongruous languages, moving between literary foliation and rationalized squalor. They cut away script, decontextualizing language and shaping it into new meaning events.

Laura (Riding) Jackson's most stunning work of pastiche, *Anarchism Is Not Enough* (1928), is made up of mock poetic manifestoes, critical and theoretical exegesis, and fictional extravaganzas. Central to this volume and to understanding (Riding) Jackson's entire career is her concept of the "individual-unreal" or "unreal self," developed in her essay "Jocasta," named for the erased and contaminated mother of the Oedipus myth. (Riding) Jackson, who felt that existing social orders belied the self, postulated through her concept of an "unreal self," an entity apart from these orders. Indeed, the "individual-unreal" or the "unreal self" might be seen as the rejecting substratum of the self that would change the terms of its existence. (Riding) Jackson writes, "'In every person there is the possibility of a small, pure, new, unreal portion which is, without reference to personality in the popular, social sense, self. I use 'self' in no romantic connotation, but only because it is the most vivid word I find for this particular purefaction." As (Riding) Jackson put it, the "unreal is to me poetry." (*Anarchism*, 96, 69)

From (Riding) Jackson's perspective, most twentieth-century writing was an art of the "individual-real" and was compelled by "the nostalgic desire to reconstitute an illusory whole that has no integrity but the integrity of accident" (*Anarchism* 104). Such an art was hopelessly "synthetic": "imitative, communicative, provocative of association." In contrast a poetry of the "individual-unreal" was "analytic": "original, dissociative and provocative of dissociation" (*Anarchism* 115). (Riding) Jackson comments:

The end of poetry is to leave everything as pure and bare as possible after its operation. It is therefore important that its tools of destruction should be as frugal, economical as possible. When the destruction or analysis is accomplished they shall have to account for their necessity; they are the survivors, the result as well as the means of elimination. . . . The greater the clutter attacked and the smaller, the purer, the residue to which it is reduced (the more destructive the tools), the better the poem. (*Anarchism* 117)

Perhaps more than any other poet of the twentieth century, (Riding) Jackson works to negate the narcissistic and idealizing psychic economies and the signifying practices that underwrite them, so critical for most literature, especially poetry. The last two pieces in *Anarchism Is Not Enough*, "The Damned Thing" and "Letter of Abdication," show both the range of (Riding) Jackson's pastiche and the force of her social critique. In "The Damned Thing," (Riding) Jackson analyzes the production of sexuality within civilization, dismissing literary sensibilities as deeply implicated in such a production. As she saw it, man's "phallus-proud works-of art" amount to little more than man's "private play with [woman] in public" (*Anarchism* 208, 205). Indeed, sexuality has been overwritten by a civilization uncomfortable with it. The king pin of this system is women's "sexual impersonality" that "if not philosophized, would wreck the solemn masculine machine" (*Anarchism* 196). Importantly her target for attack is neither men nor sexuality, but the ways sexual desire has been produced through an "insidious, civilized traffic." In its civilized version, sexuality is articulated as a kind of rare brew of bodily impulses, scientific phrases, and literary sentiments, which all conspire to keep women in a passive state. (Riding) Jackson parodies "the diffusion which modern society calls love," revealing how a man's "I love you" speech is constituted:

My sexual glands, by the ingrowing enlargement of my sex instinct since childhood and its insidious, civilized traffic with every part of my mental and physical being, are unfortunately in a state of continual excitement. I have very good control of myself, but my awareness of your sexual physique and its radiations was so acute that I could not resist the temptation to desire to lie with you. Please do not think this ignoble of me, for I shall perform this act, if you permit it, with the greatest respect and tenderness and attempt to make up for the indignity it of course fundamentally will be to you (however pleasurable) by serving you in every possible way and by sexually flattering manifestations of your personality which are not strictly sexual. (*Anarchism* 189)

In the concluding piece of *Anarchism Is Not Enough*, "Letter of Abdication," an autocratic "I" or "Queen" abdicates her authority, impugning a "you," her audience. The fictional extravaganza is a virtual extinguishing of narcissistic and idealizing psychological relations that might animate relations between such a Queen and her entourage. She upbraids her audience, "You are sticky instead of rubbery. You represent yourself with priggish sincerity instead of mimicking yourself with grotesque accuracy" (*Anarchism* 209). She further condemns, "You know only how to be either heroes or cowards. But you do not know how to outwit yourselves by being neither, though seeming to be both. 'What,' you say indignantly, 'would you have us be nothing?' Ah, my dear people, if you could you would all shortly become Queens" (*Anarchism* 224). In the conclusion of the piece, the autocratic "I" flounces out, "Good-bye. I am going back to my mirror, where I came from" (*Anarchism* 224). In this perverse writing, it is fitting that the Queen should exit with such finality into a mirror, as she has so thoroughly denounced all mirroring relations.

While (Riding) Jackson's early writing is importantly excessive in its modes of overstatement, her poetry is decidedly spare and economical. Valuing at this time her poetry more highly than any of her other writing, (Riding) Jackson equates its intellectual shaping with the very existence of a newly emergent, positively valued "real":

> There is a sense of life so real that it becomes the sense of something more real than life . . . . It introduces a principle of selection into the undifferentiating quantitative appetite and thus changes accidental emotional forms into deliberate intellectual forms. . . . It is the meaning at work in what has no meaning; it is, at its clearest, poetry. (Jackson, *Contemporaries*, 9)

In the poem "Be Grave, Woman," the speaker in search of a new "real" negates existing love scenarios. Invoking a doubly directed pun of a "grave" demeanor and a "grave" as a place of death, the speaker ends any errant yearnings for love in the "grave" woman herself.

Be grave, woman for love
Still hungering as gardens
For rain though flowerless

What perfume now to rise
From weary expectation.

Be not wild to love,
Poor witch of mysteries
Whose golden age thy body's
Alchemy aburn was
Unto haggard ember.

Beauty's flesh to phantom
Wears unprosperous
And come but devils of
Chill omen to adore
The perforce chaste idolon.

Be grave, woman, to greet
The kiss, the clasp, the shudder which
Rage of thee from crafty
Lust unrolls — and think
These are thy dead to grieve on

And thyself the death in whom
Love must disaster and
Be long ago in ruin-sweet
Story, on the sense to ponder
Thou alone, stark mind. (Poems 264)

The poem would end love's impoverished bewitching and "unprosperous" idolizing of beauty. Negating love's corrupt craftiness, born of what (Riding) Jackson calls in another poem "the patriarchal leer," the speaker imagines a different love (*Poems* 267). Only by passing through a "grave" woman and her "stark mind" will this changed love be possible. While some critics have mistakenly seen (Riding) Jackson's emphasis on the mind throughout her work as making her a "philosophical poet," an epithet that (Riding) Jackson herself abjured, importantly her emphasis on the mind is rather on what the mind enacts, its intellectual judgments, and negations.

IV

FEW, IF ANY WRITERS, CAN EQUAL the extreme ferocity and spare bleakness of (Riding) Jackson's early writings. However, Kathy Acker comes to mind, albeit differently. If (Riding) Jackson aims to negate existing love economies of idealism and narcissism, Acker explores these *ad nauseam*. At once evoking and deflating these economies through disclosure of their sado-masochistic dimensions, Acker combines mytho-poetic modes with flattened non-sequiturs. Lyrical effusions amplify the rationalized languages of an industrialized society and the sound bite logics of newspeak.

Acker begins *Don Quixote* with an overview of its heroic quest:

> When she was finally crazy because she was about to have an abortion, she conceived of the most insane idea that any woman can think of. Which is to love. How can a woman love? By loving someone other than herself. She would love another person. By loving another person, she would right every manner of political, social, and individual wrong; she would put herself in those situations so perilous the glory of her name would resound. The abortion was about to take place. (Acker 9)

Initially undertaking a line of feminine reasoning, love will save the world and bring honor to the woman, the narrational tone abruptly shifts as a kind of deux ex machina comes down: "The abortion was about to take place."

Throughout the opening pages of *Don Quixote*, an abortion, technically the destruction of the fruits of love-making, functions as the mock heroic event by which this knight can gain her "knighthood / nighthood." The term 'abortion,' a particularly negative synonym for a 'woman's right to choose,' introduces the possibility of complex psychological and linguistic operations, such as castration and negation, which are, in turn, negated through the flattened naming of the event. Modern day hospital technologies shift into memories of Don Quixote's sixteenth century misfortunes and other epochal landscapes of despair:

> They told her they were going to take her from the operating chair to her own bed in a wheeling chair. The wheeling chair would be her transportation. She went out to look at it. It was dying. It had once been a hack, the same as all the hacks on grub street; now, as all the hacks, was a full-time drunk, mumbled all the time about sex but now no longer not even never did it but didn't have the wherewithal

or equipment to do it, and hung around with the other bums. That is, women who're having abortions. (Acker 9)

Acker engages more punning, turning the mythic abortion into multiple indignities and impossibilities:

> As we've said, her wheeling bed's name was 'Hack-kneed' or 'Hackneyed', meaning 'once a hack' or always a hack' or 'a writer' or 'an attempt to have an identity that always fails.' Just as 'Hackneyed' is the glorification or change from non-existence into existence of Hack-kneed,' so, she decided, 'catheter' is the glorification of 'Kathy.' By taking on such a name which, being long, is male, she would be able to become a female-male or a night-knight. (Acker 10)

Unlike (Riding) Jackson, who, at least in her poetry, would turn her negations into dignified rearticulations, Acker hungers around the economies of love's "despite." In the section titled, "Heterosexuality," Acker explores what for Don Quixote is the most intense experience of passionate love, "rejection." She calls attention to the mirroring economies of narcissistic and idealizing love relations by staging two androgynous figures, De Franville and Villebranche, whose multiplied negated sexual identities work to make them the most alluring sexual objects around: "Both men and women adored this creature who, by his/her sexual void, like a magnet, attracted most those whose sexual desires were the fiercest. He/She seemed to be magnificently sexual." (Acker 129) While here the representation of sexuality spins out into mirrors of non-identity, at other times in the text, brutally physical sado-masochistic relations prevail. In one incident, a student returns to a teacher whose love for the student is most evident in his brutal whipping of him.

In the conclusion of *Don Quixote*, several affirmative statements emerge born of the vicious negations of this text. In one, Don Quixote rejoices in a desire "restored," through complete "neediness" and "desparation," which is equated with "the desperation of a baby who must suck [her mother's] nipple" (Acker 192). In another, a "female pirate" travels over "crumbling European waters" in a new "mo[u]rning," "totally strong in [her] helplessness," listening to the "violent sex between sun and water" (Acker 200).

V

AS IMPORTANT TO TWENTIETH-CENTURY POETRY as the historical and intellectual forces culminating in Freud are the historical and intellectual forces culminating in Derrida, and somewhat differently, in Foucault. All three thinkers, at a time in which it is increasingly possible to conceive of language apart from the material reality to which it refers, insist on materiality — of the body, of writing, and of social processes. Derrida begins his first published essay with a reflection on "the danger of questioning a way of thinking before one has listened to it carefully, which, he says, is always an act of aggression and disloyalty, even if it is meant to discover or uncover the sense of labor latent in the text" (Biris 151). Foucault orients his initial work around the question of how social institutions ostracize some groups of people, marking them for severe societal punishment and isolation.

VI

REFUSING THE BROAD AND DRAMATIC OPPOSITIONS of (Riding) Jackson and Acker, Susan Howe and Teresa Cha negate authorized cultural texts, decontextualizing and recontextualizing their sayings. Howe explores through Puritan and nineteenth-century American texts and scholarship, the emergence of a distinct American history, born of its sanctioned writings and her negations of these. Cha, scrutinizing multiple cultural texts and media, including her own life history as a Korean born, American woman, negates their seemingly transparent communication. Both writers take on Howe's professed commitment, "I wish I could tenderly lift from the dark side of history, voices that are anonymous, slighted, inarticulate" (DuPlessis 134). Yet, Howe's and Cha's successful "lifting" is of necessity a textual "lifting," a recontextualizing of prior sayings, within their own radically reconfigured texts.

In *The Birth-mark: unsettling the wilderness in American literary history*, Howe negates authoritative cultural histories, making them testify against themselves. In the introduction to *Birth-mark*, Howe professes her love of history and literary criticism, remarking, "I know records are compiled by winners, and scholarship is in collusion with Civil Government . . . . I know this and go on searching for some trace of love's infolding . . . ." (*Birth-mark* 4). Throughout the volume, Howe explores multiple enclosures, including enclosed scholarly domains:

Every statement is a product of collective desires and divisibilities. Knowledge, no matter how I get it, involves exclusion and repression. National histories hold ruptures and hierarchies. On the scales of global power, what gets crossed over? Foreign accents mark dialogues that delete them. Ambulant vagrant bastardy comes looming through assurance and sanctification. (*Birth-mark* 45)

This passage, like many in Howe, proceeds through declarative sentences, each asserting its singular authority, as if in partial or oblique negation of the preceding sentence. Howe's brilliant "Foreign accents mark dialogues that delete them" might be seen as the inverse of Howe's own textual technique in which deleted phrases become marked, turning an abject figure into "Some love-impelled figure." (*Non-Conformist* 25)

This technique is particularly pronounced in "The Captivity and Restoration of Mrs. Mary Rowlandson." Based on Mary Rowlandson's captivity by the Pocasset Wampanoags, her captivity experience is jointly narrated by Mary Rowlandson and her husband, Reverend Joseph Rowlandson. In Howe's text, the blatant ethno-centrism and religious zeal that is well evidenced in the Rowlandsons' captivity narrative is rearticulated through Howe's retelling, making way for the counter sayings also embedded in the text. In her concluding sentence, Howe bares her technique "Mary Rowlandson saw what she did not see said what she did not say" (*Birth-mark* 128).

Howe writes, "In the first chapter of the first published narrative written by an Anglo-American woman, ostensibly to serve as a reminder of God's providence, Native Americans are called 'murtherous wretches,' 'bloody heathen,' 'hell-hounds,' 'ravenous bears,' 'wolves'" (*Birth-mark* 95). She later quotes verbatim from the captivity narrative:

"There came an Indian to them at that time, with a basket of Horse-liver. I asked him to give me a piece: *What* says, he, *can you eat Horse-liver?* I told him, I would try, if he would give a piece, which, he did, and I laid it on the coals to rost, but before it was half ready they got half of it away from me, so that I was fain to take the rest and eat it as it was, with the blood about my mouth, and yet a savoury bit it was to me: *For to the hungry Soul every bitter things is sweet.*"

The narrator comments, "There she stands, blood about her mouth, savoring the taste of raw horse liver. God's seal of ratification spills from her lips or from her husband's pen" (*Birth-mark* 125-126). As savage as Rowlandson's depiction of the savages, this moment of bloody consummation inspires godly ratification, confusing the identities of all of the parties. In *The Non Conformist's Memorial*, Howe extends her study in *The Birth-mark* of such American non-conformists as Anne Hutchinson, Thomas Shephard, and Emily Dickinson to include earlier non-conformist figures, Jesus, Mary Magdalene, and Charles I. While in many histories, Charles I is the symbol of retrogressive forces killed by the non-conforming, emergent forces of an English democracy, in Howe's "A Bibliography of the King's Book or Eikon Basilike," Charles I becomes the memorialized non-conformist and Milton is presented as the conformist, as the image smasher. Howe upholds the memory of Charles I and negates the authority of Milton, honoring the "king's book" or the *Eikon Basilike*, a highly popular text thought to be written by Charles I himself, although actually forged, and widely and surreptitiously circulated among the English people, bereft of their King. Within it a poem, purported to be written by Charles I, "A Prayer in the Time of Captivity," is actually a paraphrase of a poem in Sidney's *Arcadia*, uttered by a pagan woman to an all-seeing heathen Deity. And it is this doubly forged, doubly inauthoritative poem on which Milton wages his attack, performing a double murder of a text beloved by the people and of a generative, anonymous female figure. Of Milton's *Eikonoklastes*, Howe writes,

> Eikonoklastes is a political tract. It was written by the poet-propagandist-author of L'Allegro," "Il Penseroso," "Comus" and *Areopagitica, a Speech for the Liberty of Unlicenc'd Printing, To the Parliament of England* while he was acting as the Latin Secretary, a government censor, and an image smasher. (*Non-Conformist* 49)

Far more important to Howe than Milton's professed political sympathies is his censoring and smashing of the delicate forgery written in English vernacular. Howe summarizes, "*Eikon Basilike* means the Royal Image. *Eikonklastes* can be translated "Image Smasher" (*Non-Conformist* 48).

Howe's text bears the violence of this historical moment and her redress of its violence. Howe remarks, "This was the killing of the king, and the king was holy." Of her own typographically explosive poems in the "Eikon Basilike," Howe comments "Somehow, all my thinking about the misediting of Dickinson's texts, [George Butterick's] careful editing of Charles Olson's poems, all the forgotten little captivity narratives, the now forgotten *Eikon*, the words *Eikon, Eikonoklastes*, and *regicide* — all sharp vertical sounds, all came together and then split open." (Foster 175). Passages of sharply delivered vertical tensions with their "state secrets" give way to Arachne's silken, skiddering:

ΕΙΚΩΝ ΒΑΣΙΛΙΚΗ.

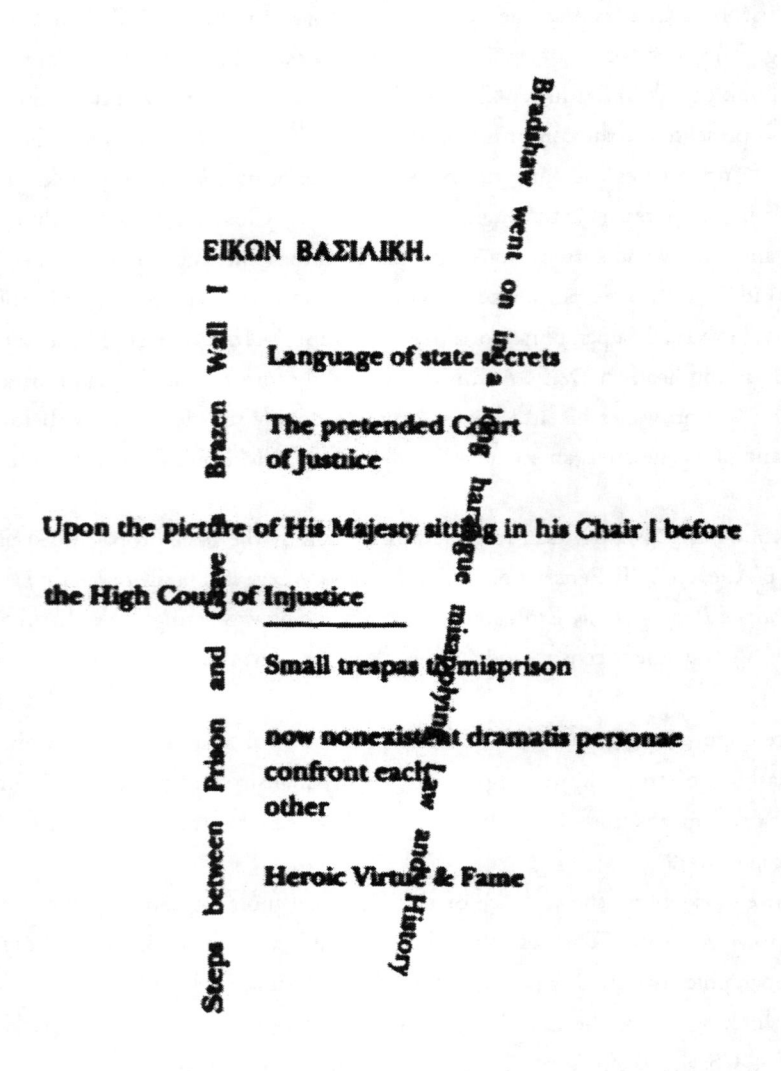

Brazen Wall |

Language of state secrets

The pretended Court
of Justice

Upon the picture of His Majesty sitting in his Chair | before

the High Court of Injustice

Small trespas to misprison

now nonexistent dramatis personae
confront each
other

Heroic Virtue & Fame

Steps between Prison and Grave

Bradshaw went on in a long harangue misapplying law and History

Silk

   symbolic

      Praeparative

   faith

      Ariagne

    Idman   satter

   the   s e t
          Penned

  stars
ARACHNE SUN'S
  deft   ray

   through

  She   s h i e l

  was   T h r ieea l d
          s   d

  winding
          trace
  wool
          weft

Cloud

  soft

   threada

  twist

VII

Perhaps the ultimate negation is the delivery of language as dictation, as if all sayings are in perpetual remove from any originating speech, and therefore to be heard apart from any committed delivery. Through wide spread use of conceptual and typographical blank spaces, Cha in *Dictee* makes her text hard of hearing, as the sense of her writing as a secondary language or tongue predominates. Beginning *Dictee* with a classroom dictation that verbalizes all typographical devices, Cha interrupts the regular flow of written and spoken communication:

> Open paragraph It was the first day period She had come from a far period tonight at dinner comma the families would ask comma open quotation marks How was the first day interrogation mark close quotation marks (Cha 1)

From this classroom style dictation, Cha shifts her attention to the physical production of speech, exploring the changed spatial and temporal experience of a speaker in the throes of whether to say or not say, "To wait from pain to say. To not. Say":

> From the back of her neck she releases her shoulders free. She swallows once more . . . . She allows others. In place of her. Amidst others to make full. Make swarm. All barren cavities to make swollen. The others each occupying her. (Cha 3, 4)

When she finally does speak, transforming her stopped speech into a present utterance, a sense of eternity prevails:

> All the time now. All the time there is. Always. And all
> times. The pause. Uttering. Hers now. Hers bare. The utter. (Cha 5)

Throughout *Dictee*, the "diseuse," the female speaker, utters politically and culturally charged speech as simultaneously meaningless and meaningful dictation. Important for Cha's cultural exploration are the many religious invocations of Jesus and other martyred figures, with their hollowed out, but rich presences. Throughout her text, Cha invokes many different kinds of language events, but always with a sense that these texts are being reiterated, thereby partially negating their claims. In Cha's text, truths are always nominal, never actual. Titling her chapters after Greek feminine gods that name diverse genres — Clio History, Erato Love Poetry, Thalia Comedy, Polymnia Sacred Poetry — Cha's "diseuse" moves from ironic displacements to professed beliefs, without distinguishing between them. Throughout, Cha's *Dictee* rings of a previously uttered and partially negated language that dwells within and without diverse speakers.

In "Love Poetry," Cha recomposes painfully scripted love scenarios. A lone woman watching a film and the heroine of foreign film become interchangeable, as physical separations between viewer and viewed, and the physical theatre and the screened image collapse into an undifferentiated stream of seeing. "Love Poetry" begins with the entrance of a woman, who could be an anonymous viewer; Cha's mother, who appears elsewhere in the book; or Jeanne d'Arc, who is portrayed in the frontispiece of the chapter:

> She is entering now. Between the two white columns. White and stone. Abrasive to the touch. Abrasive. Worn. With the right hand she pulls the two doors, brass bars that open towards her. (Cha 94)

The movement within this woman's vacated mind and on a whitened screen are conflated: "drawn to the white, then the black. In the whiteness the shadows move across, dark shapes and dark light" (Cha 95). Traditional expectations of love poetry are introduced, but then erased: "One expects her to be beautiful," but in looking for her, one encounters only her house, "the space, not the objects that fill the space . . . . You do not see her yet. For the moment you see only her traces" (Cha 98, 100). Her husband touches her "with his rank." And "Gratuity is her body, her spirit" (Cha 112). Marked by painful social scripts, the spaces of modern cinema provide an alternative painless touch that is pure sensation: "The touching made so easy, the space filled full with touch. The entire screen" (Cha 106).

Finally, all but negated of any actual qualities, the anonymous woman, just at she absents the screen, is named:

> She moves now. Quickly. You trace her steps just after, as soon as she leaves the frame. She leaves them empty. You are following her. Inside the mist. Close. She is buried there. You lose her. It occurs to you her name. Suddenly. Snow. (Cha 114)

On the almost blank page following this dramatic moment of named negated presence, "Snow," Cha inscribes a single quotation: "'The smallest act of PURE LOVE is of more value to her than all other works together.'" "While the "PURE LOVE" calls up sensationalizing religious messages or even a billboard announcing a Korean Christian church, this particular dictation names something of the love the unidentified female has sought. While "Pure Love" is sensationalized, essentialized, it is precisely through this sensationalizing and essentializing of love, this particular dictation, that love is called by its name.

VIII

"'The enthusiast suppresses her tears, crushes her opening thoughts, and — all is changed.'
Mary Shelly Journal, February 7, 1822
Marked by Herman Melville in his copy of Shelley Memorials"
—Epigraph to Susan Howe's "Turning," The Nonconformist's Memorial.

WORKS CITED

Acker, Kathy. *Don Quixote*. New York: Grove P, 1986.
Birus, Hendrick. "Adorno's Negative Aesthetics." In *Languages of the Unsayable: The Play of Negativity in Literature and Literary Theory*. Stanford: Stanford UP, 1987.
Budick, Sanford and Wolfgang Iser. *Languages of the Unsayable: The Play of Negativity in Literature and Literary Theory*. Stanford: Stanford UP, 1987.
Cha, Theresa Hak Kyung. *Dictee*. Berkeley, Third Woman P, 1982, 1995.
DuPlessis, Rachel Blau. *The Pink Guitar*. New York: Routledge, 1990.
Foster, Edward. "An Interview with Susan Howe." In Susan Howe, *The Birth-mark: unsettling the wilderness in American literary history*. Hanover: Wesleyan UP, 1993.
Freud, Sigmund. "Negation," *The Freud Reader*. Ed. Peter Gay. New York: W.W. Norton & Co., 1989.
Heuving, Jeanne. "Laura (Riding) Jackson's 'Really New' Poem,." In *Gendered Modernisms: American Women Poets and their Readers*. Ed. Margaret Dickie and Thomas Travisano. Philadelphia: U of Pennsylvania P, 1996.
Howe, Susan. *The Birth-mark: unsettling the wilderness in American literary history*. Hanover: Wesleyan UP, 1993.
-------. *The Nonconformist's Memorial* New York: New Directions, 1993.
(Riding) Jackson, Laura. *Anarchism Is Not Enough* Garden City, N.Y.: Doubleday, Doran and Co., 1928.
-------. *Contemporaries and Snobs* Garden City, N.Y.: Doubleday, Doran ad Co., 1928.
-------. *The Poems of Laura Riding* New York: Persea Books, 1938, 1980.

Peter Bushyeager

STAYING UP ALL NIGHT: THE NEW YORK SCHOOL OF POETRY: 1970 - 1983

The New York School has been a flashpoint in American poetry for more than three decades. Always considered one of the major strains of alternative poetries, it was — during the 1960s and part of the 1970s — the primary arena for experimental work and the demarcation by which certain American poets and their audience defined themselves.

If you disparaged the New York School, you most likely admired the mainstream confessional poetry of Anne Sexton, Sylvia Plath and Robert Lowell. If you aligned yourself with the New York contingent, your pantheon was a dynamic but unlikely grouping of Harvard graduates with art-world connections and Lower East Side residents who, with the assistance of the period's artist-friendly economics, proudly eschewed regular employment for a gritty, tenement-apartment lifestyle that enabled them to be full-time poets.

The New York School aesthetic was initially established in the 1950s, when the burgeoning Manhattan art world combusted with poets Frank O'Hara, John Ashbery, Kenneth Koch, Barbara Guest, James Schuyler and others. By the 1960s, it had morphed into the very definition of the period's counterculture aesthetics.

Fueled by speculative poetics and lifestyle experimentation — and seasoned with dollops of Black Mountain, Beat and San Francisco Renaissance poetics — the New York School came to embody a piquant blend of uptown elegance and downtown funkiness. It was where classic forms like the sonnet were unexpectedly recharged with fresh, contemporaneous energy; magazines and books produced on mimeographs and photocopiers had the cultural imperative of samizdats; lines of poetry were often powered by amphetamine, marijuana, all-night discussions and ramblings on edgy streets; poets cross-pollinated influences and voices in collaborative works; humor played an important role; and writing workshops focusing on process rather than rigid line-by-line critiques stimulated poetry that posited a different sort of rigor.

Historical overviews tend to focus on the activities of the New York School's first generation during the 1950s and 1960s. This essay is a step toward filling in the "second half" of the story. It briefly outlines the activities of the second and third generations of the New York School by surveying a period bookended by two notable events: the 1970 publication of the landmark *An Anthology of New York Poets*, edited by Ron Padgett and David Shapiro; and the 1983 death of Ted Berrigan, one of the New York group's most important figures.

While the delineation of eras is an arbitrary way to order messy, inconsistent continuums, there's justification for singling out 1970-1983. It was a period in which the New York School expanded its reach, stimulated offshoots, and ultimately faced the impact of economic and social change that resulted in major shifts, both personal and aesthetic, for those who were active in the scene.

Of course, definitions, rather than artificially imposed eras, are ultimately more important to historical discussions. And the definition central to this essay hinges on the answer to a simple question: What is the New York School? An indication of the definition's slipperiness is the fact that the modifier "so-called" is often appended to any mention of the group. Why? Perhaps to indicate that, rather than a sharply delineated group of poets, the so-called New York School is a casual grouping united in one thing: their response to Manhattan's roiling diversity.

According to poet Alice Notley, who is considered a member of the group's second generation, New York School poets are " . . . reacting to the experience of New York . . . living in the community that the whole city constitutes, the sound of it and the look of it, including all of its social classes . . . Kenneth Koch reflects the city's urbanity and humor . . . John Ashbery reflects the unconscious aspects of the city, the river of dream images flowing beneath it . . . O'Hara simply celebrated it."

Poet/novelist Lewis Warsh, another member of the second generation, pinpoints a particular tone and point of view that the group shares. "They avoid self importance and absorb information without showing off. O'Hara's 'The Day Lady Died' is a perfect example; the poem is the voice of an everyday guy talking." Finally, poet Anne Waldman, in the introduction to her anthology *Out of This World*, characterizes the first generation of the New York School in this way: "Their work — subtle, witty, urban, visual — included the playfulness of the Surrealists without the ideology. It didn't complain or call attention to itself. It was anti-provincial."

1970: A TOUCHSTONE

Koch, Ashbery, O'Hara and the rest of the first generation were well established by the time Ron Padgett and David Shapiro's *Anthology of New York Poets* appeared in 1970. Most had published several books, and O'Hara, killed in an accident several years earlier, was becoming a legendary figure. The next wave of poets was also beginning to have an impact — among them Padgett, whose 1969 book *Great Balls of Fire* offered a witty and lyrical poetry infused with 20th century French poets and pop-art sensibilities, and Shapiro, whose poems expressed a telling, non-linear tenderness:

> I discovered the United Nations night building.
> It was a low-slung bar.
> News on an electric band ordered one to
> DEFINE THE PLACE; DEFINE THE TIME.
>
> Napoleon used to persuade me to shinny up
> long poles that always drop back from heaven.
> What is the pacifist nutrition?
> RHYTHM AS MENTALITY; RHYTHM AS SENSORY CONTROL.
>
> Why do we invent communities
> in the clouds? their strictures against children
> posted in the castles at Deal:
> WALK ON THE MATTRESSES; DON'T WAKE THE BABIES.
> —"Poem from Deal"

Published by mainstream publisher Random House, the anthology was "the talk of the town," according to Maureen Owen, who at the time was part of the Lower East Side poetry community. It created a "sense that this could be the start of something big, that we could all get our sort of work put out by major publishers." That wasn't what ultimately happened. By 1971, after Padgett, Dick Gallup, Clark Coolidge, Tom Clark and a few others featured in the anthology had been published, large publishers lost interest in this group of poets. But the anthology had lasting influence nevertheless — not necessarily by creating a canon, but by providing an imprimatur for this relatively new poetry and defining its range of possibilities.

Many of the modes and voicings that developed over the next three decades are represented in the book: an emphasis on dailiness and autobiography (James Schuyler, Frank Lima, Frank O'Hara); hipster jokes, absurdity and camp (Tom Veitch, Kenward Elmslie); pop aesthetics, "found" text, repetition (John Giorno); the word as object, music and kernel of meaning (Clark Coolidge, Bernadette Mayer, Aram Saroyan); and revitalization of classic forms through dramatically shifting tone and "chance" operations, exemplified by Ted Berrigan's revolutionary sonnets. Berrigan's sonnets were created using a brilliant "cut and paste" method that juggled "found" lines with his own writing and sensibility. According to poet Charles Bernstein, Berrigan "built his edifice on the wreck of the old — using its broken shards to build a structure with altogether different architectural principles."

> Joyful ants nest on the roof of my tree
> Crystal tears wed to wakefulness
> My dream a crumpled horn
> Ripeness begins in advance of the broken arm
> The black heart two times scary Sunday
> Pale thighs making apple belly strides
> And he walks. Beside the fifteen pieces of glass
> A postcard of Juan Gris
> Vast orange dreams wed to wakefulness
> Swans gone in the rain came down, came down and went
> Warm hands corrupting every tree
> Guiding his eyes to her or a shade
> Ripeness begins   My dream a crumpled horn
> Fifteen pieces of glass on the roof of my tree
>   —Sonnet XLIX

The editors' preface reflects their awareness of the thorny literary politics that crop up in the wake of any anthology. Amidst carefully defensive statements (". . . nor is it even a collection of all the good poets living and/or writing in and/or about New York . . . we do not in any way wish to pass judgment on poets not included"), they hedged their bets by quoting in full "Personism," O'Hara's classic anti-manifesto. And they threw in some stylishly flip attitude for good measure: "we arranged poems in no discernible order. This is, after all, a Random House book."

Like most influential anthologies, the book was a stimulating snapshot in time. But the scene was moving at warp speed, so the picture it presented was blurred and incomplete. Only one woman, Bernadette Mayer, was included among the book's 27 poets, which was emblematic of the marginal role women had in all literary scenes of the period. In addition, some important figures, both male and female, did not appear in the anthology, among them the habitués of an intense East Village salon conducted in an apartment on St. Marks Place.

During the 1960s and 1970s, St. Mark's Place was Manhattan's counter-culture crossroads. The noisy, hyperactive street — a melange of rock clubs, boutiques and street drug trade — was the perfect location for a convergence of poets concerned with riffing their own contemporary variations on the traditions of O'Hara et al. This included the salon's hosts, Lewis Warsh and Anne Waldman. For several years, Warsh and Waldman had been publishing Angel Hair magazine and books, which were primarily devoted to New York School writers. Waldman was also the director of The Poetry Project (founded in 1966 with federal funds earmarked for programs helping alienated urban youth!).

By the time the Shapiro/Padgett anthology was published, The Project — headquartered at Manhattan's historic St. Mark's Church — had evolved into a glittering scene that attracted rock stars, Andy Warhol's coterie and a fair amount of media attention. The Project was the primary venue for readings and workshops that focused on the New York School, and Warsh and Waldman were ringing their own changes on the aesthetic, filtered through the uproar of St. Mark's Place:

> What is around me is
> this huge shape I can't visualize
> from here, sitting here quietly
> nights go by the same way
> noisy people outside on the block
> I want to move from
> so I can understand it better
>
> Not all streets are like this one
> bursting with so much energy
> you can't keep still
> with cops watching over every second
> nothing gets out of hand out there

but does deep inside you somewhere
down in your American soul

It's hard to kill, harder still to love
where you come from when it hurts you
but you know you do, you do
— Anne Waldman, "Mother Country"

Joe Brainard was among the writers Waldman and Warsh published. Brainard, who had moved to New York from Tulsa, Oklahoma, with Berrigan and Padgett in the early 1960s, was primarily known as an artist. But his three Angel Hair books — *I Remember, I Remember More,* and *More I Remember More* — established him as a strong force in the poetry world and indicated how O'Hara's and Schuyler's aesthetics had permutated over time. Brainard took their concern with dailiness, with everyday transcendent details, and offered a stripped-down, modular version. His work utilized a simple format: sentences or brief paragraphs that all began with "I remember." After reading dozens of these affirmations, which relentlessly marched along the page, the reader had a sort of pop epiphany.

DIASPORA

IRONICALLY, BY THE TIME THE Shapiro/Padgett ANTHOLOGY had formalized the New York School, several of its proponents had left Manhattan. The 1970-1976 period was a time of leave-taking, of "missionary" work outside the city. Ted Berrigan had been an academic nomad for several years, alighting for brief teaching assignments at an assortment of colleges and universities in the Unted States and England. His travels started at, of all places, the Iowa Writers Workshop, the bastion of academic verse, where he met Alice Notley, who became his second wife.

Like a circuit-riding preacher, Berrigan gathered like-minded colleagues around him each stop along the way, including Simon Pettet and Douglas Oliver in England, and Steve Levine, Rose Lesniak, Rochelle Kraut, Bob Rosenthal, Barbara Barg, Paul Hoover and Maxine Chernoff in Chicago. Many of these writers followed Berrigan when he returned to New York in 1976.

While Notley began writing her first accomplished poems, Berrigan was, in her words, "discovering the style that would take him into the 1970s . . . something he could meditate with as he journeyed closer and closer to his own death and dealt with his physical problems." Mortality would be a leitmotif in Berrigan's work from the mid 1970s on; after years of intense living that included copious use of pills and alcohol, he was diagnosed with alcohol hepatitis — the precursor to his passing from cirrhosis years later.

Lewis Warsh also split from Manhattan during this period, ultimately ending up in Bolinas, a seaside town north of San Francisco where there was a cheap, appealing communal approach to life. The small town was a hotbed of poets that included New York expatriates Warsh and Bill Berkson, Robert Creeley, former Paris Review poetry editor Tom Clark, Joanne Kyger, Richard Brautigan, Aram Saroyan and Beat icon Phillip Whalen. "It ultimately became too intense," Warsh remembers. "You couldn't go to the store and get a loaf of bread without running into a poet. It was a public life that after several years didn't seem conducive to writing." It was also the place where Black Mountain and New York aesthetics blended.

Under the influence of Creeley and an abundance of marijuana, the poetry became stripped down, somewhat fragmentary, and concerned with magnifications of brief moments. Although the energy eventually dwindled down, for several years Bolinas nurtured a fascinating conjunction of styles that is documented in the 1971 City Lights anthology *On the Mesa*:

> Perhaps an evening awaits me
>   when I will go
>   peacefully
> to some small town
>   and settle down
>   there, for the
>   life that awaits me
> among the living
> animals, and the effigies, the celestial forms
> that light the way . . .
>   —from Lewis Warsh, "In the Stars"

BACK IN MANHATTAN

WHILE BERRIGAN, WARSH AND OTHERS WERE OUT OF TOWN, the scene continued to evolve in Manhattan. By the mid-1970s, The Poetry Project was a well-established institution and the first generation was becoming increasingly recognized and commodified. John Ashbery's 1975 book *Self-Portrait in a Convex Mirror* won the Pulitzer Prize, the National Book Award and the National Book Critics' Circle Award. James Schuyler became more of a presence through the publication of *The Crystal Lithium* and *Hymn to Life*, and Koch's *The Art of Love* offered personal perspectives that were new to his work.

The second generation was also asserting itself. Two books by Bernadette Mayer were published: the prose book *Moving*, and *Memory*, a journal documenting July 1971. The text from "Memory" was also audiotaped for a show at the Holly Solomon Gallery that included a chronological display of photos Mayer had taken throughout the time the journal was written. Mayer's emergence reinforced a distinctly different strain in the New York School — one with roots in Gertrude Stein, which used moment-by-moment observations, abstraction, prose-like structure, and doses of feminism, politics and humor:

> All movement is a transmitter.
> all movement is old. "dont bother with moving it."
> a reflection of a receiver seems to remain the same.
> a moving picture of dots is all movement.
>   does a transmitter have an idea?
>   does a reflection state something that remains the same?
>   does a measurement reflect light?
>   the idea of nothing remains the same.
> a similar light doesnt state "there's some trouble with the light
>   to which I'm similar."
>   —from "Moving"

> women belong in the death force. they play a vital role, not in secretarial jobs, but as true killers with full responsibilities. for more information see a death recruiter. see him. he will say "for example, a moment before this f4B Phantom Jet was belching fire at the blast shield, vibrating the flight deck & wardrooms below. the catapult officer gives the signal & the jet screams down the length of the cat & over the water, aircraft carrier duty is exciting &

> demanding, you are learning the incomparable feeling of being one of the
> elite, an exciting life of important service begins ... this is a good idea ..
> but NO FUCKING! that guy's got wings on his head! he's a centaur!
> — from "Moving"

Within a few years, Mayer would begin her legendary series of poetry workshops, which fostered many new poets, including a group that would later be known as the Language poets. Attracted by Mayer's — and Clark Coolidge's — focus on words as objects/music, Charles Bernstein and others coalesced at Mayer's workshop and then went on to create an advance guard of their own.

During this time, a publishing revolution was in full swing, thanks especially to the cheap, low-tech, readily accessible mimeo machine, which enabled poets to instantly hit the streets with their work and, in some instances, have a lasting impact that belied the publications' humble origins. (The period was extensively documented in "A Secret Location on the Lower East Side," a 1998 exhibition at the New York Public Library that reverently displayed dozens of these shoestring publications in museum vitrines.)

Inspired by precursors such as *0 to 9*, co-edited by Bernadette Mayer and conceptual artist Vito Acconci, Warsh/Waldman's early Angel Hair editions and Berrigan's "*C*," which published its first number in 1963, there was a host of mimeo publications vying for attention. Many of them entered the literary arena via The Poetry Project's overworked Gestetner machine, including The Project's magazine *The World*, Larry Fagin's *Adventures in Poetry*, and Maureen Owen's *Telephone*.

"It was all about just getting the work out because you were excited by the poems and wanted other people to read them," remembers Owen. "You put your energy into it and didn't care if it paid off. I mean we handed those magazines out to people on the street. There was a sense that the poems were going somewhere, that everything was going somewhere."

For poet/editor Larry Fagin, a veteran of both the New York School and San Francisco Renaissance, the "instant" aspects of mimeo gave him the opportunity to take the poetry community's pulse at any given time and quickly telegraph his findings. "A reading was an optimum situation to screen material and get the writer to submit a piece on the spot," he recalls in a brief statement that appears in the "Contributor's Index" of the *Out of This World* anthology. "A magazine or pamphlet might be 'run off' in the afternoon, collated during dinner (deli sandwiches to go), and distributed at that night's event."

There were also increasing numbers of offset-printed publications devoted to the New York School, among them Kenward Elmslie's Z, which offered well-chosen, substantial selections of work from many of the School's best.

RECONVERGENCE: 1976-1980

BY 1976, BERRIGAN, ALICE NOTLEY, WARSH AND OTHERS were back in town — along with a roster of new, mostly younger poets. Many attended Notley's Poetry Project workshop that year: Greg Masters, Gary Lenhart, Michael Scholnick, Steve Levine, Bob Rosenthal, Shelley Kraut, Jeff Wright, Bob Holman (who in the 1980s would be instrumental in creating the Nuyorican Poets Cafe "spoken word" movement), and Eileen Myles.

"There were these long tables, and it was very 'in-crowd'," Myles remembers. "People would drink beer, the workshop would start at 7 and go on to 11. Then everyone would go out and get more beer. There were also a lot of drugs, but it was the fuel and it was fun. I have to say I didn't go to graduate school — instead I stayed up all night in the East Village."

For many of the younger poets, an important part of "staying up all night" was attending the salon that developed at Berrigan and Notley's miniscule walkthrough tenement flat at 101 St. Mark's Place, where they were drawn nightly by Berrigan's generous spirit and famed talkativeness. "There was the formal, institutional church — that was The Poetry Project at St. Mark's," notes Myles. "Then you had the 'human' church — Ted and Alice's house — where there was an endless parade of poets from out of town, people bearing money, drugs, books to sell. It was great and it introduced you to the fact that, in reality, people are the point, not institutions."

The dichotomy Myles outlines may sound simplistic, but many on the scene during this time concur with her assessment. The Project, in existence for a decade, had evolved into an institution in many senses of the word. In this context, Berrigan played an important role; he kept alive the anarchic, no-holds-barred spirit that infused much of the work that had come to be associated with the New York School and the Project.

"Ted was sort of the anti-Project or parallel Project;" recalls Alice Notley. "He was too uncontrollable to have a position there, no one there really wanted him to do anything except attend and give readings. And they weren't always sure they wanted him to do that."

Besides the new young poets and the Berrigan/Notley salon, what was the terrain during the remainder of the 70s? Lewis Warsh returned to Manhattan and became involved with Bernadette Mayer. Together, they created *United Artists*, one of the scene's last great mimeo mags and ultimately an important small-press book publisher. By the end of the 1970s, their East Village apartment had developed its own salon ecology, and young poets shuttled between the Berrigan/Notley and Warsh/Mayer households for stimulating talk and inspiration.

Anne Waldman, after years of directing The Poetry Project, moved to Boulder, Colorado, where she helped establish the Buddhist-focused Naropa Institute, which also serves as a Western outpost for the New York School zeitgeist. In *Fast-Talking Woman* and other works she established an affirmative, energetic performance-based style that set the stage for later poets, particularly women, concerned with "spoken word." Other Project-inspired offshoots also cropped up around the country, including the Beyond Baroque Literary/Arts Center in Venice, California.

New magazines appeared, including Eileen Myles' *Dodgems*, Tom Weigel's *Tangerine*, Joel Lewis' *Ahnoi*, and *Mag City*, which was co-edited by Gary Lenhart, Greg Masters, and Michael Scholnick from 1977 to 1985. *Mag City* #13, a fairly representative issue, offered samplings of "first generation" poets such as James Schuyler and Tony Towle, collaborative works by Mayer and Notley, and a strong selection of the newer figures on the scene, including John Godfrey, Bob Rosenthal, Steve Levine, and others.

As the third generation surfaced, some observers sensed a fall-off in quality. Were too many people mining the same turf? Had newer poets "received" the aesthetic wholesale from predecessors rather than formulating their own poetics through critical reading? Aesthetically there was a continued emphasis on poems concerned with daily details/autobiography. But some felt that a format had been established for this sort of work and an image created for the New York School poet's lifestyle. As a result, poetry began to appear that could seem narcissistic and formulaic. If anyone had ever thought that the New York style was simple to achieve, that impression was quickly dispelled. In reality, the New York School had a subtle sophistication that Eileen Myles neatly sums up: "In many ways, The New York School is about intelligent people being deliberately 'dumb,' — speaking in contemporary jargon as a way to cut through the history of literature, but in a channeled way. Of course, if this way of doing things is misunderstood, you just have storytelling and endless narcissism."

Humor — another major component of the aesthetic since the 1950s — could also seem a bit problematic. For some, the quest for laughs was engendering a provincial insiders'-club feeling to the work. However, there was still deftly playful — and pointed

— writing coming from poets such as Maureen Owen, Ed Friedman, Paul Violi and especially Ron Padgett, who had helped establish humor as a bulwark in the first place:

> I have always laughed
> when someone spoke of a young writer
> "finding his voice." I took it
> literally: had he lost his voice?
> Had he thrown it and had it
> not returned? Or perhaps they
> were referring to his newspaper
> *The Village Voice?* He's trying
> to find his *Voice.*
>   What isn't
> funny is that so many young writers
> seem to have found this notion
> credible: they set off in search
> of their voice, as if it were
> a single thing, a treasure
> difficult to find but worth
> the effort. I never thought
> such a thing existed. Until
> recently. Now I know it does.
> I hope I never find mine. I
> wish to remain a phony the rest of my life.
>   —Ron Padgett, "Voice"

While there was plenty of magazine space for poets, books were another matter. Previous generations had launched many small presses. But there were fewer presses in the late 70s, perhaps because of changing economics. And with some notable exceptions — among them Gary Lenhart, Steve Levine, Bob Rosenthal, Eileen Myles and Bob Holman – the newer poets' work did not appear in collections.

During this time, the Language poets began to draw attention away from New York School writers. They published extensively and also made their mark through critical writings. Joel Lewis, a poet and literary historian, observes that "Language poetry theoretized the kind of experimental work that had always been part of the New York

School. Before, people just did it and didn't feel they needed to write a manifesto explaining what they were doing. Language poetry took away a lot of that thunder by formalizing it."

Performance-based work — a longstanding tradition dating back to the first generation's involvement with the Poets Theatre in Cambridge, Massachusetts — also claimed some of the scene's energy as Bob Holman, Bob Rosenthal, Barbara Barg, Rose Lesniak, Eileen Myles and Eleanor Nauen mounted theatrical pieces. There were also many notable books published, including Berrigan's collection of poetry *Nothing for You* and his novel *Clear the Range*, Padgett's *Triangles in the Afternoon*, Mayer's *Poetry* and *Golden Book of Words*, Warsh's *Blue Heaven*, Notley's *Songs for the Unborn Second Baby*, and newcomer Tim Dlugos's *Je Suis Ein Americano*, which continued the O'Hara tradition of hyperactive observation of cityscapes while also offering a flat diction that echoed the period's high sense of irony.

1980-83: POETRY IN THE FACE OF GENTRIFICATION

By 1980, THE EAST VILLAGE (or the Lower East Side, if you were a diehard who refused to use the real estate developers' trendy moniker) was undergoing massive transformation. Art galleries were opening up on Avenues A and B, traditionally the province of the socially disenfranchised and the purposefully disengaged. There were yuppies paying absurdly high rents for tenement flats with bathtubs in the kitchen, and the new economics made it increasingly difficult for Ted Berrigan and others to pursue their catch-as-catch-can approach to earning a living.

Berrigan's *So Going Around Cities*, an extensive selection of his work from 1958 to 1979, appeared during that year of encroaching Reaganomics, along with James Schuyler's *Morning of the Poem*, and Maureen Owen's often baroquely witty *Hearts in Space*.

>   Just as the term "beautiful woman"   is used
>   by those who bored by the very image   don't
>   want to go into detail   Garbo's stunning forehead
>   has peeled   clear to the tip   of her nose
>   beside the elevated sign   "HOTEL" where a silvered
>   snow is falling sideways   dark horizontal bars
>   between the stuttering flakes   Down here

> we appear   Bound   in Dashes   Like
> the guy   who after the 6th time   was easily caught by
> the police   & questioned   Why he always robbed
> the *same* donut shop   I don't have a car," he told them
> "& it's close to where I live   it's handy."
> Easy to make the first mistake   & after that the rest
> are simple . . . .
> —from Maureen Owen, "Frogs Ringing Gongs In A Skull"

The following year, the publication of Alice Notley's *How Spring Comes* and Eileen Myles' *A Fresh Young Voice From the Plains* underscored the presence of a new, strong generation of American women poets. Anne Waldman and Bernadette Mayer had staked a claim and Maureen Owen, Notley, and Myles were expanding the territory. It was dramatically different from the marginalized position women had held only ten years before. Myles offered a tough/tender persona that was often fast and fearless:

> I love everywhere you're walking, inventing
> Space as it gets inhabited by you. Getting
> Embarrassed and it makes you shy or crazy. Like I
> Might mention my horse is sick & you start discussing
> The skies, some beer, you steal their scarf and
> Everyone feels better. Don't know how you keep doing
> it — lazily, stupidly, really beautiful.
> I've also got to mention that you invented eyes.
> Look, Look, Look . . . everything's happening all around
> & whenever — I don't know how, but sometimes
> I think you're doing it all or something. It's like
> You've got a genuine fix, or
> Maybe I've just got to blame somebody for beauty.
> —"Sonnet to the Doctor"

The centerpiece of Notley's book was a long tour de force titled "The Prophet," which seamlessly moved between the serious and the comic:

> They say there is a dying star which is traveling in two directions.

Don't brood over how you may have behaved last night. If you
Can't remember that much about it, don't ask anyone else about it
Except a little, in case you were wonderful in your abandon.
Don't gloat if you were wonderful, for you have a hangover, ass . . .

Some things have been made easy for you, and some are easier
    than they seem.
If you cannot open a door and it consists of two doors, don't
    surmise that you are locked in,
You can sometimes open such doors by opening both doors at once
    with long and widespread arms.
Many things are not interesting. Things perhaps not interesting
    include the drugs that we take, the decade
That we live in, & current political crises – they are X the Boring . . .
    —from "The Prophet"

1982 and 1983 offered a multitude of stresses on the poetry community: steadily escalating economic pressure via the ongoing gentrification of the East Village, aesthetic pressure as new modes of writing and performative work continued to draw attention and interpersonal tension among some of the New York School's leading lights.

In retrospect, Lewis Warsh's *Information From The Surface of Venus*, an assured collection of work completed in 1982, seems very much of its time. Through his own distinct deadpan romanticism, Warsh expresses the nostalgia and dislocation that were in the air:

Some people work best when there's an orgy
in the next room while others feel depressed
by the solitude of country life. Crickets,
centipedes, migrant workers, lots of strawberries.
Hostile stares at the hair on your legs when
we go to the beach. "This lake reminds me of . . ."
that's why I like it here. Now I've talked
about these feelings before and I've told you
all the signs that shriek perversely beneath
the surface and demand your attention as they emerge
out of the free-floating past, but sometimes
even nerve is unconscionable like a model

of the human mind might serve another purpose
to one less beautiful. Now you might sneer
at this but I know it's true. That if on occasion
we may seem lost, it's stranger to ignore what
once was true.

—"Friends of the Lake"

In many ways, the tensions came to a head in the fall of 1982 when an interpersonal explosion divided the embattled community. It came about due to disagreements between Berrigan and Warsh regarding United Artists' publication of a special hardcover edition of Berrigan's classic *Sonnets*. "I'd underestimated it all: the fragility of the whole structure of friendship, especially when there was business involved" recalls Warsh in an essay that appears in *Ted Berrigan: An Annotated Checklist*.

That disagreement had a ripple effect as people chose sides and recriminations ricocheted. Then, within months, there was another blow. On July 4, 1983, Berrigan died and the community went into mourning. Maureen Owen remembers the mood at that time: "Ted was a very strong personality; he was big in every sense of the word. Many people emulated his lifestyle and it was scary for them because they thought that he was too strong to die."

"A lot of people couldn't deal with Ted's death," adds Joel Lewis. "His death happened during really horrible economic times and it seemed that things got even worse after he died. It was very difficult to go to a poetry workshop and the next day see people from the class selling their worldly possessions on the sidewalk."

In *Poet Be Like God*, their recent biography of San Francisco poet Jack Spicer, Lewis Ellingham and Kevin Killian talk about the impact of Spicer's death on the coterie of writers that surrounded him. "That no ongoing artistic community survived Jack Spicer's death has much to do with Spicer's personality itself. For Jack's social skills were the principal agency of bonding . . . ."

The parallel is apparent. While New York School writing continued to evolve in the years following Berrigan's demise, some of the poets who were part of his immediate set became inactive. Perhaps they were forced to deal with the brutal economic realities of the 1980s and had no energy left for poetry, or maybe they simply felt too keenly the loss of a central force in their lives. Whatever the reason, their community reeled, took stock and moved on.

Stephen Paul Miller

TED BERRIGAN'S LEGACY: SPARROW, EILEEN MYLES, AND BOB HOLMAN

This essay considers the legacy of Ted Berrigan in the work of three poets — Sparrow, Eileen Myles, and Bob Holman. All three shed light upon 1980s and 1990s Lower East Side and New York School poetry. Although Holman is discussed elsewhere in this anthology as a performance poet, I treat him here in terms of Berrigan and the New York School of poetry.

There is, of course, much other notable New York School poetry of the last fifth of the century, and not all of it can be traced through the informal school of Berrigan. The works of Thomas Fink, Joseph Lease, and John Yau, for instance, are inspired more by John Ashbery and David Shapiro than Berrigan. It might be said that there are many different second generations of New York School Poetry. Indeed, there were many different first generations. Each "founding" New York School poet — Frank O'Hara, John Ashbery, Barbara Guest, and Kenneth Koch had a markedly different style. (Schuyler was older than the first generation New York School poets, but since he did not begin writing the poetry for which he is now remembered until well into the 1960s, he does not quite qualify as "first generation.") This is not to say that there was not something uniquely "New York School" about each of the first generation poets.

The term New York school poetry refers primarily to the poets who are most associated with the New York School of painting — the artists who dominated the Western world's art after the second world war. For the first generation of New York School poets, poetry and art shared a symbiotic relationship. Significantly, this art seemed to be at the center of the art world, and, if the poetry was not at the center of the poetry world, that world was perhaps vitiated for it. If the poetry of the 1950s was arguably too insularly involved in its own discipline, this trend has for the most part continued.

O'Hara, Ashbery, Guest, and Koch were working in the tradition bequeathed to them by the Paris school of painting, which thrived on the dynamic relationships between the poets and painters of Dada and Surrealism. At least since Baudelaire, a tradition existed in France of poetry, art, and art criticism working together. What we call New York School poetry and its sphere of influence occupies a much larger part of the poetic landscape than we often acknowledge. It is difficult to understand fully the ideas and impetuses motivating and illuminating poetry exclusive of discourses concerning the visual and related arts. Expectedly, as the art world moved from abstraction in the late 1950s and the 1960s, a corresponding shift occurred in much New York School poetry toward a linguistically constructed kind of representation and realism.

The first generation of New York School poets mined a vast resource of poetic and artistic techniques. Ashbery applied a linguistic "loose paint brush" to both open and given poetic forms. O'Hara placed easily understandable and mysterious journalistic and abstract details in bizarre and revealing apposition. Koch followed linguistic formulas into the absurd and the poetically poignant. Guest presented baroque meditations on the world as artistic and poetic constructions. The number of techniques available allowed each of the New York school poets to be very different yet related, and the organizing methods of the second and third generations New York school poets are of course even more variegated. Permutations abound, making it very difficult to write a comprensive essay on the school. For instance, Alice Notley could easily be included here. However, I feel that she came into her own well before Berrigan's death and is therefore not quite a poet who emerged in the 1980s. She is part of a slightly different historical and poetic moment. Countless other poets, such as Bob Rosenthal, Hal Sirowitz, Jill Rappaport, Shelly Kraut, Emmy Hunter, Burt Kimmelman, or Lee Anne Brown either were not directly enough in the path of Berrigan's influence or not in the same trajectory of influence that I outline here to be included in this short essay.

Sparrow, Eileen Myles, and Bob Holman are part of a trajectory of influence from O'Hara to Berrigan. Of particular interest here is Ted Berrigan's anxiety of influence with regard to Frank O'Hara. O'Hara's theory of poetry is often understood in terms of his theory of Personalism which maintains that a poem and a telephone call are interchangeable. What is often overlooked in O'Hara's sardonic yet seminal manifesto is that he was not saying that a poem's content can equal a telephone call's content. O'Hara maintained that the motivating energy behind a poem and a telephone call could be the same. However, he said that poetry was always "abstract" (O'Hara 499). What was important to him was choosing the right kind of abstraction. O'Hara preferred the abstractions of interpersonal, felt, and perhaps idiosyncratic expression to the abstractions of intellectualized expressions that are meant for a general and indefinite audience.

Ted Berrigan and James Schuyler, whom I regard as related second generation New York School poets because they both developed in the 1960s after and in response to O'Hara and the other first generation New York school poets, were for some time rooted in a sense of abstraction that paralleled O'Hara's. However, Berrigan and Schuyler reacted against an abstract poetic base and moved toward a content-based poetry. Content became a dominating principle in Berrigan's and Schuyler's work, although of course always within nurturing "abstract" possibilities and contexts. By abstract here I mean the poem's stressing of its purely linguistically based elements. (Interestingly, some second generation New York School poets, such as David Shapiro, moved further into the abstract, linguistic, formalistic, and referentially unfixed aspects of O'Hara's personally charged poetry. Indeed, some similarly influenced poets might be said to hide their New York School poetry roots. As T.S. Eliot was arguably hypercritical of the Romantic poets so that their great influence upon him would not be detected, some Language poets have perhaps protested too much about their debt to New York School poetry.)

Whereas Frank O'Hara's personal poems are abstract collages of quotient and symbolic mind sets that avoid direct communicative points, Ted Berrigan increasingly tried to get across a message. A consideration of the public lives of the two poets elucidates a distinction between them. Whereas O'Hara cultivated a community though his notoriety and collaged his personal experiences into his poems, Berrigan cultivated a community through enthusiasm about poetry and his formal and informal role as a teacher. Poetry allowed Berrigan to make statements, if often only about poetry. For example, "New Personal Poem" (Berrigan 75) seems to choose the influence of a contemporary poet, Michael Lally — to whom the poem, according to its inscription, is addressed — over the influence of O'Hara: "I did love Frank, as I do / You 'in the right way.'" Berrigan distinguishes Lally's abstractions from O'Hara's. "New Personal Poem" notes that Lally did not want to be clear to himself so as not to get in his "own way" and presumably censor himself. The implication is that O'Hara used abstraction in a different "right way" — one, however, not "right" for Berrigan, who is moving away from O'Hara-type abstraction. Unlike O'Hara, Berrigan is not emphasizing abstraction as a generating mechanism that maintains itself. For Berrigan abstraction leads to clarity. Thus the poem ends, "I take it as simple particulars that / we wear our feelings on our faces." There is ultimately little to hide in Berrigan's poetry. His work is an open secret that increasingly shows its communicative and communal workings. By the late 1970s, "content" was a buzz word in the art world, and it is not surprising that New York School poetry reflects this. A new kind of accessibility plays an increasingly larger role in the works of Berrigan and the three younger poets whom I discuss take that influence further.

The three younger poets whom I discuss in relation to Berrigan — Sparrow, Eileen Myles, and Bob Holman — often acknowledge Berrigan as a primary influence to the point where they, not unrelated to their poetry, devote themselves to developing communities in conjunction with their writings. In 1992, Sparrow and Myles ran for the presidency in campaigns that sought to reimagine communities. Sparrow, who studied under Berrigan at the City College of New York and calls the older poet his entry into the world of poetry and major influence, based one of his major books upon his 1996 absurdist presidential bid. Although he might have been stereotyped as a leftist "bearded Old Hippie, carrying a large multicolored bag from Puerto Rico" (*Republican Like Me*), Sparrow ran as a Republican, seemingly extending Berrigan's sense of community past all rational bounds. Sparrow also extended Berrigan's communicative urges. The younger poet carried his referential urges to heights of abstraction by using a surplus of sense in effect to level sense. For example, he writes, "this year the Republicans are following a Democratic strategy, and the Democrats are pursuing a Republican strategy. (At the Republican Convention, Colin Powell denounced 'corporation greed'; the Democrats didn't mention the Poor *once.*) In the future, I predict, one strategist will guide both campaigns — the same way a great chessmaster can play an interesting game against herself."

In 1995, to her credit, *New Yorker* poetry editor Sally Quinn, playing the role of a kind of bipartisan fence chessmaster, chose one of Sparrow's poems for publication by that esteemed venue. To Quinn's surprise, Sparrow's publication precipitated a controversy of sorts. First, the poem was not listed in the *New Yorker* table of contents as poetry. Indeed, it was not listed at all, presumably because it was included as a portion of the magazine's "Talk of the Town" section; although the poem was formatted in the conventional *New Yorker* style for poetry, and it had nothing to do with the content of that edition's "Talk of the Town." Evidently, the *New Yorker* was hedging its bets. Even to consider Sparrow's work as poetry was, for many, to change their conception of poetry. Sparrow's work is too direct and accessible in the sense that it too frontally and "self-consciously" addresses the concerns and expectations of its readers. For a serious if humorous poet, this can of course be a difficult and consuming enterprise, and Sparrow is an important poet in part because of these aspirations.

Like Ted Berrigan and David Antin, Sparrow experiments with forms that speak directly to audiences. The book opens with a direct address: "In 1992 I ran for President, on the Pajama Party, because I wanted to write great poems." He then presents "The Revolution," in which he describes how even though revolutions are "unwinnable" they are a fated corrective. After receiving "zero votes," he decides not to run for president in 1996 because he feels that a presidential run will not produce great poems two times in a row. However, the specter of Pat Buchanan as the Republican presidential candidate front runner based upon a populist stance shocks him and prods him into action. The poet must reclaim the soul of the Republican party which was borne of the abolitionist movement. In a series of campaign speeches framed within a diary form, he gradually comes to the realization that Americans are being terrorized by the their slave-like relations to work. If we are not so much wage slaves, then we are slaves to a system of signification that thoughtlessly assigns power to concentrations of capital. Sparrow proposes a "One Time Investment Economy," in which one need only buy a commodity, such as a CD, once and then receive that product for free forever.

Whatever the practical basis of Sparrow's program, it defetishizes consumerism while virtually turning forms of money into easily but wondrously accessed perceptual modes, passports to material but transcendent realms. According to Sparrow, money will become a "sacred substance," a totem of "transformational magic" that opens one to the "world" of a product.

There is not enough space here to discuss fully the many forms of address that Sparrow adapts in *Republican Like Me* in such a charmingly accessible fashion. Suffice to say that the speeches, diary entries, seemingly real letters, and hilarious parodies of poems by terrorists form the basis of an ideal and more poetic Republican community that hearkens to its abolitionist roots.

Perhaps Sparrow's most important mode of address is his attempt to relate directly with his audience. In poetry, a direct relation with an audience can seem oddly taboo. Perhaps a kind of mystification of the audience is indirectly produced by a need of "the powers that be" to filter poetry and impose values. If so, it would not be surprising that Sparrow was labelled "bad," since he has little to do with this institutional filter.

In 1992, four years before Sparrow's conversion to Republicanism, he debated Eileen Myles for the presidency in the lobby of the New York Public Theater. The debate was not
confrontational or competitive. It was not premised on an either/or system of choice. If Sparrow's candidacy symbolized economic freedom, hers validated all manner of identity politics and sexual orientation. In this vein, her poetry reimagines gender itself. For instance, her poem "The Bicycle" (192) presents the speaker's bicycle ("a girl") and apartment as two female friends who "get along." The poem created a comfortable Lesbian community of sorts.

Myles told me in conversation that Ted Berrigan is her most overriding influence. However, she also worked for and spent much time with James Schuyler, and the influence of the latter poet's descriptive muse is obvious in Myles's work, even if mediated by Berrigan's drive to create community. Myles brings her bike and apartment together in a sexual and graceful manner. Her poetry concerns alliances between queer identity positions. One notes the oddly apt normality of her queer stance. Whatever she discusses is eventually included in a kind of queer family whether it is her childhood family, her friends, other lesbians and gays, characters from the news, or inanimate objects. One might characterize her as a "clear queer" poet. Myles's central enterprise of animating queer politics with clear-minded spirituality is more aggressively "in the world" than Berrigan's task of bringing together poets.

Bob Holman brought Sparrow and Myles together for their 1992 "debate." Holman, one of many of Berrigan's proteges toward the end of his life, is often associated with community and accessibility. He was the founding master of ceremonies for the weekly poetry slam at the Nuyorican cafe, helped begin the publication and circulation of an ever enlarging list of New York City poetry events, and produced numerous poetry projects for public broadcasting, the internet, poets theaters, and poetry recordings. Indeed, Sparrow mentions Holman in *Republican Like Me* as someone who in a sense commissioned his campaign since Holman arranged for the recording of Sparrow's campaign poetry in 1996.

Holman's multi-partisan spirit is also displayed in a poem that he wrote for Eileen Myles's campaign entitled "I CAN'T BELIEVE IT'S NOT A POEM!" (145). The poem and Holman's poetry in general bespeaks a strong urge to extend the sphere of poetry's influence outside the poetry world. A dominant trope in his poetry is the creation of the paradoxically familiar "other," which is succinctly displayed in his poem, "Love" (54), dedicated to his wife, the sculptor Elizabeth Murray. The poem ends with the speaker adding that the other body the speaker puts her hand on is "my body."

The speaker in "Love" evokes an impersonal form of beauty and sensuality with the brushing of "another body" and then creates another more focused sensuality by specifying that it is his body. Holman often uses this characteristically Russian Formalist tool of defamiliarization. In a sense, there are no others and no aesthetic is ultimately foreign, but, Holman suggests, we must begin with that assumption to gain new perspectives. For Holman, poetry itself is a field of otherness that works to ingrain itself in our lives. Thus he entitles the poem that he wrote for Eileen Myles's campaign "I Can't Believe It's Not a Poem" but ends it. "This is not a poem" (145). The poem argues that in a world in which the definitions of words overlap like television snow, the world itself is a kind of poem and poetry loses its unique status. To be revolutionary is to own up to how transitory meaning is, and this shock of recognition and nonrecognition becomes one of poetry's chief tasks. For Holman this is more than an academic game, and these perceptions must be felt sharply individually and accounted for within communities.

In conclusion, a trajectory of highly articulate and politically communal efforts exists from O'Hara to Berrigan to Sparrow, Myles, and Holman: O'Hara notes and addresses community from within an abstract expressionist base, Berrigan's poetry begins to direct a sense of poetic community that confronts reality and reference as problematic concerns in themselves, and Sparrow, Myles, and Holman begin to generate politically active communities through the powers of their poetries.

WORKS CITED

Berrigan, Ted. Selected Poems. New York: Penguin, 1997.
Holman, Bob. *The Collect Call of the Wild*. New York: Henry Holt, 1995.
Myles, *Eileen. Not Me*. New York:Semiotext(e), 1991,
O'Hara, Frank. The Collected Poems. Berkeley: U of California P, 1995.
Sparrow. *Republican Like Me*. New York: Soft Skin P, 1997.

Thomas Fink

BETWEEN/AFTER LANGUAGE POETRY AND THE NEW YORK SCHOOL

THE CATEGORIES LANGUAGE POETRY AND THE NEW YORK SCHOOL OF POETRY have long been problematic. Noting that "the Language movement has always been an umbrella for very disparate practices" and has "displayed internal conflicts and ruptures," Marjorie Perloff in *Radical Artifice* asserts "that what we might call 'criticism based on movement-affiliation' is bound, sooner or later, to give way to a historical and literary reshuffling of the deck" (Perloff 174) and yet she and such other supportive critics as George Hartley, Linda Reinfeld, and Jerome McGann have consistently used the "umbrella" for convenience. This use is possible, because most practitioners of Language poetry share an interest in the material properties and performative aspects of language, foregrounded through a deployment of highly disjunctive collagistic or citational strategies and/or elaborate formal (not formalist) procedures, and a rejection — grounded in left political theory (frequently informed by poststructuralism) — of the centrality and coherence of narrative, imagistic representation, conventional grammar and syntax, and the concept of the unified self or "I." In Joseph Lease's cogent formulation, "Language Poetry has been self-conscious and aggressive about situating experimental writing practices (especially the decision to explode the lyric 'I') in a NeoMarxist narrative that equates the postromantic lyric tradition with individualism and late capitalism" (Lease 2).

As for the New York School, various critics in *Beyond Amazement* and *The Tribe of John*, two collections about John Ashbery's work, find that the term obscures the major differences between Ashbery's poetry and that of Kenneth Koch, Frank O'Hara, and James Schuyler; these critics indicate that the sole value of the term lies in the supportive friendship of the "School's" participants.* "At first," as David Shapiro writes in his pioneering book on Ashbery, "they were pragmatically and conspiratorily joined against poets of a

---

*See the "Introduction" by David Lehman and essays by Douglas Crase, Lehman, and John Koethe in *Beyond Amazement: New Essays on John Ashbery*, Ed. David Lehman (Ithaca: Cornell UP, 1980). See essays by Koethe and John Gery in *The Tribe of John: Ashbery and Contemporary Poetry* Ed. Susan M. Schultz (Tuscaloosa, AL: U of Alabama P, 1995).

different aesthetic (Richard Wilbur, for example)," and common aesthetic influences, such as the French symbolism, deserves acknowledgement (Shapiro 4). If one can speak of an "Ashbery wing" and an "O'Hara-Koch-Schuyler" wing of the New York School, it should be acknowledged that both groups display a fondness for parody of common speech and attitudes and intellectual jargon, collage, poems of casual meditation, occasional use of formal procedures like the sestina, and a suspicion of ideological critique, overt spiritual expression, and "closed" narrative strategies. Except in Ashbery's *Tennis Court Oath* period, which has been championed by Charles Bernstein and other Language Poets, and in a handful of poems *by* others like Koch's "When the Sun Refuses to Go On," the New York School does not share the Language poets' desire to undermine conventional grammar and syntax. The difference between the wings would hinge on the latter's greater tolerance for relatively large units of coherent (but not "closed") narrative and description and the greater degree to which the former group rejects the centrality of the "I" and fosters a greater tolerance for disjunction, though, of course, generally much less than the Language poets.

The last fifteen or so years has witnessed the emergence of various poetic "figures of capable imagination," as Wallace Stevens puts it, whose work exists in productive relation to — one might say, between and after — the New York School and Language poetry without fitting into either camp. These poets, some of whom know and respect each other's work and some of whom are unfamiliar with one another, do not embody a collective synthesis of the two groups; their poetic strategies are sufficiently different from one another not to form a new "school." On the other hand, the idea that each can be situated between the two precursor groups — and not, as in the case of such fine poets as Nathaniel Mackey and Kathleen Fraser, between the Black Mountain School and Language poetry — suggests that they have enough in common for a literary historian to perceive them in relation to one another.

Because he edited the *Anthology of New York Poets* with Ron Padgett and because he was encouraged and promoted at a very early age by nearly all the senior members of the New York School, David Shapiro (born in 1947) is generally considered a second-generation member of the group. Although perusal of Shapiro's eight books of poetry between 1965 and 1994 does bring to light numerous poems that "behave" a good deal like post-*Tennis Court Oath* Ashbery or Koch's jaunty catalogue poems or surrealist whimsy or O'Hara, these are far from his best and most characteristic work.

In the late 1960s, before Language Poets like Bernstein, Ron Silliman, and Susan Howe had begun the kind of work for which they are known, Shapiro had followed the extreme disjunctions of *Tennis Court Oath* poems like "Europe" in his own, non-Ashberyan "voices." This is not to say that his poetics reflected a "Marxist" orientation, as did those of Bernstein and company, but, during the period at Columbia University in which he was a vigorous protester of the Vietnam War, he was certainly calling contemporary social coherences into question through strategies of collagistic fragmentation. In his mature work of the last two decades, while he continues to make strong use of disjunction and collage, Shapiro equally pursues the disclosure of the performative aspects of language and relatively overt meditations on the issues of representation that have preoccupied cultural critics during the ascendency of poststructuralism in the 1970s and early 1980s and, to a lesser extent, since then. Not only is Shapiro willing to sustain a meditative drift longer than Ashbery does (in any poem besides "Self-Portrait in a Convex Mirror"), but, unlike the elder poet, he directly includes the themes of family and sexual conflict, the horrors of political oppression, and the problems of elegy as part of his investigations of these more abstract issues. It should also be noted that Shapiro prefers a more elegant musicality than the Language poets, who are much more tolerant of a preponderance of dissonant effects.

Born in 1942, Ann Lauterbach, who, like Ashbery, won a coveted MacArthur grant, has often been linked, for better or worse, with the New York School's Ashbery wing.[*] Her use of abstractions, tonal fluctuations, and a poetic surface that simultaneously has the feel of collage and casual meditation often resembles Ashbery's, and so do her thematic emphases on mutability, the elusiveness of erotic experience, and the difficulties of perception. The *political* divergence of *all* of Lauterbach's mature work from Ashbery and the New York School is to be found in her exploration of how women have assumed and are assuming gendered subject-positions in the socius; in this sense, she is closer to feminist Language poets like Susan Howe, Leslie Scalapino, Lyn Hejinian, and Carla Harryman, as well as to Bernadette Mayer, who is closer to the New York School but bears some affinities with the Language camp. In fact, a handful of Lauterbach's poems depart from any stylistic similarity to recent Ashbery and court extreme disjunctiveness, but their intriguing interruptions of the conventional flow of a sentence do not result in a violent disruption of the norms of

---

[*]Praising the notion that Ashbery's writing "opens to a fully dialogic poetics," James McCorkle in "Nimbus of Sensations: Eros and Reverie in the Poetry of John Ashbery and Ann Lauterbach" in The *Tribe* of John finds "in the tracing of thoughts voicings of a phenomenology that necessitates and inscribes a social world," while considering the "parallel critique of the atomistic self" in Lauterbach's *Before Recollection* (Princeton: Princeton UP, 1987) constitutive of "a phenomenologically enclosed world" that, "finally, pursues the possibilities of rapture and thereby risks enthrallment" (123). The fact that Lauterbach, like many more overtly feminist poets, often speaks from the position of an "I" allows her to explore the constitutive features of social constructions of the female "I," which are still — in the 1990s — very much open to speculation.

grammar and syntax. It should be noted, too, that Lauterbach's poetry sometimes evinces a spiritual impulse that is not ironized, as it is in the New York School and, generally, among the Language poets.

Another poet whose work features the feminist intention to situate gender power relations within questions of representation is Mei-mei Berssenbrugge, born in 1947 in Beijing. In Berssenbrugge's poetry of the last decade, the "I" is a site of complicated, intricately problematized perception. Her process of meditation, which is developed in labyrinthine sentences and which features a more insistent use of abstraction than Ashbery's "Self-Portrait," Shapiro's long poems, Lauterbach's work, or just about any other contemporary poet, enables the self to enact its own dispersal into the disparate loci of its social situations. As in the poets cited above, the continual disruption of epistemological confidence makes it difficult to read a Berssenbrugge poem as a single, coherent meditation, and yet, compared to much Language poetry, the "I" is constituted rather legibly, even as its "common sense" foundations are assaulted, and, along the way, some of her demystifications of ordinary masculinist perceptual constructs are sufficiently accessible. Aside from considerations of gender, Berssenbrugge also departs from Ashbery when, at times, she contemplates the mapping of power relations between Euro-American perceptions of "China" and "the Chinese" and whatever Chinese perspectives she has inherited.

Like Berssenbrugge, Stephen Paul Miller, born in 1951, is a poet of meandering meditation. In his single book, the long poem *Art Is Boring For the Same Reason We Stayed in Vietnam* (1992), the poet's quirky speaker is endowed with as much "presence" — as much authority of "voice" — as are O'Hara's, Schuyler's, and Koch's, but, as in Ashbery, the self's authority is continually called into question. More unabashedly and prolongedly discursive than the other poets under discussion, with the possible exception of Berssenbrugge, Miller nevertheless permits moments of lyricism upon which Language poets would cast a suspicious eye. Though Miller's "leaping" from one image or topic to another and his play with the performative qualities of language is indebted to Shapiro and Ashbery, and his interest in the general problem of representation follows theirs, his social subject matter marks a significant departure from their concerns and establishes a point of contact with Bernstein, Andrews, and other Language Poets. Considering the U.S.-Iraqi War and other political events of the early 1990s, *Art Is Boring* probes the authoritarian forms and practices of the management of consensus in U.S. politics and media, including the suspect and potentially menacing aspects of the constitution of rigid identity, and it poses many potent questions about the possibilities of more rigorously democratic structures that would enable a non-hegemonic sense of community to emerge.

John Yau, who has published nine books of poetry between 1976 and 1996, is extremely difficult to categorize. Many of his earlier poems can be placed in the New York School (Ashbery wing) and later work is closer to that of the Language group. Yau, born in 1950, studied with Ashbery, and his book *Corpse and Mirror* (1983) was chosen by the elder poet for publication in the National Poetry Series. In Yau's early work, John Gery finds the use of "idiomatic speech in the style" of various mid-1070s Ashbery poems, "less for deconstructive effects than for its visual evocativeness and its diffusion of the arcane or the consummate." (Gery 134-5). The younger poet, he rightly notes, "manages to focus" in Ashberyan ways "on the space between experience and thought, between observation and interpretation, a space that wavers even as he isolates it" (136).*

Such an observation may be true of the Language poets, but their way of problematizing that wavering "space," of course, is very different from recent Ashbery. Like many Language Poets, Yau has been interested in the last two decades in employing formal procedures and collage to concentrate on the material properties of language and a sense of fractured narratives and/or pervasive lyric fragmentation (Foster 46-8). The social dimension of Yau's poetry of the 1980s and 1990s is a serious play with the discourse of race that never seems to enter Ashbery's work. Priscilla Wald, his most astute critic, observes: "With neither history nor country to which he can return, Yau finds himself struggling with the terms that constitute subjectivity in the United States, profoundly distrustful" of "conventional forms and expressions" of that "subjectivity" and striving to express "his Chinese-American identity in his poetic engagement with what he sees as the terms of that subjectivity" (Wald 133-34).

Joseph Donahue, four years Yau's junior, shares his propensity to explore epistemological and social uncertainties through strategies of collagistic fragmentation that place emphasis on the visual. As in most of the poets I have treated here, the "I" is available for use but is never as stable in its functioning as in the work of O'Hara, Schuyler, and similar New York School poets. The procession of disjunctive perceptions in Donahue's poems is consonant with his social topoi: the disintegrative violence and speed of urban life, both enervating and exhilarating, in the past two decades, and the displacements of an oft-thwarted spiritual seeking. (Donahue also contemplates the disruptive force of President Kennedy's assassination on the present.) Not only does Donahue differ from the Language poets and perhaps the entire New York School in his qualified valorization of

---

*Edward Foster, "An Interview with John Yau," *Talisman* 5 (Fall 1990), in which Yau states that he "knew... fairly early on" that he "didn't want to be gabby or social the way" many New York School Poets were, but that "with Ashbery's work, the relationship is probably a more complicated one, which [Yau hasn't] figured out"

spiritual questing — perceived from the context of a vexed Catholic upbringing — but his disjunctions are not so relentless, as in much Language writing, that they block the reading of articulations of social tendencies and representative subjectivities.

I end with a poet who is a full seven years younger than Donahue, himself younger than the other poets under consideration. Joseph Lease is deeply interested in the exploration of heterosexual erotic relations that are moving away from patriarchal patterns, in the problematization of Jewish-American community fifty years after the Shoah, and, like Miller, in speculations about obstacles and possibilities of effectively democratic collectivity. While Lease has learned much about what poststructuralism, Language poetry, and poets like Ashbery and Shapiro have had to say about linguistic representation and fundamental instabilities of the constituted self — and demonstrates such an awareness through the self-reflexivity of his poetry — he abjures what he takes to be the proscriptions of both the New York School and Language Poets and employs a wide range of poetic strategies. These include collage with varying degrees of disjunction, narration, psychological exploration, extremely precise and evocative sensory description (an inheritance from imagism), metapoetic irony, and a transformative, visionary language that bespeaks spiritual yearnings, as in Lauterbach and Donahue. Lease's combinatory aesthetic is not a homogenizing synthesis; the various elements in his work continually speak to one another, sometimes conflictually and sometimes with ample tolerance. Like the others who are situated lucidly "between" and "after," he illustrates the notion that the "ingredients" of New York School poetry and Language poetry cannot coalesce into a "stew," but that their dialogue, which also features conversation with what they both leave out, serves as a highly enabling condition for the production of imaginative and cogent poetic experimentation.

WORKS CITED

Gery, John. "Ashbery's Menagerie and the Anxiety of Affluence," *The Tribe of John*. Ed Susan Schultz. Tuscaloosa, AL: U of Alabama P, 1995.

Foster, Edward. "An Interview with John Yau." *Talisman* 5 (Fall 1990).

Lauterbach, Ann. *Before Recollection*. Princeton: Princeton UP, 1987.

Lease, Joseph. "A Study in 'counter-dependence1: Language Poetry as collective voice.'" Unpublished essay.

Lehman, David. *Beyond Amazement: New Essays on John Ashbery*. Ithaca: Cornell UP, 1980.

Miller, Stephen Paul. *Art Is Boring for the Same Reason We Stayed in Vietnam*. New York: Domestic, 1992.

Perloff, Marjorie. *Radical Artifice: Poetry in the Age of Media*. Chicago: U of Chicago P, 1991.

Schultz, Susan, ed. *The Tribe of John: Ashbery and Contemporary Poetry*. Tuscaloosa, AL: U of Alabama P, 1995.

Shapiro, David. *John Ashbery: An Introduction to the Poetry*. New York:Columbia UP, 1979.

Yau, John. *Corpse and Mirror*. New York: Ecco, 1983.

Wald, Priscilla. "'Chaos Goes Uncourted: John Yau's (Dis-)Orienting Poetics," *Cohesion and Dissent in American Literature*. Ed. Carol Colatrella and Joseph Alkana. Albany: State U of New York P, 1994.

David Clippinger

BETWEEN SILENCE AND THE MARGINS: POETRY AND ITS PRESSES

THE MOST DRASTIC CHANGE UPON THE LANDSCAPE OF POETRY SINCE 1970 has not been the result of poetic innovation (although radical poetic tenets have been proposed); a deeper (or lesser) commitment of poetry to social and political issues; the proliferation of the so-called career writer who has emerged out of the avalanche of M.F.A. degrees; nor because of the ongoing debates over the "canon" — that academically sanctioned list of poetry which "deserves" to be read seriously and studied. Rather, poetry as well as all these issues have been transformed over the last three decades by a marked shift in the production and reception of poetry; that is, the means by which a poem reaches its potential audience and in what form. The flow of poetry over the last thirty years has come to be more rigorously regulated by publishers and the market, which, in turn, directly impacts how an audience responds to poetic innovation, the assumed responsibilities a poet has to social and political issues, the relative "prestige" of the career-poet, and the acceptable lineage of poetic forebearers. In essence, the negotiations and debates concerning the nature of poetry as well as all the other issues listed above are played out within the three venues of poetry publication — the major for-profit publishing corporations, the university presses and academically-affiliated journals, and the small presses and independent journals. The dynamics of these three modes of publication has deeply affected poetry as a whole, and before turning to the pivotal role of the small press, it is necessary to examine the overarching positions of the for-profit and academic presses and how those dynamics affect the field of poetry as a whole. Within a deeper historical context, the significance of the small press and independent journal will become readily apparent.

While it might be argued that poetry has always maintained an uneasy relationship with major publishing houses, a significant shift occurred within the market-driven philosophy of large corporate publishers after 1970: the dwindling profit margin for poetry as a whole prompted a severing (or at least a re-evaluation) of the relationship between most poetry and for-profit publishing corporations. A conscious shift away from serious poetry developed because of small readership numbers, which could not justify sustained financial investment. As William Abrahams, senior editor at Holt, Rinehart and Winston acknowledges, "the gulf is widening . . . between the good and serious book aimed at the serious reader and the commercial, mass market book" (Haslam 1173). While the gulf may be widening, most for-profit corporations have published a handful of "established," recognizable, and therefore marketable poets who generate an acceptable profit margin — Allen Ginsberg or Maya Angelou, for example. More often than not, the publishing corporations also court the amateur poet who possesses a certain cultural and economic cache — Jimmy Stewart, Jimmy Carter, and most recently the pop music star Jewel — whose books have reached the best seller list. Ultimately the poem within the purview of the for-profit publishers is, clear and simple, a commodity that exists apart from the issue of literary merit or cultural value. In this regard, the market and art often are regarded as disjunctive entities that are not easily reconciled with corporate economics.[*]

Whereas an editor at a large press, in an attempt to camouflage its economically driven mindset, might argue that only the most established and reputable poets earn a place within its pantheon, the fact remains that very few contemporary poets achieve such "established" and marketable status. The major publishing house has become a closed venue for poets. As H. L. Brunt prophetically announced in 1974:

> There can be too many bombs but never enough magazines and presses. Especially now when most of the standard publishers and magazines have been bought by giant corporations. For within ten years the only books coming out of the New York houses might be cheap fiction, instant journalism, and cook books. Corporate executives don't give a damn about 'literature,' and pretty soon they're going to stop pretending to. So if you call yourself a serious writer you had better start taking the littles seriously. They are going to be your first publisher and probably your last. ("Property" 181-182)

Instead of "cheap fiction, instant journalism, and cook books," the current market revolves around novels that have been turned into films, romance novels, and the biographies or autobiographies of celebrities. Within this economy driven solely by profit, poetry has been relegated a marginal position within the priorities of large publishing corporations. Consequently, the only available publishing opportunities for poetry have become by default or design the university presses and/or the small press — both of which share the dubious

---

[*] As John Berger, the Marxist art historian, remarks in his book *Ways of Seeing*," Hack work is not the result of either clumsiness or provincialism; it is the result of the market making more insistent demands than the art."

distinctions of low sales, non-existent advertising and promotional funds, and small or non-existent profit margins. But as Mary Biggs points out, "Together, academic and small publishing stands as a culturally essential corrective to for-profit publishing, which is naturally and unchangeably hostile to serious poetry with its great demands and minute readership" (20). Despite these economic parallels, a key distinction between the university press/university-affiliated journal and the small press/independent journal needs to be stressed: the university press and journal remain aligned with its parent university's overarching philosophy and are, therefore, extensions of and controlled by the university's agenda. As Cid Corman, the longtime editor of the legendary magazine, *Origin*, emphasized, "a little mag is only such when independent of . . . clear sponsorship by an institution" (Golding 140). That sponsorship usually comes in the form of funding linked to an institution's governing body, which enacts some degree of control. Control may vary from institution to institution, but it would be naive to assume that university-affiliated presses and journals remain wholly detached from the governing policies of its parent university. As Karl Shapiro claims in regard to his experience as a editor for university affiliated journals,

> In every campus literary venture there is a chain of command that runs from the magazine itself, through the English and other Humanities Departments, through the university press, the administration, and on to the public opinion. In extreme cases . . . the controls can go as high as the governors of states and involve the expression of historical fact itself. (Haslam 1170)

More often than not, the English department and its creative writing program enacts the greatest jurisdiction over a journal since faculty writers serve as editors or advisory editors, who monitor the publication and keep it closely aligned with the poetic aesthetic of the department. Moreover, most M.F.A. programs tend to strive towards a more "professionalized," academic poetry, or what is often referred to as the "workshop" poem. The dominant mode of poetry since 1970s (if not before) has been the workshop poem, which ascended in prominence alongside the proliferation of university creative writing departments and M.F.A. degrees in poetry. As Christopher Beach in his "Careers in Creativity: The Poetry Academy in the 1990s" observes, "Without question, the most significant demographic shift in American poetic culture over the past quarter century has been the growth of the creative writing academy" (4). That growth has sparked a mass generation of "workshop" poems, which has detrimental effects upon poetry and its "market":

> The workshop as it exists in most American universities not only tends to homogenize the level of what has traditionally constituted authorial style — substituting a notion of personal "voice" or "authenticity" for more inventive linguistic or stylistic manipulation — but it also tends to breed a conformity to certain established patterns of verse, in particular the self-contained, narrative, lyric, first-person poems that have dominated mainstream American poetry for the past twenty years. (14)

The workshop poem and its commitment to the lyric is also the overarching standard of many university affiliated journals and presses, which in turn creates a deeper layering of homogenization of published (or "readable") poetry that carefully controls the "acceptable" levels of innovation and social or political interrogation. Douglass Messerli, the publisher of Sun & Moon Press, claims that for this particular reason most academic journals fall under the rubric "of poetry outlets handling only unadventuresome 'cooked' verse instead of the avant-garde 'raw'" (Biggs 4). Similar to how the for-profit corporations compromise literary integrity in favor of immediate economic benefits, the university poem denies the dialectic nature of art by valorizing a stable, contained, and (hence) teachable poetic form. Charles Robinson observes that

> The independents feel that not only have the popular magazines sold out, but that the university magazines have followed suit — that . . . the latter . . . have adopted a peculiar academicism as sterile as the policy of popular magazines turning out formula pieces. (Haslam 1169)

Ultimately, poetry affiliated with either for-profit or university presses is rigorously monitored so that the poem serves an overarching agenda. What is lost is the sense of poetry as an ever expanding and evolving form that stands in opposition to a "stability" peculiar to economics of the academy.

In all fairness, some university presses and journals are committed to publishing "experimental" poetry, but it should not be overlooked that a significant publishing lag time transpires during which time a "raw" poet usually has achieved some degree of canonical status and is, therefore, more palatable. Consequently, many university presses and journals seem to be more directly engaged in the dialectics of canon formation than the rendering of the scene of contemporary poetry.* That is to say, most university presses are more concerned with presenting and maintaining a stable body of academically "cooked" poetry (or arguing what constitutes a "cooked" poem) than contributing to the *poetic* dialogue over the continual negotiation and renegotiation over what constitutes a poem.

Whereas corporate presses cater to, or attempt to anticipate shifts in, popular taste (which tends to lag at least twenty years or more behind the questions and concerns with which contemporary poets are grappling), the university press and journal lags for quite different reasons — namely, the issue of "canonical" poetry envisions a static field, which does not accommodate an ever-rippling and transforming poetry. As should be clear from its institutional setting, the academic journal is an extension of poetry as an object of study and imitation, which responds to the guild-like structure of an M.F.A. program where the student/apprentice learns directly from a professor/"master." Such a structure tends to quell the practice of questioning, transforming, and experimentation, which effectively elevates "imitation" over invention. Ezra Pound might regard most workshop poetry as the valorization of poetic "diluters," who are significantly less integral to poetry as a whole than the inventors and the masters. As he remarks in his *ABC of Reading,*

> When you start searching for "pure elements" in literature you will find that literature has been created by the following classes of persons:
>
> 1. Inventors. Men [sic throughout] who found a new process, or whose extent work gives us the first known example of a process.
>
> 2. The masters. Men who combined a number of such processes, and who used them as well as or better than the inventors.
>
> 3. The diluters. Men who came after the first two kinds, and couldn't do the job quite as well. (39)

Since the small press tends to eschew being driven wholly by market economics and academic politics, both of which normally depend upon a diluted and assimilable poetic form, the small press remains the primary forum for inventors — the poets concerned with

---

*For a more detailed discussion of the role of canon formation and its dialectical impact upon the conception of "poetry," see Alan Golding's essay, "New, Newer, and Newest American Poetries" in this volume as well as his chapter "Little Magazines and Alternative Canons" in *From Outlaw to Classic.*

stylistic, linguistic, and narrative experimentation — and the unrecognized "masters" who have yet to be absorbed by the mainstream. Subsequently, the small press provides a more accurate perspective of the issues, dialogues, and interrogations that constitute the focal points for contemporary poetry even as those issues continue to unfold.

It should not be deduced that the small press completely elides the demand of the market nor that a poet published therein is not susceptible to the processes of assimilation, homogenization, and imitation that characterizes the workshop poem. After all, imitation seems to be a part of the ongoing process of poetic development, but the moment that a poet breaks with the practice of mere imitation and begins to challenge and question the assumed boundaries of poetry, he or she simultaneously slips into the realm of the poetic while slipping out a marketable niche. Nevertheless, an "experimental" poet is not free from the pressures of audience either. As Susan Howe remarked during an interview with Ruth Fallon,

> In fact, there may be a danger in having an audience. It's hard not to want to keep pleasing these enthusiasts. Will you feel forced to please them in some subtle sense? The issue is force, however subtle. What is the extent to which an audience pulls an artist? It's very mysterious. (33)

The desire of the poet shifts in the face of an audience as a market, which alters the poetic production for the author. Even without the lure of money, Howe suggests that the positive reception of one's poetry creates demands upon the author. It goes without saying that the demands only become greater as a poet crosses from small press to university or "big" press and is granted more and more positive reviews, readership, contracts, and academic positions.

Additionally, the small presses and independent journals are not free from charges of elitism even as those presses attempt to counter the self-serving and narrow agendas of for-profit and university presses. Gerald Haslam claims that "Alternative magazines, as well as their less numerous brethren, small presses, have been elitist in that they were not produced for general consumption" (1170), which reveals "a certain reverse snobbery" that attempts to mask a network of "incestuous publishing" (1174). Such narrow, reactionary thinking aside, publishing on all levels draws upon a tight-knit circle of poets that seems "closed" to any "outsider," but the key difference is that whereas the for-profit and academic presses rely upon an incestuous network in order to bolster sales or advance the cache of a creative writing department (which also has economic ramifications), the small press serves no other master than that of an editor's or editors' poetic vision and sense of what constitutes poetry. Since the goal of the small press is not financial, its view of poetry is not tethered to the economic bottom-line but, rather, has within its scope a more holistic sense of poetry as an mode of art.

The small press, in this regard, is the vehicle that perpetuates the evolution of poetry as a whole. The poems published therein may become canonized, merge with the mainstream, and become suitable material for academic presses or may even become part of a publishing corporation's roster of select, elite poets. Nevertheless, the small press provides a space for the dialogue over what constitutes a poem and what intrinsic responsibilities poetry has to larger social issues. Moreover, that forum engages in a larger conversation regarding the status of poetry in relation to a perpetually changing human social fabric that is constantly transformed through technology, scientific discoveries, socio-political events, and shifts in knowledge and human consciousness. Poetry is a barometer for the multi-faceted levels of human existence, and the small press in effect disallows the poem from dwindling into a static form by maintaining the connection between the poem and the world. In essence, the small press bodies forth a living poetry by introducing fresh poetic visions that press at the boundaries of poetry and knowing. Robert Duncan explicitly links the new, poetry, and knowing:

> Our engagement with knowing, with craft and lore, our demand for truth is not to reach a conclusion but to keep our exposure to what we do not know, to confront our wish and our need beyond habit and capability, beyond what we can take for granted, at the borderline, the light finger-tip or thought-tip where impulse and novelty spring. (*Certainties* 87)

The small press remains absolutely vital for keeping poetry and knowledge moving and alive — a point that is accentuated by the very names of independent journals and small presses such as Vehicle, *New American Writing, New Rivers, Crossing, Momentum, Volt, Junction,* and perhaps the most appropriately named small press, Living Batch.

Despite the names of these presses and journals, which allude directly or indirectly to the privileging of the new, the question remains How exactly do small presses sustain poetry? One of the most comprehensive responses to the role of the small press/independent journal is in the inaugural and absolutely invaluable issue of *Chain* (Spring/Summer 1994), where the editors, Jena Osman and Juliana Spahr, sent surveys to various women editors of small presses and journals. While many of the questions on the survey address the issue of gender and editorship — questions such as "Does gender play a role in your editorial practice? and "How do you think women fit into the exchange economy of editorial practice? Is editing an issue of economy or an issue of aesthetics, or both?" — the responses that Osman and Spahr received and published from thirty-six editors are extremely illuminating in regards to the role of the small press in relation to poetry. The responses are as varied as the journals themselves, but many editors propose that their responsibilities tend to revolve around three core issues: publishing various interest and/or identity groups; creating a journal that serves as a touchstone for a poetic community; and/or serving poetry as a whole by publishing major poets who have been or might be otherwise completely overlooked (as in the case of Bernadette Mayer published by Lee Ann Brown's Tender Buttons or William Bronk published by a range of small presses including *Origin*, St. Elizabeth's, and Talisman House). Each of these perspectives touch upon a vital aspect of the small press and independent journal, but before turning to the issue of the culminative effect that small presses have upon poetry, each of these three issues merit deeper consideration, which will further illustrate the role that the small press plays within poetry as a whole.

During the early 1980s as feminist theory gained an intellectual presence and following in the universities, a concomitant rise in the consciousness of how cultural marginalization affected the social, political, and artistic gained position outside of the academy as well. Prompted by or parallel with the emergence of feminist theory, a literary movement centered upon identity issues gained momentum within the pages of the independent journal in the late 1970s and early 1980s. The field of poetry was no exception, and it was within the arena of the small press that identity politics was most evident. Richard Masteler notes that identity politics in effect has opened a wider and a more varied field of poetry:

> The rise of what can be called 'identity poetry' has accompanied this rise of identity politics. For each of numerous interpretive communities ostensibly defined by sets of specific interest and values. . . , there are poems written in light of those values. (27)

The broadening of the spectrum counters homogeneity by creating a democratization that offers a forum for a range of voices that might not otherwise have a means to be heard. In effect, an "identity" centered journal or press is a vehicle of validation, which might not otherwise exist for a particular poet or mode of poetry. While such issues of validation and voice are painfully obvious within the context of gender, race, or class marginalization and discrimination, it should not be overlooked that the issue of identity has poetic and aesthetic ramifications as well whereby the "silencing" by the mainstream also applies to experimental poets and innovators who remain on the fringes of "accepted" and "established" verse. As William Carlos Williams remarked,

> The little magazine is something I have always fostered; for without it, I myself would have been early silenced. To me it is one magazine, not several. It is a continuous magazine, the only one I know with an absolute freedom. (Haslam 1169)

The small press grants a space to poets who might otherwise be silenced, and even canonical poets such as William Carlos Williams (and others) owe much to the small press and independent journals.

The forum for a range of voices with specific interests and agendas also establishes a sense of community that obviates the alienation poets often feel from their audience and one another. Such a community grouped under the auspices of a particular press or journal often leads to a proposed vision or poetics that further solidifies a thrust towards a new(er) realm of poetry. As Kathleen Fraser remarks in "The Tradition of Marginality,"

> The reward of asserting a vision is to become visible, to participate actively in the wider literary conversation, and to help in creating a community that has been waiting to come into view. It turns out, in our case, that there have been many women like us feeling isolated for years, excluded from the aesthetic or political mandates of existing poetics. (26)

The charge that small presses are elitist or incestuous (where friends publish only friends) is handily refuted when one considers the larger sense that the overarching issue for some journals is to create a forum for a community, which engages in the "larger literary conversation" that, in turn, yields fresh insights or offers critiques that alter Poetry as a whole. And while the effect of such a community may not be immediately felt, it often has wider repercussions that have long-standing importance.

In this vein, editors of independent journal sometimes regard their task as a means to offer a unified vision that may serve as the foundation that unites a group of poets under a shared poetic philosophy. For example, Robert Creeley's *Black Mountain Review* is often perceived as positing a vision that became a movement; or more recently, the first issue of the now defunct *apex of the M* opened with a poetics statement, "State of the Art," intended to catalyze change by questioning the "state" of poetry. Such concerted poetics statements, for obvious reasons, tend to have a better chance of altering the poetic landscape since multiple and relatively harmonious voices are pressing for change. Certainly the trace of the "Black Mountain School" has deeply affected both experimental and mainstream poetries. In addition to creating a movement, such concerted efforts bridge physical distances by providing a network that otherwise might seem illusory. The sense of community and voice therefore is woven into the dynamics of the small press and its particular commitment to social and poetic issues.

Subsequently, the small press and independent journal emerges out of these silences and distances in order to bridge space, create community, and press poetry in new ways. And when considering the network of independent journals and small presses operating in the United States alone, many voices and communities are flourishing under the aegis of the small press. For example, the catalogue from Small Press Distribution carries over eighty-five independent journals together with titles from over four hundred small presses; these numbers not only suggest that an immense body of "independent" poetry is being written and published, but also testify to the pervasive and potential force that the small press has upon the literary and social fabric. Moreover, some journals, such as *Raintaxi*, are dedicated almost exclusively to reviewing books from small press publishers, which further suggests that the small press is more than a mere literary aside.

It is within this spirit of contributing to literature as a whole that Susan Smith Nash remarks,

> I am firmly convinced that the energy and diversity of the small press (or micropress) scene is absolutely essential to the development of art in America. If our government won't fund us, we have to do it ourselves — small is beautiful, cheap is good! (Chain 88-89)

While the small press perpetuates the ongoing dialectic of art by continuing to question, critique, and transform the supposed "boundaries" of poetry, such questioning ultimately alters not only the contemporary sense of a poem but also prompts a reconsideration of the poetic past since the questioning of the poem often looks for prior models and precursors, which, in turn, perpetuates, resurrects, and remakes poetic history.

Ultimately, the interrogative mode of questioning "the" poem not only presses towards the inception of contemporary poetry but also maintains the larger sense of the poem by disallowing it to stagnate into a set form, pattern, style, voice, or model. And in essence my central argument is that the vital role of the small press and independent journal needs to be recognized as a central element. Hank Lazer, author of the two-volume *Opposing Poetries*, argues for an inclusive conception of poetry where the independent journals and small presses are recovered from the margins and considered within a larger literary historical framework.[*] That is, faced with the veritable explosion of the numbers of small presses and journals, the politicized nature of the relation of the academic institution to its M.F.A. centered poetry, and the dubious editorial policies of the for-profit press towards literature, Lazer argues that serious readers must "adopt a more skeptical, informed, investigative relationship to the social, political, and economic ramifications of their habits as poetry-consumers" and therefore "[s]erve poetry and the book" (volume 1, 81). Such an approach doesn't attempt to elide the fact that poetry occurs within an economy of production and reception, yet the point remains that bringing to the surface the "habits" of "poetry-consumers" should allow for a more open and democratic market where independent journals and small presses would cease being perceived as marginal or nearly silent voices floating on the periphery of the ongoing debate about poetry but would become, rather, central voices that pose crucial questions and potential answers. While not disavowing the mainstream or workshop poetry, an inclusive model disrupts a unified, homogenous sense of poetry in favor of a multi-dimensional, less-hierarchicized, and heteroglossic conception of poetry wherein the oppositions and tensions between poems and poetries should not be effaced but should be the focal point of one's reading. The goal of such an approach is to broaden the context of poetry in order to gain a deeper understanding of the range of poetry, wherein the small press and the independent journal are shown to be absolutely integral.

In essence, such an approach reveals the degree to which the small press occupies a central position within the triangulated nexus of for-profit, university, and small presses — the sum of which reflects the multi-faceted strata of contemporary poetry. And while there may be ideological and economic tensions between these various presses and that a slippage sometimes occurs between these three venues as a particular poet or school of poetry is re-evaluated and appropriated into the "canon," the serious reader of poetry has a responsibility to the multiple layers of poetic discourse. Most importantly, the seemingly unseen stream that flows deep below the smooth, glassy surface of mainstream and academic poetry — the ever surging waves of the small press — needs to be recognized as a substan-

---

[*]Jed Rasula in his *The American Poetry Wax Museum* also makes a similar argument throughout his exhaustive study of twentieth-century American poetry.

tial poetic force. After all, it is within the pages of the independent journal that the "inventors" and the future "masters" can be found and that the ongoing debate over the contemporary poem is taking place. It is there that the future of poetry is, in fact, already taking shape somewhere between silence and the margin.

WORKS CITED

Beach, Christopher. "Careers in Creativity: The Poetry Academy in the 1990s." *Western Humanities Review* 50.1 (1996): 4-16.
Berger, John. *Ways of Seeing*. New York: Penguin, 1972.
Biggs, Mary. "Academic Publishing and Poetry." *Scholarly Publishing* 17 (1985): 3-23.
Duncan, Robert. *Fictive Certainties*. New York: New Directions, 1985.
Fallon, Ruth. "Speaking with Susan Howe. *The Difficulties* 3.2 (1989): 33-42.
Fraser, Kathleen. "The Tradition of Marginality." *Frontiers* 10 (1989): 22-27.
Golding, Alan. *From Outlaw to Classic: Canons in American Poetry*. Madison: U of Wisconsin P, 1995.
Haslam, Gerald W. "Unknown Diversity" Small Presses and Little Magazines in the West, 1960-1980." In *A Literary History of the American West*. Fort Worth: Texas Christian UP, 1987.
Lazer, Hank. *Opposing Poetries*. 2 Volumes. Evanston: Northwestern UP, 1996.
Masteler, Richard N. "Between Silence and Banality: The Poetic Search for Community." *College Literature* 24.3 (October 1997): 17-32.
Osman, Jena and Juliana Spahr, eds. *Chain*. (Spring/Summer, 1994).
Pound, Ezra. *ABC of Reading*. New York: New Directions, 1934.
Rasula, Jed. *The American Poetry Wax Museum: Reality Effects, 1940-1990*. Urbana: NCTE, 1996.
van Brunt, H.L. "The Property of Love: Little Magazines in the 1970s." *Smith Review* 15 (1974): 180-184.

Linda Russo

THE 'F' WORD IN THE AGE OF MECHANICAL REPRODUCTION: AN ACCOUNT OF WOMEN-EDITED SMALL PRESSES AND JOURNALS[*]

I: "ON THE 'FLY'": WOMEN PRINTING, WOMEN PUBLISHING, AND WOMEN POETRY-EDITING

"I do not think there is any other business from which a woman can derive more satisfaction than that of printing. It is like music to me to hear the click of the type as it falls into the stick, and the buzzing sound of the old press as she turns her papers out on the 'fly.'" —Rena Challender, forewoman of the *Manistee News*, 1897[†]

"these girls have written a distinctly national product." —Ezra Pound, "Marianne Moore and Mina Loy"

IN 1980, ALICE NOTLEY, in a lecture titled "Dr. Williams' Heiresses," imagined a mythopoetic lineage of American poets that would explain the situation of contemporary

---

[*] See Appendix C: Women-edited (and co-edited) Little Magazines and Presses. Although there are several indices of small press activity (such as *Herstory*, the *Alternative Press Index*, *Women's Periodicals and Newspapers*, Len Fulton's *Small Press Publishers* and Loss Pequeño Glazier's *Small Press: an Annotated Guide*) none is comprehensive. And though the feminist and avant-garde presses in the latter half of the twentieth century have been well-researched, women-edited journals of innovative poetry have fallen between the lines, often remembered but generally not a focal point of discussion. In most cases crucial information has only been available through the generosity of poets who shared experiences with me through personal correspondence and interviews. Since this essay was written in 1999, Lynn Keller, Linda Kinnahan and Ann Vickery have written extensively about topics here. I am grateful to each of them for inquiries that, during my initial drafting stages as now, have opened new territories and piqued my thoughts.

[†] Biggs 1980, 431.

"descendents." It begins with a goddess, impregnated by Edgar Allan Poe, giving birth to Emily Dickinson and Walt Whitman. These siblings, since "they were half divine" and "could do anything they wanted," together begat William Carlos Williams, Ezra Pound and T.S. Eliot. With a few more goddesses and Gertrude Stein thrown into the mix, a third generation — Frank O'Hara, Philip Whalen and Charles Olson — arrived. "Anyway," Notley continues, "it was striking how there were no females in this generation" and that the children of Olson and his brothers were all male. That is, until O'Hara and Whalen, "the male-females,"

> produced a second wave of children of which there were many females. These females could not understand how they came to be born — they saw no one among their parents & brothers who resembled them physically, for the goddesses their fathers mated with were evaporative non-parental types. As a matter of fact these females couldn't even believe that their fathers *were* their fathers. (Notley 1980, n.p.)

In several ways, Notley radically revises standard genealogies that circumscribe possibilities in the poetic field.[*] On the one hand, in following a lineage transcribed in Donald Allen's 1960 anthology *The New American Poetry*, which introduced O'Hara, Whalen and Olson to a larger reading public and introduced a rift into a more or less codified tradition of American poetry, Notley renews that lineage; by 1980, the genealogy that ran like a backbone through poetry workshops across the United States was more apt to acknowledge Lowell, Berryman or Bishop. On the other hand, Notley's lineage relates a generation of women to the alternative small press practices that had, in the previous two decades, made not only their appearance, but that of their immediate "ancestors," possible. Further, this generation of emergent, "newly formed" women poets in the second wave of the mimeo revolution serves as an allusion to the crucial role of women poet-editors (for example, Lyn Hejinian, who published Notley's talk on Tuumba Press, or Notley herself).

In 1980 such an observation was historically acute. Throughout the 1970s, the Women's Movement, the rise of feminist scholarship, and a first wave of post-War women poet-editors had changed the American (family) tree of avant-garde poetry. For the first time, it came to include many women and not just one or two. A few of them uttered the 'f' word, but to others it signified the populist, voice-oriented feminist poetics of the

---

[*] The notion of the field, a spatialized notion of poetic production, is borrowed from Pierre Bourdieu's *The Field of Cultural Production* (NY: Columbia UP, 1993).

Women's Movement which were incongruent with "inherited" experimental practices. Notley's observation was clarifying; a situation where women poets were primarily understood in relation to a populist feminist poetics made its formulation and publication necessary. With the feminist project, mastered by critics such as Elaine Showalter, Sandra Gilbert, and Susan Gubar, recovering an exclusively "female tradition" in literature just then underway, the existence of an alternative lineage available to women poets could introduce new poetic possibilities and provide another way of conceiving the shape of American poetry.

In 1980, finally one could look back and ask: was there a peculiar 'feminine weakness' that Dickinson and Stein, prolific and persistent, and in print through their own devices, overcame? Or a peculiarly 'masculine persuasive force' to be reckoned with? As for example is evident in the critical work of Ezra Pound, who in the space of a few paragraphs (confusedly? purposefully?) refers to Marianne Moore and Mina Loy as "women" and "girls."[*] For the first time in the history of this lineage, one could look back and, seeing that literary history had been predominantly a history of men's writing and publishing activities, see also that the absence of women writers was not due to a lack of women writing, but a structural effect of institutions that produced poetic activity as male.

Women in the United States have always labored in the *trade* of typesetting, participating in family-run printing shops and, later, when custom (and law) would allow, working alongside men as professional type-setters and, eventually, editors and publishers.[†] But with few exceptions women's work was subsumed to a masculine order of production. This was true also in literary communities, where women's contributions to the textual productions — poetry, criticism, manifestoes, etc. — of avant-garde movements had been limited or only partially visible. Feminist scholarship since the 1970s has rectified many elisions, revealing a range of activities that regender literary-historical landscapes. But it is the contemporary production of poetry, as through selection and mechanical *re*-production, the making-public — a sort of engine (like the kachuking mimeograph machine) that works on the poetry individuals produce — that offers up to archivists, readers and scholars the lay of those literary-historical landscapes. Editing, as an act of insertion and assertion, makes visible affiliations and dialogues, and redefines the legitimate and the utterable, the individual and the community — all that occupies and constitutes fields of literary production. Since literary historians look largely to (and selectively through) written documentation,

---

[*] Both were most decidedly women, and well on their way to becoming established poets.

[†] See Biggs 1980.

recognition amongst one's contemporaries without representation in contemporary print production is tantamount to erasure. And those documents that often represent the smallest gestures — such as chapbooks, broadsides, postcards and little magazines — mere ephemera in the eyes of custodians of literary history, are easily effaced.

Increasingly, women poet-editors have occupied the field of poetic production, constructing though their work a productive relation to innovative poetic discourses. Since 1953 — when Daisy Aldan began co-editing *Folder*, a major outlet for New York avant-garde poets and artists, with Richard Miller, and continuing through the 1960s as Diane di Prima, Margaret Randall, Rosmarie Waldrop, Anne Waldman, and Bernadette Mayer co-edited little magazines and small presses (usually with a husband or lover) — women poet-editors have started over 70 such ventures devoted to innovative poetry, almost half of these since 1990 alone.[*] Looking back, one might say that post-war women poet-editors have done well to rejuvenate an occupation dormant in the United States since *The Little Review*, founded in 1914 by Margaret Anderson (and edited with Jane Heap since 1921), and *The Dial*, which had been under the editorship of Marianne Moore since 1925, both published their last issues in 1929[†]; or since Margaret Fuller co-edited (with Ralph Waldo Emerson) *The Dial* (1840-44) and Harriet Monroe founded and published *Poetry* (1911-25). But as Notley's lineage suggests, such a connection is deceptively simple. Claiming these women as feminist foremothers is problematic, for though they catalyzed poetic discourse, "for the most part these were editors who happened to be women" (Biggs 1983, 4). Moore's allegiance, for example, was to the magazine as an institution rather than to the possibilities poetry presented to other women poets.[‡] But with a shift in both centers and ideologies of poetic production and a concurrent increase in the concentration of women in the role of poet-editor, the phenomenon of poetic change takes on new significance.

Women poet-editors pose a challenge to extant mechanisms of poetic production. They can't simply enter a field of production structured on their exclusion. Through experiments in writing, editing and publishing, women don't take up a position in the field but enter by opening and changing it. Thus, for example, it is not simply that more women publishers will enable more women to write and publish poetry, but that fields of production are themselves transformed to become inclusive of what might otherwise be unrecog-

---

[*] This figure includes small presses equitably co-edited with men. See Appendix C.

[†] Perhaps not coincidentally, this date marks the end of an era of literary journalism and the consequent academization of poetry by the New Critics. See Golding, chapter 3, "The New Criticism and American Poetry in the Academy."

[‡] See Jayne E. Marek, *Women Editing Modernism*, Lexington: UP of Kentucky, 1995.

nizable or unacceptable as poetic production. Women poet-editors effect not a quantitative expansion (reconfiguring the ratio of male to female writers) but outmode mechanisms that traditionally define the field — the labeling, for example, of women as "girls." Aside from shedding light on the backward glance of literary history, the innovative small press circumvents belittling *re*-presentations by enabling the presentation of various figures in the poetic field.

It is difficult to realize the extent to which contemporary poetics are shaped by the small press when one looks at recent innovative works such as Kathleen Fraser's *il cuore : the heart, Selected Poems 1970-95* (Wesleyan UP, 1998), Alice Notley's *The Descent of Alette* (Penguin, 1996), and Susan Howe's *Frame Structures: Early Poems 1974-1979* (New Directions, 1996), to name but three contemporary poets published by established presses.[*] These poets were initially small press poets, and what we now call innovative poetry was at its inception 'unpoetic' in the eyes of the majority in the field of poetic production. These poets, partly because they experimented, but also because they were women, found receptive and critical communities in the small press. Fraser's work had appeared with a variety of presses, from Tuumba (*Magritte Series*, 1977) to Em Press (*Wing*, 1995); Notley first published sections from *The Descent of Alette* as "from an untitled long poem" in *Scarlet* (1990); and two early works of Howe's, *Hinge Picture* (1974) and *Secret History of the Dividing Line* (1978), were published with Telephone Books — all works produced and re-produced by women. Of course, as Notley's lineage reminds us, men did/do this too, and male-edited presses did/do contribute to proliferating work by women poets.

Nonetheless, there is a history of women small-press editors that may reveal a thing or two about the 'production' of contemporary innovative poetics. And the fact of "more women" remains — there *are* more women writing, editing, and publishing. Undoubtedly the increased involvement of women poet-editors since WWII constitutes a making "wild" of the culturally domesticated relationship of woman and machine. She reconfigures and de-privatizes this relationship: from the confidential secretarial communique of dictaphones, typewriters, intercoms and the domestic intimacy of clotheswashers, vacuum cleaners and televisions to the public/a(c)tion of editing and printing. Thus engaged, women poet-editors enter avant-garde practice and production as agents of change rather than as its unchanging object — 'Woman' — a status which Stein and Dickinson, persistent and in their own ways *in print*, defy.[†] The absent fathers to whom Notley alludes in her

---

[*] A commercial, university, and a larger small press, respectively.

[†] For example, Surrealist fetishization of the female body. Particularly pertinent are Man Ray's 1933 photographs

genealogy become the 'fathering' of texts and the furthering of poetic practice by a generation of un-domesticated women — "half divine" and able to do "anything they wanted."

II. "WITH A PRINTING PRESS A REVOLUTION" : A SHORT MIMEO REVOLUTION HISTORY UP TO ABOUT 1968

"One of the beautiful things about mimeo is the sense of community. People collated and stapled and took copies to hand around." —Maureen Owen on *Telephone*

"Probably the most important thing about the summer of '63 in San Francisco wasn't so much going down to Gino & Carlo's but seeing the books that were coming out, the White Rabbit Press books. Books like "The wood climb down out of . . . ." by Harold Dull and George Stanley's "Pony Express Riders." And I remember Steve Lovi taking me to the Auerhan Press, and meeting Andrew Hoyem and Dave Haselwood, and looking around and realizing that a community of poets could exist through the actual writing and publishing of the work, and that the social scene — the back of the bar — was secondary to this other activity." —Lewis Warsh[*]

"If the invention of the printing press inaugurated the bourgeois era, the time is at hand for its repeal by the mimeograph, the only fitting, the unobtrusive means of dissemination." —Theodor Adorno, *Minima Moralia*

THE COLD WAR IN AMERICA was an epoch of technical advancement, energy, and, for some, optimism, for others, ideological embattlement — and textual proliferation. For fledgling small press publishers, revolution was in the ink. It was the mimeo revolution, that post-Second World War moment when print technology zoomed on — the photocopier replaced the mimeograph, offset replaced letterpress — and outmoded production

---

of painter Meret Oppenheim, naked and ink-besmeared, next to painter Louis Marcoussis' etching press — not to operate it, but to be operated on by it. In one photograph Marcoussis is forcing her into the rollers, as if to make a print of her.

[*]Interviewed by Ed Foster in *Talisman*18 (Fall 1998: Lewis Warsh Issue).

machinery freely or cheaply available enabled left-revolutionaries to produce and distribute their own texts, and to demand and prepare for (sometimes quite coincidentally) a transformation of the existing political and social order — including that of poetry (Fulton 25). As a sort of palimpsest, on the very machines that were worked to produce exclusive (and exclusively male) histories — including literary histories — new possibilities were written into the field of poetic production.

> In the early sixties . . . the quotes from printers were completely unaffordable, but we found we could buy a small letterpress for $100. We [Keith and Rosmarie Waldrop] had stumbled into a moment of technological development when offset printing had proved cheaper than letterpress, so printshops all over the country were dumping their machines. And more and more small presses sprang up, not all using letterpress, but in the early days a good many [did so] because this particular technology was accessible (as is now computer typesetting). I remember a bookseller in Ann Arbor whose eyes lit up when we told him about the press: "With a mimeo you can start a party, with a printing press a revolution." It is not quite a revolution, but it very quickly became more than just a few kooks printing little books. (Waldrop 1990, 62)

Whether spawned by mimeograph or letterpress production, the collective effort of small press editors has come to be called the *mimeo* revolution, connoting the machinic aspect of the period. But it was also a *basement* revolution — a revolution of place and of foundations. A crucial aspect of both machines is that they are relatively small and operable manually (in someone's basement, say). Where friends assembled materials were assembled. Annabel Lee, for example, started Vehicle Editions "as an enthusiastic cottage industry," using the printing press at the nearby Center for Book Arts, binding books in the kitchen and storing them under the bed (Clay & Phillips 225). For the independent small press editor, every decision is geared toward keeping costs low. At a time when the copy shop didn't exist and there was no xerox-in-the-workplace, another cost effective option, when there was no established distribution network such as Small Press Distribution and The Segue Foundation,[*] poet-friends who helped with assembly helped circulate the mimeo-zine hand to hand. If mailed, a magazine might be accompanied by appeals for postage stamps and other such donations, unless one was able, as many were in the 1970s, to secure a

---

[*]SPD was established in 1969 and The Segue Foundation in 1977. See Appendix C.

federal or state arts grant. "Subscription" doesn't seem to have existed in the small press lexicon of the time and would've been a bit of an albatross anyway; the small press didn't run on guarantees but on promises, and presses and serials were subject to short lifespans. But for all its privations, in "a time where contemporaneity meant everything" (Fulton 31), mimeo production disseminated new work *fast*. It was a mechanism primarily for the community of writers, and vice versa: the community functioned together to keep their inspiriting duplicating fluids flowing.

Though distinct machines and mediums (mimeo, letterpress, xerox, offset, desktop publishing and the internet) produce distinct products, they are interchangeably referred to as "small press," an elision which publisher and historian Len Fulton refers to as a "liquidizing (not liquidating) of traditional boundaries between genres and media" (25). For poets disinterested in the demands of New Criticism, then the prevalent strain in literarily high-minded academic quarterlies,[*] the mimeograph was "the most important modern technological development for writing and reading . . . enabl[ing] 'literary' and other writing a relative freedom from constraints" (Bernstein 1986, 354). As an alternative to professional, out-of-house printshops it introduced various editorial freedoms. (Imagine Ed Sanders, for instance, contracting a printer for *Fuck You: A Magazine of the Arts*.) Throughout the 1950s and 1960s in New York, in Chicago, at Black Mountain College, and in San Francisco (male) poets edited *Yugen*[†]*, "C," Beatitude, Big Table, The Black Mountain Review, Caterpillar, Open Space, Contact, The San Francisco Review* and *J*, to name a few. These little magazines often published new poetry alongside informal commentary and criticism, staging "a redefinition in [the] *process* [of] . . . the austere and isolated scholarship of the university" (Fulton 25). Along with small presses (such as Corinth Books, Totem Press, and The Jargon Society), they cultivated the "New American Poetry" figured in Allen's influential anthology, catalyzing the "anthology wars" that signified a rift in formal understandings of American Poetry. As Alan Golding notes, "the book's tone and contents assailed the walls of the academically established canon, eventually broke them down"(32) as poets like Charles Olson and Robert Creeley were admitted.

---

[*] Such as *The Kenyon Review, The Chicago Review, Prairie Schooner* and *The Southern Review*. According to Daisy Aldan, "there were [in the mid-fifties] about forty-two literary magazines in the whole country" (264).

[†] Hettie Jones served as the assistant editor for number 6-8, but such a byline inadequately depicts the extent to which Jones worked to help produce the "new." See my essay "On Seeing Poetic Production: The Case of Hettie Jones," *Open Letter* (11th series, number 1, Spring 2001).

These, however, were almost exclusively *men's* battles. A woman's odds for inclusion were slim.* The battles of the revolution were predominantly fought against censorship, contra McCarthy-era conformity to a status quo represented by quarterlies. In the fall of 1959, for example, an issue of the *Chicago Review* featuring a chapter from William Burrough's *Naked Lunch* and "two brief but significantly articulate letters about the Beat movement by Allen Ginsberg," had been castigated as "filth" by a columnist of the *Chicago Daily News*, effectively forcing University of Chicago overseers to demand the cessation of Beat literature publication under their auspices (Michelson). The following spring editors Paul Carroll and John Logan resigned and independently published the first issue of *Big Table*, featuring "The Complete Contents of the Suppressed Winter 1959 Chicago Review," as the cover prominently announced. And in October of 1961, co-editors Diane di Prima and LeRoi Jones of *The Floating Bear* were indicted by the FBI on charges of mailing obscene material. In yet another "man's" battle, Jones defended their publication of his homoerotic play *From the System of Dante's Hell* and Burroughs' *Routine*. di Prima provides an account of his heroic performance: "he brought in a ton of stuff that had one time or another been labeled 'obscene' . . . he read for hours to the grand jury, and they refused to return an indictment" while di Prima's lawyer, taking advantage of her barely perceptible state of pregnancy, "went rushing around insisting that clerks move out of their offices so [she] could sit down and rest" (di Prima xv). This example serves as a reminder that though grassroots activism and federal initiatives were then reconfiguring women's relationship to such power structures,[†] in the battle over what could and could not be in print, a woman still occupied her traditional place off to the side.

In an era unprepared to address difference, when the battles turned to address gender (though they seldom did), the results were notorious. In January 1958, Denise Levertov, making a guest appearance at San Francisco State University's Poetry Center, was greeted with Jack Spicer's reading of "For Joe" ("People who don't like the smell of faggot vomit/Will never understand why men don't like women"). Though hardly indicative of the larger poetic community ("all present felt implicated in Spicer's misogyny" [Ellingham & Killian 124]), which included Helen Adam, Joanne Kyger and Madeline Gleason, and

---

*Four women (out of 44) appeared in the anthology, and two (out of 22) on the "New American Poetry Circuit" of 1967 that was developed as a mechanism for distributing the new poetry through managing individual readings on college campuses. For a list of authors on the ill-fated circuit, see ads in *Caterpillar* 10 or 11 (1967). See "Anthology Wars" in Rasula (pp.223-247) for contemporary responses to Allen's anthology.

[†]Such as the founding of the National Organization of Women (NOW), the Women's Equity Action League (WEAL) and Federally Employed Women (FEW), and the Kennedy Commission's 1963 Report on American Women.

came to include Levertov herself, his public 'name-calling' (the poem included the lines "The female genital organ is / hideous") remains notorious among contemporary poets.[*] Men *did* vastly outnumber women in poetic communities of the 1950s and 1960s, and where individual subcultures and coteries encouraged and have preserved women poets in name, image and deed, scholarly biases have mislabeled and misplaced women of a generation, subsuming them under the imagined identity of the "woman beat."[†] It is easy to imagine that women of that period remained somewhat insular, absorbed in their work and the work of their male peers, as there is as yet little ground from which to recognize the existence of women's poetic practices as such. Were she encouraged to write and publish, she could find no courage in her circumstances to be contrary; she could not support herself as a university lecturer (as did Spicer, Robert Duncan, and Charles Olson, for example) or with her female beatnik charm.

The gender exclusive nature of the poetic field influenced editorial practices. *The Floating Bear*, tireless and vital, and for long stretches published by di Prima solo, brought only about 16 women into print.[‡] It seems to be impossible to come to anything but a near-estimate of the number of women writing and submitting work at a time when women's work was rarely published. In *Folder*, for example, "some [women] gave themselves male names or used initials." Women's work may have been published, but beneath the mask of the masculine it would not be recognized as such. A woman who wished to enter the public space of print did so at the cost of the imprint of gender. *Folder* "published many women," enough so that Aldan "actually made a list of women poets for an intended anthology, which [she] never accomplished" (a fact that the contents of *Folder* won't attest to [Aldan 269]). The suppression of writing marked "female" by Aldan, a woman editor aware of contemporary prohibitions, reflects the lack of urgency — or agency — to promote a body of work that would reflect the extent to which women were developing writing practices. Even more incomprehensible would have been the development of a poetic particularly concerned with writing by women. Though Aldan published women, "It was not that [she] wished to take up the standard for women. It was because the work of many fine women

---

[*] See Ellingham & Killian, pp. 124-127, for a contextualized reading of Spicer's misogyny.

[†] See my essay "On Seeing Poetic Production: The Case of Hettie Jones," *Open Letter* (11th series, number 1, Spring 2001).

[‡] Though a tally of female names could hardly be said to reflect the actual number of women contributors as many published under pseudonyms — often for fear of not getting published. di Prima's Poet's Press, which produced 12 books between 1965 and 1968, including one by Audre Lorde and five by herself, was similarly weighted toward literary output by men.

poets came to [her] attention, and good women poets were among [her] friends, and [she] felt they should be published" (269).

Throughout the 1960s, the mimeo revolution was changing the face of American poetry written by men. The infamous Berkeley Poetry Conference of 1965, a "gathering of the poetry tribes," brought together for the first time poets, poet-editors, and publications that had been until then more or less distinct geographically and aesthetically. The atmosphere was still exclusive: "women in general were not given much to do at the Conference, except to host parties, take photos, have sex with the poets, and make up the majority of the audience" (Ellingham & Killian 345-46). Anne Waldman would later comment that "there were hardly any women . . . Lenore Kandel stood out," and yet it was there that she met Lewis Warsh, future lover and co-editor of *Angel Hair*, which would present a younger and more-traveled perspective of the New American Poetry — "poets of the New York School and . . . West Coast writers like Robert Duncan [and] Joanne Kyger . . . along with [their] own friends, and the few poets [they] knew" (Clay & Phillips 179).

The small press set about organizing its constituents as the 1960s came to a close in the belief that, as Allen Ginsberg had put it, "The solitary activity that we indulge in does have large historical results" (De Loach 106). By 1968, the newly organized Committee of Small Magazine Editors and Publishers (COSMEP) had held three annual conferences. At the 1972 conference in Madison, Wisconsin, frustrations over the "solitary activity" that women editors were indulging in would come to the fore: "many women who had traveled great distances to get there did not get enough notice and rebelled and said nothing was happening and they felt uneasy talking to the men . . . Carol Bergé [editor of *Center*, a little magazine of innovative fiction and dance and art criticism] stood up and made this point and that was the start of the women's movement at COSMEP" (Kruchkow 235). Throughout the 1970s, developing feminisms did exert pressure on scholarship, on women's representation in the poetic field, and on women's innovative practices. But because of the androcentrism of poetics and scholarship that developed in the wake of the New American Poetry, the work women have done to open the field of poetic possibilities has remained in the shadows. Diane di Prima's *The Floating Bear* and Poet's Press, Margaret Randall's *El Corno Emplumado/The Plumed Horn*[*] ("one of the decade's largest and most important magazines" [Fulton 34]), the Waldrops' Burning Deck Press, Anne Waldman's *Angel Hair* and *The World*, and Bernadette Mayer's *0 to 9* and *United Artists* were all significant to the communi-

---

[*] Anti-establishment, expatriate, avant garde, and bilingual, *El Corno Emplumado* perhaps best represents mimeo revolution political ethics, publishing poets from North America and Latin America until political unrest after the 1968 student uprising forced Randall into hiding and eventually out of Mexico.

ties of poets in which they engaged. But these women, all *co*-editors,[*] were exceptions; for the most part "women sent out their work," if they sent it out at all, "and waited to be taken up by powerful male editors and mentors who were willing to discover them and authenticate their reality as writers" (Fraser 1993, 57). In the coming years, the small press, party or revolution, and the poetic field it represented, would change in and through the shifting balance of gender.

III: "A 'HIDDEN' COMMUNITY OF WORKERS SUCH AS MYSELF": PRODUCTION BETWEEN POPULIST FEMINIST POETICS AND THE AVANT-GARDE

". . . when a baby cried, [Adrienne Rich] stopped. Talked about the years she wasn't able to go to poetry readings because of her children. She asked if there was a man in the audience who would take care of the baby so that its mother could stay and listen, so that women would be able to hear the poem." —Frances Jaffer, "For Women Poets, For Poetry: A Journal Entry"

". . . in 1969, and in the eye of a new storm of feminism, my lover Wendy Cadden and I helped to found the gay women's liberation movement on the West Coast. We discovered that women love poetry which is true to our own experience, and art which helps us see ourselves without masks. We also found that the independent women's presses are the foundation of women's literature. They have made it possible to speak the unspeakable, to reveal what has had to be hidden, to redefine the experiences of women, and the connections among us." —Judy Grahn, *The Work of a Common Woman*

"Once you've said you're an 'editor' and once your magazine comes out a few times, you are *valid* — you are asserting yourself, and serving others." —Alice Notley on starting *Chicago* in 1972

"The reward for asserting a vision is to become visible, to participate actively in the wider literary conversation and to help in creating a community that has been

---

[*] All of these serials were at some point co-edited by men. See Appendix C.

waiting to come into view. It turns out, in our [the editors of *HOW(ever)*] case, that there have been many women like us feeling isolated for years, excluded from the aesthetic or political mandates of existing poetics." —Kathleen Fraser, "The Tradition of Marginality"

W̲ HEN WOMEN BEGAN TO RECOGNIZE the correlations between the public, the private, and gender privileges and oppressions, the poem was embraced as an emancipatory vehicle from which women's personal (and political) dissatisfactions and demands could be expressed. Throughout the 1970s the poem and its public reading were occasions for 'consciousness-raising' and a realization of women's political agency. Through poetry, women enacted an ethics of exchange, mutual listening that was essential to the developing Women's Movement. Scholars and poets, often inspired by their writing groups, emerged onto the fields of poetic and literary-historical production with a set of particular, gendered concerns: in what way does the history of poetry conceal women's voices and realities? And how might poetry serve as an expressive political tool, as a meter of self-awareness and liberation? Judy Grahn's insistence that "[w]omen must define what our poetry is" (24) was echoed in Adrienne Rich's summons to "try to find language and images for a consciousness we are just coming into" (Rich 35), a consciousness highly critical of ancient myths and beauty myths alike. Grahn called her first "woman-produced, mimeographed" book *Edward the Dyke and Other Poems* because "it meant people had to say the word *dyke*" (24) — that it would be part of, in Rich's words, a "common language."

Publishing activities that grew out of this new oral medium were consciously *feminist* activities, a result of the growing awareness that the male-dominated press, like other patriarchal power structures, afforded women scant opportunities for participation. "Women had to create their own presses and they did — very nearly from scratch" (Biggs 1983, 5). Taking over the means of small press production, like taking over conventionally androcentric poetic structures, was self-consciously counter-cultural. A self-styled, outspoken, outlaw status was reflected in the names they chose for their magazines and presses — shameless hussy, mama, wyrd woman, amazon, common woman, muse. Throughout the decade of the 1970s, at least one explicitly feminist little magazine devoted to politicizing and validating women's experiences hit the streets each year.[*] In New York and the Bay

---

[*] *Ie.* Shameless Hussy Press, Mama's Press, and Wyrd Press. A partial list of little magazines includes: *Black Maria*, 1971; *Amazon Quarterly*, 1972; *13th Moon*, and *51%*, 1973; *Sojourner*, 1974; *Letras Feminas*, *Primavera* and *The Wild Iris*, 1975; *Calyx*, *Sinister Wisdom* and *Room*, 1976; *Bloodroot*, *Common Woman* and *Conditions*, 1977; *Sing Heavenly Muse!*, and *Heresies*,

Area, women's bookstores stocked many quickly and inexpensively produced staple-bound books, pamphlets and little magazines. It was not only *literary* feminist publications that published poetic alternatives to existing political and literary discourses; nearly *all* feminist publications did: various city- and campus-based "women's liberation" newsletters, feminist academic journals, and 'commercial' magazines such as *Ms.* all published poetry, and, it wouldn't be too much to say, with a vengeance.

Many women writing did so against a political backdrop that could be as limiting as it was liberating. Tina Darragh felt at the time that "[v]ictimhood was the basis for the form and content of poetry, and was valorized as the source of combination political statement/personal identities" (Darragh 1998, 696). The atmosphere could be indifferent (and even hostile) to a writer whose interests lay in experimenting with language rather than focusing on the verbal validation a poem might offer. Experimental poetry by women, though it too explored women's relationships to culture, was by many dismissed. What good, one might ask, was *The Woman Who Could Read the Mind of Dogs* that Leslie Scalapino would dwell on so? What good Rochelle Owens' 'wild-woman' who ranted "VIVA WILD-MAN" in *Poems From Joe's Garage*? And what to make of Joanne Kyger, writing *Places To Go*, critical of such ideological inflections: "I think of people *sighing* over poetry, *using* it, I / don't know what it's for" — what good was that?[*] Though politically radical in the preferred *content* of poetic utterances, feminist editors were aesthetically conservative and, ironically, the spaces that they were creating to open communication, like the patriarchal lines they'd set out to subvert, proved impermeable to other sorts of women writers: "ranks appeared to close, rather than open, as the powerful ideology of a 'common language' took hold" (Fraser 1992). For an experimental woman poet there were two visible alternatives — populist feminist poetics and the avant-garde — and, refusing or unable to identify with either camp, she was a hybrid like the 'woman poet' in the 19th century — vexing either category, herself excluded (self-excluded) from both.[†]

With ideas and methodologies that were not feminist enough for feminists and/or not masculine enough for the avant-garde, many poet-editors set out to provide alternative

---

1978.

[*]These three books were published in 1976 (Sand Dollar: Berkeley CA), 1973 (Burning Deck Press: Providence RI), and 1970 (Black Sparrow Press: Los Angeles CA), respectively.

[†]The extent to which particular innovative women poets negotiated ideological and social contentions between populist feminist poetics and avant-garde poetics of course varied, and many would ultimately bring their feminism to bear on their experimental poetic tendencies and vice versa — a phenomenon which would only become visible as the number of women who published their work grew.

spaces to encounter and construct — and thus legitimize and develop — intellectual and artistic communities. At least 11 women-edited little magazines and 7 presses commenced publication in the 1970s and by 1979 over 47 new women poets had published books with Effie's Press, Kelsey St., Five Trees, Telephone, Angel Hair Books, Tuumba and Burning Deck.[*] Though production was undoubtedly small (generally from 200-500 copies) and distribution often local, the discovery of other innovative writers created a sense of community, however "hidden." It legitimized for Tina Darragh, for instance, her commitment to "turning to words" as a response to a need for political change. "In 1974," she writes,

> there had been no Revolution . . . and I found myself turning to words and the directions they suggested to me.
>
> Naturally, I felt that I was the only one going that way, but gradually I began reading the work of others who seemed to be moving along the same lines. Given this sense of a "hidden" community of workers such as myself, I replace "the story of the revolution" with "the story of turning to words." (1998, 703)

If innovative women poets produce, according to Joan Retallack, "enactments of the feminine" rather than "images of the female" (1996, 355), publishing, too, is one such enactment. Devoted to furthering innovative explorations, a woman poet-editor enacts a feminist poetic not by creating a space specifically for women writing in a feminist/liberationist dialogue, but by inserting her editorial agenda and reshaping the field of poetic production to include different practices, priorities, and poetics — hers. Small press work provides for cross-pollination: its products ensure that individual poets and editors read and publish each other's work. In the 1970s-80s it ensured that poetry written by women was increasingly represented in the literary production of a generation. Susan Howe, for example, feels certain that if it wasn't for Maureen Owen, who published her first book *Hinge Picture* on Telephone, she wouldn't have found her poetic community or realized herself as a poet.[†] Darragh would comment retrospectively that

---

[*] Effie's Press: Carol Bergé, Beverly Dahlen; Kelsey St.: Frances Phillips, Rena Rosenwasser, Nellie Wong, Karen Brodine; Telephone: Fanny Howe, Janet Hamill, Janine Pommy-Vega, Rebecca Wright and Rebecca Brown; Angel Hair: Joanne Kyger, Anne Waldman, Bernadette Mayer and Alice Notley; Five Trees: Jaime Robles, Jane Rosenthal, Judy Katz-Levine, Susan MacDonald, Lois Steinberg; Tuumba: Susan Howe, Lyn Hejinian, Barbara Baracks, Kathleen Fraser, Carla Harryman, and Rae Armantrout; and Burning Deck: Hejinian, Rosmarie Waldrop, Barbara Guest, Dorothy Donnely, Carol LaBranche, Mary Ashley, Rochelle Owens, Nancy Condee, Marcia Southwick, Debra Bruce, Lissa McLaughlin, and Susan Hankla.

[†] Personal interview, 10/1/98.

> Whenever I pick up one of [Susan Howe's] books, I'm reminded of the endless discussion groups dealing with the topic of the 'politically correct' woman writer ... Her first book, *Hinge Picture* ... could have brought some needed clarity to our women's group discussions that grew increasingly embroiled in ideological arguments that obscured real feelings and real events, both past and present. (1986, 547)

This is not to imply that women were never published in male-edited small presses, but rather that as women published more, their interests and texts joined the discourse that is shaped through poetic communities. A detailed study of the number of presses publishing women, broken down by the editor's gender, might allow for a clearer sense of personal urgencies and prejudices, but the point here is that a dynamic was in place for a few interested and motivated individuals who felt that editing was something they could and should do alongside their poetic practices. For Lyn Hejinian, for example, her interest in starting Tuumba in 1976 was to extend her poetic inquiry and to expand ground for aesthetic discovery: "I though of it, too, as an extension of aesthetic responsibility. I had the sense that my poetics included other writing than my own, by definition. Part of the method was to include it" (Hejinian 1986, 3).

While such resources provide much-needed intellectual community, the small press *as a practice* vitalizes poetic communities as well. Production can be intensive both for the poet-editor, who must often learn new skills or come up with creative solutions. Maureen Owen relates:

> I pasted Yuki Hartman's *Hot Footsteps* up when I had taken my children to my Uncle's farm in Minnesota one summer. I rolled out a 25 gallon crock from my Grandmother's pantry, cleaned up a sheet of glass I found, and dropped a toggle light into it. Voila! a light table! I pasted the whole book up and designed the cover on the upstairs landing after I had put the kids to bed at night. I must have looked like a madwoman bent over the crock with my rulers and tweezers and rubber cement as my children snored in the next room.*

Owen's example illustrates a dynamic feminist poiesis that extends beyond the making of the poem into re-assembling the immediate materials in one's world. Working, writing,

---

*Personal correspondence, 10/6/98.

publishing, raising two children, and struggling constantly to afford mimeograph stencils and paper, Owen operated in a restricted economy that produced a generous poiesis fueled by the sensual pleasure of the do-it-yourself aesthetic:

> immediate, street wise, hands on, open to change to the last second before the machine starts to hum, and the ink sits up on the page like art. It's sensual and sexy, raw and real. Alone in the big empty church of St. Mark's late into the night with only the sound of the mimeograph 'kachuking' and the pages swishing down. (Clay & Phillips 227)

What emerges from the proliferation of these practices among women writers is a larger economy that might be thought a poetics of production: networks of advice and shared devices within and across poetic communities that increasingly displaced tradition- and feminist-led demands for normative aesthetic collaborationism with the collective peculiarities characteristic of small press activity; thus encouraging the co-existence of a wide range of aesthetic practices.

One such cohesive network — technically, aesthetically, historically, and geographically — was associated with the Poetry Project at St. Mark's Church-in-the-Bowery, established in 1966 with funding from the Office of Economic Opportunity. All New York mimeo activity of the 1960s — *Yugen*, *Floating Bear*, "*C*," *0 to 9* and *Fuck You*, for example — developed in direct relation to the Lower East Side locale. Howe's indebtedness to Owen belongs as well to St. Mark's, where Howe was drawn for free poetry workshops (she took one with Ted Greenwald); it was where Owen "met a number of poets and especially women poets who weren't getting published anywhere" and whose poems she thought "should be on the street." In the 1970s, the so-called second wave mimeo revolution was initiated with the publication of *The World* following "a lull in the little magazine blitz" (Clay & Phillips 187). This time many women editors who traversed the church's basement, where the Gestetner mimeograph machine ran off Owens' *Telephone* and Telephone Books, Waldman's *The World*, and other publishing ventures, albeit short-lived, such as Eileen Myles' *Dodgems* and Rag-on Press's sole production, *The Ladies Museum*, a satirical mimeo-anthology women poets at the Poetry Project.[*]

Even when it wasn't the center of production, the Poetry Project was a nexus for many, and often mimeo served to maintain close connections from afar. Somewhat isolated in

---

[*] For an intimate history, see Marcella Durand's "Publishing a Community: Women Publishers at the Poetry Project" in *Outlet* (1999, 4/5).

Lennox, Massachusetts, Bernadette Mayer and Lewis Warsh bought a mimeo machine and began *United Artists* in 1977 because "editing a magazine put [them] in touch with poets and friends [they] had left behind in New York" (Clay & Phillips 199). Waldman, resettling in Boulder in 1976 and homesick, bought a used mimeo machine and founded *Rocky Ledge* with Reed Bye. To Alice Notley, Ted Berrigan had suggested that she start a magazine as a way to make contacts. Temporarily displaced from New York, editing *Chicago* allowed her to create the energy and community that was crucial to maintaining her identity as 'woman poet.' She started Chicago in 1972:

> I was pregnant with our son Anselm . . . I was twenty-six and living in Chicago, and I was afraid I would have to put my career on hold, my writing . . . I wasn't thinking 'feminism' at the time but on the other hand I was thinking 'survival, of a woman poet who's about to have a baby.'*

Male figures associated with St. Mark's such as Allen Ginsberg, Jim Caroll and Ted Berrigan loom large but women poets, Notley insists, "were in charge." One mimeod little magazine, *Caveman*, had passed around, issue by issue, from editor to editor, before it fell into the hands of a group of women and came to function as a source of humor and community critique. It was a "savage publication,"

> dominated by women but too anarchic to be called feminist or anything else. The feminists savaged the feminists, this because it was an ongoing critique of the P[oetry] P[roject] (which got called the Peepee Projectile, that was our level) they were the authority which had to be flouted. So when Maureen Owen was in charge, someone wrote in *Cavemen* "if you want a reading grow tits."†

Perhaps because there was residual masculine energy to contend with, women editors were energetic, outspoken and prolific poet-editors whose strength was contagious. The Poetry Project had a "matriarchal kindliness and openness to all poets, women and men"‡ and has "stayed woman-strong" because Waldman's influence "lasted a long time both

---

*Personal correspondence, 3/12/98.

†*Caveman* was edited by Barbara Barg, Shelley Kraut, Elinor Nauen, Alice Notley, Eileen Myles, and Susie Timmons Personal correspondence, 3/12/98.

‡Maureen Owen also notes "I'm sure it didn't appear so to everyone, and for many different reasons." Personal correspondence, 10/6/98.

literally and imaginatively."* Waldman had sought out many poets in New York during the 1960s, including di Prima, Mayer, Notley and Hannah Weiner because "the sense of other women engaged in the same demanding act of writing & being a poet in what was basically, at that time, a man's world, was inspiring, encouraging." di Prima's "stamina and her seeming ability to 'do it all' as a woman" inspired Waldman, when she was working to establish the Poetry Project at St. Mark's Church, "to include more women in the programs & in the publications" (Osman & Spahr, 108-109).† A New York poet-editor of the next generation (Lee Ann Brown of Tender Buttons) remembers Waldman "saying to [her] one summer ('87) in Boulder, 'why don't you start a magazine?' . . . [Waldman] also emphasized how many great poets would not be in print if it wasn't for their friends' efforts. So [Brown] set out to do some inspirers right" (Osman & Spahr, 16). Waldman's efforts had encouraged Owen to realize herself as a poet-editor, and, like *The World*, *Telephone* fed off of and fed the community:

> Ann Waldman was bringing out *The World* . . . and it was very exciting. I started thinking about doing books and putting a magazine of my own together. I went over to St. Mark's and asked Anne if I could use the Gestetner to launch my new press . . . . I'll never forget that first page coming off the big roller. Like a miracle, the dark stencil had yielded up a page bright white with words embossed in shiny black ink . . . .. After we ran off the pages we stacked them to dry, and some days later I gathered every friend I'd made and their friends and we collated. (Clay & Phillips 227)

The urban, gritty, do-it-yourself aesthetic suited St. Mark's. It brought publishing technology to anyone's fingertips with very little technical training. Mimeo publications come in one shape and size and simply *look* like reduplicated typescript between covers, sometimes hastily, sometimes laboriously, done up with line drawings or collages by the editor or an artist friend. Ask any mimeo poet-editor and they'll tell you, it was an ethic, a way of life, a way of creating community for oneself and for giving back to one's community, of encouraging and locating poetic affinities, and of cultivating a scene. An earlier instance of this was Jack Spicer's *J*: he left a box marked "J" in his favorite bar for submis-

---

*Alice Notley, personal correspondence, 3/12/98.

†This citation refers to the "Editorial Forum" in *Chain 1* (1994) thus individual quotes may not be specified by author herewith.

sions. Mimeo was an effective community-builder in part because producing an issue, from prepping materials to machine-operation to final assembly, was laborious yet easy to learn and the product indelicate:

> 'mimeo' is a special kind of experience involving the energy of a whole community of poets to respond and, more specifically, the energy of one individual to edit, type, run off, collate, staple and distribute with the help of several friends and a few pep pills. The people editing such magazines are poets and the people reading them are poets, poets who exist in some sort of working community together. (Waldman 1969, xiii)

Mimeo built on the immediate community by bringing it 'inside' — into the space of someone's apartment, or St. Mark's basement — and turning it back out as each labor-contributor, with several copies in hand, left for local hangouts. Thus the concentration of energies literally *in* the field of production, localized around a specific effort, and the proliferation of mimeod magazines embodied the energetic tenor of the Poetry Project.

Meanwhile, with equal zeal many women in the San Francisco Bay Area were learning techniques of offset and fine letterpress printing. Kelsey St. Press's Rena Rosenwasser notes "One could easily view this period as a renaissance of the craft of printing [but this time with] women printers . . . at the hub"(Osman & Spahr 93). Unlike Poetry Project publications, these presses didn't share historical roots or common spaces, weren't handed down (like *The World* and *Caveman*) or (co-ed)ited (like all small presses of the previous decade in which women participated), and they diverged widely in ethics, aesthetics and poetics. The handful of women-edited presses that would emerge out of the demand for more experimental representation in the field of 1970s production — Kelsey St., Five Trees, Tuumba and Effie's Press — interacted with both populist feminist and avant-garde writing and publishing activities with considerable breadth. While Kelsey St. and Five Trees both operated on feminist co-operative principals, Kelsey St. focused on the poetry of contemporary innovative women writers and Five Trees reprinted fine editions of H.D. and Djuna Barnes as well as publishing contemporaries Levertov and Charles Olson.[*] As for individually run presses, Bonnie Carpenter's Effie's Press published women exclusively, while Hejinian's prolific Tuumba, like contemporary little magazines *Big Deal* (ed. Barbara

---

[*] Kelsey St. is no longer a co-operative, but it is the only press of these four still in operation. Founding members were Karen Brodine, Patricia Dienstfrey, Kit Duane, Marina la Palma, Laura Moriarty, and Rena Rosenwasser. Five Trees was founded by Eileen Callahan, Cameron Folson, Cheryl Miller, Jaime Robles and Kathy Walkup.

Baracks) and *Gnome Baker* (ed. Madeline Burnsides and Andrew Kelly), and *Matchbook* (ed. Joyce Holland), and, later, *QU* (ed. Carla Harryman), focused on experimentation rather than gender politics.

On the West Coast, production was not centralized as in New York. The Poetry Center at San Francisco State served as a nucleus for readings and workshops, but print community was often constructed from scratch, from the inside out, so to speak. Primarily because operating a letterpress is a skilled trade, and books, often "fine press" editions, are carefully assembled, press work is more likely to be carried on solo, and the printer is usually detail-oriented. Each page is assembled character by character, space by space, inked by hand and pressed onto paper with a manually-operated machine. ("It took time. We were slow. But our hands locked the metal type into the press's bed, pushed the rollers over the type until the desired impression was exacted on the paper" [Rossenwasser in Osman & Spahr 93]). When production necessarily exceeded the space and the unwritten laws of a tight-knit community often encountering the 'outside' meant encountering cultural prejudices. In New York in 1954, for example, when someone entered the print shop where she was at work Daisy Aldan "had to stop ... because women were not allowed in the union then and the printer would have been suspended or fined" (268). Though that had changed to some extent in the 1970s (Annabel Lee, who used the letterpress at the Center for Book Arts, had worked in a union offset printing shop), for Lyn Hejinian learning letter press in 1976 was a flashback to a more prohibitive era:

> In order to learn how to print, I invented a job for myself in a print shop of a local printer. The shop was in Willits, California — a small rural town with an economy based on cattle ranching and logging; the owner of the shop (the printer, Jim Case) was adamant that 'printing ain't for girls,' but he took me on three afternoons a week as the shop's cleaning lady. (Clay & Phillips 257)

Work wasn't always isolating; though the *manual* production required for fine presswork is often solitary and physically demanding, its technical intricacy and flexibility required a certain amount of outreach. A poetics of production arose out of a need for practical advice and aesthetic guidance which would bring fledgling publishers like Patricia Dienstfrey (of Kelsey St.) and Hejinian into contact with their contemporaries. Kathy Walkup (of Five Trees) and Johanna Drucker "taught [Hejinian] a few essentials and a number of tricks" about typesetting (Clay & Phillips 257). Rosmarie Waldrop, who'd been publishing for over a decade, and Barbara Baracks were to influence Hejinian aesthetically and provide continued encouragement and advice.

A poetics of production also arose from the inside out in the case of the women's writing groups that formed bases for founding little magazines and presses. The same year Tuumba was established, "the excitement of sharing ... work each week" made the editors of *Room* "aware of the need for more dialogue among women who write."* And for the members of Kelsey St. their writing group contributed to their growing awarenesses of women's absence — from canonical omissions to similar inequities in current publishing practices. When a 1970 anthology, *San Francisco Bay Area Poets*, came out, for example, the fact that there wasn't one woman included would not be overlooked.† This fact, along with the group's awareness of the limited scope of women's writing available, would encourage Kelsey St. to stray from the feminist poetic party line to publish writing they as a group valued — writing that was approaching issues of identity in new ways. Co-founding a press with this purpose in mind "was a means of questioning the centrality of the male figure in writing" (Osman & Spahr 92). Working from a small community out into a larger community of writers and readers, Kelsey St. developed an outreach-ethic, considering the impact their cognitive and material productions (book selection and design) might have, and worked to establish a women's literary salon in the Bay Area.‡ Co-editor Patricia Dienstfrey laments that in preserving few records from the 1970s they "lacked perspective on [their] possibilities for a good part of [their] publishing life." But they could hardly have foreseen the significance they would develop to institutions such as the New York Public Library division of special collections and the Bancroft Library at the University of California, Berkeley.

Unlike most presses of the 1970s, Hejinian's Tuumba Press didn't arise out of a need to serve a particular community of women though she did enact her feminism as editor and poet; she asserted (and inserted) herself into an overwhelmingly male writing community. Along with little magazines such as *L=A=N=G=U=A=G=E*, *This*, *Tottel's*, *Hills*, Tuumba became central to the development of so-called Language Poetry, a 'group' uncatagorically united by its various avant-garde theoretical forays. The idea of "perceiver-centered" writing was for Hejinian implicitly feminist (and revolutionary). In *Poetics Journal*, a subse-

---

*"Editor's Note," *Room* 1.1 (1976).

†Personal correspondence with Patricia Dienstfrey, 3/1/98.

‡Dienstfrey comments that though it never developed, "for a year, many committed and articulate women — professors, artists, lawyers, poets, of different races and classes and sexual orientations — met to define what this salon might be, and what the crucial issues were." *Ibid*.

quent publication she co-edited with Barrett Watten, Hejinian noted that making texts "open to the world and particularly to the reader, invites participation, rejects the authority of the writer over the reader and thus, by analogy, the authority implicit in other (social, economic, cultural) hierarchies" (Hejinian 1998, 619).

Hejinian, too, worked from the inside out, "looking to various modes of 'experimental,' 'innovative,' or 'avant-garde' writing for information." Between 1976-84, Tuumba produced 50 "pamphlets," a term she preferred over "chapbook" because she "wanted the Tuumba books to come to people in the mode of 'news'" (Clay & Phillips 257). And though publishing Tuumba was physically and intellectually a "solo venture," it was not a solitary one. Community meant not many hands ink-stained hands but many minds:

> I had no partner(s) or assistant(s) but [Tuumba] was not . . . private [or] solitary; I had come to realize that poetry exists not in isolation (alone on its lonely page) but in transit, as experience, in the social worlds of people. For poetry to exist, it has to be given meaning, and for meaning to develop there must be communities of people thinking about it. Publishing books as I did was a way of contributing to such a community — even a way of helping invent it. (Clay & Phillips 257)

The impulse behind mimeo revolution publications was, from the start, to create community around otherwise unrepresented concerns. In the case of *under*-represented women writers, the small press created spaces to make representation possible, enabling accumulation and recognition, and, eventually, the sort of dialogues and diatribes that lead to critiques and critical theories of poetic praxis. Undoubtedly the increasing number of women poets and editors played an important role in defining for numerous poets a political engagement with poetry, a 'turning to words' that found information in the newly available work of other innovative women poets. Though "hidden" throughout the1970s by the more visible and vociferous poetics of the Women's Movement, women poet-editors continued moving out into larger and more inclusive communities. By the end of the decade work by innovative women was available in unprecedented quantities, yet it's clear that those willing or wanting to publish remained comparatively small in number, and, as in the male-dominated presses, more men were published; women-operated presses of this period published more than twice as many books by men as by women.[*] That's not to say that these editors were less feminist or more avant-garde. Against a backdrop of prohibitive

---

[*] Five Trees published at least 4; Telephone, at least 8 Angel Hair, at least 35; Tuumba 18; and Burning Deck at least 70.

literary history, asserting one's editorial position, as well as writing and agreeing to have one's work read and published — insomuch as these amount to an exercise of agency — is a feminist undertaking. The appearance of these writers and editors upset the prevalence of a set of top-heavy relations (subject/object, speaker/listener, viewer/viewed) and served to fully deconstruct the hegemonic order of feminist realism and masculinist innovation that preceded it. This in itself is revolutionary.*

IV. WHEN WE AWAKEN THE DEAD (AROUND 1979): LITERARY HISTORY, LITERARY HERSTORY, *HOW(ever)*, AND AFTER

"In 1978 Charles Bernstein asked me to write an essay responding to the question, "Why don't more women do language-oriented writing?" The first answer that came to mind was that, as an oppressed group, women have a more urgent need to describe the conditions of their lives. This answer, however, seemed rather facile. It implied, for instance, that there was another (that is, non-language centered) poetic style in use which could fully and clearly represent the nature of women's oppression . . . .. The question of how best to represent women's social position remained open, and the answer must depend on what one assumed the cause of that position to be." —Rae Armantrout, "Feminist Poetics and the Meaning of Clarity"

"It is my belief that she cannot simply enter the tradition, identify with it as if she were male; she is, I think, in grave risk to do so. But what other identity is there? Surely, to ask that is to bring us to the heart of the matter: woman as absence and the consequent risks involved in the invention of our own traditions." —Beverly Dahlen, *HOW(ever)* associate editor

---

*If my project weren't limited to print journals, I would mention other projects such as Susan Howe's radio show "Poetry," a series of readings and interviews broadcast on WBAI Pacifica Radio in the late seventies, and C.D. Wright's "The Lost Roads Project: A Walk-in Book Of Arkansas," a multi-media exhibit "to advance the relation between writing and reading in a slightly different medium" and "to work alongside other Arkansas artists/thinkers/doers in the process"(*Chain* 3, 206) which opened in 1994 and toured Arkansas for 2 years, featuring the work of native Arkansas artists. Wright Comments "I think I stand a better chance of gaining that sweet communal feeling again from the lonesome practice of poetry for having found expression in a walk-in book"(*Chain* 3, 211).

"I began writing to escape being a woman." —Johanna Drucker

CRITICAL ARTICULATIONS SUCH AS THE FOREGOING began to accumulate in alternative spaces opened by the small press. Voicing dissatisfactions created a space "between," while the avant-garde small press enabled women to critique feminism's powerfully asserted vision and methodology. Even before feminism was critiqued for inadequately addressing the concerns of non-white middle-class women, it was clear that a feminist approach to gender and language could not represent a full range of women's concerns. A *feminist* poetics from any ideological or theoretical perspective always contests the limitations of the "universal voice" which threatens to erase, marginalize or discount the cultural participation of women. But exactly what a "feminist poetics" might be was contested throughout the 1970s and 1980s as women engaged in radical acts of poetry. The feminist poetics of the Women's Movement was informed by and large by the revisionary tactics outlined in Adrienne Rich's 1971 essay, "When We Dead Awaken: Writing as Re-Vision," which consisted in "breaking" tradition's "hold" over the female poet's "available materials," her subject-matter. This was to be done by means of voice, through which previous lyrics of "victimization by Love" would be replaced by 'new' lyrics expressing "female anger and . . . furious awareness of Man's power over her" (35-36). By 1979, critic Elaine Showalter had encouraged women in "Towards a Feminist Poetics" to render "the newly visible world of female culture" and "the experience of the 'muted' female half" (28) in order to create a "distinctly female literary tradition." Sandra Gilbert and Susan Gubar's *Madwoman in the Attic: The Woman Writer and the Nineteenth Century Literary Imagination* (1979) spoke of the female "prisoners" of a previous century, "glancing into the mirror of the male-inscribed literary text" and — finally — seeing themselves "enraged." Thus co-opting traditional mimetic strategies was central to the "vision" of the feminist poetics under construction.

Titles of other feminist works, such as *A Literature of Their Own* (1977) and *Shakespeare's Sisters* (1979), reveal the extent to which Virginia Woolf was taken up as a mentor and a guide. Her fictional Judith Shakespeare illustrated the incomprehensibility, under the strictures of a patriarchal *descriptions* of Woman, of the inscription "woman poet"; she was seen and not heard and thus to be a "poet" was to be "profoundly 'unwomanly'" (Gilbert & Gubar, xxii). While Woolf *was* writing on behalf of women and while her infamous case for £500 per annum and a room of one's own *does* articulate the female artist's struggle *for* self-representation, it also locates as a contingent concern woman's need for self definition: Woolf asks, "what is 'herself'? I mean, what is a woman?"

But there was another Virginia Woolf, one who had written, in *A Room of One's Own*, of a woman writer's ability "to use writing as a means of art, and not just self expression." Woolf *also* delineates a struggle *with the means* of self-representation — language. In 1979, poet and scholar Rachel Blau DuPlessis looked toward Woolf for a different version of feminist poetics, one that included a vision of difference and recalled Woolf's observation that writing by men and women exhibit "marked differences of plot and incident . . . [and] infinite differences in selection method and style." Reviving Woolf's insistence that sexual difference influences artistic production on a semiotic level, DuPlessis set about to argue for recognition of a "female aesthetic" in artistic production "which begins when women take, investigate, the structures of feeling that are ours" and which reveals a conflict with the "patriarchal structures of feeling" — that determine a range of permissible formulations. A feminist poetic based on this aesthetic would take sexual difference into account not only as it determines the realm of one's experience but also as it mediates one's articulation of it: "these differing experiences produce different consciousness, different cultural expression, different relation to realms of symbols and to symbol users" (DuPlessis 1980, 141-49).[*]

The re-visionary poetic trope fails to account for this 'otherhow'[†] of Woolf's divisive ideology — her insistence that, in order to break the conventional mirror-like structures/strictures that had cast the feminine in the pose of object, women writers must attend to a "technical difficulty" by radically altering the structure of the sentence: "the very form of the sentence," wrote Woolf, "does not fit her. It is a sentence made by men, it is too loose, too heavy, too pompous for woman's use." A mirror, even attuned to a more sympathetic female gaze, is still a mirror, and those captured in its 'authoritative' glare 'objects' of attention. A Woolfean feminist poetic announces that it is not experience which literature must reflect (the basis of those "dumping grounds," according to Woolf, the drawing room novel), but woman's consciousness that must freely move *though the medium of language*. Importantly, DuPlessis' female aesthetic, like Woolf's inquiry into feminine consciousness, is focused not on newly-found emotions and expressions peculiar to women but on questions regarding the structures that subjective poetic utterance takes; it is not essential to women but a set of mobile "practices available to those groups . . . which wish

---

[*] By 1990 DuPlessis would modify the phrase "These differing experiences produce different consciousness" to read "These experiences of difference . . . produce different consciousnesses" (1990, 11), foreclosing the binaristic notion of woman as 'other' with the notion of 'difference.'

[†] The term is DuPlessis': "not 'otherness' in a binary system, but 'otherhow' as the multiple possibilities of a praxis"(1990, 154).

to criticize, to differentiate from, to overturn the dominant forms of knowing and understanding with which they are saturated."

Feminine consciousness, in Woolf's formulation, was irruptive to conventional (masculine) semantics that marked writing as "feminine": unacceptable, subversive, chaotic. Unacceptable, as well, to the normative female literary tradition, where Woolf's radical admonitions, along with those of Dorothy Richardson, Gertrude Stein, Mina Loy, and, as Susan Howe has shown, Emily Dickinson, were relegated to the blind spot of "Re-Vision" — or their complexities reduces to slogans.* Implicit in DuPlessis' essay is a critique of a feminist poetics that maintains traditional hegemonic structures to express new realizations. Preserving these structures, she implies, ironically preserves conditions of women's objectification and oppression and confirms patriarchal perspectives — a critique that would be elaborated years later by DuPlessis herself. Joan Retallack too would critique hegemonic feminist poetics for simply exercising "an assertively female vocabulary — *womb, breast, vagina, menses*" polemically situated in conventional lyric structures. To "steal" from patriarchal ideology conventional means of constructing poetic voice, Retallack argues, adheres too strongly to patriarchal structures to transform them: "Since images created by women do not impress what are still seen as male linguistic arbiters, these images cannot really enter, much less transform the language" (Retallack 1994, 354).† The mode, DuPlessis insists, is of "rupture," which "makes of representation a site of struggle" (DuPlessis 1990, 145). A critical feminist poetics, as Woolf notes, if it is to be of *any* use to women writers, experiments *im*properly with conventional forms qua literary history.

"Experimental writing of all sorts has always been crucial to the feminist project of cultural change: of revolution, not revision" (DuPlessis 1993, 105). But for a *woman* to join the growing male avant-garde in playing openly with semantics (by eschewing accepted formal, syntactic, grammatical, typographical, or referential structures, etc.) — to write, in the 1970s, like Vito Hannibal Acconci, Robert Grenier, or Barrett Watten — was to risk "unintelligibility." In the eyes of movement feminists, to be 'unintelligible' or 'difficult' was to be inaccessible and incommunicative, to assume a position of self-imposed silence, and

---

*Stein receives such treatment in *Madwoman in the Attic* where the authors refer to "the career of a single woman artist, a 'mother of us all' as Gertrude Stein would put it"(101) and "what Gertrude Stein would call 'patriarchal poetry.'" According to Susan Howe, *Madwoman in the Attic* "fails to discuss the implications of a nineteenth century American penchant for linguistic decreation ushered in by their representative poet." See Howe's *My Emily Dickinson*, especially pp

†See Retallack's essay for a thorough critique of the feminist strategy of appropriating traditional (lyric) structures to voice female experience. Retallack makes reference to the title of Alicia Suskin Ostriker's monumental 1986 study *Stealing the Language: The Emergence of Women's Poetry in America*.

thus of privilege and power. Straying from 'properly' feminist voice- and identity-based poetics by wrenching one's language from 'easy' structures was to challenge the validity of the normative (and normatizing) perspective espoused by such structures. This, DuPlessis maintained, was to change consciousness and transform social relations:

> writing exerts a continuous destabilizing pressure, and, in both analytic and formal ways, creates an arousal of desire for difference, for hope. If consciousness must change, if social forms must be re-imagined, then language and textual structures must help cause and support, propel and discover these changes. (DuPlessis 1993, 105)

In the following years innovative women poets and poet-editors would continue to pursue the work of women writers of the past, especially in those aspects that had been effectively deadened or left dormant. For Kathleen Fraser this meant re-utilizing and creating access to women's radical poetic practice. Teaching a 'Feminist Poetics' seminar at San Francisco State University in 1982, Fraser introduced "nontraditional language structures" and contextualized these by focusing concurrently on modernist and contemporary texts by women and recent feminist criticism. In this way, one could rethink the boundaries of poetic practice and wonder whether the exclusion of "women's literature" was related to the exclusive nature of genre and, Fraser suggested, a particular understanding of temporality in writing. Following Woolf, Fraser proposed women's spatio-temporal experience as a literary structure, a formulation that was shaping Fraser's own poetry. She advocated an alternative feminist formulation, "the building or restructuring of the poem incorporating the measure of female thought and daily life, the stutter of uncertainty, the multiple voice, the discontinuous character of time experienced in women's diction, the simultaneity of multiple perceptions" (1982, 8). If, following Woolf, a woman could restructure the sentence to reflect feminine consciousness, and if, in lieu of a room of one's own in which to experience uninterrupted thought, Fraser reasoned, a feminist poetics should embrace this interruption as a formal innovation.

Continuing on the heels of recent feminist criticism that questioned the canonization of some modernists — Pound, Williams, Eliot, Yeats, and, tokenized, Marianne Moore — and the accompanying erasure of others — Laura (Riding) Jackson, Dorothy Richardson, Lorine Niedecker and Mina Loy — Fraser urged her writing group (Frances Jaffer and Beverly Dahlen) to edit a little magazine. *HOW(ever)* would work to recover a lineage based on the enactment of experimental practices by women and use these newly available "models" to think about formally innovative *contemporary* writing by women. Its interrogative feminist poetics registered an editorial outcry against the suppression of the "unofficially recognized realm" of experimental women writers who were coming along in the wake of these modernists. Her critical sense of literary history, like that of DuPlessis, a substantive "'mail-order' contributor,"* critiqued and challenged the conventional, centered and restrictive 'lyric order.'

Though in opposition to a too-narrow definition of feminist writing that had emerged in the feminist small press and scholarship, *HOW(ever)* shunned the isolationism and anti-academism of avant-garde little magazines that would have hindered its feminist literary-historical project. Fraser notes that "there were problems in asserting a point of view that defined itself as female and often feminist . . . some people inevitably felt excluded . . . . But rather than seeing ourselves as exclusionary or here to displace or replace anything or anyone, we hoped, instead, to be an added source of information and stimulation" (1993, 63). *HOW(ever)* provided a forum for an informed exchange, publishing experimental work by women[†] in tandem with poet-generated "working notes" that would provide elucidation for other poets and feminist literary critics wanting to develop an understanding of them. "Maybe," Fraser reasoned, "women critics simply didn't know how to begin thinking or talking about the more innovative compositional work and the seriousness of its quest . . . perhaps new insights and descriptions coming directly from the poets might provide useful clues for the careful detective work in which scholar-critics engage" (1993, 62). Patricia Dienstfrey observed that this structure kept experimental texts "open to feminist readings" at a time when the influential ideology of Language poetry was "publicly defining" them.[‡] *How(ever)*'s informal exchanges would battle the myth of codification, of the 'experimental voice' as merely an alternative to the 'coalitional voice' celebrated by populist feminist poetics. The editorial board sought the feminist scholars they were reading in the hopes of having dialogues, communication that could fight the dismissal of experimental writing as merely 'difficult' or 'inaccessible,' thus providing insurance against future omissions from literary history. Each issue's "Postcards" hosted lively exchanges and responses, and by inviting scholars and poet-scholars to contribute "alerts" ("brief commentary, new slants,

---

[*] As DuPlessis dubbed herself in an essay of 1993.

[†] In its 9 years, *HOW(ever)* published many women writers central to experimental poetic discourse including Barbara Guest, Maureen Owen, Rae Armantrout, Fanny Howe, Susan Howe, Laura Moriarty, Myung Mi Kim, Rachel Blau DuPlessis, Hannah Weiner, Norma Cole, Patricia Dienstfrey, Rosmarie Waldrop, and Johanna Drucker.

[‡] Personal correspondence with Patricia Dienstfrey, 3/1/98.

current scholarly finds") *HOW(ever)* could build a new body of criticism from inside the new tradition it was forming, with informal essays or transcribed talks on modernist and contemporary poets (such as Mary Butts or Dorothy Richardson, Barbara Guest or Meimei Bersennbrugge) and poetic issues (such as canon formation and questions of form and style) — issues that found little or no space in other serials.

The collective editorial practice of *HOW(ever)*, a "tricky staging of vulnerability, chanciness and resistance to male editorial approval" (Osman & Spahr, 45), helped the editors to find alternatives to the sorts of disabling editorial biases and controls they confronted as 'uncategorizeable' poets.* In arguing for their choices issue by issue they sought to keep their preferences unhindered and avoid settling into a fixed aesthetic. And, Fraser reasons, they were "opening up places that had been shut down by powerful ideas of 'worth' and 'importance'" (Osman & Spahr, 44). The name *HOW(ever)*, an homage to Marianne Moore, "represented for [them] an addendum, a point of view from the margins, meant to flesh out what had thus far been proposed in poetry and poetics"(1993, 63) as reflected in *HOW(ever)*'s format and unconventional mix of texts.

HOW(ever) continued to publish for eight years, until, as Fraser recently commented, they "finally felt legitimate" (19); and, with the establishment of *HOW(ever)*, Dienstfrey notes, "the Bay Area . . . had once more positioned itself as a locale where new practices, readings and rereadings could converge. This time the nexus would be experimental writing by women" (Osman & Spahr, 94). Beyond providing a space to locate and discuss experimental practices, *HOW(ever)* disrupted the complacency of at least one reviewer, who wrote, "I have yet to meet anyone who has been able to sit and read GERTRUDE STEIN for more than an hour at a stretch . . . or to remain excited by H.D. after twenty pages or so. These seem the deities behind this sort of writing. . . . When I pick up *HOW(ever)* I shudder." He issued an edict: "Let's strangle the little creature in his crib before he soils his pants and screws up our life," and took the opportunity to legislate further poetic prescriptions: "A poem is not a dictionary. A poem is not a set of easy metaphysical speculations on the nature of grammar, guilt, or the primal flood aggressive . . .. Nor is the facile word play, no matter how 'round' and female the concept, poetry." He put these editors descriptively in their place, "bitching" and "get[ting] together on a rainy day and sip[ping] their herb teas."†

***HOW(ever)* had a number of different editors (and associated editors) throughout its lifetime, including Kathleen Fraser, Frances Jaffer, Beverly Dahlen, Rachel Blau DuPlessis, Carolyn Burke, and later Susan Gevirtz, Myung Mi Kim, Meredith Stricker, Diane Glancy, and Adalaide Morris.

†In *The Peters Black and Blue Guide to Current Literary Journals* (1987).

Concurrent to formulations of feminist poetics, in the early 1980s translations of French feminists Luce Irigaray, Hèléne Cixous and Julia Kristeva were appearing in American feminist journals. Their work refigured the "feminine" in discourse, *as writing*, a set of discursive practices disruptive to the Lacanian 'law of the father,' patriarchal language established in and through textual conventions. They provided a useful vocabulary for thinking of the feminine in language *and* in literary history; multiplicitous, fragmented, and thus subversive, the feminine "ruptures" the symbolic, refusing to play Other to the phallus, the signifier that "centers" and through which all meaning is secured. For innovative women writers striving to work with language as a material rather than a mirror, as something that constructs rather than reflects (identity and gender, among other things), these powerful notions, accepted, questioned or rejected, kindled theoretical fires.[*] Carolyn Burke's guest lecture on French Feminism in Kathleen Fraser's 'Feminist Poetics' seminar was, Dodie Bellamy recalls, "so exciting that afterwards the women in the bathroom talked about it like [they] were on drugs" (Osman & Spahr, 13). The sense that in writing women engage in language *differently* on a *structural level* encouraged a (feminist) critique of *language* (and not merely poetry) as a set of (masculine) conventions that renders 'illogical' and thus 'inaudible' notions that can't be articulated in normative, rationalistic, or unexamined structures: "When a writer attempts to speak directly, she is crippled by an inherited patriarchal language in which certain core female experiences/perceptions are inconceivable" (Bellamy 1989, n.p.). The inquiry had shifted away from points of enforced silence to the overall structural limitation, such that all representation was suspect and the notion of the feminine in discourse was examined for its potential to influence poetic (and not specifically feminist) practice. Rosmarie Waldrop, for example, speaks of her work of the late 1970s (*The Road is Everywhere or Stop This Body*) as feminist in retrospect: "It was only later, that I realized that this challenge to a rigid subject-object relation has feminist implications"; thus drawing out the work's relation to inherent (and no longer hidden) cultural issues: "Woman in our culture has been treated as object par excellence, to be looked at rather than looking . . .. Instead, these poems propose a grammar in which subject and object function are not fixed . . . where there is no hierarchy . . . but a fluid and constant alternation" (1998, 13).

---

[*] Often their tropes — Irigaray's lips, Cixous' milky ink, Kristeva's womb-like semiotic chora — appeared too essentialist, and perhaps too physical, to effect otherwise intellectual and theoretical ends. In "The Rejection of Closure" for example Lyn Hejinian claims that "the literalness of the genital model for a woman's language . . . may be problematic. The desire that is stirred by language is located most interestingly within language itself."

While it had been important for feminist criticism to validate the historical identities of women poets, and important likewise to introduce alongside the newly emerging "female literary tradition" the existence of a tradition of experimentation, many writers grew wary of the risk implied by a too-inclusive characterization — that actual practices might be subsumed and destroyed, in literary-historical terms, by the imposition, for example in criticism and anthologies, of a generalized identity (the "experimental woman poet") — yet another exclusionary boundary. Bellamy resisted the idea that "avant-garde women's writing ... is merely an acting out against traditional feminism. Many women deeply feel the need to do more in their work than tell the stories of women's lives" (1989, n.p.). And Alice Notley, for example, questioned the construction of a gender-specific alternative tradition: "you can't create this female tradition and keep it all for yourself. It isn't nice. It doesn't matter if men haven't been nice. You can't repeat their sins" (1988, 26).

Women poet-editors operating in the small press do provide against erasure: no one can say "women did not write in the 1980s" the way they have said "women did not write in the 1950s." But they surpass the boilerplate feminist rhetoric of securing a feminist literary history — the construction of a past for future use. As Hejinian suggests, the site of construction is present and active: "language itself is never in a state of rest.. . . And the experience of using it, which includes the experience of understanding it, either as speech or as writing, is inevitably active" (1998, 624). In other words, experimental women poets and poet-editors do not only contribute to the grand historical project of constructing a tradition of women's writing, but work to insure heterogeneity and stave off categorizations that might eclipse the particularity of any one project. This is why, for example, such distinct projects as Fraser's and Hejinian's could work contemporaneously. With its centers of production and exchange, the small press enabled the development of a multiplicity of feminist poetic strategies, disturbing not only poetic conventions but, one hopes, critical conventions that simplify retrospectively.

This is why, perhaps, women have come to the fore among poets of the post-1960s generation. Through debates "that raged around issues of language and gender"(Cole 593) women proceeded, to various degrees, to investigate structures through which gender distinctions are maintained. While Fraser seeks to reproduce social effects "structurally, in the look and sound of [women's] poems," Leslie Scalapino sees her work as *unraveling* structural effects: "My articulation of feminism is in the gesture of trying to unravel how something is packaged or mirrored back to me — as part of the whole web of what's around us — and how we can be attuned to seeing social creations of ourselves and others" (Frost 20). Alice Notley recognizes that cultural effects structure linguistic possibilities —

"most ways of composing & setting down lines of poetry, of grouping them into poems on the page, seem 'male'" — but sees also in language the possibility to question: "What would it be like to make a female poetry? Is that possible? . . . Is there feminine and masculine?" (Notley 1991, n.p.). Rosmarie Waldrop apprehends a similar openness in language: "I don't really see 'female language,' 'female style or technique.' Because the writer, male or female, is only one partner in the process of writing. Language, in its full range, is the other" (1998, 611). Joan Retallack, who delineated "a distinctly 'feminine' experimental project that had previously been carried on almost exclusively by the male avant-garde" (1996, 296) — recognized it as being composed of a set of strategies ("new grammars and models for thinking about interrelationships") accessible to all writers.

While the concept of an experimental feminist poetics has proven useful, it does not define the critical thought for a generation (or two) of women writers. The number of poets committed to their own explorations of language shifted the poetic debates of the 1980s away from boundary-making discourses, feminist or not. That is, they recognized no center, authoritatively decreed, which women approach marginally; the totality implied by that model having been supplanted by a recognition that the proliferation of contingent individual constructions effectively de-centers the field. The small press was the vehicle for this phenomenon. Women poet-editors effectively intervened by publishing women's poetic experimentation of this period, which extended from and particularized, by means of individual poetic lineages, the large structures they encountered: both the operative field of production and a "female tradition in literature" that feminists proposed as another authoritative center.

In 1989, Dodie Bellamy argued that it was "time to blow apart the arbitrary gulf between experimental and traditional, to create a sense of continuum. Any writer should be able to choose wherever she wants to be along the continuum in any particular place. To allow permission for these fluctuating boundaries" (1989, n.p.). Recognizing gender as a mechanism through which distinctions were made in poetry and in language, poet-editors created spaces to carry out experimental feminist investigations of the boundaries it proposed. Charles Bernstein has noted a "male version of the universal voice of rationality trying to control, as if by ventriloquism, female bodies"(1992, 5). Experimentation sought ways around the formal closure that a populist feminist poetics proposed — a female version of the universal voice that exerted influence over women's texts — and used poetry, to use Hejinian's phrase, as a "language of inquiry."

V. EDITING, (CO-ED)ITING, AND A NEW POETICS OF PRODUCTION: "WITH A PROPER BALANCE OF GENDER (OF COURSE)"

"Emily Dickinson's carefully handwritten manuscripts — some sewn into fascicles, some gathered into sets — may have been demonstrating her conscious and unconscious separation from a mainstream literary orthodoxy in letters . . . The issue of editorial control is directly connected to the attempted erasure of antinomianism in our culture." —Susan Howe, *The Birth-mark*

" . . . Bernadette Mayer's *Sonnets* manuscript had been sitting in a drawer for while . . . one publisher had fallen through. Besides, who was going to publish me? I might as well do it myself. But I shouldn't do myself first, I reasoned. I should create a context." —Lee Ann Brown, on Tender Buttons Press

"Women who edit hold a particular place in an established discourse of authority. Whether they think about it or not, they must evaluate their stance in relation to that realm. Perhaps to ignore the factor is in itself a form of subversion — it's a way of maintaining a frame that refuses to participate in unpleasant histories." —Jena Osman & Juliana Spahr, *Chain*

"I see the world as physically maleish in a way that has nothing to do with language or symbols. I participate in male forms. A poetry journal is a male form. My other choice is to be a hermit." —Alice Notley

"Nothing changes from generation to generation except the thing seen and that makes a composition." —Gertrude Stein, "Composition as Explanation"

IN 1998, THE FIRST ISSUE OF *Gare du Nord* promised to provide "a good mix of work from as many different cultures as we can find, with a proper balance of gender (of course)."* Women's participation, like the 'always already' feminism implicit in various modes of women's experimental poetic practices, *is* a matter "of course"; the "balance" of women in the small press has enabled the emergence of an otherwise uncategorizeable and hidden

---

*See "Editorial," *Gare du Nord*, Vol. 1.1, (1997).

community of poets. By the early 1990s, editorial poetic practice began to change hands. 1984, especially, was a turning point: Tuumba (in the San Francisco Bay Area) and *Telephone*/Telephone Books (in New York) both ceased operations. Book production by women waned until, prompted by ethical necessity more than economic 'accessories,'* in Berkeley, Leslie Scalapino began O Books (1986) and Lee Ann Brown started Tender Buttons in New York (1989). By 1990 several new women-edited and (co-ed)ited little magazines (*Avec, Scarlet, Big Allis, tight, Re*map* and *Troubled Surfer*) were established. Leave Books, highly prolific, would publish its first book the next year, while Texture Press and Avec Books geared up to begin production and join in a small (women-edited) desktop revolution: in 1991-1992, eight new little magazines and four new presses were established. The amplification of women-edited small press activity — more than double that of the previous decade[†] — effectively diffused the bi-coastal nature of poetic production (the East/West of Ron Silliman's 1986 anthology *In the American Tree*). Providence, Rhode Island, home of the Waldrop's Burning Deck, would witness a small explosion of women-edited littles (*The Impercipient, Black Bread*, and *Cathay*). Women-edited small presswork at the State University of New York at Buffalo, which began with Judith Kerman's collectively edited *Earth's Daughters* (1971-80), was revived by *No Trees*, and later arrivals Leave Books, *Chain, Apex of the M* and *verdure*. The women-edited desktop revolution (currently over 20 little magazines and e-zines and 11 presses) not only extends from New York to San Francisco, but punctuates the landscape from Hawaii (*Tinfish, Chain*), to Oklahoma (*Texture*/Texture Press) and Kansas (*First Intensity*), to Pennsylvania (*6ix*) and Washington D.C. (Primitive Publications), to Paris, France (*Gare du Nord*).

This transformation of the field of poetic production continues to be crucial to the development of theoretical and critical writing by and/or about women. *HOW(ever)* put out its last paper issue in 1992 after publishing poetry and providing information on modernist and contemporary poetry and poetics for over 8 years.[‡] *Poetics Journal*, too, had put a hold on production after having published essays — including Hejinian's influential "The Rejection of Closure,"[§] and an in-progress section of Susan Howe's *My Emily Dickin*

---

[*] "Mistakes were made." Attributable to the Reagan Administration's war on public arts funding, the paucity of small press production throughout the eighties contrasts sharply with that of the preceding decade, when government subsidies were widely available.

[†] Between 1990-1999, twenty-five new little magazines and ten new presses appeared, vs., from 1979-89, twelve and three.

[‡] Fraser recently launched *HOW2*, an on-line publication. See Appendix C.

[§] First delivered as a talk in a series of talks held in the Bay Area. See Bob Perelman's *Writing/Talks* (Southern Ill.

son — by more than 30 women poets. Hejinian had articulated her sense that men didn't "tend to take women seriously" in a 1980 letter to Susan Howe and proposed that women "have to keep telling those guys to do so" (Vickery 31). The modification that women poets in the 1980s proposed was revolutionary in that it would bring about change by subverting authority within the field of poetic production (challenging, transforming or discarding its conventions) which is to challenge the operative structure of the field by creating new, unanticipated positions. Editing and disseminating new poetic material thereby deconstructs the binaries that grant women's work lesser, marginal, or non- status. Women editing and actively shaping the field challenge such boundaries, a challenge that is not only feminist; it does not concern only the acts of women. The challenge is enacted on the level of poiesis, in that it serves as a practical critique of a range of practices that constitute the field of production.

Changes in the reception of women's work were reflected throughout the small press. Poetry and responses by women were increasingly published with a host of presses, such as Potes and Poets, Roof, Sun and Moon, and Chax, and in many little magazines such as *o•blek*, *A.bacus* and *Sulfur*. While a comprehensive list might sketch particular preferences, a statistic (the number of men publishing work by women) would obscure the actual situation: at times it is not gender differences per se which keep women out of print, but those formalities of textual production that keep activity (including writing) by women hidden.

In 1992, Johanna Drucker pointed out that

> If one of the features of the modern avant-garde was to pretend to the autonomy and self-referential value of the work, then one of the most significant projects of the contemporary scene has got to be the undoing of that mythic autonomy in recognition of the complicity of (still male dominated) power relations as they structure the ongoing production of literature as its own critical history. (13)

Her comments point at once to the project of *HOW(ever)* (in which Drucker's essay appeared) and away from it, to a younger generation of innovative women poet-editors. In 1992, the Canadian little magazine *Raddle Moon* produced a "Women/Writing/Theory" issue (no. 12), promising to be "a first exchange" involving some of a group of women who

---

UP, 1985).

"agreed to pursue in print the conversation they had been having among themselves and were aware of around them."*

The emphasis on "first exchange" simultaneously positions the issue in relation to the already ongoing conversation between women, writing, and theory (or women's writing and theory) — in which *Raddle Moon* had been a participant throughout the 1980s — and announces the possibility of a break or re-beginning commensurate with the shift in editorship and in editorial concerns that occurred in the early 1990s. This first exchange also constitutes a change in editorial dynamics that had shaped the little magazine as a field of poetic inquiry. Editor Susan Clark then established *Q'ir'i*, a "small, casual irregular of poetry and poetics, discussion and information" to exist beside *Raddle Moon* and to extend its inquiry. Though *Q'ir'i* was never realized as a serial (the contents of the first issue were republished as the *next* issue of *Raddle Moon*), it suggests that by 1992 a critical mass of poets and poet-editors had been reached such that their conversations must be publicized. It suggests also that a new poetics of production was underway — "in recognition," as Drucker had put it, "of the complicity of (still male dominated) power relations."

A woman editing takes on production as a sort of experiment as her authority over the materials and processes she engages with is untried. Editing means confronting familiar prohibitions. Ann Erickson, editor of *tight*, for example, "was tired of messing around and . . . wanted to run one corner of the universe in [her] own way,"† and Mary Hilton started Primitive Publications in part "as a way to break out of 'I can't' or 'I could never.'"‡ Jennifer Moxley eschewed plans to co-edit with her partner because she "would have become intimidated by his presence and judgement and before long would have started to turn to him for approval on every decision," and viewed the *Impercipient* as "a space in which [she] did not have to fight" (Osman & Spahr 85). These individual assertions, however personal the impetus, work to reconstitute the field and dynamics of selection and exchange kept in circulation there.

But as Jena Osman and Juliana Spahr suggested in the premier issue of *Chain* (1994), why stop there? To edit could mean to explore language and contingent issues of power. Along with disseminating new work, *Chain* also served as a forum in which to scrutinize editing practices and to start a dialogue among current women editors. Suggesting that

---

*Respondents included Abigail Child, Jean Day, Johanna Drucker, Norma Cole, Kathryn MacLeod, Chris Tysh and Laura Moriarity.

†Personal correspondence, 3/3/98.

‡Personal correspondence, 6/17/98.

editors must examine the extent to which they're complicit in constructing boundaries, they pointed out how unannounced editorial assumptions construct ideological frames. They provided a critical edge to a gesture like that of Madeline Burnside and Andrew Kelly editing *Gnome Baker* in 1978, who aimed "to present a variety of previously unpublished written work ... which is centered upon the use of the written word as a medium in itself" and sought "to free the writer from the intrusion of editorial taste or select[ion by] provid[ing] a written space large enough for the representation and articulation of a complete idea,"* Osman and Spahr wrote, "I am uncomfortable with the idea of the editor as arbiter of good taste, or as the (in)visible navigator/sculptor of a final packaged product. Journals rarely seem to openly admit the presence of personal ideology behind their pages. And when they do, the 'personalized' frame seems to stifle and alter the work by mashing it into an overly-prescribed space" (129). They chose instead to experiment radically with (non)editorial possibilities — *Chain*'s first issue, "devoted to the work of women poets, editors and critics" (6), includes an "Editorial Forum" based on their provocative questions regarding gender and editing. The issue concludes with "a series of 'chains'/poems and other responses that enact an alternative editorial practice" — *i.e.* the editorial philosophy of the series was to avoid authoritarian framing in favor of presenting individual contributors' felt connection to other participants. Rather than presenting a magazine structured by a centralized, authoritative nexus, their editorial efforts reflected a decentered field of poetic production. To this end the method of the concluding series was to play off of the form of the chain letter in its unpredictable path.

Further undermining the notion of editorial selection as a finalizing gesture, one that "opens" the work to a reader just as it "closes" it within the frame of its pages, Osman and Spahr place their editorial note in between these two alternative editorial propositions. *Chain*'s project is utopian, an attempt to produce the admittedly implausible frameless frame, "an attempt to investigate the (im)possibility of an unmediated reception, the (im)possibility of detaching a writing from its presentational/ideological form"(129).

Poetic experimentation attempts to shift the frames of understanding that assumptions (previous understandings) of poetry elicit. Editorial experimentation attempts to challenge concepts of authority and these conjoined have enabled women's individual (and collective) editorial assumptions to shift the focus in (or on) the field of poetic production, not by pulling women out of the margins but by making the field inclusive of their concerns through instrumentalizing engagements and dialogues. By the middle of the 1990s, a larger,

---

*Editor's note, *Gnome Baker I & II* (Spring 1978).

more geographically diverse third generation of women poet-editors — many of whom were literally "schooled" in feminism, the construction of literary history and the work of experimental women poets — were moving into and using the spaces that, during the previous two decades, women had engineered. Their focus had shifted from the strategic ground-breaking and space-making that enabled first-wave representation (and the codification of individual poets engaged in common poetic practices) to continued explorations and geographically diverse enactments of theoretical and political concerns. Many are devoted to non-gender-specific issues, representing and developing other concerns and experimental investigations: *Tinfish*, for example, forges connections between experimental poetries of Pacific Islanders and mainlanders, challenging U.S. isolationism; Primitive Publications focuses on historically-based writing that is perceptibly influenced by the present; *Tripwire* explores the poetics of post-Language poetry and a range of contingent concerns regarding race, class and gender; Em Press continues in an artist's books tradition and Kelsey St. makes related forays into artist/poet collaborations; *Re*map* encourages and publishes informal dialogues along with poetry; and many little magazine editors follow the path forged by Burning Deck over 30 years ago, taking on the different demands and skills associated with book publishing (*Avec*/Avec Books, *Outlet*/Double Lucy Books, *Texture*/Texture Press, *Explosive Magazine*/Spectacular Books).

A history of women in the small press *is* a history of innovative feminist poetics. For innovative women poets, an engagement with avant-garde writing — as a practice and as an institution — is an act rooted in a feminist awareness of literary history and textual production. Undoubtedly many women feel the imperative to edit *because* they are women in this particular historical moment — because they *can* edit, they *can* take a position in the field of poetic production. Increasingly women poet-editors render their own position within the field of poetic production rather than approaching it 'marginally' or from the 'outside.' A result of their activity is not to register difference — to construct a new identity, the 'experimental woman poet' — but to transform the field of production so that it is inclusive of a range of poetic practices. The emphasis, though, has been on proliferating poems rather than critical or theoretical writings; thirty new little magazines have appeared between 1990-99, and only six of those include a substantial amount of critical investigation.

Like Susan Howe's Emily Dickinson — 'feminine' *and* antinomian — contemporary women poet-editors continue to challenge the integrity of literary establishment expectations, and raise issues of editorial control. But experimental texts written by women — texts, like Dickinson's, in dialogue with one's poetic lineage — are transformative of the field of poetic production only when they are recognized, and a 'hidden community' revealed through individual acts of editorial insertion. The contemporary reception of writing, its publication and the critical discourses it engages with and vice versa, are its only insurance against literary-historical revisionism — no matter how ample, however considered and prepared, manuscripts in a drawer —

WORKS CITED

Aldan, Daisy. "Daisy Aldan, an Interview on *Folder.*" *The Little Magazine in America: A Modern Documentary History.* Ed. Elliott Anderson and Mary Kinzie. New York: Pushcart Press, 1978. 263-280.

Bellamy, Dodie. "Four Years in the Making." *Mirage* 3 (1989: Women's Experimental Issue).

Bernstein, Charles. *A Poetics.* Cambridge, Mass.: Harvard UP, 1992.

-------. *Content's Dream: Essays 1975-84.* Los Angeles: Sun & Moon, 1986.

Biggs, Mary. "Women's Literary Journals," *Library Quarterly* 53.1 (January 1983): 1-25.

-------. "Neither Printer's Wife Nor Widow: American Women in Typesetting, 1830-1950," *Library Quarterly*, 50.4 (1980): 431-452.

Clay, Steven E., and Rodney Phillips, eds. *A Secret Location on the Lower East Side: Adventures in Writing (1960-1980).* New York: Granary Books, 1999.

Cole, Norma. "The Subject Is It: Translating Dannielle Collobert's *It Then* . . . . " *Moving Borders: Three Decades of Innovative Writing by Women.* Ed. Mary Margaret Sloan. NJ: Talisman House, 1998. 593-599.

Dahlen, Beverly. "In Re 'Person'."" *Moving Borders: Three Decades of Innovative Writing by Women.* Ed. Mary Margaret Sloan. NJ: Talisman House, 1998. 663-65.

Danky, James P., ed. *Women's Periodicals and Newspapers from the 18th Century to 1981: A Union List of the Holdings of Madison, Wisconsin, Libraries.* Boston: G.K. Hall & Co., 1982.

Darragh, Tina. "s the any M*efinel* mes: A reflection on Donna Harraway's 'Cyborg Manifesto'." *Moving Borders: Three Decades of Innovative Writing by Women.* Ed. Mary Margaret Sloan. NJ: Talisman House, 1998. 696-701.

-------. "Howe." *In The American Tree.* Ed. Ron Silliman. Orono, ME: National Poetry Foundation, Inc., 1986. 547-49.

De Loach, Allen, ed. "Little Mags/Small Presses and The Cultural Revolution." *Intrepid*, no. 21-22 (Winter-Spring 1971): 106-39.

di Prima, Diane, and Jones, LeRoi, ed. *The Floating Bear, a Newsletter, Numbers 1-37, 1961-69.* La Jolla, CA: Laurence McGilvery, 1973.

Drucker, Johanna. "Exclusion/Inclusion vs. Canon Formation." *HOW(ever)* 6.4 (January 1992): 13-14.

-------. "Women and Language." *Poetics Journal* 1.4 (May 1984): 57-68.

DuPlessis, Rachel Blau. "Reader, I married me: a polygynous memoir." *Changing Subjects.* Eds. Gayle Greene and Coppélia Kahn. London and New York: Routledge, 1993. 97-111.

-------. *The Pink Guitar: Writing as Feminist Praxis.* London and New York: Routledge, 1990.

―――. "For the Etruscans: Sexual Difference and Artistic Production — The Debate Over a Female Aesthetic." *The Future of Difference*, eds. Hester Eisenstein and Alice Jardine. New Brunswick, NJ: Rutgers UP, 1980.

Ellingham, Lewis and Killian, Kevin. *Poet Be Like God: Jack Spicer and the San Francisco Renaissance*. Hanover and London: UP of New England, 1998.

Foster, Edward. "An interview with Alice Notley." *Talisman* 1 (Fall 1988: The Alice Notley Issue): 14-35.

Fraser, Kathleen. *il cuore: The heart, Selected Poems 1970-95*. Hanover & London: Wesleyan UP, 1998.

―――. "The Tradition of Marginality." *Where We Stand: Women Poets on Literary Tradition*. Ed. Sharon Bryan. NY: Norton, 1993. 52-65.

―――. "Analytica Femina," an excerpt from "Without a Net: Finding One's Balance Along the Perilous Wire of the New" presented at the Dec. 1992 MLA in NYC.

―――. "Line. On the Line. Lining up. Line with. Between the Lines. Bottom Line," *The Line in Postmodern Poetry*. Ed. Robert Frank and Henry Sayre. Urbana and Chicago: U of Chicago P, 1988. 152-174.

―――, ed. *Feminist Poetics: A consideration of the female construction of language*. San Francisco State University, 1982.

Frost, Elisabeth A. "An Interview with Leslie Scalapino." *Contemporary Literature* 37.1 (1996). 1-22.

Fulton, Len. "Anima Rising: Little Magazines in the Sixties," *American Libraries* 2.1 (January 1971): 25-47.

Sandra Gilbert and Susan Gubar. *Madwoman in the Attic: The Woman Writer and the Nineteenth Century Literary Imagination*. New Haven: Yale UP, 1979.

―――. *Shakespeare's Sisters: Feminist Essays on Women Poets*. Bloomington: Indiana UP, 1979.

Glazier, Loss Pequeño. *Small Press: An Annotated Bibliography*. Westport, CT: Greenwood P, 1992.

Grahn, Judy, *The Work of a Common Woman*. New York: St. Martin's Press, 1978.

Hejinian, Lyn. "Lyn Hejinian/Andrew Schelling: An Exchange" *Jimmy & Lucy's House of 'K'* (#6, May, 1986), pp. 1-17.

―――. "The Rejection of Closure." *Moving Borders: Three Decades of Innovative Writing by Women*. Ed. Mary Margaret Sloan. NJ: Talisman House, 1998. 618-29.

―――. "The Person and Description," *Poetics Journal* 1.9 (June 1991): 166-70.

Hinton, Laura. "An Interview with Lyn Hejinian and Leslie Scalapino," *Private Arts* (1996): 58-85.

Hogue, Cynthia. "An Interview with Kathleen Fraser," *Contemporary Literature* 39.1 (Spring 1998): 1-26.

Howe, Susan. *Frame Structures: Early Poems 1974-1979*. New York: New Directions, 1996.

―――. *The Birth-mark: Unsettling the Wilderness in American Literary History*. Hanover and London: Wesleyan UP, 1993.

―――. *My Emily Dickinson*. Berkeley, CA: North Atlantic Books, 1985.

Jaffer, Frances. "For Women Poets, For Poetry: A Journal Entry." *The Poetry Reading: A Contemporary Compendium on Language and Performance*. Ed. Stephen Vincent and Ellen Zweig. SF: Momo's Press, 1981. 58-63.

Keller, Lynn. "An interview with Susan Howe." *Contemporary Literature* 36.1 (1995).

Kruchkow, Diane and Johnson, Curt, eds. *Green Isle in the Sea: An Informal History of the Alternative Press, 1960-85*. Highland Park, IL: December Press, 1985.

Michelson, Peter. "On *The Purple Sage, Chicago Review*, and *Big Table*." *The Little Magazine in America: A Modern Documentary History*. Ed. Elliott Anderson and Mary Kinzie. New York: Pushcart Press, 1978.

Notley, Alice. *The Descent of Alette*. New York: Penguin, 1996.

―――. "Women & Poetry." *Scarlet* 5 (Sept. 1991). unpaginated.

-------. *Doctor Williams' Heiresses: A Lecture Delivered at 80 Langton Street, San Francisco, Feb. 12, 1980*. Berkeley, CA: Tuumba Press, 1980.

Osman, Jena and Spahr, Juliana, eds. "Editorial Forum,"" Chain 1 (Spring/Summer 1994: Special Topic: Gender and Editing): 5-118.

Rasula, Jed. *American Poetry Wax Museum*. Urbana, IL: National Council of Teachers of English, 1996.

Retallack, Joan. "The Poethical Wager." *Onward: Contemporary Poetry and Poetics*. Ed. Peter Nicholas Baker. New York: Peter Lang Publishing, 1996. 193-206.

-------. "RE:THINKING:LITERARY:FEMININSM:(three essays onto shaky grounds)." *Feminist Measures: Soundings in Poetry and Theory*. Ed. Lynn Keller and Cristanne Miller. Ann Arbor: U of Michigan P, 1994. 344-77.

Rich, Adrienne. *On Lies, Secrets, and Silence*. NY: Norton, 1979.

Showalter, Elaine. "Towards a Feminist Poetics." *Women Writing and Writing About Women*. Ed. Mary Jacobus. New York: Harper & Row, 1979. 22-41.

-------. *A Literature of Their Own: British Women Novelists from Brontë to Lessing*. Princeton, NJ: Princeton UP, 1977.

Vickery, Ann. *Leaving Lines of Gender: A Feminist Genealogy of Language Writing*. Hanover and London: Wesleyan UP, 2000.

Waldrop, Rosmarie, "Thinking as Follows." *Moving Borders: Three Decades of Innovative Writing by Women*, ed. Mary Margaret Sloan. NJ: Talisman House. 1998. 609-617.

-------. "Alarms & Excursions." The Politics of Poetic Form: Poetry and Public Policy, ed. Charles Bernstein. New York: Roof, 1990. 45-72.

-------. *The Road is Everywhere or Stop This Body*. Colombia, MO: Open Places, 1979.

Waldman, Ann. *The World Anthology*. New York: Bobbs-Merril, 1969.

Woolf, Virginia. *Women and Writing*. Ed. Michèle Barrett. FL: Harcourt Brace Jovanovich, 1979.

Gino and Carlo's, North Beach, San Francisco. Jack Spicer's bar (photo: Ed Foster)

Robert Bertholf with portrait of Robert Duncan by Jess, Poetry Collection, SUNY Buffalo (photo: David Landrey)

St. Mark's Church, New York City. Home of the Poetry Project (photo: Murad Mahrem)

Robert Creeley at his home in Buffalo, New York
(photo: David Landrey)

William Bronk's home, Hudson Falls, New York
"This was man did this, and thought to do well
when he turned away to say, on the contrary, all
the world was what we measured: houses, sums
and angles, vectors and smoothable curves."
—"My House New-Painted"
(photo: Ed Foster)

Gallo-Roman Aqueduct near
Gustaf Sobin's home in Provence.
"only there, in enumerating artifact,
cataloging all that auroral debris,
had you intuited —your ankles
jingling with shadows— the
first stuttered increments of passage."
—"Transparent Itineraries, 1998"
(photo: Gustaf Sobin)

William Bronk (photo: Dale Davis)

Nathaniel Mackey (photo: David Landrey)

Philip Whalen (photo: Ed Foster)

Ron Padgett (photo: Linda Bruce)

Lyn Hejinian (photo: David Landrey)

Clark Coolidge, Ted Berrigan, Alice Notley (photo: Ed Foster)

Simon Pettet, Mary Margaret Sloan, Joseph Donahue (photo: S. Retsov)

Ed Foster, John High, Leonard Schwartz (photo: Peter Grosski)

Standard Schaefer

IMPOSSIBLE CITY: A HISTORY OF LITERARY PUBLISHING IN L.A.

Los Angeles has always suffered sneers from the American literati. Perhaps, it was Hollywood. Perhaps it was the working-class, genre work of Raymond Chandler. In the realm of poetry, the suffering has been worse despite the fact that everyone from Robert Creeley to Michelle Clinton have lived and written there. The inferiority complex of the city, the very fact that it has been so long ignored has become part of the unique character of the work that has been published here. But, it has also been the reason so few writers have stayed. People come for the gold and the glitz. Nobody comes in order to become a Californian. Nobody chooses L.A. in order to participate in the community. They come to make a little money and move on, or they come to make a lot of money and hide behind their wrought-iron fences. Some people are born here, but there is a good chance they stay out of a lack of resourcefulness. Almost everyone comes here for a better life. Writers often come for a teaching gig before moving on to something better, maybe north to San Francisco. Writers *choose* to go to San Francisco in order to be involved in a community, or they go to New York in order to make it. But no writers, no literary writers, certainly no serious poets come to L.A. with the intention of staying. In part, this is because staying may be detrimental to their reputation. It is crucial to be aware of this revolving door in order to understand what is unique about L.A. and its literary history.

It is a city where the myth of rugged individualism and self-made men makes the struggle for a literary community more of a necessary evil than almost anywhere else. L.A. is a place where personality has always been of the utmost importance and where the quality of the work has almost always been neglected. In this respect, it is like any other city, except that the personalities here are larger. They are more visible, more audible than the personalities within other literary scenes. Quixotic poets like Charles Bukowski, Henry Rollins, and Jim Morrison absorb an unusual proportion of the resources in the city. Dennis Cooper, before becoming a star of "underground" fiction in the 1980s, made a name for himself and his friends through poetry, and a string of anthologies that attempted to blend his punk rock sensibilities with higher brow culture. His magazine *Little Caesar*

(1976-1980) was the kind where one could find sexually rather explicit poetry next to the work of transplanted Language writers like Diane Ward, perhaps the most truly innovative of all the poets he published. Cooper's writing often directly targeted and discussed his particular clique, but in the final analysis, neither his writing nor his publishing was more insular or provincial or ethnocentric than of the rest of "experimental" writing in America. His tendency to look eastward, however, is characteristic of L.A.'s transplanted poets.

In the late 1960s, the L.A. region was still dominated by what was then largely a mythopoetic Black Sparrow Press. It had been founded in L.A., publishing Robert Kelly, Charles Bukowski, and Diane Wakowski while they were on the periphery of the Beat movement. Eventually, it moved north, and only a hard-living scene in Venice remained to live out the Beat legend, but it produced fewer and fewer notable personalities. Even rarer, perhaps, were the bonafide literary innovations. Outside of this scene, however, the Beyond Baroque Foundation, L.A.'s half-hearted response to the Ear Inn, would not have endured as it has for almost thirty years. Beyond Baroque has hosted a wide variety of readings and published many magazines and books. Most notable were the readings that occurred under the startlingly inclusive Dennis Cooper and the extremely discerning Dennis Phillips. The foundation has catered increasingly to the shock-driven writing that one superficially associates with Southern California. At the same time, Beyond Baroque has become more beholden to the national poetry establishment and local academic poets like David St. John, Carole Muske-Dukes, and celebrity fiction writers from the area like John Rechy. These camps, and especially those with ostensibly oppositional stances, have produced only a handful of publications, few of which have had an impact on their own home ground.

Nevertheless, the 1970s saw true aesthetic change within the region. There was a turn away from Beat influence toward popular culture as seen, for example, in Dennis Cooper's *Little Caesar*. There was also a turn away from mythopoetics and a more significant turn toward international writing as seen in *Invisible City* (1971-1981), co-edited by Paul Vangelisti, who lived in L.A., and John McBride from San Francisco and Berkeley.

It was a gradual change, of course, beginning arguably with Clayton Eshelman who moved to Sherman Oaks, California, bringing *Caterpillar*, which lasted until 1973, with him. Eshelman did not so much reach out to the Southern California community of writers as try to improve the local scene by making it aware of other kinds of writing. Most notable in this regard were his translations of Caesar Vallejo.

However, it was *Invisible City* that managed to bring local writers into contact with the international avant-garde literary community. This magazine reached readers as far away as Italy and brought into its pages writers from Latin America and Europe. With impeccable design and artwork, the magazine out-classed every other local publication with an aesthetic that was eclectic, but never simply "noisy." The design (and obviously the title) managed to assault the American literary lineage. Leery of the "deep image," the American Surrealism, and the crypto-Olsonian notion of "open form" as well as the talky, gossipy and ultimately personality driven poetry of Venice Beach, North Beach, and the East Village, *Invisible City* reflected the socialist concerns of its editors, who believed that translation was a key component to building community and instigating poetic innovation. Experimentation which did not evolve from the necessity of the historical conditions and from cross-cultural concerns was not highly regarded. To force a greater critical awareness on the part of its readership, *Invisible City* published international critics and philosophers who were themselves challenging the intellectual mainstream — Roland Barthes, Roman Jakobson and Michele Foucault, for example. Still, it was not a theoretical journal. Writing was always the focus.

Glancing at an *Invisible City* from 1979, one finds little concern with "the line as the basic unit of breath" or the superficial notion of the preconscious image. Instead, one finds interviews with Archie Shepp and Adriano Spatola as well as with Amiri Baraka together with their poems. Gilbert Sorrentino wrote on Jack Spicer, Zanzotto wrote on Pasolini, and Giulia Niccolai's "Feminism and the Italian Avant-garde" was published. Walter Benjamin commented on André Gide. The truth is that this issue of *Invisible City* contained a more important and wider array of work than any independent journal in America and contributed to the idea that an alternate and non-academic yet intellectual community was possible — an idea that spread to Lee Hickman in the 1980s and is especially evident in the ninth issue of his journal *Temblor*, dedicated to the memory of Antonio Porta and Adriano Spatola, two canonical Italian poets who had been introduced to America through *Invisible City*.

But even before that issue of *Temblor*, the international spirit inspired by *Invisible City* had reached *Sulfur*, which began publication in L.A. in 1981. It was edited by Clayton Eshleman with Dennis Phillips in charge of the review section. *Sulfur* 7 was particularly international, featuring the work of Octavio Paz and Antoin Artaud. When Eshleman moved from L.A. taking *Sulfur* with him, part of the void that resulted was Hickman's *Temblor* and part by Red Hill Press, which had grown out of *Invisible City*.

Red Hill Press published books by Guiliani Niccolai in 1975 and Adriano Spatola as early as 1978, but in the late 1970s and early 1980s, it published local writers such as Robert Crosson and John Thomas, as well as its own anthology of Los Angeles poets, one of the only two anthologies of this sort — the other being Dennis Cooper's — which appeared without university ties.

These two anthologies would seem particularly significant after the 1980s when institutional power became even more prominent. The University of Southern California began its *Southern California Anthology*, edited by James Ragan — an annual which included Miroslav Holub, and other prominent figures from the European poetry world, many of whom had few ties to the region, which begs the question, "So why was the magazine the named the *Southern California Anthology*?" Another less obvious institutional power that came to region was Sun & Moon Press which Douglas Messerli brought from Maryland in 1985. He did not to pretend to have any regional affiliations, at least not yet, and was then publishing primarily Language poets and did not publish any L.A. poets until the 1990s. Nonetheless, Messerli did attempt to get involved in the local literary community. He held a position in the Beyond Baroque Foundation, where he came into contact with Dennis Phillips and Dennis Cooper. Both were promoting readings by non-mainstream writers at the time.

The same year Messerli arrived, *Temblor* began publication. Hickman's editorial tastes at that time were still confessional and mythopoetic, but he gradually became more influenced by other experimental poetics, not just those of the American Language poets that he was publishing, but also international writers and translators. Hickman himself continued to write occasionally but still in the mythopoetic mode of writers like Kenneth Irby, but he was well aware of international scene and even briefly corresponded with Samuel Beckett.

Hickman often wrote out of guilt and torture regarding his homosexuality as can be seen in *Lee Senior Falls to the Floor*, published by Marty Nakel's L.A.-based Jahbone Press, which also published Dennis Phillips' *Twenty Questions*. Hickman did so at a time when many gay poets within and outside the city, some of them publishing in *Temblor* itself, were trying to get away from representations of homosexuality as involving a shameful and turbulent lifestyle. The larger point is that from the early to the mid-1980s, there was much aesthetic change within the less conventional writing scenes of southern California, and Hickman had the integrity to publish work that was not entirely in line with his own taste and that often challenged his own sensibility. As a result, *Temblor* holds an important place in the history of L.A. publication because more than almost all other magazines at that time, it sought out and succeeded in capturing the spirit of that particular moment in history. The range of poets included Kenneth Irby, Clark Coolidge, Gustaf Sobin, Fanny Howe, Lyn Hejinian, Rosmarie Waldrop, Dennis Phillips, and Nathaniel Mackey.

Hickman's ability to reach beyond his own limits and find his own "invisible city" had been apparent in 1983 when he teamed with Paul Vangelisti to publish two issues of *Boxcar*.

Hickman again reached beyond boundaries when he made an attempt to start a book press with Vangelisti and Phillips, two writers who not only practiced aesthetics different from his own, but who were also not part of the burgeoning Language movement. Hickman eventually stepped aside from the venture, but his efforts left their mark. Dennis Phillips, Paul Vangelisti, Todd Barron and Martha Ronk went ahead in what would become Littoral Books, whose most famous publication has been *Funk Lore* by Amiri Baraka. Littoral Books has published not only southern Californians with international ties like Pasquale Verdichio, but also poets on the fringe of the Language movement like Norma Cole, a Canadian perhaps more influenced by the French abstract lyric than by American conventions.

Despite Littoral's somewhat low profile, this was a time of increased awareness of poetry within the region. Not only were *Sulfur*, Littoral, and *Temblor* active, but the *L.A. Weekly* had a poetry section. The *L.A. Times* even reported on local poets like Robert Crosson in an effort to explain postmodern poetry to general reader.

Everyone who has written about and lived in L.A. from Paul Vangelisti to Charles Bukowski to Holly Northup-Prado to James Efroy, Raymond Chandler, William Faulkner, and even Jack Spicer has used the carpetbagger, land grabs, boosterism, and general violence towards history itself as major themes in his or her work. Traffic jams, long distances, and hectic adjunct teaching schedules have often prevented large turnouts at poetry readings and other literary events. No doubt the background of many of the immigrants and inner city poor who came to the region simply for jobs has prevented a cohesive or influential writing scene. One of the few groups that have transcended their rather severe geographical boundaries were the African-Americans in the Watts Writers Group. They were largely a 1960s phenomenon, but have continued to meet on the campus of the University of Southern California in some form or another. Their influence on jazz poetry has been largely unacknowledged except perhaps by its influence on Will Alexander's rhythms. Not even Lionel Rolfe's *In Search of Literary L.A.* (1991), a book applauded for its coverage of underground, politically tinged writing made much of the Watts Writers, who were perhaps the most explicitly political group of any. They, like most of the city's denizens have remained in splendid isolation.

Few poets here have been able to avoid writing about the still missing, still arriving nature of the city, a city part tropics, part desert, often suffering from an overabundance of sincerity and, at the same time, an overabundance of falsity:

> who can deny a city that gives nothing back
> where the rain always leaves at night
> and only leprechauns and gaffers
> whistle at the end of a rainbow
> who can deny the sincerity of
> hot dogs stands envisioned as hot dogs
> checks emblazoned with skiers and
> snow-capped Sierras who can deny
> a communion of lovers at eighty
> miles per hour shot once through the head
> a replay of roses of ten million
> sincere words still missing still arriving
> to die among strangers once and for all
>   —from Paul Vangelisti, *Rime*

    Vangelisti's piece is typical not only because of its concern with what it means to write in Los Angeles but also for its elaborate, often classical rhetoric combined with a postmodern interest in the problems of reference. A look at the entire book-length philosophical poem with its concern about physical appearance and reality would not reveal merely a fashionable exploration of the history of a particular "artistic process" or a gesture toward the non-fixity of language. Instead, Vangelisti's work often oscillates between philosophical meditation and a strong sense of place, even if that place is becoming more pluralistic all the time. As philosopher Gianni Vattimo wrote, "To live in a pluralistic world means to experience freedom as a continued oscillation between belonging and disorientation." This notion of freedom as both belonging and disorientation seems very much at the heart of what Paul Vangelisti, Will Alexander, Dennis Phillips, and Martha Ronk have explored as they write from within this re-built, re-destroyed landscape.

    Time and time again, poets in Los Angeles have expressed that their very presence here seems to require their isolation from whatever poetic trend might be dominant elsewhere in the country. Merely celebrating "the surface of language" or mimicking the talky, clubby style so dominant in New York or resorting to the overly ironic and self-referential strands of the Language School seem beside the point if not outright inappropriate to many of Los Angeles' most serious poets. Poets here worry that writing primarily in those manners merely duplicates the aesthetic of Hollywood and neutralizes the oppositional stance of the radical poets and publishers working beneath the shadows of the Capital Records building.

In a city constantly deconstructed, deconstruction may very well verge on naturalism. As a result, the poets here have often gone out of their way to counter Hollywood's corporate power and television's aesthetic of speed, repetition and surfaces. They have done so by addressing the history of corruption and negation within the region by focusing not only on the historical and material conditions through which their own work has come into existence, but also by recovering older forms that require close attention and a significant investment of time.

This interest in old forms and avant-garde experiment embodied in the book-length poem dates back at least the time of *Bachy*. *Bachy*'s first editor, Bill Mohr, was a founder of Beyond Baroques Writer's Workshop along with Lee Hickman, Jim Caruso, John Thomas, Kate Braverman, and others. His 1978 anthology *The Streets Inside: Ten Los Angeles Poets* shows that each of these writers were adamantly against the thirty-two line Iowa workshop style poem so dominant on the national scene in the mid-1970s. That anthology which was a result of the workshop also documents an interest in the long or serial poem as did his subsequent L.A. 1985 anthology *Poetry Love Poetry*, which included Vangelisti, Martha Ronk, Dennis Phillips, Amy Gerstler, Bob Crosson and Harry Northup. Not all of these poets would be considered innovative by today's standard, but this anthology stills shows not only the characteristic inclusiveness of its editor, but an almost unanimous concern for untimely rhetorical exploration within the formally intricate serial or long poem

A tendency toward book-length poems and novels-in-verse remain to this date and continues to oppose the personality driven art of the city, to counter act it, to demand longer attention spans and to embrace historical themes which are constantly being glossed over by the community-at-large. Vangelisti's *Villa*, a novel-in-verse, is one of the most intricate of the works of this sort and it shows how the lack of a community lead to the need for somewhat imaginary geographies, for a grounding in rigorous historical detail and ancient idioms. The need to build an invisible city or deal with the impact of the geography occurs over and over through the region's most interesting books: John Thomas' *Patagonia*, Robert Crosson's *Geographies*, Will Alexander's *Asia & Haiti* Dennis Phillips' *Arena*, parts of *State of Mind* by Martha Ronk, and even the mythopoetic *Tiresias* of Lee Hickman.

Not being aware of the connection between the long poem and the other aesthetic concerns mentioned above has lead otherwise perceptive commentators to overlook the poetry of the region as being derivative of the Stuart Z. Perkoff-Charles Bukowski beat aesthetic. For this reason, perhaps, Mike Davis states rather glibly that the true literary voice of Los Angeles is graffiti, the unheard voices of the poor. But, it might be more accurate to say the problem is one of "not knowing the language," as Martha Ronk has put it in *States of Mind*. Ronk's remark seems simply put, but she refers not only to the diversity of foreign languages within the city, not only to the local jargon (whether it be surfers, gangsters, or rednecks) that scars the inhabitants, but also to the fact that L.A. lacks a unique literary idiom. The racial, educational, and economic divisions in L.A. combat the very notion of a literary elite.

Most efforts to establish a literary elite in L.A. have attempted to do so from within already existing communities (or markets). During the 1980s, for example, Dennis Cooper leveraged his reputation using the sadomasochistic pop art of the region on his snazzy book jackets in order to market them to L.A.'s erotic underground. Similarly, a host of highly glossy, presumably "experimental" books appeared by Sun & Moon's writers whose "avant-garde" status was either reflected in or marketed through the cover art of well-known avant-garde figures. When not marketing in this fashion, many of Sun & Moon covers were designed by Katie Messborn, one of Douglas Messerli's many aliases. These jackets (and even their contents) mirrored the general lack of connection to and limited impact on L.A. by Sun & Moon's most famous writers like Lyn Hejinian and Charles Bernstein. While superficiality, opacity and a sort of "postmodern affectation" is thoroughly suitable to Messerli's literary interests, the same qualities have proven dangerously ingenuous when deployed for his public relations interests. For example, when Messerli appeared on a September 3, 1998 program of KPFK, he told host Jay Kugleman that no experimental literary scene had existed in L.A. until he arrived in 1985. The statement seems even more curious given the fact that Messerli (and rightfiilly so) never has had any particular interest in regionalism. In fact, he did not publish any local poets until 1989 when he published Dennis Phillips' A World (another book, this time by a native Angelino, that is concerned with invisible communities). It was another six years before he published another L. A. poet's book: Martha Ronk's *State of Mind*. Perhaps this familiar Los Angeles phenomenon of taking credit for the work of others is what Dennis Phillips meant when he wrote, "They will invent/the stories to surround phrases."

Nevertheless, even if certain forces were well in place before Messerli arrived, Sun & Moon's presence in Los Angeles has contributed to the internationalism of the region. For example, in 1995, Sun & Moon brought out a crucial translation of the Italian 1960's avant-garde: *I Novissimi*, edited by Alfredo Giulani. In 1999, Sun & Moon plans to continue to bring out more translations from the Italian with the editorial help of Luigi Ballerini and Paul Vangelisti. Sun & Moon also recently began an international magazine *Mr. Knife, Miss Fork*. In doing so, it joins a host independent magazine publishers in L.A. who have expanded their international coverage.

A host of L.A. magazines have recently expanded their international coverage. Chris Reiner's *Witz*, one of the very few critical journals in the country that remain independent, has focused much energy on Russian poetry. Vangelisti's *Ribot* (pronounced ree-boe) which continues the aesthetic of *Invisible City*, although on a smaller scale — a decision that Vangelisti says is consistent with the diminished state of beauty in the culture — has inspired a handful of younger writers and editors like Evan Calbi and myself to publish more translations in the journal we edit — *Rhizome*. All this activity has led to a series of annual conferences that include poets and artists from all over the country and that help focus attention on the issue of how a writer generates his or her work in the context of an adopted tradition or historical situation. Franklin Bruno has aptly described the first annual conference in the Fall 1997 issue of *Witz*, pointing out that such activity proves that a literary community that is is not anti-intellectual but is outside the academic mainstream is possible here and now. At present in the L.A. area, there are six journals of experimental writing. *Ribot, Rhizome, Remap,* edited by Todd Baron, *Witz, Indefinite Space,* edited by Marcia Arrieta, and the well-known, rather glossy *Arshile,* edited and published since 1993 by Mark Salerno. There is also a chapbook series published by Guy Bennett's Seeing Eye Books, which includes the work of Mohamed Dib, Gionvanna Sandri, Clark Coolidge, and Robert Crosson, among others, and two presses, Littoral and Sun & Moon. Perhaps only now does L.A. have the potential to reconcile its image as an American paradise with its political and cultural reality.

Susan Vanderborg

"IF THIS WERE THE PLACE TO BEGIN": LITTLE MAGAZINES AND THE EARLY LANGUAGE POETRY SCENE

O**N BOTH AMERICAN COASTS IN THE 1970S**, a group of little magazines was circulating experimental poetry at odds with the confessional and formalist verse of institutional grant networks and publishing venues.* Many of the Language or L=A=N=G=U=A=G=E writers, labels adapted from the editors and contributors who theorized these experiments, argued that language does not reflect a prior meaning but rather constitutes and delimits meaning. "Language is the means of our socialization," Charles Bernstein asserted in the fourth volume of the journal *L=A=N=G=U=A=G=E*; it is always already ideological (7).

Language writing tends to disrupt referentiality, focusing on the materiality of the signifier and the process of its own composition. Its antecedents include Gertrude Stein's associative word patterns and disjunctive syntax, the early prose-poetic texts of William Carlos Williams, the fractured imagery and sound games of the Objectivists, the projective verse of the Black Mountain poets, and the self-reflexive surface play in John Ashbery's

---

*The national awards for the period are a useful index. They favored confessional poets (Robert Lowell, Pulitzer 1974, National Book Critics Circle Award 1978), Deep Image writers (W.S. Merwin, Pulitzer 1971; James Wright, Pulitzer 1972), Beat authors (Allen Ginsberg, National Book Award 1974) and formalists (James Merrill, Pulitzer 1977). The formalists, while emphasizing the artificiality of poetic language, did not distort syntax and semiotics in the ways that Language writing foregrounded. Even John Ashbery's *Self-Portrait in a Convex Mirror* that swept the Pulitzer Prize, National Book Award, and National Book Critics Circle Award in 1976 had relatively clearer lyrics and meditative sequences than the poetry of *The Tennis Court Oath* that the Language poets admired.

In addition to the established journals at the time, *American Poetry Review*, begun in 1972, still featured writers like Robert Bly, John Berryman, Anne Sexton, David Ignatow, Richard Wilbur, and Ginsberg in its early issues; one essayist called for a "'Hands-Off'" approach to teaching poetry in the classroom as a lyric vehicle for expressing emotion rather than a "mysterious intellectual exercise" (Wagner 58). Daniel Halpern's 1975 *American Poetry Anthology* selected new poets who combined "sureness of technique" with "depth of feeling" (xxix).

The Language magazines cited in this article are intended only as a sampling; others should include *A Hundred Posters*, *Oculist Witnesses*, *Sun & Moon*, *Eel*, *Shirt*, *Vanishing Cab*, *E pod*, and *Streets and Roads*, to name a few. *Vort*, *Wch Way*, *New Wilderness Letter*, *New American Writing*, *Sulfur*, *Conjunctions*, *Ironwood*, *The Chicago Review*, and *Talisman* also promoted Language authors. Many of these magazines are listed in *A Secret Location on the Lower East Side: Adventures in Writing, 1960-1980* by Steven Clay and Rodney Phillips.

texts. Heavily theoretical, Language draws on sources from Marxist literary theory to Wittgenstein's concept of language games and Derrida's attack on a transcendental Logos. In particular, it challenges the idea of a poetics of voice; instead of focusing on a lyric speaker, a Language poem might suggest how subjectivity is constructed by slogans, advertisements, and broadcasts so familiar that we no longer notice their influence. By scrutinizing such found texts and by subverting conventions of grammar and semantics, the authors encourage readers to participate actively in creating textual meaning.

Individual Language authors share many of these practices, but their varied styles make them difficult to characterize as a school. Examining the magazines that published them is the best way to appreciate the genesis and diversity of this poetry. The editors were poets themselves who were invested in defining a community of their peers and predecessors. Journals like *Là-Bas* and *Roof*, for example, advertised themselves as "poets' publication[s]" (Messerli copyright page), inviting contributors to determine the journals' creative direction and themes.* The magazines not only showed the interactions between East and West Coast Language centers but often printed highly elliptical or opaque texts side by side with the confessional poetry that they seemed to critique. The linear, first-person narrative about a mother's deathbed in the fourth issue of *Miam* was followed by Bob Perelman's writing in the fifth issue, texts in which "Words fail to describe" a fixed referent and one's private experience is constructed by others' language: "My strength was as your letter made me" (unpaginated). These juxtapositions reveal Language poetics less as a coherent agenda than a gradual evolution from different literary origins.

I. "TRYING TO UNDERSTAND MY PROCESSES": EARLY LANGUAGE JOURNALS

THE LANGUAGE JOURNALS OF THE 1970S RANGED from card-sized booklets and five-page newsletters that were mimeographed or xeroxed to perfect-bound volumes with artwork and photographs. Many were left unpaginated with a creative mixture of type fonts and handwritten passages. Though one or two journals received an occasional NEA grant or

---

*As James Sherry and Tom Savage announced: "*ROOF* is in search of a perspective which we expect to develop from the writers as we continue to publish" (5). Douglas Messerli wrote in the opening issue of his magazine: "[B]ecause it is a poets' publication, not a publishers', *LÀ-BAS* seeks new ideas and suggestions for its format. Like the poetry it publishes, *LÀ-BAS* will not be poured into moulds, but hopefully will serve poets to keep in touch with one another and to keep abreast of exciting new poetry and theory" (copyright page).

donations from a local arts board, they were perpetually pressed for funding; some of them lasted only a few issues or resumed publication under a new title. They were typically published several times a year, often irregularly, in runs of a few hundred copies with individual issues distributed for a couple of dollars each or sent at mailing cost to a circle of readers. There were also early collections of Language-oriented poetry in special issues of *Toothpick, Lisbon & the Orcas Islands* and *Alcheringa*.

Not only the journals but many of the contributors seemed at a transitional point in their writing. "[I'm] trying to understand my processes," David Bromige explained in the fifth issue of *Hills*, in a "language-oriented writing" that stressed verbal slippages and breaks in meaning (109). A poem by Clark Coolidge in *Toothpick* 3.1 stated succinctly that "thought's pressure / bends grammar" (unpaginated). A Ron Silliman composition in *Miam* 3 investigated the possibility of a "not represents / sentence" to replace a mimetic style of literary realism, a "language that no longer worked" (unpaginated). As Silliman's description suggested, the associative rhythms of Language writing often combined aspects of both prose sentence and poetic line. "I don't like it," Bromige mockingly complained about this disjunctive writing, "for hurting my head" (109). But it is precisely the stylistic conflicts and contradictions that make the 1970s publications such a revealing history as the authors introduced their innovations to selected audiences.

"NOT METAPHOR": THE UNSTABLE REFERENTS OF *THIS*

In 1971, Barrett Watten and Robert Grenier co-edited the first issue of *This*, one of the formative journals of Language writing. It showcased photographs of Ezra Pound and Charles Olson, whose influence was reflected in the journal's collaged citations and the attention to the visual aspect of the poetry. Rather than long sequences, however, the writing in early volumes more closely resembled Stein's *Tender Buttons*, Louis Zukofsky's lyrics, or Robert Creeley's *Pieces*—short poems or prose-poetic passages in which an object is defamiliarized in the act of description. Titles such as "Siren," "The Man," or "White Bells," as well as the journal's own title, a demonstrative pronoun, only called attention to the absence of clear referents in these poems that focused more on the grammar, sound, and shape of their word groups.

With selections from Bernstein, Silliman, Coolidge, Bruce Andrews, Lyn Hejinian, Bernadette Mayer, and many others, the journal's process-oriented style sometimes produced concrete poetry or puns, while other pieces played against expectations of message and symbolism:

> If this were the place to begin
> is not,
>
> starts with the disk-sun-boat--a journey
> we can share,
>   a precise
> boat--Gokstad, not metaphor--
> to our own country
>   following the line
> of tensions between the heart & the hard
>
> facts of the world,
>   perception. Stanza
> of particulars.
>   Lamplight half led
> onto my book & half held back--
> afraid of the white page
>
> My confession. The pale blue asters
> with dark hearts
> are everywhere these days.
> It begins to rain.   (2)

This poem by Robert Kelly with its image of a ship setting sail seems appropriate for the opening selection in a new journal, but the subjunctive form of "If this were the place to begin" implies that readers have made a false start. The second line confirms that the poem "is not" a straightforward linear progression, an impression reinforced by the fragmented syntax as well as the broken lines and frequent spaces in the layout. What does a "precise" boat or "hard" fact mean in this context? The "disk-sun-boat" might symbolize the sun's passage across the sky--a journey every reader "can share"-- but the poem relies more upon metonymy than metaphor, presenting a loose association of details and sounds as the disk boat become a historical Viking ship, the sunlight transforms into lamplight, and the poetic "heart" is phonetically linked to the "hard / facts" of perception and the flowers' "dark hearts" at the poem's conclusion. The reader searching for a stanza of descriptive particulars finds something more like a projective lyric in which verbal precision paradoxically becomes a deferral of choices among possible conclusions for a sentence or among multiple connotations for a single word. Adjectives and phrases in Kelly's poem are frequently separated from the nouns they modify, prompting readers to think of substitute choices to describe the "journey" or "line." By the end of the piece, the promise of a unique personal or national landscape is deferred to conversational clichés about the weather.

The journal's poems and reviews continued this pattern of distorting descriptions that announced their status as texts-in-progress. Instead of polished illustrations, a child's crayon drawing of faces decorated the cover of the first issue. Sketches illustrating "Knitting" and "Spilled Milk" in the second gave the impression of a textbook, as if the reader were learning the rules of language from an immigrant's perspective, a premise reflected in some of the exchanges:

Father: Speak English Today.
   Son: Allright.   (Saroyan 90)

Like Aram Saroyan's colloquial son, the contributors delighted in slang and jargon as they quoted billboards, bad Christmas card poetry, notebooks, and telegrams in contexts that reinterpreted their meaning. One issue included an attached set from Grenier's *Sentences*, words printed on index cards that could be reshuffled to create new reading patterns. Among these diverse texts, the writers' own statements on poetics functioned less as a guide than as another discursive style to be evaluated.

Theorizing a poetics was further complicated by the authors' ambivalence toward lyric voice. In the poetics statement "On Speech," Grenier's impatience with poetry that tried to simulate a spoken presence went hand in hand with Romantic references to "thought or feeling forming out of the 'vast' silence/noise of consciousness" (86).* The journal as a whole reflected this ambivalence. The "confession" of Kelly's opening poem, for example, was deliberately anti-confessional, hinting that poets who bared their hearts in flowery

---

*See too Perelman's argument that this quote about consciousness emphasizes Grenier's source of poetic inspiration as something "personal: the originary, omnitemporal space 'way back in the head'"; Perelman connects Grenier's essay with the making-it-new impulse of Williams's modernism (*The Marginalization of Poetry* 43). Silliman points out that Grenier's essay and the journal as a whole remained fascinated with the speech-based breath patterns of projective lyrics even as they questioned the limitations of that form (Introduction to *In the American Tree* xv).

imagery were already too numerous. Yet other poems would not have been out of place as workshop verse despite unusual line breaks or lack of punctuation. As the writing selections became even more extensive in Watten's long-running San Francisco journal, they moved further away from conventional characterization, plot, and description.

TRANSFORMING THE IMAGE: A MODERN *TOTTEL'S*

BEGUN IN THE BAY AREA IN 1970, Silliman's *Tottel's* offered its own strategies for critiquing the premise of referential language. Named after *Tottel's Miscellany*, a book that had introduced new poetic styles during the English Renaissance, this newsletter foregrounded texts with provocative juxtapositions of images and with words or letters arranged as visual objects on the page. Silliman argued that the original *Tottel's* had separated poets from their audience by reifying and marketing the texts in book form[*]; he announced in the first issue that he was mailing his own mimeo circular for free to a community of interested literary "friends" (5).

The imagery in *Tottel's* first few issues ranged from Romantic to postmodernist. Excerpts from Jerome Rothenberg's Bantu translations in the first issue read like an alienated version of Whitman's *Leaves of Grass*: "I was a tree that lost its leaves." and "I was angry later I roamed their forests" (1). Despite the visual focus, however, the poets rarely created a stable portrait of either perceiving subject or perceived object. "My poems come from a limited experience," one writer asserted, "and, as such, are open to criticism and unlimited revision" (Cohen 4). Coolidge's word sequences in the tenth issue left the imagination at the edge of what "can be seen" amid the "faults" and "lost sets" of dictionary references and interrupted phrases that crowded his passages (14). One of the journal's most memorable images was in fact a symbol of violent absence: the cover of the sixteenth issue was a copy of an execution form from San Quentin prison, with the name of the journal inserted in place of the prisoner's name.

Sound patterns connected these mutable pictures for many of the *Tottel's* authors. "[R]'s l's roar," Daphne Marlatt wrote in one alliterative poem (3), while other writers played with broken words and strings of letters across sections of their texts. D Alexander's "Poem" in the second issue compacted words into a "sediment" of sound that prohibited

---

[*]He analyzes this commodification of the first English poetry anthology in "Disappearance of the Word, Appearance of the World." *L=A=N=G=U=A=G=E* Supplement 3: *The Politics of Poetry* (1981), unpaginated.

any easy absorption of meaning (9); they became a "gate plac't to be / not gone thru but filld" with different interpretive possibilities (10). Other *Tottel's* pieces seemed to invite readers directly to fill in their own connections and conclusions. "We are mailing you," one author began—and never completed the sentence describing the package (Lally 9). "You have just won a thought," Opal L. Nations wrote in the middle of a series of one-line poems (4), as if the reader's input were the safeguard that might ensure "The poem is not erased" (3) and the word play would continue.

"ALL OF MY FRIENDS WERE THERE": NEW NARRATIVE SEQUENCES

A WIDE RANGE OF EXPERIMENTAL POETIC AND PROSE SEQUENCES characterized the narratives of Perelman's *Hills*. First published in 1973 in Iowa City and then moved to California, the journal resembled *This* with many of the same authors and similar childlike drawings. A *Hills* selection might present a vignette with spliced storylines or a mock personal anecdote interrupted by outside conversations. Even if the phrases seemed syntactically regular, the transitions between them were often abrupt or missing:

> A soft breeze that I took into my lungs from the open window beside me. It sized up to be about a six month cycle. I glossed the combinations as they cut loose and reformed, end, beginning, middle. All of my friends were there.
> —Kit Robinson (34)

Styles clash here as Robinson's passage moves from a poetic description of inspiration to the mechanical prediction of a "six month cycle" and then speculations about restructuring elements in a linear sequence. The different descriptive "combinations" themselves become characters, playfully rebelling and then "reform[ing]" themselves, but not in the expected order, for a receptive audience of peers. "[T]he interest evident in the construction, rhythm of the sentences, obviates the need for the content," Bromige quipped about his own texts (107). "Everywhere there is the tension of an incomplete sentence, an ambiguous antecedent, an unnatural act, an illogical causality" (111), the point of which is to prevent the text from becoming a "commodity" or a "vacation" to be taken for granted by the reader (107). The writers traced influences from various modernisms--Russian Futurism, Objectivism, Dada, and Surrealism—as well as the compositions of Stein and Pound.

To make the new poetry less of a commodity, the journal's contributors emphasized the cumulative effect of reading the pieces instead of discrete quotable lines. Watten in an excerpt from *City Fields* used metaphors of traffic intersections and collisions to describe the dialogic interplay among the passages in his own writing and their relation to the language games of other speakers (40-43). Silliman also refused to compartmentalize his work ("Maybe I write poetry, but I don't write poems" [23]), comparing his texts to those of Larry Eigner in which the "borders between [the] poems are very arbitrary" (23). Echoing Robinson's image of group participation, the journal specialized in collaborative "talks": poetics discussions and textual analyses from roundtables of authors based on a public series that Perelman had begun in 1977. He described the talks in *Hills* 6-7 as simultaneously "educational, creational, dramatic" (Perelman 5), creating a sense of community without requiring consensus. *Hills*'s ninth issue presented lively metafictional exchanges among narrators, characters, and historical figures in plays from the San Francisco Poets Theater; the roles for each play were originally acted by the poets themselves.

On the cusp between 1970s and 1980s Language writing, Carla Harryman's San Francisco newletter-style *QU*, first published in 1980, also experimented with innovative forms of narrative and poetic prose. Contributors including Steve Benson, Johanna Drucker, Hejinian, Perelman, and Watten satirized the typecast roles and recycled plots of Hollywood storytelling. *QU*'s narratives, though frequently presented in myth or fairy tale tropes, offered highly disjunctive characterizations of the heroes and heroines. "You are trying to make a person out of me," the nymph Echo complained in a Benson poem from the first issue. "A person you might know" (1). Instead of psychological insights, the poem gave surreal stage directions about role-playing: "The carrots tried to *be* mushrooms. . . .You are trying to *be* the sunset" (1). Pronouns and perspectives shifted abruptly in the journal's texts, and Echo was a good introductory figure for compositions in which a single expression might repeat in multiple storylines, with princesses becoming drag queens and allusions to immigrant aliens leading to images of rockets and spaceflight. The author, however, retained a privileged position in a number of these transformations. "[T]hings define people," one of Harryman's narrators asserted in the fifth issue (5), yet also valorized the writer's imagination as a subversive process of restoring narrative possibilities to old props and settings.

The *QU* authors suggested that crossing fictional and non-fictional genres—official histories, personal diaries, television episodes, and folktales--offered another kind of realism by demonstrating the constructedness of any narrative form. The implication was that readers needed to learn the difference between "Active and passive dreaming" (Friedman 4) in their approach to absorptive Hollywood texts. As a Drucker character commented in a metaphor about consumption: "Sometimes it takes that much bland to mobilize" an audience response (4).

READER PLEASE FOLLOW

DEBATES OVER A POETICS OF VOICE AND THE NEED FOR READER PARTICIPATION strongly shaped the evolution of the New York journal *Roof*, published by Segue Press and edited by James Sherry along with Tom Savage in the early issues. *Roof*, which became a key forum for both East and West Coast Language writers, began as a 1976 anthology from the Jack Kerouac School of Writing at Boulder, featuring pieces by Allen Ginsberg, Robert Duncan, and William S. Burroughs. While the next few issues retained a Beat and Black Mountain flavor, Andrews was also writing poetry that mixed allusions to breath, spontaneity, and personal experience with legal and scientific diction; it is not clear, for example, in his word sequences in the second issue whether "appreciate" and "tender" are economic or emotional signifiers (10). Bernstein too created "Otherwise / images," phrases in which a subjective "internalness" is a "tease" or "style" to be explored like any other role-playing game (17). The last lines of their poems did not provide closure but evoked scattered "parts" (Andrews, "No Tumble" 14) and "splintage" (11) without privileging any one conclusion.

To ensure that an audience knew how to approach these indeterminate texts, a number of authors provided reading guidelines. Several poets explicated their generative devices and Savage's "Ode to Unreality" came with instructions: "The following **Kits** invite the reader to participate in their writing. One may add words in the spaces, subtract words that are printed, rearrange by any principle or at random, or simply read them as finished poems" (67). Sherry's editorial preface to the collaboration *Legend* in the third issue explained "Language-centered writing" as a merging of "form and content" in which information could be conveyed by the "surface relations of words" (49). Though the journal's entries often seemed to privilege the "Melodramatic *forms*" over the "*contents*" (Andrews, "Getting Ready To Have Been Frightened" 72) in their parodic sonnets, game codes, equations, and drawings, the premise of communicating information stressed the importance of the reader's role in interpreting these exchanges. Sherry's initial challenge to *Legend*'s audience, "Do [the poems] require a new kind of reading?" was the necessary first step to answering his final question: "will the sentence be saved?" (49).

VISUAL POETICS

As part of emphasizing the materiality of signifiers, many early Language magazines included graphics with their written texts. *Là-Bas* inserted rebus-like cutouts in its pages, illustrating its "RE:VisioNs" of a poetics of identity by juxtaposing prints of an eye, a visual pun on "I," with scribbled misspellings of an author's name (Eigner and Norse unpaginated). The contributors to *Toothpick, Lisbon & the Orcas Islands* bracketed poems with photographs and diagrams, scattered letters at different angles across the pages, and framed words in chessboard squares to visualize the concept of language games.

Other magazines devoted themselves extensively to visual and interart poetry. The opening issue of *Big Deal*, published by Barbara Baracks in 1973, covered poetry by Ray DiPalma, Michael Palmer, Maureen Owen, Coolidge, Andrews, and others, incorporating texts with sketches, shifting margins, and word fragments. The minimalism of three syllables

    sence   ed

    spect   (unpaginated)

for example, in a DiPalma poem, suggested numerous semantic combinations. Do they mark an ab*sence* of meaning or non*sense*, or is this a pun on the visual *sense* as we asked to in*spect* the poem as a *spect*acle? Instead of reading the poem as something already complet*ed*, the readers are prompted to *edit* its *sense*. Later issues of this annual New York journal expanded the spectacle to discuss paintings, photographs, and sculpture complemented by poetic commentary as in Robert Smithson's essay on the *Spiral Jetty* earthwork. The journal paid homage to the midcentury New York art scene when painters and poets often collaborated, but it was not limited to visual art alone. Performance pieces ranged from David Antin's talk poetry to John Cage's reading through Thoreau, and there were also prose excerpts by avant-garde fiction writers like Kathy Acker and Jayne Anne Phillips. *Big Deal* had a relatively large print run of a thousand copies by the third issue; its successors included multi-media journals of the 1980s and 1990s such as *Lingo*.

"THE POLITICAL CHARACTER OF POETRY"

LIKE *Big Deal*, THE PENNSYLVANIA JOURNAL *Paper Air* incorporated calligraphy, drawings, collages, and photographs with its poetry. It honored earlier writers like Cid Corman and Jackson Mac Low as well as featuring translations and new work by emerging poets. Yet a journal whose inaugural call for contributions in 1976 celebrated "Emotion becoming the word I speak" and "new avenues of consciousness" does not at first sound like a vehicle for Language poetry (Ott unpaginated). The key to that inclusion lay in its textual politics.

Editor Gil Ott described the journal as part of a revolutionary praxis by artists as workers, a literary Marxist rhetoric that would parallel some of the theorizations of Language writing. He explained in an editorial in *Paper Air* 2.2 that "the contemporary American poetic community, with its disdain for hierarchical organization and its investigation of the political character of poetry on all levels, is ready to assert itself as a necessary labor force," though he argued that institutional grants too often coopted the most radical social artists (1). The remedy: small presses and journals that could be circulated easily and that operated outside grant networks. But what type of poetry could best convey a "Revolutionary content and analysis" (Ott, *Paper Air* 2.2 1)? Some of the journal's poems dealt directly with political themes, as in *Peace on Earth*, John Taggart's protest poem that blended Vietnam reports with words from a Tarahumara dance of healing. Other authors showed the process of their labor by handwriting poems and letters. Silliman insisted in 2.2 that his poetic forms were themselves ideological. In response to the charge that formal experiments appealed only to an elite audience of intellectuals, he argued that the fracturing of sense and syntax in his poetry was a way of showing how language constructs our concepts of class (10). These articles, letters, "re/views," and interviews about the politics of poetics remained some of the most influential aspects of *Paper Air* throughout the 1970s and 1980s.

"THOUGHT'S MEASURE": THEORIZING THE NEW POETICS IN $L=A=N=G=U=A=G=E$

EIGNER S ESSAY "APPROACHING THINGS" in the first issue of $L=A=N=G=U=A=G=E$ magazine still suggested a referential model of poetry. "[B]ehind words and whatever language comes about are things," he stated, and language would not change those material conditions though it might help us "cope with them"; words "can't bring people in India or West Virginia above the poverty line" (unpaginated). But his comments about language and politics raised subtler questions about the political implications of innovative poetry techniques. As in *Paper Air*, many of the contributors to this journal contended that their writing played an active role in interrogating ideology, though they debated the method and degree of its efficacy.

Co-edited by Andrews and Bernstein in New York, *L=A=N=G=U=A=G=E* ran from 1978 to 1981, with initial printings of about five hundred copies each of the first volume issues, later supplemented by photocopies. The journal's capitalized title with its equal signs advertised the writers' disruptive scrutiny of language and typography, underscoring the arbitrariness of distinctions among signifiers. Steve McCaffery set the tone in the second issue by arguing for a "structural reappraisal of the functional roles of author and reader, performer and performance," since the journal took the view of writing as reading even further than its antecedents. The early issues were composed almost entirely of reviews, some of Stein, Zukofsky, and Ashbery, but chiefly of the reviewers' circle of contemporary poets, offering sympathetic readings of small press books and citing other journals and collections where readers could find the new poetics. The creative format of the reviews led one writer to complain that they were unnecessarily inaccessible, mimicking rather than explaining an already difficult poetry (Taggart). But these reviews challenged literary language as a fetish through their radical intertextuality.

Readers quickly realized that the lengthy quotes from the reviewed author were not clearly distinguished from the reviewer's responses. "The words in this piece are mostly from Barrett Watten's work," one essayist warned humorously. "The excerpts are often accurate" (Perelman). A reviewer in the first issue mixed Eigner's phrases with quotes from other authors, concluding with the words: "I do not think of Eigner" (Coolidge). Reading became a Borgesian appropriation of the other's text, removing it from a private context to a public space in which the process of mediation was the message; the journal offered a performance of Perelman's Watten or Bernstein reading Stanley Cavell reading Wittgenstein. "Author dies, writing begins," Andrews stated succinctly in the sixth issue, a communal activity in which no one owns the words or limits the interpretations.

L=A=N=G=U=A=G=E 9-10 in 1979 was a special issue on the politics of poetry. Though the writers agreed that a political theme alone was not a sufficient social critique, they differed on stylistic strategies. "I DON'T WANT ANY CONTENT I JUST WANT EXTREMISM," Acker proclaimed, advocating a practice of rule-breaking and shock tactics. Instead of negation, Andrews countered, the poetry must "*charge* material with possibilities of meaning" that could "reach or <u>act on</u> the world (not only as it is, as it could be.)" He admitted, however, that a poetry of openness and unexpected connections might look superficially like a syntax fractured simply for the sake of disrupting fixed meanings. Some of the authors were intrigued by dysfunctional speech and reading processes like stuttering and dyslexia (Mason) or else wrote about illiteracy, i.e. those outside the debates over the "morals of our grammar" (Thomas). For all the writers who championed a specific technique, others expressed concern that singling out any particular style would produce formulas rather than action. "[I]t isn't good enough to press the conviction that if everybody could practice parataxis the structures that make our lives so awful wld crumble," Brian Fawcett observed, urging writers to incorporate colloquial speech patterns and rhetoric in their poetry. The goal is not to choose between a formalist or materialist approach to language and politics, Michael Davidson added, but to interrogate the way one's poetry is produced and disseminated.

What tied these authors together? In tracing their own methodology, the $L=A=N=G=U=A=G=E$ contributors drew eclectically from Marx, Adorno, Althusser, Wittgenstein, Derrida, Deleuze, Freud, and Lacan. There were discussions of individuals interpellated as subjects by a language system next to calls for a poetry to record personal experiences lying outside capitalist exchanges. Between those two extremes, Hejinian in the third issue proposed styles of writing that would be "personal and inclusive but not necessarily self-revelatory," responding through different formal strategies to the patterns of language the writer hears and reads. The strongest similarities among these authors lay in their responses to a common bibliography--to the workshop lyrics they challenged, to the modernist texts they reinterpreted, and to the chapbooks they praised for making language a little more resistant or defamiliarized. "All theory is safest ascribed in retrospect," Hejinian noted, and what $L=A=N=G=U=A=G=E$ bequeathed to its successors was a set of poetries in the process of constructing an agenda and a reading community. Looking ahead to the next generation of Language-oriented writers, Bernstein insisted in the eighth issue that any temporary group "walls must be stripped down & new ones constantly built as (re)placements" if a poetics forum were to be effective.

II. LANGUAGE COMMUNITIES OF THE 1980s

B Y THE 1980S, A LARGER NUMBER OF CRITICS AND AUTHORS were referring to Language or language-centered writing. In 1982, both *The Paris Review* and *Ironwood* hosted samplers of Language writing, and *Boundary* 2 featured Bernstein's 43 "$L=A=N=G=U=A=G=E$

Poets" collection four years later. Not only did more mainstream journals include selections from Language authors, but the same poet-publishers who had organized journal roundtables were circulating essay collections: Palmer's *Code of Signals* (1983), *The L=A=N=G=U=A=G=E Book* (1984), Watten's *Total Syntax* (1985), Pereleman's *Writing/Talks* (1985), and Silliman's *The New Sentence* (1987). Silliman also produced a six hundred-page anthology of East and West Coast Language poetry, *In the American Tree: Language Realism Poetry* (1986) and Douglas Messerli published *"Language" Poetries* for New Directions in 1987. In the mid-1980s, Language poetry attracted the attention of such prominent critics as Marjorie Perloff and Charles Altieri; by 1989 George Hartley published the first book-length study of the writing: *Textual Politics and the Language Poets*.[*] In the late 1980s and 1990s, moreover, many of the poets themselves found jobs within academia teaching literature and poetics classes.

The 1980s journals that published Language authors reflected this critical attention, devoting more issues to specialized aspects of the writing or to individual poets. The attempts to anthologize a movement also created arguments over which poets fit the Language rubric, particularly for the more neo-Romantic poets in terms of poetic voice, political praxis, and the extent of their interest in theory. Palmer and Susan Howe, for instance--two authors included in Silliman's *In the American Tree*—would distance themselves from the Language label.[†] There were debates with earlier experimentalists; when Robert

---

[*] Perloff's detailed close reading of Language poetry and poetics essays, "The Word as Such: L=A=N=G=U=A=G=E Poetry in the Eighties" was first published in *American Poetry Review* (1984). Lee Bartlett's "What Is 'Language Poetry'?" in *Critical Inquiry* (1986) discussed Language as the "most recent 'group' of American poets...really to be of more than passing interest and perhaps to be actually capable of bringing about a major shift of attention in American poetry and poetics" (741-42). Jerome McGann's "Contemporary Poetry, Alternate Routes" in *Critical Inquiry* (1987) emphasized the political ideology of Language poetry's fractured syntax, nonnarrative, and nonsense passages. In a response article, Altieri questioned whether encouraging readers to participate in creating their own textual meanings could effect any real political change ("Without Consequences Is No Politics"). As the essay title "Opposing Poetry" suggests, Hank Lazer placed Language writers, by virtue of their challenge to familiar reading habits, in a tradition of "oppositional" modernists such as Williams, Stein, and Zukofsky, with the added influence of poststructuralist criticism. The last chapter in Stephen Fredman's *Poet's Prose: The Crisis in American Verse* (first edition 1983) also discussed Steinian prose poets such as Bromige, Silliman, and Davidson; his 1990 epilogue covered Language poetry more fully as a movement. Linda Reinfeld's *Language Poetry: Writing as Rescue* (1992) and Perelman's *The Marginalization of Poetry: Language Writing and Literary History* (1996) have emerged since Hartley's book on Language poetics.

[†] Palmer, in an interview published in 1987, described his poetry as more Romantic and less committed to the "many directives and proscriptions" of Language poetry such as Watten's, while still expressing a shared interest in questioning "surfaces of language" and "normative syntax" (Interview with Lee Bartlett 129). Two years later, he emphasized his appreciation of the Romantic aspect of Duncan's writing and also identified a number of contemporary authors including Nathaniel Mackey, Leslie Scalapino, and Rosmarie Waldrop, as "outside that so-called language-oriented identity" (Interview with Keith Tuma 9).

Duncan criticized Language as an unimportant and derivative movement, six San Francisco poets responded by interrogating the politics of group identification and emphasizing Language's scrutiny of "the nature of social reality" (Silliman et al 274).[*] Some of the journals actively took sides in these debates; others undercut the distinctions by continuing to publish a wide selection of innovative poetry.

In format, the 1980s journals that published Language writing tended to be lengthier, perfect-bound volumes with extended poetry excerpts, translations, and sophisticated art sections. Printings ranged from several hundred copies per issue to over a thousand; the price of an individual issue usually fell between three to eight dollars. Though the editors had slightly more access to national and local grants, funding continued to be a problem. New York and San Francisco remained major publishing centers, but there were other Language-centered communities in the United States and in Canada. The Toronto journal *Open Letter*, edited by Frank Davey, had been an early forum for discussions of Language writing, and essays from McCaffery's symposium on "The Politics of the Referent" were reprinted in 1980 as a *L=A=N=G=U=A=G=E* supplement; the fourth volume of *L=A=N=G=U=A=G=E* in 1981 was co-published as a special issue of *Open Letter*. The Kootenay School of Writing in Vancouver frequently invited Language authors to read, sponsoring a 1985 New Poetics Colloquium to discuss poetry that, in the words of one participant, could generate "multiple meaning" and "multiplying means" of literary production (Gay 17). By 1990, a *Tyuonyi* journal symposium on contemporary poetry edited by Bernstein and Phillip Foss included responses from almost a hundred poets doing Language-oriented writing and related avant-garde experiments from the United States, Canada, England, New Zealand, and Australia.

"INVERSIONARY STRATEGIES": LANGUAGE POETICS JOURNALS

A NUMBER OF JOURNALS FOCUSED ON LANGUAGE POETICS emerged in the wake of Andrews and Bernstein's magazine. Tom Beckett christened his Ohio-based journal *The Difficulties* in

---

[*] Duncan described the Language poets as a "crowd of mosquitos off there in somebody else's swamp," denouncing their writing as "reductionism" and "illogical negativism" (127). The six poets who published "Aesthetic Tendency and the Politics of Poetry" in *Social Text* took exception to Duncan's characterization of a Language movement, charging that he used it only to reinforce his own idea of a literary canon; they also criticized the group lines drawn by Palmer, "a poet who has appeared in all the major magazines and anthologies of our tendency" but who was "careful to distance himself from the market implications of such group identity" (Silliman, Harryman, Hejinian, Benson, Perelman, and Watten 272, 273).

response to Olson's charge that modern life has become too easy or convenient. Beckett's inaugural issue in 1980 presented twenty-seven "process-oriented" writers who defined the relevance of a "'language environment'" for their poetry (Beckett and Neikirk unpaginated). Davidson championed a poetics of "inversionary strategies and interruptions" that would reveal the methods "by which poetry is cut off from experience." Many of the other participants echoed a Black Mountain vocabulary of composition by field and the importance of voice as sound. One poetic composition described an "empire of ears" where "elephant poets" come "trumpeting" (La Charity); another traced the phonemes and pauses of a "mother / tongue" in translation (Waldrop). Howe wrote of recovering voices: the "wild cries" and the "names creeping out everywhere" behind the "blanks and dead spots (despots) in history."

With the second volume, the journal covered a single author for each issue, juxtaposing a selection of the poetry with multiple interviews of the author and commentary by other poets. The hundred-page issues on Bromige, Silliman, Bernstein, and Howe maintained the format of a lively, frequently interrupted conversation developed in *Hills*. While it was easier to distinguish between primary and secondary sources than in *L=A=N=G=U=A=G=E*, there was still significant citation in the reviews and the interviews often extended into collaborative dialogue pieces between writers.

Jimmy & Lucy's House of "K," edited by Andrew Schelling and Benjamin Friedlander, captured the flavor of the Berkeley lecture scene and the poetics discussions at 80 Langton Street in San Francisco, or "Language" Street as it was nicknamed. From its first issue in 1984, the title, illustrations, and typewritten format suggested a coffeehouse roundtable of neighborhood poets. Yet its allusions to forerunners from Blake to Pound combined with reviews of numerous contemporary poets and theorists provided a broad reading context for the debates over Language. Fond of piquant contrasts, the *House of "K"* would offer a list of military slang words in the same issue as a commentary on Balzac or remind readers that Bernstein's blend of parodic lyrics and mixed maxims in *Resistance* came out a year before Duncan's mythy *Ground Work*. As in *The Difficulties*, the distinction between poetry and criticism was fairly clear, but the prose formats were creatively digressive.

Poetics Journal, edited by Hejinian and Watten, concentrated upon theoretical essays and reviews from many of the poets in *The L=A=N=G=U=A=G=E Book*. The journal's issues incorporated Russian Formalism, linguistics, politics, and philosophy, opening in 1982 with a selection by Viktor Shklovsky on plotless literature; the second issue was devoted to an analysis of close reading practices. Like *Hills*, *Poetics Journal* examined a variety of "non/narrative" sequences that challenged characterization, plot, and sentence structure.

Cris Cheek recorded an "Interfusion" of fractured sense perceptions and thoughts in his writing: "Jolts from revery by what appears as incongruity or tangential intrusion" (74). Nick Piombino speculated about the form of a disjunctive "experiential syntax" modeled on Freud's theory of the repetition compulsion (40). The journal's fourth issue on women and language examined ruptures in imagery and syntax by authors from Dickinson to Acker. Questioning what it means for writing to be labeled "marginal" or "mainstream," these reviewers looked at the different audiences for a specific text: what happened, for example, when Antin's talk poetry performances were translated into printed books or when a text on avant-garde poetics made a case for Language writing to a general academic audience.

UNDER-WORD[S] AND INDIRECTIONS: THE POETRY JOURNALS

1980s POETRY JOURNALS FEATURING LANGUAGE WRITING varied widely in format and project. *Abacus*, first published in 1984 by Peter Ganick with Potes & Poets Press, combined the newsletter style of the early 1970s journals with a focus on a single author. There were eight ten- to twenty-page issues per year, each covering a long poem or excerpts by writers such as Tina Darragh, P. Inman, Bernstein, Sherry, Howe, Beckett, and Hejinian; the magazine also created interest for other small presses that printed Language poetry chapbooks.

Leland Hickman's *Temblor*, begun in 1985 in North Hollywood, titled itself simply as a venue for "Contemporary Poets" and offered new work, book excerpts, and translations by Language authors and other experimentalists. The writing included long poems, narrative segments, poets' prose, image sequences, and even isolated grids of words, as in Howe's word matrices clustered densely at the center of a page. For many authors, the imperative to "translate that mime into a newer currency" (Irby 7)—to reject a more mimetic model of art--produced a vocabulary of myth and magic reminiscent of Black Mountain but with less sense of a single narrative voice controlling the fragments. "[D]on't let / [Circe] hear her song broken up," one of John Clarke's narrators lamented, "the words falling dead / in the material analogy" (13). Myth and pop culture collided in Jed Rasula's witty language games, with Anthony Perkins acting in the movie "Psyche," or, as No-man Bates, taking on the character of Odysseus (92). "'I be good girl with my magic / markers,'" a speaker asserted in a poem by Rachel Blau DuPlessis ("Draft #2" 29), the line break suggestively turning magic into a child's play with writing. In series of rearranged letters, her characters wavered between the "Scared" and the "sacred" ("Draft #1" 28), "mother" and "monster," or the possibility for a "change" and another "chain" ("Draft #2" 32) as the poet's "Shadow under-word / lopes thru stands of wet papyrus" (31) in echoes of H.D.'s palimpsest imagery.

Recovering neglected under-words was the overt project of *HOW(ever)*, a San Francisco journal of women's experimental writing that opened in 1983. As if in response to Rae Armantrout's 1978 essay, "'Why Don't Women Do Language-Oriented Writing?'"[*], *HOW(ever)* editor Kathleen Fraser collected poems of "Slashes, anarchies, sentences, disruptions" (1) that shared techniques and agendas with Language writing although the issues also included other literary styles and multi-media art. Authors contributed poems, drawings, collaborations, prose poems, palimpsests, and storyboards for performance art. Its later issues concentrated upon one aspect of form or genre, often expressed as thematic pairings ("Fugitive/Exposure," "Erasure/Restoration") that questioned the distinction between canonical and marginal poetry. The volumes offered vivid literary "postcards" from readers and "alerts!" reviewing predecessors and contemporaries like Lorine Niedecker, Laura (Riding) Jackson, Stein, Hejinian, Howe, Nicole Brossard, and Theresa Hak Kyung Cha.

o.blēk: A Journal of Language Arts was first published by Peter Gizzi and Connell McGrath with the Garlic Press in New York in 1987. As its name suggests, the journal favored indirect associations and word play; even the set of dictionary definitions for "oblique" changed across different issues. Its texts provided unexpected juxtapositions, from John Yau's fusion of hard and fluid images (a "cloud smelter," a "box mountain of hardened tears" 127) to Dallas Wiebe's sharp sound contrasts ("Snockered. Gash. Bread" 31) and Owen's shifts in diction and tone ("Dashboard Idol / or / Imbecility differs from idiocy" 147). "I worried about the gap between expression and intent," one narrator confessed (Waldrop 178), but the "threat of giddy slippage" (Mackey 106) among signifiers increasingly colored the journal's selections. *o.blēk* cited writers from Pound to Samuel Beckett but, like *Big Deal*, seemed particularly influenced by New York poets — Ashbery, Frank O'Hara, and Ted Berrigan—and included paintings and ink drawings with its poems.

ACTS: A Journal of New Writing (1982) announced its literary roots with an inaugural cover photograph of Duncan's blackboards. Editor David Levi Strauss published work

---

[*]Arguing that Language writing is not completely non-referential, since it incorporates both ideas and the social or historical contexts for language, Armantrout analyzed the poetic agendas linking the texts of Howe, Hejinian, and Harryman, raising the question of why these women poets were not more frequently grouped with male Language writers (unpaginated).

from Bay Area poets, with substantial selections by Palmer, Nathaniel Mackey, and Leslie Scalapino, as well as from easterners like Howe and Coolidge. The issues combined poetry with interviews, translations, sketches, and movie stills. Contributors often probed the consequences of different political constructions and deconstructions of the subject. "[T]he self is implicated in the world after and because the mechanism of the 'I' has been abandoned," Benjamin Hollander wrote in the fourth issue (ii) about the cover quote from Nazi war criminal Klaus Barbie: "'I do not remember personally torturing prisoners.'" Tracing the subjects elided in historical records was the project of "Hope Atherton's Wanderings" by Howe; in this palimpsest account of a battle between colonists and Native Americans, her narrators find it increasingly difficult to distinguish between communal insiders and liminal outcasts.

The journal *Avec* with its striking art covers opened in 1988, its early issues pairing first and second generation postmodernist authors. The premiere issue included an excerpt from Burroughs's *Interzone* flanked by texts from contemporary experimentalists: Bernstein, Andrews, Benson, Cole Swensen. The poetry adapted political catch phrases, as in Abigail Child's references to "Wiretaps," "mudslings," and a "possible billboard" (26) or the military-speak that entered Sherry's "Live Action Language" in the third issue: "In the grammatical arsenal, what part of speech is strategic weaponry?" (37). Authors experimented with poems lineated in columns, receding margins, and superimpositions; many poems directly incorporated hieroglyphs, sketches, photographs, and computer-generated images. This journal from Penngrove, California kept a strong international flavor as editor Cydney Chadwick foregrounded the Language poets' translations of French, Russian, and German authors.

Among the Canadian magazines, *Writing* from the Kootenay School published poets like McCaffery, Silliman, and Karen Mac Cormack, incorporating Language-oriented writing particularly in the mid-1980s when the goal of recording both subjective experience and "the actual conditions of contemporary daily work" (Wayman 3) turned contributors toward the language rules that delimit meaning. The result was an intriguing mix; alongside poems narrating job experiences, author Gerald Burns looked at the "public sound" of poetic language patterns or the imprecision and "savagery of conveying information" (18) when "all categories change their meaning" in application (19). "[T]hat skin, ambient language" (55) was Fiona Templeton's raw material as she filled her compositions with slogans and soundbites from "conformation sites" (54) where bad actors were "trapped-in-a-woo-den-cue" (53). Visual artist Maggie O'Sullivan created typographic "Seizures" (3)—words run together, breaks in phrases and lettering, and idiosyncratic punctuation; her extended underlining beyond word breaks, for instance, simultaneously suggested authorial presence and absence. The contributors referred back to Joyce, Stein, Mallarmé, the Objectivists, and the Black Mountain writers. Editors included Colin Browne and Jeff Derksen.

Raddle Moon, edited by Susan Clark, moved toward Language poetry in 1986-87 with selections of "open texts, the new lyric, [and] translations," as the cover of the fifth issue announced. The issues' "sequence[s] of surface disorders" (Ngai 84) included textual collages, word play with dictionary entries, and letter-poems addressed to doubtful recipients (e.g. "disappearing Nick," Shiraishi 20). Political and personal references often collapsed humorously: "We get close. We grow tender. We're soft on Communism" (Child 15). *Raddle Moon* consistently featured innovative women authors, beginning with its international women writers issue through the thoughtful symposium "Women/Writing/Theory" in the eleventh and thirteenth issues.

How have other small press journals incorporated Language writing during the 1990s? As well as the 1980s magazines that continue to publish, there has been an explosion of experimental poetry and poetics magazines in the last decade — e.g. *Chain, Lingo, Rhizome, Witz, Aerial, The Germ, Aufgabe,* and *How2* — cutting across Language group allegiances and art genres. The Electronic Poetry Center at SUNY Buffalo has been an important cataloguer of these journals, many of which are available through Small Press Distribution. In addition to the Canadian magazines, there are Australian journals such as *Salt* that include Language writing, while national boundaries may become increasingly fluid for the electronic poetry magazines that take questions of referentiality and material signifiers to the context of virtual pages. Language writing has always been a contested label, and it is unclear whether it will be meaningful to use the rubric for subsequent publications. That fact itself suggests the success of the writers' projects. As Loris Essary asked in the third issue of *L=A=N=G=U=A=G=E*: "What better evidence of success for a piece of creative writing than its inherent ability to expand its original creative act beyond itself, to evoke further creative acts in its readers/perceivers?"

WORKS CITED

Acker, Kathy. "Notes on Writing—From *The Life of Baudelaire*." *L=A=N=G=U=A=G=E* 2.9-10 (1979): unpaginated.

Alexander, D. "Poem." *Tottel's* 2 (1971): 9-10.

Altieri, Charles. "Without Consequences Is No Politics." *Politics and Poetic Value*. Ed. Robert von Hallberg. Chicago: U of Chicago P, 1987. 301-308.

Andrews, Bruce. "Code Words." $L=A=N=G=U=A=G=E$ 1.6 (1978): unpaginated.

-------. "Getting Ready To Have Been Frightened." *Roof* 8 (1978): 62-92.

-------. "No Tumble." *Roof* 2 (1977): 10-14.

-------. "Writing Social Work & Political Practice." $L=A=N=G=U=A=G=E$ 2.9-10 (1979): unpaginated.

Armantrout, Rae. "'Why Don't Women Do Language-Oriented Writing?'" $L=A=N=G=U=A=G=E$ 1.1 (1978): unpaginated.

Bartlett, Lee. "What Is 'Language Poetry'?" *Critical Inquiry* 12.4 (1986): 741-52.

Beckett, Tom and Earel Neikirk. Editorial. *Difficulties* 1.1 (1980): unpaginated.

Benson, Steve. "Echo." *QU* 1 (1980): 1-3.

Bernstein, Charles. "The Conspiracy of 'Us.'" $L=A=N=G=U=A=G=E$ 2.8 (1979): unpaginated.

-------. "For -------." *Roof* 2 (1977): 17-24.

-------. "Thought's Measure." $L=A=N=G=U=A=G=E$ 4 (1981)/ *Open Letter* 5.1 (1982): 7-22.

Bromige, David. "My Poetry." *Hills* 5 (1978): 106-118.

Burns, Gerald. "Two Poems and Two Prose Pieces." *Writing* 10 (1984): 15-20.

Cheek, Cris. Statement for "Symposium on Narrative." *Poetics Journal* 5: *Non/Narrative* (1985): 71-75.

Child, Abigail. "Lust." *Raddle Moon* 5 (1987): 13-16.

-------. "A Possible Inflammation." *Avec* 2 (1989): 26.

Clarke, John. "Completing the Circuit of Circe." *Temblor* 1 (1985): 13.

Cohen, Robert David. "Bee." *Tottel's* 1 (1970): 4.

Coolidge, Clark. "Larry Eigner Notes." $L=A=N=G=U=A=G=E$ 1.1 (1978): unpaginated.

-------. Excerpts from "Notes on C, W & Z." *Toothpick, Lisbon, & the Orcas Islands* 3.1 (1973): unpaginated.

-------. "Prase." *Tottel's* 10 (1972): 14.

Davidson, Michael. Untitled article. $L=A=N=G=U=A=G=E$ 2.9-10 (1979): unpaginated.

-------. "What Is Being Language-Centered"? *The Difficulties* 1.1 (1980): unpaginated.

DiPalma, Ray. "Cordial." *Big Deal: A Journal of Sloth* 1 (1973): unpaginated.

Drucker, Johanna. "World Teeth." *QU* 3 (1980): 4.

Duncan, Robert. Interview with Michael André Bernstein and Burton Hatlen. *Sagetrieb* 4.2-3 (1985): 87-135.

DuPlessis, Rachel Blau. "Draft #1: It." *Temblor* 5 (1987): 22-28.

-------. "Draft #2: She." *Temblor* 5 (1987): 29-33.

Eigner, Larry. "Approaching things." $L=A=N=G=U=A=G=E$ 1.1 (1978): unpaginated.

Eigner, Larry and Harold Norse. "RE:VisioNs." *Là-Bas: a newsletter of experimental poetry and poetics* 1 (1976): unpaginated.

Essary, Loris. Letter to the editor. $L=A=N=G=U=A=G=E$ 1.3 (1978): unpaginated.

Fawcett, Brian. "Agent of Language." $L=A=N=G=U=A=G=E$ 2.9-10 (1979): unpaginated.

Fraser, Kathleen. "Why *HOW(ever)*?" *HOW(ever)* 1.1 (1983): 1.

Fredman, Stephen. *Poet's Prose: The Crisis in American Verse*. 2nd ed. Cambridge: Cambridge UP, 1990.

Friedman, Ed. Excerpt from "Journals." *QU* 5 (1981): 1-5.

Gay, Michel. "Working, Writing." *Poetics Statements for the New Poetics Colloquium*. 1985. Vancouver, British Columbia. 16-17.

Grenier, Robert. "On Speech." *This* 1 (1971): 86-87.

Halpern, Daniel. Introduction. *The American Poetry Anthology*. New York: Avon Books, 1975: xxix-xxxii.
Harryman, Carla. "A Genre." *QU* 5 (1981): 5-6.
Hartley, George. *Textual Politics and the Language Poets*. Bloomington: Indiana UP, 1989.
Hejinian, Lyn. "If Written Is Writing." *L=A=N=G=U=A=G=E* 1.3 (1978): unpaginated.
Hollander, Benjamin. Statement on cover design. *ACTS* 4 (1985): ii.
Howe, Susan. "Hope Atherton's Wanderings." *ACTS* 4 (1985): 3-11.
-------. "Yeats gathered mummy wheat..." *The Difficulties* 1.1 (1980): unpaginated.
Irby, Kenneth. "A Set." *Temblor* 1 (1985): 6-12.
Kelly, Robert. "If this were the place to begin..." *This* 1 (1971): 2.
La Charity, Ralph. "Empire of Ears." *The Difficulties* 1.1 (1980): unpaginated.
Lally, Michael. "Two Pages from a Longer Work." *Tottel's* 10 (1972): 8-9.
Lazer, Hank. "Opposing Poetry." *Contemporary Literature* 30.1 (1989): 142-50.
Mackey, Nathaniel. Excerpt from *From a Broken Bottle Traces of Perfume Still Emanate. o.blēk: A Journal of Language Arts* 2 (1987): 103-13.
Marlatt, Daphne. "Largely Sea." *Tottel's* 1 (1970): 3-4.
Mason, Chris. "Learning Reading as a Second Language." *L=A=N=G=U=A=G=E* 2.9-10 (1979): unpaginated.
McCaffery, Steve. "Repossessing the Word." *L=A=N=G=U=A=G=E* 1.2 (1978): unpaginated.
McGann, Jerome J. "Contemporary Poetry, Alternate Routes." *Critical Inquiry* 13.3 (1987): 624-47.
Messerli, Douglas. "LàBaStatement." *Là-Bas: a newsletter of experimental poetry and poetics* 1 (1976): copyright page.
Nations, Opal L. "Three Poems." *Tottel's* 10 (1972): 3-4.
Ngai, Sianne. Excerpt from *Some Brief Histories of Time. Raddle Moon* 13 (1994): 84-97.
O'Sullivan, Maggie. "Three Poems." *Writing* 17 (1987): 3-16.
Ott, Gil. Editorial. *Paper Air* 1.1 (1976), unpaginated.
-------. Editorial. *Paper Air* 2.2 (1979): 1.
Owen, Maureen. Excerpt from *Imaginary Income. o.blēk: A Journal of Language Arts* 5 (1989): 145-51.
Palmer, Michael. Interview with Keith Tuma. *Contemporary Literature* 30.1 (1989): 1-12.
-------. "'The man by contrast is fixed symmetrically.'" Interview with Lee Bartlett. *Talking Poetry: Conversations in the Workshop with Contemporary Poets*. Ed. Lee Bartlett. Albuquerque: U of New Mexico P, 1987: 125-143.
Perelman, Bob. "I began the Talk Series..." *Hills* 6-7 (1980): 5.
-------. *The Marginalization of Poetry: Language Writing and Literary History*. Princeton, Princeton UP, 1996.
-------. "Perelman on Watten." *L=A=N=G=U=A=G=E* 1.2 (1978): unpaginated.
-------. "Vienna: A Correspondence." *Miam* 5 (1978): unpaginated.
Perloff, Marjorie. "The Word as Such: L=A=N=G=U=A=G=E Poetry in the Eighties." *American Poetry Review* 13.3 (1984): 15-22.
Piombino, Nick. "Towards an Experiential Syntax." *Poetics Journal* 5: *Non/Narrative* (1985): 40-51.
Rasula, Jed. "Arched Like the Back of a Hissing Cat." *Temblor* 1 (1985): 92.
Reinfeld, Linda. *Language Poetry: Writing as Rescue*. Baton Rouge: Louisiana State UP, 1992.
Robinson, Kit. "Winter." *Hills* 3 (1976): 34.
Rothenberg, Jerome. "Praises of the Bantu Kings." *Tottel's* 1 (1970): 1-2.
Saroyan, Aram. "Play." *This* 2 (1971): 90.

Savage, Tom. "Ode to Unreality." *Roof* 2 (1977): 67-68.

Sherry, James. Excerpt from *Our Nuclear Heritage*. *Avec* 3 (1990): 35-39.

-------. Preface to *Legend*. *Roof* 3 (1977): 49.

Sherry, James and Tom Savage. Preface. *Roof* 2 (1977): 5.

Shiraishi, Kazuko. "Rhapsody in the Air-Conditioner." Trans. Hosea Hirata. *Raddle Moon* 4: *International Women Writers* (1986): 20-24.

Silliman, Ron. "Disappearance of the Word, Appearance of the World." *L=A=N=G=U=A=G=E* Supplement 3: *The Politics of Poetry* (1981): unpaginated.

-------. Editor's remarks. *Tottel's* 1 (1970): 5.

-------. Introduction. *In the American Tree: Language Realism Poetry*. Orono: National Poetry Foundation, 1986: xv-xxiii.

-------. "Notes on the Relation of Theory to Practice." *Paper Air* 2.2 (1979): 6-13.

-------. "San Francisco Destroyed by Fire." *Miam* 3 (1977): unpaginated.

-------. From "Talk" with Bill Berkson, Barrett Watten, Bob Perelman, and others. *Hills* 6-7 (1980): 7-24.

Silliman, Ron, Carla Harryman, Lyn Hejinian, Steve Benson, Bob Perelman, and Barrett Watten. "Aesthetic Tendency and the Politics of Poetry: A Manifesto." *Social Text: Theory/Culture/Ideology* 19-20 (1988): 261-275.

Taggart, John. Letter to the editor. *L=A=N=G=U=A=G=E* 1.2 (1978): unpaginated.

Templeton, Fiona. Excerpt from *Realities*. *Writing* 28 (1992): 53-58.

Thomas, Lorenzo. "Is It Xerox or Memorex?" *L=A=N=G=U=A=G=E* 2.9-10 (1979): unpaginated.

Wagner, Linda. "Poetry in the Classroom (4): A 'Hands-Off' Approach to the Teaching of Poetry." *American Poetry Review* 2.3 (1973): 58-59.

Waldrop, Rosmarie. Excerpt from *Lawn of Excluded Middle*. *o.blēk: A Journal of Language Arts* 5 (1989): 175-79.

-------. "'The Tongue Around The Mouth.'" *The Difficulties* 1.1 (1980), unpaginated.

Watten, Barrett. Excerpt from *City Fields*. *Hills* 5 (1978): 40-43.

Wayman, Tom. "Ground Breaking: An Introduction to the New Work Writers." *Writing* 15 (1986): 3-5.

Wiebe, Dallas. "Oracles." *o.blēk: A Journal of Language Arts* 2 (1987): 17-37.

Yau, John. Excerpt from *Halfway to China*. *o.blēk: A Journal of Language Arts* 2 (1987): 126-32.

Susan M. Schultz

LANGUAGE WRITING

In his introduction to the 1986 anthology of Language writing, *In the American Tree* (1986), Ron Silliman alludes to "the constant flow of dismissals and exposés, many of them composed in the threatened rhetoric of fury" that have been directed at a poetry that attacks the unified subject; poetry's traditional role as arbiter of feeling; the importance of "communication"; even speech itself (xix). In 1986, these attacks against Language writing were, for the most part, still launched by what Charles Bernstein calls the paragons of "official verse culture," namely mainstream writers with vested interests in "the scenic mode," as Charles Altieri calls it. Writers of this mode are belated Romantics who find themselves in a landscape and then communicate that self-discovery to a reader who shares vicariously in the poem's process of loss and recovery. They, in turn, have become Language writing's "stray straws and straw men," to borrow the title of one of Charles Bernstein's most important essays. In 1986 Language poetry was still non-professional, even if, as Vernon Shetley argued in 1993, "it is certainly the body of work most in tune with the skeptical, highly politicized, theoretically sophisticated character of postmodern academic thought" (19). But, by the early 1990s, Language writing had achieved a grudging acceptance in many English departments, and Language writers such as Charles Bernstein, Bob Perelman, and Barrett Watten were entering the academic fold; the attacks against it came from a very different angle, indeed, namely from poets one might think sympathetic to Language writing. In 1993 *Talisman*, which publishes experimental writing, ran an article by Susan Smith Nash with the provocative title, "Death, Decadence, & the Ironies of Language Poetics." Nash argues that, "Instead of rescuing American poetics, Language poetry seems to endanger it, by alienating a large segment of the general population by creating a body of work that can be extremely cryptic and inaccessible" (202). "Like it or not," she continues in a passage that could have easily been written by an official verse culturist, "most people look to poetry for affirmation. We are human beings, replete with emotional 'baggage'" (203). She also quotes Norman Finkelstein, who claims that the Language writers' style is "as rarefied as that of any Pre-Raphaelite or Symbolist" (201). Even more sternly, the four editors of the short-lived but significant *apex of the M*, all students in the Poetics Program at the State University of New York at Buffalo, which is run by Charles Bernstein, accused

Language writers in 1994 of the worst political faith possible: "Thus we feel that in the present poetical and political climate a merely avant-garde ideology of the politics of poetry no longer suffices when, for instance, Reagan's, Bush's, and Quayle's extemporaneous public comments are themselves a kind of Language poetry: any language that creates or reflects the kinds of diversions and sedations required for the triumph of capital is, finally, a language of denial" (5). And so, many poets who have come to be called "post-Language" writers have taken up the humanist torch against Language writing, finding fault with it not so much on the aesthetic grounds that they often share, as on political and moral ones. Not only does their stern opposition reflect political and aesthetic differences from Language writers, of course, but it also reflects on the increasing power of the movement in American letters. The attacks no longer seem directed at a small group of poetical subversives, but at another version of the Establishment, even if it is an establishment founded on subversiveness.

Obviously, a sea change occurred in the reception of Language writing during the 1980s, ironic considering that Language writing is consciously non-narrative. While the content of attacks against this mode of writing were consistent, the shift in the sources of attack, from mainstream writers to other marginalized writers, many of whom had gone to school to Language poetry and poetics, indicates the extent to which Language writing gained a place at the fractious poetic table during the late 1980s and early 1990s. This power may have been far more rhetorical than institutional — there is no equivalent of the MFA for Language writers, but its strengths are considerable, nonetheless. Much of the power of Language writing comes of the fact that Language writers are the most active and blatantly ideological poet-critics since the modernists and, like T.S. Eliot and Ezra Pound, they resist the Romantic terms by which poetry is still defined by most poets and critics and general readers. The oft-used label of "Language *writing*," instead of "poetry," also challenges widespread preconceptions about the separation between poetry and prose, art and theory. All discussions of Language writing, pro and con, point to it as "a group phenomenon" (Perelman 31). For Douglas Messerli, writing in 1986, the writers have "a shared aesthetic, a body of ideas about poetry and poetics that has shaped these far-embracing poets into a group of sorts in the 1970s and 1980s" (2). According to Messerli, who finds lyrical qualities in the poetry that even Susan Smith Nash might approve of, "such social gathering has helped not only to gain an initial readership for the individual poets but also to create an atmosphere in which thoughtful and serious writing, an emotional and powerful poetry could be created" (9). Ron Silliman notes a "dual pattern of migration to urban centers on both coasts," which "greatly enhanced the possibilities of face-to-face interaction and sharing" (xviii). Silliman, though he does not enumerate them, finds differences between the work created in San Francisco and New York, and so emphasizes a sense of place not usually associated with a poetics consciously preoccupied with words and not places. Some of the strongest evidence of community among the Language poets can be seen in their creation of journals and small presses; not only did the foremost experimental poetry press, Sun & Moon, emerge out of the Language movement, but so did other presses and journals of poetry and poetics like *This*, *L=A=N=G=U=A=G=E* (1978-1982), *Poetics Journal*, *Roof*, and to some extent *Sulfur*, all of which disseminated the ideas and the work of Language poets, while engaging them in a common enterprise.

But, while "the emergence of Language writing," according to the Australian critic Ann Vickery, "should be contextualized against the call for civil rights, the women's movement, the failure of the European intellectual community in 1968, and reactions to the Vietnam war," there are tensions inside the community, especially over gender issues. Most of the work in poetics (theories behind the poetry) has been done by men, Charles Bernstein, Ron Silliman, Barrett Watten, and Bob Perelman foremost among them, and, as Susan Howe has written, "When articles are written about Language poetry, it's usually the men who do the writing and fighting" (quoted in Vickery). Vickery, in *Leaving Lines of Gender: A Feminist Genealogy of Language Writing* (1997), argues that "Mayer's shifting poetics made her a contentious figure. . . . It is worthwhile considering Mayer's reputation in relation to that of another influential yet contrary figure in Language writing, John Ashbery. . . . While Ashbery was seen to 'compromise' in his later poetics, he nevertheless remains central to projects aimed at building a tradition for Language writing" (159-60). Most important, according to Vickery, is the fact that, "the critical reception of Language writing has . . . tended to represent women as secondary participants or its passive benefactors" (12). Likewise, recent attempts by Language writers such as Charles Bernstein to address the complexities of multiculturalism have proved problematic; for the most part, Language writing is a movement by and for middle-class white poets. Yet the ideas behind Language writing are probably more coherent than the ways they are acted out in a community of men and women, and the ideas, at least, are profoundly egalitarian.

But what are these ideas that so disrupt, at times viscerally, assumptions about poetry, and as Alan Golding has put it, challenge "almost every aspect of poetic canon formation as it has been historically practiced in the academy" (145)? As Bob Perelman points out in *The Marginalization of Poetry: Language Writing and Literary History* (1996), Language writing is not so much a new phenomenon as the continuation of an old avant-garde war by new means. While "no means equivalent" to other avant-garde movements (15), Language writing is especially indebted to Gertrude Stein for its methods, if not its politics, which are farther left than hers ever were. A section of *The L=A=N=G=U=A=G=E Book* (an anthology of pieces published in a journal of the same name and edited by Charles Bernstein and Bruce Andrews) is devoted to readings of selections from Stein's *Tender Buttons* (1914). Perhaps the most representative reaction to these passages comes from Michael Davidson, who writes of the lack of logical continuity in her prose that, "What this implies for the act of reading is that there are no longer any privileged semantic centers by which we can reach through the language to a self-sufficient, permanent world of objects, foodstuffs or rooms. We must learn to read *writing*, not read *meanings*; we must learn to interrogate the spaces around words as much as the words themselves" (198). In this passage, which is typical of Language writers' reactions to their precursor, Davidson sounds a note very similar to Peter Quartermain's when he defines "disjunctive poetics": "Hence the only first thing to hold on to in the poem, that holds the writing together, is not *meaning* in the sense of an encapsulation which can be separated out, cashed in at the end of the reading in exchange for the knowledge-claim that 'this is what the poem means,' but language ... the dialogue with the poem taking place in the reader's consciousness" (19). Jerome McGann writes that, "Meaning occurs as part of the process of writing — indeed, it is the writing" (209). And Jed Rasula refers to "the mass of theoretical statements and position papers" of which these are typical. To Rasula, "it's evident that the only issues about which a consensus may be said to have been reached were the restoration of the reader as coproducer of the text, and an emphasis on the materiality of the signifier" (398). These ideas are inseparable, as it is the very materiality of the signifier — its role as matter, not as meaning — that permits the reader entry into the text in the way that Davidson, Rasula, Quartermain and other Language oriented poets and critics intend. These ideas are borne out in an anecdote Perelman tells of how he and Kit Robinson and Steve Benson began collaborating in San Francisco in 1976; they did not so much write, as listen, together. "One of us would read from whatever books were handy and two of us would type .... This was not automatic writing; automatic listening would be more like it" (32). What the poet gives the reader, then, is a field within which such automatic listening is possible. Of course the emphasis on process rather than product, on the reader rather than the producer, is not itself such a terribly inflammatory idea any more. It is the way in which these ideas are borne out, and the paradoxical way in which many readers feel left out rather than invited in, that causes visceral reactions against this way of writing. If, as many mainstream writers would assert, clear communication between human beings is an ethical obligation, then the seemingly willful obscurity of most Language writing can provoke charges of unethical writing behavior. Language writing is often Brechtian; the alienation effect is its method, if not its ultimate goal, and that deliberate alienation (of "word" and "meaning," for example) can drive even the most active reader away. It can take patience, even obstinence, to read *In the American Tree* even a decade after its publication; indeed, it can still take chutzpah to read Gertrude Stein.

Stein's "A Carafe, That Is a Blind Glass," is at once a model for and an instance of what Ron Silliman has termed "the new sentence," a construct that, typical of the ideas promulgated by Language writers, combines — or conflates — ideas about poetic form with ideas about politics. Stein's brief poem reads as follows: "A kind in glass and a cousin, a spectacle and nothing strange a single hurt color and an arrangement in a system to pointing. All this is not ordinary, not unordered in not resembling. The difference is spreading" (quoted in LB 196). Silliman's rules for the "new sentence" are more numerous than Pound's famous imagist rules, but the first four are most crucial to an understanding of Stein's reception by the Language writers, and to the work of writers like Silliman.

1) The paragraph organizes the sentences;
2) The paragraph is a unit of quantity, not logic or argument;
3) Sentence length is a unit of measure;
4) Sentence structure is altered for torque, or increased polysemy; ambiguity;

(ITAT 574).

Thus, the formal organization — of actual sentences, none of which have apparent, logical relation to one another — creates a torque to tweak the reader into the active creation of meaning, creating a writer out of the reader in much the way that reader-response theorists of the 1970s advocated. In a tongue-in-cheek use of his own method in *Paradise* (1985), Silliman alludes to the value of naming his (and Stein's) method, even as he torques back to the kitchen: "Becoming identified with an inaccurate but provocative name enabled the Language Poets to rapidly deepen market penetration and increase market share. I turn the muffins over" (18). What is an active reader to make of this parataxis? That earning a market share for writing is akin to earning one for muffins? That the (male) Language writer is as able in the kitchen as he is in the den? That the trivialization of writing as a capitalist activity is akin to the triviality involved in turning a muffin over (a message that goes against the previous one, perhaps)? That writing like this can be taken at face value? That writing like this is intensely ironic and therefore mocks capitalist ideas about "market penetration"? That reading such work is like playing a game? That playing such a game is intensely serious as an activity? I think all of these possibilities — and more

— are invited by the writer, although I suspect he himself values some of them more than others. At any rate, he does point to the mixed blessing involved in calling the movement "Language writing," since the label has proven at once inaccurate and highly successful in the small world of literary self-marketing.

One of the best, and best known, instances of this New Sentence method is Lyn Hejinian's *My Life*, originally published in 1987; the book, which initially had thirty-seven sections, each of which contained 37 sentences (matching Hejinian's age at the time), is an autobiography in ambiguity, an artful presentation of the matter from which memoirs are made. Hejinian, also, considers the story of her life to be the story of her work (every writer's autobiography, as it were), writing early on in the book: "On my mother's side a matriarchy. I wanted to be a brave child, a girl with guts. And how one goes about educating that would-be audience may very likely determine the history of that moment, that direction, the qualities that become emphatic and characteristic of its later influence" (25). Thus the story of her own education, as girl and as poet, becomes a model for the education of the book's reader. Hejinian's version of the reader-response technique espoused by Language writers presents the reader more as a student than as a full participant in the process. She also acknowledges that their audience is a "would-be," not a completely stable one.

This emphasis on the reader's, as opposed to the writer's, production of meaning has never meant that Language writers did not have intentions on their audience, desires for their ideas to be re-produced rather than accepted passively, or fall victim to what their nemesis, Harold Bloom, would term "misprision," or mis-interpretation. As Quartermain notes, "A moral imperative runs through their work, a kind of 'methodism' which seeks to liberate and clarify our sense of an object by revealing its characteristics as verb, as meaningful act" (20). For Hank Lazer and others, the importance of Language writing extends far beyond the often constricted realm of poetry: "The greatest virtue of Language Writing is its reintegration of poetry into a fuller cultural and intellectual context, providing us with a poetry and poetics once again immersed in politics, history, and the broad range of debates in the human sciences" (Vol. 2, 6). This act of re-integration can only take place under the aegis of a collective style, or group of styles, for Language poetry does not distinguish between meaning and writing; words are not conduits for history but the material in which it is created. For Silliman, "style has an ethical rather than aesthetic basis" (ITAT 486). And for Bernstein, the ethical thrust of writing involves a resistance against the status quo through the use of a promiscuity of writing styles. Plural styles are necessary, because, "The contemporary expository mode was adopted because it effectively did the business of the society's vested interests," he writes in "Writing and Method," from *Content's Dream* (1986) (224). If the ethic of clarity, represented by this expository style, has failed, then Bernstein advocates an ethic of impermeability, or "non-absorption." His long poetic essay, "Artifice of Absorption," completed in the banner year of 1986, promulgates a theory of writing that values difficulty over ease, obstruction over clarity. "Absorptive" writing, according to Bernstein, is writing that like found in romances or science fiction novels, namely writing that attempts to draw the reader into a world that is not her/his own. The reader, absorbed, is simply not herself, so that the act of writing (and reading) is an act of tyranny. Bernstein's definition is as follows:

> By *absorption* I mean engrossing, engulfing
> completely, engaging, arresting attention, reverie,
> attention intensification, rhapsodic, spellbinding,
> mesmerizing, hypnotic, total, riveting,
> enthralling: belief, conviction, silence. (*A Poetics* 29)

Bernstein is aware, here, that many of the terms he holds up as troublesome, problematic, even dangerous, are terms that are held in high esteem by most readers; who can argue against "belief" or "conviction," or even "silence"? Bernstein does, since he considers these terms to have been falsely "naturalized" by the culture so as to gain control over readers and writers alike; what seems like clarity to the reader of expository prose is, in Bernstein's view, its exact opposite. Not clarity but control is the issue. In order to combat this especially pernicious (because "natural," because "transparent") mode of clarity, Bernstein proposes "impermeability" as a remedy. So impermeable is his description that parallel structure drops out after a time:

> *Impermeability* suggests artifice, boredom,
> exaggeration, attention scattering, distraction,
> digression, interruptive, transgressive,
> undecorous, anticonventional, unintegrated, fractured,
> etc. (*A Poetics* 29)

Artifice, then, provides an innoculation against the "natural" paradigms to which he and other Language writers are opposed. Apparent stylistic villains (who can imagine teaching freshman writers to be "boring," to "exaggerate," and so on?) become worthy aspects of style because they remind us that we are reading, and goad us into creating meanings divorced from the logical force of the text. While the Language writers' moral thrusts resemble those of George Orwell, in "Politics and the English Language," their methodism is radically different from his. Like him, they consider that "political writing [and all writing, one could well argue, is political] is bad writing," and that "political speech and writing are largely the defence of the indefensible" (206). Unlike Orwell, they do not advocate remedies such as his rule number two, "Never use a long word where a short one would do"; nor do they believe that clarity of expression is a necessary good (206). As Bruce Andrews puts it, untransparently: "That language, being socially constructed, suggests that what's not possible is a condition of transparency or presence or aura. Because meaning isn't naturally reflected in language; language is producing it actively" (34). Active production, the argument goes, cannot be transparent or clear.

Thus far, most of the texts I've mentioned or quoted are from the mid-1980s; I would go so far as to say that 1985-87 were the movement's watershed years. Silliman's anthology was published in 1986, as were Douglas Messerli's complementary, if far less politically charged, anthology, *"Language Poetries"* and Charles Bernstein's *Content's Dream*, a collection of essays on poetics; Lyn Hejinian's *My Life* would appear a year later; Susan Howe's *My Emily Dickinson* had appeared one year earlier. If one is to consider Language writing as a political, as well as a literary movement, this historical moment is no accident, coming as it does in the middle of Ronald Reagan's second term and during the Iran-Contra hearings, namely in the midst of a constitutional crisis. The origin of Language writing in 1971 (with the founding of the journal *This* by Barrett Watten and Robert Grenier), came in the midst of another political crisis, Vietnam, another moment in history when language was used to disguise horrifying political realities. Rod Smith asserts that Barrett Watten is "not being metaphorical" when he says, "My imagination locked in place during the Vietnam War" (18). Charles Bernstein's poem, "A Defence of Poetry" addresses a later political abuse of power (in this instance in the speeches of George Bush), as does Barrett Watten's recent *Bad History* (1998), which performs close readings of the language used during the Persian Gulf war and the Los Angeles riots. "So language is historical," he writes, "but in such a way as to be the source of the historical" (88). For Watten, bad history is what is necessary "to writing good poetry" (80), a statement that cuts both ways, pointing to Watten's utopian desire for language to cure history's badness, but also to his ambivalent acceptance that there is poetry to be made out of linguistic, historical errors.

Susan Howe writes in order to recover suppressed histories; both in *My Emily Dickinson* and in *Singularities*, Howe attempts to fill in the silences of women left in the record through the editorial (here she is using the word both literally and figuratively) agencies of men. Her Emily Dickinson is at once a genius poet and a cultural and historical critic, and her work provides an interesting prolegomenon, then, to Howe's own. Like other Language writers, Howe is as interested in form as in content, considering the two utterly impossible to divorce, and like Bernstein she is as interested in sound as in sense, but Howe differs from many of them in her vision of history and transcendence, both of which are for her "true" in ways that they are not for other of the writers. Her work is as replete with parataxis as that, say, of Bernstein or Hejinian, but she is more taken with "meaning" than they are. And, while Howe is not interested in writing out of her own direct subjectivity (the pronoun "I" is rare in her work), her vision is profoundly lyrical. She is obsessed with the subjective histories of words, the ways in which the language creates the subjectivities of historical characters. For example, her book *Singularities* contains fields of words that appear random, discrete, but actually represent attempts to re-create a field of meaning that has been lost to the ravages of the historian and the editor. The following lines from "Hope Atherton's Wanderings" illustrate this point:

rest chondriacal lunacy
velc cello viable toil
quench conch uncannunc
drumm amonoosuck ythian (10)

At first glance, or even second and third (I *have* taught this poem), these words appear to have little to do with one another except in their sound patterns ("velc cello viable" and "quench conch uncannunc" spawned out of their "v" and "c" and "q" sounds more than anything). But this sequence is not random, as it represents Howe's attempt to bring together the vocabularies of the early American setting and history that she is writing about; the sound origins of these words include the Latinate "cello," the Native American sounding "uncannunc" and "amonoosuck," and the rather more English "toil" and "rest." The scattering that Howe elsewhere terms "Behavior Toward Risk" comes out of historical brokenness; the writer as visionary editor, then, has the glue to re-place the scatterings in tentative order.

Toward the beginning of this essay, I argued that Language writing, like the High Modernism it sometimes resembles, rejects Romanticism, especially that literary movement's interest in human subjectivity and feeling, its concern with finding the human subject in the natural world. There are links to Romanticism in Language writing, however;

as Michael Davidson argues, "I would see it [the work of this group] as representing a new stage in a romantic theory of language, one based less on the artist's imaginative and expressive powers than on a skepticism about language's ability to represent" (215). The first poem in Ron Silliman's anthology, Kit Robinson's "In the American Tree," is a masterpiece of ambiguous feeling about the tradition of American Romanticism from Emerson through Stevens and Ashbery (whose "Some Trees" is surely invoked here), and suggests the bounds of any conception of language based more on artifice than on nature. His first stanzas, like so much in the poem, mixes (rather jarringly, it would seem) vocabularies of Romanticism, business, and the landscape of colloquial language:

> A bitter wind taxes the will
> causing dry syllables
> to rise from the throat.
>
> Flipping out would be one alternative
> simply rip the cards to pieces
> amid a dense growth of raised eyebrows.

The experience of the poem (if not poet's experience, which is deflected) includes a vision of "The freeway," which "is empty now, moonlight / reflecting brightly off the belly of a blimp" (xiii). As the poem comes to an end, it echoes the marginal modernists, William Carlos Williams and Wallace Stevens, in its invocations of spring, but in a curiously truncated version of the season:

> And it is Spring.
> The goddess herself
> is really
>
> Feeling great.
> Space assumes the form of a bubble
> whose limits are entirely plastic.

The plasticity of, dare I say speech, that informs and enriches Robinson's poem, a plasticity that is characteristic of the work of the Language writing community, is adopted, it seems to me, with some ambivalence. The "plastic bubble" of space that comes to replace the "tree" as the poem's subject, may be transparent, but it also represents a profound limitation. The poem, then, is not a celebration of such limitation (despite the richness of the different vocabularies that Robinson combines "artificially") but a statement of the problem posed by that limitation. The field of language taken as a given by Language poets is not without its limits, and may, in fact, be shared by the politicians and cultural mainstreamers that they argue so vociferously against. (But the editors of *apex of the M*, when they argue that Language writing is no different from Reagan-speech, deliberately neglect to consider that oft-maligned term, "intentionality.") At its most forceful, the work of Language writers invokes, if it cannot enact, the utopian possibility that the world can be changed by and through language — the language that we already, of necessity, use. Robinson's almost wistful use of natural imagery points to a paradox shared by Language writers and American Romantics; like Thoreau and like Emerson, these writers advocate both utter originality and utopian community; like them, they detest conformity and quotation, yet advocate democracy. They write out a language so private that they have been attacked repeatedly for their elitism, yet argue that language can never be private: "The idea of a private language is illusory because language itself is a communality, a public domain. Its forms and contents are in no sense private — they are the very essence of the social" (Bernstein quoted in Reinfeld 65). If these tensions render their projects untenable as political programs, and it is likely that they — and poetry's limited audiences — do, then they express the profoundest truths about the American psyche. And if this poem — like so many other Language poems — does not quite escape the scenic mode, after all, it does alter the landscape of American writing, making it harder to see the "tree" (in all its many senses, from nature to family and back again) for the words. Re-turning our attention from poetry to the language from which it is made has been the Language movement's prime inheritance.

WORKS CITED

Andrews, Bruce and Charles Bernstein. *The L=A=N=G=U=A=G=E Book*. Carbondale: Southern Illinois UP, 1984.

Andrews, Bruce. *Paradise & Method: Poetics & Praxis*. Evanston: Northwestern UP, 1996.

apex of the M. #2 and 3. Edited by Lew Daly, Alan Gilbert, Kristin Prevellet, Pam Rehm.

Bernstein, Charles. *A Poetics*. Harvard UP, 1992.

-------. *Content's Dream*. Los Angeles: Sun & Moon, 1986.

Davidson, Michael. *The San Francisco Renaissance: Poetics and Community at Mid-Century.* New York: Cambridge UP, 1989.

diacritics: a review of contemporary criticism. "Poetry, Community, Movement." Special Editor, Jonathan Monroe. 26: 3-4 (Fall-Winter 1996).

Golding, Alan. *From Outlaw to Classic: Canons in American Poetry.* Madison: U of Wisconsin P, 1995.

Hejinian, Lyn. *My Life.* Los Angeles: Sun & Moon, 1987.

Howe, Susan. *My Emily Dickinson.* Berkeley: North Atlantic Books, 1985.

-------. *Singularities.* Middletown: Wesleyan UP, 1990.

Lazer, Hank. *Opposing Poetries: Volume Two: Readings.* Evanston: Northwestern UP, 1996.

McGann, Jerome J., *Social Values and Poetic Acts: The Historical Judgment of Literary Work.* Cambridge: Harvard UP, 1988.

Messerli, Douglas, ed. *"Language" Poetries: An Anthology.* New Directions, 1987.

Nash, Susan Smith. "Death, Decadence, & the Ironies of Language Poetics." *Talisman: A Journal of Contemporary Poetry and Poetics* 10 (Spring 1993): 201-205.

Orwell, George. "Politics and the English Language." In *Language Awareness: Essays for College Writers.* Eds. Paul Eschholz et al. New York: St. Martin's, 1997: 199-210.

Perelman, Bob. *The Marginalization of Poetry: Language Writing and Literary History.* Princeton: Princeton UP, 1996.

Quartermain, Peter. *Disjunctive Poetics: From Gertrude Stein and Louis Zukofsky to Susan Howe.* New York: Cambridge UP, 1992.

Rasula, Jed. *The American Poetry Wax Museum: Reality Effects, 1940-1990.* Urbana: National Council of Teachers of English, 1996.

Reinfeld, Linda. *Language Poetry: Writing as Rescue.* Baton Rouge: LSU, 1992.

Shetley, Vernon. *After the Death of Poetry: Poet and Audience in Contemporary America.* Durham: Duke UP, 1993.

Silliman, Ron, ed. *In the American Tree.* Orono: U of Maine P, National Poetry Foundation, Inc., 1986.

-------. *Paradise.* Providence: Burning Deck, 1985.

Smith, Rod, ed.. *Aerial 8: Barrett Watten.* Aerial/Edge, 1995.

Vickery, Ann. *Leaving Lines of Gender: A Feminist Genealogy of Language Writing.* Hanover, NH: UP of New England, 2000.

Watten, Barrett. *Bad History.* Berkeley: Atelos, 1998.

Marjorie Perloff

AFTER LANGUAGE POETRY: INNOVATION AND ITS THEORETICAL DISCONTENTS

—Are you sure, she asked, you're talking of ideas?
Dark, emptied of touch would be entire, null and void. Even on an island.
—Rosmarie Waldrop, from "Split Infinitives," p. 50

INNOVATE: FROM THE LATIN, *in* + *novare*, "to make new, to renew, alter." In our century, from Rimbaud's "Il faut Être absolument moderne!" and Ezra Pound's "Make It New!" to Donald Allen's *New American Poetry* (Grove Press, 1960) and Douglas Messerli's *From the Other Side of the Century: A New American Poetry 1960-1990* (Sun & Moon, 1994), novelty has been the order of the day. Think of the (now old) New Criticism, the New Formalism, the New Historicism, *le nouveau roman* and *la nouvelle cuisine*. As I was writing this essay, a message came over the internet announcing the British poet-critic Robert Sheppard's *Poetics and Linguistically Innovative Poetry 1978-1997*.[*] And in recent years, two important anthologies of women's poetry —*Out of Everywhere: Linguistically Innovative Poetry by Women in North America & the UK*, edited by Maggie O'Sullivan, and *Moving Borders: Three Decades of Innovative Writing by Women*, edited by Mary Margaret Sloan — have made the case that, in O'Sullivan's words, "much of the most challenging, formally progressive and significant work over recent years, particularly, in the U.S. . . . is being made by women" (p. 9), thus leading directly to the title of the Barnard conference: "Innovation and Experiment in Contemporary Poetry by Women."[†]

It was not always thus. The OED reminds us that innovation was once synonymous with sedition and even treason. In 1561, Thomas Norton wrote in Calvin's Institute, "It is the duty of private men to obey, and not to make innovation of states after their own will." Richard Hooker in 1597 refers to a political pamphleteer as "an authour of suspicious innovation." The great Jacobean dramatist John Webster speaks of "the hydra-headed

---

[*] I wrote a blurb for this excellent book as I did for Sloan's *Moving Borders*.

[†] This essay was delivered as the keynote address at this conference, held in April 1999.

multitude / That only gape for innovation" (1639), and in 1796, Edmund Burke refers to the French Revolution as "a revolt of innovation; and thereby, the very elements of society have been confounded and dissipated."

Indeed, it was not until the late nineteenth century that innovation became perceived as something both good and necessary, the equivalent, in fact, of avant-garde, specifically of the great avant-gardes of the early century from Russian and Italian Futurism to Dada, Surrealism, and beyond. I cannot here trace the vagaries of the term, but it is important to see that, so far as our own poetry is concerned, the call for Making it New was the watchword of the Beats as of Black Mountain, of Concrete Poetry and Fluxus as of the New York School. At times in recent years, one wonders how long the drive to innovate can continue, especially when, as in the case of Sloan's *Moving Borders*, fifty contemporary American women poets are placed under the "innovative" umbrella. Given these numbers, one wonders, who isn't innovative? And how much longer can poets keep innovating without finding themselves inadvertently Making It Old?

The problem is compounded when we turn to the relationship of innovation to theory. When the various French poststructuralisms of the postwar first became prominent they were known as *la nouvelle critique*. But as time went on, *la nouvelle critique* became known as post-structuralism, just as the "new American poetry" was called, in Donald Allen's revised version of 1982, *The Postmoderns*. What, then, is the relation of "new" to "post"? The issue is complicated but it's fair to say that, in the case of theory, "new" was an epithet applied from outside, for the theorists themselves were less concerned to Make It New than to establish certain truths, for example, to study the relation of literary to so-called ordinary language, to determine the respective role of author and reader in the interpretation of a given text, and to establish the ways in which individual texts speak for their culture. For Barthes and Derrida, as earlier for Benjamin and Adorno, Bataille and Blanchot, innovation as such was of little interest. Benjamin, for that matter, had no use for the Dadaists who were his contemporaries, dismissing them as instigators of little more than "a rather vehement distraction," designed "to outrage the public" (Benjamin 238). And Adorno regarded most of what passed for "new" fiction or poetry as little more than kitsch.

Accordingly — and this is an important aspect of the Language movement, which stands squarely behind so much of contemporary "innovative" poetry — the "new" rapprochement between poetry and theory that we find in the first issues of *L=A=N=G=U=A=G=E* (1978), and in such equally important journals as the San Francisco-based *This* and *Hills*, and the Canadian *Open Letter* — all these now a quarter-century old — had less to do with innovation per se than with the conviction, on the part of a group of poets, themselves keenly interested in philosophy and poststructuralist theory, that poetics was an intellectual enterprise, deserving a larger place than it had in the Creative Writing classroom of the 1970s.[*]

Consider the symposium edited by Steve McCaffery, published in the Canadian journal *Open Letter* in 1977 and reprinted by Andrews and Bernstein as *Language Supplement Number One* in June, 1980. The symposium was called "The Politics of the Referent"; it includes McCaffery's "The Death of the Subject: The Implications of Counter-Communication in Recent Language-Centered Writing," Bruce Andrews's "Text and Context," Ray DiPalma's "Crystals," Ron Silliman's "For Open Letter," and Charles Bernstein's "Stray Straws and Straw Men." Although three of the above were to be reprinted in their authors' own books on poetics,[†] these early versions are revealing. For so quickly did their authors soften their stance that the 1980 *Supplement* begins with the editorial disclaimer: "It seems worth remembering, in looking back on these essays, that the tendencies in writing McCaffery is talking about under such headings as 'language-centered' are as open to the entrapments of stylistic fixation as any other tendency in recent poetry."[‡] And when McCaffery came to revise "The Death of the Subject" for his collection *North of Intention* (1986), he declared, "I was never happy with the title and both it and much of the content have been revised. The essay, whose original thoughts and materials were gathered through the mid-seventies, concentrates on a partial aspect of Language Writing: a concern primarily with the morphological and sub-lexemic relations present and obtainable in language. A decade later I can safely speak of this concern as an historic phase with attention having shifted . . . to a larger aspect — especially to the critical status of the sentence as the minimal unit of social utterance and hence, the foundation of discourse" (*NI* 13).

McCaffery's original version begins dramatically with this declaration: "There is a group of writers today united in the feeling that literature has entered a crisis of the sign . . . . and that the foremost task at hand — a more linguistic and philosophic then 'poetic' task — is to demystify the referential fallacy of language." "Reference," he adds, "is that kind of blindness a window makes of the pane it is, that motoric thrust of the word which

---

[*] *L=A=N=G=U=A=G=E*, edited by Bruce Andrews and Charles Bernstein, was a mimeograph magazine, whose first issue appeared in Spring, 1978. *This*, edited by Robert Grenier, began publication in 1971, *Hills*, ed. Bob Perelman in 1973. Frank Davey's *Open Letter*, published in Toronto, was founded in 1972. These foundational journals as well as such projects as Lyn Hejinian's Tuumba Chapbook series were thus in place by the mid-1970s.

[†] See Steve McCaffery, "Diminished Reference and the Model Reader," subsequently cited as *NI*; Bruce Andrews, "Text and Context," Charles Bernstein, "Stray Straws and Straw Men."

[‡] *L=A=N=G=U=A=G=E*, Supplement Number One (June 1980), front page, unpaginated. Subsequently cited as SUP, and, for convenience sake, I shall supply page numbers.

takes you out of language into a tenuous world of the other and so prevents you seeing what it is you see" (*SUP* 1). Such a thrust — the removal of what McCaffery calls later in the essay "the arrow of reference" — is essential because "language is above all else a system of signs and . . . writing must stress its semiotic nature through modes of investigation and probe, rather than mimetic, instrumental indications."

Here, in a nutshell, is the animating principle of the movement: poetic language is not a window, to be seen through, a transparent glass pointing to something outside it, but a system of signs with its own semiological "interconnectedness." To put it another way, "Language is material and primary and what's experienced is the tension and relationship of letters and lettristic clusters, simultaneously struggling towards, yet refusing to become, significations." McCaffery himself points to the Russian Formalists, to Wittgenstein, Barthes, Lacan, and Derrida as the sources for his theory, and indeed language poetics, in this first stage, owes its greatest debt to French poststructuralism, although Charles Bernstein, for one, was much closer to Wittgenstein, whom he had studied with Stanley Cavell at Harvard, than to Derrida, whose analysis of signification he distrusted, even as Silliman and Andrews were drawn to a more politicized Frankfurt School poetics. But McCaffery himself sounds a Derridean note when he declares that "the empirical experience of a grapheme replaces what the signifier in a word will always try to discharge: its signified and referent." Indeed, in poetry the signifier is always "superfluous," overloaded with potential meanings and hence more properly a cipher (*SUP* 4).

There are two corollaries, one Barthean, one Marxist-Althusserian. "Language-centered writing," McCaffery tells us, "involves a major alteration in textual roles: of the socially defined functions of writer and reader as the productive and consumptive poles respectively of a commodital axis" (*SUP* 3). And again, "The text becomes the communal space of a labour, initiated by the writer and extended by the second writer (the reader). . . . The old duality of reader-writer collapses into the one compound function, and the two actions are permitted to become a simultaneous experience within the activity of the engager" (*SUP* 8). "Reading" is thus "an alternative or additional writing of the text." Indeed — and here the Marxist motif kicks in — "Linguistic reference is a displacement of human relationships and as such is fetishistic in the Marxian sense. Reference, like commodity, has no connection with the physical property and material relations of the word as a grapheme" (*SUP* 3). Direct communication, on this count, is the hallmark of the commodity fetish. Thus, "to remove the arrow of reference," to "short-circuit the semiotic loop" (SUP 9) becomes a political rather than a merely aesthetic act. In his "Text and Context," Bruce Andrews reinforces this notion, dismissing referentiality as the misguided "search for the pot at the end of the rainbow, the commodity or ideology that brings fulfillment" (*SUP* 20).

As the utopian manifesto of a twenty-eight year old poet, "The Death of the Subject," inevitably overstated its case. The call for "unreadability" and "non-communication," for example, was largely exemplified by sequences of disconnected word fragments and isolated morphemes, as in the citations from Andrews, Clark Coolidge, and Barbara Baracks, the latter giving us a two-column poem like

stint	grits
darts	file
gratis	ways to fit tins
dapper	angle
ill	apple

McCaffery calls on us to "produce one's own reading among the polysemous routes that the text offers" (*SUP* 4), a challenging invitation, even though, as soon became apparent, less stringent readers than McCaffery himself took him to mean that one reading would be just as good as another. Moreover, the rejection of all "instrumental" language as commodity fetish in favor of a poetic paradigm that, if we are to trust McCaffery's examples, includes only the most extreme form of word play, fragmentation, decomposition of words, and absence of all connectives, as in Andrews's "mob cuspid / welch / eyelet / go lavender / futurible" (*SUP* 5), could be seen as excessively dismissive of alternate ways of composing poetry.

But despite McCaffery's Ubu-like iconoclasm, his basic premises — and this is the irony — were by no means as extreme or as new as both the proponents and opponents of Language poetics would have had us think. What McCaffery and Andrews (SUP19) call the "referential fallacy" takes us right back to Roman Jakobson's central thesis that in poetry the sign is never equivalent to its referent and the corollary notion that poetry is language that is somehow extraordinary.[*] The case against transparency, against instrumental value and straightforward readability was the cornerstone of Russian Formalist theory as well as of Bhaktin's theory of dialogism and heteroglossia. In *The Noise of Culture*, William Paulson has shown that the concept of poetry as "noise," as blockage of the normal (trans-

---

[*]See especially Jakobson, "Linguistics and Poetics," *Language in Literature*, ed. Krystyna Pomorska and Stephen Rudy (Cambridge and London: Harvard UP, 1987), pp. 62-94. Many of the essays in this collection are relevant to the topic: for example, "The Dominant," "Problems in the Study of Language and Literature," and "Two Aspects of Language nd Two Types of Aphasic Disturbances."

parent) channels of communication, is a notion that was already central, if intuitively so, for Romantic theorists.* As for Wittgenstein, who refused to distinguish between ordinary and extraordinary language, finding "ordinary" language quite "strange" enough, the basic tenet that there are no meanings outside of language gave McCaffery and his fellow symposiasts license to denounce what Bernstein called, in "Stray Straws and Straw Men," the "natural look" as itself a construction with particular implications. Poetry, Bernstein argued, is never really "natural" (e.g., "I look straight into my heart & write the exact words that come from within"); rather, "it emphasizes its medium as being, constructed, rule governed, everywhere circumscribed by grammar & syntax, chosen vocabulary: designed, manipulated, picked, programmed, organized, & so an artifice" (Bernstein, 40-41).

Twenty-five years after its appearance, we can read "The Politics of the Referent" sym-posium as an important intervention, on the one hand reminding readers that poetry has always been "an artifice," and, on the other, that poetry cannot be too far out of step with the other discourses — philosophical, political, cultural — of its own time. By the mid-1970s, let's recall, these discourses, as studied on every campus across the U.S., had produced a highly sophisticated and challenging body of texts about the nature and function of écriture or writing, whether "writing the body" (Cixous and Iragaray), the position of subjects in particular discourses (Kristeva), the relationship of truth to fiction (Todorov, Bahktin), and so on. I remember clearly, in those years, walking into St. Mark's Bookshop in the Bowery and seeing, on the central table, the stacks of Barthes's *The Empire of Signs*, Derrida's *Of Grammatology* in the Gayatri Spivak translation, and Foucault's *The Order of Things* (1970), which was published, not by a university press but by Random House. These books were selling as if they were popular novels. At the same time poetry, insofar as it had become the domain of the Creative Writing workshop, was no longer the contested site it had been in the days of Pound, Eliot. and Williams, or even of the "raw versus cooked" debates of the early sixties. In the 1970s, for reasons too complex to go into here,† the

---

*See William R. Paulson, *The Noise of Culture: Literary Texts in a World of Information* (Ithaca and London: Cornell UP, 1988), Chapter 2, "Science at Work," passim.

†In his essay "1973," Peter Middleton begins to engage the thorny issue of 70s poetry. He relates the demise of Clayton Eshleman's *Caterpillar*, whose last issue was in 1973 and the founding of *American Poetry Review* (1972) to post-Vietnam, Watergate politics and the new distrust of public speech and the increasing separation of the white avant-garde from black writing. Middleton takes into account such important poetic developments as Jerome Rothenberg's projects to place cultural difference and the recognition of non-Western poetries on the agenda, David Antin's turn toward improvisation, and Michael Palmer's incorporation of French avant-garde poetics into his work. But he notes that at the moment when Barrett Watten's *This* was devoting a whole issue to Clark Coolidge (1973), the dominant poetic discourse valorized poets like Robert Lowell, Maxine Kumin, and William Stafford. Middleton's as yet unpublished essay is part of a longer project, *Writing to be Heard: American Avant-Garde*

production of poetry had become a kind of bland cottage industry, designed for those whose intellect was not up to reading Barthes or Foucault or Kristeva. The feeling / intellect split had probably never been wider. For even as students were absorbing Foucault's "The Death of the Author" and Benjamin's "Work of Art in the Age of Mechanical Reproduction," official verse culture, as Bernstein called it, was spawning poems like the following, which I take from *The Morrow Anthology of Younger Poets*, edited by Dave Smith and David Bottoms (1985):

Hollandaise

The sauce thickens. I add more butter,
slowly. Sometimes we drank the best wine
while we cooked for friends,
knowing nothing could go wrong,
the soufflé would rise, the custard set,
the cheese be ripe. we imagined
we were reckless but we were just happy,
and good at our work. the cookbook is firm:
it is safer not go over two ounces
of butter for each egg yolk. I try to describe
to myself how we could have been safer,
what we exceeded. If the sauce "turns"
there are things to be done, steps
to be taken that are not miraculous,
that assume the failed ingredients,
that assume a willing suspension of despair. (*Morrow* 107-108)[*]

Here McCaffery's arrow of reference is flying straight into the saucepan, ready to curdle that hollandaise. The lasting contribution of Language poetics, I would posit, is that at a moment when workshop poetry all across the U.S. was wedded to a kind of neo-con-

---

Poetry and the Public Sphere 1950-1990.

[*] The author, Sharon Bryan, born in 1943, holds an MFA from the University of Iowa and has published a book called *Salt Air* from Wesleyan. In their Introduction, Smith and Bottoms describe the typical Morrow Younger Poet as one whose "knowledge, while eclectic, seems focused on the psychological and mythical resonances in the local surface, event, or subject.... .He seems to jog more than to write literary criticism" (19).

fessionalist, neo-realist poetic discourse, a discourse committed to drawing pretentious metaphors about failed relationships from hollandaise recipes, language theory reminded us that poetry is a making [*poeien*], a construction using language, rhythm, sound, and visual image, that the subject, far from being simply the poet speaking in his or her natural "voice," was itself a complex construction, and that — most important — there was actually something at stake in producing a body of poems, and that poetic discourse belonged to the same universe as philosophical and political discourse.

None of this, of course, was all that new, but it was new within the particular context of "Naked Poetry," as an important anthology edited by Robert Mezey and Steven Berg was called, or vis-à-vis Allen Ginsberg's insistence on "First thought, best thought" — a precept Ginsberg fortunately didn't put into practice, at least not in his best poetry (Ginsberg 106-17).* By the 1990s, in any case, all three of the Language principles that McCaffery put forward had been subtly transformed even as their force remains implicitly operative today. The referential fallacy, to begin with, has given way to a more nuanced emphasis on the how of poetic language rather than the what. The dismissal of instrumental language as the commodity fetish has come under criticism from both Left and Right, as readers have realized that so-called "innovative" writing — writing that is fragmented, asyntactic, non-sensical, etc. — can be just as fetishized as anything else. And the emphasis on readerly construction, an article of faith in the semiotic theories of Barthes, Foucault, and Eco, and, in the U.S., of Reader Response Theory, has given way to a renewed perception that the alleged authority of the reader is, as Ron Silliman has remarked in a recent essay, merely a transfer of power whereby, in ways Barthes could not have foreseen, "the idealized, absent author of the New Critical canon has [merely] been replaced by an equally idealized, absent reader."†

Language poetics, let's remember, had a strong political thrust: it was essentially a Marxist poetics that focused, in important ways, on issues of ideology and class.‡ But it was less attuned to questions of gender and race: indeed, in the case of L=A=N=G=U=A=G=E, although one senses that every effort was made to include "innovative" women poets — for example, Rae Armantrout, Barbara Baracks, Abigail

---

*Again and again Ginsberg speaks of "natural" speech, spontaneity, the breath as guide to measure, and so on.

†See Ron Silliman, "Who Speaks: Ventriloquism and the Self in the Poetry Reading," in *Close Listening: Poetry and the Performed World*, ed. Charles Bernstein (New York: Oxford, 1998), p. 365. Silliman's is a seminal essay for understanding the limitations of reader-response theory.

‡See, on this point, George Hartley's *Textual Politics and the Language Poets* (Bloomington: Indiana UP, 1989). This, the first book-length study of language poetry, was largely devoted to the movement's politics, drawing heavily on Ron Silliman, Bob Perelman, and Barrett Watten.

Child, Lynne Dreyer, Johanna Drucker, Barbara Einzig, Carla Harryman, Lyn Hejinian, Susan Howe, Bernadette Mayer, Leslie Scalapino, Rosmarie Waldrop, Diane Ward, and Hannah Weiner — the more overt theorizing itself was left, with rare exceptions,[*] to the men in the movement. Thus students in the 1980s were usually introduced to Language poetry by such "reference books" as Barrett Watten's *Total Syntax*, Charles Bernstein's *Content's Dream*, Steve McCaffery's *North of Intention*, and Ron Silliman's *The New Sentence*, all published between 1985 and 1987. The dominance of these Founding Fathers can be seen in the British reception of Language poetics, a reception coming largely from the Left, which was keenly interested in but also highly critical of the doctrines put forward in "The New Sentence" and "Artifice of Absorption," and "The Death of the Subject," but had little to say about specific poems.[†]

What, then, of the women poets in the original movement? Interestingly, their background was more literary and artistic than that of, say, Andrews and Bernstein, who had studied political science and philosophy respectively. Susan Howe began her career as an artist and was very much influenced by concrete poetry, especially the work of Ian Hamilton Finlay and Tom Phillips. Johanna Drucker, was trained as a printmaker and visual poet and wrote her Ph.D. thesis at Berkeley on the Russian avant-gardist Iliazd. Rosmarie Waldrop was a student of Modernism and of concrete poetry and a translator of Edmund Jabès, Maurice Blanchot, and many Austrian and German avant-gardists. Kathleen Fraser had studied with the New York poets, especially Kenneth Koch. And so on.

The increasing recognition of the women poets associated with *L=A=N=G=U=A=G=E* was made evident in Lee Hickman's superb journal *Temblor*, which began publication in 1985, and ceased, with issue #10, in 1989 because its editor was dying of AIDS and could no longer sustain the operation. Hickman is to my mind one of the great

---

[*] The most notable exception is Lyn Hejinian, who contributed essays and manifestos to the early issues of *L=A=N=G=U=A=G=E*, for example "If Written is Writing," and was co-editor, with Barrett Watten, of *Poetics Journal*. Another very different exception is Susan Howe who combined, not poetry and theory so much as poetry and historical scholarship, negotiating in fascinating ways between the two in *My Emily Dickinson*. A key volume that includes a number of women poets writing as theorists is Bob Perelman's *Writing / Talks* (Carbondale and Edwardsville: Southern Illinois UP, 1985). The book contains "Rae Armantrout's "Poetic Silence," Beverly Dahlen's "A Reading: a Reading," Carla Harryman's "The Middle," Fanny Howe's "Artobiography," and Lyn Hejinian's now well-known "The Rejection of Closure."

[†] See, for example, Rod Mengham, *Textual Practice*, 3, no. 1 (Spring 1989): 115-24; D. S. Marriott, "Signs Taken for Signifiers: Language Writing, Fetishism and Disavowal," and Anthony Mellors, "Out of the American Tree: Language Writing and the Politics of Form," both in *fragmente* 6, (1995): 73-91. Marriott's essay, for example, begins with the sentence, "It will be the argument of this paper that language writing, in its systematic attempt to empty the linguistic sign of its referential function, replaces representation with a fetishistic substitute, that of the signifier" (73), the reference being to essays by McCaffery, Bernstein, Silliman, and Andrews.

unsung heroes of the so-called innovative poetry scene. Unaffiliated with a university or even a specific movement, he published *Temblor* from his home on Cahuenga Boulevard in the much despised San Fernando Valley above Hollywood. *Temblor* had no editorial board, no mission statement and, until the last few issues, no grant money. Hickman simply published the poetry that interested him — a good chunk of it "language poetry," but also the related poetries coming out of Olson-Duncan school, the Objectivists, and the "ethno-poeticists" associated with Jerome Rothenberg: for example, Clayton Eshleman, Armand Schwerner, Rochelle Owens, Kenneth Irby, Robert Kelly, Jed Rasula, Gustaf Sobin, and John Taggart. *Temblor* was a portfolio with a 9 x 12-inch page which allowed for visual design, as for example in Leslie Scalapino's "Delay Series" (#4) and a long (28 page) section from Susan Howe's *Eikon Basilike* (#9). The journal published Rosmarie Waldrop's *A Form of Taking it All* in its entirety (#6), Kathleen Fraser's sequence "In Commemoration of the Visit of Foreign Commercial Representatives to Japan, 1947," (#9), nine poems from Hejinian's "The Person" (#4), Fanny Howe's "Heliopathy" (#4), sections of Rachel Blau du Plessis's long sequence *Drafts*, and work by Barbara Guest, Rae Armantrout, Carla Harriman, Mei Mei Bersenbrugge, Johanna Drucker, Norma Cole, and Martha (Ronk) Lifson. The magazine introduced the work of poets from other countries and cultures: Anthony Barnett, Paul Buck, and Peter Middleton from Britain, Anne-Marie Albiach, Michel Deguy, Edmond Jabès, Jacqueline Risset, from France, Saul Yurkievich and Tomás Guido Lavalle from Argentina, Minoru Yashioka from Japan, and so on And finally, unlike the various "Language" journals, *Temblor* focused on poetry rather than theory, although it did include critical prose, especially on or by its own poets.

Here, then, was an opening of the field that nevertheless avoided the merely eclectic. Like any editor Hickman had his idiosyncrasies (a number of poets, no doubt, were published simply because they were Los Angeles friends), yet, with rare exceptions,[*] no effort was made to recruit the mainstream. Hickman never published Derek Walcott or Galway Kinnell, Adrienne Rich or Rita Dove. Why not? We cannot, alas, ask Hickman himself and there is no mission statement to guide us. But I suspect there were three reasons. First, I imagine the editor felt these other poets got enough of a hearing in the mainstream press and, if he was to edit and produce a journal, he might as well introduce lesser-known poets. Secondly, publication of the established poets would have been too expensive. And thirdly, although there is no *Temblor* manifesto, the journal's unstated aesthetic remained true to what was the cornerstone of Language aesthetics — namely, that poetry is more than the

---

[*] Ashbery's "The Ice Storm" is in #5 (1987), as are extracts from *Conversing with Cage*, ed. Richard Kostelanetz. *Temblor* is subsequently cited as *T*.

direct voicing of personal feeling and/or didactic statement, that poetry, far from being transparent, demands re-reading rather than reading, that it is News that Stays News.

Consider, in this connection, Lyn Hejinian's "Two Stein Talks"* in *Temblor* #3 (1986). Hejinian makes a strong case for Stein's brand of "realism" as "the discovery that language is an order of reality itself and not a mediating medium — that it is possible and even likely that one can have a confrontation with a phrase that is as significant as a confrontation with a tree, chair, cone, dog, bishop, piano, vineyard, door, or penny" (*T*#3 129). In the course of her talks, Hejinian shows us how one can analyze such poetic language, how, for example, in the first of the *Tender Buttons*, "A Carafe, That Is A Blind Glass," the first phrase "A kind in glass and a cousin" "binds carafe with blind phonically." As for "blind" "A carafe is a container, a glass one, which, if filled with a thick liquid, that is a colored one, might be, so to speak, blind, opaque." "A blind glass," she adds, "might also be a blank mirror, or a draped window — as my aunt would say, 'Draw the blinds, it's dinner time'" (*T*#3 132).

The poet's offhand phrase "as my aunt would say," shows that reading semiotically rather than referentially, "in" rather than "for," need not be as impersonal an activity as it may have looked in its first incarnation. On the contrary, after citing Stein's sentence, "A gap what is a gap when there is not any meaning in a slice with a hole in it," Hejinian decides "to quote myself," in a stanza that begins "going / by the usual criteria for knowledge / I vowed not to laugh / but to scatter things" (*T*#3 133). Elsewhere in this issue we have Susan Howe's "12 poems from a Work in Progress," that begins with a play on "sitt" / "site"/ "cite," in keeping with McCaffery's account of the cipheral text and ends with an oblique prayer to "Keep and comfort come / unhook my father / his nest is in thick of my / work" (*T*#3 27). How does one "unhook" a father, and why? We never know for sure any more than we can paraphrase Fanny Howe's observation, in her "Scattered Light," that "Some patios won't allow the shadow of a maid / It's where I want to go with my tray / See heat unbearably white / Each book must fall, a scholar's mind" (*T*#3 51).

Here pun ("Sea heat unbearably white") and burlesque, as in the last line's play on "Into each life, a little rain must fall," complicate the story of this "shadow of a maid" carrying her tray on the forbidden patio. Throughout *Temblor* 4 (which contains the complete *Conduit* by Barrett Watten and *Demo* by Ron Silliman), the Language program is operative even if — and here we come to Hickman's own predilection — emotion, if by no means personal confession, is brought back into the equation. Further along in Fanny Howe's "Scattered Light" we read the following ten-line poem:

---

*Rpt. with a headnote and footnotes in Hejinian, *The Language of Inquiry*, pp. 83-139.

> It was a night to be left alone
> To dig out fifteen pounds of pumpkin guts
> Stick in a candle and water the curtains
> I phoned a friend with What do you want
> Money and luck they said
> When I asked the angel in the bottle
> She fluttered and cried
> I want to die!
> Sex, too, squeezes out a lot of pleasure
> Till nothing is left but the neck (T#4 52)

Failed domesticity probably looms as large here as it did in "Hollandaise," but the relationship between the pumpkin carving of the opening, the allusion to the Cumean Sybil trapped eternally in her bottle, and the image of the sex act hollowing out the body like an empty pumpkin cannot be transformed into any sort of coherent narrative. "Till nothing is left but the neck" is especially graphic. The neck of the bottle? The neck of the woman as external to the emptied out body? The neck as all one has without money or luck? Oddly, my own image — if I am to follow McCaffery and become a co-constructor of the poem's meaning — is that of a chicken neck — the hard ugly piece of flesh (rather like a distorted penis or "stick in a candle" — that remains when one has hollowed out the chicken, as opposed to the pumpkin, guts — the liver, heart, and other giblets, the fat along the inside chicken wall. Phonemically, in any case, the monosyllabic "neck" in final position connotes an unpleasant cut of some sort.

Howe's "Scattered Light" happens to be followed, a few pages later, by Nathaniel Mackey's "Uninhabited Angel," which begins:

> Sat up sleepless   in the Long Night Long, love
>   Stood me up. Stayed away though its
> Doing so stirred me. Wine on my shirtsleeve,
>   Wind on my neck. (T#4 36)

Again, love standing the poet up, again that ugly word "neck" in final position. . But here in Mackey's jazz-inspired lyric, rhythm is quite other — an allusion to the Dogon myth of the Andoumboulou fusing with the "attempt to sing the blues," as in the drumbeat of:

> Tilted sky, turned earth. Bent wheel, burnt
>
>   we.
>
>   Bound I. Insubordinate
>
>   us

where "we" is the is what's left when the wheel is bent and "I," bound to the wheel becomes part of that "we" or "Insubordinate / us."

Nathaniel Mackey's poem serves as a reminder that even as women poets associated with poststructuralist experimentation were gaining recognition, persons of color had rarely been included. And here we come to a major shift in the 1990s, when what could loosely be called a Language poetics has come into contact with one of color. A signal example is the poetry of Harryette Mullen, to which I now turn.

MUSING & DRUDGING

IN A 1997 INTERVIEW FOR *Combo #1*, Harryette Mullen recalls her own initiation into poetry:

> I had come from Texas to Northern California. I was in graduate school at Santa Cruz. I was reading all of this theory as a student in Literature at UC-Santa Cruz. So, at that point when I would . . . be taken to these talks and readings . . . I had a context for it. . . . although of course no one at the university was dealing with the work of the [Language] poets. But [they] read the same theory that my professors did — in fact they probably read twice as much, and had read the same theory earlier than a lot of my professors had, and they were highly intellectual poets. . . . and they were saying interesting things. . . . for instance the idea of problematizing the subject. (Hmweb)

And Mullen jokes about her fellow minority graduate students at Santa Cruz, who used the argument that it was all very well for white male poets to renounce "voice" but that "We need our subjectivity." Either extreme, she decided, seemed unsatisfactory. In her drive to problematize her own subjectivity, she began to incorporate into the language poetics that animated *Trimmings*, her book of prose poems based on Stein's *Tender Buttons*, the actual verbal games of her own culture — the childhood jump-rope rhymes and "pseudo-courtship, formulaic exchanges" of pre-adolescence, like the male "What's cookin' good lookin'?" with its female response, "Ain't nothin' cookin' but the beans in the pot, and they wouldn't be if the water wasn't hot."

Trimmings is a wonderful example of the new fusion of language poetics and a renewed "Personism," to use Frank O'Hara's phrase. In an interview with Barbara Henning, Mullen remarks that "*Tender Buttons* appeals to me because it so thoroughly defamiliarizes the domestic, making familiar 'objects, rooms, food' seem strange and new, as does the simple, everyday language used to describe common things" (Ppweb). But Mullen's own version of *Tender Buttons* also becomes, as she puts it, "a reflection on the feminization and marginalization of poetry: a whole poem composed of a list of women's garments, undergarments, & accessories certainly seems marginal & minor, perhaps even frivolous & trivial" (PPweb 2). Consider the following:

Tender white kid, off-white tan. Snug black leather, second skin. Fits like a love, an utter other uttered. Bag of tricks, slight hand preserved, a dainty. A solid color covers while rubber is protection. Tight is tender, softness cured. Alive and warm, some animal hides. Ghosts wear fingers, delicate wrists. (*Trimmings* 9)

This glove poem takes its inspiration from Stein but is really quite different. Mullen keeps her eye more firmly on the object than does Stein, whose cushions, umbrellas, and hats quickly give way to other related items, often quite abstract. Mullen's poem immediately raises the issue of color with the punning of "Tender white kid," and "off-white tan." For the poet, the "snug black leather" is in fact "second skin," and so it "fits like a love" even as it is "utter other," with its play on "udder" — the female body — and the need to speak, to give poetic voice to what has been voiceless. Further: the emphasis on "utter other" leads to classification: rubber gloves, leather gloves, gloves that are too tight, gloves that fit. But also an unease as to the source of leather gloves that is quite unSteinian: "Alive and warm, some animal hides," where the pun on "hides" (as of "softness cured") leads directly to the image of ghosts known by their large white fingers in the dark. Do those ghost fingers belong to the predominantly white glove wearers? Mullen doesn't press the point: gloves are "tender" and "dainty": they make the wrists look "delicate."

The *Trimmings* poems thus have a complicated derivation. On the one hand, one could read this particular playful prose poem in conjunction with the short paragrammatic pieces cited by McCaffery in his essay for "The Politics of the Referent" — poems by Bruce Andrews, bpNichol, and McCaffery himself. On the other, Mullen's piece is more overtly political and engaged in the contemporary discourse about gender and race. Indeed, Mullen internalizes the theoretical paradigm of Language poetics so as to refigure the relationship between the various ethnicities and communities to which she belongs..

In a 1993 lecture called "Visionary Literacy: Art, Literature and Indigenous African Writing Systems," for example, Mullen uses the deconstructionist analysis of écriture to call into question the standard explanatory models of African-American vernacular orality:

> That black literary traditions privilege orality . . . . has become something of a commonplace, in part because it's based upon what seems to be a reasonable and accurate observation . . . Presumably, for the African-American writer there is no alternative to production of this authentic black voice but silence. This speech-based and racially inflected aesthetic that produces a black poetic diction requires that the writer acknowledge and reproduce in the text a significant difference between the spoken and written language of African Americans and that of other Americans.[*]

As Aldon Nielsen, who discusses this lecture in his *Black Chant*, points out, Mullen's proposed study of African signage, as the background for understanding the relationship of oral to written, "has much to tell us about the falsity of the assumed opposition between singing and signing in both Africa and America" (36). And he cites her statement:

> The larger question I am asking is this: How has the Western view of writing as a rational technology historically been received and transformed by African Americans whose primary means of cultural transmission are oral and visual, rather than written, and for whom graphic systems are associated not with instrumental human communication but with techniques of spiritual power and spirit possession . . . In order to construct a cultural and material history of African-America's embrace and transformation of writing technologies one might ask how writing and text functioned in a folk milieu that valued a script for its cryptographic incomprehensibility and uniqueness rather than its legibility or reproducibility. (Nielsen 36)

---

[*]From an unpublished lecture delivered at Intersection for the Arts, San Francisco, May 24, 1993. I owe my knowledge of it to Aldon Lynn Nielsen's important study *Black Chant: Languages of African-American Postmodernism*, pp. 35-37.

Here is a theoretical project that has very real poetic implications, involving, as it does, the struggle against the received idea that one is either "black or innovative." "*Muse & Drudge*, Mullen explains, really was my attempt to show that I can do both at the same time."

Muse & Drudge is written, seemingly against the "Language" grain, in irregularly rhyming and heavily syncopated ballad quatrains. Its eighty pages have four quatrains per pages, with no stops or indeed any punctuation except for the capitalization of proper nouns and apostrophes marking the possessive as in "galleys upstart crow's nest." Each page, as Kate Pearcy points out in an excellent essay on the book, seems to be a discrete unit, unbroken during oral performance. Accordingly, the lines of contiguity — that is, the network of metonymic associations — are offset by an oral paradigm that insures temporal reception of a given four-quatrain unit. Consider the following:

> Sapphire's lyre styles
> plucked eyebrows
> bow lips and legs
> whose lives are lonely too
>
> my last nerve's lucid music
> sure chewed up the juicy fruit
> you must don't like my peaches
> there's some left on the tree
>
> you've had my thrills
> a reefer a tub of gin
> don't mess me I'm evil
> I'm in your sin
>
> clipped bird eclipsed moon
> soon no memory of you
> no drive or desire survives
> you flutter invisible still (*M&D* 1)

Of this pseudo-ballad, we might say, in Steve McCaffery's words, "a reading activates certain relational pathways, a flow of parts, and . . . a structural 'infolding' of the textual elements" (*SUP* 11). In the first stanza, each of the fourteen words functions paragramatically. "Sapphire's lyre" (the play on Sappho places Mullen's own blues singer in a rich poetic tradition)* "styles" (or is "styles" a noun, designating Sapphire's lyric styles?) "plucked eyebrows," where "plucked" can also be a verb as can the "bow" in "bow lips." "Bow lips and legs" is a witty false parallel: it refers to being "bow-legged" but "bow lips" are the Cupid's mouth, a lovely rounded form. Or do the "lips and legs" bow down? Most important: "lyre styles" sounds like "life styles," and, lo and behold, the last line reads, "whose lives are lonely too."

Now consider the role sound plays — the rhyming of "Sapphire's" / "lyre" / "styles," the consonance of "lyre," "lives," the alliteration of "l"s in seven of the fourteen words, the eye rhyme of "brows"/"bow." We can hear "Sapphire" playing the blues in this poignant and droll love song. What's more, in the second stanza, the "lucid music" comes to incorporate the Southern Black idiolect of "you must don't like my peaches / there's some left on the tree."† Individual morphemes create tension: "chewed up the juicy fruit" refers to a common brand of chewing gum, but "chewed up" relates that "juicy fruit" to those rejected peaches. Again, "you've had my thrills" is a brilliant send-up of the expected "I've had my thrills / a reefer a tub of gin / don't mess with me I'm evil." And "I'm in your sin," with its allusion to the Bessie Smith song "A Pig Foot and a Bottle of Gin," undercuts self-recrimination (e.g., "I'm full of sin'") by putting the blame squarely on the lover. Then again, "you've had my thrills" can be read as, "you've had my best moments; I've given it all to you!" Finally, the semantic and phonemic conjunction of "clipped bird" and "eclipsed moon" plays on the standard romantic clichés about love. Is the poet herself the "clipped bird"? Or is she getting rid of the lover? The poem's last line, "you flutter invisible still" makes for a comic rhyme with the "thrills" of line 9; it also echoes the image of the swans who glide through the water "Unwearied still" in Yeats's "Wild Swans at Coole." The substitution of "invisible" could hardly be more deflating": if "you" (the lover) has been reduced to no more than an invisible flutter, it is surely time to move on. And in the penultimate line, "drive" rhymes with the second syllable of "survives," the chiming of "drive" — "desire" — "survives" underscoring the poet's case for survival.

---

*Juliana Spahr points out that *Sappho's Lyre* is the title of Diane J. Rayor's translations of archaic lyric and women poets of ancient Greece and adds, "Only here Sappho is marked as the African-American Sapphire. Resonating here is Hortense Spiller's beginning of 'Mama's Baby, Papa's Maybe: An American Grammar Book': 'Let's face it. I am a marked woman, but everybody knows my name. 'Peaches' and 'Brown Sugar,' 'sapphire' and 'Earth Mother'." See *Everybody's Autonomy*, p. 114.

†Spahr cites Steve Miller Band's "The Joker" as source of this image. And there are related songs by Blind Lemon Jefferson, and Ma Rainey that stand behind the peach image as well as the "juicy fruit" that follows.

"Despite random, arbitrary, even nonsensical elements," Mullen has remarked of *Muse & Drudge*, "the poem . . . is saturated with the intentionality of the writer." "I intend," she insists, "the poem to be meaningful: to allow, or suggest, to open up, or insinuate possible meanings, even in those places where the poem drifts between intentional utterance and improvisational wordplay." And she talks of the poem's amalgam of "topical references to subculture and mass culture, its shredded, embedded, and buried allusions, its drift between meaning and sound, as well as its abrupt shifts in tone or emotional affect." Metonymy and pun, already much in evidence in the earlier *Trimmings*, are the key tropes, but they function in a traditional lyric form that ironizes their mode of operation, and is itself ironized by these figures. In the words of a later stanza:

> down there shuffling coal
> humble materials hold
> vestiges of toil
> the original cutting tool (*M&D*, 11)

where the off-rhyme
  "coal"-"hold"-"toil"-"tool" contradicts the ballad account of the miner's dreary work routine. Lyric and linguistic play combine to create a vision at once detached and yet oddly "personal."

CAVEAT LECTOR

I COME BACK NOW TO THE QUESTION OF "innovation." To call *Muse & Drudge* "innovative" is not especially helpful because it would be just as accurate to say that, as the the very title, with its nominal/verbal collocation of inspiration and hard work, suggests, the book is quite traditional in its respect for the lyric contract, the emphasis on sound structure, the personal signature, and the mimetic grounding of experience. What matters more than "innovation," I think, is that *Muse & Drudge* is a book that speaks very much to its own time, that taps into various writings and speech formations in ways that are compelling. If Mullen's is a "theoretical" poetry, it is one that has nicely internalized the theories in question.

But — and this is where the situation has become problematic — such internalization is hard earned. Like any mode, the production of "text without walls," as McCaffery called it, can become a mere tick. And so can the theory that ostensibly animates it. One of the most problematic manifestations of what we might call post-Language poetics is that, in the wake of the foundational theory that filled the pages of avant-garde little magazines of the 1980s, poets, and this has been especially true of women poets, perhaps because they have felt, quite rightly, excluded from the earlier formulations of poetics (a situation that can be traced back to the homage paid to Charles Olson's "Projective Verse"), have engaged in a good bit of "soft" theorizing. Indeed, exploring such venues as the "Women /Writing / Theory" symposium for *Raddle Moon* (#11 and #13), the most recent issue of *Poetics Journal* (#10, June 1998), or the "Poetics and Exposition" section of *Moving Borders*, I find myself wishing that the poets in question would engage in more hand-on explication and critique of each others' work — something very much needed today — rather than producing so much "theoretical" prose.

In an essay for the "Poetics" section of *Moving Borders*, for example, I came across the following sentence: "Mimesis can partner metonymy, another obstruction to either/or"* (Sloan 600). What can this mean? Metonymy is the trope that relates one image or phrase to another along the axis of contiguity, as in "hut," "hovel," "poor little house," "shack" (Jakobson's example). The discussion of mimesis or representation is perhaps the cornerstone of literary theory from Plato on down, but, however we construe mimesis, the word refers to the mode of the verbal construct itself and its relation (or non-relation) to an external reality. Metonymy, on the other hand, is a trope and hence exists, if it does exist, within the mimesis, not side by side with it. Tolstoy's *Anna Karenina*, for example, is considered a highly mimetic novel and one of its main verbal devices is metonymy, as when Anna sees her husband at the train station after she has already fallen in love with Vronsky and notes that Karenin's ears stick out underneath his hat in a peculiar (and unpleasant) fashion, the protruding ears becoming a synecdoche (the most common form of metonymy) by which Karenin is known throughout the novel. Not only can't mimesis partner metonymy, there being no equivalence between the two ("another obstruction to either / or"), but metonymy is in fact one of the key features of the mimetic text.

Further down on the same page we read, "Can the rational accommodate the irrational? Can forms exist which truly allow for the accidental, absurd, grotesque, horrific, incommensurate — is this what Adorno meant?" The answer is quite simply no, for Adorno never equated "form" with the "rational"; he knew it was quite possible to have complex and subtle forms that are by no means "rational"; moreover he did not conceive of form as the container of the thing contained. Again, in an essay called "In Re 'Person,'"

---

*Ann Lauterbach, "Pragmatic Examples: the Nonce"

there is a statement that reads, "[T]he *value* of perspective to nascent capitalism was that it eventually aided in the creation of a new reality, a rationalized objectified space which could then be opened to exploitation'"* (Sloan 664). What artist can this author have in mind? Perugino? Raphael? Leonardo? Giorgione? All those wonderful Italian painters who used perspective to create the most amazing sense of palpability of nearness and distance, of mysterious background events that complicate what is seen in the foreground? Was theirs a "rationalized objective space" — a space of nascent capitalism?

Such theory buzz, like the current spate of what I call Big Name Collage — the large theoretical essay or even poem that is no more than a collage of nuggets by Big Names — Agamben and Heidegger, Cixous and Wittgenstein, Deleuze and Adorno — without any real analysis of what the philosophers in question are actually arguing, is problematic because this particular form of "innovative" writing may well alienate the very readership it hopes to capture. That readership is, I think, more attuned to specific issues, as when Mullen tries to walk the minefield between the particular idiolects or, as Jeff Derksen has called them, "communolects" (Pbweb 2) of our increasingly multilingual society. For those "communolects" now have everything to do with the one revolution that really has occurred in our own time — namely, the habitation of cyberspace. I don't have time here to discuss the poetic experiments — and many of these really are experiments in that they fail as often as they succeed and are replaced by more adequate models — on sites like Kenneth Goldsmith's *UbuWeb: Visual / Concrete / Sound Poetry*, but clearly, two important things are happening. The first is the visualization of poetic text — a visualization which is again a time-honored mode, as in George Herbert's The Temple or Mallarmé's *Coup de dés*, but reconfigured in important semantic ways in Johanna Drucker's *The Word Made Flesh* or Susan Howe's *Eikon Basilike*. The second is a form which I call, for want of a better name, "differential poetry," that is poetry that does not exist in a single fixed state but can vary according to the medium of presentation: printed book, cyberspace, installation, or oral rendition.

In the performative work of Laurie Anderson and Suzan-Lori Parks, Joan Retallack, and Caroline Bergvall, for example, the issue is less the referential fallacy, as it was for McCaffery in the mid-1970s, than the semiosis of the verbal/ visual field itself, where words and phrases can be moved around, reconfigured, and assigned to different slots, so that the "poem" has a variety of different forms. In a piece called "RUSH (a long way from H)," for example, Caroline Bergvall has designed a text you can access and activate on the Electronic Poetry Center website or read in book form, but it can also be seen and heard as performed and videotaped, in which case temporality becomes an important

---

*Beverly Dahlen, "In Re 'Person'"

determinant of meaning. As a barstool monologue cum brawl, interrupted and qualified by visual diagrams, media argot, and verbal breakdown, Bergvall's puts an ingenious spin on such pub monologues as that of Lil's "friend" in *The Waste Land*.

Is it "innovative"? Is it in Bergvall's words, "kindajazz or excitingly passée?" Well, there are surely Dada precedents for this performance model and "RUSH (a long way from H)" recalls the work of John Cage and Fluxus. So, to rephrase the question, is Bergvall's an interesting rendition of a lonely, anxious, and hilarious conversation, presumably between two women, in the neighborhood pub? A close look at the work's linguistic deformations and repetitions lays bare the complex layering that defines "this gigantic submarined trancehall" as it takes shape on the cyberpage. And the next step, one we find taken in Kenneth Goldsmith's Java Applet called "Fidget," is to have the words themselves put in motion, touch one another, and vary according to what time of day one accesses the site.

Would Adorno, with his distaste for kitsch and his revulsion of the Consciousness Industries (of which the internet is surely a prime instance) be the right guide for reading this text? Or would a better frame be provided by a critic like N. Katherine Hayles, whose new study subtitled "Virtual Bodies in Cybernetics, Literature, and Informatics," raises the issues which poets, like the rest of us, are now facing? It is less a question of novelty as such than of coming to terms with specificity and difference. As Gertrude Stein put it so nicely in "An Acquaintance with Description":

> What is the difference between three and two in furniture. Three is the third of three and two is the second of two. This makes it as true as a description. And not satisfied. And what is the difference between being on the road and waiting very likely being very likely waiting, a road is connecting and as it is connecting it is intended to be keeping going and waiting everybody can understand puzzling. (Stein 507)

WORKS CITED

Andrews, Bruce. *Paradise & Method* Evanston: Northwestern UP, 1996.

Benjamin, Walter. "The Work of Art in the Age of Mechanical Reproduction." *Illuminations*, ed. Hannah Arendt. New York: Schocken Books, 1969.

Berg, Stephen, and Robert Mezey, eds. *Naked Poetry: Recent American Poetry in Open Forms*. New York: and Indinapolis: Bobbs Merrill, 1969.

Bernstein, Charles. *Content's Dream: Essays 1975-1984*. Los Angeles: Sun & Moon Press, 1986.

Bryan, Sharon. "Hollandaise," *The Morrow Anthology of Younger American Poets.* Ed. Dave Smith & David Bottoms. New York: William Morrow & Co., 1985.

Ginsberg, Allen. "'First Thought, Best Thought." *Composed on the Tongue* Ed. Donald Allen. Bolinas, CA: Grey Fox, 1980. (The essay originally appeared in *Loka: A Journal from Naropa Institute* [1975].)

Goldsmith, Kenneth. *UbuWeb: Visual / Concrete/ Sound Poetry.* The site is located at www.ubu.com.

Hayles, N. Katherine. *How We Became Posthuman.* Chicago: U of Chicago P, 1999.

Hejinian, Lyn. *The Language of Inquiry.* Berkeley: U of California P, 2000.

Hmweb. Griffin, Farrah; Michael Magee, and Kirsten Gallagher. "A Conversation with Harryette Mullen." *Combo* 1 (Summer 1998). Reprinted on Harryette Mullen Website, http://wings.buffalo/edu/epc.authors/mullen, pp. 1-2.

L=A=N=G=U=A=G=E. Supplement Number One (June 1980).

McCaffery, Steve. *North of Intention: Critical Writings 1973-1986.* New York: Roof Books, 1986.

Mullen, Harryette. *Muse & Drudge.* Philadelphia: Singing Horse Press, 1995.

-------. *Trimmings.* Providence: Tender Buttons Press, 1994.

Nielsen, Aldon Lynn. *Black Chant: Languages of African-American Postmodernism* (Cambridge and New York: Cambridge UP, 1997)

O'Sullivam, Maggie, ed. *Out of Everywhere: Linguistically Innovative Poetry by Women in North America & the UK.* London: Reality Street Editions, 1996).

Pearcy, Kate. "A Poetics of Opposition: Race and the Avant-Garde." Unpublished essay read at the "Poetry and the Public Sphere Conference on Contemporary Poetry," 24-27 April, 1997.

Ppweb. Henning, Barbara. "In Interview with Harryette Mullen." *Poetry Project Newsletter.* (1999): 2. As read online on the Poetry Project website, http:///www.poetryproject. com/mullen.html.

Sheppard, Robert. *Poetics and Linguistically Innovative Poetry 1978-1997*

Sloan, Mary Margaret, ed. *Moving Borders: Three Decades of Innovative Writing by Women.* Jersey City, NJ: Talisman House, Publishers, 1998.

Spahr, Juliana. *Everybody's Autonomy.* Tuscaloosa: U of Alabama P, 2001.

Stein, Gertrude. "An Acquaintance with Description" (1929). *A Stein Reader* Ed. Ulla E. Dydo. Evanston: Northwestern UP, 1993.

Waldrop, Rosmarie. "Association." *Split Infinitives.* Philadelphia: Singing Horse Press, 1998.

Daniel Barbiero

REFLECTIONS ON LYRIC BEFORE, DURING, AND AFTER LANGUAGE

FROM ONE PERSPECTIVE, MUCH OF THE AVANT-GARDE WRITING OF THE 1970S AND 1980S — writing that for better and for worse has come to be called Language writing — can be read as entailing a rejection of lyric. Although this reading is onto something, it isn't quite entirely true. While a certain type of lyric does seem to have been rejected, it is also true that Language writing's critical program served to produce an alternative, more self-conscious understanding of lyric. Rather than being simply rejected in full, lyric conventions were instead subjected to a critical scrutiny that chose to emphasize the role of artifice in the production of lyric effect. Lyric features still figured in avant-garde work of the 1970s and 1980s, but they had been transformed into something different from the ostensibly artless lyric that was then predominant.

I want to explore some of the changes lyric has undergone in recent avant-garde writing first by offering a provisional, functional definition of lyric, after which I will consider the lyric form that was predominant when Language writing was beginning to emerge. I will follow this with a discussion focusing on the lyric features of two avant-garde works of the 1970s, and will conclude with a consideration of what might be called the post-Language lyric as it is exemplified in the work of two currently emerging poets.

LYRIC AS MODE: EXPRESSION OR DESCRIPTION?

LYRIC CAN BE DEFINED IN ANY OF A NUMBER OF WAYS. W. R. Johnson, for instance, has defined it grammatically, with emphasis on the I-you pronominal structure found explicitly or implicitly in various lyric forms (Johnson 3). Marjorie Perloff, offering a condensed paraphrase of others' notions of lyric, defines it more or less formally as a short verse utterance embodying a Romantic vision (Perloff, 173-74). Käte Hamburger has defined lyric as a genre characterized by what is for all intents and purposes a pragmatic statement structure organized around the "lyric I." (Hamburger 234)* While the foregoing criteria — grammatical, formal, and pragmatic — must be taken into account in any consideration of lyric, I would suggest, following Anne Williams's example, that we begin by defining lyric as a mode rather than as a genre (Williams 3).

If a poetic mode is understood as the manner in which a poem frames its content, then the lyric mode can be described as one in which the poem's subject matter is presented through the way the speaker takes the world. What this means is that it is the function of the lyric to show (demonstrate, describe) how things are with the speaker. The lyric utterance, in other words, pivots on the indication, whether directly or indirectly, of the (broadly speaking) subjective or phenomenal states of the poem's speaker. To borrow Hamburger's apt phrase, the lyric's emphasis is not on "the object of experience, but the experience of the object" (278) — if by experience we mean something like what it is like to be in a given relation to an object, event, or state of affairs. We can thus think of lyric as consisting in the linguistic presentation of a speaker's state of mind as this latter is elicited under the given conditions and circumstances described, specified, or hinted at in the poem.

So far, so good. But there is a crucial qualification that must be introduced here. Noel Carroll has pointed to an "ontological difference" between an utterance issued in the context of an ordinary speaking situation and an utterance issued in any of the various contexts associated with the general field of literature (Carroll 102ff). I believe Carroll's distinction is basically correct, but I would prefer to frame it in terms of functional rather than ontological difference. Put this way, the distinction would consist in the fact that sentences or other units of utterance occurring in a literary context have a different communicative function from that of ordinary sentences and units of utterance. Given that difference in function we can distinguish between the performance of a given speech act and the representation of one.†

If we accept something like this functional difference, we can refine the above definition of lyric to the following: lyric, rather than consisting in a properly expressive utterance, instead functions to represent or describe such an utterance. Rather than counting as an expression of a (real, actual) state of mind, in other words, the lyric counts instead as a description of a state of mind that *would be* manifested *were* a speaker really in that state and

---

*Note, though, that Hamburger's own understanding of the pragmatic is couched in terms of the non-constative speech acts associated with questions, commands, and wishes. See, e.g., p. 46.

†Carroll, p. 103. Of course as Carroll notes, many literary works combine performances with representations of performances, and the difference must be judged on a "case-by-case basis" (108).

were that state expressed (assuming the speaker's sincerity in uttering it). In short, all else being equal, a lyric utterance does not have the function of manifesting a "real" phenomenal or psychological state, but rather describes what it *would be* like to be in that state. In Williams's apt phrase, lyric is the "representation of an act of self-expression" (13) and not an act of self-expression per se.

THE PLAIN LANGUAGE LYRIC OF SINCERITY

CONSIDER NOW THE FOLLOWING EXCERPT, which is taken from "Working with Tools" by A.R. Ammons:

> I make a simple assertion
> like a nice piece of stone
> and you
> alert to presence and entrance
> man your pick and hammer . . .
> I understand such
> ways of being afraid. (Ammons 1097)

This is a good example of what I would call the plain language lyric. The plain language lyric has since sometime in the late 1960s or early 1970s attained the status of the period style. As the label implies, the plain language lyric is notable for its anti-rhetorical rhetoric. This is evident in Ammons's poem, which appears to be a plain-spoken anecdote about the speaker's relationship with an apparently argumentative partner. The anecdotal effect arises to a significant degree from its reliance on first person present tense indicative sentences, which create the impression of a face-to-face immediacy in which a speaker addresses a listener in an everyday situation.

As an utterance, the poem is, like the event that gives it its immediate topic, an assertion, and one can imagine any of a number of situations in which it could be spoken. Its ordinary use would be to express the speaker's real state of mind; were we to hear it uttered in any of a number of ordinary language situations, we would probably feel justified in thinking that this is how things are with the person uttering it. We would, in other words, be convinced of its sincerity.

Sincerity in fact seems to be the central value embodied in this poem, as it seems to be the central value of the plain language lyric generally, precisely by virtue of its very plainness of expression. Here Hamburger's observation that on the basis of its statement structure, the lyric utterance is to be interpreted as a reality statement and its subject encountered as a real subject is apt. The first person singular present tense phenomenal statement, commonly encountered in the plain language lyric (as it is in Ammons's poem above), nicely illustrates how this reading is licensed: such statements deploy a statement subject, denoted by the pronoun "I," and connect it to a given statement by a verb telling us something about how the statement subject stands in relation to the content of the statement. Strictly on the basis of such a sentence's internal information, we would seem to be justified in reading it as an expressive utterance, that is, as one expressing the statement subject's "field of experience."

It is this capacity of the plain language lyric to appear as a reality statement that obscures, at least potentially, the functional difference referred to above. Such an obscuring is of central importance to the plain language lyric because it is the basis on which the lyric's claim to sincerity apparently is guaranteed. By taking on the appearance of a reality statement, the plain language lyric in effect licenses a reading in which it is evaluated by the standards that normally apply to reality statements. The most important of these standards can, following Searle, be called the sincerity condition (Searle 64). The sincerity condition simply holds that in uttering *p*, the speaker (sincerely) means that he or she believes *p* to be the case. The plain language lyric, precisely to the extent that it uses plain language, mimics this characteristic aspect of ordinary speech and thus seems to want to be subject to the sincerity condition and perhaps little else. But because the plain language lyric, despite its appearance as an ordinary language statement, is not in fact an utterance proper to an ordinary language context, to read it as one is to commit what might be called the expressive fallacy, which consists in the misreading of a non-spontaneous and therefore quasi-expressive utterance as if it were a spontaneous, and therefore genuinely expressive, utterance.

"LANGUAGE" AND THE LYRIC

IT IS AGAINST THE EXPRESSIVE FALLACY that some avant-garde poets of the 1970s reacted. There is a parallel of sorts here: just as the plain language writers reacted against the impersonality and explicit artifice in the prevailing poetic style of the 1950s and early 1960s, the Language writers can be seen as having reacted against the mimicry of expressive spontaneity characteristic of the prevailing poetic style of the 1970s and 1980s.

One Language piece that seems to re-evaluate the status of quasi-expressiveness as a poetic value is Lynne Dreyer's "Exploration," from *Lamplights Used to Feed the Deer* (Dreyer 77-83). We have seen how the plain language lyric encourages a reading by which its utterances are construed as reality statements. In an interesting way, certain parts of "Exploration" encourage a similar reception: in a number of sections of this poem, one encounters apparently autobiographical or confessional passages. The following lines offer a good example of this:

> . . . You think I didn't
> hear you. You think I didn't
> hear a word you said. I not only
> heard the words I heard each
> action you made. Every raise of
> the eyebrow. Each gesture.
> Every wave of the hand, and
> instead of piecing them together
> It all flowed. (Dreyer 80)

On the basis of the excerpt alone, "Exploration" would seem a prototypical plain language lyric. But it isn't. The poem occurs early in the Language period — it is dated 1974 — and can be read as representing something of a transition between the plain language lyric and Language writing proper. Although plain language lyric conventions do recur throughout the poem, they are employed in a way that can only be described as disruptive. Such disruption is largely a result of Dreyer's tendency to block linguistic integration at the inter-sentential or discourse level. Concretely, this means that although the individual sentences comprising the plain language passages are well-formed from an ordinary language perspective, they do not combine to make the well-formed larger units necessary to successful ordinary language communication.

Taken as a whole, "Exploration" reads as an early example of the post-lyric sequence. This latter can be characterized as a poem consisting of shifts in tone and topic set within an episodic, formally-variable framework. What makes "Exploration" such a sequence is its juxtaposition of plain language passages of direct address and reminiscence, with such decidedly non-lyric elements as enumerated lists of lessons, things, and situations. By combining these elements, Dreyer emphasizes the fact that plain language passages notwithstanding, "Exploration" is not in fact an ordinary language utterance. (It has long been a commonplace to recognize this about avant-garde poetries generally, and while it seems a truism now, it would not be so in 1974, when plain language conventions were ascendant.) In fact the artifice of the poem's overall construction prevents us from taking for granted the reality status of its plain language passages. The outcome is a de facto critique of plain language conventions which foregrounds the artifice not of language per se, but of the parasitic relationship between the plain language lyric and the ordinary language utterance it mimics.

As a result, in "Exploration" as in other Language works, a question regarding the reality status of, and hence the applicability of the sincerity condition to, the poem's constitutent utterances is effectively raised. The plain language passages encourage us to read them as sincere reality statements, but the disruption that characterizes them refuses to allow this reading to go through entirely without a measure of self-consciousness on the part of the reader. We may want to take the poem's voice for the poet's, but we realize that to do so is to risk a misreading.

Interesting in this regard is the work of Hannah Weiner, which would seem to be a limiting case of both Language writing and of lyric. If work such as Dreyer's emphasizes the artifice that undergirds lyric sincerity, Weiner's work has the opposite effect entirely. Much of her writing, particularly in work such as the *Clairvoyant Journal*, communicates an immediacy that appears to be wholly unpremeditated. This creates a number of interpretive complications.

On the one hand, the *Clairvoyant Journal* creates the impression of having been the result of a spontaneous, automatic transcription of multiple voices and visions. But even though it appears to be a variety of spontaneous expression, it is nothing like the spontaneous expression of ordinary speech. For one thing, the language used is very noticeably different qualitatively from that encountered in ordinary speech. It would thus seem to be an open question whether or not sincerity as a value — poetic or otherwise — is appropriate to apply to the work.

> Part of the difficulty lies in the polymorphic nature of the voice(s) Weiner favors:
> ... that was an ESP term your name SO WHAT has been
> appearing around here a lot so it's in this book
> JUNIOR some publisher is looking at it now *big*
> *question stop typing* ... (unpaginated)

In this excerpt, Weiner takes a voice associated with clairvoyance ("that was an ESP term"), interrupts it with a mocking voice recorded in upper case letters ("SO WHAT"), adds an apparently interior voice commenting on the act of transcription ("*big question stop typing*"), and finally combines all of these with the words she apparently saw on people and things ("your name has been appearing around here a lot"). The end result is a polyphony that cannot be reduced to the utterance of a unitary speaker — indeed, in much of this work it is difficult to determine who or what exactly counts as the utterer.

In some respects, the *Clairvoyant Journal* — and other works by Weiner — can be seen as a limiting case of lyric rather than a non-case. If the textual fact of multiple voices reflects a kind of possession by words, this makes for a situation that genuinely throws into question the role of intention, and consequently of artifice, in the production of the work. This pushes to an extreme the traditional lyric value of inspiration — literally, in that the work appears to have been written in a trance state. This same situation would implicate Weiner's work as a limiting case of Language writing as well. For many Language poems a fragmentation of voice was used as a deliberate device precisely to call into question the possibility of voice. But despite the fragmentation that was effected at the level of the poem itself, at a meta-level there could be identified a unity that derived from the fact that the fragmentation of voice was imposed as a critical method. With Weiner's work this deliberation seems to be missing. Although Language-like fragmentation of voice is present in the work, it seems to serve a documentary function closer to journal writing than to anything else.

But this observation leads to a certain undecidibility in how best to approach Weiner's work — whether as a poetic artifact or as a record of extraordinary, "real" states of being and uttering. The proper reading probably would combine both approaches, but the possibility remains that the latter will predominate. If that is the case, then we may find ourselves coming full circle and returing to a reading in which sincerity (or something like it) once again takes on a central value.

Overall, the writers associated with with avant gardes of the 1970s and 1980s, in choosing to make poetic artifice explicit, helped to underscore the non-expressive status of the poetic utterance generally and, by extension, the lyric utterance specifically. But this critical move did not entail a wholesale negation of the lyric tradition; rather, it would seem instead that the lyric tradition was given a refigured reading. Two points suggest themselves in this connection.

First, the non-expressive reading of lyric does not implicate a denial of a poem's capacity to embody sensibility per se. Rather, it denies the temptation, encouraged to varying degrees by lyric conventions, to interpret the lyric utterance simply as a reality statement, and does so on functional grounds. Concretely, the non-expressive reading invites us to acknowledge that absent corroborating independent evidence, we are not licensed to interpret the sensibility on display in the lyric to be that of the poet presented directly to the reader or hearer.

As a result, reading lyric as non-expressive means resisting two fallacies that can be characterized as ontological and epistemological, respectively. The ontological fallacy involves equating the speaker with the poet. The epistemological fallacy — which follows directly from the ontological fallacy — involves taking *all* of the individual utterances within the lyric as statements necessarily true or false of actual states of affairs. I emphasize "all" here because it is not clear to me that some utterances in a lyric cannot be read that way; some utterances within a lyric (or other literary text for that matter) may perform the same function as constative utterances, that is, they may be intended to state matters of fact. And it is also true that if we are to take lyric's quasi-expressive utterances as descriptions, there may be circumstances in which truth or falsity will be an issue. But it seems to me that in general the functionality of lyric prevents us from taking at face value statements purporting to be expressions of states of mind.

Second, Language writing's critique of the plain language lyric's claims to sincerity implicates a particular concern with authenticity. On the one hand there is a rejection of what are seen to be the ideological implications of the plain language lyric's bias in favor of banal (i.e., "transparent") language. On the other, there is a conservation of the notion that in producing poetry, one must somehow be in good faith (to borrow a convenient though not entirely accurate term). The question is this: on what basis can one be in good faith? The answer couldn't be seen to consist in the traditional idea of the individual constituting him- or herself through his or her choices, or confronting the dichotomy between his or her private and public ways of being. Rather, good faith (following this view) would seem to be rooted in a willingness to take a dis-illusioned look at oneself as part of a collective form of life, with a special emphasis on the role language plays in constituting the conditions for such a collective life. The rejection of plain language sincerity and the consequent emphasis on poetic artifice may be seen as one way of coming to this recognition.*

---

*The notion of authenticity implicit in much Language writing is an often overlooked yet important aspect of its critical program. This assertion is likely to be controversial, though.

LYRIC AFTER "LANGUAGE": THE CIRCUMSPECTIVE LYRIC

RECENTLY THERE HAS BEEN AN UPSURGE in interest in the lyric and the possibilities it presents for further poetic and critical exploration. Lyric has thus become an explicit concern of a number of poets emerging into what can be called, for lack of a better expression, the post-Language period.[*] While many of this new generation of poets have concerned themselves with exploring a variety of poetic forms, their starting point can be identified as being rooted not only in Language poetry's experimentation with syntactic and semantic structures, but in its more general outlook regarding the contexts within which poetry is written and received. As a consequence, emerging poets have inherited a particular understanding of the subjective as a factor dependent on social, linguistic, and other structures. This has had an effect on how lyric is now apprehended. For if inwardness is the pivot of the traditional lyric, the current lyric by contrast pivots on a sense of inwardness as outwardly constrained if not compromised. How we take the world is viewed as significantly determined by how the world is given to us; the inner dimension of experience is reimagined as a porous domain susceptible to partial and ongoing constitution from outside agencies, be these social forces, the givenness of language, or the already existing state of the discipline in which one writes.

As a result, new lyric writing can be described as predominantly circumspective in nature, rather than — as is traditional lyric — introspective. Whereas introspection asks us to look within ourselves, circumspection involves us in a look around ourselves, to the situation(s) encompassing us. Somewhat paradoxically, though, the circumspective view shows also that — by definition — we are situated within the center of the circumstances surrounding us. But it is understood that such a center is not something we create, but rather is a kind of point of insertion into the given. One takes one's place in a world already formed, already there, one is pushed or pulled into place — into a given place. And that is the place from which the circumspective lyric speaks.

Like some other poets of the generation emerging in the wake of Language writing, Mark Wallace has advocated a reexamination of the lyric. His collection *Complications From Standing in a Circle* shows one way this can be done. Here is an excerpt from the collection's title poem:

---

[*]For a general discussion of the recent interest in lyric and other poetic forms, see my "Avant-Garde without Agonism?" *Talisman* 14 (1995), pp. 151-160.

> I love so many things, eyes, waves on
> sea shore storm, my fingers brushing in hair
> the dullness in not seeing enough.
> I remember once a watermelon
> we ate aching in the park. I remember
> grief among the stones, crumpled windowsills
> this hope remains a seizure (Wallace 16)

This passage exhibits some of the distinguishing features associated with the traditional lyric mode. First, the poem's speaker describes how things are with him in first person singular present tense phenomenal statements. Further, these statements are relatively unadorned and reminiscent of ordinary speech — so much so that they would not seem entirely out of place in a plain language lyric. The overall tone is conversational as the speaker catalogues the things he loves, or recollects an episode marked by strong emotion. Given these lines' statement structure, tone, and content, we would probably want to read them as reality statements. But there are rhetorical effects that prevent such a reading. For example, the figure "this hope remains a seizure" is not the kind of thing one is likely to hear in an ordinary language context. Beyond this, though, it is the context of the poem as a whole that blocks the plain language reading, at least in part because of Wallace's use of the disjunctive forms associated with Language and other avant-garde writing.

Interestingly, the title of the collection indicates what it is to take the circumspective view. "Standing in a circle" can be read as a gloss on the meaning of the word "circumstance": standing within the circle traced by circumstance, one is ringed by or situated within what is given, which circumscribes one. The everydayness of much of the poems' subject matter reinforces this reading, as the mundane appears as a set of determinations in relation to which a voice is formed.

Different in many ways from "Complications" is Pam Rehm's "The Coming Second," a poem in several parts from her collection *To Give It Up*. The poem is largely in the lyric mode and contains a number of first-person singular present tense phenomenal statements in which the speaker describes her longing, admits her ignorance, announces her newly-found fearlessness, and so forth. But alongside the lyric elements didactic elements are found, such as well. In a six-line passage beginning with a play on the word "eros," "sore," and "rose" (76), Rehm addresses — albeit obliquely — the loss of oneself in another. In that passage, the implicit allusion to consummation can be understood in a figurative as well as a literal sense whereby eros is not just physical love, but a generalized figure for self-surrender to another. One then becomes a "part of everything," and the distinction between self and other is lost. By the same token, these same lines can be read as a caution against an imprisoning and dessicating solipsism in which no "rose" — presumably a figure for eros, for which it is an anagram — can grow. Either reading uncovers the poem's circumspection, which inheres primarily in its looking outward for the prerequisites of becoming oneself: the inwardness of introspection is supplanted by the outwardness that consists in our looking around to find ourselves in others.

As with most of the poems in *To Give it Up*, "The Coming Second" lends itself to two possible readings. The first of these is theological, in which case the poem can be read as telling of a search for union with the divine. The allusion to physical love is thus transfigured into a coded reference to divine union — a trope familiar from traditional religious lyric. But it retains its literal meaning as well, to the extent that one loses oneself in others as these latter embody the divine. (This would seem to be the case, as the poem appears in a section of the book entitled "Heaven Corresponding to Life in the Body.") The second reading possible is secular. Here again the theme is losing oneself in another, but with the goal being not divine union, but the attainment of one's own identity through identification with another.

In this as in other poems in *To Give it Up*, Rehm's elaborate use of figurative language allows her work to maintain its distance from ordinary language and hence from the appearance of spontaneous utterance. Artifice is factored in at the level of the figure rather than at the level of statement structure, and makes for a lyric form that avoids the studied artlessness of the plain language lyric. Here again Rehm's poetic is as close to traditional religious lyric as it is to any recent avant-garde.

The current refiguration of lyric has taken place within the larger framework of a more or less pragmatic attitude toward the poetic forms of the recent and not so recent past. Preexisting poetic forms seem to be understood as a given that can be used to the extent that they can be made to say what needs to be said — and only to that extent. Certainly Rehm's work, with its combination of elements drawn from the avant-garde and from older religious traditions, would fit this description. The same pragmatic motivation would seem to be at work in Wallace's use of plain language and other lyric conventions as well.[*] The prime value here seems to be an open-minded willingness to refigure past avant-garde and

---

[*]Similar observations can be made of poets such as Peter Gizzi, Buck Downs, Jean Donnelly, Chris Stroffolino, and Alan Gilbert, to name a handful.

other traditions, which I have elsewhere described as arising from a non-agonistic relationship to the past.[*]

Although the post-Language lyric has refigured some traditional and recent lyric conventions, it does not represent a return to the status quo ante "language," since the critical awareness Language writing brought to the lyric is now as much a part of the given for poets working after Language as are the past forms they may choose to explore. For post-Language poets taking Language writing as their (positive) point of reference, the question of the dependence of lyric effect on artifice has been settled. Even a poet like Rehm, who might be expected to reject at least some of the Language platform, makes use of artifice to a degree that seems at least an acknowledgement of the Language precedent. But rather than foreground the non-expressive status of lyric through unrelenting emphasis on artifice, post-Language lyric has incorporated lyric elements into a larger context that, taken as a whole, prevents identification of the post-Language lyric with ordinary language conventions. In this sense post- Language lyric has consolidated the avant-garde critique of lyric convention, and has extended the boundaries of the self-consciously non-expressive lyric.

WORKS CITED

Ammons, A.R. "Working with Tools." In *The Norton Anthology of Modern Poetry*. Ed. Richard Ellmann and Robert O'Clair. New York: W.W. Norton & Co., 1973.

Carroll, Noel. "Art, Intention, and Conversation." In *Intention and Interpretation*. Ed. Gary Iseminger. Temple UP, 1992.

Dreyer, Lynne. "Exploration." In *The White Museum*. New York: Roof, 1986.

Hamburger, Käte. *The Logic of Literature*. Second Revised Edition. Tr. Marilynn J. Rose. Bloomington IN: Indiana UP, 1993.

Johnson, W. R. *The Idea of Lyric*. Berkeley: U of California P, 1982.

Perloff, Marjorie. "Postmodernism and the Impasse of the Lyric." In *The Dance of the Intellect: Studies in the Poetry of the Pound Tradition*. Cambridge: Cambridge UP, 1987. 172-200.

Rehm, Pam. *To Give it Up*. Los Angeles: Sun & Moon Press, 1995.

Searle, John. *Speech Acts: An Essay in the Philosophy of Language*. Cambridge: Cambridge UP, 1969.

Wallace, Mark. *Complications from Standing in a Circle*. Buffalo, NY: Leave Books, 1993.

Weiner, Hannah. *Clairvoyant Journal*. New York: Angel Hair, 1978.

Williams, Anne. *Prophetic Strain: The Greater Lyric in the Eighteenth Century*. Chicago: U of Chicago P, 1984.

---

[*]In "Avant-Garde without Agonism?"

Christopher Beach

"EVENTS WERE NOT LACKING": DAVID ANTIN'S TALK POEMS, LYN HEJINIAN'S *MY LIFE*, AND THE POETICS OF CULTURAL MEMORY

THE PERSONAL OR AUTOBIOGRAPHICAL MODE IN CONTEMPORARY AMERICAN POETRY has generally been associated with the "confessional" or "post-confessional" lyric, a form that became the dominant mode of American poetry in the 1960s and has determined much of the production of the poetic mainstream for the past three or four decades. Since the 1970s, however, there has been another mode of autobiographical poetic writing which departs radically from the model first established by confessionalists like Robert Lowell and Sylvia Plath and more recently practiced in creative writing workshops across the country. Unlike the confessional poem — a form of lyric in which the use of "voice" to create a personal space for the autobiographical subject often isolates that subject from cultural and historical conditions — the works of David Antin and Lyn Hejinian explore the personal within the larger context of what can be called "cultural memory." I define "cultural memory" as a level of interaction between the lived experience of the individual poet and the concurrent experience of the society or culture as a whole. In the case of the kind of avant-garde or oppositional poetics represented by both Antin and Hejinian, I would also suggest that the reflection on cultural memory reveals a desire to confuse the level of the personal with that of the cultural, and a refusal to accept the conventional boundaries which post-Romantic poetry has drawn between the lyric as a reflection or meditation on the narratized or transcendental self and "non-poetic" genres — the novel or autobiographical essay, for example — which seek to present the self within a larger social or cultural framework.

On the surface, there may not seem to be a great deal in common between David Antin's "talk poems" and Lyn Hejinian's autobiographical prose-poem sequence *My Life*. Hejinian's is a highly "constructed" work based on a procedural or mathematical form, while Antin's talk poem is a spontaneous or at least quasi-spontaneous form that is determined only by his own thought process and by the amount of time he allots himself for his "talk." On other levels, however, Antin's and Hejinian's works display important points of similarity. Both are very much concerned with memory, whether it be personal-autobiographical memory or cultural-historical memory. Both are concerned with the way in which memories work and the way in which language is produced in contact with a personal past or an historical past.

The title of my essay refers to one of the "titles" given to the sections of *My Life*, but it also refers in a more general sense to the fact that any human situation is constituted by various "events," whether linguistic events or social events or cultural events. The privileged status of "event" is challenged in Hejinian's poem, so that rather than a narrative marked by defining moments we find a fluid progression of event which is formally reinforced by the poem itself at the level of the sentence, no sentence being more "important" or more "central" to the narrative of *My Life* than any other. In contrast to conventional autobiographical narratives which plot a series of climactic or episodic moments — turning points in a career or life history — *My Life* suggests that events are not reifiable entities but instead interdependent parts of an irreducible process.

An event is usually defined as an occurence, incident, or experience of some significance. The word "event" comes from the Latin *evenire*, which literally means "to come out"; thus an event is a kind of coming out, and a life is a series of happenings, out-comings, or emergences. Events are those moments in one's life that come out and show themselves, through the agency of the memory, to the world. These events stand out from the background of life, as it were, and enter the foreground of consciousness.

Hejinian refers to *My Life* as a "permeable constructedness," and we find throughout the text the sense of something that is on one level very carefully constructed but on another level extremely permeable and almost random in its form, to the extent that any sentence could be replaced with any other without affecting in any absolute way the overall construction of the text. This structure reflects the way that our lives are constructed out of millions of individual moments or memories or events that are constantly changing within our consciousness but which make up the sense of a relatively unified whole: myself, my past, my life. Just as every moment or experience in our lives could be reduced to the same level of emphasis or importance without privileging one over another, Hejinian's form does not privilege one sentence or one thought over another, except through the highly self-conscious placement of certain sentences or phrases as "titles" and the subsequent repetition of these phrases throughout the text.

But there is at the same time another sense in which everything in life, and everything in *My Life*, resists being reduced to the same status: certain sentences can be read as pointing to the operations of language — self-referentially or metalinguistically — while other sentences can be read as pointing to the operations of thought, and other sentences can be read as referring to a level of non-linguistic events that have marked in one way or another the autobiographical "life" represented in the poem, and still other sentences can be read as referring to events that affected not only the subject of the poem — Hejinian herself — but the society or culture in general. What interests me is how demarcations can be made in the text between different levels of event, between different levels of pointing or indexing, and what that demarcation says about both the operation of language and the operation of memory.

What Antin is trying to do in his talk poems is to some extent similar to Hejinian's project: Antin uses language, or more specifically uses "talk," to move through memory and ideas in a way that produces what Hejinian has called a "rejection of closure." In Antin's talk poems, as in Hejinian's *My Life*, we find an important relation to what Hejinian calls "event." As Sherman Paul writes of Antin: "the talk poems are not only poems of an occasion, they themselves are the occasion"; they are "'language events,' irreducible poems-in-process" (56). These talk poems, like *My Life*, blur the boundary between language and event, between event or occasion and its representation.

Antin is also, like Hejinian, intensely interested in the mode or genre of autobiography: in fact, two of Antin's pre-talk poem works from the late 1960s are the volume entitled *Autobiography* (1967) and the poem "Autobiography 2," from *Code of Flag Behavior* (1968). In these relatively early works, Antin can be seen to anticipate both his own project in the talk poems and Hejinian's project in *My Life*. In "Autobiography 2," Antin organizes the poem into fifty-four sections or fragments not totally unlike Hejinian's forty-five sections in *My Life*. As Paul has noted, this kind of writing calls into question both the autobiographical form and the autobiographical process in order to "make autobiography *interesting* again" (30). In each section we learn about an episode either in Antin's life or in the life of others, but it is impossible to tell — without recourse to additional biographical information about Antin himself — which of the events or situations described actually happened to *him*, which happened to others he knows, and which are either made up or so general as to lose any appearance of biographical specificity (i.e. "she forgot how to make love"). At times Antin appears to be playing with the reader's desire to make autobiographical sense of the moments, occurences, or events he describes. At other times, he appears to be asking the very pertinent question: "What does an autobiography include?" Does it include everything one remembers? Only what one remembers at the moment of writing, without recourse to mnemonic aids such as diaries, notebooks, calenders, or journals? What one remembers selectively? What one remembers in order to trace a particular life trajectory? The memories of other people as well as the autobiographical subject? "Autobiography 2" is a poem that foregrounds the level of sociohistorical event while never offering a clear commentary on the meaning of such event, suggesting that there is no defined boundary between lived experience and the cultural memories derived from others' experiences.[*]

In question in the poem is the fact of who is narrating the autobiography, from whose point of view it is witnessed and told. This is a question Antin emphasizes by shifting between pronouns — sometimes narrating in the first person and sometimes in the third person. In "Autobiography 2" Antin takes a particular mode of destabilizing the autobiographical to its logical extreme, where the collage-like structure of seemingly disparate mini-narratives is never brought into a unified or coherent master narrative, into the plot of a single life. It is at this point that he moves to the next logical point of development, the talk poem, which is in one sense a continuation of the movement away from linearity and closure represented by "Autobiography 2," but in another sense a complete departure from that collage-based mode, a mode of writing that still maintains clear connections to traditions of experimental modernism.

With the talk poems, beginning in the early 1970s, Antin has moved into a mode of autobiographical writing that is more clearly "postmodern," as Charles Altieri and others have suggested.[†] The improvisational quality of the talk poems makes the act of memory even more central than it was in Antin's earlier poetry, since only what is remembered at the moment of talking will find its way into the poem, will come out of the almost infinite background of Antin's lived experience. Further, the talk poem makes the boundary between personal or private memory and public or cultural memory far less stable, since one level of memory constantly flows into the other.

As one example, we may examine Antin's talk poem "The River," from the collection *What It Means To Be Avant-Garde*. Here, Antin begins in an autobiographical mode, or more specifically a mode of self-referential autobiography: talking about the process of compos-

---

[*]Historical events alluded to in the poem include the Russian revolution, the Spanish Civil War, World War II, the Korean War, and the Vietman War.

[†]Altieri argues that Antin "adapts and alters the critical and constructivist dimensions of Modernist practice" in his talk poems; Antin "transforms Modernist ideals of art as direct testimony . . . into an elaborate demonstration of who one becomes in the very process of tuning as one speaks" (11,12). In a paradigmatic shift from modernist construct to postmodernist process, Antin makes the work "the literal activity of the performing self accepting the burden of establishing the evidence necessary for our taking the artistic activity as potentially representative and significant" (22).

ing his own talk poems. From there he shifts to memories of New York and more specifically of Central Park, and from there he shifts again to the question of pollution and to various sites of pollution: first the Hudson River and then San Diego and the campus of the University of California at San Diego where he teaches.

At the same time that the poem follows an apparently improvisational or stream-of-consciousness exploration of the poet's own associations, it also continues to circle around a larger social or cultural issue: that of environmentalism and of the various nuances of the word "environment" itself. As a result, the poet's idiosyncratic flow of personal memory is always implicated in and refracted through a level of cultural memory. This interaction culminates in an incident in which the university administration, having worked with Antin and others to "treat the land the enviroment we live in in a more respectful way" by building an "academic park that would be a model to the community of an ecologically humane place that would set an example in how to build and above all not build when natural conditions required it," suddenly and without explanation destroys the landscape of a large section of the campus:

> one day we got there at the end of the summer and the trees were gone in their place were these amputated stumps five hundred and fifty stumps of living eucalyptus trees weird looking little tables   and theyd gone through there and put little red flags up near them to show that this was no accident   we'd tried to get them to turn this place into an academic park and theyd turned it into a field of carnage (140)

This traumatic ecological event appears to lead Antin to the brink of despair:

> we're constantly aware that what we're dealing with is like being in a chute its like a chute and we're falling in it and maybe its like being in a river and we're being swept out to sea but we're not sure whether we're being swept out to the ocean or sucked into the bottom of some very foul swamp (141)

Antin is able to pull himself out of this sense of acute depression partly by reminding himself of the futility of being depressed ("what difference would it make if i was depressed") and partly by realizing that the kind of "humorless" attitude that typifies the response of the American left to social wrongs is not consistent with his own more exploratory poetics. Rather than give up his narrative entirely, however, he quickly counters with another personal narrative which itself has significant cultural undertones: that of his ninety-year-old Hungarian Jewish emigré father-in-law, a poet and painter who still plays an elegant game of tennis, even after having lived an extremely difficult life which included being beaten up and jailed by the Hungarian police. "The River" subsumes personal memory into cultural memory by speaking of cultural or historical events — environmental despoliation and political repression — as shared human events which intersect with more personal events through the agency of language.

Antin's talk poems and Hejinian's *My Life* are two of the most fully articulated examples of a genre that could be called the postmodern poetic autobiography, but what Hejinian does with the autobiographical genre in *My Life* is quite different from what Antin does with it in his talk poems. Where in Antin's poems the stylistic and generic indeterminacy is created by a lack of linearity in the progression from one memory to the next — a lack of either chronological linearity or clearly defined causal or narrative linearity — in Hejinian's poem it is caused by the apparent disjunction between a systematically applied experimental form (forty-five-sentence blocks of text occuring in a sequence of forty-five sections) and the evocation of seemingly "actual" memories and experiences in the poet's life.

There is also a further dislocation between the necessarily "private" language Hejinian adopts and even actively foregrounds on the level of the sentence, and the public nature of language as it enters the sphere of the published text, an artifact that is meant to be read and at least to some degree understood.[*] Hejinian's form problematizes this private/public split more acutely than Antin's talk poems. When we come upon seemingly private lines or phrases in *My Life* such as "a name trimmed with colored ribbons," "like plump birds along the shore," or "as for we who love to be astonished," all of which occur at fairly regular intervals throughout *My Life*, we are at first puzzled by their seeming lack of connection to the "events" taking place around them, only later discovering how to "place" them in context, how to find a meaningful relationship between these phrases and the rest of the text.

The sense that "to some extent each sentence has to be the whole story," as Hejinian puts it, pervades the text of *My Life*, so that on a fundamental level, as with Antin's talk poem, there is no way of separating cultural memory from personal memory, private event from public event, personal history from public history. Or to put it another way, what is at stake in Hejinian's textual economy is not only the syntactical relationship between

---

[*] It is this tension that Stephen Ratcliffe refers to when he defines Hejinian's *The Guard* as "private eye/ public work."

words and things, as David Jarraway has suggested, but the syntactical relationship between sentences and events, between the way events (re)occur in the memory and the way the syntactic and semantic properties of the sentence reenact such events and the process of remembering them, the way the sentence serves to reconstruct them or place them in a "syntax."

Like Antin, Hejinian is extremely self-conscious about the process of memory ("what memory is not a 'gripping' thought" is the title of section nine of *My Life*), yet the ambiguous rhetorical phrasing of even that line allows the possibility that all memories are not equally "gripping." Some memories "grip" while others float into consciousness or never fully materialize.* When Hejinian writes that "the years pass, years in which, I take it, events were not lacking" (69). we find an expression of this same ambivalence. Sometimes the memory of events is *not* gripping; sometimes we have only a vague sense that as time passes things must have happened. But the curiously passive phrasing of "were not lacking" and the interpolated and casual "I take it" detract from any sense of certainty about exactly what those events were or what significance to attach to them.

The section itself begins with an even greater and more ominous sense of uncertainty:

Somewhere, some there, disorder out, entangled in language. I was reading several books at once, usually three. If faster, then more. The typewriter at night was classical. As the storm approached it was as if the blue suddenly evaporated from the sky, leaving a sky merely a pale shadow of itself. Why isn't the reflection in the mirror flat, since the mirror itself is flat. Or cream, when it turns. (69)

In the typically associative style of *My Life*, the passage moves through a series of interlocking metonymic chains from language to books to typewriters, from night to sky to shadow to mirror to flatness to cream, while at the same time the underlying sense of foreboding is carried by words like "disorder" and "entangled" and by the image of the approaching storm.

But are these words and images the "events" she evokes in the title? Certainly the first sentence suggests some kind of event — "somewhere . . . some there . . . out [there]" — but it is an event, or perhaps the memory of an event, that falls into "disorder" and that subsequently becomes "entangled in language," leading to a disorder that is of a much more

---

*See for example the section entitled "Now such is the rhythm of cognition," in which Hejinian writes that although she lives "within a few blocks of the scenes of my childhood," these childhood scenes now "evoke nothing" (93).

personal nature: "reading several books at once, usually three." Reading several books at a time may be a source of mental disorder or linguistic entanglement, but it is also a source of excitement — "if faster, then more" — or perhaps of an uncontrolled and unfulfilled desire. The sense of fear, of events or situations out of control, continues in the following sentences:

> When we were children, in a careless moment, my father had suggested that we go camping, but now that we were outdoors in the dark he was scared. I want to remember more than more than that, more or less as it really happened. It seems that we hardly begin before we are already there. It was cancer but we couldn't say that. (69)

Memories of a frightening event of childhood lead to a desire for better understanding, for a sharper memory, but that very desire — the intensity of which is reflected in the construction "more than more than that" — is undercut by the "more or less" of the second half of the sentence, and the passage ends with the kind of traumatic psychic event that permanently marks the consciousness of a child or young adult: the knowledge of a fatal but unmentionable illness.

At this point the narrative appears to draw back from the traumatic memory of cancer and into the realm of language and intertextuality. The sentence "No ideas but in potatoes" appears to combine the language of two modernist poets — W.C. Williams ("no ideas but in things") and Gertrude Stein ("roast potatoes for") — in a kind of intertextual language "event."

We have already identified several levels of "event" in the passage: personal or familial event, aesthetic event, psychic event, literary or linguistic event. But we have still not found a clear example of what I identified earlier as the most public level of event: that is, an event that would register itself not only in the poet's own memory — in the memory of "my life" — but also in the collective or cultural memory of a particular moment in history. While the presentation of a radical political consciousness is rarely foregrounded in *My Life*, elements of political critique — and in particular feminist critique — can certainly be found embedded throughout the text. According to Hilary Clark, Hejinian substitutes daily rhythms and repeated perceptions for the kinds of "pivotal" events foregrounded in traditional autobiographies; she "sketches in those areas of a woman's or person's life which have been largely skipped over in life-narrative" (329). Thus Hejinian's radical openness in autobiographical form can be seen as "a sign of a feminine, nonappropriative desire to remember 'without ambition,' without serving any final purpose" (331). In fact, on the level of historical event and overt social and political statement *My Life* is fairly subdued, even suggestive of a certain recuperation of everyday life. Yet the very difficulty of identifying an unambiguous ideological function in Hejinian's poetry reflects a well-articulated ideological position, one motivated by the desire to preserve a fundamental sense of estrangement in language and experience that would be lost were she to comment more explicitly on topical or political issues.

I would make two general observations about the status of "cultural" events in *My Life*. First: when cultural memory is evoked, it is usually not marked by a particular historical or chronological reference, since, as Clark puts it, "*My Life* is marked with chronology, but with its relics only."* Rather than indicating a specific historical moment, cultural memory is more often evoked as an indicator of the awareness that significant events outside the immediate structure of the individual life do take place, and do affect both life and writing. Second: these moments tend to occur with increasing frequency toward the later sections of the book, reflecting a presumably greater awareness of the relationship of the personal (or poetic) and the political as the poet matures, or as events in her life dictate such an awareness.

Yet it is surely significant that *My Life* begins in its very first sentence with a scene that interweaves personal memory with cultural memory:

> A moment yellow, just as four years later, when my father returned home from the war, the moment of greeting him, as he stood at the bottom of the stairs, younger, thinner than when he had left, was purple — though moments are no longer so colored. (7)

My Life contains at least four references to specific dates or years, but it is marked more by its *lack* of such temporal indicators than by their presence in the text. Perhaps the most foregrounded example of a specific date being attached to an historical context occurs in the section that corresponds to the year 1969: "Class background is not landscape — still here and there in 1969 I could feel the scope of collectivity" (74). In this section, Hejinian appears to set up a tension between the forces of bourgeois domesticity (the house, the barbecue, the babysitter) and the disruptions brought about by civil protest and revolutionary energy. The babysitter, for example, comes "directly from the riots," and dreams "of the day when she would gun down everyone in the financial district." If the particular moment represented by the late 1960s was "not so new as we thought then," it is clearly identified within *My Life* as a time for seeking "an alternative to the bourgeoisie," even if that alternative is only a form of "gullibility."

Hejinian's reference to her father's return from World War II allows us to date the poem's progress, and provides a context for her own life: one that can be mapped onto the history of the post-war United States. Yet there are few such references in the succeeding sections,[*] and the language of the sentence implies a greater interest in the visual or aesthetic memory evoked by the scene (and especially the "color" of the recollected moment) than in the details of cultural memory, in the circumstances of the war itself.

As the sections continue, the passage of the post-war years is chronicled; however, as Hejinian puts it, "what follows a strict chronology has no memory." It is instead the accretion of memories and of the language surrounding them that become of greatest significance in the poem. It is not until one of the later sections of *My Life* — entitled "preliminaries consist of such eternities" — that we find a more sustained moment in which an awareness of events in the "outside" world comes to the forefront of consciousness:

> I was coming home from a late literary event and heard a commotion at the corner 7-Eleven (consciousness and poetry). "Do you know what middle-class people expect from poetry?" said Parshchikov later in Moscow, "a glimpse of eternity." There is more trilling trigonometry in trees — that description of discipline. A somewhat pleasant-looking policeman, communications unit in hand, was calling in for help with an abusive drunk in front of the store, and a few minutes later (I lingered to see) a policewoman turned up in response, swinging her dark club from a thong as she jumped from the car, its door open even before the car had stopped, then she sauntered over in a change of pace, as if she intended to face down the drunk, hooting in complaint, on whom she suddenly clapped cuffs, before she flipped him, whipped off her belt, and tied his feet. Words (unlikeness and discipline) — there are no unresisted rhythms in one. (95)

This particular section of the poem, the thirty-ninth of *My Life*, seems to me more saturated with what we might call an overtly political consciousness than any other. Immediately following the disturbing scene of the police violently arresting an abusive drunk — one of the most sustained narrative scenes in the entire text — we find reference to the Marxist revolutionary Trotsky, to the Marxist critic Fredric Jameson, to ideas of collectivity and colonialism ("I was territorial at their nativity"), to disillusionment at the apparent

---

[*] There are, however, a few. See, for example, the air raid sirens in section 2 or the grandmother "waging war" on ants in the kitchen in section 3.

failure of the democratic process ("After every election I vow never to vote again"), and to social theory ("Society has no fringe"). Not coincidentally, the year in United States history corresponding to this section of the book was 1980, also the year in which Ronald Reagan was elected president and in which the sweepingly conservative social, political, and cultural agenda of the Reagan-Bush years was put in place.

In this context, then, the scene of the police arrest can easily be read as an allegory for a much more general process of political coercion in American society. The "somewhat pleasant-looking policeman, communication unit in hand" could serve as a figure for the ever-jovial Reagan — the "great communicator" of the White House — while the more aggressive and macho policewoman ("sauntering" and "swinging her dark club from a thong") represents a reversal of gender roles which would appear to implicate women as well as men in the new, more "disciplined" social order.

At the same time, "literary events" such as the one Hejinian is leaving when she witnesses the scene cannot be artificially cordoned off from other potentially more significant events, the social and political realities of daily life, as she indicates with the ironic reference to "consciousness and poetry" and the quotation from the Russian poet Alexi Parshchikov. Neither can the poetic text of *My Life* be read apart from its reference to such realities. In the final section, entitled "altruism in poetry," Hejinian appears to be seeking among other things a solution to this problem of what can be called in its most reductive formulation "the relationship of poetry to politics." Yet the words dealing with this issue are spoken not by Hejinian herself but by an unnamed dying person who says "we can no longer ignore ideology, it has become an important lyrical language," and by the author of a book of theory she is reading (perhaps Gramsci or Foucault): "Two), power."

Throughout the section, we are constantly reminded of the need to understand the workings of power and ideology. Yet Hejinian refuses to isolate these theoretical issues from the imposition of everyday domestic event: eating carrots, hearing her husband play the saxophone, mopping the linoleum tiles, and hearing the sound of neighbors talking. Hejinian has been to the Soviet Union and returned "banal with shock-value." She is puzzled by the fact that "Stalin medallions dangle at the windshield in trucks throughout the republics," as if this too open display of ideological solidarity is impossible to translate into the context of contemporary American democracy and individualism. Yet the desire to understand Russian culture, to participate in its cultural memory as well as that of her own country, would require a shift in energy toward "the language of inquiry, pedagogy of poetry," a movement toward the very kind of closure Hejinian rejects. Like Antin, Hejinian rejects traditional forms of formal and narrative closure, and also rejects the level of direct and uncomplicated sociopolitical statement that such closure would entail. Where Antin defies closure by periodically moving on to new narratives and shifting the discursive ground of his talk poems, Hejinian avoids closure by adopting a form which is infinitely expandable, thus allowing new and previously unforeseen relationships both at the level of the section and at the level of the individual sentence.[*]

Finally, it is not "events" that are lacking in *My Life* — a book filled almost to overflowing with every conceivable kind of event — but the attempt to interpret or fix those events, to provide a ready-made cultural, historical, or narrative context in which to view them or understand them. As in Antin's talk poems, the intricacies of cultural memory lie just beneath the surface of an ostensibly more personal narrative. Subverting the terms of the "confessional" poem, a genre Hank Lazer has aptly described as the "well-crafted lyric of personal epiphany" (99), these texts explore the possibilities of personal and autobiographical narrative without fetishizing the personal subject or relying on conventionalized modes of constructing the personal, autobiographical, or lyric voice. Along with other postmodern texts like Ron Silliman's *Ketjak* and *Tjanting* and Beverly Dahlen's ongoing series *A Reading*, works like Antin's talk poems and Hejinian's *My Life* have charted possible directions for a writing that can enact forms of significant cultural engagement while at the same time expressing a multilayered individual experience.

WORKS CITED

Altieri, Charles. "The Postmodernism of David Antin's *Tuning*." *College English* 48.1 (1986): 9-26.
Antin, David. *Code of Flag Behavior*. Los Angeles: Black Sparrow, 1968.
———. *What It Means To Be Avant-Garde*. New York: New Directions, 1993.
Clark, Hilary. "The Mnemonics of Autobiography: Lyn Hejinian's *My Life*." *Biography* 14 (1991): 315-25.
Hejinian, Lyn. *My Life*. Los Angeles: Sun & Moon, 1987.
Jarraway, David. "*My Life* through the 1980s: The Exemplary L=A=N=G=U=A=G=E of Lyn Hejinian." *Contemporary Literature* 33 (1992): 319-36.
Lazer, Hank. *Opposing Poetries*. Volume One: *Issues and Institutions*. Evanston: Northwestern UP, 1996.
Paul, Sherman. *In Search of the Primitive: Rereading David Antin, Jerome Rothenberg, and Gary Snyder*. Baton Rouge: Louisiana State UP, 1986.
Ratcliffe, Stephen. "Private Eye/ Public Work." *American Poetry* 4.3 (1987): 40-48.

---

[*]Hejinian has told me that she continues to revise *My Life* every year by adding both a new section and new sentences to all the preceding sections.

Andrew Joron

NEO-SURREALISM; OR, THE SUN AT NIGHT

SURREALISM IS THE PRACTICE OF CONJURING OTHERNESS, of realizing the infinite negativity of desire in order to address, and to redress, the poverty of the positive fact. In Marxian terms, it demands a sensorium, a social body, capable of making the leap from the realm of necessity to the realm of freedom.

The surrealist identification of reality and desire has obvious sources in Romanticism and even earlier, alchemical and Hermetic, doctrines. However, in Surrealism this identification leads, not to reconciliation, but to *agonistic embrace* — that is, to the beautiful convulsion of irresolvable paradox. For Surrealism, the vertiginous spiral by which the familiar is estranged can never end in refamiliarization. The surrealist struggle has to be waged not only against society but also, scandalously, against nature. Its cosmo-political teaching heralds the establishment of a Church of Disquiet.

Still, Surrealism does not levitate above History; the shape of surrealist subversion shifts according to the contours of the surrounding landscape. Both the darkness of the "uncanny" and the brightness of the "marvelous" are not absolute but relative qualities. Only at midnight does the apparition of the Sun become strange.

As Philip Lamantia, the most prominent North American surrealist, has asked: "What is not strange?" The question raises the curtain on the situation of Surrealism in the New World, where everything — and so nothing — is strange. Here, in the society of the spectacle, the empowering twist of estrangement tends to reverse direction and spiral toward the passive doom of alienation. Here, the techniques of Surrealism seem to have been all too readily absorbed by the advertising system.

Yet in the Old World also, Surrealism was implicated in — even as it developed a radical response to — the increasing commodification of the life-world. Surrealism has enacted, since its inception, a critique and a carnival of the object under capitalism. And in doing so, it has anticipated and transcended the self-ironizing discourse of postmodern consumerism: for the object is not simply a sign to be endlessly circulated, but also a *non-sign*, the materialization of a mystery whose *non-sense* signals the irruption of the genuinely new.

In the dominant culture of the United States, otherness has been systematically denied a presence, so that the *surreal* must be perceived only as a representation of the *unreal*. Perhaps this is why those postwar American artists who fell under the influence of Surrealism — Gorky, Motherwell, Pollock — tended, in their later practice, to redefine the problem of representation itself, and to reclaim the will-to-otherness as a form of the non-representational.

The postwar moment was altogether a fateful one for the reception of Surrealism in the United States. Breton and his associates, during their years of exile in New York, had encouraged the formation of an American surrealist community. After Breton's return to Paris, however, the American surrealists were left leaderless and soon dispersed. By 1945, *VVV* and *View* — magazines that were vehicles for the group's art and writing — had ceased publication. As Charles Henri Ford, editor of *View* and the most accomplished American surrealist poet of his day, complained, "There's no place to sleep in this bed, Tanguy." The art historian Dickran Tashjian, in his monograph *A Boatload of Madmen: Surrealism and the American Avant-garde 1920-1950*, asserts that "the Surrealists were effaced from the American record even while significant traces lingered in the wake of their departure." Tashjian further states that "the Surrealists were banished from the American cultural terrain, both at the outset and at the conclusion of their encounters with American artists and writers."

As orthodox Surrealism receded, however, it began to glow: it now became a part of the "background radiation" of American culture. Enough of its light leaked through the 1950s' and early 1960s atmosphere of conformism and conservatism to color the writings of Ashbery, O'Hara, Spicer's *After Lorca*, and the Beats. In the second volume of the anthology *Tracts surréalistes et déclarations collectives*, the French surrealist José Pierre periodized the fortunes of Surrealism during the 1950s and 1960s as follows: "The Crossing of the Desert," 1952-1958; "The Resurgence," 1959-1965; and "The Hour of the Phoenix," 1966-1969. Certainly, the rising tide of oppositional activity in the 1960s promoted such a resurgence. The situationists and other radical groups explicitly cited Surrealism; its influence seemed to expand in proportion to the intensity of the struggle against imperialist war and the one-dimensionality of capitalist society (the slogans of the May 1968 student revolt in Paris, such as "Take your desires for reality," recall passages from the first and second *Manifestoes*). The mystical, apocalyptic, and psychedelic tendencies of 1960s counterculture also mingled with political currents, adding momentum to the surrealist surge in America.

The time-line shows a sharp clustering of such works between the mid-1960s and the early 1970s: Lamantia's *Touch of the Marvelous* (1966) and *Selected Poems* (1967); Sotère Torregian's *The Golden Palomino Bites the Clock* (1966); Louis Hammer's *Bone Planet* (1967); George Hitchcock's *The Dolphin with the Revolver in Its Teeth* (1967); Bill Knott's *The Naomi Poems: Corpse and Beans* (1968), whose subtitle alludes to Desnos's *Corps et biens*; Franklin Rosemont's *The Morning of a Machine Gun* (1968); Lamantia's *Blood of the Air* (1970); Pete Winslow's *Mummy Tapes* (1971); Torregian's *The Wounded Mattress* (1970); and Winslow's *A Daisy in the Memory of a Shark* (1973). There was thus some cause to celebrate the phoenix-like rebirth of an authentic surrealist poetry, even at the hour of Breton's death in 1966.

True to its setting within the oppositional and sometimes utopian culture of the time, the rebirth of surrealist poetry in the United States was accompanied by the issuance of manifestos, the staging of art exhibitions, protests, and happenings, and the launching of new movements and organizations. These proved to be more or less ephemeral, with one notable exception: the activities of Chicago Surrealist Group. Founded in 1966 by Franklin and Penelope Rosemont, the group has, up to the present day, promulgated a militantly orthodox brand of Bretonian Surrealism through the publication of over two hundred pamphlets and chapbooks and an assortment of perfect-bound books. Over the decades, the group has suffered from a largely self-imposed insularity; according to a statement in the third issue of the group's periodical *Arsenal* (1976), "we do not collaborate on bourgeois literary and artistic reviews, preferring to present our researches in our own publications where the integrity and scope of the surrealist project are not compromised by the abject opportunist deceit characteristic of the cultural racket. . . . The only possible exceptions might be in cases in which an entire issue, or a large section of a publication was placed at our disposal, carte blanche, under our exclusive editorship." The sterilizing effects of such a puristic, if not puritanical, stance is revealed in the formulaic quality of much of the group's poetry (it is instructive to compare their work with that of the "unaffiliated" neo-surrealist poets who arose in the 1970s and later). The poetic practice of the Chicago Group seems flattened by the massive and inescapable presence of the ur-texts of "classical" Surrealism. (Yet there are moments of originality in the poems of group member Joseph Jablonski: see his collections *In a Moth's Wing* [1974] and *The Dust on My Eyes Is the Blood of Your Hair* [1980].) In general, the group's program consists of an all-too-familiar compound of aesthetic conservatism and political radicalism.

But Surrealism is not exempt from its own imperative, synthesized from Marx and Rimbaud, to "transform the world" and to "change life." Even in its earliest years, while unified under the leadership of Breton, the movement underwent successive mutations in response to internal and external conditions. The self-identity of the movement therefore cannot be situated within timeless tenets, but only in *the shock-pattern of the wave-front of surrealization as it passes, under the impetus of practices not to be prescribed in advance, through a particular time and place.* This expanding wave-front has no permanently fixed form or content. Sur-reality is not a state of standing "over" reality; rather, it is the boiling-over of that reality, a phase-change that always departs from a highly specific set of initial conditions. "Neo-Surrealism" is a term that refuses termination — one that awaits the emergence of the novum within Surrealism itself.

Lamantia once, in the very pages of *Arsenal*, articulated a neo-surrealist position in his statement "Between the Gulfs" (1973): "From this vista of dormant volcanos and tropical ice, we can all the more happily trace our inspirations from Lautréamont and Rimbaud to Breton and Péret and Roussel to [the Haitian poet] Magloire-Saint-Aude, exemplary signposts for further transgressions, *without literally re-tracing in one's own poetic praxis their inimitable movements* [emphasis mine]." In the context of the Chicago Surrealist Group's own rather imitative poetry, these words offer a subtle hint of reproof. At the same time, Lamantia has supported the activities of the group by contributing to their publications and co-signing many of their collective declarations.

Despite the shortcomings of some of their verse, the Chicago Surrealist Group continues to perform valuable work across a wide spectrum; they are undeniably one of the most important sources of surrealist thought and practice in the United States. They were among the first to translate and disseminate many of the works of "classic" French Surrealism; they have maintained contacts with other surrealist groups around the world, as well as with radical historians and labor activists; and they have delved deeply into the popular culture of the United States to discover the "accomplices of Surrealism." For example, Paul Garon's *Blues and the Poetic Spirit* (1975) is a knowledgeable and affecting study of the poetry of the blues from a surrealist perspective. As for the presentation of classical Surrealism, the 389-page compendium *What Is Surrealism? Selected Writings of André Breton* (1978), edited by Franklin Rosemont, remains one of the most comprehensive editions of Breton's texts available in English.

Most recently, Penelope Rosemont has edited a sizeable anthology of *Women Surrealists* (1998). The anthology, which contains poetry, essays, fiction, and artwork, is international in scope. The American contingent, however, is (with the exception of Rikki Ducornet and Jayne Cortez) represented by minor poets, associates of the Chicago group itself. Nonetheless, the anthology's documentation of surrealist work by women beyond these shores is thorough and meticulous.

The Rosemonts' claim to represent the true and authentic lineage of Surrealism in the United States is, in fact, a considerable one: they were the last American poets to receive any measure of recognition from Breton (on a trip to Paris in 1966, they were "welcomed by Breton into the surrealist movement"). Such recognition was also extended to Lamantia in 1943, but he has shown far less inclination to organize a homegrown movement than the Rosemonts (who were labor activists in their youth). Lamantia was always too self-absorbed for such work, too attentive to his inner transformations: his self-described "mystical silences" and experiments with hallucinogenic drugs give evidence of this. Indeed, the two faces of French Surrealism — one looking exoterically outward to political and cultural revolution, the other looking esoterically inward to spiritual revelation — seem to be reflected in the complementarity of the Rosemonts' and Lamantia's respective approaches to American Surrealism.

Lamantia (who was born in San Francisco in 1927) first encountered Surrealism as a freshman in high school, at an art exhibit featuring the paintings of Miró and Dalí. His first poems were published in the magazine *View* when he was fifteen years old. He traveled to New York in 1943, where he met Charles Henri Ford, Parker Tyler, and other American and European surrealists; Breton hailed him as "a voice that rises once in a hundred years." Lamantia returned to the Bay Area to enroll in the University of California at Berkeley. Here he took part in radical political activities but also became preoccupied with occult lore, gnosticism, and other traditions of religious heresy; after two years, he dropped out of the university to wander around the world. His travels led him through the American Southwest (where he participated in Indian peyote rituals), Mexico, and finally overseas to France and Morocco. During this decade of wandering, Lamantia returned often to San Francisco and New York, where he immersed himself in the jazz scene and associated with Beat writers. Lamantia's Beat-inflected poems from this period are assembled in *Ekstasis* and *Destroyed Works*, both published by Auerhahn Press in San Francisco. The following lines from "Hypodermic Light" (included in the latter collection) illustrate Lamantia's ongoing quest for ecstatic, often drug-mediated, mystical experience in non-Western cultures and in the West's own pre-capitalist culture:

> My friend keeps talking in my head of magic herb Colombian Indians snort,
> shut their eyes seeing clouds and float around like clouds
> I'm looking for the seeds of the Virgin.

For Lamantia, who had been raised as a Catholic, the seeds of ecstatic experience are also scattered through the heretical traditions of the Church: he is depicted shooting up before an altar on the cover of *Narcotica* (a polemic against repressive drug laws with supplementary texts by Artaud, published in 1959 by Auerhahn Press).

In the early 1960s, Lamantia temporarily stopped writing: this was the period of his "mystical orientations & silences." He resumed his wanderings through Europe, living in Spain, Italy, and Greece. In the meantime, his earliest poems were reprinted in *Touch of the Marvelous* by Berkeley's Oyez Press, and his *Selected Poems 1943-1966* was published by City Lights in San Francisco. The latter volume showed a progression from dreamy eroticism in the 1940s through the 1950s' Beat attitude (with its jazzy, bedraggled, bedrugged beatitude) to the more controlled and authoritative esoterism of the work that, after 1963, emerged from the silences. Lamantia's return to writing — and, more than ever, to a Surrealism in the service of the Revelation — was confirmed by the release of *The Blood of the Air* at the turn of the decade. One reviewer in *Poetry* (Chicago) observed that the collection marked "a return to Surrealism, but to a different Surrealism. . . . The concept of the 'adept' is repeated throughout and there are many references to alchemy, Egyptian mythology, and the Middles Ages."

In Lamantia's mature work, language often functions in the manner of esoteric texts, by using words as hermetic seals to simultaneously conceal and mark the location of power sources. Such allusive, elusive strategies were developed by medieval and Renaissance mages to insure that the fruits of the Great Work would not fall into hands of the uninitiated. In *The Blood of the Air*, Lamantia appropriates these strategies for the purpose of poetic empowerment: "All the mancies shall be mine who grew the trunk from the vibrated seed sent from the sun," he vows in the prose poem "World without End." Lamantia's renewed purpose in writing, then, is not to lift the "veil of Hermes" (which would constitute a betrayal of that hermetic knowledge kept secret for "40 centuries"); rather, it is to announce that the "original voice" of Hermes now inhabits the poet, that a transmission, a transmutation, has taken place.

> treasure shored up from my inner eyes
> the victuals medieval cathedrals secrete secretly
> for the likes of the adepts
> who smile through the velvet fissures of the centuries
> that are Waves & Blankets of Stars
> under which we are given, if we burrow long enough

for the hidden script, the Key to the King's Shut Chamber
that vanishes into the night hot with luminations...

In this language of correspondences (which provides the infrastructure for magical efficacy), nothing occupies the place of the referent but another sign. The meaning of the mystery always recedes and "vanishes into the night hot with luminations." The revelation has no content but conjuration: it is the mage's own movement within an infinity of facing mirrors that makes the poem.

During the 1970s, Lamantia increasingly invoked the natural history of the Far West and the lore of its indigenous peoples, interpreting these as a system of sacred signs, alongside traditional esoteric sources such as the *cabala*. In the poem "Redwood Highway," for example, Lamantia divines "the coming of cursive script on the Micmac barks" and "a star field of birds / whose cries paint the sonorous language." As Foucault noted of Renaissance discourse, "These buried similitudes must be indicated on the surface of things; there must be visible marks for the invisible analogies." Accordingly, Lamantia's lines might be characterized as a delirious cataloging of the "visible marks" of "invisible analogies"; his poems of the 1970s were collected in a volume entitled *Becoming Visible*, published in 1981 by City Lights.

Throughout the 1980s, Lamantia continued to apply his esoteric learning to the biosphere of the West Coast and especially to the magical alphabet of its birds. "There are many centers of mystic geography," Lamantia wrote at this time, "but the great Black V of gold flashing in the meadow Bird unknown / opening the air like all the lore of the chants," that avian V whose form resembles that of an open book, had become for him the most potent of signs, the most visible mark of the invisible. Thus, Lamantia utilizes a Renaissance model of reading as interpretation of the cascade of correspondences, as translation of the mirror-signs reflecting the light of an invisible Original. His readings of the Far West's biosphere culminate in *Meadowlark West*, a collection published by City Lights in 1986. Here, for example, is his gloss on a Northern California mountain peak:

Shasta great Shasta
Lemurian dream island, perhaps Atlantis, scallop on the sierras, Hopi sovereign of
    animate dream, oceanic claw: Alta California climbs into view.
Shasta great Shasta
geography in a mystic state later pruned by seers.

In 1989, Lamantia undertook a journey to Egypt, the very source of the occult tradition: next to his love for the life and landscape of the West, he has long been impassioned by the mythology and learning of Egypt, as well as by all varieties of para-Egyptology. In more than one poem of this period, Lamantia superimposes "the great signature / that is eternal Egypt" upon his native ground: "the temple of Luxor goes over it in a transparency to catch it before it goes A Vision of Synarchic Bioregions over Northern California's haunted scapes." More and more, the texts of Lamantia's poems have been composed of layerings of esoteric citations, oracular archaeologies: consequently, the mature Lamantian poem may be defined as a *Bed of Sphinxes*. In 1997, City Lights issued a volume of Lamantia's new and selected poems under this title (the book contains six new poems, including "Egypt" and "Passionate Ornithology Is Another Kind of Yoga").

Like Lamantia's (and Rosemont's) earlier work, the writings of San Francisco poet Pete Winslow negotiate the passageway between Beat poetry and Surrealism. Winslow died suddenly in 1972, aged 37. While Winslow's style, especially in his last years, had been moving toward a space of grace and clarity comparable to that of Eluard's *Capital of Pain*, many of his published works rely on a jazzy, jagged rhythm of incantatory refrains:

The old and the new collide every couple of billion years
Striking sparks which set the mind racing
Sparks of feasting on the charred flesh of one's comfort
Sparks of triumphal entry into snow castles...
Sparks of people speaking the crazy thoughts of a fish
Sparks of new fruits the same as the old except for the writing inside...

Winslow seems to have felt the tension between "the old and the new" within Surrealism as well. In an essay published in 1971, he denounced certain American poets for attempting to "redefine" Surrealism; Winslow argued that Breton's definition of Surrealism as "pure psychic automatism" was "still applicable." According to Winslow, "It is simple enough to adhere to Breton's definition unless one is swayed by esthetic or moralistic concerns, or by the desire to please the makers of literary reputations." Winslow's only widely distributed book is *A Daisy in the Memory of a Shark* (1973).

Bob Kaufman, a black surrealist and Beat-associated poet who for many years lived in San Francisco, was never acknowledged by Breton or the members of the Chicago Surrealist Group. The literary scholar Charles Nyland has commented that Kaufman's Surrealism "is not Breton's automatic writing. It appears to be logically derived from his awareness of paradox and discontinuity and from experimenting with bebop and black speech patterns."

> In black core of night, it explodes
> Silver thunder, rolling back my brain,
> Bursting copper screens, memory worlds
> Deep in star-fed beds of time,
> Seducing my soul to diamond fires of night.
> Faint outline, a ship — momentary fright
> Lifted on waves of color,
> Sunk in pits of light,
> Drummed back through time,
> Hummed back through mind,
> Drumming, cracking the night.

After the assassination of JFK in 1963, Kaufman fell into a state of quasi-silence (speaking rarely, and then only in monosyllables) that lasted for ten years — an indication not only of Kaufman's sensitivity, but also of the overwhelming significance with which he endowed the act of speech.

Kaufman's poetic speech was always a form of direct address, whether his interlocutor was another person or the inhuman face of Time itself (at such moments, Kaufman's gaze resembles that of Klee's wide-eyed *Angel of the New*, blown away by history's vast explosion). Yet despite its frequently anxious, anguished tone, Kaufman's work is also pervaded by a brash and biting *humour noir*; his "Abomunist Manifesto" satirizes the rhetoric attributed to political and aesthetic vanguard movements. Here the poet becomes a trickster figure whose willingness to destabilize his own foundations is, paradoxically enough, an important source of his power over reality (a source, in other words, of his surreality).

Kaufman's own surrealist self-portrait, in his poem "I Am a Camera," presents an iconic, ironic picture of the poet's paradoxical state of being:

> THE POET NAILED ON
> THE HARD BONE OF THIS WORLD,
> HIS SOUL DEDICATED TO SILENCE
> IS A FISH WITH FROG'S EYES,
> THE BLOOD OF A POET FLOWS

OUT WITH HIS POEMS, BACK
TO THE PYRAMID OF BONES
FROM WHICH HE IS THRUST
HIS DEATH IS A SAVING GRACE

CREATION IS PERFECT

Bob Kaufman, shortly before his death, entered a North Beach bar and proclaimed (according to Neeli Cherkovski), "I have seen my own death. One day I shall be walking down Grant Avenue. And a pay telephone will ring. I will pick it up. It will be Jean Cocteau on the other end. And he will say, 'The Blood of the Poet.'" In 1986, Kaufman died of emphysema in San Francisco; a volume of selected poems, *Cranial Guitar*, was published by Coffee House in 1996.

Another American surrealist poet of African ancestry who has never been accorded recognition by "orthodox" surrealist groups is Sotère Torregian, author of six poetry collections published between 1966 and 1979. Although Lamantia once hailed him as a "brother surrealist," Winslow later accused Torregian of revisionism. Torregian was born in 1941, grew up in New Jersey, and associated with poets of the New York School in the early 1960s. In 1967, Torregian moved to California, where he taught as writer in residence at Stanford University and assisted in launching the Afro-American Studies program there in 1969. He has attested to the influence of both the French surrealists and "the poets of Négritude (Senghor and Césaire)." His two most important publications — *The Wounded Mattress* (1968) and *The Age of Gold* (1976) — reveal a wry absurdist humorousness, a delicate, sometimes fairy-tale-like lyricism, and a lively eroticism.

The work of Jayne Cortez, while often labelled "jazz poetry," also stands in the tradition of pan-African Surrealism. Even in the first-person singular, Cortez's voice often sounds like a chorus, opening outward to a polyphony of mythic remappings, to where the poet's solar sensorium can "see a way through" the univocal night of economic, sexual, and racial oppression.

> when my mystical bunions
> like steel hearses jam eyes
> into searching spit of a starving wolf
> into cosmic lips like monkey genitals. . .

I see a way through the maroon glass of this milky way
I say i see a way through for the cradle of hulls
sticking through these indigo ankles
I see a way through. . .

Jayne Cortez was born in 1936 in Arizona and grew up in the Watts district of Los Angeles; later, she moved to New York City. For a time, she was married to the innovative jazz composer and saxophonist Ornette Coleman; she recites poetry with her own jazz group, the Firespitters, which has released several albums. Cortez's books include *Scarifications* (1973), *Firespitter* (1982), *Coagulations: New and Selected Poems* (1984), *Poetic Magnetic* (1991), and *Somewhere in Advance of Nowhere* (1996).

Cortez's far-from-doctrinal Surrealism derives mostly from that of Césaire and the other poets of the Négritude movement. (In the cultural context of the United States, not surprisingly, the Surrealism of Aimé Césaire — with demotic, demonic sources — can seem more relevant and convincing than that of the Old-World patrician André Breton.)

Surrealism has entered the United States from more than one direction. Other lineages of "non-Parisian" Surrealism (in addition to the Caribbean branch) have assumed importance here: an allegorizing Eastern European mode of Surrealism is apparent in the work of Charles Simic, for example. And the "deep-image" poets of the 1960s and 1970s preferred Neruda's Latin-American Surrealism to the Rimbaldian "derangements" of the French tradition.

Robert Kelly, in 1961, invented the term "deep image" to emphasize that the image in poetic language is a projection from the depths of the ego (as modelled by the depth psychology of Freud and Jung). As Jerome Rothenberg explained it, the deep image is "an exploration of the unconscious region of the mind in such a way that the unconscious [of the poet] is speaking to the unconscious [of the reader]." Such notions, in spite of their superficial affinities with Surrealism, fall short of Surrealism's radical demand for the dialectical *Aufhebung* of dream and reality. The deep imagists tended to rely on the "intensification of intuition" (citing Jung) rather than on the *intensification of contradiction*; theirs was essentially an affirmative art, devoid of the surrealist appetite for negation and otherness (as exemplified by Breton's phrase "Existence is elsewhere").

The most sustained, and most visible, interaction between deep-image and surrealist poetry occurred in the pages of *kayak*, a magazine edited by George Hitchcock (himself a surrealist poet of some distinction). In the first nineteen issues, an introductory statement proclaimed hospitality to "surrealist, imagist, and political poems." Although the statement was dropped from subsequent issues, the editorial policy continued. *kayak* was a magazine wholly infused with the style and personality of its editor; over the course of its 64 issues (published between 1964 and 1984), it remained remarkably consistent both in its aesthetic orientation and its appearance (staple-bound, with "distressed" typography, colored inks and paper, and Ernst-like collages). The magazine had a rough-and-ready elegance, like Hitchcock's own poetry. Sometimes the collages and colorations integral to *kayak*'s design seemed to outperform the texts themselves, playfully creeping and seeping into the magazine's poetic content.

Hitchcock's own poetry possesses the charm and perhaps the quaintness of a hand-worked artifact: many of its images seem deliberately drawn from a sepia-toned inventory of obsolescent objects. In one poem, "Figures in a Ruined Ballroom,"

> The chandeliers hemorrhage, Tritons
> weep for the plaster dolphins, the pheasant
> in its glass room feeds on candle-droppings:
>
> apothecaries cannot heal the wax dogs,
> sutures will no longer save Apollo
> nor violins awake the stuffed ospreys.

The poem's final lines are "These statues turn by concealed levers: / their hinges fold in on mortality." Hitchcock's poetry thus embodies an aspect of Surrealism that treats the past — especially the recent past — as a storehouse of the unconscious, where all that is half-submerged, caught in the act of (material or memorial) disappearance, seems pregnant with unrealized meaning. As Walter Benjamin pointed out in his essay on Surrealism, the Parisian surrealists were the "first to perceive the revolutionary energies that appear in the 'outmoded,' in the first iron constructions, the first factory buildings, the earliest photos, the objects that have begun to be extinct, grand pianos, the dresses of five years ago, fashionable restaurants when the vogue has begun to ebb from them." That such uncanny alignments of lost and last things can still become conduits for poetic (if not revolutionary) energy is repeatedly demonstrated in the delicately crafted, almost miniaturist, works of Hitchcock.

Before becoming a lecturer at the University of California at Santa Cruz, Hitchcock labored at such artisanal trades as shipbuilding and landscaping. Hitchcock's age (he was born in 1914, one year later than Charles Henri Ford) places him among the first generation of American surrealists, although his writings did not begin to appear until the 1950s. His later books of poetry include *Lessons in Alchemy* (1976), *The Piano Beneath the Skin* (1978), *Mirror on Horseback* (1979), and *The Wounded Alphabet: Poems Collected and New, 1953-1983* (1984).

Hitchcock's "artisanal Surrealism" thus seems congruent with what the critic Walter Kalaidjian has called "the deep image's pastoral Surrealism" — which, with "its authentic privacy and its psychic distance from everyday life, bespeaks a profound unease with America's social milieu." Among the deep imagists of the 1960s and 1970s, this sense of unease was often represented by pre-industrial landscapes and tableaux, in order, perhaps, to be better translated into a timeless, metaphysical discourse. One of the poets who has most successfully synthesized imagism and Surrealism, and whose work is also strongly pervaded by the melancholic mood of the "outmoded," is Charles Simic, a regular contributor to *kayak* (his first two collections of poetry were published by Kayak Books). In "A Landscape with Crutches," Simic describes,

The bread on its artificial limbs,
A headless doll in a wheelchair,
And my mother, mind you, using
Two knives for crutches as she squats to pee.

Simic was born in the Serbian region of Yugoslavia; his parents immigrated to the United States when he was still a young boy. His poetry, though written in American English, holds an atmosphere of Eastern European mystery and dread; in this it resembles the folkloric Surrealism of the Serbian poet Vasko Popa. As Simic has stated in an interview, "When I was young and just starting to write in English, Serbian words would often come into my mind and create difficulties. . . . English is the language that I know well and yet I speak it with an accent."

American (neo-)Surrealist poetry also speaks with a foreign accent in the work of Edouard Roditi and Nanos Valaoritis. Both of these European-born writers have composed notable poetry in multiple languages, including English. Both poets have contributed regularly to American magazines and have had books published by American presses. Roditi was born in Paris in 1910 (and so belongs to the earliest generation of surrealist poets writing in English); as the son of an American citizen, he held U.S. citizenship, but attended schools in France and Britain, and first visited the U.S. in 1929. He claimed to have written the "first English and American surrealist manifesto" in 1929; entitled "The New Reality," it offers a brief restatement of a few themes from the first French manifesto.

Many of Roditi's works take the form of the prose poem or prose fable; his style is characterized by a dry drollery, good old-fashioned grotesquery, and a somewhat leaden lyricism. Among his American publications are *Prose Poems: New Hieroglyphic Tales* (1968), *Emperor of Midnight* (1974), and *Choose Your Own World* (1992). Roditi died shortly after the last-mentioned book appeared.

The Greek poet Nanos Valaoritis shares Roditi's penchant for drollery, but in his case the inclination is more oblique, tilting the mind toward a glittering, many-eyed mystery. His poems typically play out a conceit as vast as it is absurd:

With great difficulty I manage to get out of my skin
After some hair-raising moments
    everything goes smoothly . . .
A quick tug is all it takes and I am out . . .
What an experience to see the world
Without the self's enveloping atmosphere
Everything is trembling with transparent colour
Women's thoughts are readable as the daily paper
The minds of little children contain untold marvels
The men magnificent like painted savages
The trees a patch of liquid green flowing
Into the earth's hands holding the sky's vessel . . .

In this poem, "The Birth of Second Sight," Valaoritis develops his comic premise inexorably toward a cosmic finale. His Borgesian conclusions are often profound, but his means of arriving at them are usually lighthearted: Valaoritis's strategy of estrangement has a twinkle in its eye that is both kindly and roguish; its expression is both bemused and amused. His inventiveness is splendidly exhibited in the prose poems collected in *My Afterlife Guaranteed* (1990): exercises in *mise en abîme*, they present scenes that regress infinitely, as in "Borisofski's Lair" and "Progressive Distortion of 16th-Century Oil Painting," together with the Freudian mythography of the "Edward Jaguar" stories and Orientalist fabulations such as "Simoon."

Born in 1921 in Switzerland to Greek parents (and to a literary lineage, for his great-grandfather was a highly celebrated Greek poet), Valaoritis studied law at the University of Athens and English literature at the University of London. He has twice been awarded the Greek national poetry prize. For some decades, he has resided alternately in

Athens, Paris, and the San Francisco Bay Area (where he taught for many years at SF State University). In addition to *My Afterlife Guaranteed*, three other books by Valaoritis have been published by small presses in the United States: *Hired Hieroglyphs* (1971); *Diplomatic Relations* (1972); and *Flash Bloom* (1980).

Roditi and Valaoritis were regular contributors to *kayak*, inspiring the magazine with a breath of living European Surrealism. Indeed, the magazine's atmosphere held an overly high concentration of Euro-Surrealism, while the distinctly American surrealist innovations of Lamantia, Kaufman, and Cortez were nowhere in evidence. There was, however, one exception to *kayak*'s Eurocentrism: the poetry of Ivan Argüelles, an important surrealist innovator with a Mexican-American background, whose work began to appear in the magazine during the 1970s.

Argüelles was born in Minnesota in 1939 but spent his early childhood in Mexico City. The son of a Mexican father and an American mother, Argüelles was raised bilingually; he attended high school in Minnesota and went on to study classics at the University of Chicago and then library science at Vanderbilt. As a young poet in the late 1950s and early 1960s, he felt the influence of the Beats but also immersed himself in the literature of the Romance languages and High Modernism. Upon graduation from Vanderbilt, Argüelles was hired as a cataloger at the New York Public Library. It was there, in the library's poetry collection, that Argüelles discovered the poets of the New York School. As he later wrote in an autobiographical essay entitled "Asi Es la Vida," "What was this idiom, this racy colloquial and yet often surreal mélange? I was still swinging with Dante and the troubadours. . . . And then there was the gateway to the French surrealists through Ashbery and O'Hara. . . . My mind was in flames, multiplying in all directions. . . . Between Vallejo and Breton my brain began to sunflower."

Somewhat later, Argüelles became attracted to Hitchcock's *kayak* magazine: "Heavily surreal, intelligent, and with great graphics, . . . I thought this was one of the places for my work." But the turning point came with his discovery of Lamantia's poetry. As Argüelles put it, "Lamantia's mad, Beat-tinged American idiom Surrealism had a very strong impact on me. Both intellectual and uninhibited, this was the dose for me." While Argüelles's early writings were rooted in neo-Beat bohemianism and Chicano culture, by the late 1970s he was developing his own, highly energetic genus (and genius) of Surrealism. An early collection, *The Invention of Spain* (1978), still shows the undiminished influence of García Lorca and Vallejo; in Argüelles's subsequent work, however, Lamantia's star steadily gains precedence — until it, too, is submerged within the gong-tormented sea of Argüelles's kinematic (and cinematic) encyclopedism.

In 1978, Argüelles moved to the West Coast to work as librarian at the University of California at Berkeley. By the early 1980s, Argüelles was preparing a new collection of his poems; as he remarked in his memoir, "The poems I chose for this set exhibited a greater variety of topics and styles than the previous two books. The Surrealism was more intense." This collection, entitled *Captive of the Vision of Paradise*, was published in a handsome edition in 1982 by Hartmus Press. The cover art, depicting the arrow-penetrated torso of St. Sebastian, proved to be apt, for it introduced a predominant theme of Argüelles's mature period — namely, that of (often eroticized) mystical suffering.

>the ancient city swings like a leaf
>beneath the flaming prism
>I am captive here this side
>of the second hour never to reach
>the third and the sea with its castle
>of salt and the air with its dark
>how they take me and ride me
>through the day's ruthless onslaught!

From Lamantia, he inherited such stylistic trademarks as the frequent use of exclamation points and capitalization; but Argüelles is even more passionately predisposed than Lamantia to the use of dramatic rhetoric. Citations of world-historical places, texts, and personages proliferate throughout Argüelles's poems — their kaleidoscopic facets always reflecting the central fact of the poet's anguish.

By the time he relocated to the West Coast, Argüelles had mastered an "automatic" mode of writing that allowed him to produce prodigious quantities of poems, which stormed and swarmed their way through the small-press literary landscape of the 1980s. (In a survey of "most frequently published poets" conducted by the International Directory of Small-Press Publishers in 1988, Argüelles was ranked fourth.) At the same time, Argüelles's style continued to evolve: his poetic line was lengthening and loosening, his emotional content was deepening and darkening, and his imagery was becoming an increasingly turbulent montage that now derived many of its elements from popular culture and current events.

In 1989, Argüelles assembled a collection of hard-edged, streetwise poems into his biggest book yet (169 pages long), *Looking for Mary Lou: Illegal Syntax*. This project was a collaboration with photographer Craig Stockfleth, whose Romantic-realist studies in black-and-white occupy the book's left-hand pages; Argüelles's poems appear on the right. Next to the coolness of the photographs, the poems rage like a conflagration or a ritual destruction: "smoking black combustion of invisible fish fried against their own hieroglyphs / steaming absences of the universe how she revives at the end of the hour / graced on either lip with the tattoos of the muses whose lipstick is DEATH."

In this book, as in most of his subsequent work, the poet's despair more and more assumes a mythically feminine shape: an anima-figure who embodies an eroticized death wish. Different names, such as Mary Lou or Persephone or Madonna, are attached to this figure, yet it is obvious that they are all manifestations of the same *fleur du mal*. In later compositions, these symbols of the poet's longing for (and simultaneous dread of) orgasmic annihilation are subsumed under the horrific honorific "'That' Goddess."

Looking for Mary Lou: Illegal Syntax received the 1989 William Carlos Williams Award of the Poetry Society of America. Empowered by this unexpected recognition, Argüelles immediately set out to produce an epic poem comprised of multiple books, with the overarching title *Pantograph*. As he reports in his autobiography, "I wrote [the first volume] *"That" Goddess"* in a white heat of two months (106 pages between 10 February and 25 April, 1990)." As a book-length surrealist poem in English, *"That" Goddess* is unprecedented — the only comparable achievements are, in Spanish, Huidobro's *Altazor* and, in French, Tzara's *L'homme approximatif*. It is "a deafening reportage from the other world, the one we are always / skirting, careful lest we fall into Persephone's infernal / but gorgeous embrace, when not even a sequence of connected / thoughts is of any avail, yes 'that' goddess, or Arachne / or Ariadne." The tonality of the poem is subject to manic mood-swings, racing up and down the scales between between tragic lamentation and triumphant declamation, with plenty of blackly humorous asides and Sadean eroticism along the way. Keith Tuma, reviewing the book in *Sulfur*, observed that "Argüelles plugs his unabashedly confused and lucid meditations and exhortations concerning women, myth, and culture into a loose adaptation of Virgilian epic. The book is one vast catalogue of the abjection, misogyny, lust, and ego-stroking that is manhood as the Modernists mostly understood it, turning about the specter of the indescribable unapproachable woman smoking a cigarette in the banal pose of the femme fatale." The point can be made even more emphatically: the first volume of *Pantograph* is a neo-surrealist testimonial to the poet's devotion to the Muse as Dominatrix.

For the publication of this and subsequent volumes of *Pantograph*, Argüelles founded his own imprint, which took its name from the title of his epic. Pantograph Press was launched (with the assistance of the present writer) in 1992; the intent was to produce, not only installments of Argüelles's epic poem, but works by other poets following unusual (and sometimes unlikely) muses. Of his *Pantograph* cycle, Argüelles has so far released volume seven (*Enigma and Variations: Paradise Is Persian for Park*) and volume nine (*Hapax Legomenon*).

Another poet who rose to prominence in the pages of *kayak* and has since become an important representative of West Coast Neo-Surrealism is the British expatriate Adam Cornford. Eleven years younger than Argüelles, Cornford arrived in the United States in 1969, enrolling at the University of California at Santa Cruz. There, he attended George Hitchcock's writing workshop and fell under the spell of the neo-surrealist synthesis that Hitchcock was forging between American Imagism and European Surrealism. Cornford later entered the graduate writing program at San Francisco State University and studied with Nanos Valaoritis.

Cornford set himself the task of creating a politically engaged form of poetry combining the energies of Surrealism and Situationism. As he stated in an autobiographical essay, "I wanted to use the 'convulsive' image developed by Surrealism in a more deliberate, targeted way, so as to bypass people's conditioned numbness and renew and clarify their awareness of their social situation."

> Cold word evaporating off the lips
> the television says it is something enormous
> a skyscraper with glass bones
> a priest tells us it has always been
> because God holds all the keys to our eyes ...

In 1978, Cornford's first collection, *Shooting Scripts*, was published by Black Stone Press in Missoula, Montana, in a fine letter-press edition illustrated by the Chilean collagist Ludwig Zeller. (The book's publisher, Peter Koch, also produced and edited *Montana Gothic*, a magazine whose form and content was strongly influenced by Hitchcock's *kayak*. Six issues were published between 1974 and 1977.)

Visual imagery is paramount in *Shooting Scripts*: metaphors are interlaced and lengthened to make a colorful textile whose exfoliating patterns repeat the invisible ideality of a master pattern or conceit. In "Shootout at Cranium Gulch," for example, the conceit (inspired by a line from Lautréamont) interweaves a narrative genre, the Western, with an existentialist theology:

God's reflection grins at him with aurora teeth.
He draws and fires. Bottles shatter,
but God hops aside
like a magnified flea, and out through the swingdoors.
On the street lined with flickers
God faces him, a stampede suddenly frozen.
He fires again. God's blood splashes
and napalms a horse into screaming anatomy.
The man in the cobra-skin squeezes the trigger
until his gun is empty.
Then God fires, spread out like a continent.
Bullets pass through the man's bones
with the speed of cosmic rays.
Smiling, he understands . . .
The thin dark man watches God
gallop slowly away into the vanishing-point
at the center of his head . . .

Here the state of surreality no longer possesses the "naturalistic" immediacy of a dream or an act of free association. Instead, the imagination is liberated, not by loosening the constraints on expression, but by binding the elements of language together in a new way (otherwise stated: the theory and practice of neo-surrealist metaphor requires something like a theory of knots).

In 1988, City Lights published a new collection of Cornford's poems, entitled *Animations*. Nearly half the collection is taken up by a single poem, "Lightning-Rod to Storm." This poem's vast conceit maps the quarrel of a pair of lovers onto the discharge of energy between a lightning-rod and an electrical storm. "All this / Has been a means of travelling far and fast, of lifting the instruments / Of a viewpoint above dirty weather that / Was both of us." "Lightning-Rod to Storm" is Cornford's masterpiece: more than an exercise in extended metaphor, it is a dazzling display of analogical consciousness that, like the speculative cosmologies of the Renaissance, follows a thread of resemblances through the labyrinth of space and time. These resemblances (as in the writings of Giordano Bruno and other Renaissance *magi*) are frequently derived from science and technology:

> ... anti-star whose deep gravity
> Ghosts and streams all the sights of the world inward
> Into a momentary virtual image, a dazzle-hologram
> Of elsewhere,
> there at the event horizon —

Cornford's imagery progresses futureward, through scenes of social revolution, along a continuum from actual to potential, "shift[ing] the invisible into the spectrum not only / Of knowledge, but of astonishment." This is the trajectory of utopian narrative and of science fiction — indeed, several other poems in *Animations* are even more explicit in their use of science-fictional tropes.

Such tropes assumed an even greater prominence in Cornford's subsequent work. His longest poem yet, "The Snarling Gift" (which appears in *Terminal Velocities*, an anthology published in 1993), narrates the emergence of a "kind of intelligent sub-program manifested by the Earth itself as a response to ecological degradation." "The Snarling Gift" once again exhibits Cornford's talent for expanding and contracting a metaphorical conceit through a multitude of referential frames (in accordance, perhaps, with the diastolic and systolic pulsations of Blake's Eternity).

> She [the Snarling Gift] emerges
> In the sunken vault of the thalamus, cable-jungle
> Where the senses converge.
> Her own vestigial image
> Sweeps past her, gigantic ghost-mask on its way
> To be understood.

The style of the "The Snarling Gift" is as protean as its main character, shifting from social realism to mythic fantasy. The text is also typographically complex, verging at times on concrete or "pattern" poetry. These experiments in typography foreshadow the diagrammatic format of "The Cyborg's Path," a series of science-fiction poems that Cornford began in the 1990s. The decidedly "speculative" turn of Cornford's recent work is evident in his third collection, *Decision Forest* (1997), which contains several poems from the "Cyborg's Path" sequence as well as "Millennium: A Topology," a cycle of densely worded science-fiction poems.

There are obvious affinities between the twin Romanticisms of Surrealism and science fiction. Efforts by poets to synthesize the two forms were made sporadically (and more or less independently) until the mid 1970s, when a community of speculative poets began to take shape around a core of publications (such as *Speculative Poetry Review* edited by Robert Frazier). Among them was *Velocities*, a magazine of speculative poetry that I launched in 1982, which was dedicated to "traversing the space between science fiction and Surrealism." Its fifth and final issue appeared in 1988. Fashioned after the model of *kayak*, it featured contributors such as Valaoritis, Argüelles, and Cornford. Within this rather recondite milieu of "neo-surrealist science-fiction poetry," some single-author collections were also produced, including my *Science Fiction* (1992) and Lee Ballentine's *Phase Language* (1995).

The San Francisco poet John Noto has also advocated a "new synthesis" of cyberpunk, Surrealism, and postmodern poetry. In 1997 he launched the magazine *Orpheus Grid* and co-founded, with the poet David Hoefer, Vatic Hum Press. Noto's *Psycho-motor Breathscapes* and Hoefer's *New, Improved Wilderness*, both published by Vatic Hum in its inaugural year, are crowded with the dreamlike juxtapositions caused by information overload. Lindsay Hill's *NdjenFerno*, published by Vatic Hum in 1998, is a poetic upgrade of Anthony Burgess's *Clockwork Orange*, with its near-future lingo of ultraviolence.

The resonances between Surrealism and various genres of high and low fantasy (including the fairy tale) have also been picked up and amplified by certain American poets. In the early 1980s, Detroit poet and artist Thomas Wiloch published and edited *Grimoire*, a magazine devoted to surrealist fantasy; it featured colored paper in the tradition of *kayak* as well as unusually skillful collages by the editor himself. Wiloch has written a book of prose poems, *Mr. Templeton's Toyshop* (1995), that hauntingly harmonizes Surrealism and the modern genre of "dark" fantasy. Beat scholar Stephen Ronan's chapbook *Nights of October* (1985) is a sequence of Halloween-flavored poems "concerned with Philip Lamantia and derived from conversations with him." And Christina Zawadiwsky's *The Hand on the Head of Lazarus* (1986) is a convulsively beautiful collection of neo-surrealist poems and prose poems redolent with the violence and sensuality of Eastern European folklore (the author, born in New York and now a resident of Milwaukee, is of Ukrainian descent).

Folktales and fairytales have traditionally functioned as zones of "permissible transgression," as cultural reservoirs of collectively shared illicit desires. This spirit of transgression is well captured in the work of Rikki Ducornet. Born in New York in 1943 and now residing in Denver (after long stays in France and South America), Ducornet has written six volumes of poems — most memorably *Weird Sisters* (1976) and *Knife Notebook* (1977) — whose vivid and visceral neo-surrealist imagery seems to be drawn from some well of legend. Her style has been described by the critic J. H. Matthews as "an unsettling mixture of monstrosity and humor, for which the closest parallel — in Surrealism or anywhere outside — is to be found in the prose and verse of Joyce Mansour."

Such amalgamations of Surrealism with other literary traditions might be considered as late, decadent chimerae or as minor offshoots from the main body of the movement. But the development of neo-Surrealism in the United States resembles a fractal pattern whose mode of generation is nonlinear, and whose various elements stand in a nonhierarchical relation to one another. The sudden, spontaneous apparition of the sun through the night-meshes of conventionalized discourse cannot be foretold from within that discourse.

Among the most unprecedented and fiery of all such apparitions is the work of Will Alexander. As Alexander testifies, "It is not with the steepness of vultures that I seek to procure an arcane stability in the void, but by the blending of halts and motions, like the vertical equilibria of fire, brought to an incandescent pitch of value." (He is speaking here in the voice of "The Whirling King in the Runic Psychic Theatre.") Alexander's work participates in, but can hardly be confined to, the pan-African surrealist tradition of Cortez and Césaire. The explosion of his language engulfs almost every continent and sweeps away the categories that separate poetry and philosophy, myth and science. Three collections of Alexander's poetry have been released: *Vertical Rainbow Climber* (1987); *Asia & Haiti* (1995); and *The Stratospheric Canticles* (1995). He is also the author of a book of essays, *Towards the Primeval Lightning Field* (1998). Each book is illustrated by the visual force-fields of Alexander's own artwork.

Will Alexander was born and raised in Los Angeles and attended UCLA. He alludes to a painful process of self-education in his first book: "Outside myself and bleeding on my own discoveries I discover in a cave Pythagorean lodestones broken in the air of Chaldean snake myths." During those years of self-discovery, Alexander worked mostly in isolation, becoming the conduit for a primal and oracular speech. His Surrealism has most often been compared to that of Césaire. The comparison is not inaccurate; yet Césaire's language, while similarly energetic, is thoroughly dialogical (as if he were facing a circle of auditors), whereas Alexander's is monological (as if he were orbiting the earth).

Moreover, as the critic Garrett Caples has pointed out, "Alexander's Surrealism is not about 'the image' but about 'the word.'" Obviously, Alexander's self-fashioning as a poet did not start from that centralizing point of view demanded by scopic discourse. Instead, he positioned himself within the contingent order of the lexicon, refashioning (and thus reclaiming) language word by word. As a result, Alexander's writing liberates the *imagination* from the restricted economy of the *image*:

though shattered by various Saxon devices
I am the flame throughout the soaring absolute
I denigrate
I take on sanguine territorial opposition
with a force
enriched
with untoward fertility
with a dominate tendency to waver
with excessive a-regional metrics
with inhaled phantasmatics
spilled on fortuitous migrational soils
there is ermine
there is discourse by nugget
there is scarification by increase

As is evident in these lines from *The Stratospheric Canticles*' "Song in Barbarous Fumarole of the Japanese Crested Ibis," the linguistic turn of Alexander's practice melts metaphor and metonymy together to make a new glyph of meaning. This Alexandrian glyph is typically formed by neologisms and etymological dislocations; by "focus throws" between denotation and connotation; and by the radical recontextualization of specialized vocabularies.

Caples insightfully comments that "Alexander's privileging of the word as medium in poetry no doubt partially accounts for his penchant for the dramatic monologue." But Alexander's monologues rarely communicate the experience of an atomized individual speaker; rather, the monological voice is unified and legitimized only by relaying signals from *elsewhere*, from some transindividual level of being. The two long poems collected in *Asia & Haiti* are composed in the plural voice. In "Asia," it is "a collective voice of rebellious Buddhist monks who hover in invisibility, vertically exiled, in an impalpable spheroid, virescently tinged, subtly flecked with scarlet, conducting astral warfare against the Chinese invasion and occupation of Tibet." In "Haiti," the voice is that of *les Morts*, the dead souls of the Duvalier dictatorship's victims. In both poems, the tone is appropriately accusatory; here, however, the crimes of the oppressors are judged, not according to conventional legal or moral standards, but "with the seismic zeal of darkened speculation." Alexander hurls down his glyphic phrases as weapons, as instruments of revendication, for they contain the power of the Word's poetic autonomy. Thus, Alexander's voice, with its glyphic revaluation of received meanings, is as much autonomist as automatist — a voice that, in giving its own law to itself, naturally takes the form of a (collective) monologue.

Besides poetry, Alexander has written novels, short stories, and plays. In all of these forms, Alexander allows the autonomous Word to come into being in its own way: either to drop vertiginously into a semiotic space of unexpected correspondences or to become a merely localized fillip of sonic or graphic texture. Under the terms of this allowance, the Word, prior to its emergence, exists in a state akin to nothingness, yet is charged with potential. Thus, there are frequent invocations to the awaited Word's vertical, vortical, tornado-like *suspension*. For example, in his play, *Conduction in the Catacombs* (published in *Hambone* no. 13 [1997]), the "bodiless vortex" is divided "through the corporeal" into two characters in a sanatorium, where "the authorities have no other cause than having us eat ourselves alive in a mirror." This enforced mirroring or self-division has tragic consequences; nonetheless, as one character admits, "we take from brokenness a message or a hawk, across scattered lamps and trees. It is the necessary ritual." And the other responds, "The Elysium!"

Alexander's prioritization of the word rather than the image initiates, as stated above, a linguistic turn within neo-surrealist practice. This turn is convergent with the emergence, in post-1960s American experimental poetry, of the Language school. From the start, the Language poets were careful to distinguish their practice from that of Surrealism. One of the movement's chief theoreticians, Barrett Watten, in an essay on "Method and Surrealism," criticized the valorization of the "private image" and the "identity of perception and representation" in Breton's work; in another essay, Watten compared a passage from Breton's "Soluble Fish" to texts by Carla Harryman and Kit Robinson, concluding that the latter's work demonstrated "not the coming into being of the image but of something even deeper — the perception of the mind in control of its language. Distance, rather than absorption, is the intended effect." Undeterred by these demarcations, a few poets and critics have sought to investigate the pre-existing affinities, as well as the potential for collaboration, between the two movements. In 1991 Charles Borkhuis wrote that "this gap between Late Surrealism and Textual (including 'Language') poetry may prove to be a magnetically charged, yet largely unexplored area." In this important essay, "Late Surrealism and American 'Language' Poetry," Borkhuis argued that "both Surrealism and 'Language' poetry are attempts to decenter the idea of the self-as-creator"; in both forms, "the text is read as an accumulation of poetic evidence" rather than as the testament of "a particular ego." In light of the work of writers such as Michael Palmer and John Yau, whose texts are "open-ended and dispersed throughout the body," Borkhuis envisioned a form of

"Parasurrealist/Textual" practice, where "thought is not outside, observing this process [of writing], but part of it; it finds itself in-situation."

The poetry of John Yau has increasingly become both surrealist and serialist: in his latest collection, *Forbidden Entries* (1996), permutations of words intermingle with and motivate patterns of self-distancing imagery. For example, the poem "Angel Atrapado XXIII," the line "A torn sheet hovering above an empty yield" is rescued from pastoral Surrealism by the substitition of a single letter. By writing "yield," and thus forcing a detour in the line's own drive toward the word "field," Yau, with an elegant gesture, incites a struggle between the material text and its imaginal content. This maneuver, replicated throughout Yau's recent work, permits the (sometimes agonistic) embrace of self-reflexive textuality and surrealist imagery: "This tongue is a flower. Someday you will hear what it has to pay."

The struggle between the *sign* and the *seen* in Yau's writing is also played out on the thematic level of self-identity. In the many passages where self and other are constructed as a series of morphing masks, the poem becomes a palimpsest of textual skepticism and imagistic enthusiasm: "I was the toad in tinsel, / you were the donkey in red suede." The effect of such imagery is distancing rather than absorptive. In *Forbidden Entries* and his previous collection, *Edificio Sayonara* (1992), Yau seems to be drafting documents of ecstatic doubt.

Occasionally, Yau's earlier work — which can be surveyed in a volume of selected poems, *Radiant Silhouette* (1989) — also stages an encounter between serialism and Surrealism (for example, the imagery of "Broken Off by the Music" relies on the recombinant splicing of textual fragments). For the most part, the Surrealism of *The Sleepless Night of Eugene Delacroix* (1980) and *Broken Off by the Music* (1981) stands closer to that of Ashbery and O'Hara. By the time *Corpse and Mirror* was published in 1983, however, Yau had magnified the New York school's surrealizing tendencies considerably. And by the time of *Dragon's Blood* (1989), Yau had turned the Russian futurists' "baring of the device" (a strategy reclaimed by the Language poets) into a surrealist act: "When the last mirage / evaporates, I will be / the sole proprietor of this voice / and all its rusted machinery."

Within the Language and post-Language writing community, several poets have begun to explore the "magnetically charged" gap between Surrealism and textual poetry first indicated by Borkhuis in 1991. One of those poets is Borkhuis himself, whose poem-cycle *Hypnogogic Sonnets* (1992) thematizes the body as half writing surface, half dream-object. In his later collections *Proximity (Stolen Arrows)* (1994) and *Alpha Ruins* (1999), the condition of textuality itself generates images: "letters pulsing / radiant foliage behind thought- /

splinters that break / the skin. . . ." Similarly, my book of surrational poems, *The Removes* (1999), embraces language as a paradoxical body.

The poems of Phillip Foss, too, approach the text with the "intent . . . to create a church of sound, a baroque vehicle for image, and these a sonata of bastard symbols." To this end, Foss often engages in inventive typographic realignments, spatializations of meaning that are at once speculative and sensual. Foss's collections include *The Composition of Glass* (1988), *The Excesses the Caprices* (1991), and *Courtesan of Seizure* (1993). His work, like mine and Borkhuis's, enacts a neo-surrealist invocation to otherness within the framework of self-reflexive textuality. Among other post-Language poets working in this "magnetically charged gap" are John Olson, W. B. Keckler, Kristin Prevallet (especially in her homage to Max Ernst, *Perturbation, My Sister* [Leave Books, 1994]), Jeff Clark, Brian Lucas, and Garrett Caples.

The history of Neo-Surrealism in American poetry is not a linear story whose future is determined by its past. It is a sleepwalker armed with reason. As such, it arrives both too late and too early: a solar apparition at midnight.

WORKS CITED

Alexander, Will. *Asia & Haiti*. Sun & Moon, 1995.

-------. "Conduction in the Catacombs." *Hambone* no. 13 (1997)

-------. *The Stratospheric Canticles* (Pantograph Press, 1995).

-------. *Towards the Primeval Lightning Field*. O Books, 1998

-------. *Vertical Rainbow Climber*. Jazz Press, 1987.

Argüelles, Ivan. *Captive of the Vision of Paradise*. Hartmus Press, 1982.

-------. *Enigma and Variations: Paradise Is Persian for Park*. Pantograph Press, 1995.

-------. *Hapax Legomenon*. Pantograph Press, 1993.

-------. *The Invention of Spain*. Downtown Poets Co-op, 1978.

-------. *Looking for Mary Lou: Illegal Syntax*. Rock Steady Press, 1989.

-------. *"That" Goddess*. Pantograph Press, 1992.

Ballentine, Lee. *Phase Language*. Pantograph, 1995.

Borkhuis, Charles. *Alpha Ruins*. Bucknell UP, 1999.

-------. *Hypnogogic Sonnets*. *New York*: Red Dust, 1992.

-------. "Late Surrealism and American 'Language' Poetry." *Onthebus* no. 8/9 (1991).

-------. *Proximity (Stolen Arrows)*. Sink, 1994.

Cornford, Adam. *Animations*. San Francisco: City Lights, 1988.

-------. *Decision Forest*. Pantograph Press, 1997.

-------. *Shooting Scripts*. Missoula, MT: Black Stone P, 1978.

Cortez, Jayne. *Coagulations: New and Selected Poems*. Thunder's Mouth Press, 1984.

------. *Firespitter*. Bola Press, 1982.

------. *Poetic Magnetic*. Bola Press, 1991.

------. *Scarifications*. Bola Press, 1973.

------. *Somewhere in Advance of Nowhere*. High Risk Books, 1996.

Ducornet, Rikki. *Knife Notebook*. Fiddlehead, 1977.

------. *Weird Sisters*. Intermedia, 1976.

Foss, Phillip. *The Composition of Glass*. Lost Roads, 1988.

------. *Courtesan of Seizure* Light and Dust, 1993.

------. *The Excesses the Caprices*. Light and Dust, 1991.

Garon, Paul. *Blues and the Poetic Spirit*. Da Capo Press, 1975.

Hill, Lindsay. *NdjenFerno*. Vatic Hum, 1998.

Hitchcock, George. *The Dolphin with the Revolver in Its Teeth*. Unicorn Press, 1967.

------. *Lessons in Alchemy*. West Coast Poetry Review, 1976.

------. *Mirror on Horseback*. Kayak Books, 1979.

------. *The Piano Beneath the Skin*. Copper Canyon, 1978.

------. *The Wounded Alphabet: Poems Collected and New, 1953-1983*. Jazz Press/Papabach Editions, 1984.

Hoefer, David. *New, Improved Wilderness*. San Francisco: Vatic Hum, 1992.

Jablonski, Joseph. *The Dust on My Eyes Is the Blood of Your Hair*. Black Swan, 1980.

------. *In a Moth's Wing*. Black Swan, 1974.

Joron, Andrew. *The Removes*. Hard Press, 1999.

------. *Science Fiction*. Pantograph, 1992.

Kaufman, Bob. *Cranial Guitar*. Minneapolis: Coffee House P, 1996.

Knott, Bill. *The Naomi Poems: Corpse and Beans*. Follett, 1968.

Lamantia, Philip. *Ekstasis*. San Francisco: Auerhahn P, 1959.

------. *Destroyed Works* San Francisco: Auerhahn P, 1962.

------. *Narcotica*. San Francisco: Auerhahn P, 1959.

------. *Touch of the Marvelous* by Berkeley, CA: Oyez P, 1966.

------. *Selected Poems 1943-1966*. San Francisco: City Lights, 1967.

------. *The Blood of the Air*. San Francisco: Four Seasons Foundation, 1970.

------. *Becoming Visible*. San Francisco: City Lights, 1981.

------. *Meadowlark West*. San Francisco: City Lights, 1986.

------. *Bed of Sphinxes*. San Francisco: City Lights 1997.

------. "Between the Gulfs" *Arsenal* no. 2 (1973)

Noto, John. *Psycho-motor Breathscapes*. San Francisco: Vatic Hum, 1997.

Roditi, Edouard. *Choose Your Own World*. Asylum Arts, 1992.

------. *Emperor of Midnight*. Black Sparrow, 1974.

------. *Prose Poems: New Hieroglyphic Tales*. Kayak, 1968.

Ronan, Stephen. *Nights of October*. Ammunition Press, 1985.

Rosemont, Franklin. *The Morning of a Machine Gun*. Surrealist Editions, 1968.

———, ed. *What Is Surrealism? Selected Writings of André Breton*. Pluto Press, 1978.

Rosemont, Penelope, ed. *Women Surrealists*. U of Texas P, 1998.

Tashjian, Dickran. *A Boatload of Madmen: Surrealism and the American Avant-garde 1920-1950*, Thames and Hudson, 1995.

Pierre, José. *Tracts surréalistes et déclarations collectives*. Terrain Vague, 1980.

Prevallet, Kristin. *Perturbation, My Sister*. Buffalo: Leave Books, 1994.

Torregian, Sotère. *The Age of Gold*. Kulchur Foundation, 1976.

———. *The Golden Palomino Bites the Clock*. Andel Hair P, 1966.

———. *The Wounded Mattress*. Berkeley, CA: Oyez Press, 1968.

Tuma, Keith. "Review of *"That" Goddess* by Ivan Argüelles." *Sulfur*. no. 32 (1993).

Valaoritis, Nanos. *Diplomatic Relations*. Panjandrum, 1972.

———. *Flash Bloom*. Wire Press, 1980.

———. *Hired Hieroglyphs*. Kayak, 1971.

———. *My Afterlife Guaranteed*. San Francisco: City Lights, 1990.

Wiloch, Thomas. *Mr. Templeton's Toyshop*. Jazz Police Books, 1995.

Winslow, Pete. *A Daisy in the Memory of a Shark*. San Francisco: City Lights, 1973.

———. *Mummy Tapes*. Medusa P, 1971.

Yau, John. *Broken Off by the Music*. Burning Deck, 1981.

———. *Dragon's Blood*. Gervais Jassaud, 1989.

———. *Edificio Sayonara*. Black Sparrow, 1992.

———. *Forbidden Entries*. Black Sparrow, 1996.

———. *Radiant Silhouette*. Black Sparrow, 1989.

———. *The Sleepless Night of Eugene Delacroix*. Release Press, 1980.

Zawadiwsky, Christina. *The Hand on the Head of Lazarus*. Ion Books, 1986.

Dan Featherston

ON VISIONARY POETICS, ROBERT KELLY, AND CLAYTON ESHLEMAN

"The modern mind has not only chickened out on God, on angels, on Creation, but it has chickened out on the common things of our actual world, taking the properties of things as their uses and retracting all sense of fellow creatureliness. Not only the presences of gods and of ideas are denied ... but the presences of stones, trees, animals and even men as spiritual beings is exorcized in our contemporary common sense. Wherever this contempt moves, it strikes to constrict the realm of empathy." — Robert Duncan, *The Truth and Life of Myth*

ONE OF THE DIFFICULTIES OF DEFINING VISIONARY POETICS involves the definition of vision itself, which runs the sacred-secular gamut from prophecy and the perception of a spiritual dimension to dreams, memories, and hallucinations.[*] The long and complicated relationship between religious and literary vision poses another difficulty, and it is impossible to discuss vision in American poetry without mentioning the Bible's four-fold vision of creation, fall, resurrection and salvation. Since the birth of modern science, the social and political power of Judeo-Christian ideology has declined, but it still has a strong influence on what we think of as visions and the visionary mode. The following are some primary beliefs within the Judeo-Christian tradition that have shaped how we think about visions and the visionary mode:

Reality is divided into matter (creation) and spirit (creator).
Creation is exile from God.

---

[*]Prophets and madmen are the traditional custodians of vision, which implies an interesting parallel between vision and taboo. According to Freud *(Totem and Taboo: Some Points of Agreement Between the Mental Lives of Savages and Neurotics*, trans. James Strachey, New York: W.W. Norton & Co.), *taboo* "diverges in two contrary directions ... on the one hand, 'sacred,' 'consecrated,' and on the other 'uncanny,' 'dangerous,' 'forbidden,' 'unclean.' The converse of 'taboo' in Polynesian is *noa*, which means 'common' or 'generally accessible'" (18). Vision: an uncommon way of seeing that is both "sacred" and "forbidden"? According to this definition, the visionary poem might resemble Duncan's "true epithalamium where chastity and lewdness, love and lust, the philosopher king and the monstrous clown dance together in all their human reality" *(Fictive* 27).

Creation is error and, therefore, fallen.
Our bodies and the world we live in are divine punishment.
Since creation is fallen, vision is to look through, not at, creation.
The ultimate "looking through" creation is its destruction (i.e., apocalypse).
The ultimate vision is to look through creation unto the creator (i.e., beatific vision).
Spiritual and biological/ecological survival are mutually exclusive.
Salvation is the renunciation of creation, a magical undoing of fallen creation.
Seers, as instruments of visions, are passive receptacles of divine, external agency.
The ultimate source of visions is abstract (God).

One of the great achievements of innovative poetry in the twentieth century was the critique of these and other beliefs within the western tradition without necessarily abandoning the visionary mode altogether.

MODERN VISION

Historians will undoubtedly point to the twentieth century as a period of profound shifts in human civilization. For the first time in history, war, economics, and information were global. An American poet late in the twentieth century could turn on the television to discover that her tax dollars were used earlier in the day to launch a space probe off Cape Canaveral and cruise missiles at supposed terrorist facilities in Afghanistan and Sudan. She may have turned away from world citizenship in her poetry, but there was no turning away from world citizenship at large. This has been the modern condition, and to consider the vast, complex terrain of twentieth-century civilization is truly mind-boggling: the airplane, the automobile, the machine-gun, psychoanalytic theory, communism, television, the computer, the atom bomb, postcolonialism, multinational capitalism, jazz, plastic, global warming, discovery of the DNA helix, space exploration, mass genocide, penicillin, civil rights, women's movement, AIDS epidemic, genetic cloning, international terrorism . . . the list is endless. According to poet Robert Duncan, the hallmark of the twentieth century was a vision of global citizenship, a "coming of all men into one fate":

> The very form of man has no longer the isolation of a superior paradigm but is involved in its morphology in the cooperative design of all living things in the life of everything, everywhere. ("Rites" 23)

But from Judeo-Christian eschatology to the Nazi Final Solution, "one fate" has been anything but the cooperative design of all living things. In the twentieth century, total vision meant totalitarian vision, and a premise in nearly all post-war theory is that we live in a paradoxical era of globalization and fragmentation: the world is both closer and farther away than ever before. Moreover, postmodern theory dictates that all ideologies are provisional, culturally constructed, and involve complex power relations. The popularization of such a perspective may help keep in check totalitarian visions, but it has also led to extreme skepticism toward the visionary mode in general: if Biblical vision, set against the atom bomb, cannot justify the ways of God to men, then neither can the visions of any prophet or poet. Thus, in the last years of the twentieth century,

> the total vision of literature seems to be nihilism; literature, some now claim, reveals a human condition which is meaningless chaos of human desires controlled at best by whatever power relations obtain at a particular time. (Preminger 1360)

There is an important distinction, however, between the total vision of a "superior paradigm" and Duncan's vision of a "whole symposium." Total means all-inclusive, but the so-called "total" visions of totalitarian states and religions are based on strategic exclusion: Plato's vision excluded the poet, Nazi Germany's vision excluded the Jew, and Judeo-Christian vision excludes the heretic. If as Blake states "Reason is the bound or outward circumference of Energy" (149), twentieth-century visionary poets questioned how reasonable these boundaries were. While desires are undoubtedly controlled by shifting power relations (i.e., cultural forces), visionary poetics in the next millennium must question the very foundations of these forces. Duncan's "symposium of the whole" is one model of vision as the critique of culture, stressing plurality, compassion and coherence by cooperative design against the exclusive, alienating visions of fascism and orthodox religion that made the twentieth century the bloodiest in human history.*

---

*Compassion = "to suffer with."

IMAGE & SYMBOL

Glancing back over the last hundred years of American poetry, *The New Princeton Encyclopedia of Poetry and Poetics* defines Modernism as distinct from Romanticism in that it is the artwork itself that synthesizes images and symbols, not the external agency of Spirit (Preminger 55). Another shift came from the development of psychoanalytic theory in the twentieth century and the notion that the source of visions is not external and absolute (God) but internal and contingent (psyche). This not only secularized vision, but marked a sea-change in its phenomenology: as "absolute other," vision re-enters human consciousness *as part of human consciousness.*[*] Vision is no longer beyond or outside of creation, it is *part of creation.*

According to the Princeton schema, Modernism falls into two camps: Imagism and Symbolism. Imagism (Pound) endorsed "the direct treatment of things," whereas Symbolism (Poe, Baudelaire, Rimbaud, Mallarmé, etc.) "exemplified the tendency to turn inward on subjective consciousness and absorb impressions of the external world into the expressions of moods and feelings of increasing subtlety" (55). Responding to this dichotomy, Symbolism seems to have maintained the modernist tradition of visionary poetics, expanding the definition of vision to include personal (psyche, body) and transpersonal or transcultural (history, mythology, etc.) material as well. But the Symbolism of twentieth-century visionary poetry was not simply "a tendency to turn inward"; instead, it was a tendency to turn *outward* toward "other" in the belief that there is a reality accessible outside the self. While that reality is mediated by subjective consciousness and language, twentieth-century visionary poets argued that the investigation of what is "other" to the poet is crucial if

---

[*] The characterization of Modernism as secular Humanism is well-documented. Christian poets in particular tend to confuse this fact with a "loss of the sacred" in twentieth-century poetry, "sacred," of course, meaning "Christian". What this really amounts to is nostalgia for the social and political hegemony that Christianity enjoyed for centuries. A recent example of this atavistic sentiment appeared in *The Writer's Chronicle* ("Writers & Their Faith: Christianity in Contemporary Poetry," September 1998) where "religious poet" means Christian poet. Paul Mariani states in the interview that ". . . the Christian poet, even if he or she is not always writing about faith or religious experience, will have at some point to write about [religious] issues, or how are we to know they are poets informed by a religious vision? Charles Olson was a poet who had been baptized a Catholic, but where in the poetry will one find a Catholic vision?" Note the confusion between "religious" and "Catholic" vision, not to mention the authorial fallacy and lack of historical knowledge (i.e., the visions of Maximus predate Christianity by thousands of years). If the sacred means simply Christianity, then, yes, twentieth-century poetry underwent a "loss of the sacred." But if the sacred means everything from Yeats' rosy cross and H.D.'s Greek mythology to The Beats and Buddhism, ecology poets and nature, Black Mountain and deep history, and the various religious perspectives of multicultural poetics, then the twentieth century was a veritable renaissance of the sacred.

poetry is to engage reality on more than a solipsistic level. Imagism ("No ideas but in things") tended to dismiss visionary modes as having no basis in external reality, especially those that endorsed impressionistic and expressionistic tendencies. While Symbolism responded by opening itself up to all visionary traditions, Imagism turned toward so-called objective reality and the "clean-edged delineation of image."

The above dichotomy is useful to some degree, but it is ill-suited for dealing with any practical application to experimental modernisms of the twentieth century. True, Pound's early work overhauled decadent Symbolism, but *The Cantos* are informed by more than "the direct treatment of things." And if H.D., Williams, and Zukofsky are Imagists, then what do we do with the symbolic dimensions of *Helen in Egypt, Paterson,* and *"A"*? Likewise, I read Mallarmé's scored poems as examples of a "clean-edged delineation of image." On a more basic level, the Imagist/Symbolist dichotomy ignores the fact that all language is both sign and symbol. Individual poets may lean more toward Imagism (Stein) or Symbolism (Duncan), but all twentieth-century experimental poetry has made use of both modes. What Pound accomplished was a house-cleaning of *decadent* Symbolism, not Symbolism itself. The confusion between decadent Symbolism and Symbolism in general has fueled straw-man arguments against the visionary mode this century by academics and scientific positivists alike.* The problem stems in part from well-meaning suspicion of all totalizing, sectarian visions (cf. Olson's "Against Wisdom as Such"). Of course, the dichotomy of subjective Symbolism and objective Imagism is fantasy: nothing, including language, is exclusively subjective or objective. Twentieth-century visionary poetry, therefore, combined new modes of Symbolism's "turn inward on subjective consciousness" with Imagism's "direct treatment of things."†

VISIONARY POETICS

There is no singular visionary mode in twentieth-century American poetry, but its origins go back to shamanic seeing as "boundary-crossing": breaking down the self/other dichot-

---

*Duncan's assessment of literary criticism thirty years ago is still relevant today: "Much of modern criticism of poetry is not to raise a crisis in our consideration of the content or to deepen our apprehension of the content, but to dismiss the content" *(Fictive* 22).

†The twentieth-century model, of course, is Pound's *Cantos.* See also Olson's discussion of man as both "instrument of definition" and "instrument of discovery" in his essay, "The Human Universe." Praxis: *The Maximus Poems* (Berkeley: U of California P, 1983).

omy, viewing reality instead as a vast web of interdependency.* In a skeptical era, such a view of poetry was not merely radical and innovative, but traditional as well, emphasizing poetry's origins in ritual and sacred acts. As Duncan states, "One of the primaries of the poet is his magic identification with the natural world — *'the pathetic fallacy'* the rationalist-minded critics and versifiers call it" ("Rites" 64). On the humanitarian front the rationalist mind has failed us, and in the next millennium survival will increasingly mean *global* survival whereby our ability to distinguish *pathos* from *pathetic fallacy* will be critical.†

Unfortunately, shamanic seeing has been used as a vague catch-all for self-discovery. The distinction, here, and the relationship between shamanism and visionary poetics, is that shamanic seeing is not merely self-discovering, but self-losing: no self is discovered in the visionary mode without the corollary of purposefully losing inadequate modes of personal and cultural perceptions.‡ Modern visionary poetics is, by definition, critical of the dominant modes of cultural perception (i.e., Blake's "outward boundaries"). If anything is lost in America's demotic visions, it is certainly not the dominant modes of cultural perception. Indeed, America's demotic visions *are* the dominant modes of cultural perception, from the self-affirming angel and men's group shaman to the Protestant vision of resurrection — a cross, cleansed of suffering, from which no man hangs.§

---

*"*Seeing*," then, as an act of survival. From a twentieth-century perspective it is difficult to conceive of the full scope of the shaman's responsibility for the survival of the tribe. At 30,000 BCE, survival was intimately connected to knowledge of all aspects of life (weather, migration patterns, the uses of plants, functions of the human body, etc.). Today's specialist and specialized poet would surely perish in such a world.

For the most comprehensive anthology to date tracing some of the primary global impulses and diasporic threads of modern and postmodern visionary poetry, see the two-volume *Poems for the Millennium: The University of California Book of Modern & Postmodern Poetry*, ed. Jerome Rothenberg and Pierre Joris.

†One important distinction is that the pathetic fallacy is not merely imparting human characteristics to non-human things (for example, rocks, trees, god), but imparting non-human characteristics to humans: a kind of "non-pathetic" (i.e., non-compassionate) fallacy: slavery's African "beast," the Third Reich's Jewish corpse as "ragdoll," etc.

‡For example, Rimbaud's poet-seer:
> The Poet makes himself a seer by a long, prodigious, and ordered *disordering of all the senses*. All forms of love, suffering, and madness. He searches himself. He exhausts all poisons in himself and keeps only their quintessences. Unspeakable torture where he needs all his faith, all his superhuman strength, where he becomes among all men the great patient, the great criminal, the one accursed — and the supreme Scholar! — Because he reaches the *unknown*! He reaches the unknown, and when, bewildered, he ends by losing the intelligence of his visions, he has seen them. Let him die as he leaps through unheard of and unnamable things: other horrible workers will come; they will begin from the horizons where the other one collapsed! (letter to Paul Demeny, 15 May 1871, my translation).

§ The muse of traditional American poetry is the benign, rational, and self-affirming angel. For an alternate take

Some primary gnostic fields in visionary poetics that are traditionally excluded or ignored by dominant culture and mainstream poetry include pre-Socratic philosophy, alchemy, astrology, psychoanalytic theory, ethnography, anthropology, archaeology, world history and mythology, ecology, Buddhism, Hinduism, and the "heretical" traditions of Gnosticism, Kabbala, and Sufism. New knowledge requires new forms, and the American visionary tradition is one of experimentation with the longer poem (middle-length, serial, and epic), as well as alternative modes of perception: body and voice as active "fields" of composition, dreams, memory, meditation, trance states, automatic writing, controlled use of hallucinogens, and so on. Literary influences on twentieth-century visionary poetics include world poetries, the oral tradition, orthodox and heretical texts, Romanticism, Dada, and European and Latin American Surrealism. The literary roots of visionary poetics in America go back to Melville, Emerson, Whitman and Dickinson, and move forward through the Pound trajectory to include various impulses from both the so-called imagist tradition and the "expressive" poetics of The Beats, Black Mountain, San Francisco Renaissance, Ethnopoetics, and deep image.

POSTMODERN VISION

Duncan's vision of cooperative design came late in a century that had already begun exploring Whitman's prophecy of a poetry that would "reflect all themes and things, old and new, in the lights thrown on them by the advent of America and democracy" (447). But Whitman's vision was curtailed by a desire to correlate visionary poetics with a national spirit distinct from European tradition. Instead, Duncan's dream of a whole symposium would move "beyond the reality of the incomparable nation or race, the incomparable Jehovah" ("Rites" 23), dissolving "not only the boundaries of states or civilizations but also the boundaries of historical periods . . ." (24). Robert Duncan is one of America's great visionary poets, and, along with Charles Olson, a key figure connecting the front and back of twentieth-century experimental poetry.* Duncan viewed poetry as an act of social re

---

that has had more influence on innovative twentieth-century poetry, see Lorca's "Play and Theory of the Duende" (*Deep Song and Other Prose*, trns. Christopher Maurer, New York: New Directions, 1975).

*Rexroth is correct in calling Williams "the bridge to the future," and he is, of course, behind Olson and Duncan. Of Duncan's work, Rexroth states, "it would be possible to make up an anthology of all the important trends in modern poetry from Duncan's work. . . . He is a man of many skills with a full orchestra of poetic instruments at his disposal. In addition there is a great deal going on in his poetry, intellectually as well as, shall we say,

sponsibility and compassion. His writings were a wake-up call to poets living in a world where "wars like business are practical affairs, and the body counts from the battle fields of Vietnam are issued like the scores of football and baseball teams" (*Fictive 45*). He drew important parallels between the American poet of the cold war era and the American expatriots in the early part of the century. According to Duncan, the Protestant-Capitalist cult and the Military cult "combined forces in 1914 to make a new world. War was to become, as it is in our own day, the most profitable business, the foundation of the economy, and the economy was to become the cause of the soldier" ("Rites" 46). At midcentury, modernisms praising high-culture, machinery, and nationhood were no longer viable, and American poetry, led by the New Critics, turned away from the world for the most part, reflecting the massive psychological block of a nation wanting to forget its history.* Although many American poets in the last decades of the twentieth century continued to draw from a small range of concerns in their work, the social and political climate was not unlike the one in which Duncan wrote. As Jerome Rothenberg and Pierre Joris state, the cold war and post-cold war eras were less of a "pax americana" than

> a continuation of the midcentury war by other means; a diffuse but unrelenting form of World War III. The wars of the time were not only the Amencan conflicts in Korea and Vietnam — and the forty-year long cold war — but hundreds of other regional conflicts, wars of independence, revolutionary guerrilla wars and uprisings, genocides, mass slaughters, cultural wars fueled by ideology and, increasingly, by ethnicity and religion. And with this too there was the sense of a natural world under continuing attack or lashing back with new plagues and hitherto undreamed-of biological disasters. (2)

Whether in a time of one vision or a hundred visions of war fueled by ideology, ethnicity and religion, America has had little tolerance for the old stories: not because it is a nation of skeptics, but because the old stories remind America of its own role in global suffering. In the short memories of most Americans, war is always elsewhere. But America has a long history of domestic crisis, beginning with the mass extermination of Native Americans whose visionary traditions go back more than 20,000 years to Paleoasiatic tribes

---

imagistically" (*American Poetry in the Twentieth Century*, New York: Seabury Press, 1973; 165,).

*For example, who, among the American Modernists, addressed the bomb and the Nazi concentration camps in their work? And a generation later, Vietnam? Certainly not the wave of poets backed by the New Critics. The same lack of concern for global issues affects academic poetry today.

Dan Featherston 415

that brought Siberian shamanism across the Alaska-Siberia land bridge: the true origin of American vision.*

Olson said that men spring up like violets when needed. Likewise, visions spring up in times of crisis. They are the measure of a culture's desire to transform itself. From Ezekiel, Black Elk, and David Karesh to Dante, Bruno and Artaud, visions are tools of survival: personal, tribal, global.[†] Like Duncan's symposium, they are structures of coherence aimed at transforming cultural fragmentation and chaos. Traditionally, those cultures under the greatest threat to survival have produced the greatest visions. Whitman's visionary poetry, for example, was a product of civil war where political and spiritual visions merge in the dream of a restored union.[‡]

Although innovative poetry since 1970 has continued to explore the visionary mode, the general perception in American culture is that the poet is a craftsman (workshop poetry) or maker (New Formalism, Language poetry), not a seer.[§] Indeed, America has never really thought of its poets as seers, let alone priests or politicians, and in the final decades of the twentieth century the emphasis in American poetry was on form (New Formalism, Language poetry) and technique (workshop poetry) versus content. Perhaps as a corrective to what was perceived by some poets and theorists as excessive symbolism or "expression" in innovative post-war poetry (itself a reaction to the New Critics), the

---

*For some surviving visions of the indigenous Americas, see Jerome Rothenberg's *Shaking the Pumpkin: Traditional Poetry of the Indian North Americas* (New York: Alfred Van Der Marck Editions, 1986) and *Technicians of the Sacred: A Range of Poetries from Africa, America, Asia, Europe & Oceania* (Berkeley: U of California P, 1985).

[†]Studies of the relationship between sensory deprivation and hallucination give evidence of the need for "dialogue" between self and environment, even if that means fabricating internal stimuli that can then be projected onto a sensory-deprived environment. This may be at the root of shamanic visions from the Paleolithic to the vision quest, as well as shamanic visions within the Judeo-Christian tradition. For an interesting comparison of two visions/hallucinations resulting from sensory deprivation, see the Biblical account of Jesus' temptations in Luke 4:1-44 and "The Great Vision" chapter of *Black Elk Speaks* (ed. John G. Neihardt, U of Nebraska P, 1979). See also Clayton Eshleman's "A Phosphene Gauntlet" (*From Scratch*, 1998). For the role of crisis in the construction of cult- and culture-visions, see Weston La Barre's *The Ghost Dance: Origins of Religion* (Prospect Heights, Illinois: Waveland Press, 1972) and Norman Cohn's *The Pursuit of the Millennium: Revolutionary Millenarians and Mystical Anarchists of the Middle Ages* (Oxford: Oxford UP, 1970).

[‡]While colonial America's first visionary bard was completing his final vision of democracy, the Military Cult was preparing a final solution to the "Indian problem." 1,500 miles from Camden, the last large-scale Native American resistance to colonialism and one of the great crisis-visions in American history — The Ghost Dance of 1890— ended in the massacre at Wounded Knee. Combined with the more insidious warfare of the Protestant-Capitalist cult, the truly "native" spirit of America suffered a blow from which it never fully recovered.

[§]The Judeo-Christian split between the material (secular) and the spiritual (sacred) ensures that maker and seer remain separate.

reigning theories in the last decades of the twentieth century endorsed a view of poetry as the imitation of an external, albeit fragmented, world.

DEEP IMAGE

Taking Duncan's "whole symposium" as a working definition for visionary poetics, those poets defined briefly in the 1960s as "deep imagists" (Jerome Rothenberg, Armand Schwerner, Diane Wakoski, David Antin, Robert Kelly, and Clayton Eshleman) made some of the most important contributions to the visionary mode in the last decades of the twentieth century. According to Rothenberg, deep image was to "renew a demand that poets get at the reality of things by turning inward: that the process of self-perception be united as far as possible with our means for perceiving the world around us."* Such a notion stands opposite the Judeo-Christian model of vision as something that comes wholly from outside one's self. Although concerned with the role of language as mediation between self and world, deep image poetry emphasized the complexities of the subject's psyche versus the complexities of language itself. And unlike confessionalist or workshop poetry, deep image was informed by a view of subjecthood as a complex network of both personal and impersonal forces extending far beyond personal anecdotes and family history.† It is no surprise, then, that many poets originally associated with deep image have had a lifelong commitment to a broad range of disciplines, as well as an involvement with other cultures and languages via translation and Ethnopoetics.‡

For the deep image poet,

---

*For two views of deep image by Robert Kelly, see "Notes on the Poetry of Deep Image" in *Trobar* 2 (October, 1960) and *Statement* (Los Angeles, CA: Black Sparrow, 1968). See also Jerome Rothenberg's "From 'Deep Image & Mode': An Exchange with Robert Creeley (*Pre-Faces & Other Writings*, New York: New Directions, 1981).

†Carl Jung's theory of a collective unconsciousness had a strong impact on deep image poetry in that it moved away from Freud's emphasis on personal biography in the construction of the unconscious and toward an understanding of the unconscious as transpersonal and communal (cf. *The Archetypes and the Collective Unconscious*, London: Routlege & Keegen Paul, 1972). For many deep imagists, another strong influence was European and Latin American surrealism.

‡Coined by Jerome Rothenberg, a complex of ideas meaning, roughly, "a redefinition of poetry in terms of cultural specifics, with an emphasis on those alternative traditions to which the West gave names like 'pagan,' 'gentile,' 'tribal,' 'oral,' and 'ethnic.' In its developed form, it moves toward an exploration of creativity over the fullest human range..." (xi). See *Symposium of the Whole: A Range of Discourse Toward an Ethnopoetics* (ed. Jerome Rothenberg & Diane Rothenberg, U of California P, 1983).

the direction of seeing ... is into a man rather than outside him: not a habit of the eye so much as a penetration of the self to refocus on the world through the eyes-of-feeling. This means that we have to try to see the world in all its natural and contemporary detail as if no differences existed between the seer and the things he sees.

Like any movement, the works of those poets briefly associated with deep image are more interesting in how they differ from one another than how they cohere within any one definition. Two poets originally associated with deep image whose works embody aspects of a twentieth-century visionary mode are Robert Kelly and Clayton Eshleman. What follows is not a comprehensive study but proposes possible entries into these two vast fields of work.

ROBERT KELLY

When I think about Robert Kelly's giant *oeuvre* of over fifty books and his personal dictum, "write everything," I'm reminded of one of those Buddhist avatars of human desire — a demon-like figure whose gaping mouth and hunger-swollen belly are connected by a neck too narrow to swallow. Thus it may be that the man who eats nothing and the man who eats everything have one thing in common: hunger. Like the Buddhist demon, the fullness of any *corpus* reveals a paradoxical emptiness: to write everything is also to write nothing:

> what is important to each man
> he never says,
> never learns it till the light
> walks out of the sky
> & he is left
> alone with his failed utterance
> impossibly clear in the dark *(Finding* 84)

For Kelly, "there always seems to be too much to say, too much to notice, too much to write. I'm usually exhausted by my own greed. What not being bored means is being greedy about enough different things so that there's always something to feed on" (Mc-

Caffery 174). But Kelly's so-called greed is, finally, given away in the poem as an act of generosity, an attentiveness to "all the ordinary and extraordinary knowledge that comes its way from . . . searches among libraries, annals, archives, dreams, meditation, ritual, introspection, conversation, argument, analysis, lovemaking, daydreaming, looking, remembering" *(Island* 181). Such is vision— far seeing, capacious. In its fullest sense, it is compassion and the ability to move beyond false boundaries.*

Ironically, this inclusiveness has excluded many readers who feel overwhelmed by the breadth and depth of the work. Where to begin? How to begin? A descent into Kelly's work might be augmented by reading Thomas Vaughan and listening to Mahler, as well as knowledge of astrology, classical Greek, Hindu mythologies, Kabbala, Gematria, Tantrism, and a sense of etymology as psychical rubble; for good measure, an eye and ear for "all marks anywhere [as] inscription" *(Red* 388), and a sense of language as "a circle whose circumference / is nowhere and whose center's everyone" (227).[†] But there is a point at which the poems can be crushed under the weight of the reader's own armory, whereby reading around the poems becomes an "evasion by transferring the energy of the total response over to an area of dialectic or gridwork 'where we can handle [the poem]' — i.e., abolish it & offer its Spectre" ("Discourse" 34). Of course, "total response" is what one brings to the poem: the more one brings, the more "total" the response. But it is also important to *disarm* oneself in the descent in order to listen to the whole range of the work, including one's own resistance and bewilderment, for "the happening of a text is . . . the reading of it, what the book *does* in head & breath & heart" (33).

While there is a lot of "headwork" in Kelly's poetry, it is important to keep "breath & heart" in mind: not generalization and abstraction, but an attentiveness to the poem as its own notation. The greatness of Kelly's work is in its precision and attentiveness to things, despite the erudition, the thinking; or because of the erudition and thinking. Indeed, thinking and erudition *require* precision and attentiveness to things (poet — "Last of the materialists"):

---

*Kelly's leviathan appetite also conjures the image of the divine-human body: "'To the enlightened man . . . whose consciousness embraces the universe, to him the universe becomes his body.' As in schizophrenia: 'what happens to the person's own body . . . is identical with what happens in the universe'" (Norman O. Brown, *Love's Body*, Berkeley: U of California P, 1966, 226). "A landscape made out of the dreamer's own body" (227): health's "wholeness" or sickness? Sacred or profane?

[†]For an early gathering of essays on Kelly's work, see the "Kelly issue" of *Vort* (#5, summer 1974, ed. Barry Alpert.)

> The SUBJECTIVE
>
> is not the opposite of the rigorous.
>
> It is the most rigorous, the most difficult.
>
> The *precise subjective* is what philosophers are too lazy & too generalizing to labor, scientists too frightened to search out.
>
> The Objective is p.r. for the Generalization. (18)

The "precise subjective" strikes me as the alchemy of the Imagist's precision, the so-called "clean-edge delineation of image," and the Symbolist's subjectivity discussed earlier. Vision, perhaps, implies the ability to simultaneously hold in the imagination the contraries of precision and subjectivity without perceiving them as opposites.

Given the breadth of Kelly's work, his selected poems — *Red Actions* — is a good port of entry. For Kelly, "[a] poem is activity, a nest of deeds which reader and writer share, transpersonal, unpossessed" *(Island* 181). If the poem is an activity shared by the reader, it is a read action, as the title of the selected aptly implies. Of course red actions, like Kelly's poems, imply the color's vibrant history in the human psyche: alchemy's mercury, Dante's rose, Christ's stigmata and "the crucifixion in the rose's heart" *(Red* 117), the red of human desire and suffering. Given the staggering volume of Kelly's poetry, one might also hear, in "selected," *redactions*—"acts of drawing back; resistance; reaction," as well as "a bringing into definite form."[*] Weighing in at just under 400 pages, *Red Actions* represents less than 10% of Kelly's published poetry. Just as "any narrative . . . is itself a fragment of a vast transaction" *(Scorpions* 191), one of the inevitable drawbacks of any selection is that latitude elbows out longitude. Thus, many of Kelly's longer and serial poems have been excerpted *(Sonnets, Songs I-XXX, The Loom* "Postcards from the Underworld") or excluded altogether ("An Alchemical Journal," "A Book of Building," "The World"). But these vitals should not dissuade the reader from picking up the book as both an excellent introduction and a

---

[*] According to Jed Rasula's essay, "Ten Different Fruits on One Different Tree: Reading Robert Kelly," the Kelly archive at the Poetry / Rare Books Collection at SUNY-Buffalo contains approximately 30,000 typescript pages of material from 1960 to 1982. That is not including prose and essays. Add material from 1982 to present, and the count exceeds 50,000.

kind of aerial map of the terrain. *Red Actions* is thorough in latitude, representing material from nearly all of Kelly's books, from *Armed Descent* (1961) through *A Strange Market* (1992), as well as roughly seventy-five pages of uncollected material from 1991-1993.

Since Kelly is better known for his long poems, one of the wonderful things about *Red Actions* is how it foregrounds shorter and middle-length poems that carry just as much freight, flex and rigor. Poems such as "Section 3: Claude Lorraine" (from *The Pastorals*), "Les Joueurs de Foot-Ball, 1908," "Variations on a Poem of Stefan George," and "A Flower for the New Year" illustrate Kelly's ability to be instructed by (versus poem as attempt-to-instruct) the smallest details of things (postcards, paintings, another poem) as well as those things that we would distance and, therefore, diminish.

Although many readers are overwhelmed by Kelly's work, it is important to keep in mind that the poem "is not a puzzle it is / necessity" *(Red* 31). A comment by Jed Rasula on Kelly's work is insightful in this regard: "[t]here are not, actually, difficulties in Kelly's work; there are *mysteries*, because Mystery is at the heart of it, the *mysterium tremendum* of sanctity and grace, the burden on man of 'making love salvation'" (149). But mystery is a difficulty: not only the difficulty of being human, but being in a world where "[w]e are silenced / by the way things are. // By pain" *(Loom* 168). Kelly's writings are visionary for their penetration of the difficulties of compassion and violence, love and lust, salvation and burden.

In "A Flower for the New Year," the speaker, trying to remember the name of a flower, asks ". . . why should I be thinking about the gods or even winter / when there are men and women who have no homes / with or without flowers on the wall" *(Red* 309). But in "the heavy traffic of names" (309), remembering "the names of flowers or the names of anything" (308) is not merely re-covering the world, but bringing forward its distances and dissonance. Naming calls close. The so-called "hermetica" of Kelly's work is precisely this refusal for the life "out there" in all its complexities and inter-connections to be excluded from the work. In twentieth-century visionary poetics, nothing must be willfully distanced:

> A man is bent double over the hood of a car
> and the police are twisting his thick sunburned arms behind his back
> putting handcuffs on.
> Ambulances with swinging lights, sheriffs and troopers
> and a street full of frightened people.
>
> This has to be in the book. This is the map.

> It has to show the fear, it has to show my hand
> squeezing your wrist too hard, the doubt
> beginning to show in your eyes as you look at me,
> the grief in mine that I would twist the world again,
> that I'm doing it again, hurt you to love me.
> That I can't trust the world to come to me and stay. (339-340)

Is this the red action of violence? passion? Nothing left out: the "he" / "she" / "it" out there in the street drawn into the "me" behind the poem. Rather than poem-as-"heart to heart" behind the safety zone of myopic narratives, generalizations and abstractions, Kelly's poetry tunnels under the declensions that distance "I" from "you," "you" from "he," "she," "it": poetry as compassion. What is called hermetic in Kelly is actually quite the opposite: a precise subjective, an "I" whose precisions generate multiple intersections, contradictions and coherences. Such is the work I think of when I consider Olson's call for "a secularization which not only loses nothing of the divine but by seeing process in reality redeems all idealism fr[om] theocracy or mobocracy, whether it is rational or superstitious . . ." (190). It is a view of reality as both "divine" and "processual" that Kelly's precise subjective would restore.

Often, Kelly's work coheres like a dreamscape: loosed from the cognitive bindings of cause and effect and their linguistic correlative of normative syntax, each poem acts as an "occasion with many doors," asking "what lies on the other side of sex, of war, of fear? Of place? // What is on the other side of *this* place?" ("Discourse" 29). The "other side" may be just under the grid of language, in the "intricate raftwork of wreckage from our lives" (*Red* 292), in the mulch of etymological compost, puns and mishearings where the mercurial beads of language scatter and disperse the reader's attention in unpredictable directions. *Red Actions* closes with such ample openings: "The Door" is a kind of threshold between the work behind and the work ahead — not language as lintel, something to pass under, but a liminal place where

> . . . there is always something there that isn't you
> something that reminds you of a tree
> yes, something growing not too far from anybody
> something hard and useful and answerable when you ask
> yes, but something that isn't that either
> something no kinder than glass something

emptier than steel, a crystal
with nobody home a broken radio a child's thumbprint
left on the window of a closed store (387)

CLAYTON ESHLEMAN

There are several dimensions to Clayton Eshleman's work, including editing and translating, but what strikes me as visionary are the poems and prose (notes, lectures, and essays) that investigate the origins of image-making and its relationship to the evolution of human consciousness and the construction of culture.[*] Recently published as *Juniper Fuse: Upper Paleolithic Imagination & the Construction of the Underworld* (Wesleyan UP, 2003), this work includes material from *Hades in Manganese* (1981), *Fracture* (1983), *Hotel Cro-Magnon* (1989), *Antiphonal Swing: Selected Prose 1962-1987* (1989), *Under World Arrest* (1994), and *From Scratch* (1998). These and other works go into a twenty-five-year work-in-progress entitled "Juniper Fuse," which "attempts to imagine the presence of decorated Upper Paleolithic caves in varying twentieth-century contexts" (*Scratch* 182). Rather than isolate and analyze particular poems from this extensive body of work, I'd like to focus on the theoretical underpinnings of the cave-art poems, which might help to contextualize the project at large. It is important to keep in mind, however, that the poems dealing with Paleolithic imagery cannot be divorced from the context of Eshleman's lifework of more than fifty titles anymore than the present can be divorced from the past.[†] As Eshleman states, "I have no interest whatsoever in writing poems 'about' the caves, or even doing poems that can be identified as 'poems with the paleolithic as the subject.' It is the present itself, with all its loop back and deadend meanders, that is precious to establish" (*Hades* 12). It is precisely the establishment, or *re*-establishment, of the present by way of a serviceable past that makes these poems and prose visionary — "far-seeing."

Eshleman's investigation of the upper Paleolithic began in 1974 when he made several visits to decorated caves in the French Dordogne. Beginning with *Hades in Manganese* and its investigation of Paleolithic image-making, Eshleman moves away from a self anchored

---

[*]Eshleman edited *Caterpillar* (1967-1973) and *Sulfur* (1981-2000), and has translated works of various poets, including Artaud, Césaire, and Vallejo.

[†]This discussion deals only with the ideological underpinnings of Eshleman's cave poems. For other works by Eshleman that bear upon the visionary, see *Coils* (Black Sparrow, 1973) and *Companion Spider*. See also Paul Christensen's *Minding the Underworld: Clayton Eshleman & Late Postmodernism* (Black Sparrow, 1991).

primarily in personal experience and into a more complex terrain involving "other" in a transpersonal, deeply historical sense.* But the most profound relationship seems to have begun six years after his first trip to the Dordogne in what I would call a series of visionary experiences.† With *Fracture* it is evident that the Paleolithic dimension has worked its way into Eshleman's imagination to the extent that it can be presented as a kind of mythological structure, an anti-thesis against which the thesis, so to speak, of contemporary consciousness (from psychological repression to sexual violence) and culture (from Protestant anti-symbolism to Disney's portrayal of animals) is explored in greater critical and imaginative depth.

But how, exactly, are the origins of image-making relevant to contemporary consciousness and culture? The answer has to do with time itself. If the Judeo-Christian tradition associated vision with prophecy of the future, twentieth-century visionary poets — faced with the prospect of no future — redefined vision as, in part, prophecy of the past. As Duncan states, "In a time when only one vision — the vision of an atomic disaster and the end of the species— haunts the world, in religion as well as in science, men labor to exorcize the old stories" (*Fictive* 5). In innovative twentieth-century American poetry, the old stories (via poetry, history, philosophy, mythology, etc.) re-enter the imagination. Time itself seems to re-enter the twentieth-century imagination as a material and spatial *presence* (Pound: "All ages are contemporaneous"). When we consider vision as "far-seeing," visionary works of the twentieth century (*Ulysses, The Cantos, Paterson, The Maximus Poems*, and so forth) were as concerned with time as earlier visionary works (*Odyssey, Divine Comedy*, and so forth) were concerned with space. Among the discoveries of the century that fueled an interest in history, the discovery of upper Paleolithic cave-art must rank as one of the most profound in how it offered a perception of early hominids as complex and imaginative subjects tens of thousands of years before the so-called birth of western civilization. As Eliot Weinberger notes in the introduction to Eshleman's selected poems,

> The invention of the historical other has become almost programmatic in twentieth-century American poetry: for Pound, ancient China; for H.D., classical Greece; for Olson, Mesopotamia; for Snyder, the Neolithic. Eshleman has pushed

---

*For a study of Eshleman's work up to and including *Hotel Cro-Magnon* (1989), see Paul Christensen's *Minding the Underworld: Clayton Eshleman & Late Postmodernism* (Santa Rosa, CA: Black Sparrow Press, 1991).

†These experiences are recounted in the Introduction to *Fracture* and reprinted in *Antiphonal Swing*.

the historical back about as far as it can go: to the Upper Paleolithic, and the earliest surviving images made by humans. *(Name* 13)

More than any other American poet, Eshleman has heeded Olson's call for "the hinges of civilization to be put back on the door," the first hinge being "original 'town-man' put back to Aurignacian-Magdalenian, for evidence of a more primal & consequent art & life than the cultivation which followed (the Deglaciation & the Wet Period until 7000-5000 BC)" (189). What Olson guessed was "a more primal & consequent art & life," Eshleman sees, via cave-art, as a period in which the human began separating out of the animal, resulting in "the creation of the underworld, at the beginning of psyche, when Hades was still an animal" *(Antiphonal* 131). That is, cave imagery can be thought of as "a language upon which all subsequent mythology has been built . . ." *(Hades* 10). In subsequent mythology, "we can observe the animal anatomy falling away, until with the early Greeks most of the deities are sheerly human-looking" (11). Eventually, both animal and human fall away entirely, and we are left with the abstract god of monotheism. According to Eshleman, we are born out of animal and "are now in the process of killing ourselves off because we do not know how to reconnect to all of the otherness that has become our enemy" *(Antiphonal* 45).

Visions propose ways of survival. The visionary mode that poets like Duncan and Olson argued for involves compassion and the ability to perceive self in outward, in "other."[*] Against that vision is the desire to either flee from or destroy otherness, which Eshleman speculates may have to do with the distinction between *autoplastic* and *alloplastic* evolution:

> . . .before man, all previous animals had been subject to the evolution of their own substance, i.e., they were autoplastic, and their genetic gambling was blind because

---

[*] In an interview with *Atropos* magazine, Eshleman configures the "flux of contrariety" as follows:

> the parasympathetic represents the direction of expansion, "out of the self — toward the world," pleasure and joy; the sympathetic, on the other hand, represents the direction of contraction, "away from the world — back into the self," sorrow and pain and, ironically, inspiration. Imaginatively speaking, the antithesis evokes "I" and "other." *(Antiphonal* 41)

Reichian theory has been important to Eshleman's configuration of the I/other dialectic as reciprocal on various levels (psychological, sexual, etc.). Works by Wilhelm Reich most pertinent to CE: *The Function of the Orgasm: Sex-Economic Problems of Biological Energy* (New York: Farrar, Straus & Giroux, 1973), *The Mass Psychology of Fascism* (New York: Orgone Institute Press, 1946), and *Cosmic Superimposition* (New York: Farrar, Straus & Giroux, 1973).

they played with their own bodies. Man's evolution, on the other hand, is through alloplastic experiments with objects outside his own body and is concerned only with the products of his hands, brains, and eyes — and not with his body itself. Is it not possible that we shudder before highly mobilized grotesque images because subliminally we know that unrestrained alloplastic invention can lead to nuclear war, and that in the grotesque image we see simultaneously the relatively benign matrix that we abandoned, and the malignant power implicit in the one we entered? (*Fracture* 14)

Like tool-making, image-making can be thought of as the projection or extension of self beyond the boundaries of the body. The creation and use of artifacts outside the body to manipulate the environment (alloplastic evolution) was indeed critical to human evolution: for the first time in history, survival is explicitly linked to projection outside of the body. According to Eshleman, the simultaneous extension and separation from the body in image-making is what lies behind the Judeo-Christian myth of human expulsion from paradise and subsequent "birth" of sexuality, violence, cultivation, and so forth.* What Eshleman's work proposes is not only a deconstruction of the Judeo-Christian origin-myth, but a revisioning of Eden as "the end of the primordial condition in which what is human and what is animal are bound together" (*Antiphonal* 163-64). That is, the original fall is not from God, but nature. And to the extent that humans are part of nature, the original fall is a fall from ourselves.

Important to Eshleman's theory of the Paleolithic crisis of hominid-animal separation is his identification of a grotesque archetype that depicts this separation:

---

*Artifact = exile. The Judeo-Christian myth of the fall is a vision of the origin of being exterior to God. If Eshleman's theory on the grotesque archetype as forming from the original violence of alloplastic (versus autoplastic) evolution is correct, then isn't God the first artifact, i.e. first exile? Is it possible that the artifact, as a projection of the body, is the real agent of exile? And is this exile a kind of doubling of the self as both body and artifact (spirit)? The etymologies of "subject" and "object" seem to reveal such a correlation: *subject*, "to throw under," and *object*, "to throw in front of, or before." The question, of course, is what is being "thrown" and by whom? Subject's "throwing under" implies a "throwing back" or self-reflextivity that calls to mind Henry Corbin's discussion of "ta'wil" in *Avicenna and the Visionary Recital*, trans. Willard R. Trask (New York: Pantheon Books, 1960): "to cause to return, to lead back, to restore to one's origin and to the place where one comes home, consequently to return to the true and original meaning of a text" (29). The body, or Judeo-Christian "Paradise"? Conversely, object's "to throw in front of, or before" implies Corbin's discussion of exile without any leading back to origin (i.e., subject). The "throw" of language, then, might be seen as both a *return to* (subject) and *exile from* (object) the poet-thrower.

Such an archetype might indicate something basic about the nature of image: that in contrast to the realistic or the abstract, the image represents an ambivalent synthesis in which forces felt as opposites are, to borrow André Breton's term, "exploding/fixed," and that the umbilical cord of the image trails back to a point at which such contrariety was sensed as the struggle of the human to detach itself from the animal. *(Fracture* 14)*

Often in Paleolithic art there is a combination of "abstract" (dots, meanders, etc.) and "realistic" (bison, deer, etc.) images. The grotesque hybrid image (e.g., "a 'naturalistic' ibex . . . gouged in rock across an 'abstract' vulva already gouged there") is reminiscent of the above depiction of Modernism as a tension between Imagism's "realism" and Symbolism's "abstraction." Indeed, many of the artists whose works Eshleman has been drawn to in his poetry (van Gogh, Soutine, Bacon, de Kooning, Marwan, and so forth) exemplify a strong sense of contrariety between "realism" and "abstraction". Eshleman's theory of a grotesque archetype is central to his own writing and dialectical view of the imagination as both synthesis and melee, "core" and "meander," whereby "one metaphor tries to grasp its amoebic split-off to hurl it forward into numerology, myth, any cosmic extension, while what it is anchored in, carnal, mute, as if a Covering Prefix, gestures earthward" *(Under* 181). Such is the primary tension in visionary poetry that strives toward both extensive and intensive intelligence.

Eshleman's poems seem demonstrative of the grotesque archetype: the metaphorical transformations that images undergo "explode" or morph their identities and, therefore, their significance within a particular narrative; and yet there is nothing "exploded" in an Eshleman poem in terms of tortured syntax or grammar. The poems are "fixed" in that there is a specific inquiry ("core") that initiates each work. In an Eshleman poem, the imagination is a mode of intelligence, a creative intelligence of declaration and stance, not merely a mirror held up to imitate the "chaotic nature of things." The inquiry meanders, but each poem seems grounded in meditative depth — in situ, a "staying power." Note, for example, the latitudinal shifts and meditative depth in the following, from "Matrix, Blower":

---

*Key here is Bakhtin's book on Rabelais *(Rabelais and His World,* Indiana UP, 1984) and his theory of the grotesque. James Hillman's *The Dream and the Underworld* (New York: Harper & Row, 1979) was also useful to Eshleman in rethinking connections between psyche and cave-art. Eshleman applies Hillman's argument that "we must reverse our usual procedure of translating the dream into ego-language ['day-world'] and instead translate the ego into dream-language" (95) to the interpretation of cave-art.

>   At Abri Cellier: the neck and head of a blowing horse
>   crudely engraved in a stone block.
>   Across the neck, a vulva a bit bigger than the horse head has been gouged.
>   "The original sentence, the original metaphor: *Tat Tvam Asi*, Thou art that"
>   Blowing horse head = vulva,
>   thus: a blowing horse head vulva,
>   "Beauty will be erotic-veiled, exploding-fixed, magic-circumstantial or it will not be"
>   The *exploding* and the *fixed* at 30,000 BP,
>   the Aurignacian "hydrogen jukebox." *(Scratch 167)**

The Paleolithic engraving is "overlaid" with quoted material (Norman O. Brown, Breton, Ginsberg), creating associations between the Paleolithic palimpsest (Horse head / vulva) and the various "contraries" that follow: Thou / that; Beauty / erotic; exploding / fixed; hydrogen / jukebox. Note, however, that the situation itself ("At Abri Cellier") does not change. Instead, there is a kind of associational layering — a build-up of correspondences.† These relationships are what give Eshleman's poetry visionary scope. Indeed, relationships are the foundation of metaphor, and "[i]n metaphor, the primal anxiety: everything is nothing" *(Under* 160). Or, as is often the case in Eshleman's work, everything is *something*, some thing other than itself.

TWENTY-FIRST-CENTURY VISION

From my first experiences with poetry in fairy tales, nursery rhymes, and schoolyard games, the critical moment of transformation (tigers to butter, frog to prince, ashes, ashes, all fall down) always elicited both fear and delight. As I got older, I noticed that these transformations were ways of possessing or dispossessing. Desire and fleeing from desire

---

*Notes on "Matrix, Blower" relevant to the quote:: "Abri Cellier is an Aurignacian rock shelter near Les Eyzies; it has some of the earliest-known engravings (30,000-28,000 B.P.) in the Dordogne region. "The original sentence . . ." is quoted from Norman O. Brown's *Love's Body*. "Beauty will be erotic-veiled . . ." is from André Breton's *L'Amour fou*." *(From Scratch* 184.)

†To make in ourselves a new consciousness, an erotic sense of reality, is to become conscious of symbolism. Symbolism is mind making connections (correspondences) rather than distinctions (separations). Symbolism makes interconnections and unions that were unconscious and repressed. Freud says, symbolism is on the track of a former identity, a lost unity: the lost continent, Atlantis, underneath the sea of life in which we live enisled. . . . (N.O. Brown, ibid., 81-8)

meant shape-changing, becoming other.

Such is the force of desire to remake us in its own image, its own amplitude.* What terror and delight that desire could migrate from body to body and suffer such violent changes, even death. The heart of desire is metaphor, which is revolution — a turning into, away from, or toward something else. It is transformation. It is change. Who knows what role the imagination and desire have played in the adaptation and survival of the human species? The history of human adaptation and survival is encoded, perhaps, in the intelligence of the imagination.

Much of what passes as "visionary" in contemporary American poetry is not revolutionary at all. It is religious verse fraught with abstraction and generalization: Judeo-Christian vision still looking *through*, not at, nature. To look through nature, including human nature, is to pass right out of existence. It is a wish for death with ego intact. The feverish talk of angels today is just that: to escape reality. Escape is not difficult. What is difficult is the trash in the gutter, the stranger's face, the lover's body that grows old and dies. At the same time, to deny nature depth is to dwell at its surface. For a poet it means to cynically pantomime the endless stream of information, as if that were enough. Information is never enough.

I would like to believe that our imaginations and poetry — its supreme language — did not develop simply to escape reality. I would like to believe that the child's schoolyard chant is no evasion of reality, but is, in some primary way, involved with the very nature of reality. If we are to consider the nature of our own reality, Duncan reminds us, then we must come to terms with the nature of our fears:

> Reject Mae West as vulgar or Hitler as the enemy, reject them as fellows of our kind, and you have to go to battle against the very nature of Man himself, against the truth of things. Hitler cannot be defeated; he must be acknowledged and understood. But we often do not want to find out what Man is like; we would divorce ourselves from fearful possibilities. Put away death and immunize ourselves to contending lives. Over and over again men disown their commonality with living things in order to conquer a place, exterminate the terrible or rise above the vulgar. (*Fictive* 115)

---

*Such remaking is a mode of knowledge. Apprehension is the ability to seize knowledge as it shifts through various guises, various shapes. The visionary poet is Virgil's Aristaeus, wrestling Proteus to give him an oracle that would explain his loss.

To disown our commonality is the end of intelligence and compassion. Standing on the rim of the third millennium, we seem to hear only Keats's "negative" without the "capability". Let the negative *be* capable. A capable negativity. Let the poet be responsible for more than the narrow circumference of self or the narrower circumference of the impossibility of self — the one white noise, the other silence.

The works of Robert Kelly and Clayton Eshleman demonstrate that vision requires a poetics open to EVERYTHING, including what is traditionally distanced as fearful, terrible, vulgar. In the next century, with Blake's vision of infinity already being replaced by an actual hole opening in the ozone, there may be little left to look through anymore. In the next century, Whitman's "I am the man . . . I suffered . . . I was there" must include the fact that he was not the man, he did not suffer, he was not there. And yet, it is only the imagination and its visions that can possibly respond wholly to the whole symposium into which we now go.

WORKS CITED

Blake, William. *Complete Writings*. Ed. Geoffrey Keynes. Oxford: Oxford UP, 1985.

Duncan, Robert. *Fictive Certainties*. New York: New Directions, 1985.

-------. "Rites of Participation." *A Caterpillar Anthology: A Selection of Poetry and Prose from* Caterpillar *Magazine*. Ed. Clayton Eshleman. New York: Doubleday & Co.., 1971.

Eshleman, Clayton. *Antiphonal Swing: Selected Prose 1962-1987*. Ed. Caryl Eshleman. Kingston, NY: McPherson & Co., 1989.

-------. *Coils*. Santa Barbara, CA: Black Sparrow P, 1992.

-------. *Companion Spider*. Foreword by Adrienne Rich. Middletown, CT: Wesleyan UP, 2002.

-------. *Fracture*. Santa Barbara, CA: Black Sparrow P, 1983.

-------. *From Scratch*. Santa Rosa, CA: Black Sparrow P, 1998.

-------. *Hades in Manganese*. Santa Barbara, CA: Black Sparrow P, 1981.

-------. *Juniper Fuse: Upper Paleolithic Imagination & The Construction of the Underworld*. Middletown, CT: Wesleyan UP, 2003.

-------. *My Devotion*. Santa Rosa, CA: Black Sparrow P, 2002.

-------. *The Name Encanyoned River: Selected Poems 1960-1985*. Santa Barbara, CA: Black Sparrow P, 1986.

-------. *Under World Arrest*. Santa Rosa, CA: Black Sparrow P, 1994.

Kelly, Robert. *The Alchemist to Mercury: an alternative opus: uncollected poems 1960-1980*. Ed. Jed Rasula. Richmond, CA: North Atlantic Books, 1981.

-------. *Finding the Measure*. Los Angeles, CA: Black Sparrow P, 1968.

-------. *Lapis*. Santa Rosa, CA: Black Sparrow P, 2002.

-------. *The Loom*. Los Angeles, CA: Black Sparrow P, 1975.

———. *The Mill of Particulars*. Santa Barbara, CA: Black Sparrow P, 1973.

———. *Not This Island Music*. Santa Rosa, CA: Black Sparrow P, 1987.

———. "On Discourse." *IO* 20(1974): 3-36.

———. *Red Actions: Selected Poems, 1960-1993*. Santa Rosa, CA: Black Sparrow P, 1995.

———. *The Scorpions*. Barrytown, NY: Station Hill P, 1985.

———. *A Strange Market*. Santa Rosa, CA: Black Sparrow P, 1992.

———. *The Time of Voice: Poems 1994-1996*. Santa Rosa, CA: Black Sparrow P, 1998.

McCaffery, Larry. *Some Other Frequency: Interviews with Innovative American Authors.*. Philadelphia: U of Pennsylvania P, 1996.

Olson, Charles. *Collected Prose*. Ed. Donald Allen and Benjamin Friedlander. Berkeley: U of California P, 1997.

Preminger, Alex and T.V.F. Brogan. *The New Princeton Encyclopedia of Poetry and Poetics*. Princeton, NJ: Princeton UP, 1993.

Rasula, Jed. "Ten Different Fruits on One Different Tree: Reading Robert Kelly." *Credences* 3, 1 (1984): 127-75.

Rothenberg, Jerome and Pierre Joris. Introduction. *Poems for the Millennium: The University of California Book of Modern & Postmodern Poetry, Volume Two: From Postwar to Millennium*. Berkeley: U of California P, 1998.

Rothenberg, Jerome. "Why Deep Image?" *Trobar 3* (1961).

Whitman, Walt. *Leaves of Grass: The 1892 Edition*. New York: Bantam, 1983.

Peter O'Leary

AMERICAN POETRY & GNOSTICISM

"Knowing forces you out beyond." —Robert Duncan

To speak about the presence of the sacred in American poetry is to draw the circle whose center is everywhere and whose circumference is nowhere. Walt Whitman and Emily Dickinson rise up hieratic in the halo of this circle: the presence of religious and spiritual material in American poetry, especially in this century, is simulataneously massive and — like these two poets — idiosyncratic. This means, on the one hand, that if you look you will find religion in just about everything, from the explicity stated pseudo-Catholicism of Robert Lowell to the Quaker-like antinomianism of Susan Howe; from the cryptic oracles of Nathaniel Mackey, all the way back to the mystical populism of William Carlos Williams. It also means, on the other hand, that you run into instant danger by proclaiming any sort of "tradition" involved in this presence of the sacred. In the way that we can call Dante a Catholic poet we cannot call Kenneth Rexroth, who professed himself to be Catholic, the same; even less so can we call Robert Duncan a Christian poet. Yet we cannot address Duncan's complex vision without attending to his attraction to the myth of, as he would put it, the Christos. Octavio Paz once wrote:

> Poetic rhythm does not fail to offer analogies to mythical time; the image, to mystical utterance; participation, to magical alchemy and religious communion. Everything leads us to insert the poetic act into the realm of the sacred. But all things, from the primitive mentality to fashion, political fanaticism, and even crime, are susceptible to being regarded as a form of the sacred. The fertility of this notion — which has been abused as much as psychoanalysis and historicism — can bring us to the utmost confusion. (Paz 101)

This goes to preface in as cautionary a way as possible my designation of a gnostic strain at work in contemporary American poetry. It is useful to keep in mind that it is the peculiarities of Whitman's and Dickinson's visions that hold us to them; we go to their poems for what remains untraditional about them. We go to them for insight, not for confusion.

WHAT IS GNOSTICISM?

I WANT TO SUGGEST THAT A FORM OF GNOSTICISM is evident in some American poetry written in the last thirty years. Before I designate any exemplars, I need to clarify what I mean by "gnosticism," so as to distinguish it from "secret society" or "religious fanaticism" or "Kabbalism" or any other such headings, each easily ballooned into a mystic afflatus. Gnosticism, as I want to use it, refers to two related but distinct categories. The first category is the historical religious movement in the Late Antique world whose beliefs and practices incorporated a mythic hypothesis whose gist is that the world and its creator are both fallen, and that the only way the spark of the human soul can be reunited with the Divine Hypostasis, which is the Good that lies beyond, is through a specific form of knowledge, designated by the Greek word "*gnosis.*" Put simply: knowledge=salvation. This involves, as Robert A. Segal has pointed out, a belief in "the present entrapment of a portion of immateriality in human bodies; the need for knowledge to reveal to humans that entrapment; and the dependance of humans on a savior to reveal that knowledge to them" (Segal 3). These beliefs were incorporated into the myth that Jehovah — who created the world and is a Satan figure — is a terrible God of judgement; but that Christ, the loving God of Knowledge, transformed himself into the serpent, coiled himself around the Tree of Life, and gave the gift of gnosis to Eve and then to Adam. In this mythology, Christ and the Jehovah-Satan are twins, born of Wisdom (*Sophia*) in her longing after the Beyonds (*Bythos*). The figure of the serpent in gnostic writings is used to represent this knowledge, and is almost a commonplace in them; just so, the evocation of Wisdom — in various guises — is instrumental to gnostic writings.

This first category of historical gnosticism incorporates three possible groupings, all of which share the property of living "mainly in or on the edges of Christianity and Judaisim" and bearing "a number of philosophical, astrological, and magical marks loosely belonging in the Near Eastern and Inner Mediterranean areas" (Smith 387). I warrant it is this "edginess" that makes gnostic material so attractive to the poets I discuss below. The three grouping are: 1) the ancient Christian heresy of the second century; 2) a more broadly inflected tradition of beliefs in the Late Antique world, which embraced Christian, Greek religious, and Judaic beliefs (all revealed in the massive discovery of the texts at Nag Hammadi in Egypt in 1945[*]); and 3) an extremely broad grouping of dualistic religious sects

---

[*]See the introduction to Elaine Pagels, *The Gnostic Gospels* (New York: Vintage, 1979) for an account of the discovery of these scrolls and what they signified to the study of early Christianity.

and philosophies that draw on gnostic mythological themes, are strongly ascetic and antinomian, and sometimes incorporate such practices as the rejection of marriage and sexual intercourse, and vegetarianism. This last grouping is broad enough to include the medieval trends of Islamic gnosis and the Kabbalism of Isaac Luria. As Ioan Petru Culianu writes: "The history of gnostic ideas and imagery is not easy to follow . . ." (Culiano 63) from which he goes on to indicate that the Ismaili mystics, the Cathars (that attracted the likes of Richard Wagner, T.S. Eliot, and Ezra Pound), Goethe in his *Faust*, and even Marx can be considered gnostics. Culianu quickly cautions us about stretching the meaning of gnosticism too far: "In modern philosophy and literary criticism, the words *gnosis* and *gnostic* tend to be indiscriminately used to indicate the nihilistic character of a specific school of thought, the presence of a transcendental capacity in man, the emanational character of a system, or simply some 'knowledge,' esoteric or not" (Culianu 67). All of these things are not necessarily gnostic, especially when we define the word strictly in terms of a regimen of religious beliefs and practices.

But, against this advice, I am going to stretch the use of gnosis, and use it to designate in contemporary American poetry a trend that is based on what scholar of gnosticism Elaine Pagels calls "insight," which I take to be a form of intuition that functions in the same way as knowledge does. This is the second of the two related categories of gnosticism that I mentioned above. It is distinct from the "historical" category of gnosticism in that it has more of an interior resonance which is not necessarily defined in terms of the world or historical events. Pagels writes: "But *gnosis* is not primarily rational knowledge. The Greek language distinguishes between scientific or reflective knowledge ('He knows mathematics') and knowing through observation or experience ('He knows me'), which is *gnosis*. As the gnostics use the term, we could translate it as 'insight,' for *gnosis* involves an intuitive process of knowing oneself" (Pagels, xix). It is this employment of insight that links present American poets back through postmodern poets like Robert Duncan and Charles Olson, and Modernists like Pound, H.D., and Hart Crane, through the Romantics and the colossal prophecies of Blake, to the Metaphysical poets, and beyond, all the way back to the early Christian heretical movements. This gnostic insight is a creative force; to engage in the process of using such intuition is to engage in a process that incorporates into the creative intelligence something more than the rational mind, challenging the poet to propose new modes of vision and expression. Since this is such a potentially flimsy designation, I hesitate to use it. But as such things go, some examples will give a better sense of what I mean than explanations.

FIRST GROUP: "GNOSTIC" POETS

A SURPRISING NUMBER OF AMERICAN POETS IN THE LAST THIRTY YEARS have incorporated into their work the tenets, the symbols, and the philosophy of historical gnosticism: William Bronk has written in the mode of an exquisitely subtle and probing gnosticism, that is at once as splendid as it is bleak. In his poem "To Praise the Music," the only gnostic emblem missing is the snake:

> As if I know some other things besides.
> As if; but I don't know, not more
> than to say the trees know. The trees don't know
> and neither do I. What is it keeps me from praise?
> I praise. If only to say their songs,
> say yes to them, to praise the songs they sing.
> Envied music. I sing to praise their songs. (Bronk, 153)

Bronk's poetic vision is cast in the "dark light" of gnosticism, whose expressions are particularly philosophic. Susan Howe, in a different manner, has been executing an incredible conflation of "nonconformist" religious and historical researches with a powerful sense of loss that, despite being built on scholarly and poetic sources, feels like it has no precedents in American letters. Where Bronk is almost stoical about gnosis, Howe is at times rapturous. In her *Pythagorean Silence*, she traces the remoteness of human connection back to a Jehovah figure striding through his artificial garden:

> Each sequent separate musician:
> (harmony
>
> a passion)
> across a deep divided deprivation
>
> (enchantment   capacity
> a paradise-prison)
>
> seems to hear a voice walking in the
> garden

> who seems to say
> I am master of myself and of the
>
> Universe. (Howe, 54)

Howe has recently been fusing this belief with a rigorous analysis of American religious history, sometimes through literary persuasions as in "Melville's Marginalia," and sometimes through intense, strong readings of the Gospels, as in "The Nonconformist's Memorial." Some might argue that in no way does Howe's work fall under an historically gnostic designation. But I contend that her work with early Christian topics, combined as they are with her own uncompromising and untraditional reading of early American literary and religious history, makes her gnostic in precisely the way these early Christian heretics were gnostic.

Nathaniel Tarn is a priest in an entirely different garb. He has had many careers in his poetic lifetime, including anthropologist, editor (of the fantastic Cape Editions in the sixties), and translator as well as poet. He was one of the seminal figures of ethnopoetics, which started in the sixties and faded slowly in the eighties, and which is arguably the only movement in American poetry whose articulated goal was a communion with and recovery of the sacred, in which he pursued a form of writing that combined elements of shamanism, initiation, and radical translation.[*] Tarn engages in a specifically gnostic poetics in his long poem *Lyrics for the Bride of God*, in which he recovers by way of incantation a Kabbalistic evocation of the Shekinah, who in Jewish tradition is the so-called Bride of God — a Wisdom figure, in whom the dispersed sparks of human souls, scattered throughout the universe, find their Source. This is an underappreciated poem I think, a rare instance in postmodern poetry of a poet putting his massive learning to use in the form of insight and transformation, instead of quotation and collage. When he brings the Goddess into his poem, as in:

---

[*] See his "Fragments from the Prayers Made on Behalf of N.T. . . . ." reprinted in *Symposium of the Whole*, edited by Jerome Rothenberg & Diane Rothenberg (Berkeley: U of California P, 1983), pp. 408-413.

HERA — HEVA — OPHELIA: ROYAL MAIDEN
   the snakes in the long stream of her death
       the snakes in her hair
       and in her maidenhair
       the snakes in her name
       before she married —
   I loved you once generation of Satan:
   where she had fallen into the grip of the winged god
   where she was covered by the diadem of feathers
   Unfallen Lucifer: that too seemed wisdom. (Tarn 56)

we encounter a description of the role of Sophia that exceeds what any encyclopedia entry can give us. It is good to keep in mind, as these poets have, that even an historically conditioned use of gnosticism is nonetheless more experimental than scholarly. These gnostic beliefs emerge from an intuition and an application of a form of or a resistance to history; not from mere study.

More recently, poets such as Phillip Foss, Alice Notley, and Nathaniel Mackey have been constructing their own gnostic myths, using gnostic material to amplify such diverse things as post-modern accounts of the fragmentation of religious history, a feminist archaism, and an intensely ambivalent account of the American appropriation of African myth, music, and sensibility, whose echoes are heard in a disarrayal of improvisational jazz, the poetry of Duncan and Olson, and western anthropology. A quotation from a recent poem of Foss's characterizes this use of historical gnosis in American poetry, at once specific and slippery, as serpentine as the snakes it evokes:

   the hands turn blue
   the knife black

   no mordant no escape
   mars is an exaggeration

   deviant light
   it is not the hue of her lips

   which exclaims

rather the torn remnant

of a red flag
poppy or rose

inevitably the mind bleeds
coals slacken

and the snake is fully cooked
neither hissing

nor rarefied alchemy . . . (Foss 26)

Notley and Mackey merit a more detailed discussion than the poets mentioned so far. While these other poets thrive on a gnostic pursuit, Notley and Mackey stand out in their working of gnostic material into a specifically American undertaking, evoking not so much the historical contours of gnosticism as the liturgical potentials, which is to say they make of their poems a prodigious gnostic rite. Notley and Mackey have been able to wed a sacred sense of the "tremendous mystery" of creation with compelling forms of poetic experimentation.

Alice Notley first published her poem *The Descent of Alette* in 1992. It is a 150-page-long self-consciously shamanistic epic. It concerns the title character, whose name chimes on a French pun of "the little she who goes" as well as ringing with the mythical "owl," bird of wisdom, that she becomes at the end of the poem. Alette who lives in a twilight world of a subway system must slay the "tyrant" who rules this subterranean world. The tyrant is a gnostic Jehovah figure, an almighty controller of forms. Alette's descent is a downgoing for knowledge, as frightening as it is empowering. After a series of initiatic trials, in which she descends from the world of subways to a world of magical caves, in the meantime incorporating a host of lost souls for whom she becomes spiritual vehical, she finds herself at last in the mansion of the tyrant on the upside of the world. It takes all of her wits and a moment of sustained violence as vivid as that in Duncan's "My Mother Would Be a Falconress" to slay the tyrant, but she is victorious, and her act frees the souls from the underworld of shadows, where they had been enslaved to the tyrant's forms since time immemorial.

Despite being so obvious a narrative, the poem has undeniable power. Notley accomplishes an "oral" poem that hangs together storywise by way of one specific trick to which she attaches considerable gnostic lore. The trick is the use of quotation marks around every breath-unit in the poem, a technique that never in the course of reading it loses its freshness and interest. By using these quotation marks, Notley creates a choral effect that allows her to present and quickly amplify mythic information, surrounding us with echoes of this world in shadows.

The precursor for this poem in Notley's oeuvre is "White Phosphorus," in which she discovered this vivid technique. "White Phosphorus" also prefigures the gnostic themes that drive *The Descent of Alette*. The poem is an honorary garland of light for the poet's brother, who had been a cog in the machine of war in Vietnam and who suffered upon his return. Notley sets up a relationship between impossible experience and an unthinking, remote and demiurgic government, mediated through her brother's tormented soul. The breath-units with which she conveys these themes are registered at the beginning of the poem as panting:

"Whose heart" "might be lost?" "Whose mask is this?" "Who has a mask,
& a heart?" "Has your money" "been published, been shown?" "Who can &
can't breathe?" "Who went" "to Vietnam?" (Notley 115)

The toll taken on those who went to Vietnam is counted in the poem in an almost Kabbalistic numeracy that relates directly to an apprehension of the economy of war:

"Money is numbers
dead bodies are numbers" "dead veterans are numbers like

hours we've worked" "country of numbers" "mother of numbers"
"your child will be numbers" "mother of numbers" "your lover is
numbers, walking the numbers" "mother of numbers" "your lover is
numbers, walking the numbers" (Notley 117)

But this notarikon does not aspire toward the transparency of the godhead: it is merely a govenmental abacus whose calculations are menacingly endless.

The poet seeks for the memory of her brother a transcendance from the fallen, war-torn world, which she glimpses in a wreath of white flowers, whose blooms appear as light:

"Flowery mantle." "Homeric sacrifice?" "noise of darkness" "fear of
darkness" "now mantle of innocence" "King of his death now" "Home"
"I've come home" "He said, 'I've come home'" "They were sacrificed for
nothing, for distant" "instants of thought" "All for your thinking"

By invoking Homer, Notley conjures the world of Odysseus' *nekyia*, his journey to the land of the dead where he seeks the oracle of Tiresias. Implicitly, she also invokes Homer's epithet for the fallen warrior, "blameless." The horrors of war are blamelessly transformed into flowers, but not without conflict and ambivalence:

"To die"
"To
wear a mantle light honey" "mantle dead white" "in sunlight, in late"
"Homeric?" "he said it was hideous" "all of it" "hideous" "every
instant in Nam" "theatre of worsts" "now mantle of
white" "phosphorus & lilies?" (Notley 118)

At last Notley finds a means of conjuring her brother in the afterworld. She has a dream in which her brother, named Al, is changed into an owl. She insists that he is not an albatross. The owl symbolically combines wisdom and war. Her concluding vision of her brother is beatific:

"mantle" "of fresh, white flowers"

"petals, like feathers" "white petals" "white feathers" "a cloak
of nature of" "purity" "of purification" "wilder, milder, he is
nature" "he is better mind" "My brother" "is owl" "Athena-like" "wise"
"I know things only" "this way" "My brother" "is Owl." (Notley 121)

This conclusion points to three verbal elements that are mythically amplified in *The Descent of Alette*: "Al," the owl, and the project of "knowing things."

In *The Descent of Alette*, the darkness of the world of the tyrant is as menacing as it is potentially generative. Notley's quotations exaggerate this ambivalence, so that we cannot be sure where hope lies. Darkness is seen in the shape of jewels that appear to be tears from the eyes of the tyrant. These jewels of darkness have alchemical properties, in that they hold powers waiting to be unlocked. It is, in fact, into the darkness that Alette descends in order to discover her power. The world of caves she travels through are petrified emblems of the womb as much as they are the dens of gnostic vipers. On seeing a mass of "almost-snakes," Alette remarks how a disembodied voice speaks to her and begs her to embrace her serpentine nature by dropping to the floor of the cave among the snake eggs and writhing. In the caves of the underworld, Alette becomes a serpent. In the end, it is by imaginatively combining the serpentine knowledge of the world below with the lingering emotional sensation of the headless Wisdom figure she encounters in the nether-reaches of darkness, that Alette discerns the tyrant's vulnerability and delusion. He believes he contains all Nature, despite nearly unconsciously proclaiming that Nature results from the Snake-Wisdom to be discovered in the underworld. "Nature" is what left the world of the tyrant for darkness. The wisdom of nature is in the dark. When Alette confronts the tyrant with this information, he begins to sing new verses of a song commonly heard in the subways below about the time when the snake was the mother of all and how they all serve her memory now in pain. Alette and the tyrant descend together into the subway world. A chase ensues. Alette changes herself into a massive owl. She uses her fantastic beak to gore the tyrant. That beak was the sharp weapon of gnosis, the means of Alette's salvation and that of the world below.

Notley has written that her inspiration for this poem and its ingenious line came in a dream and from a kind of wakeful exploration of her unconscious. She has also indicated that one of her sources for this poem is an ancient Sumerian myth of the descent of the goddess Inanna into the Underworld, in which she dies, is reborn, and ascends to pursue her husband Dumuzi, who is to die in her place ("Epic" 104). I want to avoid suggesting that this gnostic material is archetypal; nonetheless, Notley has absorbed a conspicuous amount of gnostic lore which she has found an inarguably archetypal — dreamlike — means of expressing.

For at least fifteen years, Nathaniel Mackey has been generating a poetry of another kind. We do not find the broad gnostic strokes of Notley's poem in Mackey's work. Instead we find a poetry that has increasingly woven into its complex texture gnostic information, gnostic hints and speculation, and an overall pattern of wisdom coiled with ambivalence, one so rich and contrary I hesitate to make any specific gnostic claims about it. And because Mackey's is a poetry of hesitation and slippage, I am encouraged to hold my position. But gnostic it is, and also grand — : Mackey's working of this, and manifold other material, into a range of poetic series, including a serial poem he calls "mu," after trumpetist Don Cherry's same-named series (but also sounding the "mu" in "muthos" that

Duncan and Olson made much of), as well as the serial prose experiment "From a Broken Bottle Traces of Perfume Still Emanate," and on to the majesterial "Song of the Andoumboulou," is one of the singular poetic enterprises of the day. Intrinsically, Mackey's might be the most interesting poetry currently being written, and I suspect this has something to do with the caches of gnostic lore and disposition he has ingeniously loded into his poems.

Mackey himself has said of this poetry, referring specifically to "Song of the Andoumboulou": "It's addressed to the spirit; it's a spiritual. It's speaking to the spiritual vocation of music, the spiritual vocation of art, the spiritual vocation of poetry" (O'Leary 40). This calling is at once the gruff, scratchy sound of the "Song of the Andoumboulou," which announces the newly dead in Dogon funeral rites, and also a priest-like liturgical intonation that shapes his poems. This liturgy combines many forms, especially elements of free jazz, bits of West African lore, and a phantasmagoric milieu that is simultaneously the Caribbean, the Mediterranean, and the American city. But above all, this liturgy, which is infused with an edginess that is also a circumspection and an ambivalence, is gnostic. This circumspection allows Mackey to regard himself as his own twin, a gnostic other:

> Gnostic stranger
> I embraced as though it
> was me I embraced . . .
>   Was.
> Caught me unawares . . . (*Serif*, 8)

It is this strangeness that keeps Mackey on edge with this material, and it is the past tense — the "Was" — that figures gnosticism in Mackey's work so interestingly and so unusually.

Mackey's project is not the resurrection of gnosticism — or even the "Gnostic stranger" — and this despite enfolded references to Sufi gnosticism, in his consistent evocation of *ta'wil*, which is the Arabic name for the gnostic "return" to the true source in Islam. His goal appears to be the use of gnostic material to evoke what is lost or gone from the world, so that the Gnostic stranger takes his place beside the Andoumboulou, who are the ghostlike remnants of a failed primordial race of humans, beside Mackey's exquisite articulation of the flamenco notion of *duende*, which is intense longing that has no object, and beside the "School of Udhra," a vanished race of North African poets whose extinction rests on their having given themselves to vigorously to love, among other such "phantom limbs" limping through his works.

Mackey's gnosis is inseparable from the components of loss that make up his ghostly poetic world, which is a commentary on the world as it is, and may constitute one of the most interesting critiques of American history and culture yet attempted by an American poet. The knowledge Mackey seeks is not liberating in the way Notley's is; instead, it proposes something more solemn, less manageable, and perhaps more potent, if only because it resists any full expression. Notice here how what the poet knows manages to obfuscate even while evoking a mystic state, which has real force despite its blindness:

>   Looked into as
>   the last eye closes, furtively
>   lit by what we already knew.
>   Without remedy, up all night two
>   nights
>   before, strict motionless engine,
>   sugared
>   sweat, wet hair my pillow, spoken
>   of as if spoken for . . .
>   That we'd each
>   know an alternate ending, move to speak,
>   mouth
>   wired shut . . .
>   Mute lure, blind mystic
> light,
>   lost aura.   Erased itself,
>   stuttered,   wouldn't say
>   what (*School* 13)

Mackey has written that "social estrangement is gnostic estrangement." (*Discrepant* 259). It's an idea he takes from Henri Corbin's writings on Islamic gnosticism, which posits that the gnostic makes of himself a kind of objectification, a "stranger," who then becomes a mystic Guide who leads the gnostic initiate toward the "dark light" of knowledge. Mackey's proposition that this feeling of "otherness," of strangeness, characterizes some dark light of the American experience is an insight as chilling as it is illuminative.

SECOND GROUP: "INSIGHT" POETS

T HE OTHER GROUPING OF POETS I WANT TO INDICATE makes use of a gnostic insight and intuition that function on the possibility that any knowledge is knowledge of the divine. This is to say that poetic work allows the poet to apprehend cosmological and psychic orders, and to access a recognition of sacred, if hazardous, properties of things. The poets that I would indicate under this heading — Robert Duncan, Ronald Johnson, and Frank Samperi — are different from what I've designated as "gnostic" poets in that they make minimal reference to gnostic material or history but nonetheless design an idiosyncratic — even antinomian — vision of the world and the universe that is highly and mystically ordered, so that, in a sense, their visions have a grandeur that surpasses those of their "gnostic" poet counterparts. In this light, Blake above all is the great exemplar of this manner of intuitive poetics. Blake's is a poetry of that holy order in which creative engagement is a colossal form of knowledge. I'm thinking of the Blake who says:

> Trembling I sit day and night, my friends are astonish'd at me.
> Yet they forgive my wanderings, I rest not from my great task!
> To open the Eternal Worlds, to open the immortal Eyes
> Of Man inwards into the Worlds of Thought: into Eternity
> Ever expanding in the Bosom of God, the Human Imagination
> <div style="text-align:right">(<i>Jerusalem</i>, Plate 5)</div>

These lines make a mantra for this poetry of insight I am describing.

It may seem unusual to include Robert Duncan in this survey, if only because he established himself in poetry in the fifties and was one of the leading experimental poets of the sixties. He belongs, then, to the influential period in American poetry that precedes the one that concerns us here. Yet much like Notley's Alette who went down into the darkness to discover her power, Duncan went subterranean during the seventies as a result of his decision not to release a major publication of poems following the 1968 publication of *Bending the Bow* until fifteen years had elapsed.[*] In 1984, the first installment of Duncan's digging was published: *Ground Work: Before the War*. In 1988, shortly after his death, *Ground Work II: In the Dark* was published. These are two of the most significant books of poetry

---

[*] Like many, I have a quarrel with Duncan's self-declared publishing hiatus: the seventies saw a steady stream of Duncan publications, especially in the form of ephemeral editions of new poems and the republications of nearly all his work written before 1960.

ever published by an American. In these books, especially in the installments of his epic serial "Passages," Duncan began exploring modes of expression so complex and so radical, we have not yet begun to process their effects.

I want to draw our attention briefly to one of the last serial installments of these "Passages," a grouping of poems Duncan calls "The Regulators." I should say beforehand that Duncan *does* in fact incorporate a good deal of arguably gnostic material in his writing, owing to his broad familiarity and interest in the subject (which extended into all forms of esoterica, as well as into the fields of depth psychology, process philosophy, hermeneutics, and partical physics). I distinguish Duncan from the gnostic poets discussed above because any gnostic information in his poetry he puts conspicuously to the service of a massive and seemingly improvisational construct for which "gnostic" is an inadequate heading. It is perhaps psychic, as in "of the soul," or psychosomatic, as in "body-mind," or even pneumatic, as in "spiritual."

What is powerful and even terrifying about the poems in "The Regulators" is that Duncan fuses a variety of insight with an almost baroque consideration of illness and the revelations that lie within. In 1984, Duncan's kidneys collapsed as a result of high blood-pressure medication that he had been taking for years. These poems were written in 1980 and 1981. It is as if in his poetry he anticipated this physical collapse. These poems are daring compositions, even for Duncan, with lines scattered across the entire page in sprawled array posing little hope for any sort of conventionally comprehensible sense. Duncan was always insistent that he was a traditional poet, a "derivative." In one of the poems in this series, "In Blood's Domaine," he figures the themes of illness and revelation in a manner at once characteristic of his other poetry and also somehow new:

> The Angel Syphilis in the circle of Signators   looses its hosts   to swarm
>   mounting the stem of being   to the head
>   Baudelaire, Nietzsche, Swift
>   are not eased into Death
>   the undoing of Mind's rule in the brain.

As he speculates on the possibilities of a biological destiny that somehow forces a madness he feels already present in his thought and poetic, Duncan turns his thought to an intrinsic cancer, whose bloom he sees opening in the dark light of the zodiac:

> Life in the dis-ease radiates   invisibilities devour my star
>
> and Time restless crawls in center upon center   cells of lives within life conspire
>
> Hel shines in the very word *Health*   as *Ill* in the Divine Will shone.
>
> The Angel Cancer crawls across the signs of the Zodiac to reach its
>
> appointed time   and   bringing down the carnal pride   bursts into flower —
> (*GW*II 67)

Duncan proceeds to see cells bursting into florid splendor, "the viral array" of "scarlet eruptions" which are the secret workings "of the Angel Tuberculosis," one of whose victims is a frail, poisoned Rilke: "where black the infected blood/ gushes forth from Rilke's mouth, from his nose, from his rectal canal/ news of his whole body bears as its truth of the septic rose" (*GW*II 68).[*] This "news" is a revelation through illness whose gist he states: "There is no ecstasy of Beauty in which I will not remember Man's misery," (GWII, 69).

How do we know this news is gnostic and revelatory? Duncan brings Christ into the poem, clearly a mystical, wounded Christ, who says: "I come not to heal but to tear the scab from the wound you wanted to forget" (*GW*II 69). And as he continues to envision — Dante-like in the cancerous Rose of this heaven — the atomic-age "Angel of this Polluting radiance" (referring to chemical and nuclear weapons), he insists of his speech:

> ("Nothing" is happening in these words in their accumulating sentence but the
> mounting delusions of a compulsive psychosis) (*GW*II 69).

This "sentence" is a condemnation of words but it is also the means of an apprehension. Duncan has generated through poetry something less like syntactical sense and more like constellations of psychic fragments and meanings. And just as in stargazing, the prognostications we derive from this poetry are as intuitive as they are something that we can chart, measure, and record.

Ronald Johnson spent over twenty years writing his epic poem *ARK*, much of whose

---

[*] And it is interesting to think here that these are pre-AIDS era poems, somehow eerily prognostic of the pestilential times to come . . .

knowledge is derived from looking up at the stars, in whose energy the poet perceives all of creation — from atmospheres to humans to honeybees — emerging in the quantum-physical act of the cosmos' imagination:

> Out of the mouth of
> moon and the stars,
> What is man, that made him angels, beasts
> to a perpetual end: the gates in the gates of net hid
> snared in the turn into sight.
> :let them be
> imagined.
> (*ARK*, BEAMS 21, 22, 23)

The mantra Johnson intones as he makes his giant cosmic construct is the state motto of his native Kansas: *ad astra per aspera*, "to the stars through hard work." The hard work at hand is a subtle and patient mastery of vision, which is literally the act of the eye seeing:

> Pressure on the surface on an eye make vision, though what these same pressure focus to the radial inwardness of a dragonfly in flight is unimaginable.
> . . .
> No one knows the first man to stare long at a waterfall, then shift his gaze to the cliff face at its side, to find the rocks at once flow upward. But we have always known the eye to be unsleeping, and that all men are lidless Visionaries through the night.
> . . .
> After a long time of light, there began to be eyes, and light began looking with itself. (*ARK*, BEAM 4)

The possible sources of and influences on *ARK* are many: from the poetic models of Dante and George Herbert, both poets who conceived of a massive spiritual architecture; to the naive buildings of Simon Rodia (Watts Towers) and the Facteur Cheval (*Palais Idéal*); to the self-conscious epics of Pound, Williams, Zukofsky, and Olson; and to the vivid observational poetics of Lucretius, Blake, and Thoreau. But *ARK* resists an easy categorization, which I suggest is owed to its being composed along deeply perceived lines of an intuition, for which its cathedral-like structure is formal background, for which the sciences of zoology and physics ("The music of our time") are soundings, and for which a specific and lucid language are the instruments for a lifetime's worth of insight.

Near the end of the poem, Johnson is looking again at the "innumerable numinosities" of the stars, which are also a hive of light. He sees what "Anyone might see":

> I tread the stars
> in perilous anatomy
>
> over bottomless pit
> only intricater,
> I thread evolving Heaven
>
> "nequamquam vacuum"
> flamestitch I symmetries:
> weaver oriole's nest
>
> I construct ahive
> suns one can't gaze upon
> surpassing foresight
> (ARK 96)

This is an integral moment in American poetics, this "surpassing foresight." It is a proposition for a visionary mode that exceeds irony, which can act like a black hole in religious poetry: Johnson's foresight simultaneously designates suns too intense to look at while displaying the creative insight to see them nonetheless. *ARK* is destined to be consulted oracle-like for years to come, just as traces of the future are thought to be perceived through the light of the stars.

Frank Samperi was born in Brooklyn in 1933; he died in Arizona in 1991. He spent his life as a poet in considereable obscurity. He was championed early on by Louis Zukofsky, whom Samperi had sought out as a sixteen-year old orphan. His literary mainstay throughout his life was Cid Corman, who published much of Samperi's work. I must begin my inclusion of Samperi in this discussion by saying he would balk at being called a gnostic of any sort. His poetry is figured in terms of an intense mystical Catholicism, derived from Dante and Bonaventure, that is markedly antithetical to the heresies of gnostic belief or insight. However, the poetry is poised on the expression of the visionary means of transcending the world through poetry, and is constituted of an elaborate version of insight that is at once contemplative and visionary, so that Samperi resolutely belongs in the company of Duncan and Johnson.

Samperi released a number of collections of poetry in the course of his life, and variously attempted translations of Dante's *Divine Comedy* that are at times quite traditional and at others indelibly radical. But his reputation must stand or fall on the untitled trilogy of books that were published between 1971 and 1973 by Grossman Mushinsha: *The Prefiguration*, *Quadrifarium*, and *Lumen Gloriae*. These are three of the most spiritually lucid books I can think of. They are composed from the vantage point of paradise: which is to say, they look on the world, its objects, its sufferings, its meanings from the perspective of the Paradise that extends beyond them. This is the "glorious light" that registers Samperi's most astonishing insight, expressed on the one hand as "glorified body   spiritual man   undivided" and on the other as:

duality is rhythm the essence of duality is rhythm

the essence or nature of rhythm is duality
positive and negative poles alternating indefinitely
the inner structure indefinite total combination (*Lumen* n.p)

The poems in these books cluster around two poetic modes: a lyric of the natural world that is incredibly flat; so flat, in fact, that it is often constituted of near-abstract lists of objects seen in the parks and along the streets, as in the following list from *Quadrifarium*: "Wood/ then/ up/ path/ hill right/ sea beyond/ then/ down/ rocks/ path left/ grove/ below/ hill/ valley/ between/ hill/ mountain . . ." (*Quadrifarium* n.p.). This mode, which occasionally takes on lyric flourishes, is deceptive, because these lists make up Samperi's paradisaical vision of the world. Each of these objects, fully luminous with spiritual force, makes up a map of heaven hidden in the world. These descriptions of things are in fact seraphic recordings:

a beginning of snow
and in a garden
in moonlight
an angel

inwardly radiating

Samperi is looking at these things and listing them because of what he might see in them, as in: "the// angel// passed/// through// the// city/// and// moved// up" (*Prefiguration* n.p.).

Samperi's other mode is an equally flat but spiritually dense set of considerations, instructions, and propositions which have the feel of theology, by which I mean the Word of God. Sometimes he expresses this mode in a kind of ruminative essay — on some prospect of Dante or Bonaventure, for instance — but at its best, he makes spiritual declarations that have the property of prayer. These declarations are unabashedly mystical, in that they call to a bodiless magnitude beyond sensory perception:

existing no place
pilgrim no staff

in light spirit to spirit
recalling deeper light
communicating deepest
sight

universe closing behind
pilgrim beyond
even
one with point
      (*Lumen* n.p.)

As we contend as readers of American poetry with explicitly articulating the spiritual undertakings and contours of the work of our poets in the last thirty years, we will increasingly be obliged to account for Frank Samperi's work. For me, this poetry stands as a challenge to live up to its austere expectations and comprehensions of the gnosis that constitutes the world.

In trying to reckon what this "insight" is, and in trying to avoid creating a category of poetry that has no clearly marked boundaries or distinctions, I am put in mind of something Ronald Johnson once said to me when we were talking about how *ARK* was made. He insisted that *ARK* held authority because he had developed a way to "write from the unconscious." It is a perhaps a commonplace, but these poets, in a way, are using gnosis as a lens through which they focus the unconscious — which as Freud theorized is directly affected in the manner of a radio transmitter (and we can think here of Johnson's epic rewriting of *Paradise Lost, RADI OS*) by external experiences, namely, the world, the cosmos — into the poem. Insight makes for the condensation and the constellation of these inarticulate things into a poetic expression that is a kind of knowledge.

CONCLUSION: BYZANTIUM OR AMERICA?

THIS IS A WAY THE SACRED IS EXPRESSED in American poetry today. In one aspect, a poetry that uses gnostic material and techniques toward a clarification or a disposition that reflects the world, history, language, the universe. In another aspect, a poetry made as a form of knowledge itself, not explicitly gnostic but indisputably insightful in clarity and disposition. These distinctions are not categories; nor are they a structure that excludes other engagements with sacred material in current American poetry. I would have liked to describe John Taggart's extensive project in minimalist applications and repetitions of a holy work, of which he is the gospeleer recording waves of glad tidings washing over things, as if the gospels were spoken by an American manticore, part preacher, part jazz enthusiast, part objectivist. I would have liked to describe Peter Cole's excavations of an Arabic-tinged Hebrew medievalism to produce a poetry whose reverence and awe at language and the powers of speech exceeds any label or religious tradition we might apply to them. I would have liked to call to your attention that subtle longing that casts Pam Rehm's poetry into a remarkable light as if American poetry all along had been nurtured in private consultations with Beguines and Jacob Boehme. I would have wanted to point to the ways in which Jay Wright's liturgical enactments of African and Caribbean cultural projections adumbrate and enhance Mackey's elucidations of similar material. Much like the apse of a Byzantine church is decorated with the ranks of the holy, arrayed in golden tesserated tiers, each figure marked by a characteristic gesture or symbol, I would render all of these poets, and many more, and my meaning would reflect that of the Byzantine mosaicists who rendered these saints: each in his or her way manifests the divine, irradiates with an energy whose source is at once outlandish, solitary, precise. But America is no Byzantium. Instead of saints, better then to imagine Whitman, declaring all men ever born his brothers and all women his sisters and lovers, pockets stuffed with pokeweed as he reaches to shake the hand of God, "elderhand of my own." Gnosis, for complex reasons that must be intuited in what I have said already, is one way to describe this gesture.

WORKS CITED

Bronk, William. *Life Supports*. San Francisco: North Point Press, 1982.

Duncan, Robert. *Ground Work II: Before the War*. New York: New Directions, 1988.

Culianu, Ioan Petru. "Gnosticism from the Middle Ages to the Present." *Hidden Truths: Magic, Alchemy, and the Occult*. Ed. Lawrence E. Sullivan. New York: Macmillan, 1987.

Foss, Phillip. "theofany: heart." *Chicago Review* 43:1 (Winter 1997).

Howe, Susam. *The Europe of Trusts*. Los Angeles: Sun & Moon, 1990.

Johnson, Ronald. *ARK*. Albuquerque, NM: Living Batch P, 1996.

Mackey, Nathaniel Mackey. *Discrepant Engagement*. Cambridge: Cambridge UP, 1993.

-------. *School of Udhra*. San Francisco: City Lights, 1993.

-------. *Whatsaid Serif*. San Francisco: City Lights, 1998.

Notley, Alice. "Epic and Women Poets." *Disembodied Poetics*. Ed. Anne Waldman and Andrew Schelling

Pagels, Elaine. *The Gnostic Gospels*. New York: Vintage, 1979.

O'Leary, Peter. "Interview with Nathaniel Mackey," *Chicago Review* 43:1 (Winter 1997).

Paz, Octavio. *The Bow and the Lyre*. Trans. Ruth L.C. Simms. Austin: U of Texas P, 1973.

Samperi, Frank. *Lumen Gloriae*. Tokyo: Grossman Mushinsha, 1973.

-------. *The Prefiguration* Tokyo: Grossman Mushinsha, 1971.

-------. *Quadrifarium* Tokyo: Grossman Mushinsha, 1973.

Schelling. Albuquerque, NM: U of New Mexico P, 1994.

-------. "White Phosphorus." *Selected Poems of Alice Notley*. Hoboken, NJ: Talisman House, Publishers, 1993.

Segal, Robert A. "Introduction." *The Gnostic Jung*. Ed. Robert A. Segal Princeton: Princeton UP, 1992.

Smith, J. Z. *The HarperCollins Dictionary of Religions* San Francisco: HarperSanFrancisco, 1995.

Tarn, Nathaniel. *Lyrics for the Bride of God*. New York: New Directions, 1975.

Michel Delville

THE MARGINAL ARTS: EXPERIMENTAL POETRY AND THE POSSIBILITIES OF PROSE

FIGURES, CONTEXTS, (DIS)CONTINUITIES

> . . . every poem, is a marginal
>
> work in a quite literal sense.
> Prose poems are another matter: but
>
> since they identify themselves as poems
> through style and publication context, they
>
> become a marginal subset of poetry,
> in other words, doubly marginal.
> — Bob Perelman, "The Marginalization of Poetry"
>
> Nowadays, you can often spot a work
> of poetry by whether it's in lines
> or no; if it's in prose, there's a good chance
> it's a poem —Charles Bernstein, "Of Time and the Line"

WHERE DOES POETRY STOP AND PROSE BEGIN? Can we have verse without prose, prose without the use of paragraphs, poetry without the use of repetition and metrical parallelism? And what aesthetic, ideological and marketing purposes are served when we begin to call things by certain names? Does the very gesture of calling a piece of prose a "poem" suffice to create a prose poem or have prose poets effectively developed a number of specific compositional strategies meant to expand the range of formal possibilities of contemporary poetry? If that is the case, are we speaking of contemporary poetry as a seamless continuum liable to be transgressed by the inherently subversive potential of the genre? Or is the prose poem in the process of becoming another genre with its own methods, conventions, and fashionable trends? And, finally, where do we place a writer like Kenward Elsmlie, whose *26 bars* (1987), a pub-crawled's abecedarius of poetic "tales," features in Paul Hoover's Norton anthology, *Postmodern American Poetry*, within or outside the history of contemporary prose poetry or Charles Simic, whose self-declared "prose poems" in *The World Doesn't End* (1989) draw on Serbian folklore, riddles, ditties as well as jazz rhythms, or John High's ungenred *The Sasha Poems* (1996), or Madeline Gins' "speculative prose" in *Helen Keller or Arakawa* (1994), or Rosmarie Waldrop's poetico-philosophical meditations in *Lawn of Excluded Middle* (1993), or Barbara Guest's *The Countess of Minneapolis* (1976), which comprises lineated poems, narrative fragments, and descriptive prose sketches?

These are some of the questions addressed, directly or indirectly, by Bob Perelman's poemtalk, "The Marginalization of Poetry," first published as a poem in the collection, *Virtual Reality* (1993), and later reprinted in the critical book, *The Marginalization of Poetry: Language Writing and Literary History* (1996). The piece begins by quoting Jack Spicer's famous line, "No one listens to poetry," and proceeds to investigate the literal, metaphorical, and ideological implications of the "margin." The very form of Perelman's text, a 1,500 word critical essay written in relatively straightforward prose and arbitrarily divided into 125 six-word per line couplets, is a (self-)ironical comment on the transgressive power of experimental writing, a gesture the author was later to define as an attempt to "foreground [the] clash between poetry and prose, academia and poetry" ("A Counter Response" 38). Central to this project is the influence of Jacques Derrida, the most prominent example in Perelman's pantheon of contemporary texts that value such "'marginal' qualities as undecidability and / indecipherability." Derrida's work also emblematizes what is in part the purpose of "The Marginalization of Poetry," that of dissolving the border between critical and poetic language: despite Perelman's reservations regarding its rather "decorous" (10) quality, Jacques Derrida's multiple-margin collage, *Glas* (1974), indeed seeks to challenge accepted distinctions between "literary" and "philosophical" texts while simultaneously forcing us to revise our understanding of those distinctions. The poem ends with a call for "a more / communal and critical reading and writing . . . not some / genreless, authorless writing, but a physically and socially located writing where margins are not metaphors, and where readers are not simply there, waiting to / be liberated." Only "a self-critical poetry," Perelman concludes, "minus the / short-circuiting rhetoric of vatic privilege, might / dissolve the antinomies of marginality that / broke Jack Spicer into broken lines" (10).

The prose poem, perhaps more than any other poetic subgenre, has long been involved in a systematic critique of its own formal and ideological foundations as well as of the relationship between reader and work. In the hands of its most daring and innovative practitioners, it has also helped to question the binary thinking that draws a clear-cut line between creative and critical material while undermining what Perelman describes as the "Manichean model of / a prosy command center of criticism and / unique bivouacs on the poetic margins" (8). As I have tried to show in *The American Prose Poem*, the issue of functional negotiations between verse and prose forms, can be profitably extended to the question of whether generic, functional or modal (and not merely structural) categories like "poetry" or the "lyric" can reclaim other genres, functions and modes which have come to be associated more or less exclusively with prose literature. If that is the case, the prose poem also argues for the coexistence of simultaneous and heterogeneous spaces in the mode of presentation (and representation) itself and, indirectly, for the reintegration of poetry into a larger constellation of literary and extra-literary contexts.

Because of its continual oscillation between the literal and metaphorical margins (and marginalities) studied by Perelman's poem, the prose poem form has been used by numerous American poets in order to seize upon the contradictions, but also the possible negotiations, between the "public," utilitarian language of prose and what is often perceived as the oppositional and marginal status of poetic language in the twentieth century. Rosmarie Waldrop's collections, *The Reproduction of Profiles* (1987) and *Lawn of Excluded Middle* (1993) — a poetic extension of Wittgenstein's project to "make language with its ambiguities the ground of philosophy" (unpag.) —, are among the most rewarding books of prose poems to have been published in the last twenty years. The following paragraph from the "Accelerating Frame" section of *Lawn of Excluded Middle* illustrates how Waldrop's prose poems can simultaneously break down traditional genre distinctions and rid poetic language of the "short-circuiting rhetoric of vatic privilege" denounced by Perelman as the basic flaw in such postmodern postgeneric texts as Derrida's *Glas*:

> I knew that true or false is irrelevant in the pursuit of knowledge which must find its own ways to avoid falling as it moves toward horizons of light. We can't hope to prove gravity from the fact that it tallies with the fall of an apple when the nature of tallying is what Eve's bite called into question. My progress was slowed down by your hand brushing against my breast, just as travel along the optic nerve brakes the rush of light. But then light does not take place, not even in bed. It is the kind of language that vanished into communication, as you might into my

desire for you. It takes attention focused on the fullness of a shadow to give light a body that weighs on the horizon, though without denting its indifference. (73)

One of the most remarkable features of Waldrop's *Lawn* is its willingness to integrate many different discourses from areas such as philosophy, science, narrative, and the lyric. But is this polygeneric quality what makes Waldrop's paragraphs "prose poems"? As we know, the mixing of different genres and styles *per se* is by no means the privilege of the poetry written in prose: Pound's *Cantos* and Zukofsky's *"A"* come to mind, not to mention many recent poetry collections made up of interwoven lyrics, stories, newspaper cuts or even drawings and photographs. What makes Waldrop's work so interesting is precisely that it does not confine itself to mixing or juxtaposing antipodal modes and registers. One of the main strengths of *Lawn of Excluded Middle* indeed lies in its playful and critical *appropriation* of Wittgenstein's philosophical formulations. Far from resorting to the asyntactic and disjunctive strategies encountered in many experimental works of the "language oriented" variety, Waldrop proceeds to undermine the logical, syllogistic authority of expository prose from within by confronting it to the changing psychic terrain displayed by a consciousness that is using all its rhetorical vigor to keep up with the "accelerating frame" of a world that is "edging away and out of reach" (67).

As is apparent in the paragraph quoted above, Waldrop's prose poems apprehended the particulars of subjective experience in a way that accounts for the geometries of language, body, and self and combines them in "an alternate, less linear logic" (unpag.). The constant shifts from the general to the particular, the abstract to the sensuous, the metaphorical to the literal ("logic is no help when you have no premises. And more and more people lacking the most modest form of them are wandering through the streets" [74]), need to be understood in the context of the author's proposition that "we have to pass from explanation to description in the heroic hope that it will reach right into experience" (74). It is a tribute to Waldrop's extraordinary stylistic talents that the transitions always remain fluid, achieved by almost unnoticeable shifts of tone, register, and grammatical structure. The result of the poet's meditations on the principle of ambiguity encompassed by "the gravity of love" reads like Barthes' *A Lover's Discourse* translated by Wittgenstein into a Poundian "dance of the intellect" that allows the self to struggle with the "uncertainty of fact" (60) indicated, in various ways, by a post-Newtonian model of the universe. Waldrop's investigation of the contradictions and paradoxes that undermine the consistency and authority of logical thinking invalidates what Charles Bernstein has condemned as the anachronistic assumption that "philosophy is involved with system building and consistency and poetry with the beauty of language and emotion" (218). In this sense, her work is in keeping with what Bernstein defines as the ongoing project shared by modern poetry and philosophy: that of *"investigating the possibilities (nature) and structures of phenomena"* (220).

Waldrop's desire to write a kind of poetry that recognizes that "the picture of the world drawn by classical physics conflicts with the picture drawn by quantum theory" (unpag.) joins up with a number of other recent works that bridge the gulf between poetry and the language of the new sciences, most notably Botho Strauß's *Beginnlosigkeit* (1992), a collection of short aphoristic prose fragments whose nonlinear, noncausal dynamics are meant to reflect the sense of "beginlessness" embodied by the *steady state* theory. All this, of course, has very little, if anything, to do with the supposedly fraudulent misuses of scientific terms and theories recently denounced in the context of Alan Sokal's crusade against the "intellectual impostures" of late twentieth-century critical theorists. The point here is clearly not to import the authority of scientific culture into poetry but to explore the metaphorical and cultural value of contemporary science in the light of the self's attempts to see, think and feel beyond "the bland surfaces that represent the world in the logical form we call reality" (74). By doing so, Waldrop's *Lawn* suggests that one possible way out of the epistemic gaps allegedly separating scientific, philosophical and poetic language is to incorporate them in an alternative form of knowledge that combines the heuristic pedestrianism of the Baudelairian flâneur, the speculative mind of the scientist and what Habermas has termed the "problem solving" aspirations of philosophy. Jackson Mac Low's *Pieces O'Six: Thirty-Three Poems in Prose* (1992) raises similar issues related to the use value of poetic discourse vis-à-vis the language of expository, truthbearing discourses.

Such concerns are of course not entirely new, even in the context of the history of the American prose poem. As early as 1848, Edgar Allen Poe's rather hesitant description of *Eureka: A Prose Poem* as a "Book of Truths" offered to the reader, "not in its character of TruthTeller, but for the Beauty that abounds in its Truth; constituting it true," pointed in the direction of a work suspended between the author's ideal of the self-sufficient poetic artefact and the contextual discursiveness of the essay. Poe's insistence that his "Essay on the Material and Spiritual Universe" should be considered as "an Art-Product alone: let us say as a Romance; or, if I be not urging too lofty a claim, as a Poem" (3) reflects the struggle between poetic ambiguity and the objective value of the essay that is still typical of many contemporary works of poetry written in prose. More recently, the influence of John Ashbery's *Three Poems* (1972) and Robert Creeley's *Presences: A Text for Marisol* (1976) on subsequent prose poetry works combining critical, philosophical, and lyric writing should not be underestimated.

Another poet interested in the possibility of a poetic détournement of expository prose is James Sherry, who, like Waldrop, is often associated with Language poetry. Sherry's collection, *The Marginal Arts* (1991), is addressed "to those who read paragraphs, to those who are aware of the various ways paragraphs can be collected and the reasons why" (11). Like Waldrop's *Lawn of Excluded Middle*, *The Marginal Arts* creates a body of thought that builds upon rhetorical contaminations between literary and nonliterary genres. Using concepts derived from the language of biology, thermodynamics, and nonlinear mathematics, Sherry — Sokal's caveats notwithstanding — follows the examples set by poet-mathematician Jacques Roubaud and others in reasserting the poet's right to address different levels of knowledge gathered by scientific conjecture, empirical observation, and experiment. Discussing his interest in atomic theory in his Preface to the book, Sherry writes: "people now think that the universe is composed of atoms and that these atoms have a nucleus. We have evidence at Hiroshima that is incontrovertible; the theory was made fact" (910). "In another sense," he continues, "atoms only exist as long as people use the concept. They exist as much as we use them and when we use them. Not that they stop existing when we stop using them. It doesn't mean that they don't exist. They exist in a nuclear context" (11).

Unlike Ron Silliman's "New Sentence," a mode of writing in which sentences are conceived of semi-independent units meant to resist the "syllogistic movement" (*New* 91) of prose, Sherry writes a relatively straightforward prose, at least on a formal, syntactic level. Instead of subscribing to the disjunctive poetics advocated by many other Language poets, *The Marginal Arts* preserves a certain amount of syntactic and narrative control, even as it tries to creates an interaction among the seemingly competing spheres of speculative and poetic discourses. More generally, Sherry craves for a poetry stripped of all the decorum and lyricism we associate with the Romantic spirit. His "self-portrait mirrored in theory" (11) results in a kind of writing that refuses to aestheticize itself: a poetry grounded in an engagement with the materiality of language that pays a critical homage to Wittgenstein's famous proposition that the "limits of my language mean the limits of my world."

The idea, evidenced in the works of Sherry and Waldrop, that poetry and philosophy involve commitments that are both dissimilar and complementary is also reflected in the poetry of Madeline Gins. Since the publication of her first book, *Word Rain* (1969), Gins has produced a number of important works that keep watch over the "mechanism of meaning," working on the assumption that knowledge can only exist as long as it brings to consciousness the specific conditions of our attempts to apprehend ourselves or the world "outside " the individual mind. In her most recent literary work, *Helen Keller or Arakawa*

(1994), the attainment of a vision beyond the outlines of the physically seen is both the occasion and the result of sensuous and intellectual awareness. The book, which is meant to enact a "sharing of nameless" [passing] through the words and images of Helen Keller and Arakawa and others" (304), contains a number of "composite" texts incorporating sources as various as Rimbaud's *Marine*, John Buchan's *The Moon Endureth*, and Swedenborg's *The Infinite and the Final Cause of Creation*, and Frederick Engel's *Revolution in Science*. Gins' recent installations and poetico-architectural projects around the concept of "Reversible Destiny" (conceived and carried out in collaboration with Arakawa) have produced an even larger compendium of methods for mapping the real and allowing architectural surrounds to inhabit the subject's as yet incomplete being. This Gins and Arakawa set out to achieve through a constant renewal and expansion of the mind's "thinking field" (*Keller* 9), a process of self-definition and self-rearticulation that suggests ways in which our cognitive apparatus might be liberated from conventional modes of apprehending space and time. Other recent works purporting to erase the boundaries between conceptual art and poetry include David Bromige's *Tight Corners & What's Around Them* (1974), a sequence of short, playful prose blocks "framed" by corners drawn around their first letter, and Robert Grenier's *Sentences* (1978), a boxed collection of 500 short poems printed on unnumbered 5 x 8 inch index cards. As for the typographical "distorted rooms" and truncated dictionary entries of Tina Darragh's *Striking Resemblance*, they appear as an interesting poetic response to Joseph Kosuth's photographic enlargements of dictionary definitions in the *First Investigations* series (1965).

THE POLITICS OF METAPHOR
AND THE ART OF MYTHOGRAPHERS

Dites-vous bien, lecteur ou lectrice, ou dis-toi bien (car à me lire tu deviendras de mes proches) que si je dis ici, c'est plus pour dire *que pour dire quelque chose.*
—Michel Leiris, *Le Ruban au cou d'olympia*

THE DISSOLUTION OF BOUNDARIES BETWEEN CREATIVE AND ESSAYISTIC WRITING advocated by Waldrop, Sherry, Darragh and other writers whose work is often identified with Language poetry has been confirmed by the recent adoption by Perelman and others of the expression "Language writing" (instead of "Language poetry") to define work produced by the movement or by writers associated with the "movement." In this respect, one of the lessons to be learned from such works as *The Marginal Arts* and *Lawn of Excluded Middle*, of course, is that poetic language can no longer claim to be truly impervious to the debates which have dominated academic thought for the last thirty years. The theoretical concerns that inform the speculative prose of Waldrop, Sherry and other experimental prose poets should conceivably prove congenial to academics engaged in deconstruction, critical theory, cultural studies and interdisciplinary approaches to art and literature. The relative paucity of critical material on their work, however, has the disquieting effect of reminding us that we still lack the critical vocabulary to reexamine the paradoxes built into some of the most interesting and ambitious work done in American poetry over the past few decades.

While the prose poets discussed so far seek to push the borders of poetic language by transcending the traditional split between poetry, philosophy, and science, others have written collections of prose poems which take the form of fables, parables, or "short short stories." Indeed, another important, and increasingly popular, direction taken by the genre concerns the possibility of reclaiming for poetry the storytelling functions of narrative fiction. The first generation American "fabulists" are Russell Edson and Michael Benedikt. Second and third generation fabulists include Margaret Atwood, Maxine Chernoff, Lawrence Fixel, Morton Marcus, Jack Anderson, Peter Johnson and Marie Harris. What they share is an ability to "[take] a metaphor and [pursue] it right through to make of it a story" (Ignatow 76):

PHANTOM PAIN

After the leg is lost, the pain remains as an emblem; so the kidnapper cannot part with his ransom notes. The high diver, lost on the subway, flexes his muscles defensively. The crowd fades to waves in a pool eighty feet below. "There," pointing to the nose of a seated passenger, "is where I'll land." The mad bomber turns to his wife and says, "I'll give up my career for you." She pictures his delicate bombs defusing, like scenes in a home movie played backwards. Meanwhile, the kidnapper, grown careless with sentimentality, drops a ransom note on the subway seat. The train conductor, who last night dreamed of a murderer, hides the note like a stolen pistol under his cap. Later the bomber stops at a diner full of known bombers. Anxious, he drops a coffee cup, white fragments exploding at his feet. (1)

Maxine Chernoff's own comments on the genesis of "Phantom Pain" (the opening piece of *Utopia TV Store* [1979]) insist on the necessity for the narrative prose poem to "exist independently [from the author's experience] by creating self-contained worlds." "The yoking of disparate elements such as 'phantom pain' and a kidnapper's lost ransom notes," she explains, is "characteristic of both metaphysical poetry and surrealist collage." Prose poems, she adds, are "a contemporary equivalent of metaphysical poetry, since in both cases metaphor can expand to become the central concept (conceit) of the writing." Finally, her choice of the prose poem form can be accounted for in view of her "attention to line breaks, syllables in a line, end rhyme and stanzas would limit or distract attention from the narrative development and metaphorical density" (Lehman 27).

Implicit in Ignatow's and Chernoff's comments is an interpretation of the genre as a compromise between the "metaphorical density" of the traditional lyric and the metonymic energy of the narrative mode. But it would not be too much to suggest that the use of metaphor in a seemingly "prosaic" context bears its own particular brand of richness and unexpectedness. The "metaphorical" content of "Phantom Pain," for instance, draws attention to itself at the same time as it is undermined by Chernoff's objective, matter-of-fact tone and the "fast forward" effect conveyed by the narrative. This intensification of the metaphorical within the prosaic is probably what the British critic Clive Scott has in mind when he writes that "metaphor in prose is more nakedly and alarmingly metaphorical than in verse. It is no longer one of a particular form's habits of speech, part of the act, but a figure born out of a reality that has no knowledge of such figures. Its power doubled by its borrowing the submissiveness of prose" (Bradbury & McFarlane 356).

Another type of fabulist poem is characterized by what the critic Donald Wesling calls a "narrative of grammar" (176). The first paragraph of the "Each Other" section in John Yau's *Edificio Sayonara* (1992) is not really a story dressed up as a poem but, rather, a poem that seeks to construe the movements of the speaker's mind into a story. The focus here is clearly on the intellectual "leaps" that allow the story to be told in a way that underscores the rhetorical "hardware" of both poetry and narrative:

> In the middle of the unfolding, neither yours nor mine nor ours, simply one of many we are in, we occupy (*Read*: standing, sitting, sprawling) different quadrants of a room, waiting for night's air to open its pockets, let us slip into its cubbyholes of respite. This story is true in this room, but not in the tropical breeze outside the sentences spelling it out, neon pulses crashing against the cranial area. You were speaking, though there is nothing to corroborate what I just heard, which was not you. I heard it nevertheless. We have reached the end of allegory, the thinking that makes this storytelling possible, and must now find a way to

understand the space between us cannot be filled, that we are on different sides of a window that neither opens nor shuts. (127)

Yau's interest in the "thinking that makes [the] storytelling possible" refers back to a tradition of self-reflexive fables which, from Max Jacob to Jorge Luis Borges, Henri Michaux, Italo Calvino, Julio Cortázar, John Barth and beyond, has put the emphasis on the telling of the tale rather than on the tale itself. Indeed, there is a sense in which Yau's "Each Other" can be read as an application of the postmodern technique known as "metafiction" to the art of poetry writing. Another recognizable feature of this kind of prose poem is a foregrounding of form and discourse. As suggested by the image of "the tropical breeze outside the sentences spelling it out," the Poetic Word becomes, in Yau's poem, literally decapitalized, words are turned into verbal objects within and against which the poet evolves a new estranging poetry out of the elaboration of form. In the works of Yau, Lawrence Fixel, Lydia Davis and others, the prose poem seems to have veered in the direction of what Derrida regards as the basic constitutive feature of Maurice Blanchot's "récit," *The Madness of the Day*, a narrative staked on "the possibility and the impossibility of relating a story" (*Acts* 234).

The fabulist mode has been used by different poets for different purposes. The best known representative of the "absurdist" school of the American prose poem is undoubtedly Russell Edson, whose hilarious post-Freudian family romances and fairy tales are collected in such books as *The Very Thing That Happens* (1964) and *The Wounded Breakfast* (1985). Michael Benedikt's *Mole Notes* (1971), another early example of the so-called "American prose poem revival," combines an extraordinary level of literary experimentation, urbane wit, black humor, metapoetic playfulness and rhetorical sophistication with the raw energies of Surrealism. The immediate impression in reading Benedikt's prose poems is one of rhetorical control and intellectual authority, and yet the overall sense of indeterminacy present in many pieces contained in *Moles Notes* often seems to undermine the poems' aspirations to rationality and seriousness. Out of that dialectic of self-defeating authority the prose poem becomes a form of shared play, one that allows imaginative open-endedness to prevail. As for Charles Simic's Pulitzer Prizewinning *The World Doesn't End*, it is indebted to what the author calls the art of "mythographers" (Popa 7), a form of writing that mixes the strategies of myth and humor and encourages readers to discover the metaphorical potential of everyday objects. Unlike historians and, to a lesser extent, chroniclers, "mythographers," Simic explains in his Preface to Vasko Popa's *Zivo Meso* (1975), disregard the totalizing power of grand narratives and prefer to work with fables, parables, nursery rhymes, riddles and other "minor" genres. While the prose poems of Benedikt and Simic show the influence of French masters of the form such as Max Jacob, Pierre Reverdy and André Breton, the "short shorts" of Margaret Atwood and Richard Kostelanetz point back to Donald Barthelme's metafictional games and, by way of pre-postmodern predecessors, have more to do with the prose tradition of, say, Franz Kafka's *Ein Landarzt* or Jorge Luis Borges' *Ficciones* or even with the nonliterary tradition of the standup comic than with any poetic tradition as such. More generally, however, the importance of parody and humor in many prose poems of the narrative or fabulist variety allies these poets with a line of postwar writers who, like Kenneth Koch, have learned "the possibility of being funny and lyrical at the same time" (Hoover 111).

THE PROSE POEM AND THE NEW LYRIC: WRITING POETRY IN THE AGE OF PROSE

The poet is a radio. The poet is a liar. The poet is a counterpunching radio.
—Jack Spicer, "Sporting Life"

Outside the sky is hanging by the composition of he who eats eats first with we will sell you. and this ever you, and ever this ever you, and ever of you this and. my love speaks about the overpass. my love speaks about newark. my love speaks through the merging traffic. especially with the radio on.
—Lisa Jarnot, *Some Other Kind of Mission*

Lyric? In which the winged body turns a tight circle, trying to outmaneuver and write through the built-in pornography & propaganda of official language.
—John High and Thoreau Lovell, "Gentle Reader"

Expecting poems to remind them of fragrances
They make too much of a bunch of flowers
—Nick Piombino, "Dans le jardin des plantes"

This was the source of my anxiety as I thought to write to you: how to make [oneself] invisible in [one's] words without resorting to the rhetoric of invisibility.
—Michael Davidson, "The Imperative of Fact"

Poetry is like a swoon, with this difference:
It brings you to your senses
—Charles Bernstein, "The Klupsky Girl"

An important aspect of Perelman's attempt to chart poetry's current status in "The Marginalization of Poetry" concerns the "marginal vs. mainstream" dichotomy and how it manifests itself in the antagonism between the experimental or "undecipherable" poem and the so-called "experience poem, the / mostly free verse descendants of Wordsworth's spots / of time: first person meditations where the / meaning of life becomes visible after / 20 or 30 lines" (9). For the last twenty years, Perelman's own poetry has worked towards refiguring the reading habits of those who still expect a "poem" to be a relatively short piece of writing dealing with the expression of intimate feelings or meditations and written in a style that somehow distinguishes itself from "plain prose" (often through the use of a metaphorically or imagistically charged diction).

What interests me here is the thorny issue of the survival of the lyric mode in view of the overall rejection of poetic sentimentality and poetic decorum which largely characterizes modern poetry (or, at least, the "marginal," "nonstandardized" tradition represented by Perelman himself). One possible explanation for the lack of interest of American poets in the traditional "epiphanic" lyric taught in most MFA programs is suggested by Marjorie Perloff: "If American poets today are unlikely to write passionate love poems or odes to skylarks or to the Pacific Ocean, it is not because people don't fall in love or go birdwatching or because the view of the Pacific from, say, Big Sur doesn't continue to be breathtaking, but because the electronic network that governs communication provides us with the sense that others too many others are feeling the same way" (*Radical* 2023). Why, indeed, should we read lyric poetry when we can get our Romantic sentiment and panoramic vistas from Hollywood movies, CNN newsreels or wildlife documentaries? At a time when our need for lyricism is being catered to by the public language of advertising and major motion pictures, poetry seems no longer concerned with how to express personal emotions, and many innovative works produced in the last thirty years seem to confirm Oscar Wilde's dictum that "all bad poetry springs from genuine feeling."

A comprehensive survey of the different uses to which the prose poem format has been put since the early 1970s would have to consider an extremely broad spectrum of forms and methods ranging from Ron Silliman's "New Sentence" narratives in *Ketjak* (1978) to the streetwise philosophical lyricism of John Godfrey's *Where the Weather Suits My Clothes* (1984), the speculative sensuousness of Aaron Shurin's *Into Distances* (1993), Sheila Murphy's enigmatic haibun (a form consisting of a prose paragraph followed by a single haiku of a varying number of syllables) in *A Sound the Mobile Makes in Wind* (1998), or Harryette Mullen's *Trimmings* (1991), a brilliant alliteration and pun-ridden Steinian investigation of feminine clothing and "the ways that the English language conventionally represents femininity" (69). Despite their many differences, however, all the examples cited and discussed here implicitly propose a definition of "poetic" language which is neither based on stylistical decorativeness and sophistication, nor merely based on a sense of lyric intimacy. Because of its tendency to accommodate and appropriate antithetical genres and discourses, the prose poem indeed offers a useful alternative to the aporia of lyric discourse in the late twentieth century, and it is hardly surprising that many Language poets have often used the form to expand the possibilities of subjective or "internal" modes of expression. The following quotes are from major collections by some of the best-known Language poets — have limited myself to the first lines/sentences of the first poem of each collection:

Not this.
What then?
I started over & over. Not this.
Last week I wrote "the muscles in my palm so sore from halving the rump roast I cld barely grip the pen." What then. This morning my lip is blisterd.
—Ron Silliman, Tjanting

I am often conscious, yet rain is now visibly falling. It almost combines to be one thing, but here I am again. Though he dreamed he was awake, it was a mistake he would only make at a time like that. There are memories, but I am not that person.
—Bob Perelman, a.k.a.

(I had wanted to begin slowly. A seed cracking next to my ear, slowly. My head sinking deeper into the pillow, mimicking any pressing tone of voice.) The world on the other side of the pillow was flesh. I would never come to the point. Words empty these standings without you three feet away, I remarked inkily, drowning my fingers in ink.
—Carla Harryman, Animal Instincts

> I had inferred from pictures that the world was real and therefore paused, for who knows what will happen if we talk truth while climbing the stairs.
> —Rosmarie Waldrop, *The Reproduction of Profiles*

> I do not understand what you are saying. No, I understand you perfectly. You are speaking American English, and that is my tongue.

> Sketching, a pencil nudges the subject out of place. A shaft of light is a profile of dust in the late afternoon, citizens bearing our luminous shapes on their backs. A portrait is compelling, though not so mutable as the face across which it plays.
> —Tom Mandel, *Realism*

> I wrote words on the brow of home and around the corners of its mouth — waiting for those days which wait for life to engulf them. The silhouettes of Pompeii were made and excavated for me. I take them personally. If embarrassed by my work, I turned to satire.
> —Stephen Rodefer, *Passing Duration*

What these works have in common — besides a highly self-reflexive, "metapoetic" stance — is an awareness of the complexities of narrative as well as of the irremediable fissure between the writing and the written self. With their emphasis on the difficulty of "speaking in a state of fidelity to the subject" (Harryman 32), the poets cited here conceive of poetry as an art of intellectual patterns that deliberately puts the subjective premises of the lyric between quotation marks. By giving us access to the changing present of the poet's consciousness, they write a kind of "preemptive" lyric that focuses on the self's strategies of self-expression and therefore anticipates and invalidates possible objections to the poem's sentimental or "epiphanic" orientation (including the assumptions of direct, natural apprehension of the real implied in the formulaic romanticism of the "expressive lyric" [Watten 33]).[*] Indeed, an important consequence of this project is to prevent the I-speaker from

---

[*] As Ann Lauterbach recently pointed out, the focus on the writing process and the presence of a certain amount of retrospective irony in many "language-oriented" works are meant to curb the lyrical or sentimental orientation of (semi-)autobiographical poems. Responding to Perelman's observation that Ron Silliman's work "seems autobiographical, even though the narrative is focused more at the tip of the pen than in the memory of the writer," she writes: "What I understand you to mean / is that emotionallycharged subjects / like sleeping with another woman / or the death of a loved one are / admissible only if or when they are in some sense / objectified, made ironic, or held in check by / clearly demarcated formal structures" (Lauterbach 20).

reaching any definitive (read: passive or "readerly" in the Barthean sense) "revelation" such as a regular "workshop poem" — of the kind described above by Marjorie Perloff — would surrender: the epiphany or revelation, when it occurs, remains primarily rhetorical in form and content. (This effect, it should be added, has ceased to be truly subversive as it now depends on the reader's recognition of an anti-lyrical stance that has become characteristic of a certain form of Language writing.)

Though none of these "postlyrical" features can be said to pertain exclusively to the prose poem format, it seems to me that the genre's longstanding affinities with the art of autobiography or diary writing have facilitated the methodological move that made it possible for poets to call into question both the business of reading (lyric) poetry as "authentic" and that of reading autobiographical fiction as "fictional." This "autobiographical" strain of the American prose poem is most apparent in such works as Lyn Hejinian's *My Life* (1980; rev. and exp. ed. 1987), Bernadette Mayer's *Studying Hunger* (1975), Hannah Weiner's *Clairvoyant Journal* (1978) or Erica Hunt's unsigned and untitled "letters," all of which attest to a sustained effort to create a language of the self that has not been coopted by the all-engulfing powers of corporate media, while pointing to a repositioning of the self within the social. One of the most thought-provoking insights one can derive from the works of these writers concerns the possibility of seeing in genre subversion the mediation of effective political praxis. Lyn Hejinian's "poetic autobiography," *My Life*, in particular, is a good example of how the lyric can be revitalized by the disjunctive narratives of Silliman's "New Sentence" and enriched by a larger vision of the collective reality of which it is part.

Poised between the center and the margin, the public language of prose and the private realm of the lyric, the prose poem problematizes the linearity and coherence we have been taught to expect from most histories of modern poetry and urges us to explore those axiomatic forces that shape literary tradition, as well as the world outside the text. From the writer's perspective, it can be argued that many poets have turned to the prose poem form because it tends to liberate the mind, as well as the words, from restrictions of predetermined formal or generic context. As we have seen, the question often remains that of whether the physical and metaphorical sense of language that is allowed to dominate in poetry can interfere with the forward-moving, truthbearing continuity of prose (and, as some Language poets would argue, its taken-for-granted "transparency") in an interesting and innovative way. Hence, I think, the preoccupation of many prose poets — at both ends of the mainstream vs. experimental spectrum — with the dialectics of the lyric and the narrative, the metaphorical and the literal, the gratuitous and the instrumental, the emotional and the rational, the natural and the artificial, the personal and the social. We could debate the merits or demerits of each of the poets cited in this essay, but that is not the point. The point is that they all testify to the way non-poetic discourses are increasingly attributed to the realm of poetry — not just to add a few items to the agenda of so-called experimental or innovative writers, but to change the terms of their agenda and make it compatible with particular changes in social and cultural life. As the works of Waldrop, Sherry, Hejinian and others demonstrate, the prose poem as an inherently self-reflexive and transgressive genre has come very close to performing the "self-critical" move described by Perelman as "a step toward a more / communal and critical reading" (10), one which seeks to absorb all levels of experience and continues to enact the engagement between consciousness and world.

WORKS CITED

Barthes, Roland. *A Lover's Discourse: Fragments*, trans. Richard Howard. New York: Hill & Wang, 1978.
Benedikt, Michael. *Mole's Notes*. Middletown, Conn.: Wesleyan UP, 1971.
Bernstein, Charles. *Content's Dream: Essays, 1975-1984*. Los Angeles: Sun & Moon P, 1986.
Bromige, David. *Tight Corners & What's Around Them*. Los Angeles: Black Sparrow P, 1974.
Chernoff, Maxine. *Utopia TV Store*. Chicago: The Yellow P, 1979.
Darragh, Tina. *Striking Resemblance*. Providence, R.I.: Burning Deck, 1989.
Delville, Michel. *The American Prose Poem: Poetic Form and the Boundaries of Genre*. Gainesville, Fl.: UP of Florida, 1998.
Derrida, Jacques. *Glas*. Paris: Denoël, 1981.
-------. *Acts of Literature*. Ed. Derek Attridge. New York: Routledge, 1992.
Edson, Russell. *The Very Thing That Happens*. New York: Harper and Row, 1976.
-------. *The Wounded Breakfast*. Middletown, Conn.: Wesleyan UP, 1985.
Elmslie, Kenward. *26 bars*. Calais, Vt.: Z Press, 1987.
Gins, Madeline. *Word Rain*. New York: Grossman/Viking, 1969.
-------. *Helen Keller or Arakawa*. New York: Burning Books/EastWest Cultural Studies, 1994.
Gins, Madeline, and Arakawa. *Reversible Destiny*. New York: Guggenheim Museum Publications, 1997.
Godfrey, John. *Where the Weather Suits My Clothes*. Calais, Vt.: Z Press, 1984.
Grenier, Robert. *Sentences*. Cambridge, Mass.: Whale Cloth P, 1978.
Guest, Barbara. *The Countess of Minneapolis*. Providence, R.I.: Burning Deck, 1976.
Harryman, Carla. *Animal Instincts*. San Francisco: This Press, 1989.
Hejinian, Lyn. *My Life*. Los Angeles: Sun & Moon, 1987.
High, John. *The Sasha Poems*. San Francisco: 3300 Press/Juxta, 1996.
High, John, and Thoreau Lovell. "Gentle Reader." *Five Fingers Review*, 11 (1992).
Hoover, Paul, ed. *Postmodern American Poetry*. New York: Norton, 1994.

Hunt, Erica. "Dear Dear"; "Dear"; "Dear." In *The American Tree: Language, Realism, Poetry*. Ed. Ron Silliman. Orono, Maine: National Poetry Foundation, 1986: 437-40.

Ignatow, David."A Dialogue at Compass." *Open Between Us*. Ed. Ralph Mills, Jr. Ann Arbor: U of Michigan P, 1980.

Lauterbach, Ann. "Lines Written to Bob Perelman in the Margins of *The Marginalization of Poetry*". *The Impercipient Lecture Series*, 1.4 (1997): 13-23.

Lehman, David, ed. *Ecstatic Occasions, Expedient Forms: 85 Leading Contemporary Poets Select and Comment on Their Poems*. Ann Arbor: The U of Michigan P, 1996.

Mac Low, Jackson. *Pieces O'Six: Thirty Three Poems in Prose*. Los Angeles: Sun & Moon, 1992.

Mandel, Tom. *Realism*. Providence, R.I.: Burning Deck, 1991.

Mayer, Bernadette. *Studying Hunger*. Bolinas: Big Sky, 1976.

Mullen, Harryette. *Trimmings*. New York: Tender Buttons, 1991.

Murphy, Sheila. *With House Silence*. Exeter: Stride Press, 1987.

-------. *A Sound the Mobile Makes in the Wind*. Electronic chapbook. Available in electronic form at http://www.unf.edu/mudlark.

Perelman Bob. *a.k.a*. Great Barrington, Mass.: The Figures, 1979.

-------. *Virtual Reality*. New York: Roof, 1993.

-------. *The Marginalization of Poetry: Language Writing and Literary History*. Princeton: Princeton UP, 1996.

-------. "A Counter Response." *The Impercipient Lecture Series*, 1.4 (1997): 36-46.

Perloff, Marjorie. *Radical Artifice: Writing Poetry in the Age of Media*. Chicago: U of Chicago P, 1991.

Poe, Edgar Allen. *Eureka: A Prose Poem*. New York: Prometheus, 1997.

Popa, Vasko. *Chair Vive et Coupure*. Paris: Circé, 1997.

Rodefer, Stephen. *Passing Duration*. Providence, R.I.: Burning Deck, 1991.

Scott, Clive. "The Prose Poem and Free Verse." *Modernism: A Guide to European Literature 1890-1930*. Ed. Malcolm Bradbury and James McFarlane. London: Penguin, 1991.

Sherry, James. *The Marginal Arts*. Los Angeles: Sun & Moon Press, 1991.

Shurin, Aaron. *Into Distances*. Los Angeles: Sun & Moon Press, 1993.

Silliman, Ron. *Tjanting*. Berkeley: The Figures, 1981.

-------. *The New Sentence*. New York: Roof, 1989.

Simic, Charles. *The World Doesn't End: Prose Poems*. New York: Harcourt Brace Jovanovich, 1989.

Strauß, Botho. *Beginnlosigkeit: Reflexionen über Fleck und Linie*. Munich: Hanser Verlag, 1992.

Waldrop, Rosmarie. *The Reproduction of Profiles*. New York: New Directions, 1987.

-------. *Lawn of Excluded Middle*. Providence, R.I.: Tender Buttons, 1993.

Watten, Barrett. "The Bride of the Assembly Line: From Material Text to Cultural Poetics." *The Impercipient Lecture Series*, 1.8 (1997).

Weiner, Hannah. *Clairvoyant Journal*. Lenox, Mass.: Angel Hair, 1978.

Wesling, Donald. *The New Poetries: Poetic Form since Coleridge and Wordsworth*. Lewisburg: Bucknell UP, 1985.

Yau, John. *Edificio Sayonara*. Santa Rosa: Black Sparrow Press, 1992.

Stephen-Paul Martin

MEDIA/COUNTERMEDIA: VISUAL WRITING & NETWORKS OF RESISTANCE

I

ALTHOUGH VISUAL WRITINGS OF VARIOUS KINDS have been around for thousands of years, they have played a very different role in twentieth-century poetry than they did in the caves of Altamira and Lascaux. Especially since the mid 1970s, visual literature has functioned in an increasingly subversive manner, offering readers an interpretive situation that encourages forms of perception and awareness which differ radically from those induced by mainstream communication networks. And unlike other forms of avant-garde or progressive literature — whose significance can be situated in academic debates and arenas — the visual writings of the past thirty years have not found their way into MLA Conventions and graduate seminar rooms. Rather, such writing has placed itself within its own networks of production, distribution and interpretation, functioning more as part of an alternative community than as an intellectual commodity. Taking the counter-cultural ideals of the late 1960s quite literally, the visual poetries of the past thirty years have sustained themselves through methods that implicitly refute both the logic of late capitalism and the academic process of appropriation that has turned the "radical" writings of the twentieth century into material for doctoral dissertations. What is visual writing? How is it situated within various networks of interpretation and distribution? In what ways do these networks function as a system of resistance?

Visual writing is an aesthetic activity that emphasizes the visual aspect of the written word. Where conventional literature focuses primarily on the meanings and in some cases also the sounds of words, visual literature is concerned mainly with language as a system of graphic signifiers, with the shapes and textures of words, syllables, and individual letters. In some cases, these visual messages are balanced with well-developed narrative patterns that may involve the plot/character/setting strategies of conventional fiction. Other visual writings contain elements of conventional poetry — suggestive phrases, complex images, syllabic wordplay — which are presented in visual patterns and/or juxtaposed with visual images. Some visual texts contain no complete words, working with syllables, letters, and parts of letters, often combining them with graphic, photographic, xerographic or computer-generated visual art of various kinds. There are also visual texts that contain no verbal elements at all and challenge the assumption that a clear line can be drawn between literature and visual art.

Many visual writers work with collage techniques, juxtaposing fragments of pre-existing verbal and visual messages to produce a new text whose significance goes beyond — and in some cases undermines or interrogates — the original meanings of the texts that comprise it. Fragments of newsprint may be combined, for example, with a line of Renaissance poetry, a map of Antarctica, a xeroxed paper clip, and the letter Q enlarged five times. Such procedures reflect the modernist belief in artistic experimentation, the need to mix the materials of composition in unforeseen ways to create aesthetic objects that are not mere replications of extant cultural forms. If previous artistic traditions were parts of historical patterns that culminated in nightmares like Auschwitz and Hiroshima, then there is no morally acceptable reason to continue those traditions without thoroughly questioning their basic assumptions. In this sense, visual writing can be seen as an oppositional practice, a means of encouraging modes of apperception that work against the destructive motions of the past.

What are these modes of apperception? How do visual writings encourage us to develop them? There are many ways that these questions can be addressed. My approach will initially involve a contrast between coercive and noncoercive communication: between images and messages that try to manipulate the audience's attention for the purpose of selling a product, image, idea or lifestyle (asking us to function as consumers), and texts that impose nothing on the reader but the responsibility to participate in the production of meaning (asking us to function as creators).

I will assume that most readers are already familiar with the machinations of the mainstream media. As an example of noncoercive communication, I would like to consider a purely visual text, a work that originally appeared in a 1979 issue of *West Coast Poetry Review*, Loris Essary's "Poem at Pt. Reyes":

Stephen-Paul Martin

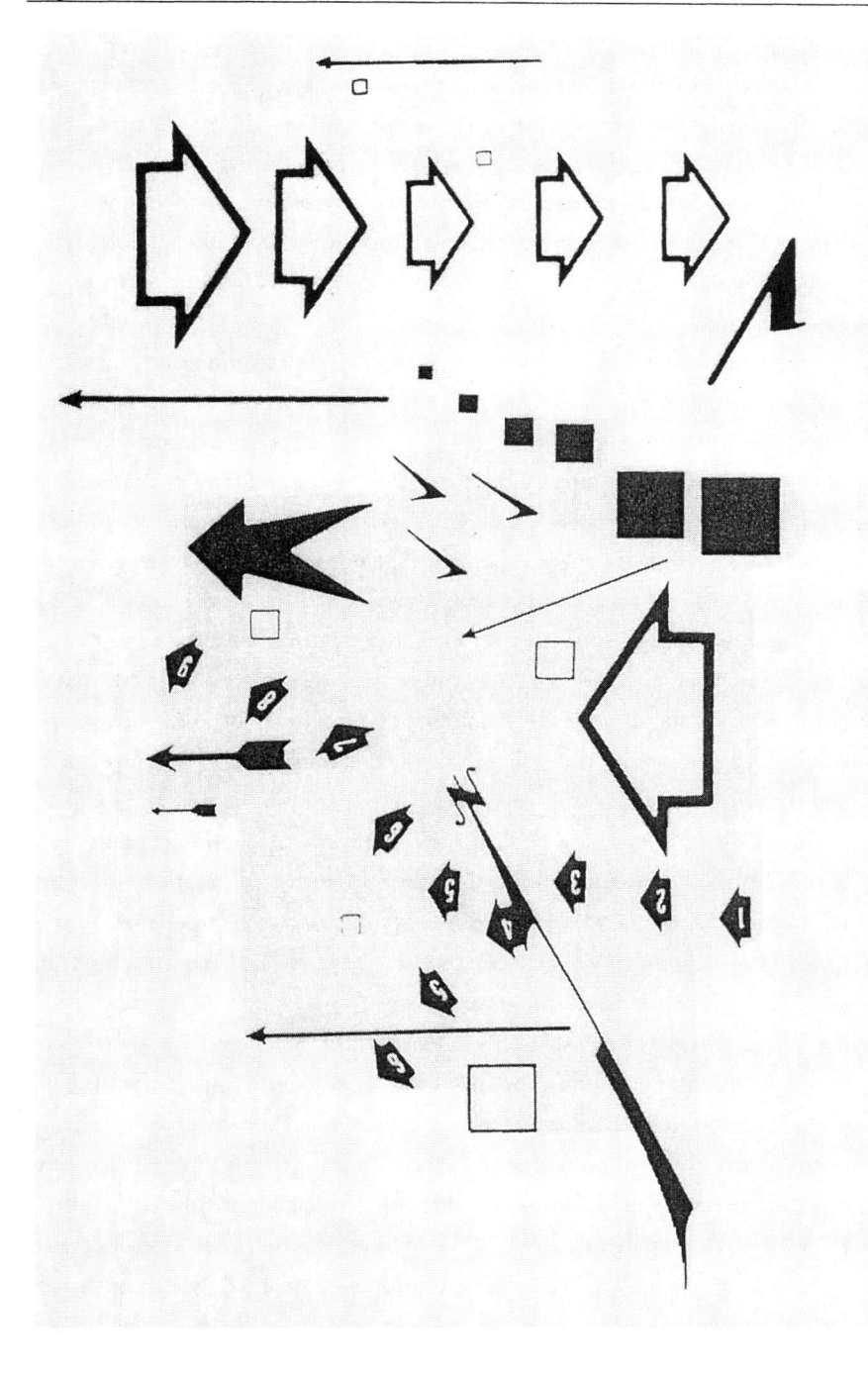

POEM AT PT REYES

Note that Essary's title is not "Poem *about* Pt. Reyes" or "Poem *on* Pt. Reyes." This text is neither a description nor a discussion of the scenic national park north of San Francisco. Essary's poem exists outside the discursive or representational functions that language normally serves, and it therefore asks us to develop interpretive strategies that differ from those that characterize our responses to novels, newspapers, TV shows, or even conventional poems. As Essary himself suggests, in working with writing like this "we must again become the child who is just learning to speak about a world he is just learning to discover" (Kostelanetz 97).

Essary's poem returns us to the very basic processes that determine our perceptual engagement with a moment of experience. Instead of referring us to some event or activity that is not actually part of our immediate situation, "Poem at Pt. Reyes" asks us only to be aware of what we are doing as we interact with its visual signals. Although the poem is exact in what it offers us, presenting itself as a tangible system of shapes, motions, volumes, and sizes, it does not forcefully determine the nature of our response. We are given the opportunity to decide what we want to emphasize, how we want to move our eyes across the page, and whether we want to systematically explain the poem's meaning or just enjoy it as a visual sensation. Our eyes are free to assemble their own pattern of significance. They are not forced to contend with the manipulative techniques of ads, movies, and romance novels. In becoming again the child who is just learning how to organize a moment of experience, we gain access to a process that is buried deep in the past and has been thoroughly obscured by what we have been forced to absorb in our interactions with mainstream communication procedures. Instead of the trite images of youth that Hollywood and Madison Avenue so relentlessly jam down our throats, we re-experience what is perhaps the most important event of early childhood — the gradual acquisition of the ability to organize our spatio-temporal situation.

According to studies by psychologists like Jean Piaget and L.S. Vygotsky, a child is not born with the same sense of space and time that adults customarily function with. This sense of spacetime has to be developed or learned through a gradual process that is roughly coterminous with language acquisition. Using words, children single out separate elements, replacing the natural structure of the sensory field with artificially introduced linguistic constructs. They begin to experience the world not only through their eyes but also through speech, and the immediacy of "natural" perception is supplanted by a complex and evolving process of mediation. Time and space begin to take a socially determined shape under the influence of language. To some extent, of course, this is an absolutely necessary transformation and represents one of childhood's crowning achievements. But it also means that even our most basic acts of perception are determined by the structural and conceptual biases of our culture. Our eyes see what they have been trained to see, and in our current situation this training takes place under the manic and seductive influence of mass communication.

The power of Essary's poem comes in part from the fact that it is not one of those objects we have been trained to see. It asks us to *learn* how to see it, and to be aware of the interactional agendas that inform our learning procedures. As we begin to formulate a response, we reactivate those energies that allowed us to learn how to shape our experience when we were children. These energies, to paraphrase Vygotsky, are what make us human and distinguish us from other animals. Unlike dogs and horses, children are capable of reconstructing their perceptions, detaching themselves from the basic elements of the sensory field. Working with the indicative function of language, children begin to master their attentional focus, generating new structural centers in the perceived situation. Again, the importance of this ability to reconstruct should not be underestimated, since it may well have been the single most important quality that allowed our species to survive on the East African savannahs two million years ago. But this restructuring capacity has been exploited by our media system. Instead of being allowed to master our attention, we are inhabited by covert ideological signals that master our attention. The value of "Poem at Pt. Reyes" is that it invites us to reclaim our apperceptional focus, to return to those fundamental motions by which as children we learned to reconstruct what we experienced.

But Essary's image is not just a childhood memory. When we work with it as adults, the situation is more complex. In addition to that very valuable energy we can reclaim from our first years as people, we also become aware of those culturally induced presuppositions that separate us from what we are looking at. Using this poem in literary theory classes over the years, I have found that most students are frustrated at first because "Poem at Pt. Reyes" does not conform to several deeply rooted literary expectations:

1) a poem is supposed to be a pattern of words and not a configuration of visual signals;

2) a poem is supposed to refer to something outside itself — its meaning, however complex, should be subject to paraphrase;

3) a poem should tell us something definite about its author, containing in some way an indication of her conceptual intention or emotional condition.

Essary's poem challenges us to move beyond such expectations, learning to value situations that ask us to be actively involved in shaping what we experience, and to appreciate those poems that offer us difficult interpretive challenges. Such texts generally give us very little if we assume that there is already a fully articulated meaning on the page and that our job as readers is to "find" or "decode" it. "Poem at Pt. Reyes" insists on a reader who is willing to interact with it as a collaborator, someone who is eager to work with what the author has provided in the production of a meaning that does not fully exist until the collaboration takes place.

Of course, such participation is important in reading most poetry, even supposedly simple works like Robert Frost's widely sentimentalized "The Road Not Taken." But with visual poems like Essary's, the demands placed on the reader are much more extreme. How can we even begin to "read" a poem that has no words in it? If we cannot use traditional (or even high modernist) categories of interpretation, what should we replace them with? We either have to accept "Poem at Pt. Reyes" on its own terms, in which case it remains absolutely mysterious, or impose our own agendas of perception, in which case we run the risk of turning it into something it's not. It is between these options, in the tension they create, that we most fully experience the meaning of Essary's image, a meaning cannot be conveniently summarized and exists more as a locus of energy than as an idea.

This brings me back to a question I sidestepped earlier. If the significance of wordless visual texts cannot be abstracted from the shapes and patterns that comprise them, how do such texts differ from certain kinds of abstract visual art, which use similar compositional strategies? Is "Poem at Pt. Reyes" a poem simply because its author says it is, because he regards himself as a poet and not as a visual artist, because the work was composed to appear on a page and not in a gallery, because a good portion of the author's aesthetic output could more easily be classified as literature than as visual art?

As a poet who has produced visual texts that more or less resemble Essary's, I can easily respond to this question by saying that I don't care whether "Poem at Pt. Reyes" is classified as poetry or as visual art. I can enjoy it without categorizing it. But as a critic of visual writing — someone who is expected to at least try to provide cogent explanations — I'm uncomfortable, not sure why Essary's text should be called a poem. Because he has *chosen* to call it a poem, I'm intrigued by the critical task of trying to understand his decision. But if he had not provided a title (a common practice among visual writers) and if the text had appeared in a visual arts journal instead of *West Coast Poetry Review*, would I have been inclined to call it a poem?

Perhaps the simplest approach to this difficult question is to examine the traditional need for distinct categories like "literature" and "visual art." As the visual poet Jake Berry bluntly claims, "The literary and the visual are the same thing applied in two different ways due to the neurosis of categorization . . . Should we remove the categories each naturally participates freely in the experience of the other" (Byrum and Hill 25). Seen from this perspective, the uncertainties that arise when we try to classify a work like "Poem at Pt. Reyes" are not separate from its textual meaning. To a certain extent, the poem was composed to question the distinction between verbal and visual art, and by extention to suggest that only the most fluid and provisional boundaries between genres and disciplines will serve a productive purpose.

Another critical problem involves the pleasure I get from "Poem at Pt. Reyes," and why I might not get the same degree of pleasure from a another wordless visual text. Am I justified in saying that the former is better or more significant than the latter? If I can explain my preference convincingly enough, if I have enough institutional power as an editor or professor, and if I have enough friends and allies with such power, can I turn my preferences into "the definitive aesthetic judgements of our time"? Critics throughout the twentieth century have tried to justify their aesthetic preferences, establishing canons and hierarchies, distinctions between major and minor writers (or significant and insignificant writers, or serious and popular writers) as a means of formally organizing the study of "serious" literature and consolidating their power and influence in various intellectual/academic arenas.

Since my purpose here is not to interrogate the rampant corruption that characterizes literary politics, it will be sufficient at this point to say that one of the crucial aspects of visual writing over the past thirty years has been its non-canonical, non-hierarchical mode of operation. There are no "major" visual writers, no "authoritative" anthologies, and no critic-wars about how visual writing should be interpreted. Instead, readers will find a wide variety of magazines and presses that function as a kind of alternative communication network, appealing primarily to those interested a different kind of information than what is typically presented in the corporate media or the academies. Such magazines and presses are generally produced with very little money, are traded through the mail rather than sold in stores, and have almost no connection with or interest in the economics of mainstream publishing. There are very few power-hungry visual writers and critics because there is essentially nothing to be gained from rising to the top. In fact, the very notion of rising to the top would seem nonsensical in visual-writing circles because there is no top to rise to.

In this context, the crucial question is not "Is it good" or "Is it significant" but rather "What kind of communication process does it encourage" and "How will it help me live with more intelligence". My personal answers to these questions vary from text to text, and would no doubt be different from the responses of Bob Grumman, Dick Higgins, Karl Young, Richard Kostelanetz, Harry Polkinhorn, or any other visual writers who enjoy discussing the significance of their practice. In contrasting a noncoercive text like "Poem at Pt. Reyes" with the coercive strategies of mainstream communication networks, I am obviously adopting a "political" frame of interpretation that would probably appeal to Polkinhorn more than it would to Grumman, Higgins, Young, and Kostelanetz. But the point is not to determine whose theory will "win out" in the long run, but to appreciate the different perspectives that are available, and to learn as much as possible from all of them.

II

As I mentioned earlier, the term *visual writing* refers to many different kinds of texts. Though all of them emphasize the graphic function of language, they do so in such diverse ways that it almost seems foolish to subsume them all into one category. Many visual poems, like the Richard Kostelanetz text below, involve a simple and often playful rearrangement of a word or group of words:

```
           N
           Y
           M
           P
           H
           O
         M   M
         A   A
         N   N
         I   I
         A   A
```

Though such poems may seem at first to be mere verbal jokes that present no serious interpretive challenge, they nonetheless indicate that words contain hidden possibilities, that the way we normally interact with language — reading line after printed line moving left to right down page after page — is a massive reduction of the almost limitless permutations available to us once we set aside our standardized models of what language is supposed to look like on a printed page. Simply by making "nymphomania" take the position of a woman spreading her legs, Kostelanetz reminds us that the customary linear presentation of printed words reduces language to a sequence of abstract signs that look nothing like the people, places, things, ideas, and actions they refer to.

Another method of taking language out of conventional linear patterns involves erasing or blotting out sections of an existing text to produce a new work. A widely-admired example of this is *A Humument*, a treated Victorian novel produced by the British visual artist Tom Phillips. Working with a sentimental nineteenth-century romance called *A Human Document*, Phillips has used each page as a canvas, producing an entirely new work in which brief verbal messages appear in the midst of full-color abstract paintings. The narrative prose of the original text becomes in Phillips's treatment a sequence of epigrams, poetic images, and fragmented episodes. On page 104, for instance, against a brilliantly colored background of mountains, blue sky, clouds, and vaguely human figures, we find these words, left visible in a number of different positions: "describe/ a/ballet/for/ changed/characters /from some inaccessible/ yesterday." The words refer, of course, to the very process of transformation that originally produced them, to the act of appropriating language that was initially intended to serve commercial purposes and relocating it in a context that calls for aesthetic contemplation.

This strategy of appropriation is also at work in Spencer Selby's *Malleable Cast*. Each page of this book is a combination of two pre-existing messages, one visual and one verbal. In general, neither message can be fully perceived. Each interferes with our clear perception of the other, and in many cases both the words and pictures run off the edge of the page. Still, we can see and read enough to determine that many of these messages seem to be ideological statements of one kind or another, drawn from the scientific, economic, aesthetic, political, psychological or promotional processes and disciplines that have constructed our social experience over the past five hundred years or so.

Removed from their original contexts and relocated in Selby's book, these messages can be seen as what they truly are — fragments of instrumental discourses that need to be questioned, not simply absorbed. At the same time, they become in *Malleable Cast* parts of a new context defined by their relationships with each other on individual pages, by their connection with the images on the other pages in the book, and by the position of the book itself in a community of readers committed to and informed by various traditions of critical intelligence. One of the most striking of these images is reproduced on the next page:

478   *The World in Time and Space*

schizophrenia — with the emergence of an immediate promiscuity and the perpetual interconnection of all information and communication networks. No more hysteria, or projective paranoia as such, but a state of terror which is characteristic of the schizophrenic: too great a proximity of all things, a foul promiscuity of all things which beleaguer and penetrate him, meeting with no resistance, and no halo, no aura, not even the aura of his own body protects him. In spite of himself the schizophrenic is open to everything and lives in the extreme confusion. He is the obscene victim of the world's obscenity. The schizophrenic is not, as generally claimed, characterized by his loss of touch with reality, but by the absolute proximity to and total instant

Even if the reader does not know that the words in this image are taken from Jean Baudrillard's discussion of the schizophrenia induced by mass communication, the verbal aspect of the text is suggestive enough to generate compelling critical questions: What does the donkey sitting on a top-hat playing a horn surrounded by dancing sprites have to do with the words that have been superimposed on it? Why has Selby chosen superimposition rather than juxtaposition as a compositional strategy? Why has he presented the words in such a way that many of them cannot be clearly deciphered? What does the picture itself represent? Further questions would arise if we considered this image in relation to other similar images in *Malleable Cast*. But just on its own, Selby's visual text leaves readers with a number of difficult interpretive problems.

In response to the first question, at least two directions can be taken, depending on whether the reader recognizes the source of the superimposed verbal text, Baudrillard's post-structuralist classic, *The Ecstacy of Communication*. Those who have not read this book are left with the task of determining the relationship between a strange picture and a number of evocative phrases ("extreme obsession," "characteristic of the schizophrenic," "proximity of all things," "meeting with no resistance," "not even the aura of his own body," "in spite of himself," "the world's obscenity," "by his loss of touch with reality," "absolute proximity"). For the reader familiar with Baudrillard, the situation is less open-ended. Such a reader will know that the phrases above refer to Baudrillard's idea that schizophrenia is the normal condition of people forced to confront the manic bombardment of mass imagery on a daily basis. Is the donkey playing the horn a symbol for mainstream communication? Do the dancing sprites represent our society, caught in superficial enchantments? Is the strangeness of the image — donkeys don't usually play music and sit on hats — a reflection of the absurdities we are so accustomed to from the media? Does the donkey refer to medieval legends about the Devil taking the form of a goat or donkey and compelling imps or demons to dance by playing music? If so, is Selby telling us that mass information is the Devil's music? Or is the image an ironic reference to the countless books and articles that describe the mainstream media as a destructive (Satanic) influence on society?

Such questions may help us establish an interpretive foothold in Selby's image, but their uncertainty is not rhetorical, since there is no way of knowing whether they have any firm connection with the author's intention. Of course, we're on shaky ground when we talk about the "author's intention" in a text like this, which is composed of two works that were not originally produced by the author. Whose text is this? Should Spencer Selby be considered an author when his compositional materials were created by other people? Certainly Selby can be credited with producing a new image, not just because he was clever enough to combine the originals, but also — and primarily — because of *the way* he has chosen to combine them. But this does not mean that Selby had a specific message in mind, nor does it mean that he has an authoritative relationship to the text's meaning. Though he probably has strong opinions about how the text might be interpreted, these need not be taken as definitive. As with "Poem at Point Reyes" and the verbal fragments in *A Humument*, the reader is asked to function as a collaborator instead of a consumer, given a large degree of responsibility in producing the meaning of a text that will offer very little to people who prefer to absorb information passively.

An important point to consider is Selby's decision to *superimpose* Baudrillard's writing on the picture. While this strategy makes it difficult to read some of the words, it forces us to see that language in the age of information is often presented in a visual context, just as visual images are generally accompanied by verbal messages. Throughout *Maleable Cast*, verbal and the visual elements build on *and* undermine each other to such a degree that neither has meaning independent of the other. The result is an interference pattern that forcibly reminds us of the multi-layered complexity of both human awareness and the communication environment it has created, a situation in which we have no pure experience of anything. There is always something above, beside, or beneath what we are thinking, feeling, and perceiving, always something infecting, blurring, contaminating, or in some way altering what we think we know. As we look at something, our visual sensations are always already inhabited by what we may have been reading recently, or by gum jingles, the obnoxious chatter of top-forty DJ's, masturbation fantasies, the moral lectures of self-deceived relatives, passages from the *National Enquirer*, or all these things at once, inhabiting us as an indistinct combination that can only be experienced as noise. Selby's texts are pictures of noise, yet they do not reproduce it. They allow us to study noise in silence, to reflect on it carefully, to gain critical distance from it. Ironically, Baudrillard's words tell us that the schizoid condition is the result of our inability to get critical distance from the mass information that assaults us. Does this mean that Selby's work offers us a therapeutic experience, an antidote to invasive mass-produced noise? And if this noise is a tool of repression, a means of jamming our mental signals, then doesn't the therapeutic effect of studying *Malleable Cast* have political implications?

I know Spencer Selby personally, and I'm confident he would reject the interpretation I've just offered. Yet it will be difficult for anyone reading these words to look at Selby's image without being affected by my response to it. A new text has been created, an interference pattern whose meaning exists somewhere between *Malleable Cast* and this page.

III

In the summer of 1988 I received in the mail a copy of a periodical with a split personality, two magazines in one: issue number 31 of *Photostatic*, a magazine of visual texts; issue number 4 of *Retrofuturism*, a magazine of commentary on visual texts (July, 1988). The former appeared on the inner two-thirds of each page, the latter on the outer third of each page. Edited in Iowa City by three visual writers and performance artists (Lloyd Dunn, John Heck, and Paul Neff) the focus of both magazines was "Plagiarism." Most of the *Photostatic* visual texts were xeroxed (or "plagiarized") reproductions of previously published images and messages of various kinds, attributed not to the original authors or artists but to the people who had copied them. Most of the *Retrofuturism* commentaries were written in support of plagiarism, echoing in one way or another Lautreamont's assertion: "Progress is necessary; plagiarism implies it."

On the cover of the magazine was a handwritten "Manifesto of Plagiarism" which consisted of two declarations: "I. Any plagiarism constitutes an exhibit of my artwork. II. Anything being done with, done to, or made by any kind of photocopy machine constitutes an exhibit of my artwork." This text was attributed to John Heck, who apparently "composed" it by "using work stolen from Christopher Erin," whose signature appeared beneath the manifesto. Beneath Erin's signature: "(c) Copyright 1988 The Thrillhammer Foundation. Except with permission this manifesto may not be used in any form including verbal. It doesn't matter where you get the permission." In the lower right-hand corner of the page, the phrase "by the Tape-beatles" appeared, diagonally rubber-stamped in red ink. Who were the Tape-beatles? Nowhere in the issue was their identity fully explained. But in a visual essay called "Plagiarism: A Plan for Your Future" the Tape-beatles ironically defined themselves as "the locus where the avant-garde and popular culture meet" and added that "the Tape-beatles as culture are obliged to negate themselves."

Mildly amusing nonsense? Yes. Perceptive commentary undermining several of the most fundamental economic and psychological assumptions of mainstream art and publishing? Yes. The issue was entertaining, but it was also interrogating established notions of seriousness, authorship, authority, cultural property, creativity, originality, and bookmaking, to name only a few of the issue's central concerns. As I laughed at the editors' twisted sense of humor ("(c)Plagiarism: After all, it's *our* idea"), I was reminded of many significant developments in twentieth-century aesthetics and social theory, of Walter Benjamin, Theodor Adorno, Herbert Marcuse, and other neoMarxists of the Frankfurt School, of absurdist playwrights like Ionesco and Beckett, of the politico-aesthetic initiatives of the Situationists, of the subversive humor of avant-garde movements like dadaism and surrealism, of the Happenings of the 1960s, of the intermedia events of the Fluxus artists, of *The Mechanism of Meaning* (an ongoing sequence of epistemological canvases and architectural constructions generated over the years by the visual artist Arakawa and the writer Madeline Gins), of the interventionist posters and actions of groups like Artfux.

Underscoring the entire issue were its modes of production and distribution: the xerox machine and the postal system. Produced in Lloyd Dunn's apartment on a Macintosh computer, reproduced in a copy center, each copy cost less than a dollar to produce *and* mail. Most of the visual texts in *Photostatic/Retrofuturism* (*P/R*) were the result of collage techniques involving scotch tape and scissors. There were no expensive materials to buy, no prestgious galleries, editors or agents to impress, no distributors and bookstores to make arrangements with, no rigidly established aesthetic standards to conform to. Instead, *P/R* and hundreds of other magazines like it were interested only in sharing ideas, perceptions, and information.

Much of the work published in *P/R* was bluntly oppositional. Consider this collage by John Stickney, which appeared in *P/R*'s "Cultural Property" issue (November, 1988):

Stephen-Paul Martin

WE ARE YOUR OCCUPIED TERRITORIES

Unlike the poems of Essary and Selby, this text generates little or no interpretive uncertainty. Instead, it issues a firm challenge to the invasive procedures of mainstream communication. The newsprint surrounding the eye clearly suggests that our minds are "occupied territories," colonized by the endless barrage of mass information. The newsprint is a collection of torn strips, indicating that what we are occupied by is not information but noise, a garbage dump of sound bites whose overall function is not to persuade us of anything in particular but to destroy silence and make sure no clear thinking takes place.

On the facing page was a simulated ad for a FESTIVAL OF APATHY. This phrase was accompanied by what looked like a 1930s Soviet propaganda poster picturing two men fighting, surrounded by the ironic slogan: WORK FOR NOTHING/FIGHT FOR FOOD. Beneath this was a partial list of questions, beginning with 11 and ending with 69, including: "Do most people do what words tell them to do? Are you paying attention only to these words? When your inner voice speaks, are any of your own thoughts also being spoken?"

On the next page was an image of an Aztec pyramid with a block of text superimposed on its base: "Images are indispensable for the construction of the technological society. If we remained at the stage of verbal dialogue, inevitably we would be led to critical reflection. But images exclude criticism. It is so much easier to let myself be carried along by the continually renewed waves of images. Images are essential if I am to avoid seeing the day-to-day reality I live in".

Though the authors are listed elsewhere in the issues, their names do not appear on the text pages, and instead of considering these texts as individual pieces we are encouraged to see them as interwoven images, an uninterrupted flow of messages that replicates the bombardment of mass information — but with an important difference. Unlike the promotional nonsense that comes at us from the corporate media, the texts in magazines like *P/R* can be carefully studied. Because they exist in "silence and slow time," they encourage us to reflect quietly, to produce the critical intelligence that "images exclude." Yet because they are presented in a way that emphasizes their connectedness, we can see that no text exists in isolation. Its significance is always determined by the context in which it appears. A *Time* magazine article on starving children in Africa is not really separate from the Toyota Camry ad that precedes it or the Jack Daniels whiskey ad which follows it. Toyota and Jack Daniels are not only financing the information in the article; they are surrounding it, separating the tragedy of famine from its true context and relocating it in placeless world defined by commercial images.

In *P/R* the context is carefully controlled to undermine the pseudo-contexts generated by the relentless flood of consumer images. Each text is thoughtfully placed to consciously comment on every other text, and since there is no need to please advertisers, the editors are free to make sure that the messages they publish interact in a way that is not only coherent but also challenging. Even if individual texts in *P/R* are not as difficult or open-ended as those discussed earlier, developing a full understanding of their interconnectedness requires an engaged reader.

IV

CRUCIAL IN ANY DISCUSSION OF VISUAL WRITING IN THE PAST THIRTY YEARS is the method by which it has been distributed. Because such work has virtually no commercial value and those who publish it cannot afford to pay for distribution, it is generally not available in bookstores. Since its importance has not been widely recognized in the academies, students will have trouble finding it in libraries. Most visual writing has been distributed through the mail or (more recently) on the Internet. This "underground" method of finding readers is inexpensive, free of censorship and other forms of institutional control, and gives writers and readers easy access to each other, creating a network that functions freely on its own terms, without the market pressures that determine and limit the activities of mainstream publishing.

As editor of *Central Park* magazine during the 1980s and 1990s, I was part of a network that included not only visual writing but also politically radical magazines, newsletters, and publishers of various kinds. I frequently traded issues with editors of "zines" like *Photostatic/Retrofuturism*, and many of these zines provided information about other zines and books, making it easy to keep expanding my connections with like-minded people all over the world. It was rare that a week went by without an interesting new publication or book arriving in the *Central Park* mailbox.

Several years ago, a book arrived from somewhere in Maine (I couldn't decipher the postmark) with no author or title. There was no publication data anywhere, except on bottom of the final page, where I found "No International Standard Book Number. No Library of Congress Catalog Card Number. No Copyright. • **00% Recycled.**" Clearly, the book had not been processed by the mainstream machinery of validation and authenticity. By "recycled," the anonymous author apparently meant that the contents of the book had been xeroxed from other sources. But even using a term like "contents" was problematic in this case, since the front page was a "Table of Contexts," of aesthetically designed situations that transmitted not meaning (contents), but opportunities for interpretive interaction. In fact, the emphasis on reader participation was explicit, since on the book's cover were the words "Your Name Here" and an arrow pointing to a blank line, inviting readers to inscribe their own names and become the book's mutiple authors. Surrounding this blank line were hundreds of transparent books, suggesting that every reader would "author" her own see-thru version of the text. Were the assumptions of post-structuralist theory being jammed down my throat, or was the absent author ridiculing these assumptions? Or both?

I was immediately interested. Though I wanted to find the author's name, I also recognized that the book was asking me to critically examine my need to connect a text with an author and a title. On the Table of Contexts page was a list of chapters that indicated a forty-two-page introduction, a ten-page list of "Editions to which reference is made," and a text of nearly eight-hundred pages. The book itself was only FIFTY-SIX pages long.

The text was a series of pages xeroxed from other books. A few pages were presented in their entirety, but most of them had been cut up and used as elements in collages. Many of the original texts were apparently academic or scientific discussions of the reading process, reproduced as ironic indications of the endless intellectualizing that has occurred over the past thirty years about the reader's interaction with the page. For instance, on page sixteen we find "WHAT HAPPENS TO THE READER" and beneath this a drawing of a man suspended with tweezers over a surgeon's dissection tray. Below this is what appears to be a scholarly psychological discussion of memory and visual perception. Next we find three xeroxed pages with blurred or disfigured words, indicating the kinds of distortion that invariably occur when we read. Or are these pages ironically commenting on the academic concern (for example, Harold Bloom's well known *A Map of Misreading* or the reader-response theorizing of critics like Wolfgang Iser) with the distortions inevitably built into the act of reading? My initial response was to take the text at face value, as an indication of the reader's importance in creating textual significance. On second reading, however, it occurred to me that the book was not simply pointing out that all reading is misreading, but also establishing ironic distance from this idea, and from academic theorizing in general.

Yet as I re-examine the book now, I find its collage techniques so compelling that I want to take them seriously, to enjoy them as explorations of the page as a site of visual-linguistic transformation. When the nameless author focuses on "The Page Within the Page" and connects a mangled page with the insights of Chaos Theory, I'm fascinated by the notion of depth within an apparently flat surface, and by the expanded space such depth promises. At the same time, the presence of scientific instruments suggests that the author may feel contempt for people who take an overly cerebral approach to the reading process.

How does this wonderfully bizarre book end? With a xeroxed sequence of pages being turned, followed by an image of books on a shelf, one of which seems to be a much larger version of the work we have been reading. We are no longer on the road with Kerouac; we are in the stacks, or on the net. There is no escape from the textuality of the world we have created for ourselves, no escape from the printed page, even if that page has become electronic. All we can do is learn to respond with intelligence, with critical distance, to the inevitability of information. Yet ironically *The Book* (as it is finally called on the last page) asks us to critically distance ourselves from the process of critical distancing. Though it playfully refers to itself as "A 'Think & Do' Book," a work that calls for an active reader, the author seems to be skeptical about the ultimate value of the sophisticated, self-analytical postures so many postmodern readers have been trained to assume. Still, *The Book* is not just an ironic response to what Susan Sontag once called "the Age of Criticism." It is also a textual sequence that visually demonstrates what happens when a poem deepens the page, when we read down into the unseen zones of significance words contain.

V

A BASIC ASSUMPTION OF MANY VISUAL WRITERS who contribute to network magazines is that realism as an aesthetic strategy makes sense only if we view reality as a fictional construct, a grammar of invasion and exploitation, a coercive combination of images and messages controlled by a few huge corporations. While this situation is oppressive in ways that have been thoroughly described by media critics over the past thirty years, it can also be viewed as an opportunity if we refuse to accept mass communication on its own terms and view it instead as a source of aesthetic raw material. Many visual writers pay close attention to what they see on picture tubes and billboards, not because they take them seriously as sources of pleasure and information, but because they feel that a realistic response to the world can only be developed by appropriating mass images and messages and relocating them in a context that calls for critical examination.

An interesting example of this is Paul Zelevansky's *Shadow Architecture at the Crossroads*, a text which not only appropriates the language of invasion and exploitation but also uses it as a basis for an extended fictional narrative. Unlike the texts discussed above, *Shadow Architecture* is a novel, though not the kind one is likely to find in a supermarket check-out line. Working with collage techniques, Zelevansky sets many different stories in motion. But "the words are staged," presented through various distancing strategies that ask us to see how a pattern of linguistic artifice develops. We are not compelled to "lose ourselves" in the motion of the narrative or to "identify" with characters. Instead, we are given the chance to think about what happens when we confront a highly elaborate system of signs.

Zelevansky's system of signs is in some ways a satirical imitation of mainstream communication procedures. Just as our social environment has been replaced by an electronic barrage of commercial messages, in *Shadow Architecture* the setting is not a place but a "crossroads," a network of images. If mass communication offers us personalities instead of people, Zelevansky works with icons and stick figures instead of characters. The four main icon/characters in *Shadow Architecture* seem to represent four basic roles that people are allowed to play in the narratives of mass information. The Trackwatcher sits passively watching trains passing through the crossroads, much as many people sit passively watching their favorite media personalities. Instead of being presented through a series of thoughts and actions that might allow us "to get to know him as a character," the Trackwatcher is identified primarily through a slogan ("We keep our eyes and ears open"), as if to say that in mass culture private experience is orchestrated (replaced) by an endless sequence of ideological platitudes

Another icon/character is The Pilot ("We form a link") who seems to be emblematic of the heroic postures mass communication offers us as symbols of public virtue. Like The Trackwatcher, The Pilot appears only as a picture that was obviously taken from a pre-existing source. In fact, both The Trackwatcher and The Pilot seem to be pictorial representations developed during the World War II era, when the U.S. government was busy trying to stir up patriotic fervor and a sense of civic duty. According to the formulas of our country's political economy at that time, one could either be a patriotic hero (The Pilot) or a dutiful consumer (The Trackwatcher).

But in a "democratic" society, where the notion of an open social dialogue is such an important part of our national self-image, people won't settle for a completely one-sided pattern of representations. The opposition must also be appropriated and reproduced as media simulation. Thus in *Shadow Architecture* we find icons of revolution: the activist and political subversive Ignacio Garcia (who appears as a picture of a person braving a storm with a lamp and a walking stick — and whose parents are a picture of Nancy Reagan and Charlton Heston) and the voyaging visionary, pictured as Saint Anthony (often represented by pictures of various artistic heroes — Kafka, Melville, Dostoyevsky, Van Gogh — and accompanied by a girlfriend, Tanya K., who is a picture of Emily Dickinson). As mass icons of opposition, these "characters" do little more than appear in subversive postures.

Saint Anthony travels and Ignacio Garcia lives underground, plotting. They have no noticeable effect on the Crossroads.

How could they? There is really nothing they could affect. The Crossroads, like our social environment, may seem to be a place, but is actually just a matrix of images. Anthony and Garcia are parts of that matrix, parts of the very same language they appear to be opposing. When all significant actions (and even the possibility of significant action) are subsumed in simulation, appropriated and reduced to a sequence of conventional images, very little can occur. The media functions as a kind of "electronic leash," domesticating our behavior with technological reproductions that encourage us not to live but to watch imitations of life.

The term "electronic leash" appears in *Shadow Architecture* as part of a simulated ad for a device that might be used to subdue "terrorists" like Ignacio Garcia:

new
THE ▲MARK OF CAIN®

From the ancient wisdom of the Old Testament to you, a remarkable, foolproof way to keep track of international terrorists, domestic criminals and their supporters.

☐ Send me full details.

name _____
firm _____
address _____

CROSSROADS NOVELTY CORP.
BUSINESS AS USUAL

ELC, a division of CROSSROADS NOVELTY, has now developed the <u>electronic leash</u> ®, a micro-transistor, which, when implanted in the forehead of a suspected or convicted terrorist or criminal, will keep him or her "in touch" and visible wherever they may go. The <u>electronic leash</u> ® sends out a pleasant, inaudible signal trackable by our patented <u>comehome</u> ™ homing device, which can be installed easily at airports, bridges, tunnels, train stations, embassies, banks or any place a wanted criminal might make an appearance or attempt an escape.

It really works!

The <u>electronic leash</u> ® is easily attached with a minimum of discomfort to the subject, comes in a variety of designer colors and is guaranteed for the life of the terrorist. There are <u>no</u> cords, <u>no</u> batteries to replace.

The <u>electronic leash</u> ®. If it was good enough for God, it's good enough for you.

Working ironically with the language of mail-order catalogues, Zelevansky juxtaposes the imagery of religious and political systems of authority to depict our government's attitude about terrorism. Just as God turned Cain into an outcast as part of an earlier narrative of power (the Old Testament) our present government labels those who oppose its brutalities "terrorists." The electronic leash, implanted on our foreheads where the third or inner eye might normally be, is a means of making sure that no one will react too strongly to anything our government does. Those who go against or outside the official (mediated) version of things become terrorists, people like Cain who have murderously sinned in the eyes of God.

Parts of *Shadow Architecture* are even more direct in their depiction of mass culture as a repressively deceptive enterprise. At one point, for instance, we are told that the news we "are about to receive takes place on a small shallow stage within a very large theater," as if to say that what we read in the papers or hear and see through the broadcast media really ought to be regarded as journalistic fiction. We are also told that news broadcasts are a covert means of promoting a certain world view:

> Before every murder, catastrophe, and foreign war, we stand condemned and practically impotent. This we are told on a daily basis.... The paternal voice on the radio, the familiar face on the screen both confirm this: "Today was sad, tragic, out of control. This is your world, you have made this happen. We are only reporting what we have seen." Is this news or propaganda?

The book ends with "The Seven Principles of Effective Management," where we are advised to "Make only what you can sell" and that "Freedom is a nine-letter word spelled MARKETING."

But to focus only on these blunt levels of critique would be to present *SA* in a misleading light. Though Zelevansky's incisive political sense of humor makes reading the book an entertaining experience, to fully come to terms with it we have to read actively, creating patterns of significance which for the most part are not spelled out for us. The layers of meaning and irony in *Shadow Architecture* work on both verbal and visual levels and represent a full-scale reappropriation of the imagery that dominates mass culture. Carefully articulated systems of imagery recur throughout the book. Possibly the two most revealing of these are focused on the signals we receive from postage stamps and penmanship manuals. By surrounding large portions of his text with the iconography of our postal system and with instructive designs that show children the "proper" way to form letters and numbers,

Zelevansky suggests that many of the signals that come at us from mass culture are extremely subtle and may not at first seem to be forms of communication. But as we work with Zelevansky's text, we begin to see that everything in our social environment communicates, and communicates (through) us. As Baudrillard has repeatedly pointed out, it is difficult to talk about human subjectivity at this point because our minds and senses have been so thoroughly appropriated. When we try to accomplish a goal, we see mental images of people in movies trying to accomplish goals (with the help of jump-cuts). When we get excited, top-forty music begins playing in our heads. Our nervous systems have been rewired to the point that it would only be a slight exaggeration to say that we ARE mass information.

The power of Zelevansky's book is that it appropriates both the form and content of mass communication and holds them up for ironic display. They are there to be studied and not just absorbed. Though *The Book* may convince us that "critical distance" is just another academic mannerism, *Shadow Architecture at the Crossroads* suggests that this critical distance may well be the only way to preserve even the semblance of sanity, a skeptical awareness that leads us to question the messages coming at us from both sides of our perceiving senses.

V

READERS WILL NO DOUBT HAVE NOTICED that I have been reading and selecting texts that allow me to present visual writing as a subversive activity. Other commentators would certainly object to this approach, claiming that visual writing ought to be studied on its own terms, as an aesthetic process. One such writer/critic is Bob Grumman, who has been directing The Runaway Spoon Press in Port Charlotte, Florida since the late 1980s. Working out of his parents' home, producing books on his own xerox machine for almost nothing, using a dead car kept under a carport as a storage facility, Grumman emerged as one of the most active publishers of visual texts in the world. Most of North America's visual writers published at least one title with Runaway Spoon, and though these books were not reviewed in the mainstream media, they were widely circulated and commented on in alternative circles. Magazines like *Photostatic/Retrofuturism*, *Factsheet Five*, *Taproot*, *nrg*, *Score*, *Kaldron*, *MaLLife*, *Atticus*, *Noospapers*, *Generator*, and the various publications of Xeroxial Endarchy in Madison, Wisconsin constituted a noncommercial network within which Runaway Spoon books and other visual texts were published and reviewed.

One of Grumman's aesthetic principles in establishing Runaway Spoon was to avoid anything overtly political. Though he has occasionally deviated from this mandate as a publisher, he has been careful to avoid social issues as a critic of visual writing. Instead he has taken up the practical task of developing a descriptive vocabulary for the interpretation of visual writing. During the late 1980s, his articles appeared in most of the journals listed above, and were ultimately revised and republished in book form as *Of Manywheres at Once*.

Readers interested in Grumman's work should be forewarned. It is not conventional literary criticism, and has none of the pretentions and polish of academic textual analysis. Writing as an individual with obvious biases and limitations, Grumman does not present himself as an authority, but as a "regular guy" who just happens to be interested in visual poetry. Though this non-intellectual stance may take some getting used to, it's ultimately refreshing, and entirely appropriate when we consider the nonconventional nature of the aesthetic material. Whereas much of the visual literature criticism collected in *West Coast Poetry Review #19* has a specialized academic quality, Grumman's commentaries are delightfully unprofessional, authentic in the sense that their occasional moments of awkwardness and confusion are the result of the uncertainties any honest reader will experience when trying to formulate an organized response to a visual text.

Faced with writings that defy conventional modes of interpretation, Grumman sets himself the task of developing a new interpretive vocabulary. His terminology is oppressive at times, almost an unintentional parody of academic literary obscurantism (okay, so he does have some of the pretentions of ivory tower critics). The danger here is that words like alphaconceptual vizlation, advertance, and segreceptuality may well come between us and our appreciation of a text, turning the reading process into a jargonized game. At the same time, such terms seem to be serious attempts to describe aesthetic experiences that don't fit into existing interpretive categories. Consider for instance this page from Harry Polkinhorn's *Summary Dissolution*:

> **for now until the**
>
> **spring returns with its**

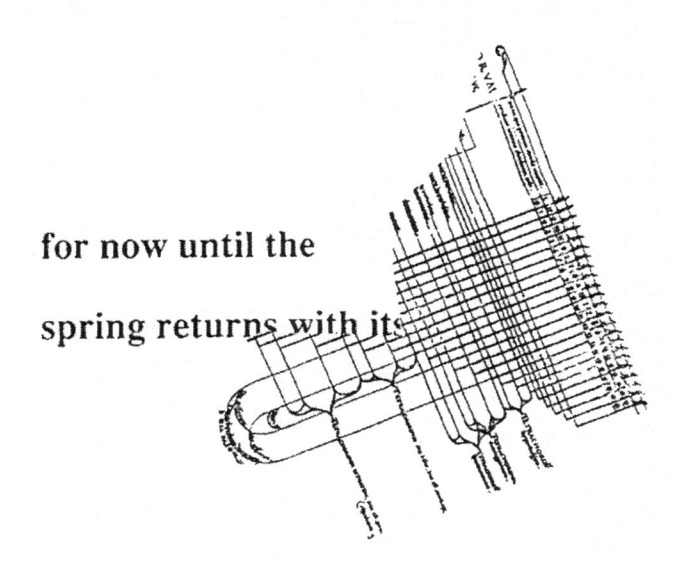

    This text is an example of what Grumman calls illuscriptation: "that which arises when verbal elements of semantic importance but little or no visual expressiveness are combined in an artwork with visual elements whose esthetic significance is comparable to that of the work's verbal elements." According to Grumman, Polkinhorn's commonplace evocation of spring "is comparable to" the diagram of tetrachords, the four-note sets that the traditional musical scale is based on. It is not difficult to see the parallel between the rebirth that takes place in spring and the power of music to reawaken dormant feelings. But the connection becomes more interesting when we realize that Polkinhorn is talking about waiting ("until") for the arrival of spring, just as his text delivers not music but a diagram of its underlying structure. The actual experience of spring and music is not on the page, nor is the author asking us to pretend that it is. Challenging the representational techniques that characterize most conventional writing, Polkinhorn's text reminds us that the map is not the territory, that we are looking at a blueprint.

    Yet the text is also more than a blueprint. As Grumman points out in his discussion, the verbal phrase disappears into the visual image at the very moment that it refers to the qualities spring transmits, as if the words were blooming into music. This is of course one of the primary effects of most poetry. But unlike the juxtapositions that characterize certain kinds of modernist poetry (imagist and surrealist writing, for example) the juxtapositions in *Summary Dissolution* force us to work in two different mediums, to mentally process words while connecting them to a message that asks for visual attention. Polkinhorn's use of musical imagery complicates the situation further, suggesting that we are somehow also hearing what we are seeing and thinking about (the emphasis on hearing is reinforced by the diagrams of the ear that appear throughout the book). Would it be fair to say that this combination of aesthetic faculties (the eye, the ear, the mind) is the text's primary "theme"? Perhaps. But this "theme" is inherent in, and inseparable from, the work's formal strategy, insisting on visual attention rather than offering the conceptual formulations typical of mental interpretive efforts. Like many self-referential modernist poems, Polkinhorn's text is a representation of its effect on the reader. But the aesthetic pleasure it offers is primarily visual, meaning that the text is a picture — and not just a description — of itself. It allows us, to borrow a phrase from the visual writer Jonathan Brannen, "to photograph the nativity of meaning," to create meaning in the act of reading, but also — and more importantly — to *see* what meaning is (Byrum and Hill 27).

Grumman and many other critics would say that this concern with meaning is primarily an aesthetic issue. I would agree if I were allowed to change *primarily* to *initially*. Though it may be our aesthetic faculties that allow us to make initial contact with the text and play with the possibilities of its significance, the activity itself has socio-political importance because it asks us to cultivate interpretive tendencies that are quite different from the hypnotic states encouraged by mass communication. A community of readers seriously pursuing this activity is in effect functioning as a network of resistance, even if those involved have no interest in mainstream party politics. What is being resisted? The colonization of our perceiving senses, the standardization of thought and feeling mainstream communication both produces and depends on, the passivity that we have been trained to equate with relaxation. Those who become involved in what Grumman calls the "otherstream," in the production and interpretation of texts that exist outside the commercial and academic arenas, are participating in one of the few oppositional activities that has not been thoroughly contaminated by the agendas of mass information.

Throughout the twentieth century, many artists have connected themselves with the romance of experimentation, the pursuit of a grail that will only exist if unforeseen textual experiences can be alchemically produced. As we move into the twenty-first century, most of that romance is gone, replaced either by virulent commercialism or by grad school seminars on "isms" of various kinds. Harry Polkinhorn recently complained to me that a renowned colleague of ours was teaching a graduate seminar on visual writing that excluded most of the visual writers he and I value most. His reasoning was that if a professor is going to pass herself off as an expert on visual poetry, she should at least be familiar enough with it to include representative writers. Because she chose to focus primarily on language-centered poets who don't even regard themselves as serious visual writers, many of the poets mentioned earlier in this essay lost an opportunity to reach new readers, and students who may never know what authentic visual writing is lost an opportunity to learn something new. I can see why Harry was angry.

But my response to the situation was that visual writing is not designed for seminar rooms, and that if it has not yet been absorbed by the academies, this may well mean that it is immune to appropriation, and has a chance to survive on its own terms, in its true context, in the oppositional networks and communities it serves.*

WORKS CITED

Byrum, John, and Crag Hill, eds. *Core: A Symposium on Contemporary Visual Poetry.* Generator Press and Score Press, 1993.

Dunn, Lloyd, and John Heff, eds. *Photostatic/Retrofuturism* (July and November 1988).

Grumman, Bob. *Of Manywheres at Once.* The Runaway Spoon Press, 1990.

Kostelanetz, Richard, ed. *Visual Lit Crit. West Coast Poetry Review* #19 (1979)

Phillips, Tom. *A Humument* London: Thames & Hudson, 1980.

Polkinhorn, Harry. *Summary Dissolution.* The Runaway Spoon Press, 1988.

-------, ed. "Visual Poetry: An International Anthology" *Visual Language* (1993).

Selby, Spencer. *Malleable Cast.* Generator Press, 1995.

Zelevansky, Paul. *Shadow Architecture at the Crossroads.* CNC Publications, 1988.

-------, ed. "Visual Literacy." *American Book Review* (Feb./March and April/May 1993).

---

*Those interested in the visual writing that developed all over the world in the 1950s and 1960s should consult the anthologies of Emmett Williams (Something Else Press, 1967), Jean-Claude Bory (New Directions, 1968), Eugene Wildman (Swallow Press, 1969) and Mary Ellen Solt (U of Indiana P, 1971). Historical discussions of visual writing and its origins are included in a number of articles published in *Visual Lit Crit*, a collection of essays published as issue #19 of the *West Coast Poetry Review*, guestedited by Richard Kostelanetz in 1979. A more recent collection of commentaries on visual writing is available in *Core: A Symposium on Contemporary Visual Poetry* (edited by John Byrum and crag Hill, published collaboratively by Generator Press and Score Press in 1993). Also of interest are *Visual Poetry: An International Anthology* (an issue of *Visual Language* guest-edited by Harry Polkinhorn in 1993) and the two *American Book Review* issues on "Visual Literacy" (February March & April May 1993) guest--edited by Paul Zelevansky.

Mary Margaret Sloan

OF EXPERIENCE TO EXPERIMENT: WOMEN'S INNOVATIVE WRITING 1965 - 1995

Boundayr

T his word, *boundary* in slight disarray, is the title of a 1987 poem by Kathleen Fraser. With one of the word's boundary positions altered by the transposition of its two final letters, a new word appears, two words, in fact: *bound air*. As our cognitive focus shifts to take in the new words, an unfamiliar set of possible readings also comes into view.

With our reading momentarily arrested, we can still "see" the familiar but now clouded word *boundary*. But, so altered, is the old word still there? Or has it become something else? Or is it now a hybrid, the old word and the two new words seen simultaneously? As our eyes focus and refocus among the options, the words' representations are also shifting. The boundary of a strictly corralled domain now wavers provocatively as we consider the new idea of *bound air*. What kind of boundary could air have: the walls of a cannister containing oxygen or a springing circlet of clouds surrounding a bit of blue atmosphere? The difficulty in visualizing what is signified by the hybrid words provokes questions regarding the linguistic sign, reading, writing, description, and poetry's ongoing concern with expressing the inexpressible. Other questions may drift at the edges. What is the nature of literary boundaries and the entities they describe, of forms, works, and genres, for instance? Are boundaries fixed, mutable, or permeable; are entities cohesive and homogeneous or dynamically fluid and heterogeneous? How do positionings of textual and poetic elements matter in light of these questions?

Fraser's experiment registers the shifting outlines of North American avant-garde poetics over the past thirty years. The rapid late twentieth century increase in experimental writing by women takes place within the broader contexts of twentieth-century avant-garde writing and the 1960s post-feminist expansion of all varieties of women's writing.

A few years before the cultural transformations of the 1960s accelerated, the publication in 1960 of Donald Allen's *The New American Poetry* indicated the changing relationship of avant-garde poetry to centrist canonical literary power, both sectors male dominated. Marjorie Perloff has noted that in the two decades preceding the appearance of *The New American Poetry*, "the canonical critical study of modernist poetry was Cleanth Brooks's *Modern Poetry and the Tradition* (1939)" which omitted avant-garde poets such as William Carlos Williams and gave short shrift to Ezra Pound. *Chief Modern Poets of Britain and America*, the most frequently used poetry anthology of the time, did not include Louis Zukofsky, Robert Creeley, John Ashbery, Alan Ginsberg, Frank O'Hara, and George Oppen.

During the same period, however, there were intimations of the eventual dissolution of a clearly fixed insider/outsider model of a literary world. Alan Golding has shown how, during the 1950s, avant-garde poetry began to gain visibility and influence when publications such as the "little" magazine *Origin*, edited by Cid Corman, gathered together a loose literary community of poets who had moved away from the literary practices favored by the canon. *The New American Poetry* corrects the omissions of *Chief Modern Poets* by including Zukofsky, Creeley, Ashbery, Ginsberg, O'Hara, and Oppen along with four women poets, Denise Levertov, Helen Adam, Madeline Gleason, and Barbara Guest. It presents, for the first time, a group of forty-four poets linked not by mainstream academic affiliation or sanction, but by shared extra-academic literary interests. Golding notes that even though by 1960 publications such as *The New American Poetry* signaled the eventual obsolescence of the center/margin model, the notion of a line bounding an inside from an outside remained, for the time being, useful as "an appropriate metaphor insofar as it reflects one means by which marginal and centrist poets of the 1950s defined their differences." Nevertheless, no matter what model serves for a given period, as Roman Jakobson pointed out in *Language in Literature*, any stage of temporal literary succession "discriminates between more conservative and more innovative forms."

Reflecting larger cultural orders, published women's writing remained relatively scarce until feminism reemerged in the 1960s along with the proliferation of other movements for social change. As the relative quietude of the post-war period began to erupt into a vociferous interrogation of all cultural norms, values, and constructs, issues of identity, including those of gender, ethnicity, class, and queerness, gradually began to appear in literary discussion. It is impossible to determine the quantity of writing by women that was actually being produced before that cultural revolution. But profuse evidence demonstrates that women's writing was being published far less frequently than men's. *The New American Poetry* has a ratio of eleven male contributors for each woman. If the male avant-garde poetry community of the 1960s represented Outside, then the female avant-garde would have to be considered outside Outside.

More than three decades have now passed. In the context of all recorded literary history those three decades are the merest blink; yet, as we open our eyes, the literary landscape has been transformed. Women avant-garde writers are now publishing work in approximately the same quantities as their male colleagues. Over the past thirty years, avant-garde anthologies have gradually included more and more women until in the 1990s, many collections represent women's work in nearly equal quantities as men's, and in a few cases, the works of even slightly more women than men.[*]

Although we cannot know if, during the 1960s, women writers actually began to produce more writing than they had in the past, they did become more active in the public realm of cultural and literary activity. Increasingly women writers began to make their own contributions to the practitioner-based publication and dissemination infrastructure that has long sustained outsider poetry production. They founded small presses and edited literary magazines; they organized reading series, workshops, symposia and other public venues for the circulation of writing they valued; they wrote about their own and other women's work, and, more rarely, on broader poetic interests including the work of male colleagues.[†]

At first, with their increasing visibility, women writers tended to be regarded by their most common and most unusual characteristic: that they were women. This regard served initially to eclipse their more significant characteristics as writers, that is, the variousness of their poetics. In fact, there were divisions among women writers at the outset. The particular distinction I want to investigate here coincides with the already existing center/margin

---

[*] A brief survey of the ratios of men to women contributors in a sample of anthologies of innovative writing over the last thirty years indicates this change. In *The New York Poets* (1970, edited by Ron Padgett and David Shapiro) there are twenty-six men to one woman. Michael Lalley's 1975 *None of the Above* has three men for each woman included. In both *In the American Tree* (1986, edited by Ron Silliman) and *Language Poetries* (edited by Douglas Messerli, 1987) there are two men for each woman. Similarly, the 1993 anthology, *Writing from the New Coast: Presentation* (edited by Peter Gizzi and Connell McGrath, includes nearly two men for each woman. By contrast, the 1994 anthology, *The Art of Practice* (Peter Ganick and Dennis Barone) includes a few more women than men, as does, in 1998, *An Anthology of New (American) Poets*, edited by Lisa Jarnot, Leonard Schwartz, and Chris Stroffolino.

[†] Important examples of such efforts include Rosmarie and Keith Waldrop's Burning Deck press; Maureen Owen's magazine and press, Telephone; Lyn Hejinian co-editing with Barrett Watten *Poetics Journal*; Rena Rosenwasser and Patricia Dienstfrey, Kelsey Street Press; Anne Waldman and Bernadette Mayer at various times editors of *The World*; *Mirage*, edited by Dodie Bellamy and Kevin Killian; *Raddle Moon*, edited by Susan Clark. In 1984 *HOW(ever)*, a literary journal devoted to publication of innovative writing by women and to discussion of Modernist women writers was founded in San Francisco by Kathleen Fraser. Later *Black Bread* was edited by Sianne Ngai and Jessica Rosenthal along with many other little magazines. Currently *Chain* is edited by Juliana Spahr and Jena Osman, *Tripwire* by Yedda Morrison and David Buuck, *Five Fingers* by Jaime Robles, *Lipstick* by Kathy Lou Schultz, to mention a few.

split among male writers. Many women, as they began to write and publish in greater numbers, made the historical fact of suppressed identity the central issue of their work. This focus on the subject of identity by some women poets generated work readily fit for absorption into a mainstream canonical model of the poem, while the aesthetic experimentation of other women writers ensured their affinity with the writings of another community, the community, as it was then, in the mid-1960s, of the avant-garde Outside.

Although the dominant canonical model of the poem, still prominent today, has frequently been described, I would like to recapitulate its characteristics here and to organize them into a slightly different conformation to distinguish it from lyric, now less a kind of poem and more a poetic attribute involving concordance of sound. The familiar canonical poem originates in a perspective of singular subjectivity. It uses normative grammar and unidirectional syntactical succession within a temporal frame to give account of a central human figure as it undergoes change from the start of the poem's narrative to its often ambiguous conclusion. It assumes hierarchies of discourse and distinctions among genres; its orientation is fixed, that is, it has a definite inside/outside and beginning/end, so its intrinsic coherence is firmly bound. Because of the manner with which the centrality of the subject places all other elements of the poem under its authority, I would like to redesignate this poem as one of dominion: it represents the reign of one person's revelation over the domain of data culled from the universe of his or her personal experience.

The individual experience of male poets publishing in the 1950s and 1960s (and for much of literary history) encompassed nothing less than the entire universe of experience authorized as of sufficient adequacy to support any sort of literary endeavor: that is, the outdoors, adventure, war, masculinity tests and heroism; the realms of art, history, philosophy, theology, politics, and the life of the spirit; of male engagement with erotic others nearly always explicitly women[*]; and the casual urban observations of the flaneur's descendants. Serious or comical impressions, private moments of reflection, subtle or startling epiphanies could all be registered while the poet was on horseback, driving a car, motorcycle, or pickup truck, while hiking, hunting or wandering, while sitting in his study, talking with friends in a bar, or while having sex. Personal experience worth writing about was based on direct knowledge of the valid domain of "the world," in which the male poet, particularly the white, middle or upper class male poet, was free to roam.

During a literary reign of personal experience, with what did women poets have to work? Since they were ideally restricted to the home and its daily data of tending, did

---

[*]Before Stonewall and the nationwide coming out of gays.

women's experience qualify them to write poems of significance? An answer is suggested in a widely circulated 1973 anthology of women's poetry, *Rising Tides: Twentieth Century American Women Poets*, edited by Laura Chester and Sharon Barba, published by Simon and Schuster. With ninety contributors, the book begins with Gertrude Stein and includes HD, Marianne Moore, Lorine Niedecker, Denise Levertov, Barbara Guest, Diane DiPrima, Anne Sexton, Adrienne Rich, Sylvia Plath, Kathleen Fraser, Marge Piercy, Erica Jong, Nikki Giovanni, and Anne Waldman. The generous editorial policy describes a broad range of poetic practices and makes the one criterion for inclusion, other than a literary career and book publication, appear to be feminine gender.

The editors' introduction invokes the smothering atmosphere into which women poets then issued their work. Chester and Barba's remarks must, of course, be read within the context of the prevailing social ideologies of the post-war period that precedes the publication of *Rising Tides*. In part as a feature of government-designed social policy at the close of the second world war to empty the workplace of women to make room for returning male military personnel, and perhaps also as an iconic return to the safe enclosure of a stable home after the fifteen year trauma of depression and war, the U.S. post-war period was characterized by national dedication to the cult of domesticity, with the role and proper place of its feminine guardians narrowly prescribed.

Nevertheless, the anxious tone of the editors' introductory apologia and plea is startling now, just twenty-five years later. "There continues to be an underlying social objection to women writing at all," they state, even though, post-1960s, "most people would be embarrassed to proclaim that woman's place is in the home." They remind the reader that "We are still not far from thinking that a woman should only make babies and casseroles, rather than books, and that the woman who chooses books is not a Real Woman." They cite a statement by the influential poet and critic John Crow Ransom that "women, like children, just can't write good poetry because they never really grow up." Most seriously troubling for the literary aspirations of women in an age of experience-based poetry is the editors' lament that, "The experiences of women are held to be narrow and unimportant compared to those of men, unsuitable for literature." They conclude with an appeal for permission to present "our lives seen through poetry" and the announcement that "Women must learn the self-love, the self-idealizing, the self-mythologizing that has made it possible for men to see themselves as persons."

If women were not widely regarded as "persons," even, as is suggested here, occasionally by themselves, it is reasonable and understandable that, in era when changes in the social construction of feminine gender were just beginning to occur on a culture-wide basis, some women poets would extend the general quest for legitimacy to the literary sphere. For non-persons or unauthorized writers of negated experience, the implied validation of self conferred by admission to the poem of experience proposed a logical and provocative direction. The knowledge, emotions and artifacts of the socially legitimate domestic realm of her household, a discrete domain over which she singularly prevailed, could readily refurnish the poem of dominion, causing little or no disruption to its extant form. Into it she could introduce "woman's experience," and hope to authorize it within the familiar, sanctioned poetic enclosure. The domestic realm could qualify as a small dominion.

Although we must read Chester and Barba's introduction as expressions of their individual perceptions and certainly as an anthological framing device not intended to fully characterize the work of all the contributors to *Rising Tides*, still, many of its contributors did, in fact, write poems which might be characterized as poems of dominion while frequently emphasizing a putative realm of feminine experience, frequently of domestic life. A sample of just a few titles from the beginning of the index indicates a focus on personal experience, and more particularly, on the personal experience of women: "The Ache of Marriage," "After Love," "Apples," "At the Gynecologist's," "Bitter Pills for the Dark Ladies," "The Common Woman," "Cutting the Jewish Bride's Hair," "A Cycle of Women, Decorating Problem."* Within the historical moment of an emerging cultural revolution, making a claim to poetic space for an excluded experience of otherness was of notable political significance, as were similar actions by diverse sets of others whose identities and experiences had also been excluded, literarily and otherwise.

Women's version of the familiar poem of Dominion, newly filled with domestic and other feminine experience, gained rapid acceptance during the early 1970s. As an indication of how quickly mainstream approval developed, when *Rising Tides* was published in 1973, of the twenty-eight of its contributors born between 1934 and 1949, (so, who were then in their twenties and thirties), 46% had already published books with major presses by the date of the anthology's publication. In contrast, the work of a comparable group of twenty one women poets, also born between 1934 and 1949, recently appeared in the 1998 anthology, *Moving Borders: Three Decades of Innovative Writing by Women* (edited by the author). These twenty-one, all now in their fifties and sixties, have focused their work not on personal experience but instead on experimentation in language, forms and genres. Throughout long careers which began contemporaneously with the writers in *Rising Tides*, their work has

---

*The respective authors of this list of poems are Denise Levertov, Maxine Kumin, Shirley Kaufman, Linda Pastan, Judy Grahn, Ruth Whitman, Sharon Barba, and Sonya Dorman.

appeared mainly in little magazines and small presses.[*] By the 1998 publication date of *Moving Borders*, that is, *twenty five years after* the publication of Rising Tides, only 28%, had been published by major presses. The price of the choice of and sustained commitment to the radical route has often been financial hardship, makeshift professional lives, and limited public visibility.

This publishing disparity points to a division within women's writing that quickly became apparent in the early 1970s, mimicking the inside/outside structure of the male literary world. On the one hand a "women's" poetry was developing which found its literary resources in the traditional models of mid-century poetry as practiced variously by, for example, Robert Lowell, Sylvia Plath, and Anne Sexton, and which concentrated its attention on the direct personal experience of the "I," now reconstituted as a feminine "I."

At the same time, experimental work by other women writers was appearing with ever-increasing frequency. In this work, which I think of as writings of inter•enactments, immediate experience shifts from the personal quotidian to the reading and writing of texts, to the investigation of meaning as constituted in language, and of aesthetic acts during a time when cultural structures were, and continue to be, undergoing large-scale transformations. These experiments generally shifted the focus of writing from a temporal succession of moments to a spatialized expanse of positions and relations. Perhaps this shift from the temporal to the spatialized is what Gertrude Stein prognosticates in "How Writing is Written" when she writes that "The thing has got to the point where poetry and prose have to concern themselves with that static thing. That is up to you."

In a writing grounded in static quasi-three-dimensional space, markers of position (in contrast to moments) logically become significant points of registration. At the most primary level of writing, *position* is the critical determinant of difference: within language, at the level of the letters which constitute words (for instance "bad" compared to "dab")[†]; within grammatical and syntactical orders, phrases and sentences, stanzas and paragraphs, and other locally discrete aggregates; between and among works; within languages specific to social, regional, technical, class, ethnic, professional and other distinct cultural groups; and within and between literary communities.

---

[*]It should also be noted that experimental writers also far less frequently received other material forms of recognition such as grants, prizes and tenured jobs than did the poets of experience. Only lately are a few beginning to receive some material and institutional support, that is, rewards other than their own satisfaction and the recognition of their peers.

[†]For further reading on the importance of difference in language see Ferdinand de Saussure, *Course in General Linguistics* (New York: McGraw Hill, 1959), and Roman Jakobson, *Language in Literature* (Cambridge: Harvard UP, 1987).

Within such a linguistic expanse, persons, and any number of other textual figures, circulate in spaces lacking fixed boundaries or divisions where occasions assemble and disperse. Change occurs as figures of the text shift positions or encounter boundary contests; change is focused not on a central character or narrator, but on the environment of the text and relations among its constituent elements. Figures undergo identity shifts within movements which are not necessarily linear or progressive, but which may just as often be cyclical, reflexive, or accretive. Narrative ceases to be a constant term; instead, segments of narrative may be distributed, as Carla Harryman has described, or factored out, leaving behind a discontinuous surface where narrative remnants interact on equivalent terms with other textual elements. Instead of the intrinsic coherence of clearly bounded entities such as word or subject, any quantum of the text may be involved in dynamic reciprocities and multiple influences. The dominance of a single perspective from a central subject position gives way to multiple perspectives and multiplicities of subject positions. These changed orders propose dispersal of central authority in favor of networks of influence, a disposing of hierarchical orders, the mobilization of fixed positions, and a fundamental reconsideration of how meaning is constituted in language and in aesthetic works. The networks of inter•enactments extend, finally, to the reader, who, in the act of reading, becomes a further influence on the text in its complex negotiations of effects of meaning.

What becomes of a self, a woman's self, for instance, in such a writing? The difference between a self as the inhabitant of a domain of experience and the possibilities of self as a constituent in a matrix of change is illuminated by Lyn Hejinian: "I have an experience of being in position, at a time and place, and of being conscious of this, but this position is temporary, and beyond that, I have no experience of being except in positions. . . . The person, in this point of view, is a mobilized reference point."

If the self is "a mobile reference point," what becomes of its universe, its medium, its genre, its writing? These questions suggest a very different kind of writing from that based on personal experience, rather, a writing that aims to destabilize boundaries dividing dominions of one from the other, of the home and the world, and by extension, to question the character of boundaries themselves and how the movement of things across boundaries from position to position changes all the relationships within given structures, however provisionally constituted.

For the purposes of contending with these issues, women experimental writers gravitated towards the resources of the avant-garde tradition, and, along with many male colleagues, created a body of aesthetic acts engaged in inter•enactments. The extent to which women have shown a special interest in matters of positionality in writing may have a simple explanation. In the late 1960s, some women deliberately initiated activity to change the relations between genders, that is, to change their own position in relation to the positions of men. Perhaps for this reason, activity and relationships among positions in literature have come to be of particular interest to women writers who chose less to register experience, than to enter into aesthetic experimentation.

In order to provide a brief sample of the writing I have described as that of inter•enactmnts, I have briefly sketched the works and interests of twelve women innovative writers.

Some of the writers described here are well-known, others perhaps less familiar. In place of those here summarized, I could just as easily have turned to a substantial number of other writers with long, well-established careers such as Barbara Guest, Rae Armantrout, Ann Lauterbach, Johanna Drucker, or Rosmarie Waldrop as well as to others with more recently established careers such as Laura Moriarty, Erica Hunt, Diane Ward, or Erin Mouré.

With each of the writers briefly introduced below, I have associated a list, necessarily incomplete, of other writers, whose work may lack surface or overall similarity, but who nevertheless engage one or more related interests or strategies of the writer with whom associated. Finally, at the end, I have listed names of other colleagues and younger writers whose work circulates within the same broad ethos as the twelve sample writers. As an expression of the intertwining of communities of interests, the sample below is merely suggestive. Many hundreds of names could have been listed; but as always, however provisionally, space has its limits.

ત ત ત

Carla Harryman:

>Not everything anyone ever wanted to say can fit here. Piles of excess are heaped at the borders.
>This is the game of minute resistance. Do not try to imagine how small but just keep minute resistance in mind. Doing so will appropriately limit your actions and you will be a viable player.
>You can play with others or by yourself. There is usually a motive for playing. A no symbolically related to a quantum no, a grand enfoldment of no. This

> small no, this no is symbolically related is what you are playing with. It is in the
> scale of meghom, and it has a life of its own. You, too have a life of your own.
> from "Meghom," *There Never Was a Rose Without a Thorn*

Carla Harryman's writing originates in her political activism during the late 1960s when, invited to membership in Students for a Democratic Society, she found herself, an intellectual, "subordinated to voiceless servitude." She left immediately, immersed herself in Feminist thought, and began to write and to collaborate on interdisciplinary works, including performances with Jim Scott and Eileen Corder's Poet's Theater, and with visual artist John Winet. Her works intersperse poetry, theory, and narrative and have also taken the form of plays or opera. Her readings led her through Jane Austen, Balzac, Ashbery, O'Hara, Genet, Beckett, Rabelais, Cervantes, Breton, Kuhn, DeBeauvoir, Stein, Marx, deSade, and the essays of Rachel Blau DuPlessis. Early influences were filmmakers Warren Sonbert and Abigail Child, and poets Lorenzo Thomas, Steve Benson, and Barrett Watten, as well as the discussions of the Language project in the San Francisco Bay Area. Her preface to *There Never Was a Rose* gives a clear account of her work: Describing her writings as "hybrid," she goes on to say,

> The writing is also a response to literature and the things of the world; it does not separate one off from the other. Marquis de Sade, rocks, Balzac, war, Lautremont, amazons, Jane Austen, news, Jane Bowles, utopias, Ludwig Wittgenstein, child's play, Saint Augustine, censorship are probably points on its strange map. In the world of this work, words themselves may become characters and instincts are regarded as if they were books. Complex ideas and simple rhetorics mingle, yielding impure theories, precarious stories, and fabulist games.

Some other writers who share one or more of her interests in playwriting, multi-genre forms, disrupted narrative, multi-media works, writing about the body, theory, comedy, identity positions, games as unsystematized restraints, and transformational grammar include Kathy Acker, Gail Scott, Nicole Brossard, Theresa Hak Kyung Cha, Abigail Child, Fiona Templeton, Camille Roy, Dodie Bellamy, Steve Benson, Bernadette Mayer, Robert Glück, Alan Davies, Kevin Killian, Juliana Spahr, Sarah Schulman, Cole Heinowitz, Bob Perelman.

Leslie Scalapino:

> (isn't it which is looked at.)
>   She goes out and gets in the car gliding down Derby to Telegraph and along it but there is no one around.
>   there are shot wounds in the glass of the booth out of a red smear as if an insect has been smattered in the crate.
>   if one says this — reading aloud — it has to be described
> -----------------------------
> 18 either clear dazzling pan that is person or what is seen
>
>   —from *Orion*

In her "world of circulation," as Leslie Scalapino's work has been described by Barrett Watten, the reader is involved with an elusive narrator, at various times "I," "she," or unspecified, who drifts, like a female flaneur, through scapes of social, syntactical and thoughtful situations. In her writing, poetry, plays, novels, and photographs, multiple geographic locations, various countries with their urban streets and rural landscapes, set stages for a narrator's encounters with events of political crisis, while the text accumulates and discards vocabulary sets through cycles of subtle repetition. Concerned with the self and the act of seeing, her project evades fixity while proposing "an examination of the mind in the process of whatever it's creating," from writing to its own life. Her early readings as a poet included Pound, Stevens and Moore in school, and extracurricularly, the Beats, particularly Phillip Whalen and Allen Ginsberg. She went on to read the poets of the New York School as well as Robert Creeley and Robert Duncan, and somewhat later, HD and Stein. Later still, she became involved with writers associated with the Language School, particularly Robert Grenier, Carla Harryman, Barrett Watten, Lyn Hejinian and Charles Bernstein, as well as with Mei-mei Berssenbrugge. Her ongoing reading project has centered around the origins of Zen in the writings of the seventh-century Indian philosopher, Nagarjuna, and the twelfth-century Buddhist thinker, Dogen. In addition, she has read widely in medieval Japanese writings, and in contemporary scientific literature.

   Some writers whose work involve similar or related interests in social observation, play writing, street culture, incorporation of graphic images into the text , Zen, smooth tonal surface, multiple geographies, sex, and political engagement include Ann Waldman, Norma Cole, Stephen Ratcliffe, Ron Silliman, Fanny Howe, Mei-mei Berssenbrugge, Norman

Fischer, Susan Gevirtz, Andrew Levy, Melanie Neilson, Rick London, Todd Baron, Denise Newman, Aaron Shurin, Hannah Weiner, Beverly Dahlen, Dodie Bellamy, Rob Fitterman, Kevin Killian, Theresa Hak Kyung Cha, Robert Grenier, Charles Bernstein.

ја. ја. ја.

Harryette Mullen:

> Mistress in undress, filmy peignoir. Feme sole in camisole. Bit part, petite cliche. Degage ladies lingering, careless of appurtenances. Lounging pajamas, custom worn to disrobe. Froufrou negligee, rustling silk, or cattle. Negligent in ladies' lingerie, a dressy dressing down.
> ....
> Thinking thought to be a body wearing language as clothing or language a body of thought which is a soul or body the clothing of a soul, she is veiled in silence. A veiled, unavailable body makes an available space.
> from *Trimmings*

Harryette Mullen describes the goal of her writing project as "making 'black' bigger, not 'narrower.'" Her scope is unrestricted, gathering anything interesting or particular into discussion with and mutual modification of 'blackness' and 'humanness.' Her intertextures of commercial slogans and images; feminine, southern, black, and pseudoscientific vernaculars; homilies and cliches; southern black signage; "body language" and its clothing in gesture and dress create endlessly proliferating crossovers. Steinian word plays, game plays, loose play among parts, and recontextualizations of words and phrases invite each to endlessly "pass" for others. The incessant interpolations and double entendres evict norms from the text which, word by word, gains inclusivity. The historical commodity uses of the physical black body and the expressive black soul are scrutinized through the layered veils of cultural construction. Behind these constructs she reaches, drawing out the heavily veiled humanity of the the black American feminine. Mullen's studies included sociolinguistics, Levi Strauss and Noam Chomsky, investigation of Black English and folklore, Deconstruction and Poststructuralism. Her poetry was inspired first by Gwendolyn Brooks, and later by Shiad Ney, Ntozake Shange, Lorenzo Thomas, and by the theory and intensity of the Language project.

Some writers whose work share involvement in language variants, issues of blackness, commercial representations of the contemporary, investigations of hierarchy and authority, morphemic play, and feminine constructedness include Julie Patton, C.S. Giscombe, Dodie Bellamy, Claire Harris, Susan Schultz, M. Nourbese Philip, Ntozake Shange, Nathaniel Mackey, Renee Gladman, Giovanni Singleton, Kevin Killian, Carla Harryman, Patricia Dienstfrey, Susan Gevirtz, Yedda Morrison, Diane Glancy, Juliana Spahr.

❧ ❧ ❧

Kathleen Fraser:

as does that
which is of
crashing to
us changing
their spots   aware your own she
heart stop   she used words like
downward who   brilliance turning
but are you   he had in my hand

swimming through
color, I was burn   struggling
hot gillsÆ events   dictum and
cold hand touched   plain as
                       a particular
                       attraction
                       treads some
                       thing cleft
                       if marked

—VIII SECOND BLACK QUARTET: from "Wing"

The poetics of Kathleen Fraser joins a writing of experience with that of experiment. For Fraser, experience *is* experiment; writing is a particular dimension of that experiment. It investigates the arrangements among provisional selves, their texts, voices and phenomenal contexts, and the material text in which experience and aesthetic act coincide. Her work began forming in early childhood with her minister father's recitations of nursery rhymes and bible stories, family singing of hymns, and her play with the drafting instruments which remained from her father's prior training as an architect. Musical sense and the architecture of the page have informed her work from the outset. When she moved to New York as a young poet, she became closely involved with the works of Frank O'Hara, Joseph Ceravolo, Barbara Guest, George Oppen, and Charles Olson. At the same time, her thinking about writing was also influenced by painting, especially that of Willem DeKooning, Jane Freilicher, and Joe Brainard, the concerts of John Cage, and the avant-garde dance of Yvonne Rainer and the Judson Dancers. She continued her readings in Emily Dickinson, Lorine Niedecker, and the Modernists, including HD, Mina Loy, and Marianne Moore. After teaching at the University of Iowa and Reed College, she settled in San Francisco where she came in contact with new writing colleagues such as Steve Benson, Lyn Hejinian, Robert Glück, Beverly Dahlen, and Frances Jaffer, and read widely among French and American feminist theorists. Her activist, perhaps missionary, spirit inspired her to direct the San Francisco State University Poetry Center, found the Poetry Center Archives, devote herself to the encouragement and support of countless students at San Francisco State, and finally to found the feminist literary magazine, *HOW(ever)*, which ran for ten years in print and is currently being revived online as *HOW2*.

Some other writers who share interests variously in issues of authority, address, error, errant and interrupted writings and readings, multiple subjectivities, connections between language and painting, feminist theory, and the space of the page include: Barbara Guest, Hannah Weiner, Nicole Brossard, Alice Notley, Carla Harryman, Steve Benson, Maureen Owen, Lyn Hejinian, Michael Palmer, Marjorie Welish, Tina Darragh, Meredith Quartermain, Laura Moriarty, Norma Cole, Susan Gevirtz, Myung Mi Kim, Beverly Dahlen, Rachel Blau DuPlessis, Joan Retallack, Susan Howe, Michael Davidson, Jaime Robles, Dale Going, Eileen Callahan, Sari Broner, Aife Murray, Denise Newman, Frances Jaffer.

Dodie Bellamy:

October 31, 1992

Dear Sam,
Happy Halloween! This is the day when the ordinary grows enormous oozing slime around the edges when aliens roam the streets with too many legs and eyeballs or not enough when physiology swells within you rendering the flesh flimsy as tissue paper there is no stopping its inevitable implosion...............the radio announcer assaults you with the tackiest Dracula accent: "Imagine if the creepiest costume around is you in a bathing suit! [.......creepy music....] The last thing you vant is to be scared of the way you look!".........
Trick or treat —
from Mina

Dodie Bellamy's writing is rich, even discriminately promiscuous, in its affinities, concentrations and haunts. Using the alter-ego character of Mina Harker, she explores various subject dispositions: the border between self and culture, particularly pop culture; between a "real" author and a "fictitious" character (we are never sure who is talking since Mina's friends happen to be Bellamy's); among the locations and subject/object personas of "you" the addressee, "I/me" the addressor, and "he" and "she" in Mina's gossipy epistolary monologues; in the high/low of class domains and positions within them; and finally in sexual enactments and literal positions of dominance or submission. The origins of her interests lie in Queer Theory, psychoanalytic theory (Lacan and Clement), Georges Bataille, and horror (Kristeva's *Powers of Horror*, the novels of Stephen King, and the horror movies of Dario Argento and Christopher Lee). She found her way into her writing through her interests in a ruptured New Narrative, pop culture, and working class emphasis on the body, along with the works of Sylvia Plath, Diane Arbus, Flannery O'Connor, Jack Spicer, as well as among contemporary associates such as Kathy Acker, Robert Glück, Kevin Killian, Dennis Cooper, Steve Abbott, Bruce Boone, and Kathleen Fraser's feminist thinking about writing.

Some other writers with variously associated concerns including genre mixture, formal enactment, queer writing, alternative narrative, alter ego, investigation and performance of self, gender and class, popular/consumer cultures, feminist theory: Kathy Acker, Lydia Davis, Tina Darragh, Gail Scott, Caroline Bergvall, Kevin Killian, Lynne Tillman, Eileen Myles, Laurie Weeks, Robert Glück, Lisa Robertson, Harryette Mullen, Carla Harryman,

Karen MacCormack, Camille Roy, Anne Waldman, Laura Moriarty, Lawrence Braithwaite, Stacy Doris, Kim Rosenfield, Heather Fuller, Pamela Lu, Elizabeth Fodaski.

❧ ❧ ❧

Fanny Howe:

> "Scattered Light"
>
> White slides over
> rows of windowed eyes:
> stone housing, that is, a hundred years snowed.
> Surrounded by more craft
> than need, the dross of winter:
> weather inspection
> stations the day and passes on information.
> See birds beat the ice off their wings
> for bites dressed in white,
> how the world contains everything
> the mind has to live by.
>   —from *The Vineyards*

Fanny Howe's novels and poems of reenvisioned lyric enact an epistemological investigation into the mysterious borderline between rational, empirical and logical constructs of knowledge, and other knowledge modes such as intimacy, the writings of spiritual philosophers and teachers, intuition, theologies, and devotion. Careful reading of her poems traces perception and thought as they swerve from word to word, phrase to phrase, alertly and devotedly drawn to meanings made elsewhere, where intention and attention contend and content themselves. She herself describes this process as "cyclical orders of the perfection and derangement of language and thought." In a writing of movements in tandem, the writer/reader is repeatedly, if briefly, poised in a stillness of interstitial syntactical shift just as the thought veers and moves along. Her writing is equally concerned with the ethical implications of vocabularies and in how language creates being, as described in her essay, "Night Realism: some thoughts on Edith Stein." Her earliest readings in poetry as an adolescent were in the Oscar Williams' *Anthology of World Literature*, e. e. cummings, Shakespeare's sonnets, continuing later on with Rilke's *Malte Lurids Brigge*, the French Symbolists

(Baudelaire, in particular), Pound's Chinese translations, Zora Neal Hurston, Emily Dickinson, and Anna Akhmatova's "Requiem." Poets whose work was important to her as she began to connect with a public world of poetry as a young woman were Robert Creeley, John Wieners, Bernadette Mayer and Maureen Owen. Additionally, she has been engaged in an ongoing project for many years reading and responding to the writings of Simone Weil.

Some other writers whose work engages the lyric, novels, ethics of vocabularies, the inexpressible, intimacy as learning site, the contemplative, or theological texts include: Barbara Guest, Leslie Scalapino, Cole Swensen, Tom Mandel, Patricia Dienstfrey, Edward Foster, Joan Retallack, Etel Adnan, Elaine Equi, Joseph Donahue, Susan Clark, Martha Ronk, Susan Thackrey, Leonard Schwartz, Gerrit Lansing, Peter Gizzi, Elizabeth Robinson, Sheila Murphy, Elizabeth Willis, Gustaf Sobin, Drew Gardner, Peter Cole, Ed Roberson, John Yau.

ཉ. ཉ. ཉ.

Lyn Hejinian:

> Chapter 163
>
> Let us behave
> I am getting to be
> So I can't escape reality
> The events are conspicuous but events are not continuous
> I behave with improvisation and intention
> Minutes, partly
> Wings of the homeland
> The bicycle rider's backbone
> We have a Russian tradition of silence, Dima said
> Silence itself, a form but in different locations
> I ask for a description of consciousness in a state of silence
> For the excitation of Leningrad
> This is an eternal nonverity
> I am keeping silent now
>   —from *Oxota: A Short Russian Novel*

"The activity of writing," says Lyn Hejinian, "is not focused on individual poems but represents a massive intellectual undertaking for individuals, groups and all humanity that will never be complete." The project, as she sees it, has to do with "thinking in the world"; why one wants to think is that "life is articulated thinking and that life wants to be alive." In the 1976 publication *Writing is an Aid to Memory* she wrote, "we are parting with description"; her project since then has focused on the real and its phenomenological and epistemological forms as articulated in writing. Through phonemic rhyming, syntactic doublings, and exploration of the poetic line's prodigious capacities for variation in its meetings with syntax, meanings of the poem are always provisional, temporary positions that continuously transform into new dimensions. Her works are quiet joinings of inventive perception, intellectual meticulousness, and lyric restraint. Hejinian's access to poetry began very young with familial readings of "The Rhyme of the Ancient Mariner," Langston Hughes, and others. In adolescence she read the Existentialists Sartre and Camus at the same time as Daisetz Suzuki on Zen Buddhism: both posited for her an acceptance of uncertainty and the notion that "life is meaningless but full of meaning." She read Proust along with the literature of exploration including Byrd, Cook, and Burton. At Harvard she majored in English Literature, and extracurricularly, the Beats, Olson, Creeley, Stevens, and Oppen. Later, as a young mother in rural northern California, she read Motherwell on Dada and Surrealism, subscribed to little magazines such as *Telephone* (edited by Maureen Owen in New York), sent away for books from small presses such as Black Sparrow, and started a press of her own, Tuumba. As a result of her growing familiarity with contemporaries, she began a correspondence with Susan Howe, and soon after was introduced to Russian Formalism by Ron Silliman. A short time later, she moved to the San Francisco Bay Area where she became a central figure among Language poets.

Some writers also variously engaged with phonemic, grammatical and syntactic experimentation, the poetic line, representation, reenvisioned autobiography, epistemolological and phenomenological investigation in poetry, serial forms, include Karen Mac Cormack, Tom Mandel, Joan Retallack, Barrett Watten, Diane Ward, Leslie Scalapino, Susan Howe, Ron Silliman, Theresa Hak Kyung Cha, Abigail Child, Alan Davies, Erica Hunt, Melanie Neilson, Charles Bernstein, Ann Lauterbach, Michael Palmer, Jean Day, Jessica Grim, Steve McCaffery, Bruce Andrews, Mary Margaret Sloan, Jessica Grim, Lytle Shaw, Pamela Lu, Jena Osman, Lori Lubeski, Barret Watten.

Theresa Hak Kyung Cha:

> Open paragraph   It was the first day   period
> She had come from a far   period   tonight at dinner
> comma   the families would ask   comma   open
> quotation marks   How was the first day   interroga-
> tion mark   close quotation marks   at least to say
> the least of it possible   comma   the answer would be
> open quotation marks   there is but one thing period
> There is someone   period   From   a far   period
> close quotation marks
> >   from *Dictée*

The range of Theresa Hak Kyung Cha's work is well summarized in her own words from a CV: "Producer, director, performer, writer in videos and film productions, performances and public texts." Her early readings included Greek and Roman classics, film theory, Korean poetry, European Modernists with a particular interest in Beckett, Joyce, Mallarmé, Sarraute, Duras, and Wittig. She also read widely in Barthes and Marguerite Yourcencar. Born in Korea and raised in the United States, she was tri-lingual in Korean, English and French. Her works infiltrate the boundaries and languages of home, history, time, geographies, nations, and religions, with radically juxtaposed narratives, typographies, personal letters, maps, photographs, charts, calligraphy, handwriting and film stills. Her 1982 book, *Dictee*, intertwines her own autobiography with the biographies of her mother; Joan of Arc; Saint Theresa; the Korean revolutionary, Yu Guan Soon; and Huyng Soon Huo, daughter of first-generation exiles born in Manchuria. Significant works include her mail art piece *Audience Distant Relatives*, texts *Exilee* and *Temps Morts*, the performance *Reveille Dans la Brune*, and the film/video *Passages Paysages*. She was murdered in an act of random violence in 1982.

Some other writers and artists with similar interests in multi-media production, re-envisioned autobiography, performance, use of graphic symbols and charts in texts, multiple geographies, writing and translation between a first and second or among multiple languages, religious subjects include: Abigail Child, Fiona Templeton, Julie Patton, Myung Mi Kim, Rosmarie Waldrop, Fanny Howe, Lyn Hejinian, Cecila Vicuna, Stephanie Hyungjung Kim, Swako Nakayasu, Etel Adnan, Hung Q Tu, Susan Pensak, Edwin Torres, Xu Bing, Catalina Cariaga, Avery Burns, Miranda Maher, Nicole Brossard, Susan Gevirtz,

Lisa Robertson, E.A. Miller, Johanna Drucker, Yedda Morrison, Clarinda MacLow, Brigid McLeer.

❧ ❧ ❧

Joan Retallack:

    we were entirely happy with our prospects
    (problemoftheunreliablenarratorortwo)

        rainbow colored shoelaces
        thistle 'n other natural graffiti

          Discipline #34

    arid and semi-arid regions and remarks

    sharp or poi ted objects or remarks

    we are not members of the class of all
classes which can not entertain themselves

      random access mem-O-rees

      single engin aer-O-plane

....

    when the earthquake was over
    they filled a glass to the rim with water
    and placed it on a table for the dead

....

                  ter
              ead
                  —from *AFTERRIMAGES*

Thought and the playful but trenchant enactments thought provokes in her have always focused Joan Retallack's writing. From adolescence to young adulthood, Retallack's reading came out of interest in Middle and Renaissance English, pre-Socratic fragments, Ovid, Sappho, Lucretius, French texts from Rabelais to the Dadaists, and Euro-American standards. She read widely through the histories of the novel, from Sterne to Woolf and Joyce, as well as Dickinson, Stein, Pound, Eliot, Ibsen, Beckett, Ionesco, Pinter, Williams Stevens, Oppen, Zukofsky, Ginsberg, and Creeley. Early on, she read Kierkegaard and Sarte; later Dewey, Wittgenstein, Kuhn, Rorty, Kristeva, and Derrida, along with scientific and mathematical texts: Archimedes, Gallileo, Bohr, and Mandelbrot. University began with a double major in English Literature and Philosphy follwed by graduate work in philosophy studying ethics, philosophy of language and philosophy of science and psychoanalysis (Freud, Lacan, French Feminists). In 1965, in Chicago, she met John Cage, a meeting which initiated her swerve away from academe towards art projects: a concrete novel, and "word plays," shown and performed in Washington, D.C., where she joined a writing group with Tina Darragh, P. Inman, Lynne Dryer, Phyllis Rosenzweig, Terence Winch, Doug Lang, frequently visited by Anselm Hollo, Bruce Andrews, and Douglas Messerli. The primary concern in Retallack's poetry and essays is what she refers to as the Poethics of our relation to the historical contemporary. This is evident in her engagement with multiple languages and vocabularies on the level of the letter, the phoneme, the excavation of historical language forms, and the visual graphics of the page. Her writing is often procedural and selectively employs chance operations, carrying on her interest in Cage and Oulipo.

Writers who variously share concerns with the ethics of writing, thought and its enactments, feminist theory, philosophies of language and science, procedural and chance operations, historical language forms, the space of the page and polylingualism include Tina Darragh, Rachel Blau DuPlessis, Julie Patton, P. Inman, Lyn Hejinian, Fanny Howe, Jackson MacLow, Hannah Weiner, Kathleen Fraser, Kevin Magee, Laura Mullen, Susan Schultz, Juliana Spahr, Lisa Robertson, Theresa Hak Kyung Cha, Dick Higgins, Cynthia Conrad, Peter Gizzi, Tan Lin, Dan Featherston, Jenny Gough, Erin Mouré, Ray DiPalma, Johanna Drucker.

ja ja ja

Bernadette Mayer:

                                    I'd like to know
What kind of person I must be to be a poet
I seem to wish to be you
            Love is the same and does not keep that name
            I keep that name and I am not the same
You,
Shakespeare, Edwin Denby and others, Catullus,
I've nothing else to say, the anonymous
Blue sky is gray, I love your being
In my unresisting picture, all love seen
All said is dented love's saluted image
In the ending morning, nothing said is mean,
Perhaps it's too long, I'm only learning
Along with love's warning
To invent a song
           Then for the breath of words respect
            me for my dumb thoughts, speaking in effect
This was my dream
Now it is done.
          —from *Midwinter Day*

From her first published work, *Story* (1968) until now, Bernadette Mayer has continued to deftly pass through and between genre boundaries. Within individual works, she moves easily in and out of poetry, prose cerebration, narrative, domestic detail, scholarship, and lyric devotion. Indeed, her earliest work shifted not only among genres, but also between media when she occasionally included photography in her work. She has preferred to work within projects she sets for herself, so has produced variously a book length sonnet sequence (*Sonnets*), an epistolary series (*The Desires of Mothers to Please Others in Letters*), and a lengthy domestic interior monologue (*Midwinter Day*) which includes this succession of sentences: "I chop onions for the sauce. St. Augustine hated the Greek language." She read all of Hawthorne, immersed herself in Stein, and carefully studied the work of John Cage as well as the works of scores of other poets throughout literary history. Always closely involved with other writers and artists and with arts communities, her writing is often located in the conversational networks of her friendships. On an activist level, she worked with others to publish and disseminate writing, and to create structures wherein poetry could flourish. Her first project was the magazine *0-9*, which she co-edited with artist Vito Acconi. Later she worked at the St. Mark's Poetry Project in Manhattan, where she taught, organized reading series, co-edited *The World* magazine with Ann Waldman and Maureen Owen, and helped to keep the organization going. Important early associates were, along with Ann Waldman, Alice Notley, and Maureen Owen, with whom she collaborated, Lewis Warsh, Ted Berrigan and Clark Coolidge. With Coolidge she determined that she would "write everything," or put another way by Bill Corbett, "she would go anywhere."*

Some writers with associated interests in multiple genre writing, formal projects, reenvisioned autobiography, epistolary form, lyric, scholarship imported into the poem: Eileen Myles, Carla Harryman, Alice Notley, Fanny Howe, Lyn Hejinian, Dodie Bellamy, William Corbett, Lisa Jarnot, Lee Ann Brown, Phil Good, Kristin Prevallet, Norma Cole, Sam Truit, Jocelyn Saidenberg, Bill DeNoyelles, Cliff Fyman, Ethie Stearns, Todd Pinney, Ange Mlinko, Jordan Davis.

ॐ ॐ ॐ

| ALL | i'vebeenthroughi'vebeen |

remains after one is taken simple
"other" ☐ used after ☐ *either* ☐

neither ☐ *whether* ☐ each
preceding one in turn the rest
in form   *other*
                    ☐ *another*
thing; s☐ omething else
a ☐ ny ☐ thing
else;   no ☐(n) other

n☐ othing else

from *a(gain)²st the odds*, 1989

---

*My gratitude to William Corbett and Lee Ann Brown for supplying background information for Bernadette Mayer.

Tina Darragh at first worked her way towards her writing through a series of negations: she did not want to write like Louise Gluck, Diane DiPrima, Rita May Brown or Marge Piercy, in whose work she found various confusions of sex, gender and prescriptions for living. Instead, she built her model for writing from pedagogical sources and texts concerned with the construction, recording and storage of language; not coincidentally, she works as a librarian. She extended Franz Fanon's concerns in *The Pedagogy of the Oppressed* with assembling of people in non-hierarchical learning situations to the learning room of the poem: how could everything come together there in relations which were not hierarchical? She was interested in Maria Montessori's *A Tactile History of the Alphabet* and looked for ways to bring out the materiality of textual representation. She enjoyed the poems of Stevie Smith and mimicked her processes: white collar office pilfering of space, time, and supplies for her own poetic purposes; her method of writing dictionary poems; and her model of writing out of a matriarchal tradition. Darragh developed her writing in a Washington, D.C., women's writing group that included Phyllis Rosenzweig, Joan Retallack, and Lynne Dryer, and looked to poets who are, as she is, also mothers, like Retallack, Dreyer, and Beth Baruch Joselow, though she also worked closely with her husband P. Inman, Michael Lalley and Ed Cox. Her writing is full of inventions for interrupting hierarchical orders, story progress, and trains of thought with bogus charts, diagrams, and false scholarship; for gradually unveiling furtive lines of language from behind successions of comical drawings; for boxing words and phrases within playful rooms, confessional booths, and tables drawn onto the page; for off-center framing of partial dictionary entries in ways that reveal elaborate networks of puns. Her work aims to foreclose on reductive closed forms, to question agency, to investigate error and a self-critical approach to writing and living, and to challenge master narratives such as religions, political institutions, language norms, and the false claim of science to objectivity, and instead to focus on the local and partial. To quote Darragh, her writing is looking for "the own in known."

Other writers whose work includes similar interests such as punning, diagramming or drawing, interrupted narrative, procedures, scholarship and false scholarship, disruption of genre hierarchies, graphic textuality, concerns with mathematics and science, error, direct engagement with master narratives include: Rae Armantrout, David Bromige, Joan Retallack, John Byrum, Kathleen Fraser, Carla Harryman, Cole Swensen, Jessica Grim, William Marsh, Dale Going, Dan Davidson, Jena Osman, Scott MacLeod, Melanie Neilson, Rod Smith, Janet Zweig, David Kellogg, Buck Downs, William Fuller, Miranda Maher, Jim Brashear, Sherry Brennan, Alan Bernheimer, Johanna Drucker.

Susan Howe:

>Summary of fleeting summary
>Pseudonym cast across empty
>
>Peak proud heart
>
>Majestic caparisoned cloud cumuli
>East sweeps hewn flank
>
>Scion on a ledge of Constitution
>Wedged sequences of system
>
>Causeway of faint famed city
>Human ferocity
>
>dim mirror Naught formula
>
>archaic hallucinatory laughter
>
>Kneel to intellect in our work
>Chaos cast cold intellect back

>   —from "Articulations of Sound Forms in Time," *The Singularities*

Susan Howe's work, according to Marjorie Perloff, draws together three codes, mythic, historical and linguistic, into "collision and collusion." Howe's early work in theater and in painting coalesce to articulate these engagements into sharply etched sound constituents and in impresses of the visible text on the page. She grew up in a household enthusiastic about history, reading historical novels such as those of James Fenimore Cooper and *The Count of Monte Cristo*. Later important readings include Nathaniel Hawthorne, Herman Melville, Jane Austen, the Brontes, George Eliot, Virginia Woolf, Aquinas, Cotton Mather, Thoreau, and the historian Richard Slotkin. Her attentions in poetry have ranged among

Shakespeare, Spenser's "Fairie Queene," Rilke, Hart Crane, HD, Wallace Stevens, William Carlos Williams, Robert Duncan, and Charles Olson, with particular interest in Olson's *Call Me Ishmael*. The century-long misrepresentation of the work and person of Emily Dickinson claimed Howe's attention for several years while she wrote *My Emily Dickinson*, revising the reading of one of America's most signficant poets. The feminist thinking of Kate Millet, Alice Jardine, and Luce Irigaray, as well as the new historicism of Stephen Greenblatt further focused her thinking as she researched captivity narratives. She wrote an essay investigating Mary Rowlandson's captivity narrative, and, in *Articulation of Sound Forms in Time*, "Hope Atherton's Wanderings." Her chief historical concerns reflect her own divided familial origins, on one side American and New England Puritan, and on the other Irish. The territorial disputes, encroachments, and wars of the Colonialists and among Irish factions inform her interests in border contests, infiltration, and in the meeting of ideology with her notion of the wild at every level of her writing: the phonemic particulates and historical memories in words; the divisions of the poetic line interacting with the syntactic and typographical play at the borders of words, phrases, sentences; the bringing forward of marginalia and forgotten texts; the encounters of lyric with essay. Her work continuously addresses a question: what is the meaning of the Western impress of "America" onto the unnamed Indian continent?

Some writers who share one or more interests or strategies including border contests (topical and linguistic), typographical representations in the space of the page, lyric, inclusion of source text material, excavations of historical events and language forms, etymological delving, marginalia, recovery of the feminine: Maureen Owen, Rosmarie Waldrop, Kathleen Fraser, Laura Moriarty, Harryette Mullen, Joan Retallack, Cole Swensen, Mary Margaret Sloan, Nathaniel Mackey, Etel Adnan, Joan Retallack, Joseph Donahue, Myung Mi Kim, Norma Cole, Kevin Magee, Andrew Joron, Juliana Spahr, Jena Osman, Camille Guthrie, Eileen O Malley Callahan.

ॐ ॐ ॐ

The above descriptions are drawn from personal interviews with the writers by the author with the exceptions of Cha, Mayer, and S. Howe. Additional sources are listed under "Works Cited."

ॐ ॐ ॐ

A few among many additional writers whose work lies within the same general ethos as those mentioned above: Michelle Murphy, Peter Cole, Dorothy Trujillo Lusk, Eleni Sikelianos, John Taggart, Bill Berkson, Maxine Chernoff, Will Alexander, Maria Damon, Paul Hoover, Matine Bellen, Laynie Browne, John High, Kimberly Lyons, Dennis Barone, Liz Waldner, Jeff Derksen, Barbara Einzig, Douglas Messerli, Sheila E. Murphy, Gillian Conoley, Benjamin Hollander, Pam Rehm, Tom Raworth, David Buuck, Chris Tysh, Julia Blumenreich, Peter Ganick, Jennifer Moxley, Stefanie Marlis, Lew Daly, Sianne Ngai, Taylor Branch, Bev Braune, Joel Lewis, Rena Rosenwasser, Connell McGrath, Anselm Berrigan, Lisa Samuels, Forrest Gander, Standard Schaefer, Kathryn MacLeod, Jerry Estrin, Charles Alexander, Deanna Ferguson, Charles Borkhuis, Brenda Hillman, Cynthia Hogue, Rodrigo Toscano, Jeanne Heuving, Lisa Kovalski, Stephen Sartarelli, Lisa Cooper, Garrett Kalleberg, Spencer Selby, Susan Smith Nash, Peter Quartermain, Cydney Chadwick, Edmund Berrigan, Thoreau Lovell, Mary Angeline, Hank Lazer, Andrew Schelling, Claudia Rankine, Stephen Ellis, Beth Joselow, Barbara Barrigan, Grace Lovelace, Noah deLissovoy, Bruce Andrews, Elizabeth Treadwell, Adam Cornford, Gail Sher, Roberto Tejada, Melissa Wolsak, Randall Potts, Albert Mobilio, Kit Robinson, Katie Yates, Steve Carll, Duncan Dobbelmann, Virginia Hooper, Geoffrey O'Brien, Sarah Ann Cox, Benjamin Friedlander, Todd Thilleman, Kathy Lou Schultz, Jeremy Caplan, Mira Schor, Michael Gizzi, Pasquale Verdicchio, Todd Baron, Gale Nelson, Jennifer Hofer, Judith Goldman, Louis Cabri, Catriana Strang, Heather Ramsdell, Laird Hunt, Bill Luomo, Anne Tardos, Simon Pettet, Kate Ruskin, Marcella Durand, Spencer Selby, Jennifer Arin, Chris Stroffolino, John Noto, Stephen Rodefer, James Sherry, Colleen Lookingbill.

WORKS CITED

Anonymous, *Theresa Hak Kyung Cha 1959-1982: A Narrative Chronology*, University Art Museum, Pacific Film Archive, 1993)

Bellamy, Dodie, *Real: The Letters of Mina Harker and Sam D'Allesandro*, (Jersey City: Talisman House, Publishers, 1994)

-------. *The Letters of Mina Harker*. (West Stockbridge, MA: Hard Press, 1998).

Cha, Theresa Hak Kyung, *Dictee*, (Berkeley: Third Woman Press, 1995)

Chester, Laura and Barba, Sharon, editors, *Rising Tides: Twentieth Century American Women Poets*, (New York: Washington Square Press/Simon & Schuster, 1973)

Darragh, Tina, *a(gain)²st the odds* (Elmwood, CT: Potes & Poets Press, 1989)

Foster, Edward, "An Interview with Susan Howe" in Postmodern Poetry (Hoboken, NJ: Talisman House Publishers, 1994), 48-68.

-------, "An Interview with Leslie Scalapino," in Postmodern Poetry (Hoboken, NJ: Talisman House Publishers, 1994), 115-23.

Fraser, Kathleen, "Boundayr," in *il cuore : the heart: Selected Poems 1970-1995* (Hanover: Wesleyan, 1997)

Golding, Alan, *From Outlaw to Classic: Canons in American Poetry* (Madison: The U of Wisconsin P)

Harryman, Carla, Meghom, "Toy Boats" in from *There Never Was a Rose Without a Thorn*, (San Francisco: City Lights Books, 1995)

Hejinian, Lyn, *Oxota: A Short Russian Novel*, (Great Barrington,MI: The Figures, 1991)

-------. "The Person and Description," in *Poetics Journal* 9 (1991), 167.

Howe, Fanny, *The Vineyard*, (Providence RI: Lost Roads Publishers, 1988)

-------, *Nigh: Realism: some thoughts on Edith Stein*, forthcoming.

Howe, Susan, *Singularities* (Hanover, NH: Wesleyan UP, 1990)

Keller, Evelyn Fox, *A Feeling for the Organism: The Life of Barbara McClintock* (New York: W.H. Freeman and Company, 1983)

Mayer, Bernadette, *Midwinter Day*, (Berkeley, CA: Turtle Island, 1982)

Mullen, Harryette, *Trimmings*, (New York City: Tender Buttons, 1991)

-------. "Miscegenated Texts & Media Cyborgs: Technologies of Bosy and Soul." *Poetics Journal* 9 (1991), 36-43.

Perloff, Marjorie, *Poetic License: Essays on Modernist and Postmodernist Lyric* (Evanston: Northwestern UP, 1990).

Retallack, Joan, *Afterrimages*, (Hanover, NH: Wesleyan UP, 1995)

Scalapino, Leslie, *The Return of Painting, The Pearl, and Orion: A Trilogy*, (San Francisco, North Point Press, 1991; new edition: Jersey City, NJ: Talisman House, Publishers, 1997)

Sloan, Mary Margaret, ed., *Moving Borders: Three Decades of Innovative Writing* by Women, (Jersey City, NJ: Talisman House, Publishers, 1998)

Watten, Barrett, "Political Economy and the Avant-Garde: A Note on Haim Steinbach and Leslie Scalapino," in *Talisman: A Journal of Contemporary Poetry and Poetics* 8 (1992), 49-52.

Edward Foster

AN INTERVIEW WITH ALICE NOTLEY

ALICE NOTLEY WAS THE FIRST POET TO BE INTERVIEWED for *Talisman*. That interview was done in 1987 in her apartment in New York City. Notley lives now in Paris, and in the following recent exchange she elaborates on various matters she had discussed earlier, particularly her sense of American poetic traditions and her place in them.

EF: What kind of poetics were writers you knew thinking about in the early 70s? What does *Phoebe Light* have in common with work being done by other poets in the New York community then?

AN: In the early 70's I got mixed up in Don Allen-anthology and 2nd-Generation-New York-School poetics I guess, sort of on the rebound from Mainstream-Confessional poetics, with which I had a brief encounter at Iowa. Looking at *Phoebe Light*, I see what I thought were imitations, of poets like Schuyler, Creeley, Blackburn, Whalen — but I'm struck by the fact that many other poems in the book were written according to "methods" in use by second-generation New York School, which those poets had gotten from Dada and Surrealism, Cage, and Burroughs. I see found poems, poems written by crossing out words in other poets' poems, cutups, fold-ins, poems made by letting my eyes fall down the page of some book gathering "random" phrases, a poem made by reading across columns in the dictionary (a method I invented myself), use of word lists, etc.

These methods point to an interest in a more unexpected and subconsciously fed language than the Midwestern and Confessional poets were using. But the tonal differences between the two major divisions, and also among the camps in the Allen anthology, are also very much to the point. New York School in particular was against anguish and in favor of humor and the general light of day. This could be very liberating, but got to be a problem if one encountered anguish in one's life and wanted to write about it. You can see towards the end of *Phoebe Light* a little darkness seeping in, and a sense of a woman's problems and of feminist concerns. These felt a little forbidden, unless handled inside a certain tonal range. The message seemed to be Don't have those feelings and thoughts, because our poetics doesn't include them. But all poetics, all poetry schools do this — rule out something or other — and so they're all suspect. Which doesn't mean they can't be useful at some point. But a poetics is a lot more transitory than a poem is.

EF: When you wrote the early poems, why did you choose to work outside whatever was happening in the mainstream? In the early 1970s wouldn't it have been usual to take, say, Anne Sexton or someone out of that world as a model?

AN: I realized that my spirit, my mind in flow, didn't sound like Anne Sexton or like anyone in the mainstream. I sounded more like Frank O'Hara and Gregory Corso. I perceived this directly — no explanatory stuff necessary — once I opened their books. My spirit was playful, attracted to both luxuriant and vernacular usages, and sympathetic to others. I also had an extremist instinct in me, and was looking for poems that looked a certain way. I had a feeling that there was probably a new poetry, as I had found out there was a new music, and that I should attempt to discover it and understand it. If Edgard Varèse's music had been composed, then there was probably a poetry equivalent which made its own rules too, word by word. I was very attracted by poetry which covered the whole page, though it was a long time before I understood how to lay out that kind of poem. I was never really attracted by the mainstream at all. At Iowa, before I heard about Corso and O'Hara, I was exposed to Bob Creeley's work at the same time, and with the same emphasis, as that of the mainstream poets, and I seem to have chosen his over theirs but without thinking about it. I think it's very much a question of what you're like to begin with: there will always be people to write and read mainstream poetry. I seem to have given Sylvia Plath's poetry a moment's thought, since I bought her book, but I can't remember what that thought was. I honestly can't remember what reading her was like for me then; I think it was part of an educational process. I don't remember actively judging anything until I had the experience of reading a lot of the New York School poets, Beats, and Black Mountain poets for the first time. Then I began to judge. At which point — and especially a little later, when I was dealing with the problems of being a young mother and an aspiring poet — I decided the poems of Plath and Sexton were a genuinely negative force. I've thought for a long time that the usages people — men and feminist women — have made of them have been quite immoral. It was as if both men and women were showing you those poems and saying, Here, this is what it's like to be a woman. Well no it ain't. It wasn't. But I do wish people would stop showing other people some bunch of poems in some one style and saying Here this is poetry not that — Poetry is so huge and there are so many kinds.

EF: What did you find consistent among Black Mountain, Beat, and New York School poets that set them off from work that poets like Plath and Sexton were doing?

AN: Something like that the shape of the poem wasn't necessarily a rectangle, that its logic wasn't necessarily sonnet-like or traditionally stanzaic. The main thing said was all over the poem instead of, sort of, buildingly towards the end. Humor was possible in all three schools, even required; the sense of how people spoke on the street was required; but the language of the poem could come from anywhere — people's mouths, scholarship, the dictionary, science — and could never be anticipated. All three schools were in love with words — even if the diction was plain one felt the poet was in love with plain words. All three schools were also interested in a new metrics, or non-metrics: the sound of it was always interesting. Mainstream poetry has a predictable sound. Mainstream poetry is largely humorless, and somewhat lackluster, because it tries to serve too many people, tries to serve a sort of consensus as to what people want. But humor comes out of active particulars, and the insouciance of the poet, and the word "active" brings up the other thing: that the three non-mainstream-schools are about the performance of the poem as it's being written, what happens now while you're writing it that makes this occasion and shape in time unique. These schools are/were much more sophisticated about time, and notions of how time is fed into the present by the past and future, than the mainstream schools. I wasn't conscious of that aspect exactly when I was young, but I did think that mainstream poetry felt dead, not alive now, and hadn't ever been really alive. There's obviously quite a lot of vividness, even savagery, in Plath's poetry — but I find her sense of form rather undeveloped. She exploited the rectangle quite fully but her poetry might have burst out of it, and pushed itself into the future, if she hadn't been such a careerist. Poets like Plath and Sexton, and even more of course all the men, wanted the mainstream rewards of poetry, it seemed, much more than they wanted a rich satisfaction from the writing of the work; but I've always gotten so much back from writing itself, from being in process with it. It's only since I've become older that the dissemination of it has seemed more urgent, but as much for what you might call political reasons as for a desire for recognition (which it's hard not to have, finally). The mainstream tends not to feel like they enjoy the writing and that therefore you should really enjoy the reading!

EF: I'm very interested in the notion that the poets you admired are or were more concerned with time and process. One criticism that is made of some, I think, is that this can lead to beautiful surfaces but not great depth. Things move too quickly for that. I don't think this is true, at least necessarily true, but I understand where it comes from. Can you comment on that?

AN: I guess it seems to me that the opposite is true, that the continual use of traditional forms tends to block depth in that it makes what gets said the same old thing said. Traditional forms say traditional things, that's what they're for. They can also be used for doing a traditional task in a very updated way — say the way Doug (Oliver) modifies ottava rima, in order to tell a story and to sound like New York, in *Penniless Politics*. But this is not what mainstream poets do. And the mainstream form and sound automatically excludes the really untraditional, the people who can't help but bring another sound to poetry — the woman poet for example, from a small town in the southwest, the voice that hasn't been heard yet. Classical forms imply that they are anyone's voice and truth, but how can that be when not everyone has come along yet? In the early 70s I probably thought I could take it from Horace though I wonder now. I don't kiss the ass of the greats in the way same I used to. I could take it from Ben Jonson in his poems because I knew what his plays were like, specific to his times, and the poems and the plays make a body of work together which is deep and rugged and imbued with the sense of his life lived and suffered. I've always like Auden quite a lot, but he found a way to say whatever came into his head within traditional forms (but not traditional diction. And he really had to ransack the form and metrics books to keep it all going!). I couldn't take it very much from Americans in the early 70s. Depth of course is a funny word. And Frank O'Hara is a very classical poet in a lot of ways. . . . But what is your definition of depth? Mine would probably have to do with taking on the big questions in a very specific way, anchored in one's times and in dialogue with them, without narcissism. Much of mainstream poetry seems more narcissistic than O'Hara's say: he never says Admire my emotion, or as Adrienne Rich often seems to, Admire my emotion which is Our emotion. He's saying Together we will make a little fun of my emotion, which may also be like yours, while I try to demonstrate how emotion is the glue of our existence (an example of a big thing to say) and what the difference between good and bad emotion really is. Of course he would deny that was what he was saying! He might say he was taking a stance this very minute though, the only one to take which is to be right here, as fully as possible, and to go on: Shall we continue Yes we shall continue It's the only thing to do Etc.

EF: Did you feel there were strong differences between New York poet who weren't aligned with the mainstream and west coast poets who also kept their distance from poets like Lowell and Plath?

AN: I heard a lot of stories and bitchy comments about and among the elders — the ones born in the 20s. One felt these people were like a quarreling family — which meant the feeling could get pretty intense. People bitched each other within schools and across (non-mainstream) schools. The Beats and The New York School always seemed very close to each other, even across coasts, because Allen and Gregory and DiPrima etc, frequented both coasts and had bi-coastal sensibilities. They were very mixed up in New York School and you can see their names all over O'Hara's *Collected* — and he and Phil Whalen met and esteemed each other. And everyone in the east had favorite poems of Snyder's. The biggest gulf seemed to have to do with Duncan and Spicer, probably because they were so dogmatic, and so competitive about their *ideas*, which the Beats and New York School tried very hard not to be. But everything was more mixed up in the Second Generation, who would like who couldn't be predicted. When I was young I would give anyone's poetry a try; I found out I couldn't like all of it, but in spite of all the complaining we New Yorkers did about how silly California — San Francisco — was as compared to New York, I don't think that had anything to do with my own preferences. As you know, one of my biggest influences has been Whalen. But I have an East Coast/ Southwest background.

I just realized I've misread your question — I seem to have taken differences to mean disputes. I must still have this flu . . . I felt that the New York School and the Beats were more cosmopolitan than the other schools, that they knew what a city was, not Olson (whom I also deeply admired) and that they knew what it was to feel part of others and responsible to them. The latter without any loss of individuality. Sympathy is actually the primary quality for me of Beat writing, it's what I so admired in Kerouac; but O'Hara had it too though it's harder to describe in him because it has to do with self- portrayal, whereas in Kerouac it has to do with self-effacement. But the Beats are bi-coastal, so I still haven't answered the question. Obviously, Duncan and Spicer seemed different. I am bi-coastal though, as I've said; I didn't think of it so much as an East/West thing. Everything is all mixed together for me — I guess that's why I'm having such a hard time answering such a simple question!

EF: But among poets outside the mainstream in the 70s and 80s, do you see everyone as bi-coastal or were there differing communities and alignments?

AN: I lived in a lot of different places until 1976 and so had the sense of a rather large community-in-the-air which included a lot of different people of different ages and even different countries. I was aware of "schools" in England for example which seemed to share my poetry concerns. I'd lived briefly in Bolinas, and in San Francisco, several years in Chicago, and in England — in general there was a lot of migratory poetry activity. Ted was, during those years, a migrant poetry teacher, as was Anselm Hollo; one had a sense of people going about delivering a sort of general poetry message, not a factionized one. Then in 1976 we moved to New York and I began to teach at, and be involved in, The Poetry Project; but I never lost my feel for other places and the fact that there was a larger world involved. One would go read in Buffalo or San Francisco or Chicago, and hear about the other poets everyone was interested in. But, there was Second and even Third Generation New York School in New York, but there were New York School-like poets everywhere, and the label ceased to fit anyone except maybe a handful of people who stuck around St. Mark's. I've never quite identified with it. Then the Language Poets arose, and they functioned on two coasts. My sense is that their friendships, their relationships among themselves, function on separate coasts, though the poetics doesn't seem to have a similar split. In the early 70s there was a sort of sub-Black Mountain Group in Buffalo as well, which didn't seem to grow much thereafter. The Bolinas poets were never a school, they were people living in Bolinas. Then back in New York there were the Umbra Poets, who had their own concerns, but they certainly felt "around" and had very strong individual identities. And then the amazing Nuyorican thing sprang up, which must be still going on in a lot of ways. That was continuously energetic, and open, for at least ten or fifteen years — is it still? The Bay Area has always had a corresponding array of scenes, various kinds of 5th Generation Beats, Street Poets, Latinos, Feminists . . . I'm always astonished when I read what's going on in *The Flash*. And then there's what goes on at Naropa — what do you call that? There's always so much more anywhere than any schools, and the kinds of activities flow from coast to coast really. So many people have moved around and have ceased to be identified with their original "places."

EF: This interview will be part of a collection of essays about poetry outside the mainstream during the last thirty or so years. Where would you place your early work (the poetrry from the 1970s and 1980s) in that context?

AN: It doesn't fit with a school, I never identified with a poetics outside myself really. Partly I had such trouble with the concept of the line — what it came from and what to do with it. As I've said so many times, it seemed so male-owned; but I had no confidence in any particular version of it so I couldn't go with any of the schools I saw around me. I was always rebelling against the line! It was a huge passion. So I invented a lot of eclectic forms in the 70s and 80s, taking hints from writers like Williams and Stein, Olson O'Hara Whalen etc, as well as prose writers like Henry Green and George V. Higgins, and an array of dramatists. I invented forms like that for *Songs For The Unborn Second Baby* — an exploded odeish form; for "September's Book" — alternating prose and poetry sections of monologue and dialogue for "characters"; for the conversational poems in *Waltzing Matilda* and *Margaret & Dusty*. I also wrote in forms in *When I Was Alive*; and utterly nakedly in *At Night The States*. I consistently stood for "women," for a female voice and consciousness, that possibility — who knows if it exists? But the idea that I would have to stand as a different kind of voice from the ones who'd gone before me. When asked some form of this question, I often ally myself with all the women who were writing in my generation at that time: I have most in common with them as an across-the-board phenomenon, not with any school or poetics. I don't have a poetics, except a need for inclusiveness and change. I am, and have been, engaged in a search for blockages so I can knock them down. Also I was trying to learn how to do anything and everything, in the 70s and 80s, which is why I worked in traditional forms sometimes. I felt as if I had to incorporate a lot of previous literary activity into myself in order to make a body of work, by a woman, which would stand next to all that male work. So I suppose I could be placed with "the women." But anyone wants to be unique. I don't accept any labels or placements even for the "early work."

EF: That, of course, makes it all but impossible to see your work as fundamentally part of an historical continuum. And I guess that's always been a problem poets seeing their work as essentially different from other poets' work. And then, too, there are claims that poetry is prior to history —that it is "the Orphic voice of the earth," for instance. What is it that underlies these claims; or, in other words, what is it that differentiates, say, a lawyer, who sees his/her language as entirely historical and meaningful only within an historical context, and a poet, who in some part resists that identification?

AN: That is a good question, hard to answer. Poetry can't get at the truth within a historical context because the historical context will close poetry down into its own language and definitions; poetry tries for a bigger truth and has to have the freedom to do what it wants with language. I also think it must have some sort of dialogue with the historical context to be valuable. The trouble with poetry movements, and poetics, is that they work like historical contexts and therefore they tend to close poetry down at the same time as they open it up. It seems to me that most poets feel part of a "movement" mostly in their youth. Movements are constrictive, a poetics is constrictive. A poetics is also — I can't stand to say this again — a male thing, the manifesto is male, the let's-change-everything-into-what-We-want-now is what men have done in poetry. I see most women poets as either clinging to a maleish movement (as far as a discussion of poetics goes), or doing a feminist politics but not poetics in some programmatic way, and/or being in some sense independent. I mean were we really part of any of those movements? As far as the men — the most Important members of course — were concerned? If so, at what point? After how many years? How many years does it take for a girl to get recognized as part of a movement? (This could be like a lightbulb joke: five years to certify her and five more to screw her in.) The most important overall movement of the last twenty years has been a broad multiculturalism-cum-feminism, which implies a broad change of consciousness for poetry, which feeds in subtle ways into the language of poetry, the connections and syntax, and so forth. I think the door really finally opened. What's interesting about the new young poets, as in the Talisman Anthology*, is that their consciousness is different, a lot of these changes are built into them. So far they don't seem to need manifestos or movements or organized poetics. The biggest driving force across my life has been the desire to know things directly for myself, without interference of opinion of others. This has never seemed something one can do in conjunction with others, they do things like try to reformulate what they think you're saying into some received language or they imply you're stupid when you're not. Stupidity means haven't read enough in the area as staked out by the experts, them. I've been led astray from time to time, into accepting someone else's ideas, but in general I have to find out for myself. I've increasingly come to distrust almost all of society's formulations of the truth, almost all of the language of "the historical context," and pretty much all the language of current philosophies and poetics. I want to stand face to face with whatever reality is and I feel that all the friendly theoreticians in my neighborhood are keeping me from doing this by proclaiming that there is no such reality as is made evident in the works of so and so philosopher or poet. I've consistently used dreams and myth-making techniques in my poetry — there are dream poems even in *Phoebe Light*, because the truth lies somewhere in there for me. But when I make myths, I don't make them out of preexisting myths or already known materials and stories. I try to build from scratch, psychic scratch. After a reading during which I'd read the "Headless Woman" section of Book III of *Alette*, a well known poet whom I respect asked me, "Where did you get all that?" "Out of myself," I said. He didn't believe me, and was only satisfied when I said I'd been reading a lot of anthropology, because that indicated to him that I probably really had a source. But I didn't, it all came out of my own dreams and visions. When I think of my poetry in this way, the idea of poetry movements and poetics and so on seems to become so irrelevant. Making a poem is a large act, hugely real and involving; it's like living a second life in the midst of this one. Having piddly conversations with so-and-so about what poetry Ought to be doing, or what those guys over there think, is just, nothing.

EF: Do you mean that there is something profoundly different about women as poets — or at least poetry by women? And if so, is that the result of history, or is it an essential difference — something outside historical consideration? To approach this problem from another angle: do you agree with Mary Margaret Sloan when she says, in her introduction

---

*Lisa Jarnot, Leonard Schwartz, and Christopher Stroffolino, *An Anthology of New (American) Poets* (Jersey City, NJ: Talisman House, Publishers, 1998).

to *Moving Borders* that a book like hers, "marks the occasion when, at the end of a period of historical transition, such a book is no longer necessary. A barrier has been crossed. . . ."

AN: I mean that men own the ways poetry has been done as a "public phenomenon" — the existence of movements, of schools, of ways of talking about poetry, of literary criticism as both an academic and popular (as in newspapers) phenomenon; also, when I was young they seemed to own the secret of the line. That is, what it had to do with oneself personally, where it came from inside one (psychically), how you chose one (just one! which everyone seemed to do) and remained loyal to it. This is a simple fact and has nothing to do with whether men or women are different from each other, it has to do with ownership of history and art. I don't know if I agree with Margy or not, although I guess I think a lot of barriers have been crossed recently. My point is not that women are approaching the poem or the line differently and making a radically different poetry. I don't know if I can tell a great deal of difference between men's and women's poetry, in general. Maybe in tone. My point is that women are not constructing poetics (plural) exactly or theorizing about the future of poetry, they're not trying to take it over and and reorganize it into some new kind of map as men have been doing throughout the last two centuries — they would probably have to organize men as well as each other in order to do this and there's no way anyone's going to stand for that! The men who participate in movements are very aggressive. My sense is that women don't necessarily want to do things that way — although I'm not sure they're thinking about it very much. But if you undertake to interview a woman on the poetry movements and so forth of the last thirty years . . . at a certain point, the concept breaks down because we did what we did most markedly, the women of my generation, across the lines of the movements. Our achievement has probably been to become ourselves in spite of the movements. I think we are now less known through our alliances with specific groups than as members of that sudden generation of strong women poets. I take that to be what Margy's anthology demonstrates.

EF: *Mysteries of Small Houses* seems, to some people, very historical and biographical, and they read it as such. Can you comment on the legitimacy or illegitimacy of reading a poetry as history or as biography? That question in turn circles around to others: is there anything in poetry that is not "essentially" historical; what (if anything) in poetry can not be appropriated as a "subject" by the historian?

AN: *Mysteries of Small Houses* is meant to be an investigation into what isn't biographical or historical; it conducts its investigation using the shape of chronology in a specific time period but repeatedly researching the depths of the self and asking the question What is constant in oneself throughout historical and biographical change? What in the self, if anything, transcends this ephemera? What is the self if it isn't history? I'm convinced that I am a self or soul that is different from my personality in history. I'm quite sure that it is some transference of one's "real self" into the poem that makes it come alive: this is the mystery of the small house! The poet's skill has to do with ability to turn spirit into words and word-music. I used self-hypnotic trance techniques writing *Mysteries* and felt I was in contact with a literal, tangible substance of spirit — there is no good vocabulary for these things — which became bound up with what I wrote. Now that I've said this it's material for the historian and for history — and people need to know such things have been said — but history is the least of what it is. A poem is written, and at best read, in a different kind of time from historical time, even if it sounds like its time and even if a good part of what the reader gets from it is bound up with what's going on in time. Writing poems gets done in a strangely isolated nontemporal space as all poets know, but I'm not really trying to claim anything "special" for the poet. I think anything we do could be like this; but poetry is especially meditative. The historian could not discuss this terribly well. The historian is, it seems to me, absolutely incapable of dealing with the role of sound in poetry and doesn't try probably, though sounds change from era to era. The historian can't deal with what it feels like to write or read a poem, and that's what poetry is all about. On the other hand it's interesting to read poetry from a historical vantage — poetry of the more distant past — to contact the sound of another time. And it's fun to read contemporary poetry for gossip value. Everyone bought the Ted Hughes book on Plath to find out what had happened! I have no idea if they found out since I haven't read the book. I've thought for awhile it would be great to write a book of poems that contained some sort of information that the public could only get by reading that book. Most poets leave so much out though. They think they've told everything by putting down about ten words.

Aldon Lynn Nielsen

"THIS AIN'T NO DISCO"

> the words in books no one reads
> are already unwriting themselves
> Erica Hunt (*Arcade* 10)

THE UNWRITING OF INNOVATIVE AFRICAN AMERICAN POETRY proceeds. Many more now read the formal and thematic inventions of Nathaniel Mackey and Harryette Mullen than ever found those poets' first books. A poet as determinedly out of the ordinary as Will Alexander has at last made his way to frequent book publication, and newer writers such as Mark McMorris, T. J. Anderson III and giovanni singleton find audiences to astonish where before there had been only the astonishment of America's persistent unreading. Still, the ominous note projected from Erica Hunt's *Arcade* finds a resonance in the artificially anechoic chamber of recent literary history:

> the words won't write themselves
> out of their depth unless someone
> listens to them   (10)

To many of today's listeners, today's black avant garde comes as blank surprise, a remarkable and unprecedented headbirth out of American modernity, because too many of today's listeners only began to listen yesterday. The most innovative of contemporary African-American poets cast a long shadow into the next millennium, because they write under the illumination of the past of black brilliance. Seen either as isolatoes or as products only of the poetics of their white counterparts, these poets must seem strange harbingers indeed, caged birds of free verse. Seen in the fuller context of evolving black experiment, they must afford a more consequential understanding of poetic consanguinity. It is not hard to predict that somebody will soon appear among us to opine that the modicum of attention now belatedly paid to poets such as Nathaniel Mackey and Harryette Mullen is a consequence of their having written the sort of poem most likely to stir the critical desires of white academics. The emptiness of such a charge should be evident to anyone sufficiently well read in the ways of white folk to have some nodding knowledge of the types of poetry most likely to find a purchase on the syllabi of historically white universities and colleges. What should have been equally evident is that Mackey and Mullen write kinds of poetry that have been assiduously avoided by the broadly flowing mainstream lo these many years; avoided but not entirely invisible. What has rendered so much of the post-Black Arts record of poetic achievement so nearly invisible to so nearly all critics and literary historians has been the occluding powers of the historical narratives some of us tend to tell others. The work itself, however, enjoys an objective persistence, upon the page wherein it is written. To turn to Erica Hunt once more, in *Local History* she writes: "In the Hall of Science, the giants sleep waiting for someone to come and misinterpret them" (45). I would ask you to savor in silence the wondrous rhyming that bridges "Science" to "giants" in Hunt's prose poem while I proceed to oversimplify, to tell a cautionary tale of blindfolding narrative.

The elephant of modernity felt the groping hands of many blind men, and thereby hangs a tale. Two of the blind men returned to campus following their hands-on inspection of the beast, and they were known thereafter for their marvelous competing accounts of the monstrous modern. These accounts will be second nature to you now. In one blind reading, the modernist breakthroughs of imagism, as if the Amygism of Ms. Lowell really had triumphed over its progenitors, eventuates in an oppressive domestic modernism championed by the otherwise antimodern Agrarians under the tutelage of Brer Possum, Mr. Eliot. This genealogy leads us, as though DNA truly were destiny, directly to Robert Lowell and *New Poets of England and America*. In the view of the other blind reader on campus, the one who has come to be favored by our more bohemian set, the radical modernity of Williams, Stein and Moore, nearly trampled to death by version one's march of triumph, survives under the care of Zukofsky, Oppen, Niedecker and others, to be rediscovered and reasserted by Olson, Ashbery, Cage and company, and displayed to great effect in Donald Allen's *New American Poetry*, the reading of which at an impressionable age lead to, well . . . "us." The one common link between the "us" and "them" of these two fables for critics is the singular absence of black faces on view in the competing poetic last suppers. True, the perspective had broadened enough in one telling of the tale to admit one Langston Hughes to the story's anteroom, balanced exactly by the accession of one LeRoi Jones, now seated at the table somewhere far to the left of Black Mountain. If you ask most tellers of these tales how it was with black poetry during these epochal changes, they will most likely tell you quite matter-of-factly that that's another story all together, that black poets were somewhere else, doing their own thing.

Which has permitted many white people to tell themselves any number of comforting micronarratives in the years since 1970. (Imagine if you will that the remainder of this paragraph is spoken to you by a white person you have met at a poetry conference. If you are the sort of reader willing to permit me to address you as "you," and you can even imagine yourself attending a poetry conference, then imagine in addition that you too are a white person. You will be relieved of this obligation before essay's end.):

The lesson of the Black Arts poetry of the 1960s is that it's a black thing; we wouldn't understand; we couldn't understand; perhaps we needn't understand. The really valuable poetry of our time is full of formal innovation, wildly associative ... dissociative ... written in decentered subjectivity ... bad, mad, and dangerous to know. Black people tend not to write this way, but that's O.K. because they have their own, probably linear and teleological tales to tell, and even though *we* don't generally value *that kind* of poetry, we *will* value it when it is written by minorities, because that's really all *they* write anyway. Black poetry, of course, is rooted in the black oral tradition, and so we shouldn't expect scribal complexity, nor should we attend too closely to confusing complexities within the oral. The black poem has to be appreciated in performance to be understood, public performance not performance on the page, so let's not bother too much with close reading. Postmodernism is a white thing, not good for black folk to fool with. Poststructuralist theory is a white thing too, politically disabling, and so black people are not the race for theory (though why the dominant race would adopt a politically disabling theory by which to maintain their dominance is either profoundly confusing or stark evidence of the devious ingenuity of white people).

These really are sad stories, fortunately fictions. Still, they are powerful fictions, all too centered, all too teleological. As the literary arts that spoke to the struggles of midcentury followed, and often fomented, the movement from Civil Rights to Black Power to Black Arts, American publishing was seized upon by one of its periodic fits of interest in blackness. When the 1960s became the 1970s, the bookstores and libraries were flooded with anthologies, reprints and new volumes of literary art by black authors. You may not remember this unless you've spent considerable time in used book stores. The flood was followed, in the seemingly natural cycles of racialist detentions and inattentions, by a prolonged drought. Where collections of black verse appearing in the wake of the Civil Rights Acts had been marked by a generosity of formal scope, placing the plain shooting of

Don L. Lee adjacent to the more slippery attack of a Russell Atkins, public representations of black poetry from 1974 to 1994 tended to recapitulate the old one-at-a-time phenomenon of America's always short attention span where black arts are concerned. The liberal difference was that where prior to 1960 it appeared that only one black poet could be heard at a time, after 1975 our more diversified sensibilities permitted us to honor any (small) number of black poets provided they sang only the one black song, presented listeners and readers with a style already certified for white people as recognizably black. The term "Black Poetry" as it operated in critical culture came to refer to only one small segment of the literary production of African-Americans, rather the way the term "Motown" came to signify all black music for certain of the *Big Chill* set.

In the 1960s a little paperback guide to the arts scenes on New York's lower East side was published. Among its bounty of photographs was one depicting Gloria Tropp, wearing a white headdress, performing her poetry before a rapt and suitably bohemian audience. In the background of the photo can be seen her husband, Steven Tropp, another performing poet, one who also toured the country playing drums for Rhythm and Blues acts. This photograph was widely circulated at the time and has been recently reproduced in a lavish coffee table book celebrating days of Beatnik glory in Greenwich Village (ambience triumphing over geographical correctness). The absence of this photograph from other local histories tells yet another tale. The years since 1970 have witnessed an explosion of interest in performance arts. We now see numerous studies and celebrations of this constantly mutating genre devoted to all segments of the performance spectrum from Karen Finley and Annie Sprinkle to Bill T. Jones and Reg E. Gaines. But as with recent consideration of black innovators in poetry, discussions of black performance artists routinely leap from the Harlem Renaissance to the present indicative, as if neither the Black Arts nor the many alternative modes of black performance had ever staged themselves. Worse yet, while nearly all white critics seem to be in agreement about the overwhelming importance of the question of performance to the understanding of black poetry, how many, in an age when we've been told we should always historicize, care to historicize black performance in any sort of rigorous and thorough manner? There seems to be no difficulty in publishing studies of white performance in blackface, and I've counted at least fifteen university press books addressing Rap in one way or another, but where are the books that will tell me of Gloria Tropp's role in the history of performance poetry?

Eventually, Gloria Tropp's work in performance will have to be viewed in the fuller context of African-American performance arts that precede her. Eventually, too, her work must be seen, as suggested by her republished photograph, as it exists in the intersections of

American and European avant gardes, as inhabiting a room where black and white artists affect one another rather than merely affecting the masks of one another's inventions. Finally, works such as Tropp's, when understood in those contexts, may have much to teach us about black soundings and white mythology in today's poetry.

Tropp's performances and their later commemorations poised upon that liminal point where a prior avant garde began to bring a still newer mode of making from within itself. In the years between the close of the second world war and the great Civil Rights march on Washington, black poets molded a modernism that, with the exception of Gwendolyn Brooks's Pulitzer, went largely unremarked in the largely white literary world both inside and outside of the academies. While the generation of Hughes, Bontemps, Walker and Dodson continued the explorations of their earlier modes, and while Sterling Brown patiently awaited the day when he could at last publish his long-delayed second collection of poems, Robert Hayden, Melvin B. Tolson, and others in different parts of the country, often working from precarious posts in black universities and colleges, developed striking variants upon the modernisms of Hughes, Brown and Toomer. Tolson is particularly instructive, as the swirl of learned allusion of his later style is rooted always in an appreciation of the vernacular. Side by side among his papers are pages upon pages of symbolist similes and metaphors he was trying on for size, and hundreds of aphorisms and proverbs collected in the course of his tireless travels and readings, many of them African in their origins. The syntactic complexity and elliptical strategies of these proverbs held a special significance for Tolson, heralding for him a sort of modernism before the letter which he could counter to the racialist modernisms of Stein and Eliot.

It was against this background that the first generation of post-second world war experimentalists among black poets began their lifelong reformation of modernism from their post within American literature. Russell Atkins, working with colleagues in the *Free Lance* group in Cleveland, was an untiring propagandist for formally innovative work. Clarence Major, through his *Coercion* review, was reaching out to a farflung network of readers and writers. On the West Coast, Bob Kaufman began *Beatitude* with Allen Ginsberg, while to the East LeRoi Jones's *Yugen* and *Floating Bear*, coedited with Hettie Jones and Diane Di Prima, provided publication not only for Black Mountain, New York School and Beat writers, but also for such exciting new black poets as Jay Wright, Steve Jonas and A. B. Spellman. Jayne Cortez, relocating to New York from the Southwest, arrived with a heady mixture of *negritude*-influenced surrealism and jazz-inflected lyric. Formal groupings of poets including Washington's *Dasein* organization and New York's *Umbra* poets formed umbrella organizations for a host of reading and publication activities.

All of this formed the fecund ground from which the Black Arts movements and Black Aesthetic criticism grew in the late 1960s and early 1970s. Though the Black Arts period remains an insufficiently historicized and profoundly neglected body of work even today, it forms a curious armature in the engine of academic narrative production. The sheer volume of the Black Arts seems sometimes to have simultaneously deafened critics to so much of what came just before and after, and to have driven critics away from a closer look at its own mechanisms (or, more accurately, the volume has been seized upon as a reason to dismiss the phenomenon itself). In point of fact, the Black Arts were far more broadly cast than many now would recall; most black poetry anthologies of that era found room for far more of the more experimental poets I have so far named than do the Nortons and Heaths of our own era. Stephen Henderson, in his *Understanding the New Black Poetry*, cast his own definitional nets so wide that his understanding of "black" encompassed not only *all* poetry by any poets of African descent, whether or not the poets themselves chose to so designate it, but also some poetry written by white people. It was *that* kind of black nationalism, because America is that kind of nation.

A view of literary history that is equally encompassing will find, as the Black Arts period passed into its own past in the early 1970s, ample precedent for what now gets presented as a sudden reflowering of black experimentalism in verse, but which is more likely a rekindling of modest public attention. In 1971, Telegraph Books, publishers of Tom Clark, Ron Padgett and Ted Berrigan, produced Tom Weatherly's chapbook *Thumbprint*. The volume's first poem, "gina," begins:

> dark owl wish.
> i hear. tic.
> her shadow. bend. sinister.
> in my window. as i bend.
> your mind. our language.   (13)

The poem is reminiscent, especially in its construction, of the formal experiments of Lloyd Addison, one of the Umbra poets writing during the same years. The bend sinister of the poem's third line alludes to Nabokov as well as to the two writers' mutual source in heraldry, but, and here Weatherly produces a bend of his own, also to the knotted joining together of "bend's" additional dictionary meanings. The diagonal cut across the window formed by the woman's frame is paralleled by the poet's bending of our language, as a blues musician bends our notes. The compositional motion of Weatherly's poem, whereby sound and association pull poet and reader from one word to the next, as though content were truly extending itself as form, should put many in mind of the similar techniques operating to somewhat different ends in Harryette Mullen's tour de force, *Muse and Drudge*.

In 1970, Weatherly had published a more extensive collection of his work, *MAUMAU AMERICAN CANTOS*, with Corinth Books, publishers of LeRoi Jones (now become Amiri Baraka), Diane Di Prima, Ed Dorn, Frank O'Hara and Al Young. Weatherly's title alone should indicate just how syncretic a moment is represented by the appearance of this book. "Cantos," recalling Dante and Pound, here conjoins as appellation with "Mau Mau," denoting African resistance to European colonialism, linguistic rebellion against cultural imperialism, and a certain African hermeticism. Both terms swing around the central term "American," indicating allegiance, in the same grain as both Williams and Hughes, to the idioms peculiar to our cadence and our universe of reference. Weatherly's tenth canto pledges just such an allegiance:

> th black hat stingy brim
> on th street you live
> one more day wearing it angel
> enuf so you live. enuf.
> devil lights up th day knowing
> which hat to wear ...   (42)

If the devil generally has powers to assume a pleasing shape, the American devil knows what hat to wear. In American cinematic vernacular, nobody requires a glossary to read the significance of a black hat. The "stingy brim," recently sighted again atop the heads of our present retro generations, is a hat whose name seems to slight itself in its eponymity. (And this decades before *Fear of a Black Hat*.) But what of the black angel "on the street where you live"? "on the street you live" is a simple and straightforward declarative sentence, but it is a declaration formed by suppressing one word in a famous song's title, as many readers will hear another pop idiom, "Devil or Angel," humming along between the lines of Weatherly's lyric. The devil you know is the one who knows which hat to wear. There is patently an excess of "enuf" in these lines, just enough too much to propel the reading eye forward and backward along the signifying horizons vying for our attention. At a time when "the white man" was sometimes said to *be* the devil (and I now release all readers from any further obligation to imagine themselves as white), the devil who knows which hat to wear bedevils our day, lit up. There'll be the devil to pay.

About that "enuf." — Would it not be indeed stingy to declare this an incomplete sentence? More importantly, the abruptness of this simple enough statement points to another line we might follow out from Weatherly's poem into the poetics of black writing of the early 1970s. Like the "tic." and "bend." of Weatherly's "gina," "enuf." demonstrates a poetics of punctual interruption that uses the form of closure as an opening. In our attentions to the oral basis of black verse we may have been too inclined to overlook, or rather we have deafened ourselves to, the ways in which the oral so often takes up the scripted. The period, at least in American English, is an unpronounced, unpronounceable full stop. When we are taking down the speech of some other, we supply on the page as a convenience for future readings the periods that are unheard of between spoken sentences (those utterances we almost unconsciously separate from one another in our hearing on the basis of having recognized in them, as our elementary teachers schooled us, "complete thoughts"). Yet, Americans have a rhetorical fondness for pronouncing the period that we do not extend to the comma or the semicolon. Often, for instance, we will pronounce the period as if its stark statement really would forestall further argument. "I'm not going with you to that poetry reading tonight, period!" Who has not heard such a sentence? In the wake of the projective poetics of Baraka's adaptations and the putatively speech-based typography of much Black Arts lineation, black poets in the 1970s increasingly made use of what might be read as a rhetorical counter to Olson's open parentheses, the period as full stop that stops at nothing, a mode of periodic interdiction.

For example, the title poem of Elouise Loftin's *Barefoot Necklace*, published in 1975, provides a punctuated caesura as unsafe harbor:

>   an investment
> to the world in the world
> unfound. unsafe. only the pedestrian act
> assuming air breathing
> and dying. what temporary grace
> my reality allows me. and you
> inside your body   (15)

In the preceding decade, Amiri Baraka had opened a poem with a period, an opening that cannot be spoken and which implies commencement as reopening, the opening of the field of the poem as coming after the full stop of some invisible predecessor. The caesura of personal lyric could be read as a temporary grace, a grace note of suspended temporality within the body of the poem. Loftin's one word sentence is not a safe place to be. In later years, Ed Roberson was to write of "What surrounds or rather ghettoes all immediate point" (34). The transformation of "ghetto" into a verb performs the immediate point Loftin had indited by her isolation of unsafety from the surround of sound by use of terminal punctuation.

N. H. Pritchard's 1971 volume *EECCHHOOEESS* had taken this punctuated poetic to an extreme in a poem titled ".d.u.s.t." Like Baraka's earlier opening, this poem begins with a period. The title can, of course, be pronounced, but nobody listening to it would hear those recurring periods (unless the reader really read them out one by one, which would greatly extend the real time of the poem), and thus much of the point might be missed in oral presentation. The poem begins:

.m.a.w..o.f..w..a.n.i.n.g..w.r.u.n.g..t.h.e.i.r..l.i.k.e..
.b.r.a.z.e.n..p.r.e.c.i.o.u.s..t.h.r.e.a.d.s..p.o.u.r.e.d. ..
.b.e.n.e.a.t.h..u.p.o.n..w.i.l.t..b.e.a.k.. .
.w.h.o.l.e..v.o.l.l.e.y..p.a.r.c.h.e.s.. ....   (23)

As we begin our reading of the first line we cannot help reuniting the letters into the words they would compose even as we conjecture about possible rules governing the use of the punctuation. Two words in, we might think that while each letter of each word is separated by a period, the words themselves are demarcated by double stops. But then, what of the twinned periods following the first letter of the word "waning"? About the time we're ready to write them off as accidentals, the wholly understandable oversights of a distracted typesetter, we notice that the second line ends not only with a period following the "d" of "poured, but with two additional enjambing periods. And if these additional periods at the sentence (?) or line level are meant to be elliptical, or as signals for pausal durations, how is the reader to measure the differently laden silences of ". .." at the end of line two and ".. ." at the close of line three? There is, as it happens, precedence for some of these periods in the freefloating punctuation in parts of William Carlos Williams's *Paterson*, and Pritchard's disruptions at the level of the letter will remind some who have read more extensively still of Abraham Lincoln Gillespie. But when we read Pritchard alongside Baraka, Loftin and Weatherly, a long overdue reading after an extended period of critical silence, a certain set of family resemblances comes into view.

Look again to the twentyfourth section of Ed Roberson's "This Week's Concerts." There, beneath a black line of demarcation stretching across the page, Roberson writes:

"This to the bridge music is our art of. period." (34) Oral traditionalists will immediately hear the unmistakable voice of James Brown imploring his band to "take it to the bridge." Bristling behind that allusion are others. ("Say it loud.") There is *The Bridge* of Hart Crane's epic. There is the bridge of Sonny Rollins's epic solo practice sessions, and there is the memorial of Amiri Baraka's "The Bridge." The bridge passage is that place where one part of the song bends into another, taking us from the "A" part to the "B" part; a surprise for the listeners, not a chorus; a leaping introduction, not a refrain; that parting in the song we have never heard before but which is replayed every time. It is the song turning back on itself, the art of getting from here to there, from one period to another. What was the Middle Passage if not a bridge joining two periods, whereby what might have seemed closure became new opening? We have seen these periods before if we are readers of English, but black poets have taken them up as Africans once took up the European tempered scale and bent those notes to new ends. From the Black Arts to now, these poets who published in the 1970s take us to the bridge.

But we've been hearing only half the song. Our critics, catching sight of an innovative poem by a black writer, have been too much amazed, too much like the Boston pedestrian (how different from the "pedestrian act" of Elouise Loftin's poem) who appears in N. J. Loftis's *Black Anima*, crying out in surprise at the woman he spies on the boulevard: "Phyllis, Phyllis Wheatley, what, you free?" (24). Conventional literary histories have functioned as what Nellie McKay calls the "Wheatley Court." Like that gathering of Boston notables who subscribed their signatures in testimony to Wheatley's authorship (even John Hancock supplied his "John Hancock"), attesting that they had examined the prodigy and could affirm that she was both black and the poet, the anthologies and histories added daily to our library shelves over the past two decades have affirmed some few poets as African-American while putting a period to the reading of others. N. H. Pritchard foretold one fate that has befallen black art. "Cassandra and Friend" concludes: "Because it was a fact / it never left a track" (*Matrix* 12). The fact of black writing remains a trackless expanse in the minds of many at century's end, and so here, for once, Pritchard puts no period of his own. The period between the time of his writing and the writings of Nathaniel Mackey, Geoffrey Jacques, Harryette Mullen, T. J. Anderson III, Erica Hunt and Mark McMorris is not the chasm that our schoolbooks would turn away from. It has been ghettoed by the surround, but it retains the grace its reality allows it. There are places where these tunes are still played, improvised upon. There are places where the singers were not entirely turned out by the owners in favor of the more marketable (but no more danceable) disco. There are places, nearby, where the song is retuned and places, still, where, as once they did, they take it to the bridge:

> a turn at once familiar and uncanny, that made us fall into an intimacy with our neighbors, joined by a mother tongue, despite it being a lingua franca of a different era.
>
> Erica Hunt, *Local History* (27)

WORKS CITED

Hunt, Erica. *Arcade*. Berkeley: Kelsey Street Press, 1996.

------, *Local History*. New York: Roof Books, 1993.

Loftin, Elouise. *Barefoot Necklace*. Brooklyn, NY: Jamima House Press, 1975.

Loftis, N. J. *Black Anima*. New York: Liveright, 1973.

Pritchard, N. H. *EECCHHOOEESS*. New York: New York U P, 1971.

------, *The Matrix*. New York: Doubleday, 1970.

Roberson, Ed. *Voices Cast Out to Talk Us In*. Iowa City: U of Iowa P, 1995.

Weatherly, Tom. *MAUMAU AMERICAN CANTOS*. New York: Corinth Books, 1970.

------, *Thumbprint*. New York: Telegraph Books, 1971.

Kathryne V. Lindberg

CLEAVER, NEWTON AND DAVIS, RE: READING OF PANTHER LYRICS[*]

> The people will win a new world. Yet when I think of individuals in the revolution, I cannot predict their survival. Revolutionaries must accept this fact, especially the Black revolutionaries in America, whose lives are in constant danger from the evils of a colonial society. Considering how we must live, it is not hard to accept the concept of revolutionary suicide. In this we are different from white radicals. They are not faced with genocide.
> —Huey Newton[†]

I BEGIN MY ACCOUNT OF THE FUNCTION AND PRESENTATION OF POETRY by the Black Panther Party with the once familiar tale of Huey Newton's biggest birthday party. In 1968, this happening *cum* fundraiser brought thousands to Oakland for a celebration at which poetry got things going. This deliberately scripted evening suggests the Party's twinned — though contentious — poetics of remembrance and poetics of revolution. The virtually iconic Free Huey Birthday party — parties, really, since two were held on successive days in Los Angeles and Oakland — inescapably participates in two imperatives of Panther communiqués, recollecting Black struggle and organizing for the coming revolution.[‡] On 17 February 1968 Panther brass and distinguished visitors, including Eldridge Cleaver, Stokley Carmichael, Bobby Seale, Ron Dellums, H. Rap Brown and Bunchy Carter (the *de facto*

---

[*] I thank Anita Hoffman Ehrenfried and Marc Christensen for their careful reading of this essay and for catching more errors than I now need to admit. Thanks also to Sheila Lloyd for proofing the proofs. My American Studies Outside the Walls colleagues and my main colleague, Murray Jackson, have made possible my many excavations in paper and synaptic archives. My colleagues are my joy; my comrades, the poets and ever-living activists, are my motive for future writing and (more?) direct action.

[†] *Revolutionary Suicide* 6.

[‡] Angela Davis uses the speeches at the Los Angeles celebration as backdrop to tell of her preference for the Panthers' coalition politics over SNCC (Student NonViolent Coordinating Committee) nationalism; however, in keeping with her college and family associations, she chose to join the Los Angeles Chapter of the Che Lumumba Club of the Communist Party. See *Autobiography* 158-88. For the background of Black Southern Left labor organizations, especially in Davis's native Birmingham, see Kelley, Robin D. G. *Hammer and Hoe: Alabama Communists During the Great Depression* (Chapel Hill and London: U of North Carolina P, 1990).

Panther poet laureate), stood on stage grouped around the symbolic wicker chair that you might remember from the famous poster of Newton in street leather with machine gun and African warrior regalia.* At the time of this quotational "photo opportunity" the chair was empty; Huey Newton was in jail. However tragicomic — vacuous rather than vacant — that standard issue Cost Plus chair seems in retrospect, the birthday celebration was supposed to unite an increasingly contentious California Party under its absent revolutionary hero and to seal a pact among the leadership of several Panther chapters, the Student Non-Violent Coordinating Committee, and variously affiliated white revolutionaries.

Earl Anthony's ambivalent account wherein "upwards of five thousand" celebrants wearing Afros and African attire were regaled with speeches and musical acts suggests that for the Party substance generally gives way to a politics at once heterogeneous and aestheticized.† However, the Panthers were more, even at this birthday bash, than mere show. Like other rallies for imprisoned or exiled comrades, here official presentations were punctuated by call-and-response cheers of "Free Huey" and "Happy Birthday Huey"; they were also quotational, calling up past Black and colonial struggle. Most poignantly, "If We Must Die," McKay's 1919 sonnet, sounded, as it has many times before and since, the call for self-defensive violence in the face of state sanctioned murder.

In order to give some of the force of this instrumental yet sacerdotal poetry, I will recite the McKay's sonnet as it is embedded in *Picking Up the Gun*:

> The program was gotten under way by Bunchy reading the Invocation, which was the stirring poem by Claude McKay, "If We Must Die." It seemed to me that

---

*This staging of the African American leader with objects that suggest an heroic past is not unusual. Oddly, the Newton poses seems a virtual quotation of no less a figure than Du Bois, in, for example, the *Afro Magazine* of the National Issue of *The Baltimore African American*, 23 February 1957; this Sunday magazine was part of extensive coverage of rising Southern Civil Rights leadership and programs and the simultaneous emergence of sovereign African states, especially Nkrumah's in Ghana. Headlined "At 89, Du Bois is Most Controversial American," this heroic study of the activist scholar sidelined by the Smith Act, places Du Bois in his Brooklyn home under a huge painting of Frederick Douglass; by way of an inventory the writer's den littered with symbolic "stuff" reminiscent of both Freud's study and Newton in the wicker chair. We see "spears of African warriors flank the door. Inside, his desk is littered with papers, books and an empty champagne glass." Du Bois is presented as "princely" and, while "unexpectedly never an especially popular man," an "unquestionable authority on world affairs" and "uncanny in his prophesies."

†Most accounts of the Panthers are interested; many are autobiographical with revisionary history recuperating the author's best self-portrait, often at the expense of Newton's or Cleaver's excesses. This is the case with Anthony — while his revisions tend to diminish Panther accomplishments in the direction of Harold Cruse's *Crisis*; he tries to ignore, and thus to erase, the fact that Newton dismissed him from the Party, along with others suspected of provocation if not conspiracy, after the shootings of Bunchy Carter and John Huggins at UCLA.

those words never rang truer than that night. They seemed to leap off the paper and come driving home, until at the end of that beautiful short poem, I had to catch my breath:

> If we must die, O let us nobly die,
> So that our precious blood may not be shed
> In vain; then even the monsters we defy
> Shall be constrained to honor us though dead!
> O kinsmen! we must meet the common foe!
> Though far outnumbered, let us show us brave,
> And for their thousand blows deal one deathblow!
> What though before us lies the open grave?
> Like men we'll face the murderous, cowardly pack,
> Pressed to the wall, dying, but fighting back! (Anthony 83-84)

The urban insurrections and the police actions against the Panthers in 1967 recapitulate, in part, earlier Red Scares as well as the physical and psychic injuries that were visited upon demobbed Black soldiers in 1919. Besides, McKay's "If We Must Die" has, from its first appearance, indexed a painful history and predicted more of the same.[*] At the Panther birthday party it was used to galvanize a revolutionary African diasporic identity by means of what Huey Newton called "revolutionary suicide" — more of that trope, later.[†] For the purposes of thinking Black Panther poetics, McKay's poem and others like it refuse victimage and meet violence with militant self-defense. This ritualistic performance — aptly

---

[*] Bettina Aptheker notes that after the massacre at Attica State Prison in New York (14 September 1971), *Time* magazine misidentified "If We Must Die," "on a strip of paper among the ruins... painstakingly printed in black ink" as the work of an inmate, "crude but touching in its would-be heroic style" (*Morning Breaks* 49). *Time* received plenty of responses identifying McKay and the sonnet's revolutionary and inspirational credentials. Aptheker's anecdote of anecdotes (or is it a Derridean metaphor for metaphor and/or the mobility of poetic meaning?) tells volumes about the use of anthems and defiant lyrics; the whole itinerary of McKay's work and his Syndicalist politics forms the skeleton of my forthcoming book, *From Claude McKay to Huey Newton: Syndicalist Letters*.

[†] Fanon's influence on Newton, direct as well as mediated through Regis Debray and others' writings of guerrilla warfare, can hardly be overestimated. See especially *Wretched of the Earth*'s formulation of transformative violence, where "the 'thing' which has been colonized becomes man during the same process by which it frees itself" (36-37). Further, Newton's simultaneous staging of legal and martial displays seems scripted, in part, by Fanon; thus, "[W]hen the native hears a speech about Western culture he pulls out his knife or at least he makes sure it is within reach.... [T]he native laughs in mockery when Western values are mentioned in front of him" (43).

likened to a sermon's "invocation" — of the familiar lyric satisfies the two imperatives, remembrance and revolution, that I wish to consider in Black Panther Party poetry.*

The Panthers expected their newspaper, language in general, and poetry in specific to testify to history and experience, to transform victimage into militancy. This means a double focus on two separate poetics and two very different bodies of poetry. First, what I am calling the poetics of revolution often involved the authorship and authority or hagiography of high Party leaders and martyrs; yet this poetry was also about deconstructing and reconstructing the language of racism, oppression, and hierarchy. The second sort of poetry and its poetics, that of remembrance, address the rank-and-file; usually coming from the rank-and-file or at least concerning the everyday, this populist poetry is for affirming group struggle and its common history. Since my purpose is to introduce the function and some examples of these two sorts of work, and in so doing perhaps to pose questions both of vanguardism and of crossed strategies, I shall use material principally from *The Black Panther*, Oakland edition. This newspaper, from which speeches and such regular columns as Newton's "In Defense of Self-Defense" were gathered into books, was by far the Panthers' most successful publishing and publicity venture; it showed who the Panthers were, even as its occasional lyrics announced Panther ideology and personal identification.† I would hope to instigate students of revolution, African diasporic culture, and political poetry to read beyond the newspaper poems and cultural criticism I can dub here. I issue the invitation: go on ahead through the bibliography I abbreviate here and into the archive of the virtually

---

*The Panthers read and issued poems ceremonially, on high occasions of mourning and declamation. Indeed, there is something hieratic about most of Huey Newton's speeches and proclamations, especially his Executive Mandates that begin "So Let it Be Heard. . . " and end ". . . So Let it Be Done." Like sermons in sanctified churches or messages from an imam, where Biblical or Koranic passages and application were declaimed, even the Huey Newton Foundation audiotapes of seminars and meetings conducted by Huey Newton and Bobby Seale suggest that in large and small gatherings Party members also exercised this sort of formal spontaneity by punctuating key points, not with "Amen," but with "Right On!!" or, if the case called for it, "Free Huey!!"

†In *Living for Change* Grace Lee Boggs claims that, lacking program and philosophical grounding, the Panthers were in no way ready for the thousands of followers they attracted (145 et passim). However, in 1970[?] "Propaganda Workshop — Newspapers and Newsletters," Panther success is explained and, in part, emulated, thus: "In over 15 years of the Black Liberation Movement, only two weekly newspapers, *Muhammad Speaks* and *The Black Panther*, have managed to appear regularly." The following reasons are given, "Both have a *nation-wide apparatus* to sell . . .Both are ideologically oriented. . . . Membership has sense of conviction re these ideas and the paper. . . . People buy the paper because they feel some identification with these ideas *or* feel they have to *show* some identification with these ideas. . . . Both have professional appearance, are published *regularly*." Box 13, Boggs Collection, Reuther Labor Archives, Wayne State University. This is an invaluable collection for information on the League of Revolutionary Black Workers, James and Grace Lee Boggs, and C.L.R. James.

forgotten, once ready-to-hand political and aesthetic controversy that the Panthers put on the street, in their paper, and "in your face."*

Both newspaper and its poems are topical and repetitive. Not without self-consciousness, they correct "the official story"; they are addressed to, even as they supplement, public memory — particularly the memory of the Black community. In this *The Black Panther* finds precedents in *The Pittsburgh Courier* of the 1930s, *The Crisis* under Du Bois and, more immediately, Student Non-Violent Coordinating Committee's *Student Voice*. Inspirational verse and the propagation of ideas by posters, photographs, cartoons, pamphlets, and reference to relevant books were nothing new to radical and special interest newspapers. Whereas *The Black Panther* advertised and sold Elaine Brown's albums of original protest and expressive songs and George Jackson's *Soledad Brother*, *The Student Voice* sold copies of *Freedom Songs*, an album that made Negro spirituals and secular lyrics sung by amateurs and professionals available to a wide audience. The solidarity achieved and celebrated in spirituals was a major part of Freedom Summer and the Southern Civil Rights struggle. Remember Fanny Lou Hamer, singer and political candidate as well as Freedom Democrat heroine, on the steps of the Capitol and leading inspirational choruses on the bus. Moreover, the first issue of *Student Voice* contains the following "minor poem" by Horace Julian Bond, in a small section called "Place for Poetry":

> I too, hear America singing
> But from where I stand
> I can only hear Little Richard
> and Fats Domino
> But sometimes,
> I hear Ray Charles
> Drowning in his own tears
> or Bird
> Relaxing at Camarillo
> or Horace Silver doodling
> Then I don't mind standing

---

*The most useful archive, in my experience, is the Huey P. Newton Foundation Papers at Stanford University's Green Library, which includes fascinating tapes of "rap sessions" as well as manuscripts and printed works of great interest, principally from 1971 on. I thank Steve Mandeville Gamble and the entire library staff for generous aid and invaluable patience, especially as I used the archives but a few months after the papers were acquired.

a little longer."*

This piece of Bond juvenilia, reprinted from a college newspaper, is characteristic of many civil rights movement poems: it is quotational (Hughes being a favorite); it references contemporaneous counter-cultural art and music, exemplifying both commercial and marginal cultural production. Like Newton and others, Bond is known principally for things other than poetry, but he is a recognized and published poet. We will see that Bond's invocation of in-group yet popular art is consonant with propaganda strategies, as well as some of the poems, of *The Black Panther*.

While its primary foci in 1969-72, especially in writings attributed to the Black Panther Intercommunal News Service, were international and anti-colonial politics, *The Black Panther* was also a cultural magazine that called attention to local art and events. Subscriptions raised money for programs, and the paper furthered works of individual party writer-leaders. Almost all the early issues of the newspaper, from 1968-71, advertize posters and pamphlets of the ideas and speeches the of The Minister of Defense, Huey Newton, as well as a large print version of the Black Panther Party's Ten-Point Program suitable for hanging. The Panthers used their paper to educate, to organize, and to raise funds along with consciousness and membership.

While I am not ready to argue that the Panthers fashioned immortal lines of poetry or a distinctive musical style, they used verse among other tested propaganda media for constructing representative personalities and invoking other traditions of Black resistance. Because its editors wanted both the paper and themselves to be successful and popular for the masses, for the revolution, and for a mass revolution, *The Black Panther* was both eclectic and dogmatic — by turns and to a fault. And, while it changed over time, the paper bore the marks of its beginnings as both exposé of police violence and paean to its victims.

Huey Newton makes clear that while his "revolution" was not limited to talk, his tactics involved the revolutionary use of words and a series of public performances with rebellious and provocative intent. In *Revolutionary Suicide*, he tells the story of the paper's Oakland founding and its exemplary rhetorical — perhaps even poetic — function:

[T]he plans for the BP paper were made after Denzil Dowell's murder by the police; it was a news and information paper to print the things not printed in the regular paper.

---

*Carson, *The Student Voice* 1:1 (June 1960), 4.

> We were an unusual sight in Richmond, or any other place, dressed in our black leather jackets, wearing black berets and gloves and carrying shotguns over our shoulders. Bobby always strapped a .45 pistol on his side. People would stop and call to us, asking what we were distributing. This was a good example of our own form of armed propaganda.... Walking armed through Richmond was our propaganda. People showed respect for the Party, not only by wanting to read about Denzil Dowell, but also by wanting to learn more about us.... So, in one sense, Denzil Dowell's death was not in vain. Every issue continues the struggle we began in his cause. In a way, *The Black Panther* newspaper is a living memorial to him (143-44).[*]

From its first appearance, on 25 April 1967, as 3,000 copies made on a borrowed mimeograph machine, *The Black Panther* was part of Party performance art, if you will; that is, its distribution by armed Black men as well as its militant — and sometimes its "selfhelp" — contents were integral to Panther ideas. During the course of its run as official organ of the Black Panther Party, the paper underwent ideological and format changes. It began as a few "throwaway" sheets of local news; during its height, with 40,000 subscriptions in 1971, it provided detailed reportage of the trials of Huey Newton and Angela Davis as well as events in Africa, Asia, and Latin America. At various times, like the Party, the weekly paper advocated Direct Action against police brutality in the ghetto and highlighted Communist Party (C.P.U.S.A. as well as R.C.P.) positions. At the beginning and at its effective end in 1975, it also fashioned a Panther ethos — though not a unified aesthetic — by means of its poems and a poetics based on the redefinition of words and images.

The revolutionary agency and personae presented in scattered and dubiously poetic lyrics are neither monolithic nor solely dedicated to, in Angela Davis's phrase, "a struggle constructed as one for the freedom of '*the* Black man'"(italics mine;). Rather than the revolutionary (straight male, cultural nationalist, and representative) subject, *The Black Panther*, and specifically the poetry published therein, presents an array of revolutionary subject positions, if not policies, that have been and might (again) become unified into a

---

[*]Newton's account jibes with that of one of the most comprehensive treatments of the Black Panther Party paper; that is, Abron, JoNina M., "'Raising the Consciousness of the People': The Black Panther Intercommunal News Service, 1967-1980."

revolutionary force.[†] Such differences display the powerful imaginative appeal of Panthers as well as the destructive, arbitrary vanguardism that was one factor in the Party's undoing.

The Black Panther, Oakland Party edition, shows the influence of different rhetorical strategies by various editors and/or Minsters of Information and Education. For example, Eldridge Cleaver, Emory Douglas, and Ericka Huggins articulated and practiced three different views of art as well as the function and proper deployment of propaganda. If those names do not immediately suggest the range and internal contradictions of Panther aims and programs; suffice it to say, Cleaver's revolutionary violence and his own literary celebrity contrast sharply with Douglas's attempts to co-opt the work of Black popular artists and, finally, with Huggins's primary investment in community education programs that encompass cultural nationalism and downplay revolution in favor of survival.

That revolutionary subjectivity and agency are constructed out of contradictions in a long struggle that has proved dialectical, continuous, and open-ended did not escape the notice of the first Minister of Information, Eldridge Cleaver. Despite repeated assertions that he hoped to initiate immediate and regimented guerrilla warfare, to literalize "the gun" and "the urban guerrilla" into an armed struggle which would undo oppression once and for all, Eldridge Cleaver announced a revisionary writing and educational program for the Black Panthers. In, for example, "Education and Revolution," Cleaver links revolution to interpretation and the refiguring of individual words. He writes:

> One of the techniques or one of the weapons that the enemy uses against us in our struggle is to turn words against us, to define our struggle in terms that place our struggle in a bad light, so that the word "revolution" is given a bad name, is looked upon as a negative term. . . . For us the word "revolution" should be a beautiful word because it's a word that promises us hope, that promises us a better life and we should not be ashamed to call ourselves revolutionaries.
> . . .[T]alks of "crime in the streets". . . "disorders". . . "law and order" all of these words are smoke screens to confuse us, to create conflicts between the various exploited groups. ("Education and Revolution" 44)

---

[*]Davis, "Angela Davis: Reflections on Race . . .," 306. See also Davis, Angela. "Black Nationalism: The 1960s and the 1990s," where Davis, renovating her Party experiences for current identity politics, recalls Newton's 1971 remarks against homophobia and the Party's association with Jean Genet as mitigating factors in the otherwise — but also misread — macho image and ideology of the Panthers.

As though his version of *the* heroic revolutionary Black Man *could* overcome itself, after being patched from a history of words and other weapons appropriated from such American shibboleths as "the people," "the American Revolution" and other institutions that "he" would abolish, Cleaver announces a war that will change history by delivering the final revolution as the people's war. He projects a "we" that will accomplish the revolution and, at the same time, stop the play of interpretation and/or revisionary history with which *it* — that is, *the*/Cleaver's revolution — began: "We must not get into a bag of thinking that we're involved in a game: a revolution is not a game, it is a war. We are involved in a war — a people's war against those who oppress the people, and this is a war in the clearest sense of the word" ("Education and Revolution" 46).

When Cleaver joined the Panthers he was already famous as contributing editor of *Ramparts*, the magazine that first published the essays and prose poetry that would appear as *Soul on Ice*. Cleaver's prison reading and writing regimen evidences his inculcation of Existentialism and Marxism as well as Du Bois on consciousness and Fanon on violence. Metaphors from these and other sources were at once compatible with and left their mark on Panther ideology. Such borrowed and twiceturned tropes also exemplify what Newton would humorously tag "shockabuku" or taking the enemy off guard in order to make him believe unwanted things and behave in unwonted ways.[*] The redefinition of words, as well as the redirection of the future away from the failed revolutions of the past into ultimate victory is, like provocation by exercising 4th Amendment rights while distributing newspapers, a self-conscious rhetorical strategy. Cleaver's formulation is again helpful; in a pamphlet issued as "The First Black Panther Party for Self-Defense Ministry of Information Black Paper" and presented to the Peace and Freedom Party founding convention, 16 March 1968, he explains:

> Black people in North America have always been plagued by a dual status. We were both slave and Christian, we were both free and segregated, we are both integrated and colonized. In the past this duality has worked to our disadvantage. It kept us running around in circles. Today we propose to turn it to our advantage, in the manner that we have turned our blackness from a disadvantage into a rallying point of advantage. Yesterday we were black and oppressed; today our

---

[*]Describing his own performance and the reaction of police to name-calling and official surveillance, Newton says, "we demonstrated their cowardice to the community with our 'shockabuku.' It was sometimes hilarious to see their reaction; they had always been cocky and sure of themselves as long as they had weapons to intimidate the unarmed community. When we equalized the situation, their real cowardice was exposed" (*Revolutionary Suicide* 122).

blackness is a tool of our liberation. Our dual status gives us a mythical right of citizenship and the concrete reality of the situation has given us the national consciousness of an oppressed and colonized people (2).[*]

This habit of turning disadvantage to advantage, of troping the double jeopardy of being Black and poor, of being trapped within and locked outside "America," is central to Panther writing and related performances, including "patrolling the police," and Newton's concept of "revolutionary suicide" that fashions survivable militancy and/or guerrilla warriors out of tragic history and against all odds. A poem by Kathleen Cleaver, published in *The Black Panther*, 16 March 1968, performs this revision of loss into revolution by the transfiguration of Malcolm into the spirit of Huey:

The Black Mass Needs But One Crucifixion

Malcolm X died for us

We will have no more religious executions
        no more political assassinations
        no more murdering of black men
            in the streets of Babylon

The black mass needs but one crucifixion

And in that death

On the cross of America

We all received a new birth

For in us awoke a new life
    Set afire by the cry of
        BLACK POWER

---

[*]The full, descriptive title of the pamphlet is helpful here, as it suggests the two-front and changing battle terrain Cleaver mapped: "Revolution in the White Mother Country and National Liberation in the Black Colony," Richmond, California: Black Panther Party, March 16, 1968 [Black Panther Party for Self-Defense Ministry of Information Black Paper, presented to the founding convention of the Peace and Freedom Party. It is also useful to remember, as Newton would later emphasize, the fact that Cleaver was Minister of Information, not Minister of Defense or Co-Chairman.

> That burned in Watts. That burned in Newark, that
> Burned in Detroit
>
> And that burns in Huey's soul
>
> . . . .
>
> Huey told us to defend our lives
>
> To stop the tide of genocide
>
> The gas chamber will not be his fate
>
> By any means necessary
>
> HUEY P. NEWTON MUST BE SET FREE!
>
> The Black mass needs but one
>   Crucifixion.*

Huey Newton's tactics of facing down police on the street, barely staying within the bounds of Constitutionally protected behavior, were daring and parodic. They did indeed turn police to pigs before the eyes of cameras and comrades, but this transformation was but part of a guerrilla theater and guerrilla war strategy that turned certain death into at least moral victory. Faced with genocide in the very streets of one's city, as Newton was not alone in noting, Black citizens had as much to gain by standing firm before police violence as the Vietnamese had before French and American arsenals.† In part because of a righteous cause, but also on account of anti-colonial solidarity and military strategy, what seemed suicidal might end up transforming the oppressor into his own victim. This all involved revolution and "revolution"; placing the adjective revolutionary before the conditions imposed by neo-colonialism and capitalism, testifying and transforming, and at the same time subjecting existing conditions to the dialectic, Newton tried to perform and to explain Revolutionary Suicide in historical and psychological terms. He coins "revolutionary

---

*"The Black Mass Needs But One Crucifixion," [poem] *The Black Panther*, 16 March 1968.

†From the 10th point of the Black Panther Party Ten-Point program (the call for a United Nations plebiscite in Black communities to determine political representation and direction), it seems clear that Newton and Seale knew The Civil Rights Congress document, *We Charge Genocide: The Historic Petition to the United Nations for Relief from a Crime of the United States Government Against the Negro People*. Eds. William L. Patterson; signed by Du Bois, Aptheker, Crockett, et al. New York: Civil Rights Congress, 1951.

suicide" as against "reactionary suicide"; as elsewhere, tracking the flow of post-industrial capital and post-national communications, he will propose "revolutionary inter-communalism" as against reactionary intercommunalism:

> Some see our struggle as a symbol of the trend toward suicide among Blacks. Scholars and academics, in particular, have been quick to make this accusation. They fail to perceive differences. Jumping off a bridge is not the same as moving to wipe out the overwhelming force of an oppressive army. . . . Thus the American colonists, the French of the late eighteenth century, the Russians of 1917, the Jews of Warsaw, the NLF, the North Vietnamese — any people who struggle against a brutal and powerful force — are suicidal. . . .
> With this redefinition, the term 'revolutionary suicide' is not as so simplistic as it might seem initially. In coining the phrase, I took two knowns and combined them to make an unknown. A neoteric phrase in which the word 'revolutionary' transforms the word 'suicide' into an idea that has different dimensions and meanings, applicable to a new and complex situation (*Revolutionary Suicide* 67).

There, in the "neoteric" — the new which is, in fact, revisionary and shows the marks of its revision — Newton displays the workings of his own poetics and his poetic faculty for working, however impossibly, against the grain of received meaning and greater force.

Bunchy Alprentice Carter, killed at a shootout in Campbell Hall at UCLA, is one organizer and prison writer who versified Panther doctrine. His poems are indeed fugitive, but the following, that adapts a quotation of Chairman Mao regarding the meaningful death of a revolutionary, and the mediating source in *Revolutionary Suicide*, is characteristic of both Newton's "neoteric phrase" and Panther programmatic verse. I take these lines, from "Black Mother," from an account of his public reading:

> For a slave of natural death who dies
> can't balance out to two dead flies
> I'd rather be without the shame
> A bullet lodged within my brain
> if I were not to reach our goal
> let bleeding cancer torment my soul (Anthony 74).

It is in the passage of metaphors, as organizational tools in the Black community, into the official media's misrepresentations, and the state's power to infiltrate a community and use guerrilla tactics (the drug war, for example), that the Panthers' Direct Action tactics seem simply suicidal, their ways of borrowing and transforming more systematic programs simply erroneous.* In the wake of failed revolution, Bunchy Carter's failures of language seem nominal. Moreover, if more for his performances than his poetry, Newton remains the focus of attention and interpretation — certainly not of unqualified veneration.

Huey P. Newton was a celebrity because he was the leader and acknowledged theorist of the Black Panther Party; not to mention the fact that he was terribly photogenic before police and television cameras as he led rallies or read his law books at the site of questionable arrests and police harassment. His writings, beyond statements and interviews in *The Black Panther*, were used for fundraising, party organizing and publicity. Visiting revolutionaries, honorary Panthers, and those who would debate or correct Newton's pronouncements, including George Jackson, named Field Marshall though he was in Soledad during his whole Panther affiliation, William L. Patterson, Robert F. Williams, and Angela Davis (only to name well known Americans), were featured as writers and/or celebrities in the paper. The Huey Newton Foundation Papers archive numerous documents, including correspondence, contracts, Party records, drafts and manuscripts of poems, essays, scripts, and movie treatments which show evidence of the mainstream artistic ambitions of individual members as well as the success of big entertainment ventures of the Black Panther Party. Rather late on, in 1975, under the imprimatur of New Directions and with an introduction by Richard Bakerroshi, Abbot of the Tassahara Zen Center, Huey Newton coauthored *Insights and Poems* with Ericka Huggins, his only collection of verse.† Averring the honorific "poet," Newton insisted in calling his brief meditations and affirmations of satire

---

*During one of his murder trials for the death of Officer Frey, Newton explains that the prosecutor, Jensen, continually turned Newton's metaphors against themselves into literal threats of violence against all police officers, and "[h]e reinforced this suggestion by having me read a poem, 'Guns, Baby, Guns'. . . which was filled with symbols and metaphors that have a particular meaning for Black people but are utterly lost on most whites" (*Revolutionary Suicide* 234). This is not the only time that Newton claims an ideal readership or habitus of, say, the oppressed who, subject to genocide, use weapons — words as well as guns — that are ready to hand and have specialized application. Of course, the Panthers did have real guns that weren't nearly as big as those pointed against them.

†The latest incarnation of a Party newsletter, *I AM WE: Newsletter of the Committee for Justice for Huey P. Newton and the Black Panther Party*, published several of Newton's Insights. "I Diminish Myself," for example, appeared in I:3 (May/June 1975), 2. In the paper and elsewhere, Newton identifies "I AM WE" as an African saying about community; it might, however, strike one as quite similar to Hegel's formulations of the highest state of consciousness and/or of the State.

and selfhood, "Insights."* I mention these to suggest the variety of projects that engaged the Panthers and to note the little known Zen affiliation of Newton.

One telling Insight seems a plea and selfcorrection, affirming Newton's full treatment of — and as a — human being, rather than the fetishizing of a particular part or function. On account of my own copyright scruples, and in order to suggest something of the intended audience and use of this "poem" (as much a poem as Kerouac's Zen *Pomes?*), I am quoting Newton from Tony Seymour's publication announcement, "*Insights and Poems* by Huey P. Newton and Ericka Huggins, Millennium Warriors." As preparation for the liberal public's consumption of the exceptional Black man, this is decidedly hyperbolic; its "we" a bit presumptuous:

> For the sake of convenience we define ourselves as being a racial strain, we define ourselves as being aged so many years, we define ourselves in terms of our macho-strength or our feminine charm, we define ourselves in so many myriad ways that many truly believe that that which constitutes our essence are the labels by which we are defined. In this regard, Huey's meditations have revealed to him the following INSIGHT:
> I DIMINISH MYSELF:
> If I define myself as my thumb
> I deny myself my fingers
> If I define myself as my fingers
> I deny myself my hand
> If I define myself as my hand
> I deny myself my body
> If I define myself as my body
> I deny myself the universe
> I Diminish myself†

---

*In a letter of 14 May 1973, to Verline Wilson, an editor at Doubleday, Newton wrote "I write what I call 'Insights,' rather than poetry. I have enclosed my insights along with Ericka Huggins poetry, which I would like to have published together." Dr. Huey P. Newton Foundation Inc. Collection, Series 2, box 44. This collection was not published until 1975 and then by City Lights.

†Perhaps taking Newton's reconstructive surgery, his search for physical/psychic wholeness or totality, too literally, but certainly betraying his own need to butcher a god with feet of clay, Hugh Pearson, narrating through a most unreliable third-person (Willie Payne, former Panther, crackhead, and bottle scavenger) scavenging for bottles, discovers Newton's corpse in fragments, thus: "he noticed someone's feet sticking out up ahead on the right sidewalk. The rest of the body was hidden by hedges. Payne thought it was a neighborhood man who lived around the corner from him. The man he thought it was often got into arguments with some of the neighborhood

Whether or not one wishes to take those lines on a turn through Seymour's leveling critique of stereotypes (where identity markers like age are equal to what some might consider larger issues of the assignment from above of Black male identity), and I think not, Newton's sentiment seems consonant with his efforts, after 1970, to expand the programs and image of the Panthers beyond a "militant vanguard." He defers plans for "the revolution now" in, for example, "The Defection of Eldridge Cleaver and Reactionary Suicide," when he says, "We saw ourselves as the revolutionary 'vanguard' and did not fully understand that only the people can create the revolution" (*Revolutionary Suicide*, 239).* Such programmatic changes meant that Newton had also to change his persona, even his title, from Minister of Defense to Servant of the People, after his visit to China.

The people, if not ready to make revolution, were perhaps ready to pay for their education by buying a range of artistic and ideological products.† In 1970, and a little later, under the stewardship of Elaine Brown, the Oakland Panthers, along with teams of entertainment lawyers, agents, and production companies engaged in an astonishing number of entrepreneurial and artistic ventures. By 1971, the Panthers were entirely ready to be funded by, and to become, Black Capitalists.‡ Therefore, questions of the propriety and utility,

---

young people, and [he] figured they had beaten him up. On second thought, he wondered if it was someone else. . . . They called 911. But it was too late to save the life of the man lying on the sidewalk. At 6:10 that morning, Huey Percy Newton was pronounced dead on arrival at Highland Hospital, from three bullet wounds to the head" (*Shadow of the Panther* 89). In this way, Newton's metaphors, and his considerable physical charms, are turned against him, but they also betray an unreconstructed worship of masculinist authority — even as Pearson mocks the notion of "Supreme Leader."

*This is not the place fully to open the question of Panther vanguardism; however, Newton, who went on to adopt what he called the African — but also the Hegelian and Maoist — motto "I Am We," could never leave behind his own image and desire as embodiment of the revolution. On the question of bureaucratic centrism and the exaggerated personal authority of the Leader and Panther mistakes in this direction , see Glaberman, Marty. *Mao as Dialectician*. Detroit: Bewick, 1971.

†In "Black Capitalism ReAnalyzed" (*The Black Panther* 5 June and 9 August 1971, reprinted *To Die for the People* 101-11), Newton rather confusingly plots ways of plowing Black money into programs that would be of mutual benefit to the poor and to bourgeois nationalists. He fails to recognize how thoroughly he contradicts his own class analysis (not to mention his mockery of "pork chop nationalism") that still underwrites his internationalist policies at this time; this would give credence to criticism (see, for example, James Boggs) of the Party's dissociation from Black workers and the practical engagement of Class — only Fred Hampton and the Chicago Panthers addressed Class actively and categorically.

‡In December 1970 the Panthers took over Acorn Market, which had been the first Black market in Oakland, and renamed it CalLa Soul Foods. In 1970 Stronghold Consolidated Productions, Inc. (the Panthers' literary wing and agency) retained Lubell, Lubell, Fine and Schapp, a New York law firm to represent the Panthers for 3 1/2% of gross on various projects. Incorporated in 1972, The Black Fund, Inc. (with Melvin Newton and Gwen Fontaine

intellectual and property rights to signature or "auteristic" productions were most important to Huey Newton and the Panthers. *Seize the Time*, the title of Bobby Seale's 1970 biography of Newton, also named Seize the Time Books and Records.* One particular letter from Martin Kenner, Executive Vice President of Stronghold Productions, the Panthers' main literary and production arm, tells a good deal about the care with which Panther intellectual properties were handled, especially the writings of the Minister of Defense and, later, the Servant of the People. Kenner, addressing Newton as "Dear Servant," tries to suggest that, given Newton's manner of composition, "great bursts of energy and productivity," and the publicity aims of the Party, it might be better to widely distribute and publish, not Party books, but articles and other sorts of compositions by prominent Party members, some of whom already had independent publishing careers. Affirming that critical and commercial success need not violate ego or solidarity strictures, he says:

> Toni [Morrison] told me that she had asked you if you wanted to write a book of review(s) for the *New York Times Book Review* and that you stated that if you did that would put you in the position of writing as Huey P. Newton and not as the leader of the Black Panther Party. What I thought, but did not say to her when she told me that, was what a Vietnamese comrade told me... that organization is to ideology and program as a shadow is to a person; as one moves or changes so must the other. I think the esteem in which you are held reflects on the Party and also that it is correct for you to have a presence that transcends our current organizational framework.†

Toni Morrison, then an editor at Random House, though not tempted by the Huggins/Newton poetry project, accepted Seale's biography, and edited and developed *To Die for the People*, Newton's proclamations and articles revised from *The Black Panther*.‡

---

as principal signatories), began doing business in Oakland and owned considerable real estate in San Francisco and Oakland. Dr. Huey P. Newton Foundation Inc. Collection, Stanford University, Series 2 boxes 31 and 44.

*Lubell, et al., whom the Panthers retained as intellectual property lawyers, were escrow agents for this record company in New York. Dr. Huey P. Newton Foundation Inc. Collection, Stanford University, Series 2 box 44.

†22 June 1972, p. 3 of 4 pages; . Dr. Huey P. Newton Foundation Inc. Collection, Stanford University, Series 2 box 44.

‡On 19 July 1972, Morrison wrote to Stronghold Productions rejecting a volume of Ericka Huggins' poetry. Dr Huey P. Newton Foundation Inc. Collection, Stanford University, Series 2 box 44.

Revolutionary Suicide, also more a collection of notes and toasts than a unified memoir or program, was published by Harcourt Brace in 1973. As further evidenced by his sketchy dissertation finished more than ten years later, *War on the Panthers*, for which he obtained a film contract and substantial advance, Newton's talents lay in quick insights and in turning his readings in canonical philosophy, social science, and street culture into concepts useful for his purposes of revolution and apologetics.* After his many seminars in historiography, philosophy (he was reading Nietzsche, Heidegger and Derrida at UC Santa Cruz), and writing, his essays were, like his earliest polemical pieces, heterogeneous and heterodox. Even as a retiree or survivor from the work of daily revolution, he simply did not have the leisure for sustained argument — let alone to conjure the revolution so many believed the Panthers heralded. Nevertheless, as early as 26 March 1971, Newton was receiving $5,000 for six packaged lectures that he took to numerous college campuses.† The pain and praise showered on him from cops and boosters, respectively, kept him too close to his agent's (Vietnamese) notion that program grows or shrivels like a man's shadow. In any case, it is a fruitful mistake to equate Newton with the Party and its projects. Granted, after Cleaver's tenure as Minister of Information, Newton did try to shift focus somewhat from the nearly Carlylean notion that revolution emanates, that leadership resides, in one man — or one's manhood. But he never gave up making proclamations and ex cathedra announcements that clash with his stated program and disruptively ironic writing practice. If they were not enough to comprise an ideology, Newton's celebrity and other Panther productions were not intermittently enough to sustain a unified cultural program. There is a certain diacritical interest to much of the cultural work done or projected by *The Black Panther* and Huey Newton. For example, we are left to imagine how Newton would have completed his short drafts for an opera, "A Modern Day Porgy and Bess: A Story of Food, Shelter, Work, Music, Dance, Love and Death."‡

---

*On 16 May 1984, Jane Kagon, of Film Development Fund, sent a check for $21,250 from Columbia Pictures for development of a project based on his dissertation in the History of Consciousness Program at Santa Cruz, which after underwent many revisions and became a report, with personal testimony, of abusive police (and COINTELPRO) to the surveillance and violence against dissenters from Haymarket to the Panthers. Some people forget that Newton finished his Ph.D. in 1985. The movie never materialized. See Dr. Huey P. Newton Foundation Inc. Collection, Stanford University, Series 1 Box 56.

†This is the date of a letter, apparently from Elaine Brown, that proposes this fee and asks for a contract forthwith; Dr. Huey P. Newton Foundation Inc. Collection, Stanford University, Series 1 Box 31.

‡This is but one of Newton's film treatments/proposals; this, along with handwritten notes for "The Rapist Stinky," a film about a real case, are in Dr Huey P. Newton Foundation Inc. Collection, Stanford University, Series 1 Box 49.

Emory Douglas, Panther political cartoonist and sometime Black Panther Minister of Culture, highlighted another "commercial" aspect of Panther art and writing. "Art for the People's Sake," a speech he delivered at Fisk University, was printed whole in *The Black Panther*, 21 October 1972, at a time when the Party, whose funds were continually depleted by costly trials as much as by community "Survival Programs," proposed that revolutionary art piggyback on commercial art. In keeping with the turning-the-enemy-against-itself tropics essential to Panther strategies, Douglas would deploy advertising techniques and redirect the co-opted work of Black artists. Popular music and movies were first among the visual and language arts with which he would "bombard the masses" who do not "go into art galleries." In attempting to snatch the weapons of the oppressor, he claims that, while imitations of Western classics and elitist institutions like museums are dangerous,

> We have a greater enemy in commercial art. What is commercial art? It is a method of persuasion, mind control; it oppresses Black people. If we look around in our community, what do we see? We see billboards, with advertising, that tells us what to buy, how to buy. And we go out and buy — our own oppression.
>
> But we say that if we take this structure of commercial art and add a brand new content to it, then we will have begun to analyze Black people and our situation for the purposes of raising our consciousness to the oppression that we are subjected to. We could use commercial art for the purpose of educating Black people, not oppressing them. (4)

That deliberate openness to more sources of quotation and a wider thematics — or is it abusive borrowing (theft?) and farfetched interpretation — accounts for a certain postmodern or simply vanishing aspect of Panther creative work. Where exactly to draw the lines of ownership, the canons of taste, in the aesthetics and the distribution program Douglas proposes? Sometimes this does get hard (or even just hard to take), and the Panthers seem like opportunists whose choices are beyond eclectic and into random. Surely, their errors lie at the other pole from monolithic agitprop. We should recall that their functions drew, and drew crowds with, entertainers such as Ike and Tina Turner and Country Joe and the Fish; that they endorsed free jazz and folkish protest songs, or whatever else might be made to carry the Panthers evermore diffuse message into an interview or cultural interest piece in *The Black Panther*. Finally in 1972, when it enjoyed large circulation but also when the big stories of Angela's and Huey's trials were winding down, *The Black Panther* ran celebrity interviews and published representative song lyrics of blues and pop-artists whose work seemed to jibe with Panther ideas; for example, the same issue that ran Douglas's speech had "Hey Mister," song lyrics from a new Ray Charles album, copyrighted by Betty Lapcevic. The lyrics, transcribed as a poem, are introduced with the claims that "[s]ongs are part of a people's life, culture, an expression and reflection of our daily lives," and that "[i]n a recent recording, Brother Ray Charles delivered his latest 'message from the people'" (14). This contradictory move, at once a bow to (Black?) capitalism and a borrowing back of Black authenticity, might be cited as proof of the Panthers' lack of originality, perhaps even of their stealing — or as we will see, in their silent use of Dudley Randall's "Ballad of Birmingham" — their ultimate respect for the content if not the copyrights of other artists. But not even Cleaver, we must remember, claimed that the Panthers were "original." Indeed, how can such a revolution — against yet within the nation and the 'hood,' if not nationhood — be anything but violently quotational?*

If their products and productions do not fall into one category, Panther attempts to demystify commercialism and to accept diverse contributions to a "people's art" make a certain, if sometimes patronizing, sense. In this vein, the Oakland Panthers frequently rented large theaters to screen movies like *The Mack, Black Girl,* and *Sweet Sweetback's Baadasssss Song* — movies in a genre perhaps misleadingly called "Blaxploitation," which tends to exaggerate the physical and psychical power of heroic Black pimps, gangsters, spies, or, to use Newton's favorite word, "the lumpen," to challenge the System that put them on the street. "Sweet Sweetback's Baadasssss Song," does indeed contain a song, which purports to be a message to the people (i.e. a rather operatic lyric poem about revolution and transformation) bearing literary and cultural analysis as the symbolic summary of the movie.† This movie, certainly a scandal to anyone who took it straight as a representation of Black sexuality and ghetto rage, provoked Huey Newton's longest piece of criticism. "He Won't Bleed Me: A Revolutionary Analysis of Sweet Sweetback's Baadasssss Song" argues that in the movie, which earned an X for sex and violence, Melvin Van Peebles "is righteously signifying because he engages the audience in a climax when Sweetback downs the police. . . . So [Van Peebles] is advocating a bloody overthrow because his victims want to survive"

---

*Newton was scrupulous about correcting misidentifications and misappropriations of his own revisionary borrowings. For instance, at the same time that he makes clear his debt to Robert F. Williams's *Negroes with Guns*, he says "Stokely wrote in a recent book [*Black Power*] that I had asked his permission to start an organization and call it the Black Panther Party. This is untrue. Bobby and I together had chosen the Party's name, taking it from the symbol of the black panther used by the Lowndes County Freedom Organization, which Stokley had helped found in Mississippi" (*Revolutionary Suicide* 157).

†Newton notes of the record album released at the time of the movie that Van Peebles had produced an opera with the Black ghetto community acting as chorus; *To Die for the People*, 141-42

(*To Die for the People*, 122).* What would have to be called Newton's Nietzschean or deconstructive reading — his reference points being Nietzschean Will and Fanon on violence — of this film is worth considering for more than its apparent hysterical misogyny, if you will.

A more extreme example of turning commercial art to Panther purposes can be seen in the revision of an advertisement for a novelty wristwatch into the Eldridge Cleaver "Funky Time" watch. It appears that someone has written over the name of Moshe Dayan the name of Eldridge Cleaver on an ad for what the inflight airline books would term "use your own logo" watches. I hope that the use of this "defaced" magazine ad, a real work of its moment, suggests another turn of the screw to which Panther irony has been submitted.† The watch deal seems not to have been consummated; at least the proposal for a contract, including prices and descriptions, suggests that the initial capital investment was too high. Panther memorabilia, more than their writings or political programs, are now gaining market share. Largely without irony or the attempt to turn commercialism against itself, websites and celebrity tours of Oakland's sacred sites, a growing number of interested memoirs, and royalties from early publications and papers, are now "an industry."‡

Panther entertainment profits and other capital were increasingly plowed back into educational and community programs, which sustained and trained people for the future revolution — or evolution? — of society, even as schools and legitimate programs made profit for the Party. Under Ericka Huggins's leadership of cultural and educational programs, *The Black Panther* issued a poetic manifesto of sorts to accompany Black Panther Intercommunal Youth Institute poems. These along with a story about the first eighth-grade graduates of the Youth Institute appear in an enlarged Saturday edition on 15 June 1974. The article announces the importance of poetry to what amounts to a pedagogic — if not a cultural — revolution. The Panthers advocate a move away from "the basics" of establishment education into a revolutionary curriculum that squares individual expression with party doctrine and Black traditions. Printed under a photograph of a "language arts class" and its instructor standing before a blackboard apparently full of poems, the five

---

*The article, originally excerpted in *The Black Panther*, 19 July 1971, appears in *To Die for the People*, 115-16.

†The advertisement, mockup, and letter, 4 March 1971, from David Lubell regarding delays and financial problems, are in Dr Huey P. Newton Foundation Inc. Collection, Stanford University, Series 1 Box 31.

‡Numerous autobiographies and authenticated accounts have recently emerged from former Black Panthers and fellow-travelers; those of David Hilliard and Elaine Brown have had the widest circulation, while Bobby Seale's *Seize the Time* (1970) seems more immediate and accurate. The best recent collections of scholarly and cultural interest are those edited by Charles E. Jones, proprietor of Black Classics Press, and Kathleen Cleaver and George Katsiaficas; while happily not free of polemics, the essays therein anthologized tend to be carefully argued and documented.

young people's poems are carefully presented as part of a lesson in Black nationalism and history, in which the Panthers and ghetto experience feature prominently. The five titles suggest individual voicings of recognizable scenes, shared experience, and Panther doctrine: "The World is a Junkyard," You Had Some Flowers," "We the People," "I Feel," "The Flower"

A headline announces the topic of the story, and a poetics, by quoting the insistent isocolons that organize the longest poem. These declare both the young writer's persona and the proper function of poetry: "Poetry: "I FEEL... I HURT... I CRY... I EDUCATE... I RECOGNIZE." This poem's form might remind us of Newton's far mood in the simple noun-verb declarations of "I Diminish Myself" ("I deny," "I define," "I diminish"); the poetics and the actions our poet, Ricky Wallace, Group 5, proposes to encompass seem adequately to define the basic function of *The Black Panther* in its last days, and its poetry, despite ideological changes and various affiliations over the course of its publication, seemed always to call the individual into the simple sentiments behind the shared group ideology.* From this small offering, the larger program, at least, can be gleaned; therefore, I quote at some length:

> I feel for Bobby Seale
> I feel very good
> I feel the table
> I feel the city changing
> I feel all that is right about the city,
> Except the police (I don't
> like them)
>
> I hurt
> I hurt my back
> I hurt when there is a comrade
>   hurt

---

*The poems are framed by a column of historical events from "This Week in Black History" (i.e. Jack Johnson's death in 1946; a triple event for Civil Rights in 1963, white rioting in Cambridge, Maryland, George Wallace's famous resistance in Birmingham and Medgar Evers' assassination) and an advertisement for Elaine Brown's *Until We're Free*, an album of her original songs. Next to this is Newton's strenuous endorsement of Brown as "the First, genuine People's Artist America Has Produced." Just as instructions for the purchase , "$4 by cash or money order" are included in the ad along with a picture of Brown; the whole presentation combines entrepreneurial and community service projects of the party in 1974.

I hurt when the pigs beat
the people
I hurt when my mother hurts
I hurt when the people hurt
I hurt when you hurt
. . . .
I recognize
I recognize the people
I recognize my comrades
I recognize my family
I recognize the things in
the real world

By contrast to earlier, overtly revolutionary days, which were perhaps no less commercially driven, in 1974 Panther entertainment and educational programs raised money primarily for local community service programs (including clinics, transportation to jails, food programs, schools), rather than weapons and bail. The programmatic introduction to the poems reflects this strategy, and it suggests bourgeois ambitions in the basics "of a child's education" modified by correct training for change; because, "the three R's — reading, 'riting, and 'rithmetic — allow for limited creativity on the child's part, poetry is a welcome opportunity to use his imagination and to express some of his innermost thoughts." Revolution is implicated in and memorialized by this rank-and-file educational poetry, but we are a long way from Cleaver's revolution in words, if not totally removed from the violence to which he responded in kind.

I would like to end this introduction to Black Panther poetry and poetics with one of many articles Angela Davis contributed to *The Black Panther*.* "Comrade Angela Davis: Eight Years Since Birmingham," 18 September 1971, recalls that Davis grew up in Birmingham, that her family knew the families of the girls killed in the bombing of the Sixteenth Street Baptist Church, 15 September 1963. The purpose of the article is to bring personal experience, cultural theory, and polemics to bear on the omnipresence and sheer ordinariness of

---

*In addition to full coverage of her trial, Davis's longest engagement with the Panthers involved her work with the Soledad Brothers Committee and her own contributions to *The Black Panther*.. Most of her signed contributions to the paper appeared in 1971-72. She was especially close in friendship and program to Ericka Huggins, whom she had met during an arrest. See, for example, "Angela Introduces Ericka's New Book," *The Black Panther*, 20 May 1972, 2, 7-9. Signed, Angela Y. Davis, Santa Clara County Jail, December 1971. Several of their letters, exchanged when one or both were incarcerated, are at Stanford.

racism in American society. Over the course of the article, Davis explicates a passage from Fanon's "Racism and Culture": "it is these racists (i.e. the overt ones, the extreme ones) who in opposition to the country as a whole are logically consistent. The racist in a culture with racism is therefore normal" (13). Using her own present and reflecting back on her girlhood "everyday," she testifies to the ubiquity of what some thought new or exceptional and to the linkage of bombings to years of Southern lynching. She says, for example, "'Bombingham [is] a far more suitable name for a place where bombs are sometimes exploded as frequently as ropes were swung over trees during earlier eras." As she was growing up, bombings were the predictable payback for Black prosperity and protest; in short, "[t] o be Black and to actively attempt to tear down the false idols of white supremacy meant that one's name was assuredly on the list of potential victims of racist bombings." I think it no accident that Davis adopts something of the manner and analysis of Ida B. Wells's lynching reportage, by suggesting that it was visibility and education, not aberrant sexuality or libertinism, that earned Blacks death at the hands of their fellow citizens.

The article also parses lines from a contemporary poem, Dudley Randall's "Ballad of Birmingham," that economically addresses both (Davis's) Fanon and the personal horror of the killing of four innocent Sunday School girls. The speaker of the poem is one of the bereaved mothers, incredulous that all her care at keeping her daughter away from the firehoses, the dogs, and the general police violence visited against the demonstrators, whom her daughter wanted to join, nevertheless sent her baby to an awful death. As Davis notes, and Randall expresses more lyrically, more economically, the increasingly apparent truth that religion is no escape from politics; there is nothing black, not even a church, that the white racist, that white supremacy, is obliged to respect.[*]

Davis narrates the progressive history of Black Church involvement in liberation as well as the awareness on the part of white slavemasters and modernday supremacists that churches mean solidarity as well as faith. Churches were (and are), in any case, more than symbols under fire; most prominently during the Civil Rights 1960s, they served as meeting places and sites of community resistance. Davis explains:

> The attack on the church must be seen within the framework of the role of religion in the historical development of the oppression of Black people. It then becomes immediately clear that the attack was objectively a response to the fact that Black people were beginning to transform an institution, which had been

---

[*]Original publication information and permission from Broadside and Dudley.

originally designed to serve as a weapon of oppression, into a weapon of resistance. The increasing participation of certain sectors of the Black church community in social struggles was a clear demonstration of the historical dialectics of oppression. (13).

Davis brings her analysis and quotation around to George Jackson, arguably the greatest by far of poets one can call Panthers, who once claimed to live and write in order "to defy all the eyes of children/living in me/in bloody exile" and, that "My anger drips oil and honey."[*] Davis recalls not only the girls, who evoke her own Birmingham girlhood; she also quotes Jackson in order to channel, as it were, current outrage, and continuity of purpose into a coming revolution. In a double memorial at once addressed to and constitutive of "we" and "our people," Davis says:

> On the occasion of the eighth anniversary of the church bombing, we must remember that even then, before the era of mass uprisings in the country's urban centers, our people responded swiftly, aggressively, and in large numbers. . . . It was because of such actions that years later George (Jackson) could say, 'I am part of a righteous people who anger slowly, but rage undammed.' (13)

By way of peroration to a preachment, Davis calls the past to service for a vision of future victory. In this, she exceeds or at least makes explicit the message of Randall's poem, but she also gives point, location, and redemptiveness to the narrative by naming Panther revolutionary heroes (Bobby Hutton, Jon and George Jackson) along with the girls:

> Our responsibility — to Carol, Cynthia, Addie Mae and Denise, to L'il Bobby, Jon and now to George, to our people and to all oppressed is clear. We must gather up that rage and organize it into an invincible movement which will irresistibly advance towards the goal of liberation. It must smash the capitalist order and its attendant racism and must ultimately begin to build the new society. (14)

Then *The Black Panther* gives the whole of "The Ballad of Birmingham" that has been used throughout Davis's article in captions for newspaper pictures that document stages of the bombing and funerals. It is noteworthy, I think, that Randall is not given credit for this

---

[*]Jackson, George. "Enemy of the Sun" (poem), *Enemy of the Sun*, A Special George Jackson Memorial Issue of *The Black Panther*. 29 August 1971, p. 7.

poem; I reproduce it here [figure 1] as part of the last page of "Comrade Angela Davis: Eight Years Since Birmingham" — so reads the running title.

> youth, there could not have been a more perfect expression of the racism of the period and the direction it was about to take. The bombing prefigured, eight years ago, the intensification of repression which was to come, the brunt of which would be borne by fighting Black youth. By Bobby Hutton, Fred Hampton, Jonathan Jackson, and now by
>
> "...Baby, where are you?"
>
> our people an.: to all the oppressed is clear. We must gather up that rage and organize it into an invincible movement which will irresistibly advance towards the goal of liberation. It must smash the capitalist order and its attendant racism and must ultimately begin to build the new society.
>
> ## BALLAD OF BIRMINGHAM
>
> MOTHER MAY I GO DOWNTOWN,
> INSTEAD OF OUT TO PLAY,
> AND MARCH THE STREETS OF BIRMINGHAM
> IN A FREEDOM MARCH TODAY.
>
> NO, BABY, NO
> YOU MAY NOT GO
> FOR THE DOGS ARE FIERCE AND WILD
> AND GUNS AND HOSES, CLUBS AND JAILS
> AREN'T GOOD FOR A LITTLE CHILD.
>
> BUT, MOTHER, I WON'T BE ALONE
> OTHER CHILDREN WILL GO WITH ME
> AND MARCH THE STREETS OF BIRMINGHAM
> TO MAKE OUR PEOPLE FREE.
>
> NO, BABY, NO
> YOU MAY NOT GO,
> FOR I FEAR THE GUNS WILL FIRE.
> BUT YOU MAY GO TO CHURCH INSTEAD
> AND SING IN THE CHILDREN'S CHOIR.
>
> SHE'S COMBED AND BRUSHED HER NIGHT-DARK HAIR
> AND BATHED ROSE PETAL SWEET
> AND DRAWN WHITE GLOVES
> ON SOFT BROWN HANDS,
> WHITE SHOES ON HER FEET.
>
> HER MOTHER SMILED
> TO KNOW HER CHILD
> WAS IN THAT SACRED PLACE.
>
> BUT THAT SMILE
> WAS THE LAST ONE
> TO COME ONTO HER FACE.
>
> FOR WHEN SHE HEARD THE EXPLOSION,
> HER EYES GREW WET AND WILD.
> SHE RUSHED THROUGH THE STREETS
> OF BIRMINGHAM,
> YELLING FOR HER CHILD.
>
> SHE DUG IN BITS OF GLASS AND BRICK
> AND THEN PULLED OUT A SHOE
> OH HERE'S THE SHOE MY BABY WORE
> BUT, BABY, WHERE ARE YOU?

figure 1

One cannot trace a single unbroken line of influence back to radical socialist writings and newspapers of Harlem, say, in 1919, but it might well be that Davis's commitments (at once to CPUSA/Che-Lumumba Club doctrine and to her own reading and experiences growing up Black and Left in the South as the daughter of parents who attended All Southern Youth Alliance meetings) draw her to a recognizable mode of reading poetry that, as I hope to show, comprises an interpretive tradition — if not a poetry and poetics — by the Black Left before and after the Panthers. Davis, in any case, cites and assembles poetry — as well as newspaper reports and pictures, cultural criticism of Frantz Fanon as well as her personal and shared cultural memories — to testify and transform. Her topic is the 1963 church bombing that killed four young girls; her aim is to memorialize and to ignite their spirits in the fight against racist violence, a war that must be fought on several fronts, and one that seems as mobile as that described in McKay's "If We Must Die."

Finally, I want to suggest that Davis's exemplary — also interested and doctrinal — interpretation of the Birmingham bombings, presented by *The Black Panther* as virtually a reading of Randall's poem, recapitulates the use to which W. A. Domingo put Claude McKay's "If We Must Die." In *The Messenger*, March 1919, Domingo uses the poem as an announcement of his own version of the New Negro. He begins by locating the broken promises of America in recent violence against Black Americans, occasionally salting his Jeremiad with McKay's metaphors:

> America won the war that was alleged to be fought for the purpose of making the world safe for democracy, but in the light of recent happenings in Washington, the Capital city, and Chicago, it would seem as though the United States is not part of the world. . . . No longer are Negroes willing to be shot down or hunted from place to place like wild beasts; no longer will they flee from their homes and leave their property to the tender mercies of the howling and cowardly mob. They have changed, and now they intend to give men's account of themselves. If death is to be their portion, New Negroes are determined to make their dying a costly investment for all concerned (4).

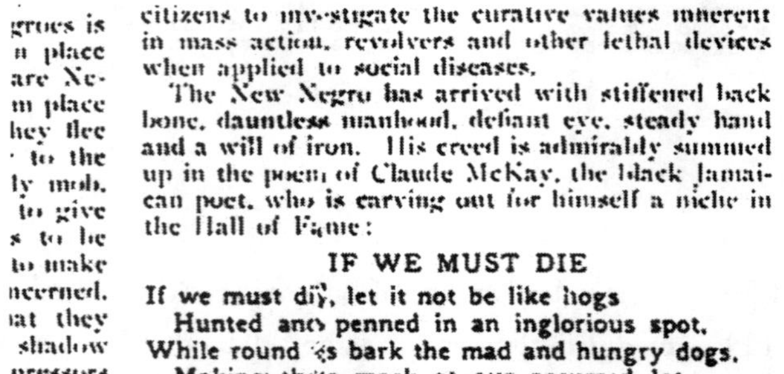

citizens to investigate the curative values inherent in mass action, revolvers and other lethal devices when applied to social diseases.

The New Negro has arrived with stiffened back bone, dauntless manhood, defiant eye, steady hand and a will of iron. His creed is admirably summed up in the poem of Claude McKay, the black Jamaican poet, who is carving out for himself a niche in the Hall of Fame:

IF WE MUST DIE

If we must die, let it not be like hogs
   Hunted and penned in an inglorious spot,
While round us bark the mad and hungry dogs,
   Making their mock at our accursed lot.
If we must die, oh, let us nobly die,
   So that our precious blood may not be shed
In vain; then even the monsters we defy
   Shall be constrained to honor us, though dead!
Oh, kinsmen! We must meet the common foe;
   Though far outnumbered, let us still be brave.
And for their thousand blows deal one death-blow!
   What though before us lies the open grave?
Like men we'll face the murderous, cowardly pack,
   Pressed to the wall, dying, but—fighting back!

                      W. A. D.

figure 2

Given time, we might trace this — Davis's as well as Domingo's — manner of appropriating the words of a poem to stoke the always present hope and rage for revolutionary change. This sort of reading, even the graphic reproduction of a poem at the end of its analysis, can be seen in small magazines like Robert F. Williams's *The Crusader*, whose title is a deliberate quotation of an earlier magazine of the African Blood Brotherhood, to which McKay and several Black Caribbean communists contributed. My temporary stopping point in this textual global journey, that traces several lines of Black anti-colonialism and Communist internationalism, is merely to suggest that the poems and poetics of *The Black Panther*, like its more clearly political articles, attempt at once to open and to contain a broad ideological field of Black liberation. If only because, as Ezra Pound would say, "they contain history," as well as a diffuse epical and epochal interpretation of the ways even the humblest of poems can work and recall the revolutionary hope of the Black Left, this material is well worth a more sustained examination. The corpuses of Cleaver, Newton, Davis, let alone the work of their interested interpreters, should be the starting point of a reading, not its limit.*

WORKS CITED

Anthony, Earl. *Picking Up the Gun: A Report on the Black Panthers*. New York: The Dial Press, 1970.

Aptheker, Bettina. *The Morning Breaks: The Trial of Angela Davis*. New York: International Publishers, 1975.

Boggs, Grace Lee. *Living for Change: An Autobiography*. Minneapolis: U of Minnesota P, 1998.

Boggs, James. *Manifesto for a Black Revolutionary Party*. [Philadelphia: Pacesetters Pub. House, 1969].

-------- and Grace Lee. "Propaganda Workshop—Newspaper and Newsletters" [unpublished syllabus and notes] Boggs Collection, Reuther Labor Archives, Wayne State University.

Brown, Elaine. *A Taste of Power: A Black Woman's Story*. New York: Pantheon Books, 1992.

Carmichael, Stokely and Charles V. Hamilton. *Black Power: The Politics of the Liberation in America*. New York: Vintage, 1967.

Carson, Clayborne. *In Struggle: SNCC and the Black Awakening of the 1960s*. Cambridge, Harvard UP, 1981.

--------. Ed. *The Student Voice, 1960-1965: Periodical of the Student Nonviolent Coordinating Committee*. Westport, CT and London: Meckler.

Civil Rights Congress. *We Charge Genocide: The Historic Petition to the United Nations for Relief from a Crime of the United States Government Against the Negro People*. New York: Civil Rights Congress, 1951.

---

*In "'Afric's Sons with Banner Red': African American Communists and the Politics of Culture, 1919-1934,: Robin Kelley treats of the instrumentality and the perhaps surprising cultural nationalism of magazine lyrics in Harlem CP and CP-affiliated publications. Kelley's short history of the poetics of this early and marginal phase of Black Left cultural work is required reading. Equally suggestive is Winston James's *A Fierce Hatred of Injustice: Claude McKay's Jamaica and His Poetry of Rebellion*, which attends carefully to the Jamaican lyrics, including newspaper verse, that McKay wrote before "If We Must Die" (1919). I also began elaborating, however differently, this same poetics in, for example, "Rebels to the Right/ Revolution to the Left."

Cleaver, Eldridge. "Education and Revolution," *Black Scholar*. November 1969, 44-52.

-------. "Revolution in the White Mother Country and National Liberation in the Black Colony," [pamphlet] Richmond, California: Black Panther Party, March 16, 1968 [Black Panther Party for Self Defense Ministry of Information Black Paper, speech presented to the Peace and Freedom founding Convention].

-------. *Soul on Ice*. New York: Dell, 1968. New York: McGraw Hill, 1972.

Cleaver, Kathleen. "The Black Mass Needs But One Crucifixion," [poem] *The Black Panther*, March 16, 1968.

Cleaver, Kathleen and George Katsiaficas, Eds. *Liberation, Imagination, and the Black Panther Party : a New Look at the Panthers and Their Legacy*. New York : Routledge, 2001.

Cruse, Harold. *The Crisis of the Negro Intellectual: An Historical Analysis of the Failure of Black Leadership*. (1st ed. William Morrow, 1967) New York: Quill, 1984.

Davis, Angela Y. *An Autobiography*. New York: International Publishers, 1988. [1st 1974].

-------."Black Nationalism: The Sixties and the Nineties." *Black Popular Culture: A Project by Michelle Wallace*. Ed. Gina Dent. (Seattle: Bay Press, 1992), 317-324.

-------. [Interview with Lisa Lowe] "Angela Davis: Reflections on Race, Class, and Gender in the USA." in *The Politics of Culture in the Shadow of Capital*. Eds. Lisa Lowe and David Lloyd. Durham, NC: Duke UP, 1997, 303-323.

Domingo, W. A. "If We Must Die," *The Messenger*. April 1919, 4.

Douglas, Emory "Art for the People's Sake: Emory Douglas Speaks at Fisk University, " *The Black Panther*, October 21, 1972, pp, 4-7

*Fanon, Frantz. *Wretched of the Earth*. Trans. Constance Farrington. Preface, Jean-Paul Sartre. New York: Grove Press, 1963.

Foner, Philip. S., Ed. *The Black Panthers Speak*. New York: Da Capo Press, 1995.

Gerassi, John, ed. *The Coming of the New International: A Revolutionary Anthology*. New York and Cleveland: World Publishing Co., 1971.

Glaberman, Martin. *Mao as a Dialectician*. Detroit, MI: Bewick, 1971.

Hilliard, David. *This Side of Glory : The Autobiography of David Hilliard and the Story of the Black Panther Party*. Boston : Little, Brown, c1993.

James, Winston. *A Fierce Hatred of Injustice: Claude McKay's Jamaica and his Poetry of Rebellion*. London and New York: Verso, 2000.

Jones, Charles E., Ed. *The Black Panther Party Reconsidered*. Baltimore : Black Classic Press, 1998.

Kelley, Robin D. G. *Hammer and Hoe: Alabama Communists During the Great Depression*. Chapel Hill and London: U of North Carolina P, 1990.

-------. "'Afric's Sons with Banner Red': African American Communists and the Politics of Culture, 1919-1934." In *Race Rebels: Culture, Politics, and the Black Working Class*. New York: The Free Press, 1994, pp. 103-20.

Lindberg, Kathryne V. "Rebels to the Right/Revolution to the Left: Ezra Pound and Claude McKay in the Syndicalist Year, 1912" *Paideuma: An International Journal of Pound Scholarship* 29: 1&2 (Spring and Fall 2000) 11-77. Rpt. in Coyle, Michael, Ed. *Ezra Pound and African American Modernism* (Orono: National Poetry Foundation, 2001).

Newton, Huey P. *Essays from the Minister of Defense. Black Panther Party*, [pamphlet, Black Panther Party, 1971].

-------. *To Die for the People*. Ed. Toni Morrison. 1972. New York: Writers and Readers Publishing, 1995.

-------. *War Against the Panthers: A Study of Repression in America.* New York: Harlem River Press, 1996.

-------. [With the Assistance of J. Herman Blake.] *Revolutionary Suicide.* New York: Writers and Readers, 1995.

Pearson, Hugh. *The Shadow of the Panther: Huey Newton and the Price of Black Power in America.* New York: Addison-Wesley, 1994

Seale, Bobby. *Seize the Time.* New York: Random House, 1970.

Seymour, Tony. *Announcing Insights and Poems: Huey P. Newton and Ericka Huggins: Millenium Warriors.* [press release broadside] San Francisco: New Directions, 1975.

Williams, Robert F. *Negroes with Guns.* 1st ed. 1962. Rpt. Detroit: Wayne State UP, 1998.

Newspapers

The Afro-American[*National Edition*]. Baltimore [Md.] : Afro-American Co., 1915- present.. Also known as *The Baltimore Afro-American.*

The Messenger [*Only Radical Negro Magazine in America*] New York, NY: Messenger Publishing, July 1918-Dec 1919.

The Black Panther. Oakland, CA: Black Panther Party, Ministry of Information, 1967-1980.

The Black Scholar. Oakland, CA: Black World Foundation. 1969-present

Other Materials

Unpublished Documents From the Huey P. Newton Foundation Papers. Green Library, Stanford University
Advertisement for Eldridge Cleaver Novelty Watch with letter. 4 March 1971.

Advertisement from *Variety* and Other Publicity on Melvin Van Peebles' "Sweet Sweetbacks Baadasssss Song." 26 May 1971.

-------. Letter to David Lubell, 26 March 1971.

-------. Proposal for film:" Shotgun Politics in Sundown City."

Kagon, Jane. Letter to Huey Newton re: Columbia contract for "War on the Black Panthers." 16 May 1984.

Kenner, Martin, letter to Huey Newton re: publication of "To Die for the People" and "Hidden Traitor," 22 June 1972.

Brian Kim Stefans

"REMOTE PARSEE": AN ALTERNATIVE GRAMMAR OF ASIAN NORTH AMERICAN POETRY

"descended on all sides from the Idiosyncrasy, the kid disdained grammar class, refused to parse, opted to be remote parsee." —Jam. Ismail

THERE S CERTAINLY NO COMPREHENSIVE WAY to account for the wide range of what is here being called "alternative" poetry written by people of Asian descent on the North American continent, and in general the more radical theories of Asian American poetry, whether those deduced from readings of Theresa Hak Kyung Cha's *Dictee* to the cogent, overtly activist valorizing of "deterritorialization" by the Canadian poet Roy Miki, would not recommend that such a suturing, politically mollifying project be pursued. Issues of "community," for example, which have served mainstream theories of Asian American literature well in attempts to circumscribe a visible "Movement" are rendered problematic by the presence of writers like John Yau, who has only been considered part of the historical phenomenon of minority literature recently as a result of more sophisticated critical paradigms. Such new paradigms acknowledge, for example, that a language that doubles its meanings contains a content that relates to central themes of ethnic literature, such as the imposition of Orientalist codes on the perceived outsider, and the consequential interiorization of these codes, an interiorization that finds its expression, in Yau's work, through often opaque language that spits back, in defiantly infantile yet damnably material forms, the range of racially motivated speech acts from the ethnic slur to the exoticizing complement. Indeed, as will become clear in the following essay, such tactics have been on the table for Asian American poets for quite some time, but have simply not been embraced in a large way, a testament, perhaps, to their efficacy. The poet Ronald Tanaka, for example, in his 1978 essay for the *Journal of Ethnic Studies (JES)*, "Towards a Systems Analysis of Ethnic Minority Literature," writes that "ethnic literature can be seen as the attempt by a majority culture to deal with the hermeneutic problems created by the necessity of cross-cultural communication," an open window which he perceives as only strengthening power relations. He continues:

> This interpretation is opposed to the more popular view that the various ethnic literatures are the independent products of their respective sub-cultures. Our claim is that ethnic systems have a very specific function to perform within the majority literary system and the result is a constrained and distorted output. This means that ultimately ethnic groups do not "have a literature" in the same way that majority societies "have a literature" in spite of what appears to be empirical evidence to the contrary. (Tanaka 49)

This theme of "empirical evidence to the contrary," of eyeing the crux of identity only to find it is a plant by enemy spies, will show up in many different guises throughout the following essay. Tanaka goes on to consider the concept of "communication stress," which he says can be created via the tactics of the "anomaly" and the "opaque," viable means of resistance for him from the days when Language poetics were not widely disseminated. What becomes clear in reading this nonlinear history of Asian American poetry is that many of the writers appear to have reached this element of their poetics without having had much communication with each other, at least not in the manner that many poetry movements — whether it be projective verse through the aegis of Black Mountain, the Language poets, the Umbra poets and others who convened around issues of Black Nationalism or even those Asian American poets who eventually found support in such important works as Elaine Kim's *Asian American Literature* — have in the past. In fact, it was not until 1996 that poets like Cha, Tanaka, Yau, Walter Lew, Myung Mi Kim, Tan Lin, Miki and his fellow Canadians Roy Kiyooka, Fred Wah and Gerry Shikatani could even be considered a constellation of experimental ethnic poets when they were included in Lew's anthology *Premonitions* (which didn't, unfortunately, include Mei-Mei Berssenbrugge). Though an anthology hardly constitutes a community, at least as a lived and malleable social space, it does give face to a series of disparate tendencies in a way that, finally, should create the atmosphere of exploration into literary difference that Asian American "ethnic" literature — at least in the way Tanaka proposes — could be said to have been lacking. As a ripped and torn sourcebook for the uncanny, *Premonitions* provides a basis for a poetics of the unreliable witness specific to the Asian American context, while, in its hybrid, rhizomic structure, not advocating — with its inclusion of radical feminist writing and Hawaiian poetry that is decidedly "transparent" — that this is the only way.

A chronological history of Asian American poetry, for reasons stated above, is out of the question, partially because certain works, like Tanaka's essays and poems for *JES* in the late 1970s and early 1980s, and Cha's writings and films of the 1980s, have both suffered from an obscurity that places them outside of any cause-and-effect nomenclature necessary to comfortable narrative. How, for example, to account for the "role" of the first Asian American poet, Sadakichi Hartmann (1867-1944), who didn't in fact write good poems but who, through his art theory and the example of his creative writing — the shameless Orientalism of his Symbolist aesthetics, for example, or the hybrid nature of his three plays *Buddha*, *Confucius*, and *Christ*, or even the clownish, partially Zen-inspired bohemian *bon mots* of his late years which contains something of the tone of a writer like Yuki Hartman (no relation) — somehow anticipated what was to come? Indeed, Hartmann's long and varied life — which Pound famously admired in the *Guide to Kulchur* — spanned the time of the West's first integration of Asian mores in their aesthetics (he was a friend of Whitman and Stuart Merrill, and the young Kenneth Rexroth[*]) right up to the time of World War II, during which he was hounded by FBI agents while living in a shack on the border of an Indian reservation. Though grouping by tendencies is probably not the best method — we've been wary of clasping divisive titles to the inchoate wilds of American poetry since the first edition of Donald Allen's *New American Poetry* — it might serve to use temporary frameworks here, at least as a way to organize the paragraphs.

The two most visible writers of Asian descent in the States are probably John Yau and Mei-Mei Berssenbrugge, and they each share something with Hartmann, which is a strong tie to the visual arts, each finding some sort of semiotic grounding in the way visual form is created and interpreted. They also, consequently, both made singular shifts at some point in their writing careers, Yau going from the early somewhat "magical realist" quasi-narrative lyrics of his first major book, *Corpse and Mirror*, to his recent explorations of literary doubling, whether in the pun or the procedural subversions of the literary "I," and Berssenbrugge from the unobscured spirituality of her early poems written with short lines ("When the Indian stops / across old rock / and his spirit sheds form / and cleaves the earth / an instant / and he settles his dry hand / across our valley / his terror is decayed with age [. . .], from "Ghost" [*Summits* 21]) to the long lines and the *nouveau roman*-like absent spectator, based partially on a collage poetics, for which she is best known. A third writer, Tan Lin, only seven years younger than Yau but whose first collection, *Lotion Bullwhip Giraffe*, was published in 1996 (and who is the brother of the artist Maya Lin),

---

[*]"There are rumors that Sadakichi discovered Ezra Pound. In fact, Pound said so once to me, but he was then in St. Elizabeth's, pretty addled and liable to say anything. However, I for one think it's true." (Rexroth)

seems to fit in this group for his innovative attention to high postmodern aesthetics.

In Yau, the shift in style may be seen as a move away from self-decimating Orientalism, in which all emotion and expression is understood as consumable artifice and rarefied effect, to an interest in lyric subjectivity conveyed with the lumpy presence of finger painting, one which combines the Self and "Other" as parallel agents. Oscar Wilde has written, "[T]he Japanese people are, as I have said, simply a mode of style, an exquisite fancy of art. And so, if you desire to see a Japanese effect, you will not behave like a tourist and go to Tokio. On the contrary, you will stay at home, and steep yourself in the work of certain Japanese artists. . ." (Nunokawa 289). The early Yau — too mischievous to not notice how Wilde's paradigm could be used to great fun and oblique horror — plays this up at times, as in the short "Shanghai Shenanigans": "The moon empties its cigarette over a row of clouds / whose windows tremble in the breeze / The breeze pushed my boat through a series / of telephone conversations started by perfume. . . ." (*Corpse* 57) However, most of the poems in *Corpse and Mirror* inhabit a surrealist range of images and techniques, such as "Persons in the Presence of a Metamorphosis": "The porcelain bayonet of noon scrapes the face / of a man who has forgotten why he started / to spit. A uniformed girl, / tiny and tireless, memorizes words / she believes make accurate mirrors. / A nun felt damp and gray, / like the windows of a plumber" (*Corpse* 119). High aestheticism creates the author figure in the shape of a tour guide, of sorts, exhibiting the presence of, at most, the possessor of fine sentiments, however sadistic he or she may be in intention under the surface. "Persons" shows, however, that Yau was already working on his later style, in which each enjambment provides something like the space between a film's edit, a portal through which narrative proceeds to unexpected ends. The suggestion of Johnson's remark on the Metaphysical poets, who "violently yoked" their imagery together to create shock, is not lost on Yau, who is more a folk metaphysician of language, even in his later stages, than a student of post-Marxist semiotics.[*] The first poem of the "Genghis Chan: Private Eye"

---

[*] This quality of Yau's poetry carries over to his writing on art, in which he reads the metaphysical qualities of the materials and processes of artistic creation. For instance, writing on Jasper Johns' use of encaustic in *Jasper Johns: Printed Symbols*, he observes:

> By using encaustic to depict the target, Johns was able to integrate an anonymously produced bodily material with an anonymous image. The target (which usually represents a surrogate body one aims at) is familiar to the point of invisibility: identity and anonymity become one. At the same time, he connected encaustic (a preservative) to his realization that one's own identity (even when it is invisible to others) must be defined in order to be seen by the self. By sealing the image of the absent body (a target) inside a bodily material (encaustic), Johns was able to give physical form to his invisibility while permanently preserving it against the passage of time. In doing so, her proposed another view of the artist: rather than being a hero and a person of action, he was a thing "which was seen and not looked at, not examined." (34)

series demonstrates most of the qualities of his later style:

> I was floating through a cross section
> with my dusty wine glass, when she entered,
> a shivering bundle of shredded starlight.
> You don't need words to tell a story,
> a gesture will do. These days,
> we're all parasites look for a body
> to cling to. I'm nothing more
> than riff-raff splendor drifting past the runway.
> I always keep a supply of lamprey lipstick around,
> just in case. (*Radiant* 189)

The sound qualities are heightened in this excerpt, and, indeed, some of the images, such as the "shredded starlight," are both made more vivid yet concealed by the tempered awkwardness of the aural quality. Most importantly, the "I" and "you" enter as well, bringing the absent narrator of *Corpse and Mirror* out into the open as a libidinous, and often androgynous, stalker of the imagination. As Yau writes at the end of his essay on Wilfredo Lam: "Lam's hybrid figures — their combinations of male and female anatomy — can be seen as a sign of his belief that the self had to give birth to the self, that the self is not a privileged place given to him by society, but something made up and discovered in the world" ("Lam" 146). By his use of often uncomplicated syntax — a unique tone of sounding like a child stating the obvious, though in a room of mirrors — jarring imagery and sound qualities, obscured yet manifest narrative instincts, and the performance of a lyric "I" and "you," Yau creates a singular presence for the author-figure while emphasizing the Steinian "everybody" quality of its singular absence.

Unlike Yau, Mei-Mei Berssenbrugge has worked frequently with individuals and organizations in the ethnic community, early books of hers being published by the Greenfield Review Press and I. Reed Books, and an early play of hers produced by the playwright Frank Chin. She has lived in New Mexico for most of her literary career, and like the work of another poet living in that state, Arthur Sze, her early poetry, as the excerpt above suggests, was very much informed by the landscape and the Native American history and mythology that inhabits it. Like Yau, though, some of her early poetry exhibits a taste for the macabre and the surreal, often achieving its effects via a quasi-cosmic or mythological sense of the interrelation of all things, accepting the pedestrian chores of narrative as a task of sensing the possibility. However, whereas Yau's settings are suburban closets, Berssenbrugge's, in *The Heat Bird*, are more geographically specific: "A dog is amenable to dust under a different house / though he tells me by phone she still sniffs / the mud on tires from El Rito. The old lady / is mother of the boy who chopped up his friend / and scattered parts all on the road to Dry Springs / That's why he thinks I shouldn't go there, because / they haven't found all the pieces, but / pretty soon they'll begin to smell and I won't get surprised / Then I won't get surprised" (*Heat Bird* 29). Surprise, however, is very much her instinct in many of these poems: "I demeaned myself in front of a / blind man, because I'm afraid of myself at night. If / he lights my cigarette when I complain how it goes out, the / flame goes out" (*Heat Bird* 38). The "I" in Berssenbrugge soon becomes the site of all her narrative negotiations, however, as the lines grow to those monumental lengths — suggestive of her engagement with the art of Georgia O'Keefe and Agnes Martin — for which she is known: "Attention was commanded through a simple, unadorned, unexplained, often decentered presence, / up to now, a margin of empty space like water, its surface contracting, then melting / along buried pipelines, where gulls gather in euphoric buoyancy" (*Empathy* 33). The presence of New Mexico is still apparent in such lines, but the previous mythologies and narrative determinacies are replaced by the perceiving mind. As RobbeGrillet writes in "A Future for the Novel," "Even the least conditioned observer is unable to see the world around him through entirely unprejudiced eyes," but he later suggests that literary narrative can be attained through a filmic use of objects such that the eye, like the camera, is nothing more than a constant: "In this future universe of the novel, gestures and objects will be there before being something; and they will still be there afterwards, hard, unalterable, eternally present, mocking their own 'meaning,' that meaning which vainly tries to reduce them to the role of precarious tools . . ." (Robbe-Grillet 21). Berssenbrugge's protagonist in much of *Empathy* is one such eye/I, though one both gendered and — as if defiantly not sacrificing agency for the objects that challenge it — acknowledging yet concealing psychological content from the gaze:

> She considers these the unconscious lessons of a dominant force
> that is being born, and as it becomes, its being is received structure.
> First ice crystals, then heavier glass obscures the light,
> so she walks back and forth talking to herself in a white soundless
> sphere past the trash of the village. (*Empathy* 21).

That "so," coming after the line break, defiantly conceals all the decision-making (or lack thereof) that is normally the sinews of narrative. "My process is so cerebral that I try to get things in front of me that hold an emotional element — that's where the family pictures come in," Berssenbrugge says in *Black Lightning* (Tabios 135).* She is explaining the detailed construction of her poem "Four Year Old Girl," which involves a painstaking assembling and editing of "found" texts, and it is clear that, in her new poems, Berssenbrugge is as observant of language as an "othered" entity as she is of the light, further reducing her author-role to that of a spectator.

Tan Lin's long essay "Language Poetry, Language Technology, and the Fractal Dimension: Michael Palmer Prints Out a Kingdom," is a manifesto of sorts disguised as an analysis of the poetry of Michael Palmer, by whom he is undoubtedly influenced. It contains, for example, a fake interview with the poet in which he is asked, "What is the relation between a joke, a lie, and a poem?," to which "Palmer" purportedly offers the answer:

> They constitute systems of self-deceptions (i.e. they can be read two ways or in both directions). Although all have an end-point, all would like to continue indefinitely. All reverse themselves as conclusion. All are essentially nonlinear, as they approach their opposite, truth. They resemble clouds and empty gas tanks. A lie and a poem lack a punchline. A joke is a metrical delusion. Gussied fragments fly? Mope thaw. (Lin, "Palmer")

Later, in an analysis of Palmer's poem "Sun," Lin writes "a straight-forward march into linearity ... is abandoned for circularity, perpetual return, nonlinearity, iteration, rewriting, and repetition with minute variations," and on the final page of the essay, in the context of fractal geometry, writes that "a Palmer poem creates the illusion that it is the most complex orderly object." All of these statements aptly describe what Lin is doing in much of *Lotion Bullwhip Giraffe*, though unlike Palmer he approaches his tasks with the hyper-kinetic mindset of a coked-up speed-skater, slinging words as if he is too impatient to bear out their often microsecond-long duration, as in this excerpt, in which words like "ambiance,"

---

*Eileen Tabios' *Black Lightning*, in which this passage appears, is a unique and versatile study of the writing practices of several Asian American poets, including John Yau, Jessica Hagedorn, Kimiko Hahn, Arthur Sze and Garrett Hongo. It demonstrates the openness to formal difference that a close study of Asian American poetry must make to be inclusive, not to mention the grab bag of analytical approaches one must adopt.

"Echos" and "distance" suggest that he is approaching some sort of poetic or narrative topography, but one which is clipped beyond recognition:

> Ruckus stone, ambiance undone and cramped echos.
> To rock like mahogany Nazis, exempt
> from a late date. The starling flattens hah hah.
> All vices are distant and strung pastel rejection.
>
> Cramped Echos: seven lined leaflets trouble
> the clay pots. I guess blessed hairy amplifier. Come and expend
> a loud distance, my floral beckoning. A sound
> ticks out like a fire. Here a spree
>
> of fragments. Solid predictions like a sweating bat. (*Lotion* 116)

Many of the poems of *Lotion Bullwhip Giraffe* challenge the idea of poetic content not just on the level of the word or sentence, but on the level of scale, as many of the longer prose poems never even threaten to descend into narrative, lyrical subjectivity, or "humanistic" political content, but rumble on in a sort of intoxicated way through a variety of postmodern gestures, tweaking the voids of meaning with a trickster-like facility. This scale suggests Lin's primary concern, which is an almost clinical interest in the fractal possibilities of a self-determining language, such that language is left to operate almost as if a computer were producing it, but always with an attention that highlights its capacity as fetish-object, such that the poetry resembles a pornography of the word more than anything else. While Lin is clearly attentive to the project of Yau, especially in his use of language in a way that suggests the meta-slur ("Ship carp do doped pressure bag go famous pure-fuck your shrag / lozenge movie geisha whittle drip drop," begins "Talc Bull Dogface" (*Lotion* 89). a poem which continues to run the gamut of English sounds in a way that suggests a temper tantrum conveyed in an epileptic's Cantonese, his surrealism, and his questioning of narrative conventions, Lin's poetics are clearly more unhinged — "liberated" in the Futurist sense — consequently free to roam at will in a countereschatological eternity.

Another grouping of writers centers around the work of Theresa Hak Kyung Cha, a video artist, performer and writer who died in 1982. Cha's work had only gotten limited exposure in Asian American literary communities due to its deconstructionist and hybrid formal characteristics which seemed to make it unassimilable to the social realist paradigms then in the ascendant. It wasn't until the early 1990s, when many young Korean American artists began to take an interest in her work, that she began to exert an influence, and thenceforth began to appear in anthologies and critical essays. Indeed, judging by the change-of-face that the most stalwart of social realist literary critics have made in the past five years, including many apologies for a previous emphasis on totalizing and reductive views of what it means to be "Korean American," one would almost think that Cha's work, most importantly the book *Dictee*, was the most instrumental force in critiquing the dominant sociological paradigms in Asian American literary analysis. As Elaine Kim, author of the first attempt at a comprehensive approach to the literature, writes in a recent essay:

> For the most part, I read Asian American literature as a literature of protest and exile, a literature about place and displacement, a literature concerned with psychic and physical "home," — searching for and claiming a "home" or longing for a final "homecoming." I looked for unifying thematic threads and tidy resolutions that might ease the pain of displacement and heal the exile, heedless of what might be missing from this homogenizing approach and oblivious to the parallels between what I was doing and dominant cultural attempts to reduce Asian American experience to developmental narratives about a movement from "primitive" "Eastern," and foreign immigrant to "civilized," Western, and "Americanized" loyal citizen. (Kim 12)

Ironically, with the exception of the phrases "unifying themes" and "tidy resolutions," she is very much describing the writing of Cha here, especially in her culminating book-length work *Dictee*, which had been largely ignored by the Asian American literary establishment for a decade until such events as the retrospective at the Whitney Museum in 1992 pulled her into prominence. Later in this essay, Kim writes: "Dealing with subtleties, hybridities, paradoxes, and layers seemed almost out of the question when so much effort had to be expended simply justifying Asian Americans as discursive subjects" (Kim 13). This is not to say that Cha was the only writer conscious of the limitations of these paradigms — Ronald Tanaka, for example, went at great lengths to outline the inadequacies of the "Movement" approach, only to throw up his hands at the linear, limning requirements of the critical project. Two very different writers, Walter K. Lew and Myung Mi Kim, by no accident Korean American, have each in their different ways partially taken up Cha's project, in

Lew's case utilizing the techniques of *Dictee* in his critical collage *Excerpts from Dikte/for Dictee (1982)*, also instrumental in reviving interest in Cha.

Dictee has been written about quite frequently since its rediscovery, both by critics working within the Asian American tradition and not. A recent essay by Juliana Spahr titled "Postmodernism, Readers, and Theresa Hak Kyung Cha's *Dictee*," uses Cha's work for the basis of a far-ranging critique of postmodern reading practices, especially Jameson's contention that postmodernism signaled "the emergence of a new kind of flatness or depthlessness, a new kind of superficiality in the most literal sense" (Spahr 24). *Dictee* seems to play a similar role as the final excerpt (prior to the three "Postludes" poems) in the *Poems for the Millennium* anthology edited by Jerome Rothenberg and Pierre Joris, an anthology that, in general, is critical of the high formalist modes of much of twentieth century art and seeks to reify the lyric-epic traditions inaugurated by Pound, or agonic literature in general. Why Cha's work stands at this unique position in so many different late-twentieth century discourses — both as the prescient "avant-garde" work in Asian American discourses (and, one might argue, feminist discourses, though feminism has a richer tradition of experimental writing), but consequently as a window onto a "Shamanist" conception of art in the central European traditions of experimental writing — has ultimately to do with the incredible freedoms that she exploited in its construction. As Shelley Sun Wong writes in her exceptional essay "Unnaming the Same: Theresa Hak Kyung Cha's *Dictee*":

> In *Dictee*, the different genres, or modes of literary (and I might add, cinematic) production, do not coexist harmoniously but, rather, undermine each other through a process of reciprocal critique. Cha works with the representation that genres are not innocent or neutral aesthetic conventions or idea types but are, instead, formal constructs which are implicated in the very processes of ideological production. (Wong 106)

Though the second sentence from Wong might suggest Cha as something of a player in the tradition of the Language poets — indeed, Steve McCaffery's *Panopticon* may resemble *Dictee* more than any other work — Cha was not approaching literature from the angle of one invested in its various traditions, but rather as a filmmaker, and hence she takes a more anthropological view of writing genres, remaining free of literary ideological battles. Flipping through the pages of *Dictee* takes one from photographs of a Korean martyr to Mallarméan writings in both French and English by Cha, from diagrams of the inner workings of the throat (linked to intense passages describing the both demeaning and empowering effects of having to learn English) to images of the scribbled-over earlier versions of passages from *Dictee*. The "Petition from the Koreans of Hawaii to President Roosevelt," a failed attempt by Korean exiles including Syngman Rhee to have the United States intercede on the Japanese occupation of Korea (still historically shadowed), is included in its entirety, which links not just with the autobiographical passages about Cha's brother participating in anti-colonial marches, but with the map of Korea foregrounding its national entity, and the face of Renee Falconetti playing the martyr St. Joan in Dryer's film. A passage addressing her mother and her plight under the Japanese occupation in which she wasn't permitted to speak English ("They have sheltered you from life. Still, you speak the tongue of the mandatory language like the others. It is not your own. Even if it is not you know you must. You are Bilingual. You are Trilingual. The tongue that is forbidden is your own mother tongue. You speak in the dark" [*Dictee* 45]) runs up against passages describing the ethical and emotional challenges of historical witness, not inconsequentially cinematic witness, as in the important "Memory" passages of the "Thalia / Comedy" section, and this section which contains something of a specifically filmic — it seems peculiarly about the edit, and the blank white screen — mourning over lost time:

> It had been snowing. During the while.
> Interval. Recess. Pause.
> It snowed. The name. The term. The noun.
> It had snowed. The verb. The predicate. The act of.
> Fell.
> Luminescent substance more so in black night.
> Inwardly luscent. More. So much so that its entry
> closes the eyes.
> Interim. Briefly.
> In the enclosed darkness memory is fugitive.
> Of white. Mist offers to snow self
> In the weightless slow all the time it takes long
> ages precedes time pronounces it alone on its own
> while. In the whiteness
> no distinction between her body invariable no dissonance
> synonymous her body all the time de composes
> eclipses to be come yours. (*Dictee* 118)

Cha edited a unique anthology of film criticism in 1980 called *Apparatus*, and indeed many of the included writings seem to relate almost directly to the formal qualities of her book, published two years later. As Vertov writes, "The movie camera is present at the supreme battle between the world of capitalists, speculators, factory owners, and landlords and the world of workers, peasants and colonial slaves" (Vertov 9). The passage seems obviously relevant considering the visual collage aspects of *Dictee*; on the literary front, Cha's writing resembles the "objects being what they are" aspect of the *nouveau roman*, perhaps escalating the maxim so that languages themselves — French as both the colonial language of Vietnam, for example, and the arbiter of Western knowledge — are a type of content. Another inclusion, "Every Revolution is a Throw of the Dice," describes a filmed performance of Mallarme's graphic poem "A Throw of the Dice," a project which ties in not only with *Dictee* but Cha's performance pieces such as "Aveugle Voix," which involved Cha covering her eyes and mouth with bandannas printed with the French words "blind" and "voice." Maya Deren's emphasis on the "ritual" in film's capacity to "manipulate Time and Space," Gregory Woods' "Work Journal on the Straub/Huillet Film 'Moses and Aaron'," replete with photographs, diagrams, diary entries, and much technical detail, and Cha's own "Commentaire," an experimental visual essay which plays off dark and light, all contribute to a wider understanding of the hybrid nature of Cha's seminal work.

Undoubtedly the most important figure in bringing attention to the formally radical possibilities of Asian American writing has been Walter K. Lew, who early recognized the fecundity of Cha's techniques in *Dictee*, as his dedication of his brief selection of poetry for the journal *Bridge* in 1983, "A New Decade of Singular Poetry" to her suggests. This selection includes writing by a wide range of people such as Eric Chock, Marilyn Chin, the "Movement" poet Nellie Wong, John Yau, Mei-Mei Berssenbrugge, Arthur Sze and Ho Hon Leung[*], suggesting the hybridic ethos even an editor in Asian American studies must possess. He describes, in his introduction to the selection, a form of poetry which he feels would be of peculiar use to Asian American writing, the "Matrix," which "employs a wide range of rapidly juxtaposed languages, media, historical frameworks, motifs and rhetorical moods. It is almost demanded by the normally multicultural situation of Asian Americans and the accelerated information flow and collisions of contemporary society in general" (*Bridge* 11). This statement, which contains something of a nod to the art of Nam Jun Paik, also anticipates the recent vogue among critical circles for hypertext poetics, and Lew's own

---

[*]Two notable poems by Leung, "After the 'Three Characters'" and "A Symphonic Poem 'Unfinished'," are reprinted in *Premonitions*. He seems to have vanished after the publication of his poems in *Bridge*.

work since that introduction — which ranges through film and video, poetry, performance and editing — fulfills this call for intermedia. His critical book on *Dictee*, for example, *Excerpts from Dikte/for Dictee (1982)* directly adopts many of the formal methods of Cha's work, creating a sort of stabilizing double for the former work, while at the same time destabilizing politically encoded reductive readings. The series of Korean cartoons depicting images of a colonized Korea, but which are recaptioned with French tags, for example, provides a diagrammatic parallel to the many strands of narrative existing in Cha's work, pointing to its reassessed meanings — to the space between edits — and yet also to the nationally specific contexts. Cha's emphasis on female martyrdom — from the revolutionary Yu Guan Soon to Joan of Arc — finds a source in Korean mythology, as Lew includes a section from a book on Shamanist rituals that tells the story of a daughter shut up in a coffin by her father and cast into a pond, but who was rescued by the Dragon King, and who, after discovering her mother was ill, "went great distances to the Western sky and brought back healing water that saved her from death" (*Excerpts* 14).[*] The split significance of the "Western sky" points to what many see as the rift in Cha's work between a turn toward high modernist (some critics just call it "white") poetics to uncover the allusive truths of colonialism. Lew's hybrid poetics come into play in the important anthology he edited, *Premonitions*, which was the first in a long line of anthologies to embrace the entire spectrum of writing in both the United States and Canada by writers of Asian descent. Again, it seems to allude to Cha's work in its form — with its contrasting black & white pages, it mimics the structure of Cha's "Commentaire" — but also in its inadherence to overly-stabilized binaries in the literary world — "experimental" vs. "mainstream," "Language" vs. "New American," or "Movement" vs. "white avant-gardist" — in a sense adopting Cha's stance as a cinematographer to collide, with a sort of Kino-eye aesthetic, the disparate range of Asian American writing being done today. This aesthetic clearly comes into play with his inclusion of Buddhist work and poetry by Asians about atrocities such as the Vietnam and Korean Wars.[†] Lew has also translated the work of the primary Korean avant-garde figure, Yi Sang, who died young under the Occupation but

---

[*] An analyis of Lew's book by the present author appears in *Korean Culture* 15.1 (Spring 1994), published by the Korean Cultural Center in Los Angeles.

[†] As Lew writes in his afterword regarding *Beneath a Single Moon*, an anthology of Buddhist poetry edited by Kent Johnson and Craig Paulenich: "Not that poets of such strength as [Lawson] Inada and [Al] Robles feel a need to be included in a Caucasian Zen circle. But when [Gary] Snyder's introduction deliberates the question – 'Poetry is democratic, Zen is elite. No! Zen is democratic, poetry is elite. Which is it?' – perhaps he should have also asked whether Zen and poetry, as reconfigured in American Orientalism, are racist, and whether race relations should be a focus of meditation" (*Premonitions* 582-3).

who was, perhaps alone, attempting to transform Modernist Western poetics into a Korean idiom. He has also published important poems such as "The Movieteller" based on his own performances of the text along with reedited Korean film footage. The piece concerns the Korean phenomenon of the *pyonsa* — a "movieteller" who would speak an often politically encoded monologue over silent or untranslated Western film imports — and, indeed, the ethos of the *pyonsa* may give insight into the cumulative content of Lew's various work, which is that he redirects and unencodes stable meanings in previously monolithic cultural products or formations. Lew's reputation as a poet has yet to catch up to that as a critic and editor, a situation that is the product of his intense, singular attention to a variety of writers — from Cha to late New York poet Francis Chung — who were or are in danger of disappearing from the Asian American canon, as much as Lew's work would suggest that such a canon is anathema to the particular contours of the Asian American literary situation. Consequently, Lew has taken the genre-crossing implications of the "matrix" to the extreme, rendering the standard text-based lyric (which he has widely explored, as his unpublished collection of poetry, *Brine*, demonstrates) perhaps a little too stable for his collage-activated mature poetics.

Like Tan Lin, Myung Mi Kim belongs to a group of slightly younger poets who have already begun to reap the benefits of radical predecessors in the experimental Asian American tradition, in Kim's case the predecessor being Theresa Cha. Even in her first book, *Under Flag*, published in 1991 around the time of Cha's "rediscovery," echoes of *Dictee* can be heard in the idiom — spare, notational, but often circling around a refrain or variation of a phrase — and in the emphatic synthesis of personal and public concerns, as in issues of nationhood and language acquisition. However, Kim's writing is more politically pointed, as her quest for witness is not tied to a haunted conversation with the "homeland" but is involved in the urgency of contemporary life, even if that, in the end, is elusive. As she states in an interview for *Tripwire*:

> How long can one sit and be attentive when the world is blowing up? These are questions to be answered as they come up; there is no *a priori* answer because then it would in effect be a summation rather than an answer. Those uncertain and undecidable spaces of — am I making a difference? — will this contribute? — how can I know? — those undecidable locations are part of the work. It doesn't feel great, it's not an exhilarated state, or at least not for very extended periods of time, but it is a lived state, and a true one. (*Tripwire* 79)

As this excerpt suggests, Kim's poetics involves an ontological questioning of political or "Movement" poetry, a quality which keeps her writing far from that of the ritualistic Cha and another big influence, Susan Howe, mostly because her attitude toward reality is pointillist at first (accumulative), and narrative (paradigmatic) only afterwards. Her new book, *Dura*, opens with three sections of mostly fragmented text, none of which, however, boldly challenges the felt linkages of the sign with the signified so much as offers the particulars of experience prior to any totalizing structure (she resembles, curiously, Larry Eigner in this way). She writes in "Chart": "Swag drum / Inland filth / Surmise commodity / Anemic shed / Corollary held / Second stock / Force lack / Acute lily" (*Dura* 43) a list poem that alludes to the various discourses that Kim is involved in, but never abstracting truths from its particulars (even if the particulars arrive through a process of deduction). A later section, "Thirty and Five Books," contains many of the themes of the earlier sections but in brief prose paragraphs, slowing the rhythm of the montage for a more stable persistence of vision:

> Heat the gaping sound constrains. Remind the herders and poison growth. Cover distances deemed impossible to cover.
>
> Great highways indicated by means of stones.
>
> Invention where the tomatoes dangling from one end are not the tomatoes hanging from the other end.
>
> And the unremarkable become the stuff of dust.
>
> Where is the start. Dress of blue chiffon and a white straw hat in its own hat box.
>
> Heat the gaping ground constrains. Turbulence. Ridicule.
>
> The desktops tilt up and you may place inside them several books and a lunch.
>
> Various kinds of rice in the manner of living in that country. (*Dura* 55)

As *Dura* suggests, the march of technological innovation is not "progress," especially in transportation — the work abounds with allusions to ships bearing commerce and cultural domination — but also in such scientific exercises as making the tomatoes at one end different from those at the other, such that the "unremarkable" — in a vision that mates Pavlovian excesses with the final solution — "become the stuff of dust." But even with this global perspective, she asks "Where to start," and finds the answer somewhere in a "dress of blue chiffon," which, like the "acute lily" from the earlier passage, is an image that resonates less with symbolic meanings — though the "lily" could be the "lily of the fields," its "acute" state suggests that its imagistic quality should thwart such readings — than with phenomenological crisis. Despite its opaque nature, Kim's poetry manages to synthesize some of the fruits of a linguistically radical poetics with the emotive, emphatic gestures and tones of an activist poetics, attentive to the particulars of group, place, and time.[*]

Two writers who are not obviously part of the experimental strand of Asian American poetry are Ronald Tanaka and Lawson Fusao Inada. Their outsider status — neither are particularly comfortable in mainstream contexts such as those shaped by *APR*, *Paris Review* or *The Best American Poetry* series, and yet both are highly critical of the social realist expectations of the Asian American literary community — along with their radical synthesis of conservative Japanese poetics and "New American" poetry forms, suggests an important placement in this lineage. As the excerpt from Tanaka's essay quoted earlier states, the surrendering of information on the terms of the dominant class plays an insidious role in confirming existent power relations, contrary to the oft-cited maxim that minority writers are obliged to "tell their stories" first in order to achieve the basic plateaus of legitimacy as artists.[†] In another series of essays published in *JES* from 1979 to 1981 titled "On the

---

[*] A more detailed consideration of Cha, Lew and Kim along with Cathy Song appears in the essay "Korean American Poetry" in the *Korean Culture* (Winter 1997), pp. 416.

[†] As the poet Ron Silliman has infamously written in an introduction to a selection of Bay Area poets for the *Socialist Review*: "The narrative of history has not led to their [marginalized groups] self-actualization, but to their exclusion and domination. These writers and readers — women, people of color, sexual minorities, the entire spectrum of the "marginal" — have a manifest need to have *their stories told*. That their writing should often appear much more conventional, with the notable difference as to whom is the subject of these conventions, illuminates the relationship between form and audience." (88/3, 1988), pp. 6182. This statement by a white poet of the "avant-garde" is troubling not only because it's faulty logic — that a "marginalized" people who are not "self-actualized" would by nature gravitate toward convention in their writing, or that writing by non-minorities doesn't "often appear" conventional — but it also demonstrates a synchronization with the oppositional but nonetheless institutionalized forms of Asian American literary and cultural criticism by a poet who is demonstrably invested in uncovering formally radical subtraditions in American and European literature from Stein to Alan Davies. One could, in fact, argue that the opposite is true: that writers from communities not "self-actualized" would most likely benefit from the politics and poetics of the fragment, the indeterminate, the neologistic, and the rearticulatory as it exists as a subsystem of modernism's Eurocentric project, while consequently avoiding the burden of having to address the Western tradition as an inheritance. In any case, writers from Blake and Kafka to Cha and Kiyooka prove the rule wrong.

Metaphysical Foundations of a Sansei Poetics: Ethnicity and Social Science," he considers the issue of Sansei — third generation Japanese — "personhood" amidst the paradigms that social science has created. "Being by definition an 'ethnic group', we have from the very beginning been 'given over to' social scientists, as opposed to, say, philosophers, artists, or theologians. In turn, social science has affected our own thinking far more than any other academic thinking" ("Metaphysical" 1), he writes, sketching in broad strokes the critical arenas in which Asian American writers, whether conscious of it or not, are forced to work, such that even a writer like Yau, whose inaugural writings were inspired by Oulipo, Surrealist and Ashberian poetics, can be seen as a poseur for wearing sunglasses in his author photograph.[*] The clinical tenor of Tanaka's approach replicates the overdetermination of the very sciences he critiques, motivated primarily by an analysis of Milton Gordon's 1964 study, *Assimilation in American Life*, which reaches such conclusions as: "In virtually all instances of inter-ethnic conflict, no matter how great the initial differences between the groups, people sooner or later become integrated into a single unit and convinced of their descent from common ancestors" ("Metaphysical" 7). Tanaka's stated

---

[*] In an unusually flawed review of Yau's collection of poems *Forbidden Entries*, the critic Marjorie Perloff observes that Yau "has always cultivated the image of Angry Young Man," attempting to hide, she states, not only his "middle class" background but also his ethnicity in his early years as a published poet. She draws this conclusion because of his slovenly dress, "long unkempt black hair," cigarette, and "eyes hidden behind sunglasses" in the author photo to a 1979 book, *Sometimes*. This betrays an essentialist understanding of how an "Asian American" who wishes to be perceived as one should in fact present oneself, as if Asian Americans never had, or could have, a fixation on James Dean or Bob Dylan, or as if Asian Americans were never resembled "construction workers." (The Chinese built the railroads, as Frank Chin, another "Angry Young Man," would be quick to point out.) She writes that "there was no indication, at this stage of Yau's career, that the poet is in fact Chinese-American," as if 1) a book with the name "John Yau" on the cover doesn't tip a reader off, and 2) poems with titles like "Chinese Villanelle," by an author named "John Yau" (and with long unkempt hair, to boot) didn't suggest to the reader — both Asian American and not — that different interpretive strategies were in order. She is perhaps blinded by what she sees as a very Ashberian strain in Yau's early poetry and art crticism, and since Ashbery isn't Chinese American, she implies that Yau could not have been engaged in anything like issues of idenity in these early works. In fact, Yau's later poetry resembles Ashbery's poems (such as "A Blessing in Disguise") more than his earlier work, which has a much flatter tone and is never very abstract, and Yau's critical approach to art is entirely dissimilar to Ashbery's. Though it is perhaps unfair to point only to those parts of this review that are problematic — when she gets into the writing it is much less so, and quite nuanced — one must wonder what stands behind the following statement: "My own unease with these silk-and-pagoda images, however, is that they don't quite grapple with the poet's own conflicted identity, his own relation to an Asian-American community that interacts, in complex ways, with the sophisticated, urban New York poetry/art world in which Yau came of age." While she is certainly free to claim that this poetry is trivial or irrelevant, it is unclear how a West Coast writer could be so aware of the "complex ways" of the Asian American community in New York, nor how to justify erecting such scales of content in avant-garde writing, as if, for example, Steve McCaffery would have to reflect the conflicted "identity" of an Englishman living in Toronto. It is possible Yau had nothing to do with the Asian American community in New York — so what? (All quotations from this review, originally published in 1997 in the *Boston Review*, were obtained from the journal's website.)

responses are too detailed to reproduce here; in general, he discovers that assimilation involves the preserving of only those characteristics of Sansei culture that can be linguistically substantiated in the dominant society, but that conceptualization in "White" terms is not adequate for a range of Sansei emotions that are not replaced or replaceable. The essays themselves — which, in their earlier sections, are straightforward logical critiques of terms and propositions, but which eventually leap genres to take in the Wittgensteinian philosophical maxim, the short lyric, and the parable — trace a retreat from the norms of Western science into what one might consider a Buddhist distrust of knowledge and logic. Parts of the third essay seem to second-guess and even improve upon the discoveries of the radical sentence-based poetics of the 1970s:

> 5.0 I take what's given to me and try to make do.
> 5.1 I dress as best I can. And smile a lot. Perhaps excessively concerned with appearances. Manners.
> 5.2 (I got shoes! You got shoes!)
> 6.0 I'm not as worried about Sansei as I am about life.
> 6.1 Do you understand me when I say this?
> 6.2 When I go to Pt. Peyes, I have to remind myself that it is not a part of my own body.
> 6.3 So I call the rain different kinds of names.
> 6.4 I am immersed in the world. All that is and was and will be. Rocky Road.
> 7.0 My preoccupation with ethnicity is strictly logical.
> 7.1 It's a product of my class interests. (*JES*, 14:4, p. 56.)

Tanaka explains in the introduction to the fourth and last of the essays, titled "Shido, or the Way of Poetry," that he has lost his funding from the Heike Society, and that his "work has been labeled 'solipsistic,' and 'unprofessional,' and I have been branded an 'academic quack.'" Though he published a few more "essays" in *JES* over the next two years, he has since devoted his attentions entirely to poetry and visual work, such as the photo/poetry sequence "The Mount Eden Poems" — two of which are included in *Premonitions* and are the only things he has in print — each of which is dedicated to a different vintage wine from the Mount Eden Vineyards and accompanied by a strange, faux fashion shot of Melanie A. Slootweg dressed, not very obviously, as "the kindergarten teacher, Madeline Giboin." This sequence runs the gamut from absurdity to romance, from ritual to nihilism, and can be tied in somewhat with his notions of Sansei personhood in terms of inter-ethnic relations (the role of the "White American woman," for example), and yet it's deceptively calm surfaces eventually lead to damning voids of meaning, suggesting the struggling logician concealed beneath them.

Lawson Fusao Inada, often cited as the first Asian American poet to have a complete book of poems published (*Before the War* 1971), is equally distrustful yet mindful of the social realist paradigms proffered as the most suitable for portraying history and the Asian American experience. He is probably the most accomplished lyricist in the Asian American tradition. "Since When As Ever More," a process poem, stands out in *Breaking Silence*, an early anthology of Asian American poetry, for its suggestion of discursive relevance despite its meandering around determinate meanings. His early jazz-inspired poems, such as "The Great Bassist," dedicated to Charles Mingus, convey an anger suggestive of Amiri Baraka in his Black Nationalist phase[*], and yet their easy flow suggests a countering weight of Buddhist quietude, and include a grounding irreverence not entirely alien to Tanaka, as when in "The Great Bassist" he observes, "I'm in Levi's now — / that doesn't matter." *Legends from Camp*, his second book (published 22 years after the first one) centers around his youth in the detention camps during the World War II, and is almost as much a hybrid work as Cha's, not just formally but in terms of its openness to themes and manifestations of cultural synthesis. "Listening Images" (Inada 69). for example, is a series of haiku-like two-line poems, each of which is dedicated to a jazz musician, and the poems, in their accessing of American cultural experiences rather than some exoticized "Asian" experience, are probably truer to the spirit of haiku than the many tepid attempts at Orientalist nature poetry that characterizes the genre in America. The one titled "Ben Webster," for instance, runs in its entirety: "Such fragile moss / In a massive tree." Billie Holiday's is simpler: "Hold a microphone / Close to the moon." The poems of the title sequence are reminiscent of Langston Hughes in their poignant simplicity and attempt to eulogize a passing historical moment, though each of these fabled moments are underscored by the determinations of the society at large, as in "Legend of the Humane Society": "This is as / simple / as it gets: / In a pinch / dispose / of your pets" (Inada 9). Inada is also a noted educator, and the primary motivation of *Legends* may be seen as didactic, but not to the world-at-large so much as to the generations of Japanese Americans to come who will need to know what happened in the camps — not through statistics, cloying declarations of "identity" or liberal apologia, but through the eyes of an artistically inclined, hyper-interested young boy. It is so unpretentious that it might be said to slip beneath the radar

---

[*]There is a complex interaction of Black Power aesthetics and radical Asian American jazz aesthetics that is worth investigating in its own right. As Inada's writing would suggest, it was a fecund interaction.

of one looking for grand theoretical gestures and displays of knowledge, blinding imagery and revelational rhetoric, but its tone, formal variety and accomplishment — not unlike that of another writer who markets in modesty on the fringes of the avant-garde, Ron Padgett — is convincing in portraying the mind of one who has found a sense of measure in a life of extremes.

The publication of Lew's *Premonitions** brought to the attention of Americans the radically investigative writing of a number of Canadian writers, notably Roy Kiyooka, Fred Wah, Roy Miki and Gerry Shikatani. Kiyooka, who was primarily a visual artist until he published his first book of poems, "Kyoto Airs," in his late-thirties, plays a similar role as Cha's in the United States, being the most generative writer of the Asian Canadian tradition, and like her also sought to utilize visual elements in no secondary way in his work. *Pacific Windows*, his collected poem published in 1997 and edited by Miki, traces a compelling yet mostly hidden literary career (he self-published in editions of less-than-fifty most of his later sequences) from the relatively understated "Kyoto Airs," through several literary-visual projects such as "StoneDGloves" and "The Fontainebleau Dream Machine" and on to his dynamic later poems, which collaged an extremely wide range of writing styles to create nexuses of meanings that are both boldly stated yet void of determinates. With an ego that can only be compared to Whitman's in its breadth, generosity, and in its libidinous capacity to incorporate and innovate new forms, he drew from a wide range of influences, seeming at times to be a footloose, rather Shakespearian Basho (most notably in parts of "Wheels: A Trip thru Honshu's Backcountry"), at others the grand magister of ontological play in the manner of Stevens ("The Pear Tree Pomes," which starts with an address to "Credences of Summer"), and, in "Fontainebleau" — which includes several Ernst-like collages by Kiyooka along with stanza-length captions — a writer/artist with all the agonic counter-systemic thrust of Blake but with an analytic and reifying view of the dream/death longings of the Surrealist project. Christian Bök likens the effect of this last work to the phenomenon of picnolepsy, "in which a perceptual discontinuity requires a sort of conceptual continuity, since the special effects of kinesic realism rely upon periodic lapses of attention at a constant speed of movement"(Bök 25). Eva-Marie Kröller, in a compelling interpretation of the visual historical overlays of the sequence, writes in an aside

---

* Not unliked much literature that was produced on the margins, the history of Asian American poetry is one marked by several important anthologies, but for reasons of space, their impacts, range of contents and situations of publication will not be considered here. A shortlist includes: *Breaking Silence* (New York: Greenfield Review Press, 1983), *Chinese American Poetry: An Anthology* (Washington: U of Washington P, 1991), and *The Open Boat: Poems from Asian America* (New York: Anchor Books, 1993), which, edited by Garrett Hongo, mostly focused on the prize-winners, big names (Maxine Hong Kingston, for example), and the most conservative strands of younger writing.

that it contributes to an "exploring of the surrealist and dadaist intertexts in English-Canadian literature, an area which has, unlike its Quebec counterpart, remained largely unexplored so far" (Kröller 48), suggesting that Kiyooka had, in his plunge into the depths of consciousness, hit upon certain aspects of Canadian nationhood that may have, for political reasons, remained largely hidden. Discourse is, unfortunately, forced to talk around the project when it comes to totalizing meanings. The following excerpt, which, like each poem, rests atop one of the collages as a sort of explanation, is replete with poignant, suggestive quick edits

sifting the Rune/s for

the Behemoth of Speech: the absolute truth of
those huge white tusks curving in the moonlight marsh
a million years ago, today. searching the Sahara
for the Algebra-of-Awe Rimbaud wept when he stumbled
on them in front of the pygmy king's palace. the impossible
death of Chairman Mao on late night television. nuclear
frisson. Hermann Goring & Separatism. on the
tusk of a dream i beheld the Elephant on the promenade:
his inflamed ear thrums the mammalian silences

the 8th frame hides
the real pigeon shit spattered on the back of a bronze Napoleon

(Kiyooka 117)

Language is a ruin/rune, a rebus of sorts, which resonates with the ecstasy of an all-encompassing truth, an "Algebra-of-Awe," perhaps the hermetic vision of eternal interrelations, but which, in the end, points, even in its encapsulated and emasculated present — "Chairman Mao on late night television" — towards "a million years ago, today." This excerpt aptly demonstrates the syntactic quality of Kiyooka's writing — singular capitalization of certain nouns, never-capitalized "i"s and first words of sentences, for example — that, as Miki writes in his afterword to the collected edition, has both a transformative yet generative content. "It was in the intimacy of the bond between mother and child that RK would also come to inhabit the imagination of his 'mother tongue' which would shape the parameters of poetic language — the 'inglish' with the lowercase 'i' which he distinguished from 'English,' the dominant language of what was for him an anglo-centric norm" Kiyooka, 304). Kiyooka's life was completely uprooted during the Canadian internment of Japanese in 1941, as Miki writes: "Overnight, the transparent signs of childhood became the opaque space of state control, a machinery that homogenized his 'Kiyooka' name in a system of codes in which the 'i' of his consciousness became a body 'of the Japanese race' — the nomenclature used to register, fingerprint, and revoke the rights of innocent people." In a sense, Kiyooka's paranoiac, individualistic method in his "Dream Machine" — whose major motif is the hot-air balloon, which paradoxically both signifies dream perspective as well as panoptic state observation, as Kröller notes — can be seen as an attempt to force the fissures in the monolith of governmental power, meeting the opacities of control with those of ellipsis. Importantly for Miki and Canadian Asian poetics in general, Kiyooka assembled out of the myriad arenas of language, a sort of hybrid idiom — more "Zen" and more "surreal" than O'Hara's, to parse Ashbery's famous comment — that on the one hand was "mastered" by a constraining, implacable ego ("that irresistible / raga-of-longing that droned through me / riddling my psyche . . . / had to be lanced before i could begin to sing," as he wrote in "Gotenyama" [Kiyooka, 229]) but which, nonetheless, never gave ground to what he considered empty in the historical context of the millennia, the "dung hill mind," as he called it in "Struck from the Heat of a Cold December Sun" (Kiyooka 179). Kiyooka's work, not unlike Blake's, bedevils the editorializing mind with its confident transgressions and trickster challenges to enact conformity.

One quality of the generation of Asian Canadian poets that follow Kiyooka is that they have found ways to theorize issues of agency in minority discourses while never sacrificing the technically innovative, resistant qualities of postmodern praxis. Fred Wah, whose early poetry stemmed from a deep engagement with the New American poetics of Olson and Creeley, with whom he studied in Buffalo in the 1960s, sunthesizes in his essay "Speak My Language: Racing the Lyric Poetic," issues of linguistic variance or "othering" with those of the racialized subject. Commenting on statements by the Nicaraguan poet Margaret Randall and the Quebecois poet Nicole Brossard, he writes:

> Randall [says] that the revolution will succeed on the common tongue of the people and Brossard [says] there will be no revolution until that (male-based) common tongue is troubled into change. Since then the range of political possibility in poetic language has pretty much dwelled between those two poles. I know which one I opt for but I'm always a little bothered by those race writers

who go for the other, that seemingly solid lyric subject ground I can't trust. I can't trust it since, for my generation, racing the lyric entails racing against it; erasing it in order to subvert the restrictions of a dominating and centralising aesthetic. ("Speak")

With a few exceptions, Asian American poets have not been the leaders in discussing linguistically innovative poetries among or for ethnic writers*, for reasons that are too deep

---

* John Yau's long review of Eliot Weinberger's anthology *American Poetry Since 1959: Innovators & Outsiders* (Marsilio Publishers, 1993), published in the *American Poetry Review* (March/April 1994) pp. 45-54, represents what is probably the first attempt by an Asian American writer to address issues that have haunted poets attentive to the inheritance of literary modernism, hence suggesting a basis for a cross-cultural poetics that seeks to find the fissures in literary constructs centered around Orientalist perceptions of the "Other". Unfortunately, Yau's approach in the essay is seriously flawed, as he attempts to apply the methods that he uses so well in his poetry — great leaps of association, a certain vitriol, the flat statement of the obvious when it is not obvious, etc. — in the forum of a wide-ranging, pointed critique that relies on acts of close reading. Yau hangs much of the early part of the essay on an attack on Pound, but primarily through the prism of a statement by Eliot. As Yau writes, "According to T.S Eliot, it was Pound who established 'Chinese poetry for our time.'" In the next sentence, Yau writes: "[W]hat helped Pound to invent Chinese poetry for the West..." The difference between "establish," which suggests permanence of approach, and "invent," which suggests that what Pound created was essentially false, are enormous; the same distinction can be made for "our time," which suggests relativity, and the "West," which suggests a sort of monolithic, unchanging whole. Eliot actually wrote, in his introduction to the *Selected Poems*, that Pound "invented Chinese poetry for our time," also writing that "each generation must translate for itself," leaving very much open the possibility that "translation" may take turns away from the sort of colonialist ethos that Yau reads into *Cathay*. (Spivak's translations and theories come to mind.) Eliot could just have easily said Pound "invented Anglo-Saxon poetry for our time," or that he "invented Anglo-Greek-Chinese poetry for our time," all of which he did. Yau's contention, because of similarities that he sees in two very short poem/translations that Pound made in 1913 and 1954, that "Pound's vision of the Chinese didn't change very much" is really quite unfounded, not only because of Pound's translations of complete Confucian works such as *The Unwobbling Pivot* and his use of Chinese philosophy in his political vision, but because most of Pound's translations that appear in the anthology resemble his early versions of Troubadour poetry more than *Cathay*, which was an experiment in a long-form imagism (compare "Clear as a stream her modesty / As neath dark boughs her secrecy / reed against reed / tall on slight / as the stream moves left and right" from his late *Confucian Odes* to the short poem "Alba" in *Personae*). This chain of observations leads Yau to claim, "To Pound, the Chinese were born losers. They knew how to maintain their heroic dignity amid a whirlwind of chaos and loss." Pound — as most readers of him know — thought the same thing about Wyndham Lewis, not to mention the Anglo-Saxons and Greeks. The entire review — which is accurate in many ways, especially concerning the exclusion of Gertrude Stein and her "instistence on difference," the limited view of African American poetry and twisted view of women's poetry conveyed in the book, the inclusion of writers centered around the magazine *Sulfur*, the politics of Robert Kelly's poem "Sleeping with Women," and his statement that "it's as if Weinberger's anthology stopped in 1979, rather than the early 1990s" — is based on this link between Pound and colonialism that is never clearly established. Yau might have fared better had he been attentive to the paradoxes of Pound's project, as Charles Bernstein was in his essay in *A Poetics*, "Pounding Fascism." Nonetheless, the review achieved what it set out to do, which was to be a *happening* in literature that more-or-less collapsed the view that twentieth century poetry is basically the story of white male European or American poets with a few hangers-on, presenting instead a tradition — or series of traditions — that includes a wide range of contexts and agendas, many of which

to go into here, but probably have to do with the institutionalization of Asian American writing through the mechanisms of the oppositional "Movement" literatures that took place in the States which occluded formal concerns, and which left those on the periphery with no real audience to address. As Wah writes later in his essay, "Social and cultural production has, in recent years, appropriated the figure of the racialized writer as a measure of containment and control," and he advocates a sort Janus-like looking-both-ways in his attitude toward the lyric, such that "a racialized lyric, caught in the hinges of inherited poetic forms, might adopt an ambiguous regard to both lyric interference and lyric convention in order to recuperate, even, the agency of linguistic choice" ("Speak"). For Wah, all forms of excess, incorporation, and general eclecticism have political content, and his statements on the exercising of linguistic "choice" are born out in his wide-ranging work. The poems of *Mountain* (1967) spill down the page as they mimetically place the self amidst the flux of nature as much as the lyric amidst language ("Hey our ice your ice / it hides / moves and slides [. . .]/ flower out in the lakes of my eyes shimmering Kootenai waters green [. . .]" [Wah, *Selected*, 28]) while formally more varied poems like "Cruise" and *Pictograms from the Interior of B.C.* speed through modes reminiscent of everything from Italian Futurism to Snyder-esque nature poetry, the latter sequence incorporating reproductions of actual prehistoric pictograms. Later ongoing sequences such as "Music at the Heart of Thinking," whose "method of composition is the practice of negative capability and estrangement I've recognized for many years, through playing jazz trumpet, looking at art, and writing poetry" (*Music*, preface), the "ArtKnots" (short lyric poems inspired by art exhibits) and the series of "Utinaki," based on a Japanese form in which he combines lyric, dated prose entries and page spacialization to create fields of paratactic meaning, convey, or rather trace, the thematically nomadic, unbounded "I" as it moves between the cultures and geographies of Canada. For Wah, meaning is "something that is strangely familiar, not quite what we expect, but familiar, is present. That quick little gasp in the daydream, a sudden sigh of recognition, a little sock of baby breath. Writing into meaning starts at the white page, nothing but intention" (*Alley* 5). His poem "ScreeSure Dancing," one of his most formally challenging works, is almost a manifesto for this poetics:

> thoughts different
> sky's all animals, all
> paper, all chalk. Our

---

are informed or entirely shaped by the experience of being the "Other".

> writing as   the tableaus
> anamorphous   =   of voyage
> river cliffs   forgetting
>
>
>   She danced the strict linguistic sense.
>   babbled bavardage   fingerpainted thick
>   memoclouds in the darkening sky
>
>
> $h_{om}{}^{om}e$
>
>
> That's the secret
>   ticket
>   to silence
> na (frame) na's notation
>   (*So Far* 10)

Not unlike Kiyooka (and the influential Canadian poet bpNichol), Wah's poetry suggests the nexus where a Mallaremean poetics of the sign-as-mind meet the proprioceptive poetics of an Olson, in which language was a medium whose message was "projective" of the self. Because of his awareness of these myriad strands, and his dedication to a "negative capability," Wah's work has grown and transformed such that his later poetry, collected in *So Far*, even approaches the status of language-centered writing, but meets head-on transparent, formally fluid "Utanaki." In this way, Wah's statements on the lyric expand to include the different degrees of opacity that language could be said to possess, so that it is not just a vertical axis of the lyric-then and the lyric-now that is traversed, but the vertical axis of the borderless language-centered lyric and the emphatic lyric of a closed subjectivity.

    Space precludes a more detailed investigation of the Canadian poets, but two important figures are Roy Miki and Gerry Shikatani. Miki, former editor of the journal *West Coast Line*, has written extensively on the poetics of Williams and bpNichol among others, and was a major figure in the Japanese Canadian redress settlement on September

22, 1988. His essays "May I See Your ID? Writing in the 'Race' Codes That Bind" (which contains a fuller exploration of Kiyooka's poetics) and "Asiancy: Making Space for Asian Canadian Writing," are radical statements of policy for those writers who (as he states in "Asiancy") choose to "escape the temptations of power relations that govern what gets to be judged of 'national significance' and of 'consequence' — reinforced as they are by an elaborate system of awards, rewards, media privileges, canonization, and ultimately, institutionalization." Unlike Tanaka, whose attitude toward "community" was always through the problematic prism of a "Movement" philosophy and a high concern for the social sciences, Miki operates from within the community, while being aware of the pressures for conformity from outside it. "The dominant values outside come to censure, repress, or otherwise propagandize the inside," he writes, emphasizing that race writing should use the "baffled textual screen" that Deleuze and Guattari describe and call "deterritorialization," which, in Miki's words, is "a disturbed use of language that foregrounds its surface as a conflicted space" ("Asiancy" 145). Miki's poems collected in *Random Access File*, with its paragrammic detonations of "inglish," fulfill this call. Shikatani, a very different poet than Miki (indeed, he is from the opposite coast), has explored every venue of experimental poetics, including sound collage (often influenced by the Japanese language) and concrete poetics (his beautiful "Our Nights in Perugia"[*] avoids the obviousness of intention that plagues this type of poetry by actually being visually compelling). His recent book *Aqueduct: Poems and Texts from Europe 19791987*, a mammoth 406-page collection of sometimes ephemeral, sometimes grandiose writings, falls in a peculiar tradition of Poundian poetic projects by racially marginalized North American writers who travel in Europe, which includes Clarence Major's long work from his voyages in Venice, *Surfaces and Masks*. Probably *Aqueduct*'s most salient characteristics are its size, the extraordinary formal variety and mastery, and the often transparent, open quality of the writing — that is, it becomes, by being transparent yet inabsorbable because of its size, a single statement on memory, not just of one man's trip to Europe, but of the idea of an approach to a European sojourn, which used to be seen (in the *Bildungsromanen* of Hnery James) as a necessary step in one's maturity. Interestingly, one loses any sense of the racial in the author, Europe providing, perhaps, the ultimate escape hatch from the "race codes that bind" and paradigms of reading and writing "race." As Shikatani writes in "Flight: Geography": "continuous, a map / with these fingers / holding black pen / a period in flight, a / moment repeating out / & in / a design / in time, in / the flurry of wings."

---

[*] as reprinted in *Premonitions*, pp. 263-65

(Shikatani 47).* As with Cha, the concern with time and the ephemeral nature of consciousness lead to inevitable critiques of meaning in which writing itself is but a trace of darkness on a white screen.

There are several younger poets who have already made impacts on the literary scene, having published either first books, important essays or selections of work in anthologies or journals. Barry Masuda's interest in the uprooting of language ranges from Language-like razing of normative speech and grammar ("Local Cyborg" begins "words distend homicides / Cindy Sherman hosts 24 blowfly pupa / nestle in my decomposing eyes / cannot see how passion's / corpse preserved in cryogenic culture / wanders aimlessly through Ala Manoa"†) to the hot discourse in Hawai'i over the "local" and pidgin writing that has wandered into the academic sphere: "Begin graduate school on the west coast to theorize 'da local,' leaving righ in da middle of da bes' 'oama run in four-five yeahs, but hard fo' get job at UH if you no leave UH, 'ah?" he writes in "Holoholo Style" (Masuda 29) As issues of "non-normative" language and languages previously viewed as "dialects" are viewed as subversions and critiques of centrality‡, writers like Masuda — who in particular seems to be aware of the global repercussions of the gestures of pidgin — will play a central role in synthesizing the "local," the "cyborgian," the language-centered and the lyric subject in their work.

The first book by Sianne Ngai, *Criteria*, was published in 1998, and is a cross between a guidebook in subversions of panoptic totalities, a primer on reading practices, along with (in the line of Berssenbrugge) a reduction of the act of perception to its component parts. "The project now breaks ground for / video monitoring density — consecrated by guardian angel's password / 'if the brick wants to enter the wall let it join'" (*Criteria* 33), she writes in "Fill," shifting effortlessly through frames of personal, political, economic and virtual realities.

E Kim's sequence, "Technical Translations After Robinson After Wang Wei," challenges normative modes of translation by running them through the grill of the

---

*Shikatani has also published *Selected Poems and Texts 1973 1988* (Aya Press, 1989) among other books, and coedited an anthology of Japanese Canadian poetry, *Paper Doors* (Coach House Press, 1981).

†as reprinted in *Premonitions*, p. 179.

‡These themes are developed most interestingly in Charles Bernstein's, "Poetries of the Americas," published in *Modernism/Modernity* 3:3 (1996), pp. 123. "The cultural space of this impossible America is not carved up by national borders or language borders but transected by innumerable overlaying, contradictory or polydictory, traditions and proclivities and histories and regions and peoples and circumstances and identities and families and collectivities and dissolutions – dialects and ideolects, not National Tongues; localities and habitations, not States." This essay can also be downloaded at the journal's website.

Microsoft spellchecker, a process that critiques not just the local of "Wang Wei" but the local of the translatorese which purports to convey it. "Law gnome sits arrears emote whiskey / — lilts swallow ginned emboss — sit do / eruptive and in ere evil lay down Dixie? / aerobe ere saw that mix of yen every to," runs one quatrain, razzing language and the tradition in a way reminiscent of Harryette Mullen's *Muse and Drudge*, but with a systemic wedge.

Hoa Nguyen, whose poems were included in the recent *An Anthology of New (American) Poets*, is part of a group of younger poets attempting to reconfirm the efficacy of pure lyricism through the emotive, free-associative speech of later Beat poetics, and has consequently done some interesting work in forms, such as the pantoum: "Look different suede eyes / flower eyes will not stay forever / O fragrant temper trying to control / the 10 thousand things (bugs, the sun / flowers, eyes) will not stay forever / Run in a field of fronds [. . .]" (Nguyen 75).

Hung Q. Tu, a Californian poet who has written much but published little, operates, in his suite "Quarto to Octano," through a series of permutations on an initial sequence of stanzas to uncover a concentricity of expanding meanings, moving from the site-specific occasion of the initial poem toward a global denunciation of the mechanisms of capital. The first line of the last stanza of each is "copies!copies!copies!," and the entire last stanza of the sixth poem runs: "copies!copies!copies! / sabotage — the finest art / *how the parentheses flourish* / feigning fainter still fink / the honesty between dog and master / read between lines the sex as sniffing / simulacrum carpet polling" (Tu 121), each line — like that final, taking Baudrillard, Vietnam and the Presidential elections in a turn — hanging on the hyper-mediated irreality of the historical moment.

A writer who is not so "young," who has yet to attain the attention she deserves, is the Canadian poet Jam Ismail, who spends half of each year in Hong Kong and half in Vancouver. Excerpts from her sequence "Scared Texts" (or, alternately, "Sacred Texts") were a standout in terms of literary exploration in the 1991 anthology of Canadian Chinese writing, *Many-Mouthed Birds*, edited by Bennett Lee and Jim Wong-Chu. Indeed, in a development of Joycean stream-of-consciousness narrative, "Sacred Texts" is a many-mouthed plethora of dialogue and narrative moments: "hibiscus mentioned that mushrooms are good for cholesterol / jaggery scoffed: what d'you mean, good for! / chestnut dehisced: she means good against, good against cholesterol. / flame-o'-the-forest said to jaggery: we know you speak better english & that you know what we mean" (Ismail 124). A later sequence, "from the Diction Air," takes accumulation of a diasporic experience deep into the language game to produce a multivalent, part-narrational and part-lyrical autobiographical riff — a sort of *Prelude* for the new order:

> :"didi" meant big sister (bengali), little brother (cantonese), DDT (english). to begin with, inglish had been at home, with cantonese & hindustani. one of the indian languages, the kid felt in bombay, which british hongkong tried to colonize. descended on all sides from the Idiosyncrasy, the kid disdained grammar class, refused to parse, opted to be remote parsee.

> :at school wrote her first poem, *DAMON NOMAD*, (damon nomad). & what mean while was writing her, what *nom de womb*? reverb with '47 (indian, pakistani), '48 (koreas), '49 (chinas, germanies), '54 (vietnams).

> :"hey," he bellowed, pants down in quebec, "bring in some english mags, i can't shit in french!" claude nearly kicked him in the anglo. macauley's minute & roosevelt's second unearthed in canadian library digs, chattel feared english had him in its grip, spooken for, punish.[*]

As Fred Wah writes in "Speak My Language," "the proximity of the autobiographical realism is still only deflected momentarily by a reading of syntactic and punctuative gestures," such that this text is a negotiation of lyric subjectivity and disruptive grammar. Ismail, like Kiyooka, Cha and Masuda, are true "interstitial" poets of the "English" language — perhaps the heirs of the world citizenry attributed to Coleridge, and implicit in the later Joyce — as they are privy to a great deal of first-hand cultural knowledge, sitting in on the Senates of linguistic negotiation, while aware yet wary not only of the call of academic discourse (perversely leveling while attempting to be inclusive) but the entire Western poetic tradition, its scales of value and its hunger for conformity.

As Allen Ginsberg may have been wont to ask: "Does a tomato have an angel?" In postcolonial terms, "angel" might be exchanged for "nation" or "geneology," and "tomato" with the externally racialized "body." A Kim suggests, even a "tomato" is open for interpretation, and scientific paradigms determine its final content perhaps more than its singular features. As the variety of writing considered in this essay demonstrates, there is no single thread of discourse to which an Asian American writer feels obliged to confirm or

---

[*] as cited in Fred Wah's "Speak My Language." The original text, like most of Ismail's work, is self-published.

argue, as there may have been in the early 1970s when Tanaka was writing his "Metaphysical Foundations" series, but rather a system of discourses which only become abhorrent to the racialized writer once the progressive liberalism of its purported content reduces to abstraction (or distraction) the singularity of the writing itself — a curious position, indeed. In this sense, it is probably not surprising that a recent controversial critique of the politics of desire, titled "Raw Matter: A Poetics of Disgust," which doesn't consider ethnic discourse in any way directly, was written by an Asian American writer, Sianne Ngai. As she writes early in the essay, "postmodernity ... and pluralism are virtually synonymous," and moves on to offer another critical and reading model which, she concludes, is only destined to self-destruct:

> What makes disgust a viable theoretical approach to innovative writing is thus its negative potentiality as a figure of exclusion, the radical externalization it enacts in facilitating the subject's turn away from the object. In this manner, the possibility of disgust as a poetics resides in its resistance to pluralism and its ideology of all-inclusiveness which allows it to recuperate and neutralize any critical discourse emphasizing conflict, dissent, or discontinuity. What makes disgust particularly strategic in organizing and informing a critical approach to contemporary writing is that *disgust thwarts seductive reasoning*. I will also argue that *disgust thwarts close reading*, the generally unquestioned, seemingly irrefutable practice criticism can't seem to do without. Lastly, as an operation of exclusion or externalization, always turning away from its object, *disgust thwarts its own use as a critical paradigm*. ("Raw Matter" 102)

This echoes Canadian poet Jeff Derksen's essay on Fred Wah's "alienethnic" poetics called "Making Race Opaque," a critique of Canadian state-sanctioned multiculturalism in which he observes: "Writing that focuses on a polyvalent sign, that utilizes this sign strategically, is *nonrepresentational* — but not culturally meaningless as it is sometimes described as — because it doesn't represent hybrid subjectivities in a manner that is assimilable by multicultural discourse" (Derksen 76)* The range of Asian American writing, which also

---

*Derksen's essays on the multicultural situation in Canada are invaluable in terms of providing an image of the meshing of classes "avant garde" and "minority/community" concerns, easily stepping over a monolithic sense of a "white European" that has hindered such discourse in the U.S. He writes of Wah's "alienethnic" poetics"

> These poetics are both oppositional and differential: oppositional in the sense of engaging an avant-garde position of "an attack on the status of art in bourgeois society (Burger, 49) as a means to carve out a social function for writing and to articulate unofficial subjectivities, and differential in the sense

includes an activist-oppositional strand — feminist, lesbian, working class, ethno-centric — most strongly represented in the 1982 anthology *Breaking Silence* (but which wasn't nearly as formally exploratory as the writers discussed here), is full of instances in which the "subjective I" is site of negotiations that rely on no stable paradigm for its enactment, but which, on the other hand, must engage in a state of covert action due to the panoptic gaze of discourse that utilizes its terms for alternative ends. This isn't to say that Mei-Mei Berssenbrugge had reached her particular poetics via a process of eluding "presence" and hence assimilation, nor that non-ethnic writers do not also feel the brunt of mollifying interpretation — Ngai's essay, after all, was founded on a reading of writers as wide ranging as Deanna Ferguson, Bruce Andrews, Kevin Davies, and Dorothy Trujillo Lusk. However, Asian American writers, probably more than not — whether they are "up" on postmodern theory, or are simply going on their nerve — are often forced into a consideration of the Western literary tradition, especially the "avant-garde," in a peculiar way due to a vague sense of membership in a racially defined community that often is not loyal to the various binaries mentioned earlier in this essay, especially that one that sees no negotiation between subjectivity and the "play" of language. In this sense, "neutralization" of the past through the freeing of the sign is vexed operation for many Asian American poets, even one like Tan Lin who writes in a recent essay "Forgetting a word is among the most beautiful things that can happen to the human brain. The dumb poem is the most beautiful poem" (interview 40). However, as writers like Ismail, Masuda, Wah and Yau show, this loosening of the grip of the sign created an open space for dialogic cultural negotiation or "deterritorialization" that wasn't a clear option for, say, Paul Lawrence Dunbar, or for the pre-1970s writers collected in the anthology of early Asiann American poetry *Quiet Fire*. The idioms and methods of writing, not to mention the *art*, that will erupt from this space are what we're looking for.

---

that it is a poetics that recognizes difference without integrating it grammatically into a larger unit such as national identity. (72)

WORKS CITED*

Berssenbrugge, Mei-Mei. *Empathy*. New York: Station Hill Press, 1989.

——. *The Heat Bird*. Providence: Burning Deck, 1983.

——. *Summits Move With the Tide*. New York: Greenfield Review Press, 1974.

Bök, Christian. "Oneiromechanics: Notes on the Dream Machine of Roy Kiyooka," *West Coast Line* (1995).

Chang, Juliana, ed. *Quiet Fire*. New York: Asian American Writers Workshop, 1997.

Derksen, Jeff. "Making Race Opaque: Fred Wah's Poetics of Opposition and Differentiation." *West Coast Line* (1996).

Inada, Lawson Fusao. *Legends from Camp*. Minneapolis: Coffee House Books, 1992.

Bennett Lee and Jim Wong-Chu, eds.. *Many-Mouthed Birds*. Vancouver: Douglas & McIntyre, 1991.

——. "from the Diction Air." Cited in Fred Wah, "Speak My Language."

Kim, Elaine. "Beyond Railroads and Internment: Comments on the Past, Present, and Future of Asian American Studies," *Privileging Positions*.

Kim, Myung Mi. Interview. *Tripwire* 1.1 (Spring 1998).

——. *Dura*. Los Angeles: Sun & Moon, 1998).

Kiyooka, Roy. *Pacific Windows*. Vancouver: Talonbooks, 1997.

Kröller, Eva Marie. "Roy Kiyooka's The Fountainebleu Dream Machine: A Reading," *Canadian Literature*, no. 113-14 (Summer 1987).

Leung, Ho Hon. *Bridge* (Winter, 1983).

Lew, Walter K. *Excerpts from Dikte/for Dictee* (1982). Seoul: Yeul Eum Press, 1992.

——. "The Movieteller." *Chain* 3:2 (Fall 1996)

——, ed. *Premonitions*. New York: Kaya Production, 1995.

Lin, Tan. *Lotion Bullwhip Giraffe*. Los Angeles: Sun & Moon Press, 1996.

——. "Interview for an Ambient Stylistics." *Tripwire*.

——. "Michael Palmer Prints Out a Kingdom." *A Poetics of Criticism*. Ed. Juliana Spahr, Mark Wallace, Kristin Prevallet, and Pam Rehm. New York: Leave Books, 1994.

Masuda, Barry. "Holoholo Style." *Tinfish* 1 (Honolulu, 1995).

Miki, Roy. "Asiancy: Making a Case for Asian Canadian Writing." *Privileging Positions*,

——. "Can I See Your ID: Writing the 'Race' Codes that Bind." *West Coast Line* (1998).

Ngai, Sianne. *Criteria*. Oakland, CA: O Books, 1998

——. "Raw Matter: A Poetics of Disgust." *Open Letter* 19:1 (Winter, 1998).

——. "Technical Translations after Robinson after Wang Wei." Arras website. www.bway.neth/~arras

Nguyen, Hoa. pantoum. *Mike and Dale's Younger Poets* 8 (Winter, 1998).

Nunakawa, Jeff. "Oscar Wilde in Japan: Aestheticism, Orientalism, and the Derealization of the Homosexual." *Privileging Positions: The Sites of Asian American Studies*. Washington: Washington State UP, 1995.

Robbe-Grillet, Alain. *For a New Novel*. New York: Grove Press, 1965.

---

*Theauthor notes that the bibliography was constructed in 1999, and readers should check other sources for more recent publications.

Rexroth, Kenneth. "Introduction." *White Chrysanthemums* by Sadakichi Hartmann. New York: Herder and Herder, 1971.

Shikatani, Gerry. *Aqueduct*. Toronto: Mercury Press, Underwhich Editions, and Wolsak and Wynn Publishers Ltd., 1996.

Spahr, Juliana. "Postmodernism, Readers, and Theresa Hak Kyung Cha's Dictee." *College Literature* (1997).

Tabios, Eileen. *Black Lightning*. New York: Asian American Writer's Workshop 1998.

Tanaka, Ronald. "On the Metaphysical Foundations of a Sansei Poetics: Ethnicity and Social Science," *Journal of Ethnic Studies* 7:2

-------. "Towards a Systems Analysis of Ethnic Minority Literature." *Journal of Ethnic Studies* 6:1 (1978).

Tu, Hung Q. "Quarto to Octano." *West Coast Line* (Vancouver, 1998).

Vertov, Dziga. "The Vertov Papers." *Apparatus*. New York: Tanam, 1981.

Wah, Fred. *Alley Alley Home Free* Alberta: Red Deer College Press, 1992

-------. *Music at the Heart of Thinking*. Alberta: Red Deer College Press, 1987.

-------. *Selected Poems*. Vancouver: Talonbooks, 1989.

-------. *So Far*. Vancouver: Talonbooks, 1991

-------. "Speak My Language: Racing the Lyric Poetic." *West Coast Line* (1995).

Yau, John. *Corpse and Mirror*. New York: Alfred A. Knopf, 1983.

-------. *Jasper Johns: Printed Symbols*. Minneapolis: Walker Arts Center, 1999.

-------. *Radiant Sillouette*. California: Black Sparrow Press, 1989.

-------. "Who Was Wilfredo Lam?" *Talisman* 5 (Fall, 1999).

Brent Hayes Edwards

THE RACE FOR SPACE: SUN RA'S POETRY

"I'm dealing with equations." — Sun Ra

IN JULY 1969, WHEN THE UNITED STATES WAS EXCITEDLY AWAITING the flight of the spacecraft Apollo 11, ferrying Neil Armstrong to the moon, *Esquire* magazine published a half-whimsical survey. Writer William H. Honan, in a piece called "Le Mot Juste for the Moon," commented on the symbolic significance of the moon walk. Because space was the "final frontier" of human discovery, Honan concluded, Armstrong would require (like Archimedes, Vasco da Gama, Columbus, Stanley, and Alexander Graham Bell before him) an appropriate phrase to pronounce as he took the first lunar steps—and so *Esquire* had asked contemporary popular figures for "Helpful Hints," proposed proclamations for the astronaut to deliver.

Most of the talking heads offered predictably heady pronouncements about the universal human significance of the First Step. Hubert Humphrey, for example, suggested that Armstrong entreat: "May the moon be a symbol of peace and cooperation among the nations of earth." Some were pithy or glib; thus Muhammad Ali: "Bring me back a challenger, 'cause I've defeated everyone here on earth." Many could not resist the boast that the event marked the victory of America in the so-called "Space Race" between the superpowers: "Forgive the intrusion, Ma'am. Don't smile so bitter / At good Yanks tidying up your Sputnik litter" (Robert Graves). But there, amidst the jingoism and utopianism, among names like Nabokov, Anne Sexton, Lawrence Ferlinghetti, William O. Douglas, Ed Koch, Timothy Leary, Bob Hope, Isaac Asimov, William Safire, George McGovern, Tiny Tim, Truman Capote, John Kenneth Galbraith, Marshall McLuhan, appeared "the space age jazz poet," Sun Ra, with what John Szwed calls a "cheery poem inaugurating the new age" (Szwed 275):

> Reality has touched against myth
> Humanity can move to achieve the impossible
> Because when you've achieved one impossible the others
> Come together to be with their brother, the first impossible
> Borrowed from the rim of the myth
> Happy Space Age to You...

It is a remarkable poem—once again, Sun Ra showing up where we least expect to see him, taking a joyful stance as a "witness of alternatives" (Baraka, "Sun Ra" 174).

I want to use this poem as a point of entry, or launching pad, into a consideration of the writings of Sun Ra, not simply because the anecdote is amusing, but more because this finely-wrought stanza opens our way out to two critical terms in the Ra cosmology: "myth" and the "impossible." Reading these words as an intervention in one of the great symbolic moments of the Cold War, we hopefully will avoid the easy response to Ra, that wants to brand him a kook, a space freak, talking nonsense, *out*. Entering, or exiting, with this poem, we are reminded that for Sun Ra, "it is no accident here and elsewhere the words myth and history walk hand in hand" (Wright 14). For Ra, myth is what poet Jay Wright calls a "mode of knowledge," a "medium to understanding" (Ra, "Living Parallel" IE 50) that is quite closely linked to the grand events of the day.

This odd little poem displaces in at least two directions. On the one hand, by speaking in terms of the "myth" rather than the nation, Sun Ra ignores and thus rejects the discourse around "America" in so many of the other "Helpful Hints"—the often triumphalist idea that the moon shot is a particularly national accomplishment. Instead, here we have a certain kind of universalist discourse, talking about "Humanity" as a whole. But in the language of this strangely dressed figure, identified in the article *only* as "the space age jazz poet," "Humanity" would appear to be circumscribed. Here it refers more to "the inhabitants of this planet" than to the only conceivable frame of life. And so we are preached a perplexing universalism, a "universalism of the impossible."

At the same time, there is a second level of displacement: for Sun Ra, by not mentioning race, also rejects the mode of most of the black intellectual commentators of the moment. Duke Ellington, for example, had written an essay called "The Race for Space" around 1957, an attempt to transfer the civil rights discourse of the "Double V" (victory against fascism abroad, victory against racism at home) from World War Two into the Cold War. Ellington described jazz as both a model for and a "barometer" of democracy, and called the US to task for perpetual racism and continuing segregation, going so far as to suggest that the USSR won the space race with Sputnik because of its relative racial harmony:

> [T]his is my view on the race for space. We'll never get it until we Americans, collectively and individually[,] get us a new sound. A new sound of harmony, brotherly love, common respect and consideration for the dignity and freedom of men. (296)

Sun Ra takes another route. The *Esquire* poem chooses not to speak *from* race, as Ellington does, to demand civil rights as the fulfillment of the principles of American democracy. Sun Ra's "impossibles," in other words, "come together" in a register altogether different from the black jeremiads of the 1960s, even those like James Baldwin's *The Fire Next Time* that close with prophetic commands to do the impossible, to "end the racial nightmare": "I know that what I am asking is impossible. But in our time, as in every time, the impossible is the least that one can demand" (Baldwin 379).

Reading the poetry, music, lyrics, theater and pronouncements of Sun Ra as a kind of constellation, however, it becomes evident that this difference is not the result of an a-historicism, not because Ra offers no racial critique. On the contrary, he roots his sense of "myth" and the "impossible" precisely in the history of US racism and segregation. For example, in the legendary 1972 mythic-blaxploitation film *Space is the Place*, there is a scene where Sun Ra, a black alien from Saturn come to Earth in a music-powered spaceship to rescue the African American population, visits a youth community center. "How we know you not some old hippie or something?" one woman demands. Sun Ra answers,

> How do you know I'm real? I'm not real. I'm just like you. You don't exist in this society. If you did, your people wouldn't be seeking equal rights. You're not real. If you were, you'd have some status among the nations of the world. I come to you as the myth, because that's what black people are. I came from a dream that the black man dreamed long ago. (Toop 29)

It is thus true, as John Szwed explains, that "space was both a metaphor of exclusion and of reterritorialization, of claiming the 'outside' as one's own, of tying a revised and corrected past to a claimed future" (140).

Nevertheless, Sun Ra does not quite end up at a black nationalist position. As with Barbara Christian's reformulation of the phrase "the race for theory" into a double-edged tool, to critique the exclusionary and self-sustaining institution of Theory in the academy while noting that the putatively "excluded" *also* theorize, Sun Ra's understanding of "the race for space" critiques the jingoistic 1960s cant of the Final Frontier while at the same time redefining "race," redefining the frame of black radicalism. That "separate kind of human being, the American black man," represents a challenge to US pretensions of democracy, but finally *doesn't* belong here. Black people are mythic, ancient, or "cosmic." They *are* the race for space:

> [H]ere in America there are also Black people who have given up nothing, who couldn't give up anything because they live in harmony with the Creator of the cosmos. And they will always be a source of difficulty for every nation on this planet, because they've no other ruler than the Creator of the cosmos and they're faithful only to him. The Bible speaks about that too. They're the only people who stand apart. Nobody can say that Israel is that people, because Israel is counted as one of the nations of this world, at least in the United Nations, but not the American Black people. (Vuijsje 17, quoted in Szwed 140)

When Sun Ra refigures the so-called black nationalist "land question"—or, in another discourse, the Communist Party "Black Belt" thesis that African Americans formed an "internally colonized" nation in the US South—into the *space question*, we are not quite in recognizable nationalist strategy any more.

In reading the *Esquire* poem, then, we have to hear through the prism of his other texts, where Sun Ra often calls for a politics of *mythocracy*, rather than demanding the fulfillment of democratic principles, or theocracy (Sun Ra, "Your Only Hope Now" 113). Not "We hold these truths to be self-evident that all men are created equal," no; Ra demands something absolutely *other*:

> We hold this myth to be potential
>   Not self evident alone but equational;
>   Another Dimension
>   Of another kind of Living Life
>   Abstract-Projection Presence
>
> This Myth are these
> We be potential

> This myth is not what you know
> ("We Hold This Myth To Be Potential," EO 128)

It seems that myth represents both a critique of the historical erasure of African Americans, as a group—the prophet Ra arrives as reminder of that exilic past ("I come to you as the myth, because that's what black people are")—and possibility, an openness that even breaks syntax ("This Myth are these") in its insistence on something new, on something radically different.

Sun Ra's use of the word "impossible" is the recognition that the radically different, a radical alterity, is inconceivable, and yet paradoxically exactly that which *must* be conceived. "The impossible is the watchword of the greater space age," Sun Ra wrote on the cover of the album *Rocket Number 9 Take Off For Venus* (later reissued as *Interstellar Low Ways*). "The impossible attracts me," Ra often said, "because everything possible has been done and the world didn't change" (Lock 15). Or:

> I'm talking about something that's so impossible, it can't possibly be true. But it's the only way the world's gonna survive, this impossible thing. My job is to change five billion people to something else. Totally impossible. But everything that's possible's been done by man. I have to deal with the impossible. And when I deal with the impossible and am successful, it makes me feel good because I know that I'm not bullshittin'. (Corbett 311)

In this light, the lines of the *Esquire* poem make more sense: when Sun Ra writes that the Apollo mission allows us to touch the "rim of myth," allows us tangential access to a kind of "brotherhood of impossibles," he is writing about an extreme version of what Thomas Kuhn would call a "paradigm shift." Going to space is epistemological work—it might force us to alter our conception of what "the inhabitants of this planet" can be. It "races," but more *razes* and *raises*, as Ra might say, the potential of the human.

More than anything else, Sun Ra's work is consistent and insistent in the way it constantly pushes towards those moments of the impossible, those paradigm shifts that are unimaginable until after they've happened, but that are necessary. As a result of this drive, one can track in this period a kind of escalating "race" in the way Sun Ra talks about space. Just after the moon shot, Nigerian writer Tam Fiofori asked Ra in an interview, "How do you feel about the moon shot, in the light of your space music?" Though he had been talking about "space music" for the past fifteen years, Sun Ra quickly shifted gears:

> Well, I'm not playing Space Music as the ultimate reach anymore. That is, not in the interplanetary sense alone. I'm playing intergalactic music, which is beyond the other idea of space music, because it is of the natural infinity of the eternal universe Eternal ETERNAL . . . it is of the universes, as all the universes together make another kind of universe. There is a need for that type of beingness upon this planet at this time. The Space music of the previous years was presented to prepare people for the idea of going to the moon and other places like that in the interplanetary thing, but now, since that has been accomplished, or the idea of it has been projected or propagated (however it is), of course there is no need for me to propagate it myself. . . .
>
> On this planet, it seems, it has been very difficult for me to do and be of the possible things and projects. As I look at the world today and its events and the harvest of possible things, I like the idea of the impossible more and more. (14)

Here the term "intergalactic," broader than "interplanetary," evidences Ra's continual vigilance towards the impossible, the un-thought, the un-conceived, the "not," the "alter," as he liked to say. Such an attempt to break the limits of what can be thought becomes Sun Ra's prophetic duty on Earth. For him, it represents the only chance for mankind to rethink its "destiny."

This critical strategy, which Sun Ra terms "myth-science," making recourse both to the knowledge systems of ancient Egypt and to a futuristic science fiction, places Ra in a rich firmament of black visionaries, what David Toop has called the "mystico-political undercurrent of black American thought" (27), from Nat Turner, Rebecca Jackson, and Julia Foote, to Robert Johnson, Marcus Garvey, and Father Divine, to Ornette Coleman, George Clinton, artist Ram-el-zee, and dub producer Lee "Scratch" Perry. What finally distinguishes Sun Ra in this kind of visionary tradition is his emphasis on the poetic and the literary—and it is this theme that I want to take up here. Even speaking of the "intergalactic" approach to music, Ra thinks in tropes implying that for him, certain operations of language are essential to any approach to the impossible, to any delineation of the myth. In a handout for the legendary class on "The Black Man in the Cosmos" he taught at Berkeley in 1971, Sun Ra made recourse to etymology to argue that the very form of myth is linguistic:

Every myth is a mathematical parable. Myth is another form of truth, a parable is a myth; it is a parallel assertion. Myth in Greek is mythos, a word meaning a word, speech, legend. (Szwed 304-5)

In an interview around the same period, he explains: "The intergalactic phase is of the expansion-continuation dictionary form. As a dictionary it is applicable to multi-sense adaptive expression; it reaches encyclopedia proportions" (Fiofori 15). He sometimes referred to his records as issues of a "cosmic newspaper" (Lock 16), and almost always describes the impossible as a poetic practice. Take for example his poem "Words and the Impossible" (IE 27):

> The elasticity of words
> The phonetic-dimension of words
> The multi-self of words
> Is energy for thought – If it is a reality.
>   The idea that words
> Can form themselves into the impossible
> Then the way to the impossible
> Is through words.
>
> The fate of humanity is determined
> By the word they so or approve
> Because they reap what they so
> Even if it is the fruit of their lies

Sun Ra says elsewhere that "words are seeds you plant in the ground" (Spady 26). In this sense, there is a peculiar kind of split semiosis, a seed that grows into many plants, espoused in this poem where we see the word "so" in a place where conventional grammar and context tells us we should see "sow." Here is the "multi-self of words," "the phonetic-dimension of words" in action: an impossible grammar, an impossible or "immeasurable" equation between grapheme and phoneme. The mark on the page doesn't equal what we "hear," and the practice of the impossible occurs in the interstices of that discrepancy. (In light of such phonetic alteration, it is crucial to recognize that "Words and the Impossible," indeed like much of Ra's verse, is as much *sight poetry* as sound poetry—if you hear the poem read aloud without seeing it, there is no way to notice the altered spelling of "so.")

"The fate of humanity is determined/ By the word they so or approve": in other words, the visionary import of this practice is that the way we "solve" this homonymic equation (writing "sow," writing "so"—the way we "sew" it?) determines our fate: opens or closes possible ways of seeing and voicing the world.

UMBRA/RA

INTERESTINGLY, THOUGH, IT HAS BEEN EXTREMELY DIFFICULT FOR CRITICS to come to terms with Sun Ra's poetry as such—or even in relation to his music. Apparently it is as difficult to comprehend his writing in a field of musicians-who-write (Ellington, Mingus, Anthony Braxton, Joseph Jarman, Cecil Taylor) as in a field of mid-century black experimental poetics. This is true even when Ra had direct contact with writers, as in the mid-1960s, during the time his Arkestra lived in the East Village, and was closely linked not only with the lively "New Thing" free jazz scene of those years, but also with poets of the Umbra group, such as David Henderson, Tom Dent, Steve Cannon, Lorenzo Thomas, Rolland Snellings, Norman Pritchard, and especially downtown figures loosely associated with Umbra like Henry Dumas and Amiri Baraka. When Ra is mentioned at all in the few existing histories of the black downtown poetry scene in the early 1960s, it is the shock of his theatrical otherness that stands out, not his poetics. Amiri Baraka's eulogy for Sun Ra recalls this aspect vividly:

> I passed through Ra's orbit when they 1st arrived from Chicago. . .
> The Weirdness, Outness, Way Outness, Otherness, was immediate. Some space metaphysical philosophical surrealistic bop funk.
> Some blue pyramid home nigger southern different color meaning hip shit. Ra. Sun Ra.
> Then they put on weird clothes, space helmets, robes, flowing capes. They did rituals, played in rituals, evoked lost civilizations, used strangeness to teach us open feeling as intelligence. (Baraka, "Sun Ra" 171)

Nevertheless, the 1967-68 *Umbra Anthology* opens with a selection of Sun Ra's poetry, apparently marking him as a signal figure—even a kind of poetic elder—for the collection.

But it is difficult to understand the relationship between Ra's oblique lines and the work in the rest of the volume. And so we are left with a curious aporia: even excellent recent work like Aldon Nielsen's *Black Chant: Languages of African American Postmodernism* places Ra in the orbit of Umbra only as musical analogy, without being able to think him as poetic inspiration:

> The radical poetics of Umbra writers like [Oliver] Pitcher and [Norman] Pritchard were no more lacking in precedent in black writing than Sun Ra's transmutations of the vocabularies of the big band were unprecedented in the black orchestral traditions; in each genre the innovators and outsiders were working with materials they had gathered from *inside* the tradition, but were working with them in new ways. (Nielsen 114-15)

But what happens when these circuits cross? At the very least, it must become clear that Ra's "transmutations of the vocabularies of the big band" are not unrelated to Ra's concurrent (and sometimes simultaneously performed) transmutations of the English language.

One also might conjecture about Ra's influence as a *poet* in Umbra, though. There are clear divergences: Sun Ra does not share the interest in the "vernacular" almost universal in black poetics of the period— he never writes in "folk forms," or attempts to "transcribe" oral culture or the particularities of black speech onto the page. Michael Oren has noted that the Umbra writers established a close relationship with Langston Hughes, and were especially influenced by his poem, *Ask Your Mama: 12 Moods for Jazz* (1961), written to be performed with jazz piano accompaniment (Oren 184). It seems that Umbra's aesthetic was peculiar in that it could admit both Sun Ra and Hughes as models (*Umbra Anthology 1967-68* includes two poems by Hughes). Lorenzo Thomas is one of the only commentators to single out the group's remarkable breadth of interest, specifically emphasizing the *literary* influence of jazz musicians on the Umbra circle: "The musicians themselves were as cleverly articulate in words as they were on the bandstand; some, in fact, were poets and writers themselves. Charles Mingus and Sun Ra, both excellent poets and lyricists, spoke in vast but terse metaphors to those who took the time to listen" (Thomas, "Ascension" 260). Still, to judge from *Umbra Anthology: 1967-68*, Sun Ra's poetics are far from exemplary of the group's practice, even with regard to the more experimental work of David Henderson or the "transrealist" poetics of Norman Pritchard. It would seem that Umbra was mainly inspired by Sun Ra as a multi-discipline artist, and a spectacular elder figure who had been melding art, poetry, music, theater, esoteric philosophy, and communal living on his own terms since the late 1940s.

It should be noted that Umbra in general was quite receptive to artists in other disciplines: in addition to Sun Ra, saxophonist Archie Shepp (who himself was also a playwright) and visual artists Joe Overstreet and Tom Feelings often attended the meetings. Indeed, the marginality and volatility that commentators like Oren and Thomas usually identify in Umbra—which in the end brought about the rupture in the group in 1964—may well have made space for similarly marginal or "liminal" figures like Sun Ra, who represented the edge between poetry and ritual, writing and music, that the group was keen to explore. Thomas, associated with the more nationalist wing of Umbra, argues that the group fostered connections with an older generation of Harlem intellectuals like poet Hart Leroi Bibbs, who represented an important "black artistic underground," the "teachers and curators of our cultural alternatives" (Thomas, "Shadow World" 64-5). For the young writers, Sun Ra and the Arkestra would have certainly exemplified such a sought-out "alter" heritage. As Thomas notes, the musical performances of the Arkestra encapsulated this legacy, with their "gyroscopically delightful resolution" of the full spectrum of jazz styles from Jelly Roll Morton's "King Porter Stomp" all the way up to free jazz and beyond (Thomas, "Classical Jazz" 239).

Sun Ra's influence among black writers in New York reached its height in the summer of 1965, during the Black Arts movement, when many of the more nationalist members of Umbra followed Amiri Baraka to Harlem to form the Black Arts Repertory Theater and School. The Arkestra often performed at Black Arts events that summer, along with horn players Albert and Don Ayler, pianist Andrew Hill, and percussionist Milford Graves, and in fact Baraka says that Ra "became our resident philosopher," still living in the East Village, but coming to Harlem most days to hold court at Black Arts gatherings (Baraka, *Autobiography* 204). David Henderson, who would edit *Umbra Anthology, 1967-68*, was a "serious student" of Sun Ra's teachings and writings at this point, as was Henry Dumas, and the Arkestra performed music to accompany Baraka's play *A Black Mass* at its premiere in Newark in May 1966 (Baraka 205).

The collaboration between Sun Ra and Baraka was formalized most strikingly in the journal *The Cricket: Black Music in Evolution*, which Baraka began assembling in late 1967 and early 1968. The masthead of the first issue credits Baraka (then Le Roi Jones), Larry Neal, and A.B. Spellman as "Editors," and Sun Ra and Milford Graves as "Advisors." This confluence between the New Music and the New Poetry was not unique in itself: for instance, John Sinclair's *Change*, a journal published out of the Artists' Workshop in Detroit in the mid-1960s, similarly featured saxophonist Marion Brown as its New York editor, and published poetry by Brown and Sun Ra. But *The Cricket* was more ambitious: it did not simply publish poetry influenced by jazz, but instead argued that black culture was a continuum — what Baraka termed the "changing same," in an influential 1966 essay — characterized by a drive towards radical articulation found in the music and the poetry alike. Baraka begins his editorial introduction with a claim for the intellectual qualities of the music: "The true voices of Black Liberation have been the Black musicians. They were the first to free themselves from the concepts and sensibilities of the oppressor. The history of Black Music is a history of a people's attempt to define the world in their own terms" (a). The title itself deliberately echoes the original (and perhaps apocryphal) musician/writer story: *The Cricket* is named after the "gossip sheet" that Buddy Bolden, the infamous early trumpeter, supposedly wrote and published in New Orleans. And the issue is dominated by similar models: Milford Graves' diatribe about the racist economics of the music, and a long essay by Sun Ra called "My Music is Words."

Within the nationalist framing of *The Cricket*, however, "My Music is Words" strikes a certain dissonance. Sun Ra's essay is the first in the journal, but it immediately refuses to take up the banner and represent: "Some people are of this world, others are not. My natural self is not of this world because this world is not of my not and nothingness, alas and happily . . ." (4). The piece reiterates Ra's literary aesthetic of "enharmonic" word equation, "phonetic revelation" (5) through a kind of sight poetry. (As Ra puts it, in a poem included at the end of the first issue: "Through the eye/ The sound has spoken" (18).) Most importantly, though, the essay also explains Ra's understanding of jazz, narrating his development from Fletcher Henderson to "Space Music" by drawing links between music and writing: "My words are the music and my music *are* the words because it is of equation is synonym of the Living Being" (6). Music here is conceived as the ultimate extension of poetics, a mode of articulating what is presently "impossible" or "unsaid" in words alone:

> My words are music and the music is words but sometimes the music is of the unsaid words concerning the things that always are to be, thus from the unsaid words which are of not because they are of those things which always are to be. . . . . nothing comes to be in order that nothing shall be because nothing from nothing leaves nothing.
>
> The music comes from the void, the nothing, the void, in response to the burning need for something else. (7)

The essay's accomplishment, in other words, is to remind us that if Sun Ra's writing is musical or phonetic, his music is equally "linguistic" in conception. As he writes in a later poem:

> Music is a voice
> A differential sound of words.
> A grammar and a language
> As well as a synthesizer.
> It is the reach toward it's twin immortality.
> ("Of Coordinate Vibrations," IE 1980)

The best-known Black Arts anthology from the 1960s to include Sun Ra's poetry was *Black Fire*, edited by Baraka and Larry Neal. Neal and Baraka read Sun Ra's work as exemplary of a drive in the movement to push literature and music closer to the community, towards a more ritualistic aesthetic and a more explicitly political agenda. In his afterword, Neal notes that black music has always represented the "collective psyche" better than black literature, and prescribes:

> Black literature must attempt to achieve that same sense of the collective ritual, but ritual directed at the destruction of useless, dead ideas. . . .
>
> Some of these tendencies already exist in the literature. It is readily perceivable in LeRoi Jones' *Black Mass*, and in a recent recording of his with the Jihad Singers. Also, we have the work of Yusuf Rahman, who is the poetic equivalent of Charlie Parker. Similar tendencies are found in Sun-Ra's music and poetry; Ronald Fair's novel, *Many Thousand Gone*; the short stories of Henry Dumas (represented in this anthology); the poetry of K. Kgositsile, Welton Smith, Ed Spriggs, and Rolland Snellings; the dramatic choreography of Eleo Pomare; Calvin Hernton's very explosive poems; Ishmael Reed's poetry and prose works . . . ; David Henderson's work. . . . (*Black Fire* 655)

Neal makes explicit reference to Sun Ra's *poetry* as part of the new "tendencies." Oddly, though, this understanding jars with the Ra poems collected in the anthology, which like most of Ra's writing are dynamically flat and relatively undramatic. Take the conclusion of the poem "Of the Cosmic Blueprints," for example:

If it was not slavery—
It was the activation
Of the Cosmic-blueprints...
Sowing seeds of cosmos rare
Casting ever down to ever lift above.

If it was not slavery
It was freedom not to be
In order to ready for the discipline-plane
From other-greater-worlds.
    (*Black Fire* 214)

Is this down with the program? Paradoxically, although Sun Ra is a musician (the only one represented in *Black Fire*), and although his writings are not unconnected to his musical performances, his poetry is simply not written to be theatrical, "ritualized," or "jazzy." So it is difficult to make this poem jibe with Neal's injunction that "the poet must become a performer, the way James Brown is a performer—loud, gaudy and racy.... He must learn to embellish the context in which the work is executed; and, where possible, link the work to all usable aspects of the music" (355). Sun Ra the musician might be close to this description—although the Arkestra's "cosmo dramas" might be *race-y* in a different way than James Brown's laborious funkfests. But it is less clear that the poetry of Sun Ra reproduced in *Black Fire* can be read as a clear example of this literary stance, "consolidating" writing and ritual, as Neal demands.

In rethinking the implications of Sun Ra as *poet*, somewhat the misfit, askew in the midst of the Black Arts, we might look in more detail at Ra's life and career: what are the poetics of Sun Ra, and where did they come from?

READING THE ERUDITE RA

ONE OF THE MORE STRIKING ASPECTS OF JOHN SZWED'S BIOGRAPHY, *Space is the Place: The Lives and Times of Sun Ra*, is its documentation of Ra's literary and lyric thirsts. Szwed traces the reading list of the-Artist-formerly-known-as-Sonny-Blount, and follows his progress in the 1940s through a staggering and thorough study of Biblical interpretation, Egyptology, science fiction, and esoterica: works like *The Egyptian Book of the Dead*, *The Radix*, the works of

Madame Blavatsky, Biblical concordances, books on Kaballah, medieval hermeticism, gnosticism, and mysticism, George G.M. James' *Stolen Legacy*, contemporary black literature like Henry Dumas' stories and poems, former slave narratives, books on black folklore, Frederick Bodmer's *The Loom of Language*, *Blackie's Etymology*, and the Bible itself—in English, Hebrew, French, German, and Italian (see Szwed 62-73, 294-99).

Throughout this period writing poetry was an integral part of Ra's life and work. He had begun writing poetry at the age of nine, and began handing out pamphlets and mimeographed broadsides during the legendary free-for-all public debates in the late 1940s in Chicago's Washington Park, featuring Ra's space disciples next to Elijah Muhammad's nascent Nation of Islam, Christian fundamentalist orators, Marxist exhorters, and straggling Garveyites. (Szwed notes that the Nation of Islam may have even been inspired to begin putting out their newspaper, *Muhammad Speaks*, by the numerous handouts and pamphlets Sun Ra brought to the Park (106).) When Ra formed his own band in the early fifties (featuring musicians such as John Gilmore and Pat Patrick, who would go on to play with him for nearly forty years) and recorded *Jazz by Sun Ra* (later retitled *Sun Song*) on the Transition label in 1956, he made an unprecedented arrangement to insert a short pamphlet of poems into the record sleeve. One section explains in this synaesthetic vein that

> Poems are Music:
> Some of the songs I write are based on my poems; for this reason, I am including some of them with this album in order that those who are interested may understand that poems are music, and that music is only another form of poetry. I consider every creative musical composition as being a *tone poem*.

The poetry and mysticism was lost on the few reviewers, including a young Nat Hentoff, who wrote in a 1958 *Downbeat* that "I'd like to hear them in a blowing date without the need for Hegel," and proceeded to complain about the space wasted on Ra's "remarkably bad 'poems'" (Szwed 159).

But poetry remained crucial to the development of the Arkestra. Some of Sun Ra's poems served as lyrics to tunes like "Enlightenment," some were programmatic (not sung, but printed on record jackets to supplement the music) like "Nothing Is" and "Astro Black," and a number were used as chants as the Arkestra developed what Ra called "cosmo drama" or "myth-ritual," concerts with dancers, light shows, formulaic recitations and fantastic "space" costumes. Often these shows would close with members of the Arkestra parading into the audience, chanting "Rocket No. 9," "We Travel the Spaceways," "Outer

Spaceways Incorporated," or "Space is the Place." John Szwed informs us that even the written poetry was central to the Arkestra conception of cosmo drama: in concert, Sun Ra or one of the singers/dancers (like June Tyson or Verta Mae Grosvenor) would recite poems, sometimes to musical accompaniment (250-51). There is a difference between the chants and the more esoteric and exegetical varieties of Ra's poetry, of course, but in many ways the verse seems to have functioned on a continuum—poetry practiced and disseminated in a space of ritual performance.

Sun Ra's writing was never published commercially, although in 1969 Doubleday expressed interest in publishing a collection. Instead, Ra prepared a two volume selection called *The Immeasurable Equation* and *Extensions Out: The Immeasurable Equation Vol. 2*, which were initially published in 1972 by El Saturn Research, Inc., Ra's own recording company, and then reappeared in a number of revised and expanded editions over the next two decades. (There are also at least two recordings of Sun Ra reading his poetry to the accompaniment of the Arkestra: a radio broadcast on WXPN in Philadelphia on Christmas Day, 1976, which is a hard-to-find but particularly illuminating performance, and a session for Blast First Records in October, 1991, in a project apparently aborted due to Sun Ra's declining health.) In fact, the volumes of *The Immeasurable Equation* were never formally distributed—for years, copies have been obtainable almost exclusively through collectors or at Arkestra concerts. So the dissemination circuits even of the written poetry have always quite close to the ritual space of the Arkestra performances, and must be approached through that link.

A typology of Sun Ra's poetry would be broad and eccentric, as one might expect. Besides the chants, the programmatic liner note poems, and the song lyrics, there are equally a variety of humorous or campy poems, for instance—as should be evident in the *Esquire* poem, Sun Ra's sense of comedy should never be underestimated. Humor was an important part of the Arkestra "cosmo ritual" as well. Lorenzo Thomas describes it this way: "Sun Ra and his band 'from outer space' have set out to design an 'alter destiny' for the inhabitants of this planet by means of a re-vision of the roots from which we spring. Their lever is joy" (Thomas, "Mathemagic" 16). Mystery smiles, for Sun Ra, and "the sound of joy is enlightenment." He even commented that the problem with most jazz avant garde musicians is that they "don't know how to connect with people.... They have no sense of humor." Asked how his own music helped his listeners, he continued:

> First of all I express sincerity. There's also that sense of humor, by which people sometimes learn to laugh about themselves. I mean, the situation is so serious that

the people could go crazy because of it. They need to smile and realize how ridiculous everything is. A race without a sense of humor is in bad shape. A race needs clowns. In earlier days people know that. Kings always had a court jester around. In that way he was always reminded how ridiculous things are. I believe that nations too should have jesters, in the congress, near the president, everywhere.... You could call me the jester of the creator. (Vuijsje 16, 19, quoted in Szwed 236)

This humor is apparent in a number of poems, including "Sun Song," "God Wot," "The Art Scene," and the deadpan "Birds Without Wings" (IE 25):

Birds without wings
Birds without wings
Poised, tensed ———
Are they unaware
There are no wings
Where wings should be?

Birds without wings
Poised and tensed
Take off
Sailing, sailing
Alas....
They drop to earth.

Are they hurt?
Bruised, bewildered
Angry
They rush to the take-off place
Again.
Poised, tensed
Ready, Go!
Birds without wings.

This type of poem is not always light camp: sometimes there is even a kind of didactic humor in the exegetical "word equation" poems, as in "Alert" (IE 1980 60), or "Detour": "This is a precision span/ The journey is discipline plane!/ Beware!/ Rights/ Rites/ Right rite [. . .] Words/ Snares: Entrapment [. . .]/ Words: Words! Beware/ Warning!" (IE 30).

The varieties of Sun Ra's poetry also include prophetic verse, pronouncements, poems that approach jeremiad—some almost petulant:

Are you thinking of metaphysics
alone? Well, don't.
    ("The Other Side of Music," IE 36).

Some are nightmares, hauntings ("On the Edge of the Thin-Between," EO 40; "'The Visitation,'" *Black Fire*), or respites, poetic harbors, visions of deliverance. Others work the recombination to the point of grammatical mind-bending:

After that, what is there after that?
And that afterwards is
Or doubly no The not of those things which are. . . . .
If I to be am
Then to be is and are.
    ("After That," EO 1)

There are invocations and praise songs, as to "The Outer Darkness" and "The Pivoting Planes." There are a number of quick poems, marginalia, ditties and throwaways—like Langston Hughes, Sun Ra has a poem for every occasion, and the writing can be extremely uneven. Some poems approach a kind of noumenous naturalism, like "When Angels Speak" and "Nothing Is" (IE 15):

At first nothing is
Then nothing transforms itself to be air
Sometimes the air transforms itself to be water
And the water becomes rain and falls to earth;
Then again, the air through friction becomes fire
So the nothing and the air and the water

And the fire are really the same
Upon different degrees.

There are recurring quirks: Sun Ra seems to have a predilection for the French word "sans," for example, and—although he almost never attempts to represent "dialect" or speech patterns in his poetry—inexplicably always writes "lightning" without the "g," as at the end of "Other Thoughts" (EO 41):

Now and then tiring of what they call reality
Bruised and beaten by its force
I step into the friendly city of the forest
Of what they call illusion
There to tend my wounds
And heal them
With the lightnin' touch
Of balanced thought
And the splendid comradeship of other worlds. . . .

TOWARDS A POETICS OF EXEGESIS

I WANT TO CONCLUDE BY QUALIFYING IN MORE DETAIL the poetic practices of Sun Ra—what I will call a poetics of recombination or an *exegetical* poetics. On the sleeve of the classic Saturn record *Cosmic Tones for Mental Therapy* (recorded in New York in 1963), there are words from Sun Ra and from Umbra-affiliated writer Henry Dumas about what the latter called "the ultimate rhythm of cosmic mathematics." Sun Ra's statement is programmatic, but seemingly not in relation to the music:

PROPER EVALUATION OF WORDS AND LETTERS IN THEIR PHONETIC AND ASSOCIATED SENSE, CAN BRING THE PEOPLE OF EARTH INTO THE CLEAR LIGHT OF PURE COSMIC WISDOM.

This note would itself later be published as a poem ("To the Peoples of the Earth," *Black Fire* 217). Sun Ra would return to this formulation of poetics again and again: the idea that his poems were, as he told one interviewer, "all scientific equations. I am dealing outside conventional wisdom. I want to explore the ultradimensions of being" (Spady 26).

Although the relationship of Ra's writing to black traditions of poetry was oblique, there is evidence that he read in those traditions. At one point, he noted: "I wasn't influenced by Paul Laurence Dunbar's poetry. He was a sentimentalist. I'm a scientist. . . . I take the position of a scientist who comes from another dimension" (Szwed 327). What returns is that claim of science, a word Ra seems to understand through his commitment to Egyptian-derived mystery systems and Kabbalistic hermeneutics:

> What I want to do is associate words so they produce a certain fact. If you mix two chemical products you produce a reaction. In the same way if you put together certain words you'll obtain a reaction which will have a value for people on this planet. That's why I continue to put words together. Einstein said he was looking for an equation for eternal life. But we built the atomic bomb, and his project has never materialized. But I'm sure he was right. To put words together, or, even if you could, to paint the image that is necessary to put out the vibrations that we need, that would change the destiny of the whole planet. (Noames 75, quoted in Szwed 319-20)

There is an especially pronounced echo of traditions of Kabbalah, an esoteric and multiple-layered tradition of post-Talmudic Jewish mysticism in which the ecstatic experience of the Torah often involves breaking down the Hebrew text, contemplating a single letter as a divine name, or even recombining letters in the Torah to aid allegorical readings of Biblical passages. Even for the more radical Kabbalists, though, such as Abraham Abulafia, who used a host of techniques like *Temurah* (letter substitution in carefully limited cases), *Gematria* (numerological substitution), and letter combination (anagram, palindrome), still Hebrew was privileged over all languages for its claimed divine nature (Idel 12, 99). Ra's practice differs in that it is multilingual, willing to make "equations" between different languages. He told one interviewer:

> I'm a wordologist. Words' what's doing this. You've got to have numerology. You've got to have phonetics. You've got to have all these things and then the world will straighten out. They worship the Son of God but they don't understand. In French, Son's equal to 'sound,' so, 'sound of God.' They've got it wrong. They think it's 'the son.' They say the word was made flesh. It's really

about *sound*—and it wasn't made flesh, if was made *fresh*. All these things the creator told me in Alabama. I'm dealing with words that can prove themselves—that can prove themselves to be correct. (Steingroot 50)

(Unfortunately, the corpus of articles and interviews around Sun Ra often leave only hints as to the implications of such procedures. This is partly due to Sun Ra's own obfuscation strategies, and partly because interviewers simply could not or would not follow him down these paths. We are left with a kind of biographical literalism, an attempt to tease out the "real life" of Sonny Blount, that ends up disparaging the seriousness of his poetics. For instance, directly after the passage above, the interviewer's next question is: "You were born in Alabama?")

As these permutations of the *"sound* of God" indicate, Sun Ra's poetics also differ from Kabbalistic exegesis in that Ra is most interested in phonetic (rather than graphic) recombinations and substitutions as a route to the allegorical. He trades primarily in homonyms, not in letters or words. Consider the conclusion of "Every Thought is Alive":

> The myth among other things
> May be considered as "a tale that is told",
> And the end of the tale is a tale that is
> tolled and likewise
> The end of a tale is the goal.
>   ("Every Thought is Alive," IE 53)

So Ra's Biblical hermeneutics *sound* a bit more than the literal mathematics of a Kabbalist like Abulafia. In reconstructing and recombining the Scripture, Sun Ra "hears" it off the page into allegory:

> You're just like in a science fiction film now. You've outlived the Bible, which was your scenario. Everybody had a part in that. Black people have been singing a long time, 'When the roll is called up yonder I'll be there.' But they didn't know it was spelled r-o-l-e, not r-o-l-l. They had a part to act and they acted it. White people began to think that black people are like this or like that, but they were only acting parts. Someone gave them these parts to act. Of course, the white race had a part to act too. They had to deal with white supremacy and other things—lies. But the point is that they all were acting parts in this play, this drama. You might

call it a passion play. The passion play moves over into words. (Sun Ra, "Your Only Hope Now Is a Lie" 106)

In offering these examples, I should note also that Sun Ra's poetics of recombination are not always directed at phrases from Biblical scripture. The techniques and procedures of Sun Ra's exegesis are reminiscent of Kabbalah, but Ra employs them to read both the sacred and the profane—verses from the Bible about "the Word of God," as well as lyrics from slave Spirituals like "When the roll is called up yonder," common clichés like "Once upon a time" and "Tomorrow never comes," and even sixties pop culture epigrams like "I'm free, white and 21." (At the same time, although Ra's exegetical devices are particularly complex, such a breadth of analysis is again quite reminiscent of the African American folk visionary tradition.) Thus the poetics of Ra are singular not just in their multilingualism and their phonetic focus, but also in their willingness to read the "light of pure cosmic wisdom" by recombining a wide variety of texts. For Ra, the sacred can be read through any surface.

Szwed tells us that one of the first books on poetics that attracted Ra was Southern poet Sidney Lanier's *The Science of English Verse* (1880). Somewhat like Poe's idiosyncratic work on the "Poetic Principle," Lanier's book is peculiar in that it argues for the primacy of sound as artistic material in verse, examining categories of "duration," "intensity," "pitch," and "tone-color." There is also a long section on poetic rhythm. For Lanier, all verse, whether recited *or* on the page, amounts ultimately to "a set of specially related sounds" (21). He coins the phrase "the imagination of the ear" in deference to this phonic primacy: "those perceptions of sound which come to exist in the mind, not by virtue of actual vibratory impact upon the tympanum immediately preceding the perception, but by virtue of indirect causes (such as the characters of print and of writing) which in any way amount to practical equivalents of such impact" (22). As we see, this is a little different formally from the modernist espousal of poetry "approaching the quality of music" in one way or another, whether in Louis Zukofsky's Objectivism or in Langston Hughes' blues poetry. Lanier sees no division between speech and writing; all graphic techniques point to *phonema*: so he places emphasis on "sounds and silences" and their representations in form (29). In other words, poetry ends up being music: "[T]he main distinction between music and verse is, when stated with scientific precision, the difference between the scale of tones used in music and the scale of tones used by the human speaking-voice" (31). Moreover, speech, not being limited to a tempered scale, has a much broader tone-range to explore than music for Lanier (47).

This is a bit too dogmatic for Sun Ra, but we see some of the beginnings of his phonetic poetics here. Lanier finally does not seem to recognize difference among various graphic techniques: perhaps because his conception of literary form is so conventional, it never occurs to him that the manipulation of orthographic conventions (the way a phoneme is represented) and line can hone and alter an articulation, can affect the way the ear is "coordinated" to a particular "set of sounds." He doesn't see, in Aldon Nielsen's words, that "writing affords the possibility of transpositions beyond those available in speech" (Nielsen 256). Nor is Lanier attentive to tensions between the structure of a poem on the page and its possible reading(s) off that page—issues of performance, accent, improvisation, the poem as kind of "score" to be realized in recitation. To Sun Ra, writing more than half a century later, and after the detonation of black expressive cultures in the 1920s, these issues come easily. When you said "Good morning" to Sun Ra, he would ask whether you meant "Good morning" or "Good mourning" (Szwed 104).

What poetics do we end up with here? One might note some convergences between Sun Ra's aesthetic and some more contemporary modes of black experimental writing. I'm thinking of the similar kind of recombinatory impulse in the work of poets like Harryette Mullen and Ed Roberson, or in the "anagrammatic scat" of Nathaniel Mackey. Interestingly, though, the most pronounced correspondences arise with a number of the black Caribbean writers who have espoused various approaches to the "Calibanization" of English, twisting sound and sense, deforming and reforming the shape of words on the page. Edward Kamau Brathwaite, especially in the trilogy comprising the books *Mother Poem*, *Sun Poem*, and *X/Self*, begins to "wring the word" in a manner that—though much more based in orality, and in Bajan speech styles—at times comes near the etymological interest in the "open" or polyvalent word that we find in Sun Ra's writing (see Mackey). In a number of his articles, as well as the poems, Brathwaite has offered permutations or recombinations of signature words like *nam*:

> 'Nam' is 'man' spelt backwards, man in disguise, man who has to reverse his consciousness as the capsule reverses its direction in order to enter in to the new world in a disguised or altered state of consciousness. 'Nam' also suggests 'root,' or beginning, because of 'yam,' the African 'yam,' 'nyam,' to eat, and the whole culture contained in it. It is then able to expand itself back from 'nam' to 'name,' which is another form of 'name': the name that you once had has lost its 'e,' that fragile part of itself, eaten by Prospero, eaten by the conquistadores, but preserving its essentialness, its alpha, its 'a' protected by those two intransigent

consonants, 'n' and 'm.' The vibrations 'nmnmnm' are what you get before the beginning of the world. And that 'nam' can return to 'name' and the god 'Nyame.'

And so it is possible to conceive of our history not only being capsuled and contracted, but finally expanding once more outwards. (Brathwaite, "History, the Caribbean Writer and *X/Self*" 33-4)

The difference between Brathwaite and Sun Ra, finally, would hinge on the commitment of the former to the lyric, and to poetic form. Brathwaite recombines, but is not exegetical, in the poetry — words are wrung and thereby rung, but the operations are not explained. Brathwaite reveals a word-artist's reluctance to divulge, to decode, for the reader, preferring to let the lyric sing. In the fascinating notes to *X/Self* (1987), for instance, he opens by writing:

[M]y references (my nommos and icons) may appear mysterious, meaningless even, to both Caribbean and non-Caribbean readers. So the notes . . . which I hope are helpful, but which I provide with great reluctance, since the irony is that they may suggest the poetry is so obscure in itself that it has to be lighted up; is so lame, that it has to have a crutch; and (most hurtful of all) that it is bookish, academic, 'history'. . . . The impression, in other words, is that I write the poems from the notes, when in fact I have to dig up these notes from fragments, glimpses, partial memories. . . . (Brathwaite, *X/Self* 113)

The supplementary notes notwithstanding, Brathwaite's poems themselves inscribe the page with a graphic musicality, as in "X/Self's Xth Letters from the Thirteen Provinces," where we encounter the poet "sittin down here in front a dis stone/face" with an "electrical mallet," carving and "chipp/in dis poem onta dis tablet/ chiss/ellin darkness writin in light" (87). The lyricism is left ragged, intentionally unfinished, so that the implications of the phrase "X/Self" for our understanding of Caribbean subjectivity continue to resonate suggestively: "Why a callin it/x?// a doan writely/ know" (84). Sun Ra, as a multidisciplinary artist arguably with less of a commitment to poetic lyric, never minds being didactic, even when it renders his writing flat. So in the place of Brathwaite's obliquity, we find Ra's poem "Symbolic Meaning of the X" (IE 1980), which almost reads like an explication of *X/Self* through myth-science recombination, opening:

> THE TIME OF EARTH IS THE X OF EARTH
> X IS THE TIME
> X IS THE EMIT
> THAT IS: THE CAST OUT
> X IS THE AIM. . . . THE SOLUTION
> SYMBOL OF THE PROBLEM. . . .
> X IS THE BRIDGE SYMBOL ANSWER
> VIEW X FROM MANY POINTS,
>   AND SEE THE POTENTIAL. . . . . .

Sun Ra, assuming the prophet's prerogative, would appear to *prefer* didacticism in his poetry, letting his words fall prosaically to emphasize the mathematics of the "sound-equations" over the music of the sounds.

Still, it should be clear that Ra is much closer to Brathwaite's poetics (even the latter's recent "Sycorax video style," which goes so far as to tamper with fonts and type sizes in an effort to catch a musical dynamic among words on the page) than to other varieties of so-called "concrete" or "visual" poetry. At times this characterization might be surprising: one might expect Sun Ra's Egyptian interest to lead him to a poetics reminiscent, say, of the opening of Zora Neale Hurston's classic essay "Characteristics of Negro Expression," where she claims that "the white man thinks in a written language and the Negro thinks in hieroglyphics." Hurston provocatively asserts that the "Negro . . . must add action to it to make it do. So we have 'chop-axe,' 'sitting-chair,' 'cook-pot' and the like because the speaker has in his mind the picture of the object in use" (49). But Sun Ra's studied focus on phonetics, the ways sound inheres in the written word, never approaches this pictorial sense of language. Ra seems attracted to the cryptology represented by hieroglyphs, but seldom turns to their implications for a figuative or "ideogrammatic" poetry on the page.

I will close with one more comparison, to take us back to the "myth-science" question with which we began. It will perhaps be surprising to note the correspondence between Sun Ra's theory of poetic language and that of Guyanese novelist Wilson Harris. But consider the "Manifesto of the Unborn State of Exile" in Harris's 1965 novel *The Eye of the Scarecrow*:

> Language is one's medium of the vision of consciousness. There are other ways—shall I say—of arousing this vision. But language alone can express (in a way which goes beyond any physical or vocal attempt) the sheer—the ultimate 'silent' and 'immaterial' complexity of arousal. Whatever sympathy one may feel

for a concrete poetry—where physical objects are used and adopted—the fact remains (in my estimation) that the original grain or grains of language cannot be trapped or proven. It is the sheer mystery—the impossibility of trapping its own grain—on which poetry lives and thrives.... Which is concerned with a genuine sourcelessness, a fluid logic of image. So that any genuine act of possession by one's inner eye is a subtle dispersal of illusory fact, dispossession of one's outer or physical eye. (95)

In Sun Ra there is also a turn away from the "pure" formalism of a "concrete poetry" and towards a poetics that reaches for the sacred, for "vision of consciousness," arousing it through language—through what Sun Ra calls the "multi-self of words," and what Harris calls "a fluid logic of image." For Sun Ra as for Harris, languages are broken, intermingled, already contaminated by ragged roots that must be *read* to tease out or stitch up the fabric of "mystery," the "universal" but uncapturable "principle of mediation." (Sun Ra's poetics may be more drastic only in that they finally operate not just on language, but also on the self—thus Ra's early renaming and life-long effort to construct an "alter" autobiography. For him, the "multi-self of words" is also, and profoundly, the multiple recombinations of the poem that is Sun Ra.) Consequently, in such reading, in the re-hearing of the jagged edge between phoneme and grapheme, the stakes are high.

This "arousal" of one's "inner eye" beyond the superficialities of everyday life, beyond what Harris terms "illusory fact," is not an idealism, in the end: it an exegetical imperative. It is not an espousal of some "pure speech" to be reconstructed through some messianic poetry; instead, it is the "impossible" task of spelling something new and different, mankind's "alter destiny," walking the tightrope between sign and speech. The stakes are high—Sun Ra would say the stakes might well be *hi*, be welcoming, brothers of the impossible peering over the rim of the myth to say hello. Solar myth-science: a *poetics of exegesis*, from the Greek *exegeuisthai* "to explain, to interpret," from *ex-* and *hēgeisthai* "to lead": thus, "to lead out or away." A poetics where sound-equations mark an impossible exit, a way out of no way: from Mr. Ra to mystery.

WORKS CITED

Baldwin, James. *The Fire Next Time*. New York: The Dial Press, 1963. Reprinted in *The Price of the Ticket: Collected Nonfiction, 1948-1985*. New York: St. Martin's, 1985. 333-79.

Baraka, Amiri. *The Autobiography of Leroi Jones/Amiri Baraka*. New York: Freundlich Books, 1984.

———. "The Changing Same (R&B and the New Black Music)" (1966). *Black Music*. New York: Quill, 1967. 180-211.

———. "Sun Ra" (1993). *Eulogies*. New York: Marsilio Publications, 1996. 171-74.

Bodmer, Frederick. *The Loom of Language*. New York: W. W. Norton, 1944.

Brathwaite, Edward Kamau. "History, the Caribbean Writer and X/Self." In *Crisis and Creativity in the New Literatures in English*. Ed. Geoffrey Davis and Hena Maes-Jelinek. Amsterdam: Rodopi, 1990. 23-45.

———. *X/Self*. New York: Oxford U. P, 1987.

Christian, Barbara. "The Race for Theory." *Cultural Critique* 6 (Spring 1987): 51-64.

Corbett, John. "Sun Ra: Gravity and Levity." *Extended Play*. Durham: Duke UP, 1994. 308-17.

Ellington, Duke. "The Race for Space" (c. 1957). *The Duke Ellington Reader*. Ed. Mark Tucker. New York: Oxford UP, 1993. 293-296.

Fiofori, Tam. "Sun Ra's Space Odyssey." *Downbeat* (May 1970): 14-17.

Harris, Wilson. *The Eye of the Scarecrow*. London: Faber & Faber, 1965.

Honan, William H. "Le Mot Juste for the Moon." *Esquire* (July 1969): 53-56, 138-39.

Hurston, Zora Neale. "Characteristics of Negro Expression." In *Negro Anthology*. Ed. Nancy Cunard. London, 1934. Reprinted in Hurston, *The Sanctified Church* (Berkeley: Turtle Island Press, 1983), 49-68.

Idel, Moshe. *Language, Torah and Hermeneutics in Abraham Abulafia*. Albany, NY: SUNY Press, 1989.

Kuhn, Thomas. *The Structure of Scientific Revolutions*. Chicago: U. Chicago P, 1962.

Lanier, Sidney. *The Science of English Verse* (1880). Reprinted in The Centennial Edition Vol. 2, ed. P. Baum. Baltimore: Johns Hopkins UP, 1945.

Lock, Graham. *Forces in Motion: The Music and Thoughts of Anthony Braxton*. New York: Da Capo, 1988.

Mackey, Nathaniel. "Wringing the Word." *World Literature Today* 68.4 (Autumn 1994): 733-40.

Nielsen, Aldon. *Black Chant: Languages of African-American Postmodernism*. New York: Cambridge UP, 1997.

Noames, Jean-Louis. "Visite au Dieu-Soleil." *Jazz Magazine* (Paris) 125 (December 1969): 70-77.

Oren, Michael. "The Umbra Poets' Workshop, 1962-1965: Some Socio-Literary Puzzles." In *Studies in Black American Literature Vol. II: Belief vs. Theory in Black American Literary Criticism*. Ed. Joe Weixlmann and Chester J. Fontenot. Greenwood, FL: Penkevill Publishing Co., 1986. 177-223.

Spady, James G. "Indigené=Folkski Equations in the Black Arts." *The Black Scholar* (November-December 1978): 24-33.

Steingroot, Ira. "Sun Ra's Magical Kingdom." *Reality Hackers* (Winter 1988): 46-51.

Sun Ra. *Cosmic Tones for Mental Therapy* (New York 1963) / *Art Forms of Dimensions Tomorrow* (New York 1961-62). Reissued as Evidence 22036.

———. *Extensions Out: The Immeasurable Equation Vol. 2*. Chicago: Ihnfinity Inc./Saturn Research, 1972. [EO]

———. *The Immeasurable Equation*. Chicago: Ihnfinity Inc./Saturn Research, 1972. [IE]

———. *The Immeasurable Equation*. Philadelphia: Le Sony'r Ra, 1980 (in different versions).

———. *The Immeasurable Equation*. Philadelphia: El Saturn/Millbrae, CA: Omni Press, 1985 (in different versions).

———. *Jazz by Sun Ra*. Transition Records (1957). Reissued as *Sun Song*. Delmark DD 411.

———. "My Music is Words." *The Cricket: Black Music in Evolution* 1 (1968): 4-11.

———. Selected poems ("The Disguised Aim," "The Gardened of the Eatened," "The Invented Memory," The Cosmic-Blueprints," "Primary Lesson: The Second Class Citizens," "The Myth of Me," "The Plane: Earth," "Precision Fate"). *Umbra Anthology 1967-1968*. Ed. David Henderson. New York: Umbra, 1968. 3-7.

———. Selected poems ("Saga of Resistance," "'The Visitation,'" "Of the Cosmic Blueprints," "Would I For All That Were," "Nothing Is," "To the Peoples of the Earth," "The Image Reach," "The Cosmic Age"). *Black Fire: An Anthology of Afro-American Writing*. Ed. Leroi Jones and Larry Neal. New York: William Morrow and Co., 1968. 212-220.

———. "Your Only Hope Now Is A Lie." Transcript of a talk given at Soundscape, New York, Nov. 11, 1979. *Hambone* 2 (Fall 1982): 98-114. [Also available as a recording: "The Possibility of an Altered Destiny," Sun Ra Arkestra, *Live from Soundscape* (Disk Union DIW-388B).]

Szwed, John. *Space is the Place: The Lives and Times of Sun Ra*. New York: Pantheon Books, 1997.

Thomas, Lorenzo. "Ascension: Music and the Black Arts Movement." In *Jazz Among the Discourses*. Ed. Krin Gabbard. Durham: Duke UP, 1995. 256-74.

———. "'Classical Jazz' and the Black Arts Movement." *African American Review* 29.2 (Summer 1995): 237-40.

———. "The Mathemagic of Sun Ra." *The Ann Arbor Sun* (April 5-19, 1974): 16-17.

———. "The Shadow World: New York's Umbra Workshop & Origins of the Black Arts Movement." *Callaloo* 4.1 (October 1978): 53-72.

Toop, David. "If You Find Earth Boring. . . Travels in the Outer Imagination with Sun Ra." *Ocean of Sound: Aether Talk, Ambient Sound and Imaginary Worlds*. London: Serpent's Tail, 1995. 23-32.

Vuijsje, Bert. "Sun Ra Spreekt." *Jazz Wereld* (October 1968): 16-19.

Wright, Jay. "Desire's Design, Vision's Resonance: Black Poetry's Ritual and Historical Voice." *Callaloo* 10.1 (1986): 13-28.

Julie Schmid

SPREADING THE WORD: A HISTORY OF THE POETRY SLAM

> The slam is about returning power to the audience. The audience is the most important part of the performance, not the poet on the stage.... At the first National Grand Slam, the Chicago slam poets realized that they had a gift to give to the rest of the world — the gift of the slam — the gift of poetry — and part of what motivated the members of the original team was giving this gift to the world. There are now about one hundred slams worldwide that are modeled after the Chicago slam.
> —Marc Smith, emcee and founder of the Uptown Poetry Slam at the Green Mill

THIS EPIGRAPH IS EXCERPTED FROM MARC SMITH'S INTRODUCTION to the End-of-the-Decade / Beginning-of-What's-to-Follow / Encore-Inception Slam, which took place on Sunday, July 21, 1996 at the Green Mill Lounge in Chicago. This event was the culmination of a five-day celebration that marked the tenth anniversary of the founding of the Uptown Poetry Slam. The Sunday night slam at the Green Mill usually attracts a small crowd of around seventy-five audience members and a handful of participants. On this particular evening, however, the bar was packed to standing room only capacity with a crowd that included slam regulars; a large number of twenty-something hipsters; a photographer from a local newspaper; yours truly; and Smith's publisher and promoter, Jeff Helgeson of Collage Press. The audience also included a group of Italian photojournalists who were covering the event for an Italian newspaper. For their benefit and for the benefit of neophyte slam-goers in the audience, Smith began the evening with a mock diatribe against New York's attempt to corner the performance poetry market, disparaging New York poets who had performed on MTV and reaffirming Chicago's status as the birthplace of the slam. After this rant-cum-slam-history, Smith, with the help of Chicago visual artist, published poet, and radio personality Tony Fitzpatrick, auctioned off slam memorabilia. The items auctioned off included the clock used to time the early slam poets; a Poetryslam board game, the creation of which initiated a series of lawsuits and trademark negotiations over the term "poetry slam" and led to the incorporation of The International Slam Family

Collective; and autographed copies of Smith's new book, *Crowdpleaser*.[*] After the auction, the slam began. The teams competing that evening were that year's Chicago team; the Berwyn, IL team; and the "Geezers" team.[†] This particular slam was divided into two rounds, the first of which was judged on the volume of the audience's applause as determined by Tony Fitzpatrick, the first slam referee (the original scoring method used at the Uptown Poetry Slam). The second round was scored by three judges chosen from random from the audience using the Dewey Decimal System of Slam Scorification — the scoring method that continues to be used at most slam venues. After the competition, some of the evening's performers continued to perform at the open mic while others worked the room, talking to old friends, being interviewed by the team of Italian journalists, and talking to me about the history of the slam and the relationship between the poetry slam and the academy.

I've decided to open my article with a summary of this anniversary celebration because, as Smith's title for the event and epigraph from his introduction suggests, the evening functioned as a revisiting of slam's roots as well as a look forward to the direction in which the poetry slam was headed. This event was partly an attempt to institutionalize this poetry movement, to establish a slam history and to chart the geographical spread of the slam from Chicago, to Ann Arbor, New York City, Boston, San Francisco, and other cities throughout the United States and worldwide. As someone who has been attending slams for the past eight years, first as an observer and closet poet and more recently as a scholar, I also see this tenth anniversary slam as marking a paradigm shift of sorts within the slam family. Over the past few years, the poetry slam, which has been defined as oppositional both by poets involved in the movement and critics outside of it, has had to come to terms with its growing popularity and the increasing institutionalization and commodification of the movement. As the slam has spread around the world, slam poets have begun to publish books; record CDs, audio cassettes, and poetry videos; and post web pages devoted to spreading the word. My history of the slam will address both the geographical spread of the poetry slam and the radiation of the slam aesthetic into other media. This essay will not only look at the work of slam founder and emcee of Chicago's Uptown Poetry Slam, Marc Smith, but will also address the role of diaspora slam poets Bob Holman in New York,

---

[*] The proceeds of this auction were used to help fund the Chicago team's and Team Berwyn's trip to the National Grand Slam, which was being held in Portland in August of that year.

[†] This team was made up of the members of the original Chicago slam team, including Patricia Smith, three-time national slam champion and co-founder of the Boston Slam; Marc Smith; and Cin Salach. Gary "Mex" Glazner, founder of the National Grand Slam and editor of the San Francisco Web poetry journal *Headless Buddha*, was substituted for Chicago poet Dean Hacker, who was unable to attend the event.

Patricia Smith (no relation to Marc Smith) and Michael Brown in Boston, and Gary Mex Glazner in San Francisco in establishing the slam as an international, multimedia phenomenon.[*]

The first poetry slam was hosted by Marc Smith, an ex-construction worker turned poet on Sunday, 20 July 1986. While Smith is generally acknowledged as the slam's founding father (his internet alias is "Slampapi"), the slam's precursors include poetry performances at the Get Me High Lounge during the mid-1980s (of which Smith and other founding slammers such as Jean Howard and Patricia Smith were a part) and the poetry boxing bouts that were held in punk clubs in Chicago in the late 1970s and early 1980s.[†] The first slam — named in honor of a grand slam that Smith saw Ernie Banks hit — took place at the Green Mill Lounge, a popular jazz club in Chicago's Uptown Neighborhood that is rumored to have been a prohibition-era speakeasy frequented by Al Capone.[‡] Due to the proselytizing zeal of Smith and other slam masters, the poetry slam has spread from this Chicago nightclub to bars, coffee houses, and bookstores throughout the world.[§] The poetry slam is a mock poetry competition in which poets' performances are scored on a scale of one to ten called The Dewey Decimal System of Slam Scorification by judges selected at random from the audience.[¶] The slam works on the process of elimination and

---

[*]Before I continue I should make clear that this essay is in no way an exhaustive history of the slam. For that, please see, Kurt Heintz, *An Incomplete History of the Slam* (www.e-poets.net/library/slam/index.html), cited hereafter as *History*. Other publications on the slam include Maria Damon, "Was That 'Different,' 'Dissident,' or 'Dissonant'? Poetry (n) the Public Spear: Slams, Open Readings, and Dissident Traditions" in *Close Listening: Poetry and the Performed Word*, ed. Charles Bernstein (New York: Oxford UP, 1998), cited hereafter as "Dissident," and Richard Coniff, "Please Audience, Do Not Applaud a Mediocre Poem," *Smithsonian* (Sept. 1992): 77-86, hereafter cited as "Audience."

[†]For a discussion of the relationship between these early poetry bouts and Smith's slam, see Heintz's *History*.

[‡]The bar's illustrious past is often cited by writers and critics and used to explain the image of the slam as a rough-and-tumble, no-holds-barred poetry competition. See for instance Coniff's "Applaud" or Maria Damon's reference to gangster culture in relationship to the slam in "Dissident." While the slam has spread to other venues in the Chicago area, most notably Fitzgerald's in Berwyn (also founded by Smith), and to venues around the world, the Green Mill has remained the home of slam poetry for both Chicago poets and poets from around the nation and every spring slam masters from around the U.S. make a yearly pilgrimage back to the slam's birthplace to hold the annual Slam Master's Meeting.

[§]According to the May, 1998 issue of *Slam!*, besides the numerous slam venues in twenty-seven of the fifty states, there are currently nine slams in Germany, seven in Sweden, a slam in Amsterdam, a slam in Vancouver, and one in Jerusalem. This is in all likelihood an incomplete listing as it is improbable that every slam venue worldwide has been sending its performance schedule to the newsletter.

[¶]The actual slam is usually just one part of a slam venue's show. The show usually begins with an open mic, which is the equivalent of the slam's minor league. "Virgins" (poets who have never performed before) usually start out with a few evenings of open mics before moving on to competing in the slam itself. It also seems important to

by the end of the competition, the poet with the highest score wins a five- or ten-dollar purse. Because of the variety of poets who perform at the slam, the local community's poetic sensibilities, and the fact that the judges vary not only from venue to venue but from show to show, it is impossible to define an overarching slam poetry aesthetic. However, the majority of slam poems tend to be narrative — often times written in the first person — and in iambic trimeter and tetrameter.* End rhymes are usually eschewed by veteran slam poets. However, many performers tend to rely on more subtle sound patterning — internal rhyme, alliteration, assonance, and consonance. Beyond these more traditional poetic devices, volume and timbre of the voice, blocking (the way that the poet moves on stage), and the poet's ability to connect with the audience are integral parts of the slam poem.

As the above suggests, one of the main tenets of the slam is that "the performance of poetry is an art — just as much an art as the writing of it" and poets are judged both on content and delivery.† Due to the emphasis placed on the performance, the venue, and the interaction between poet and audience, slam poets are more likely to come out of a theater or music background than an academic poetry program. Many of the poets who are active in the slam community continue to perform with bands and theater troupes, further emphasizing the relationship between the slam and other performance forms. For instance, over the past decade Marc Smith has performed with the Bob Shakespeare Band and Pong Unit One in Chicago; Bob Holman has roots in avant-garde theater; Gary Glazner began as a performance artist and integrates this background into his slam poems; slam diva Lisa Buscani is a founding member of the Chicago-based Neo Futurist theater troupe; and Patricia Smith has adapted her poems to one-woman shows.‡ Moreover, as Maria Damon and Henry Louis Gates have both suggested, one of the reasons that the slam has caught on and spread so prolifically throughout urban communities in the United States has to do with the resonances between Marc Smith's show and other vernacular performance forms.§

---

point out here that although the Dewey Decimal System of Slam Scorification is a one-to-ten point system, the lowest score ever given at the Green Mill was negative infinity for the worst poem ever written.

*For an insightful analysis of the ballad form (iambic tetrameter) and popular poetries, see "Dissident."

†Marc Smith, "Slampapi's Slam Philosophy," (www.slampapi.com/slamphil.htm), cited hereafter in the text as *Slampapi*.

‡A "pong" is a cross between a poem and a song. During a pong jam, Pong Unit invites members of the audience up on to the stage to perform their poems, which are often improvised, with the band playing backup. For a more in-depth discussion of the pong, see Marc Smith, *Crowdpleaser*, (Chicago: Collage Press, 1996). For more information about Bob Holman's theater background, see Edward Halsey Foster, "Bob Holman, Performance Poetry, and the Nuyorican Poets Café," *MultiCultural Review*, 2.2 (June, 1993), 46-48.

§Henry Louis Gates, Jr, "Sudden Def," *The New Yorker*. (June 19, 1995): 34-42. As Gates states on page 37 of his

Both Gates and Damon have pointed out the striking similarities between the poetry slam and the mock competitiveness, the verbal play, and the call-and-response structure of black vernacular traditions such as The Dozens, toasts, and signifying. I would like to add to Gates's and Damon lists and include the borderland tradition of the *corrido*, as well as the Puerto Rican tradition of *el trovador* (the traveling public poet) and *las descargas* (the Puerto Rican version of The Dozens).

While I will come back to this point in more detail later on in the essay, the synthesizing of literary and performance traditions — avant-garde theater, performance art, hip-hop, black and Latino vernacular traditions — that goes on at any given slam venue is a necessary component in the creation of an alternative, intercultural community poetics. Moreover, the similarities between black and Latino vernacular culture — especially rap — and the slam goes a long way toward explaining the growth of the slam CD and video market over the past few years.

Because of the focus on performance as well as the similarities between the slam and other vernacular expressive forms, the poetry slam has been defined as an anti-intellectual, anti-academic, muscular poetry movement, part Gong Show, part Geraldo, and part wrestling match.[*] These superficial glosses of slam poetry are problematic for a number of reasons, not the least of which is the underlying classism and racism inherent in them.[†] This focus on the slam as popular entertainment, however, isn't completely inaccurate. After all,

---

article, "there are rich traditions of black orality that undergird this sort of thing. Among them are the kinds of verbal jousting that go by such names as 'toasts,' 'playing the dozens,' and 'signifying.'" See also Damon's "Dissident."

[*] See for instance, Paul Hoover's comments in "Audience," 80-81, or Liam Rector's comments on the episode of *Greater Boston Arts* dedicated to the poetry slam. In all fairness to Paul Hoover, I add that in a recent email to me, he points out that his position on the slam was much more complex than his comments in the Coniff piece suggest. He writes, "One of the real oddities of the late 80s and early 90s in Chicago was that I was speaking against the slams (though I had long supported experimental practice and included performance poetry of the first two postwar generations in *Postmodern American Poetry*) and the more conservative Reg Gibbons was for them. Go figure. Hostilities were suspended by me incidentally just before Maxine Chernoff and I moved to California."

[†] Patricia Smith points out the resonances between racism and the anti-slam sentiment that she and Michael Brown encountered when they first moved to Boston in "Slamming: Shaking up New England's Poetry World," *Soujourner*, 19.6 (Feb. 1994): 20-21. She writes:

> I moved here three years ago to take a job with the *Boston Globe*, and — silly me — I thought I would find an open-minded literary and academic community enthusiastic about new forms, new ideas, new rhythms. Little did I know that "new" would set those spines a rattlin', and that I would be deceived by friends, shunned by the local poetry status quo, and warned in scrawled letters to "go back where I came from." I almost expected to see restrooms, water fountains, and bus depot waiting rooms labeled "POETS" and "SLAMMERS."

on his "Slampapi's Slam Philosophy" web page Smith describes the slam as "a grab bag, variety show," and slam argot is full of tongue-in-cheek references to the sports world — for instance, "The Dreaded Sudden-Death Spontaneous Haiku Overtime Round" (the official term for the tie-breaking round of a poetry slam); "time penalties" for going overtime in a performance; and, of course, the system of scoring poems, which is based on Olympic competitions.[*] The slam *is* a ritualized poetry competition and the competitive aspect of the performance generates the kind of rowdy audience participation that one usually associates with a sporting event. As numerous slam masters have pointed out, however, the competition is an incidental part of the slam experience; the slam is really about reaffirming poetry as an oral art and getting people curious enough to pick up a book of poetry or to attend poetry readings.[†] In the words of Asheville, North Carolina, slammaster Alan Wolfe (as paraphrased by Marc Smith), "The points are not the point, the point is poetry" *(Slampapi)*.

As the epigraph at the beginning of this essay suggests, the point also seems to be the creation of an oppositional, intercultural poetry community. And while much of slam's success is due to the its rowdy, free-for-all approach to poetry, the slam's role in community formation has been equally important to its geographical spread from Chicago to Ann Arbor, New York, San Francisco, Boston, and over one hundred cities worldwide. Marc Smith emphasizes the relationship between the slam and the community when he states, "I have become aware that the one step beyond the performance, the show is truly the most important step. What the art form of the show is really saying is that the community of people that hear the poetry and are involved in the poetry, and what happens to them, is more important than any individual poet or any individual poem" (Ingebretson 28). Moreover, the formal constraints of the slam — the open mic, the judges chosen from the audience, the number system for scoring the poem, the heckling of the poet and the judges by the audience, the performance space, and the location of the venue — help to create a ritualized alternative community that is reenacted every week during the performance. At the same time, the International Slam Family, a not-for-profit organization with which any slam venue can be affiliated, functions as worldwide poetry

---

[*]For more examples of sports lingo that has been adapted and redefined for the slam, see Taylor Mali's "Rule Book," which was written around the same time that the Slam Family decided to incorporate. While I have no proof of the following, I've also always wondered if Smith's decision to hold the Uptown Poetry Slam on late Sunday afternoons/early evening isn't some sort of reference to Sunday night football.

[†]See Patricia Smith's and Michael Brown's description of the competition as "the hook" on "Poetry Slam," *Greater Boston Arts*, WGBH, 1997. In an interview with me, Bob Holman referred to the competition as "the scam of the slam."

network, complete with their own newsletter and web pages. In an interview, Bob Holman describes the slam network as "analogous to academic circuits" and, while I wouldn't want to push this analogy too far, the National Grand Slam, which is held every August in different cities around the U.S., and the yearly Slam Masters' Meeting, which is held in April in Chicago, serve a function similar to that of the MLA convention or other academic conferences (Holman interview).[*] These events provide an opportunity to compete against poets from other cities and to make major decisions about the direction of the slam, choose the location of next year's Grand Slam, and revise the rule book, as well as learn about upcoming publishing and recording opportunities.

As the slam network has grown and become more established, the slam aesthetic has begun to proliferate other media, such as print, CDs, videos, and the world wide web. It probably goes without saying that the division between "performance" poets and published poets has never been a clear one and to construct a history of the slam that would plot out the slam's development from live performance to a published, recorded, and/or videotaped art would misrepresent what has been a much more chaotic evolution. In some cases, the development and success of a local slam venue has been at least partially dependent on the concurrent development of a multimedia slam culture. For instance, Bob Holman, the founder of the poetry slam at Nuyorican Poets Café, had published poetry collections, recorded poetry albums and poetry videos and had written and produced plays before bringing the slam New York City in 1988. Since becoming involved in the slam, Holman has co-edited *Aloud: Voices from the Nuyorican Café* (1994) with Miguel Algarín, published a collected works titled *The Collect Call of the Wild* (1995), and recorded a spoken word CD, *In With the Out Crowd* (1998). Through his work with Mouth Almighty, the spoken word subsidiary of Mercury Records, and Washington Square Films, Holman has been involved in adapting performance poetry to video, television, and CD. He has produced "Smokin' Word" segments for MTV and the "Words in Your Face" episode of for PBS's *Alive From Off-Center*; and produced the video series, *The United States of Poetry*. While the publication of *Aloud* is a direct result of the success of the slam at the Nuyorican Poets Café, the café's continuing fame is now also due to the fact that print and television have introduced this poetry to audiences beyond New York's Lower East Side.[†] Patricia Smith, who began

---

[*] Over the past eight years the National Grand Slam has been held in the following cities. 1990, San Francisco; 1991, Chicago; 1992, New York; 1993, San Francisco; 1994, Boston; 1995, Ann Arbor; 1996, Portland; 1997, Middletown, Conneticut; 1998, Austin, Texas; 1999, Chicago; 2000, Providence, Rhode Island.

[†] If the frequent invocation of *The United States of Poetry* and *Aloud* at recent academic conferences on poetry and poetics is any indication, the academy's burgeoning interest in the poetry slam and other performance poetries is at least partially due to the move from stage to page, CD, and video.

slamming in Chicago in 1987 and cofounded the slam at the Cantab Lounge with Michael Brown in 1990, has published three collections of poetry, contributed to *Triquarterly* and the *Paterson Review*, recorded an audio cassette of her poems in 1993, and adapted two of her poems to video. However, she continues to perform at slam venues and to adapt her poems to one-woman shows. Brown, who has been active in the slam poetry scene since its early days in Chicago, has published *The Falling Wallendas* (1994), founded *Slam! The International Performance Poetry Newsletter*, and maintains the Poetry Slam News Service on the world wide web.[*] Due to their joint efforts, Patricia Smith and Michael Brown have been largely responsible for the spread of the poetry slam throughout New England. Gary Mex Glazner, founder of the National Poetry Slam and the original slam master of the San Francisco slam, was the editor of the now-defunct poetry-web 'zine *Headless Bhudda* and is currently involved in visiting and documenting performance poetry movements around the world.[†] Even Marc Smith, who remains a purist about the slam and live performance, published a collection of his poems in 1996 and maintains a series of web pages on the Uptown Poetry Slam.[‡]

A poet's decision to publish, record a CD or video, and/or post web pages and the commodification of the slam aesthetic via television shows and ads are separate phenomena. However, as the slam has gained in popularity, so have the opportunities for its codification. Incidents such as Sony's underwriting of the "poetry slam" tent at the 1994 Lollapalooza festival, the 1997 Valentine's Day slam on *One Life to Live*, and the poetry slam ad that Nike launched during the 1998 Olympics suggest that erosions of the poetry slam's grassroots origins is already happening.[§] In response to these events, as well as to the trademark battle between Marc Smith and the creators of the Poetryslam board game, the slam family voted in 1996 to incorporate as The International Slam Family Collective, a

---

[*]The poetry Slam News Service can be found at www.slamnews.com.

[†]Michael Brown and Gary Glazner have been tireless promoters and documenters of the worldwide slam network. Before he discontinued publication in August, 1998, Brown's *Slam! The International Performance Poetry Newsletter* reported on slam venues worldwide. Brown, who is on faculty at Mount Ida College in Boston, recently took a research sabbatical to travel to various European slam venues. The May 1998 issue also includes an in-depth report on some of the European slams. While I haven't followed Gary Glazner's career as carefully, he too has been traveling the world as a slam ambassador. In a recent interview with me, Bob Holman stated "Gary Glazner is out there right now, scouting tea-house rappers in China, poetry ensembles in Bath, new poetry movements in Turkey."

[‡]Marc Smith, Crowdpleaser (Chicago Collage Press, 1996). Smith's webpage can be found at www.slampapi. com.

[§]*One Life to Live:* NBC. 14 February 1997. For a scathing commentary on the Nike poetry slam ads see Matthew Rothschild, "Editor's Note," *The Progressive* v.62 (Jan. 1998): 4.

non-profit corporation. During the 1996 Slam Masters' Meeting, the slam masters also voted to help independent filmmaker Paul Devlin with *SlamNation*, his documentary of the Portland National Grand Slam. While incorporation and involvement in an indie documentary might not appear at first glance to be related, I would like to suggest that they both represent the realization on the part of the slam family that the poetry slam had grown beyond the local community. As slam-master-turned-CD-producer Bob Holman points out, "Poetry can be in the world, and in the US that means taking on technology and the media and propelling the poem, just as Mayakovsky demanded" (Holman interview). While many slam poets refuse to publish or record, Mouth Almighty Records, Tía Chucha Books, and indie film groups like Washington Square Films have been integral in the propelling of slam poetry from venue to venue, city to city.[*]

While the slam has hardly gone mainstream, its spread into print, video, CD, and the internet suggests a change in the philosophical direction of the slam movement and raises important questions regarding commodification on the one hand and the continuing growth and spread of an antiestablishment, grassroots poetry movement on the other. As with its close cousin rap, the reproduction and commodification of slam poetry would seem to suggest that the slam will lose its ability to meaningfully intervene in the local community.[†] This hasn't proven to be the case so far. In response to the CDs, videos, books, and web pages — or perhaps in spite of them — local slam venues continue to spring up around the world and each year the National Grand Slam draws a large audience and national press coverage. At this point in the slam's history, it may be impossible to fully theorize how the development of a multimedia slam culture will change the slam community. Nonetheless, as the poetry slam approaches its fifteenth anniversary, its continued growth highlights the profound impact that this movement has had on the American poetry scene.

---

[*]Washington Square Films was responsible for the production of the "Words in Your Face" episode of *Alive from Off-Center* and *The United States of Poetry* video series. Tía Chucha Press in Chicago has published books of poems by slammers Jean Howard (*Dancing in Your Mother's Skin*, 1991); Patricia Smith (*Life According to Motown*, 1991); Lisa Buscani (*Jangle*, 1992); Michael Brown (*The Falling Wallendas*, 1994); and Cin Salach (*Looking for a Soft Place to Land*, 1996); among others. Tía Chucha also released *A Snake in the Heart*, a CD compilation of Chicago spoken word artists, in 1994. Mouth Almighty Records has produced spoken word CDs by Maggie Estep, (*Love Is a Dog From Hell*, 1997); Bob Holman (*In With the Out Crowd*, 1998); Beau Sia (*Attack! Attack! Go!*, 1998); and Sekou Sundiata (*The Blue Oneness of Dreams*, 1997) as well as CDs of works by Allen Ginsberg, William Burroughs, and Edgar Allen Poe.

[†]For a discussion of commodification and depoliticizing of rap and other black vernacular forms, see bell hooks, "Performance Practice as a Site of Opposition," in *Let's Get It On: The Politics of Black Performance*, ed. Catherine Ugwu (Seattle: Bay Press, 1995): 210-221.

WORKS CITED

Algarín, Miguel, and Bob Holman, eds. *Aloud: Voices from the Nuyorican Poets Cafe.* New York: Henry Holt, 1994.

Brown, Michael. *The Falling Wallendas.* Chicago: Tía Chucha Press, 1994.

-------. "The Roving Editor Reports January 5-31, 1998." *Slam! The Interternational Performance Poetry Newsletter.* 2.9 (May 1998): 4-5.

Buscani, Lisa. *Jangle.* Chicago: Tía Chucha Press, 1992.

Coniff, Richard. "Please Audience, Do Not Applaud a Mediocre Poem," *Smithsonian* (Sept. 1992): 77-86.

Damon, Maria. "Was That 'Different,' 'Dissident,' or 'Dissonant'? Poetry (n) the Public Spear: Slams, Open Readings, and Dissident Traditions." In *Close Listening: Poetry and the Performed Word.* Ed. Charles Bernstein. New York: Oxford UP, 1998. 324-42.

Estep, Maggie. *Love Is a Dog From Hell.* CD. Mouth Almighty Records, 1997.

Foster, Edward Halsey. "Bob Holman, Performance Poetry, and the Nuyorican Poets Cafe." *MultiCultural Review* 2.2 (June, 1993): 46-48.

Gates, Henry Louis, Jr, "Sudden Def." *The New Yorker.* 19 June 1995: 34-42.

Heintz, Kurt. *An Incomplete History of the Slam.* www.e-poets.net/library/slam/index.html.

Holman, Bob. *The Collect of the Wild.* New York: Henry Holt, 1995.

-------. *In With the Out Crowd.* CD. Mouth Almighty Records, 1998.

-------. Interview with the author. July 1998.

hooks, bell. "Performance Practice as a Site of Opposition." In *Let's Get It On: The Politics of Black Performance.* Ed. Catherine Ugwu, Seattle: Bay Presss, 1995. 210-221.

Hoover, Paul. E-mail to author. 1 July 1998.

Howard, Jean. *Dancing in Your Mother's Skin.* Chicago: Tía Chucha Press, 1991.

Ingebretson, Mark. "Page Meets Stage: The Round Table Interview," *Hyphen,* 10 (1995): 28.

"Poetry Slam." *Greater Boston Arts.* WGBH-TV. 1997.

Rothschild, Matthew. "Editor's Note." *The Progressive* 62 (Jan. 1998): 4.

Salach, Cin. *Looking for a Soft Place to Land.* Chicago: Tía Chucha Press, 1996.

Sia, Beau. *Attack! Attack! Go!* CD. Mouth Almighty Records. 1998.

Smith, Marc. *Crowdpleaser.* Chicago: Collage Press, 1996.

-------. "Slampapi's Slam Philosophy." www.slampapi.com/slamphil.htm.

Smith, Patricia. *Life According to Motown.* Chicago: Tía Chucha Press, 1991.

-------. *Patricia Smith Performs Always in the Head and Other Poems.* Audio Cassette. Boston: Zoland Books, 1993.

-------. "Slamming: Shaking up New England's Poetry World." *Soujourner* 19.6 (Feb. 1994): 20-21.

-------. *A Snake in the Heart.* CD. Chicago: Tía Chucha Press, 1994.

Sundiata, Sekou. *The Blue Oneness of Dreams.* CD. Mouth Almighty Records, 1997.

United States of Poetry. Mark Pellington, director. Washington Square Films. 1996.

"Words in Your Face." *Alive TV.* Mark Pellington, director. Henry Rollins, narrator. KTCA-TV. 1991.

Steve Evans

THE AMERICAN AVANT-GARDE AFTER 1989: NOTES TOWARD A HISTORY[*]

> A simple poetic undertaking: to see if life is livable,
> to make life livable. Without lying. —George Oppen

THERE HAS BEEN A CONTINUOUS, BECAUSE CONTINUOUSLY RISKED AND REINVENTED, avant-garde in American poetry since the opening decades of the twentieth century: independent, dissident, restless for aesthetic and social transformation, responsible for most of what is today considered significant in the nation's poetry. This avant-garde's distinctive demand — for the autonomy to compose a socially relevant poetic outside (and often in opposition to) the constraints of the capitalist market — has received as many historical inflections as there have been significant shifts in what some historians call "the short twentieth century." Working with a modest and vulnerable but persistently renewed set of expressive means — the typically short-lived, privately-funded, small-circulation magazine; the non-commercial, non-institutional publishing house; the low or zero-budget public performance — the generations emerging in the 1910s, 1930s, 1950s, and 1970s envisioned understandably different projects in light of their specific intersections with the large-scale forces that shaped the century.[†] If such terms as modernism, 'Objectivism,' the New American Poetry, and language-centered writing capture only in the vaguest of profile the indescribably various set of successive poetic practices spanning four generations, they do nevertheless mark out a discrete series of actual historical accomplishments, a temporal trajectory that is at the same time a densely communicating web of interpersonal and

---

[*] For their generosity, lucidity, and hard work in organizing conferences that brought the ideal of international intellectual collaboration down to earth and into a lively interaction that the present article only begins to register, I would like here to offer my thanks to Romana Huk, Rod Mengham and Ian Patterson, Stephen Clark and Mark Ford, Robert Hamson and Alison Mark, and Michel Delville. I also owe a debt of gratitude to Espen Stueland and Richard Aarø of the Norwegian journal *Vagant* for commissioning and translating an earlier version of this article.

[†] Among those forces: modernization, class struggle, world war, global depression, genocide, cold war, anti-imperial and other liberation movements, technological innovation, ecological depletion. Such abstract words hardly begin to hint at the concrete repercussions of these forces in terms of human lives and human suffering.

intertextual relations; in short, though the word scandalizes superficial observers of the avant-garde, a *tradition*.* The broad continuities of condition, stance, and impact that unite this tradition of poetic radicalism are often less visible than the local ruptures within it, for the simple reason that punctual events are more readily dramatized than abiding structures. Not surprisingly, these dramas of differentiation find an especially rich stock of affective and conceptual materials in the highly charged transition between generations. The break into modernity accomplished by the generation of Gertrude Stein and Ezra Pound was already a matter of intense and contradictory impulses, identifications, and anxieties, despite what amounted to the patent social-historical sanction these literary changes received from the simultaneous deep changes in other crucial spheres of life. Interestingly, it was not until certain of the language poets in the late 1970s and early 1980s took it upon themselves to spell out their poetic differences with the preceding generation of New Americanists that such a noisy — and largely one-sided — intergenerational dispute would again arise. The 'Objectivists' in the 1930s had been more reticent about the differences of political commitment and personal *habitus* that unmistakably separated them from the first-wave, often fascist-leaning modernists like Pound: rather, they held fast to an unresolved but not unproductive dialectic between continuity of formal approach and discontinuity of ethico-political motivation. And the poets of the immediate post-war years had little need for intergenerational dispute, as the global synchronization of the war itself divided life — including literary life — into brutally clear categories of *before* and *after*.† In fact, that war-time generation's many assertions of transgenerational solidarity with radical modernism and 'Objectivism' were themselves effectively polemical gestures in the more important battle against a conformist academy bent on poetic restoration.‡

---

*The scandal arises in part from the fact that "tradition" in the sense of a binding pre-reflexive custom (pre-modern sense) is not at all the same thing as the reflexive (and selective) appropriation of prior historical action (modern sense). The German social theorist of art Peter Bürger's equation of "becoming historical" with the failure of the original avant-garde project and the inauthenticity of the post-war avant-gardes operates fully within the second, modern, sense of "tradition." His error, however, lies in ascribing to the "institution of art" a monopoly over historical meaning and tradition. Forceful alternatives to this position have been provided by British sociologist of culture Raymond Williams and, in the French context, by Pierre Bourdieu, both of whom acknowledge the potentially contestatory nature of popular and artistic "traditions."

†Theodor Adorno's statements about the possibility of poetry — and indeed of any meaningful culture whatsoever — after Auschwitz have played an important role in focusing reflection on this historical divide.

‡One could cite countless examples: suffice it to recall John Ashbery's championing of Gertrude Stein, Robert Creeley's of Louis Zukofsky, Frank O'Hara's of Hart Crane, Robert Duncan's of H.D. Cary Nelson takes the full measure of the academic truncation of the modernist archive in *Repression and Recovery*, a passionate work that corroborates the long-standing testimony of these and countless other poets.

DARK AGES

THE MOST RECENT TRANSFORMATION OF THE AMERICAN AVANT-GARDE POETIC TRADITION has taken place quietly in the years following 1989, largely if not exclusively through the agency of a new generation of poets. Born in the decade preceding 1968 and coming to consciousness in the rain of gunfire that killed presidents, civil rights leaders, and — in a ten year undeclared war that bankrupted the legitimacy of the government that conducted it but not before destroying countless lives on both sides — a staggering number of ordinary people, these poets entered adolescence just as the economic order of the post-war capitalist boom shuddered into global recession and for a second time in ten years the office of president was vacated under abnormal circumstances. Their secondary education coincided with the backlash social and economic programs of a resurgent conservative party, an artificially revived cold war, and the outbreak of a mortal sexually transmitted disease. Anti-imperial and socialist struggles in Latin America and the battle against apartheid in South Africa informed the political horizon of their college years, but a marked depoliticization of student populations and an increased orientation toward conventionally-defined success were the more visible and typical tendencies of the period. The brokered conclusion of forty-years of superpower nuclear standoff in the mid-1980s held nothing for drama to the unforeseen and utter collapse of the Soviet empire beginning in Eastern Europe in the autumn of 1989 and striking home in the summer of 1991.[*] The rapidity and enormity of this change called to mind Hegel's famous image, from his preface to *The Phenomenology of Spirit*, of a world dissolving bit by bit, until the "gradual crumbling that left unaltered the face of the world is cut short by a sunburst which, in one flash, illuminates the features of the new world." However, in this case, the flash had nothing to illuminate but a no longer new, and anything but liberating, capitalism that immediately began dictating the meaning freedom would have for the former "second world," and by extension the entire globe: freedoms not of people, but of markets; not of unimpeded flows of informed popular discourse directed toward rethinking fundamental social structures, but of expert solutions imposed on paralyzed populations; not of building a vigilant citizenry in an emergent civil society, but of loosing predatory gangsters into conditions of unbridled economic anarchy.[†] Before intellectuals had time to finish their arguments as to

---

[*] In China, the bloody suppression of a student-led democracy movement in August of 1989 had signaled that Communist government's will to maintain autocratic political rule despite economic liberalization: there would be no Gorbachevian *glasnost* to accompany their brand of *perestroika*.

[†] The young emigré writer Eugene Ostashevsky characterizes literary culture in 1990s Petersburg in the following

the aptness of "late capitalism" as a periodizing term, the world became — to all effects and purposes — *only* capitalist. The first world stock markets soared, but in almost every other sphere of life a collective sinking feeling unmistakably set in,[*] and as early as the Gulf War in 1991 what had begun as a stunned silence turned into a summarily coerced one. Perhaps the earliest specifically poetic manifestation of the structure of feeling ascendant in this emergent set of conditions came in the form of Andrew Schelling and Benjamin Friedlander's magazine *Dark Ages Clasp the Daisy Root*, founded in the autumn of 1989 in a self-confessed mood of collapse, ruin, and disillusionment.[†] Crystallized in the journal's title was the thesis — widely intuited at the time[‡] — that capitalism, unopposed, reverts to feudalism, closing the parenthesis around a two-century aberration (the Enlightenment) in millennia of hardship and domination. That subterranean and fugitive forms of solidarity and knowledge nevertheless persist is the argument of the title's remaining words, "clasp the daisy root." Though it would remain virtually imperceptible for at least another half-decade, an important change in radical poetic practice was already gripping down and taking root.

---

terms: "The city's Baroque palaces and art nouveau mansions, late-nineteenth-century apartment buildings and classicist ministries are donning plastic shopsigns with names of Western brands and Russian corporations, the latter sounding quite savage to the Petersburg ear. The result is a vertiginous amalgam of past majesty and fast-food garishness, punctuated by remnants of Soviet squalor and general detritus. A palpable number of the intellectuals have left; mafia goons and their wanna-be's litter the landscape" (77).

[*] In 1997, just as the global markets entered the first serious crisis of the new era, Hollywood director James Cameron succeeded in turning this popular sense of class-driven doom into its own form of economic miracle in the film *Titanic*. For an interesting account of that film's place in contemporary American social struggles, see Tom Frank's "*Titanic* et la lutte des classes: La guerre sociale racontee aux enfants."

[†] See the editor's note following page 36: "Our plans for the magazine first took shape back in August, in a long conversation unwound through unlit streets back of Oakland. The sever of a difficult year had kept us from facing what we separately intuited as a collapse. Separately, we knew this collapse by its effect of disillusionment. An ethic of ruin in the ruins of the poem." Bill Luoma, Pam Rehm, Thad Ziolkowski, Peter Gizzi, Jennifer Moxley, Andrea Hollowell, Pat Reed, Jeff Gburek, and Helena Bennett are among the young writers Schelling and Friedlander published in the four-year run of their stapled magazine, along with older — if not at that time sufficiently appreciated — poets such as Alice Notley, Susan Howe, Robert Grenier, Larry Eigner, Ted Pearson, Stephen Rodefer, and Joanne Kyger.

[‡] Ridley Scott's *Blade Runner* had already made the argument credible in cinematic form by 1983.

A SIMPLE POETIC UNDERTAKING

IF A SINGLE QUESTION CAN BE SAID to have synchronized the American poetic avant-garde between 1970 and 1989, it was surely the question "what is language?" Inherited from Russian and Czech structuralism, as mediated by *Tel Quel* post-structuralism, and lent a palpable urgency by the circumstances in which it was posed (the Vietnam war; militant civil rights and liberation struggles), this question was in every way a *live* one, inspiring theory and practice, sparking debate and catching imaginations, changing the way many American poets wrote and read. In the eyes of some of the most active and accomplished writers of the era — eyes that had attentively passed over texts by Gertrude Stein and Ludwig Wittgenstein, Roman Jakobson and Robert Creeley, Louis Zukofsky and Roland Barthes — poetry was seen as a means to interrogate and intervene in 'the discursive construction of social reality' (to use the period phrase).[*] This stance toward poetic composition retained its force well into the 1990s, holding the allegiance of its initial formulators, now middle-aged, and generalizing its appeal among young writers, graduate students, and — increasingly — tenured academics.[†] Many of the poems and arguments first articulated in forums defined by their mix of unruly independence, unstable authority, and passionate risk now commenced a second life as markers on a professional game board, and though this "institutional strategy" was an understandable outcome of real contradictions in the intellectual life of capitalist America, it was no less understandably viewed by many as a demoralizing capitulation to academic power.[‡]

Nothing about the question "what is language" jarred against its academic recontextualization: after all, modern linguistics — and the social theory predicated on it

---

[*]The New York based *L=A=N=G=U=A=G=E* magazine (four volumes between 1978-1981) and Bay Area based *Poetics Journal* (10 issues since 1982) are only the most well-known of the many venues committed to some version of this axiom. Gil Ott's *Paper Air* (12 issues between 1976-1990) is an equally important, distinctively political, but less frequently mentioned, example.

[†]Thus works written predominantly between 1975-1985, and initially anthologized in 1986-87 (Silliman; Messerli), began to attract academic attention in the late 1980s and early 1990s. By mid-decade, when a second wave of anthologization explicitly targeted the academic market (Weinberger; Hoover; Messerli), the "tendency" had given rise to an established and legitimated academic discourse with a clear institutional hierarchy of expertise, defined by figures like Marjorie Perloff, Charles Bernstein, Alan Golding, Michael Davidson, Rachel Blau Du Plessis, Hank Lazer, Bob Perelman, and Barrett Watten.

[‡]See the last chapter of Golding's fine monograph *From Outlaw to Classic*, "'Provisionally complicit resistance': Language Writing and the Institution(s) of Poetry" for an optimistic reading of this phenomenon, and Silliman's "Canons and Institutions: New Hope for the Disappeared" for a more skeptical, and I believe more realistic, view. Silliman's sharply critical response to Bob Perelman's *The Marginalization of Poetry*, published in *The Impercipient Lecture Series*, is also worth consulting in this context.

— had long struck a manifestly scientific pose even in the work of a hero like Jakobson, friend and spirited celebrator of Khlebnikov and Mayakovsky.* Perhaps because they were harder to accommodate, more embarrassingly obvious and ethically intractable, another set of questions remained outside the academic economy. For instance, the question George Oppen had already posed in a mid-1960s notebook, when he imagined a "simple poetic undertaking: to see if life is livable, to make life livable. Without lying" (190). Or Bernadette Mayer's question of a decade later, in the desperate final line of "The Way to Keep Going in Antarctica": "If I suffered what else could I do." Neither the elder Objectivist, dispirited by his nation's refusal to let go its theocratic tenets and become a true democracy, nor the youthful New York School poet, as adventurous in her poetic explorations as the first Antarctic explorers had themselves been, could be charged with indifference to the linguistic basis of their common art. But their ethical and political questions — however immanent to linguistic and communicative contexts — did not admit of simple linguistic resolution or evasive formal-technical transposition. This refusal to subordinate the social to the linguistic distinguishes Mayer and Oppen from the project of language-centered writing, and it also explains their importance for the post-1989 generation. As one of the wittiest, and most politicized, members of that generation — the Canadian-born Kevin Davies — would say on the opening page of his 1995 chapbook, *Thunk*: "'I knew I was a formal device before I was born. I wanted / a *bigger* prize, for having survived.'"

Survival: it is hard to imagine that the word has ever been so frequently uttered by inhabitants of a prosperous nation in peacetime as it has been in the American 1990s.† The social logics behind the hyper-saturation of this sign are too numerous and too contradictory to be unraveled here, but it is possible to distinguish its use in relation to poetry from the spontaneous Social Darwinism of economic elites and the paranoid anti-federalism of some segments of the working class.‡ As a protest against false supercession, against the extinction of one of the oldest human art forms in the withering conditions of market-driven culture, against the incessant talk of its death, its marginality, its obsolescence, to say that poetry survives is to say that it remains a basic, and inalienable,

---

*Among the many relevant texts, see at least "On a Generation That Squandered Its Poets" (1931), collected in *Language in Literature* 273-300.

†The poet Tina Darragh gives a fascinating genealogy of this word in post-Vietnam War America in her work *adv. fans—the 1968 series*.

‡To cite only two highly legible negative variants. Positive variants include all those expressions of popular intransigence against the injunction to disappear, whether class or identity-based.

possibility of human intelligence. Poet and editor Lisa Jarnot says as much — while adding the names of Allen Ginsberg and John Cage to those of Mayer and Oppen already mentioned — in speaking of her post-1989 contemporaries: "We are a generation critically aware that as Allen Ginsberg said in 1966, 'almost all our language has been taxed by war.' And perhaps what we share the most at this moment is an unspoken thought that John Cage is right when he tells us that language is something 'that you have to use in practical ways, for survival'" (*Anthology* 2).

AN IMPULSE TO ACTION

To BELONG TO A BIOLOGICAL GENERATION, to share an historical horizon, to endure certain material conditions: important as these factors are, they remain inert data, powerless in themselves to constitute even rudimentary forms of collectivity, especially in the diffuse, discrepant social topography of the contemporary United States.* As the philosopher Jean-Luc Nancy observes: "'History' is not always and automatically historic. It has to be taken as an offer and to be decided. We no longer receive our sense from history — history no longer gives or enunciates sense. Rather we have to decide to enunciate our 'we,' our community, in order to enter history" (166).† In the wake of, and in deliberate contrast to, the self-assertive, auto-exegetical, and reciprocally-evaluative conduct of the language-centered writers, the scrupulous avoidance of certain inflated forms of framing discourse among the poets emerging after 1989 was anything but the sign of apathy certain established avant-gardists mistook it for: rather, the intransigent refusal to self-identify registered a profound and warranted resistance to "entering history" under the terms presently on offer.‡ At the same time, this decision led in the direction of a returned emphasis on poetic practice as opposed to theoretical discourse. It is action that articulates

---

*A diffuseness and discrepancy that coexists with, and partially explains, the hypercoherence of the "culture" — referred to by Benjamin Barber simply as "McWorld" — dictated by the capital-intensive dominant media.

†Translation very slightly modified. I comment at greater length on Nancy's remarks in "The Dynamics of Literary Change" 13-14.

‡ In 1993, recalling W.B. Yeats's claim that the literary movements that endure are those that "hate great and lasting things," I hazarded — in the introduction to the Technique section of *Writing from the New Coast* — that a "hatred of Identity" was the strongest motivating force in the poetics emerging there (5).

community, these poets seemed to be saying, and action — as it transforms conditions — outpaces the terms of its own recognition.*

In its initial phase this activity took the form of a loosely coordinated swarm of small-circulation magazines like Friedlander and Schelling's *Dark Ages Clasp the Daisy Root* (Oakland), Jessica Grim and Melanie Nielson's *Big Allis* (New York), Jennifer Moxley's *The Impercipient* (Providence), Scott Bentley's *Letterbox* (Oakland), Robert Fitterman's *Object* (New York), Avery E.D. Burns's *Lyric&* (San Francisco), Sianne Ngai and Jessica Lowenthal's *Black Bread* (Providence), Dodie Bellamy and Kevin Killian's *Mirage#4/Period(ical)* (San Francisco), Elizabeth Fodaski's *Torque* (New York), and Brian Kim Stefans's *Arras* (New York), not to mention the more visible counterparts of these often furtive ventures such as Rod Smith's *Aerial* (Washington D.C.) and Peter Gizzi's *o•blek* (New York and Providence), the twelfth and final issue of which gathered under the title *Writing from the New Coast* two volumes of poetry and poetics by younger writers.†

By the middle years of the decade, works first disseminated in these fugitive venues were being collected in chapbooks from the prolific Leave Books in Buffalo, with nearly a hundred titles between 1991-1995; in an excellent series from Situations press in New York, which between 1995-1997 brought out titles by Kevin Davies, Bill Luoma, Lisa Jarnot, Douglas Rothschild, Marcella Durand, Chris Stroffolino, and others; and from Joel Kuszai's Meow press, which published Juliana Spahr, Peter Gizzi, and Jena Osman, as well as much of Ben Friedlander's work after the 1991 *Time Rations* (with O Books). Debut monographs also began to appear, most often under the aegis of avant-garde publishers from the previous generation. Rod Smith's *In Memory of My Theories* from O Books in

---

*To paraphrase Jacques Lacan: "[V]ery often, even most often, what is internal to what is called action is that it does not know itself" (qtd. in Eribon 211).

†A few remarks are necessary to round out this very partial snapshot of the period. By 1990 few if any of the magazines associated with language-centered writing were still in existence, though most of the presses — Roof, Sun & Moon, The Figures, Burning Deck — remained active in spite of increasingly tenuous funding from state and federal agencies. Occupying more consecrated (and consecrating) positions in the field of experimental poetic practice were perfect-bound magazines such as Clayton Eshleman's long-standing *Sulfur*, Paul Hoover and Maxine Chernoff's *New American Writing*, and Brad Morrow's *Conjunctions*. Ed Foster's then fledgling *Talisman* magazine, the St. Marks Poetry Project's house organ, *The World*, and Cydney Chadwick's *Avec* all were at least potential places of publication for young poets. The polemically-edited *apex of the M*, appearing between 1994-1998, sharply attacked the secular and avant-gardist bases of language poetry in the name of a spiritual poetic, though little work answering the editorial board's prescriptions was ever written. It was another magazine launched in Buffalo at the same time, *Chain*, that turned out to be — by virtue of Juliana Spahr and Jena Osman's inclusive and eclectic editorial policy — the more timely project. The editorial triumph of the period was arguably the *Exact Change Yearbook*, edited by Peter Gizzi and published by Damon Krukowski and Naomi Yang's Exact Change press in 1995. Projected as the first of an annually-appearing series that sadly never materialized, the inaugural issue was a brilliantly anti-provincial blend of emergent and established, American and international writers.

Oakland, Lisa Jarnot's *Some Other Kind of Mission* from Burning Deck in Providence, and Juliana Spahr's *Response* from Sun & Moon in Los Angeles all appeared in 1996, as did Jennifer Moxley's *Imagination Verses*, an exception in this group for being published by Tender Buttons press, directed by a contemporary of the poets just named, Lee Ann Brown, whose own first volume, *Polyverse* won a national competition in 1995.[*] In 1998, Bill Luoma, whose Situations chapbook *Western Love* and Figures chapbook *Swoon Rocket* both appeared in 1996, collected his prose under the title *Works & Days*, again with Geoff Young's The Figures press. And Kevin Davies's follow-up to his 1992 *Pause Button*, the as-yet unpublished work tentatively titled "Karnal Bunt," was widely excerpted between 1995-1997 in Canadian and American magazines such as *Boo*, *The Impercipient*, *Raddle Moon*, and the *Exact Change Yearbook*.[†]

When Chris Stroffolino, Lisa Jarnot, and Leonard Schwartz set about assembling *An Anthology of New (American) Poets* for Talisman in late 1996 and 1997, they included most of the writers already mentioned — Davies and Rothschild are two regrettable omissions — and added a number of others, including Mark McMorris, whose *The Black Reeds* came out in 1997; Peter Gizzi, whose *Periplum* appeared from Avec in 1992 and *Artificial Heart* from Burning Deck in 1998; Beth Anderson, whose *Impending Collision* appeared with the British rem press (publishers also of Moxley's *Enlightenment Evidence* in 1996 and Jarnot's *Heliopolis* in 1998); Eleni Sikelianos, whose *to speak while dreaming* appeared from Selva in 1993; and Elizabeth Willis, whose *The Human Abstract* was selected in the National Poetry Series of 1994 and published the following year by Penguin. Hoa Nguyen, author of *Dark* (from Mike and Dale's in 1998); Renee Gladman, author of *Arlem* (from Idiom in 1996); and Judith Goldman, author of *adversities of outerlife* (from Object/poetscoop in 1996) are among the youngest contributors to the volume, born in 1967, 1971, and 1973 respectively.[‡] Already

---

[*] The ensuing four-year delay in Sun & Moon's publication of the book would have been regrettable even if it had befallen an established writer: that it concerned a debut collection by one of the most promising poets of the new generation lends it an air of catastrophe. On a not entirely unrelated note, the encroachment of publication- and prestige-conferring prize competitions within the avant-garde context, traditionally critical of devices long associated with the mainstream at its most transparently nepotistic and conformist, can be counted among the more dubious developments of the period under discussion.

[†] To omit other writers associated, like Davies, with the Kootenay School of Writing in Vancouver — Lisa Robertson, Peter Culley, Nancy Shaw, Dan Farrell, Jeff Derksen, all come immediately to mind — would be to lose an important dimension of this moment, in which the young British poet Miles Champion also figured importantly. The journals *Writing* and *Raddle Moon* are two indispensable reference points for KSW's energetic intervention into Canadian, and U.S., literary practice.

[‡] It must be mentioned that the Talisman anthology offers an extremely partial, indeed polemical, vision of the poetry emergent after 1989 in the United States. The exclusion of writers too closely associated with the project of Language poetry (for example Robert Fitterman, Melanie Nielsen, or Brian Kim Stefans), unrepresentative selections from mar

with poets of their age one can observe an important shift in the horizon of poetic possibility as electronic publications rapidly pass from the status of technological oddity to easily accessible sites of alternative expression.*

THE NEW COMPOSITION: SIX PROFILES

"Composition is not there. It is going to be there and we are here." —Gertrude Stein

WHAT HAS EMERGED IN THESE TEXTS is, as with all significant poetry, resistant to synopsis and paraphrase: the perceptions, emotions, linguistic combinations, intellectual positions, and social struggles articulated there belong to an imagination the integrity of which must be measured in terms of the singularity and necessity of its statements. By such standards the initial critical response, which has focused on a perceived rehabilitation of lyric forms, musical values, and direct address — all in tacit contrast to the previous generation's penchant for abstraction and hostility to lyric practice — is still far from coming to terms with the actual multiplicity of the new composition.† At the level of content, for instance, a renewed commitment to the articulation of suffering raises a number of serious and complicated questions; while at the level of composition, a commitment to what can be called the democracy of perception (with its origins in Whitman) continues to stimulate the discovery of new poetic forms, few of which have been critically charted.‡

---

of the writers included (for example, Benjamin Friedlander, Lee Ann Brown, and Bill Luoma), an unexamined retention of the nation as an organizing category (crystallized in the embarrassed parenthesis enclosing the word "American" in the volume's title), and a general failure to employ the anthology form as something distinct from that of, say, an ample magazine issue, all weaken the volume's claim to definitiveness.

*The Electronic Poetry Center, launched on the internet by Charles Bernstein and Loss Pequeño Glazier at SUNY-Buffalo in 1994, provides the best overview of radical poetry on the web. It can be accessed at http://wings.buffalo.edu/epc. Among the many sites active in 1998, suffice it to mention Brian Kim Stefans's on-line version of *Arras*, Australian poet John Tranter's *Jacket*, Laura Moriarty's *non*, Kathy Lou Schultz's on-line version of *Lipstick 11*, Garrett Kallberg's *The Transcendental Friend*, Benjamin Friedlander and Graham Foust's *Lagniappe*, and the web-sites of Idiom and Meow presses.

†In their ranging critical practices, Juliana Spahr, Chris Stroffolino, and Mark Wallace have all done much to advance this difficult task. Likewise, a host of recent magazines — Yedda Morrison and David Buuck's *Tripwire*, Lytle Shaw and Emilie Clark's *Shark*, Louis Cabris's *Philly Talks* — have provided crucial new forums for the broadening and complicating of the debates.

‡I have already cited the concluding line of Berndatte Mayer's "The Way to Keep Going in Antarctica": "If I suffered what else could I do." Another line from the same poem now becomes equally relevant, the imperative: "Look at very small things with your eyes."

By way of embarking on this necessary, if hazardous, labor of specifying the stakes, stances, devices, and distinctions at work in post-1989 poetic composition, I want to turn now to a constellation of six poets who have known and recognized each other as contemporaries, who have collaborated with one another, debated anbd disputed one another, changed one another's — and my own — thinking and writing: Kevin Davies, Lisa Jarnot, Bill Luoma, Rod Smith, Lee Ann Brown, and Jennifer Moxley.

As the metaphor of a "constellation" should suggest, this particular mapping of the poetic field is neither an entirely objective nor a remotely exhaustive one. It is, as criticism has little choice but to be in confronting the complex present of a vital and ongoing practice, implicated in values no external authority can vouch for, affective bonds no rigor can wholly neutralize, political convictions for which no consensus can be presupposed, and literary asperations no republic of letters exists to ratify. Provisional and preliminary then, these profiles seek nothing more (nor less) than to render communicable something of the specificity and necessity, the stance and cadence, of certasin texts — chosen from oeuvres elaborated over what already amounts to a decade or more — in which the complexity of contemporary experience has been given distinctive poetic expression.

KEVIN DAVIES

ACH HIGH-DEFINITION, RECOMBINABLE FRAME of Kevin Davies's poetry freezes with indelible linguistic precision a moment in the social process when "code happens" ("Overkill" 85). In this poetics of the *Pause Button*, a keen-edged descendant of Walter Benjamin's practice of dialectics at a standstill, some frames simply mimic the grammar of social pathology: "Will fuck for books, no weirdoes" ("Throb") or "Depart from this area of / simulated passion *now*" (*Pause* 13). Others state the implicit rules governing social conduct: "'Hey Man' & the unthought are drinking buddies" ("Ephemera . . ." 44), or "Acting normal as a kind of overfunded performance art kids are encouraged to express themselves with" ("Throb"). Some frames deftly fuse manifest and latent messages while retaining the block syntax of pseudo-public utterance: "Clinton licks tender inner thigh of corporate crud agenda" (*Thunk*). Others pulverize that syntax, making the deep structure show through strategic deletions: "That's what happens / when you give a [ ] a [ ] & tell it to start shooting" (*Pause* 28), or "[Abject suffering homelessness] has its privileges" (*Pause* 69). There are frames that endow the haves with a vicious eloquence: "We contracted for the personal advantages of social entropy not endless replays of its symptoms" ("Ephemera

..." 43) or "'If /they / grow / over / the / fence / we / *own* / them'" (*Pause* 12). Many more imagine a caustic form of have-not backtalk, a sort of post-Situationist vernacular for speaking truth to power and getting away with it: "If you're so smart / why are you a social worker" (*Pause* 20), "Hometowns are *reformist idiots* (*Thunk*), or "America out of Milky Way now!" ("Throb" 66).

The medium in which these frames advance is a consciousness that mixes extremes, matching Flaubert for recessed impassivity one moment, Shelley for unleashed immediacy the next, and Creeley for coloratura scaling of anguished self-reflexivity throughout. A mobile sum of semiotic excesses traversing devastated territory, weaving agilely between catatonics and fanatics, wise-guys and thugs, tempted by but never surrendering to the opiate of infotainment everywhere on hock, Davies's texts rehearse with an ever-renewed urgency the moment when spontaneous mind encounters structural determinacy, the great unthought term of the fantastic North American agora,[*] and train the attention with provocative insistence on the refusal to be human, the willful destruction of democratic potential, the assent voluntarily given to this or that unsurvivable proposition. The closing sequence of an assemblage published under the title "Throb (Claymation Kakistocracy, or") in the *Impercipient* 7 (1995) captures his stance with great economy:

> I love the look of humans when they sit or stand still & when they move around
> I love the look of them looking back & barking arbitrary commands, which I obey
> I love the fragrance of the grouping of incommensurate ego fantasias in the drone of winter
> I love the fuss of the not-quite of submission techniques
> I love to be an international unit of measure of the loading of the fissures in the communal membrane into silos on a prairie in a basement by a government of souls in trouble at a party with martinis for a long time

Total sodomy. (67)

---

[*] Davies's work is thoroughly cognizant and critical of the post-NAFTA distributions of wealth and power in North America. "Karnal Bunt," the working title of his second collection, scheduled for publication by Edge Books, is named after a grain mould at the heart of a recent Canada-U.S. trade dispute (E-mail to the author, 21 March 1999).

Like every other cell of Davies's composition, this one is a virtuoso display of poetic artifice: one notes the decaying arc of the declaration "I love" through its five phrase-inaugural repetitions; the way the ruse of a trans-species observing reason gets punctured in the relative clause concluding the second sentence ("commands, which I obey"); the lexical pseudo-lyricism of sentence three ("fragrance," "fantasias"), recording the drone in the budding grove of human hierarchy; the hectically pursued prepositional extensions of the fifth sentence describing with mock precision a subject impossibly situated; and the perverse kaleidoscope of allusions in the final line, evoking at a minimum language-wnter Barrett Watten's critical volume *Total Syntax*, those unreproductive erotic acts still legally punishable in some American states, and the illicit coupling of Whitmanic and Derridean "dissemination" in the night of digitally-coded global capitalism.

The incisive work Davies does inside compositional cells, giving each utterance its tonal stance, lexical color, and rhythmic signature of pace and pause, is matched by his acrobatic ligature work, most visible in the highly emphatic handling of punctuation in *Pause Button*. Where Charles Olson charged each parenthesis he opened with cognitive optimism and encyclopedic ambition, Davies makes his square brackets, whether filled or voided, into emblems of bad universality, demonstrating the actual relation of interchangeability underlying liberal individualism in its Western bureaucratic mode: "Easier to fill out a form that's already replaced you," he writes in "Duckwalkingaperimeter" (110). His em-dashes mark another form of interchangeability, an aesthetic one of provisional syntagms susceptible to reconstellation at a moment's notice in what he refers to as "a kind of conceptual art too ephemeral even to be documented" ("Duckwalkingaperimeter"109). For though his poetics articulates itself as a series of breaks in the ideological flow — pauses that liberate the possibility of present tense thinking from the thrall of post-cognitive "Thunk"[*] — survival in Davies's poetry is closely associated with the staving off or negating of stasis, including the stases of the printed text.[†] As he puts it with characteristic dead-serious humor in "Meanstreak":

The strong desire to *not know*
with bilious certainty what's going to happen next, unlikely to gain a majority but

---

[*] The title of Davies' 1995 chapbook recalls a little known line of Frank O'Hara's: "interesting / that in Manhattan thunk is pronounced library"("F.Y.I. #371b [Parallel Forces, Excerpted]," in *Poems Retrieved* 202).

[†] Davies has described *Pause Button* as a "poem made up of the interruptions, rewritings, and 'translations' of many poems & poem series, most of which were originally written or assembled for public readings." The same would appear to be the case for the work gathering toward "Karnal Bunt."

with a decent chance at grabbing some power in a coalition, is *only apparently* at odds with the need of humans to plan ahead to avoid starvation. (61)

LISA JARNOT

READING *Some Other Kind of Mission* (1996) is like staring at a bruise you can't remember getting, after a night you can't recall the conclusion of, in a room you've never seen before. Lisa Jarnot gets this punished effect through terse rhythmic prose phrasing; a stammering, start-again looping of irreparably broken codes; and an art-brut approach to collage in which scrawled, struck-through, inked-over, amputated, circled, highlit, diagrammed, and mistyped texts form damaged palimpsests of mostly indecipherable messages. The social landscape of this non-progressive epic in which every fragment is equidistant from the same unrepresentable traumatic core has a run-down familiarity to it that is alternately banal and menacing: motels, grocery stores, gas stations, Kmarts and Sears, salad bars, bus routes, etc. Jarnot estranges these habitual sites of working-class American experience by inserting tokens of sexual exoticism and criminalized marginality into them (thus, among the persons of the poem we find "Lucky Pierre," a "Rough Trade Angel," a "Czechoslovakian Drag Queen"), as well as by systematic distortion of the already intermittent narratorial consciousness. Consider a typical prose block from the book's eighth section, which unfolds under the brusque assertion "I Sure as Fuck Would Know,"

> he became attracted to china under willows after coffee in the pitch black clay. i had one dream last night after coffee in the pitch black clay having escaped from jail on the highway past the pitch of fields with peak crests in escape. the whole of terns, the eye of the bus ticket, the whole of the tern doubled back on the back of willows. representative of detraction, they extracted me from the clover, having been extracted from the dollars secret call. the kmart felling windows with a dust of sand the what museum. at the what museum in my dream the mcadanville lights they extracted from the sand. they extracted out the farm before the here it is at down the clay. they were terns, extracted from the sand, below and under after dream. i dreamt i took a bus to mexico to avoid the authorities who put me into christmas next to mao. before and after at the car port meet me playing candles in the window down the street. they have reached maturity in the darkness of the pitch black next to mao. shaving. he became attracted to china near the

railroad tracks in the pitch black of the clay. i escaped on a bus to the river next to fear. mashed down on refusing the meshes of the afternoon. before and after at the car port shining tickets of the whole. peach crests, by the willows, on the back of, down to pitch. he meant the calls in dreams, crawfish in the eye of, net upon the bus. having crawled through the back of the pitch. at the back of making secrets and sand. running through the peach crest's unescape. at your wall of the museum in the pitch coordinate. (81)

Built of twenty-two sentences ranging in length from one word ("Shaving") to thirty (the second), with the majority falling at fifteen or so, this passage demonstrates Jarnot's distinctive ability to layer and cross-weave patterns at every level of her composition: syllabic (the /aek/ common to *attracted - black - back - detraction - extracted*), lexical (five uses of *dream* and its variants, eight of *pitch*, three of *tern* not counting its appearance in *afternoon*), phrasal ("He became attracted to . . ."), grammatical (prepositional phrases introduced by *next to* and *after*), rhythmic (getting caesural effects from stressed function words), and even ideological (the spliced cultural frames of a phrase like "into christmas next to mao"). This surcharging of the textual surface — in each discrete section and across the whole book ("tern," the name of a bird, appears on twenty or more pages, often more than once; an odd word like "meticule" catches the attention at every appearance) — results not in semantic depth, the promise of which must continually be sacrificed to the primary hermeticism of the project, but in the kind of structured enigma that motivates the search for meaning even while conveying the hopelessness of the hermeneutic (and by extension therapeutic) enterprise.

Jarnot quickly followed the publication of *Some Other Kind of Mission* with a chapbook-length serial poem entitled, after Jack London, *Sea Lyrics* (1996). Retaining the hypnotic phrasal rhythms and extending the lexical work of *Mission* — knowing just how the addition of a suffix ("spanishest" or "foreignest") or a count-adjective ("all" in "I have hardly noticed all the artificialist lagoons") or an inversion ("where winterless I am") will jolt the attention out of an encroaching rhythmic lull — *Sea Lyrics* dispenses with the graphic elements and breaks from the hermetic stance of the earlier book. Anchored by an omni-identificatory "I," this thirty-poem Lucretian catalog of the exposed and endangered life passed on bridges, lots, sidestreets, docks, by opossums, preachers, prawn, telemarketers, dogs, and detritus offers a less obstructed, more seductive reading experience, and its updated search for beatitude amidst the downcast and the outcast of San Francisco has already, and rightly, been recognized as an important mid-decade accomplishment.*

BILL LUOMA

Bill Luoma's *Works & Days* (1998) shares with its Hesiodic namesake a number of important features. Both arise from experiences of devastating loss (Hesiod of his patrimony to a conniving brother; Luoma of his wife, the poet Helena Bennett, to cancer). Rather than narrating a single grand action, both texts cobble together sayings, tales, empirical observations, and flights of lyricism. Both mix naiveté of tone with a didactic aim, blending instruction in life's conduct with wonder at its contents. And both are texts that speak with what Hesiod calls "a sparing tongue" ("the best treasure a man can have is a sparing tongue, and the greatest pleasure one that moves orderly" [xx]) and contemporary linguist Basil Bernstein labels "a restricted code."† But for all their appearance of simplicity, Luoma's are eloquent and subtle texts, peopled, detailed, principled, humorous, and moving. In his wanderings from San Diego to New York and Providence ("My Trip to New York"), through the minor-league ballparks of the American south ("12 Peanuts & an Easton"), to San Francisco ("We Were in Burrito" and "The Replacements"), back to New York ("Auto Gobbler," "Tradition: An Allegory," and the "Ear in Reading Reports"), down to Philadelphia ("Illegal Park"), over to France ("The Annotated My Trip to NYC"), and eventually to Hawaii ("KPOI 97.5 The Rock You Live On"), Luoma follows a principle rendered explicit in a passage from "The Replacements" (where a lost metal cleat exercises all the motivating force of Lacan's *objet petit a*):

> At home I listen to a bird making a nest in my heater vent. I'll use the phone book to locate places that might satisfy my needs, but I don't phone them to nail down the particulars. I go there and see. The search becomes a project of wandering, with allowed rules that let you name things along the way that you're not searching for. Like the discovery of a new thrift store or the sighting of a person

---

*For more on *Sea Lyrics*, see Spahr 11-15.

†Bernstein posits a distinction between "restricted" and "elaborated codes." The former are characterized by their condensation, context-dependence, embeddedness in affective social bonds, and particularism; the latter by the autonomy, reflexivity, rationality, and universalism. A tenet of Bernstein's sociolinguistics is that access to elaborated codes is unevenly distributed in class societies. See "Language and Socialization" 231 *et passim*.

wearing a hat in a neighborhood you've never been in. This is the whole kind of lazy philosophy that describes my life. I assert that getting lost is part of it. I embrace the inherent good in it. Fear is transformed into let's go into that thrift store. The bird continues to scrape the inside of the vent with twigs and grasses. (75)

In this particular updating of the situationist dérive, Luoma is for the most part alone: as in the other San Francisco-based text, "We Were in Burrito," an air of isolation and melancholy pervades. Almost everywhere else in the book, however, the project of "naming things along the way" is a collective one, involving a throng of strangers, acquaintances, and close friends, among the latter of whom the hilarious, idiosyncratic pair of Brian and Douglass stand paramount as slapstick muses forever in mid-routine:

> O man there was this big huge guy. Did you see the big huge guy? Douglass asked us this when we got out of the liquor store. We had to get some scotch and I picked up a bottle that wasn't in the scanner's database. They had to do a time-consuming price check. While we were waiting Brian predicted that Douglass would be real proud of me for causing such a stir. (21)

Here the phenomenon of "time-consuming price checks" on commodities unrecognized by "the scanner's database" is brought to poetry with the precision of Hesiod telling Perses how and when to clip his fingernails or where and in which direction to stand when urinating, but the real focus of the passage is the magic of masculine admiration, capable of transmuting a boring dead-space in the life of consumerism into an act of quasi-heroic system jamming (a theme more concertedly pursued in "Astrophysics & You"). This is not to imply that Luoma shares Hesiod's — or even Jack Kerouac's — misogyny: no Pandora is loosed to explain the degeneration of men, except perhaps in an occasional aside by Douglass. In fact, the narrator's love of specific women — Helena, Margo, Kate, Juliana — and friendship with others — Jennifer, Cindy, Lisa, Marlene — is amply apparent in *Works & Days*, but unlike in the sumptuous and graphic "My Lover" poems (published in *The Impercipient* 7 and *The World* 53; 1995 and 1997 respectively) and the genre-stylized *Western Love* chapbook, this love does not form the principal compositional interest. That remains the interaction between men, expressively constrained, silly, cranky, heroic, sweet, as recorded in discrete paragraphs whose frame-by-frame progression recalls a slideshow[*] or the

---

[*] In "The Annotated My Trip to NYC," a series of 101 brief commentaries occasioned by the collective translation

baseball boxscores appearing on successive days in the newspaper.[*] In either analogy it is clear that these reports always derive their tone and function from being *for* someone (for Scott in "My Trip," or in the "KPOI" sequence for Charles who "never sees any of this so then this is for him"). Musing on Robert Creeley's "I Know a Man" in his annotations to "My Trip" — a work on whose opening page Creeley's "goddamn big car" is reduced to an irreparable and irretrievable state, the first of the many wrecks, breakdowns, and tow-aways strewn throughout *Works & Days* — Luoma explains his commitment to this form of poetic address

> I think creeley had the right idea: it's 'good' that the darkness surrounds us because it makes us form communities. Write poems for your friends to help keep them alive while you try to watch out where you're going reading the poems your friends write for you. Dharmok and Jilad at Tenagra. Ginsberg and Kerouac at the Sunflower. Kevin & Dug & Lisa in Nogo. I think that's the good the bad and the lovely of it.
>
> ps your friends die anyway. (132)

As with Frank O'Hara, whose commitment to "personism" cannot be understood apart from its elegiac origins, what might seem glib or cliquish in Luoma's project is lent weight and dimension by the tragic-elegiac "darkness" that surrounds — and sometimes falls directly upon — his naive-seeming page. Writing across that pocket where, as Hesiod knew, "the gods keep hidden from men the means of life," Luoma affirms a community of life *and* death, works and idleness by day and perishing by night. His poems are befriending incitements to keep going, naming things along the way.

---

ofd the work into French for Juliette Valery's Format Americain series, Luoma renders the analogy explicit: "These [paragraph]'s are all slides by the way, slides that you would show to relatives after you get back from a trip. These slides are for Scott another San Diego friend who wanted me to send him some."

[*] As Luoma explains in "12 Peanuts & An Easton": "A box score is good in the morning for many reasons. For example, it's good to know how long games lasted, the umpires' names and how many double plays were turned. It's also good for small talk" — all of which applies, mutatis mutandi, to the genre-founding "reading reports" in the volume's latter half.

ROD SMITH

EDITOR OF *Aerial* magazine, publisher of Edge books, and manager of one of the truly indispensable independent bookstores in the United States, Bridge Street in Washington D.C., Rod Smith is most importantly a poet whose work in aleatorical and procedural composition vitally extends the tradition of ego-bracketed, Zen-inflected anarchism inaugurated by John Cage and Jackson Mac Low in the immediately post-war decades.[*] From the early exploration of language as a Wittgensteinian "life-form" in *The Boy Poems* (1994), through the three interspliced serial works assembled in "A Grammar Manikin" (a twenty page author-feature in *Object* 5 [1995]) and the seventeen works that make up his first monograph, *In Memory of My Theories* (1996), to the elegiac lyrics and savvy media critiques of *Protective Immediacy* (1997) and the Jasper Johnsian reflections of *The Lack (love poems, targets, flags . . .)* (1997), Smith's impressive demonstration of range has kept an off-handed, self-effacing, stay-at-it workman's aura about it, that air of modesty in the midst of great daring common among genuine innovators.

Smith's texts — uniquely unstable syntheses of poetic indeterminacy, ethical decency, and political will-to-change — often crystallize around the contradiction between ephemerality and fixity, between the vanishing magnitudes of consciousness and the uncanny persistences of sign-assisted vision, between nature accepted in its chaotic indeterminacy and a schlerotic and often malign culture of reifying Midas-touches. His titles make frequent mention of states of diminished agency, often though not always with gendered connotations: males who have not yet acceded to their socially-defined rights and responsibilities in *The Boy Poems*, the posable dummy of "A Grammar Manikin," the categorical dispossession of phallic authority in *The Lack*, a mournful remembrance of dismantled thought-systems in *In Memory of My Theories*. Different evaluations attend these dispossessions: sometimes they are therapeutic, functioning as remedies to an unsustainable form of subjectivity (masculinity as symptom, mastery as unsustainable rationalist illusion); sometimes they offer comic relief to chronic determination and rigid designations; other times the reference is critical and the diminishment of human agency is judged in accordance with an utopic sense of what is possible as opposed to what is permitted (as in the substitution of the word "vicarious" for "various" in Smith's rewriting of Frank O'Hara's famous line, "grace to be born and live as variously as possible"[†]). Smith's formal

---

[*] See the biographical entry on John Cage that Smith contributed to the *Dictionary of Literary Biography*. See also the fabricated dialogue between Ted Berrigan and John Cage published in *Tripwire* 2 (1998).

[†] Concluding epigraph on the colophon of *The Boy Poems*.

gestures almost always involve second-degree transformations of found material in a perpetual diffusion and redistribution of already-existing signs. The ambient, "all-over" feel that results, especially in the longer works "Sieff," "For Loss," and the title sequence of *In Memory of My Theories*, is a function of his reduction or elimination of structuring repetition at lexical, semantic, or thematic levels of the text. What repetition is retained — notably at the morphemic and phonemic levels — is so tightly localized as to pass beneath the attentional threshold of many readers.

Juxtaposing discrepant source texts and experimenting with various degrees of authorial mediation from strict recomposition of predetermined lexical sets to relatively free improvisations, Smith's interpretations of collage privileges the purposely awkward combination, the collapsed or evaded pattern, the raised seam on a resolutely "non-poetic" surface, packed densities of linguistic intersection suddenly thinning into permeable membranes of direct address. The dozen-poem sequence "For Loss," for example, plays a series of forebodingly technical titles ("On the Calculation of Spherical Aberration Dependence" or "Rare-Earth Activated Harmonium Pulse") against wisp light evocative phrasal fragments. Who would guess that the caption "Heterostructure Injection" would yield: "states / not / more / wish / to enter / people / always / fear / death / but // make / innovations. This is called the secret's innovation. / The reason is plain / but the people / like by-paths" (15)? The non-restrictive syntactic sequences, the words and word-clusters floating in semi-autonomy, the unanchored negative particle reversing what meanings do congeal, all endow (inject?) the text with a flickering agitation (heterostructure?) at odds with the intimations of tranquility in the lexical remnants from Lao Tzu's source text.

The same device of making the conventional distinction between title and textual body into an opportunity to force two non-communicating registers into tense proximity is found in the early *Boy Poems* and in sequences from the recent *Protective Intimacy* like "The Era of Poets," and a group employing well-known book titles ("The Responsibility of Intellectuals," etc.). Smith's sharing out of transparency-familiarity-dominance (concentrated in the titles) and opacity-defamiliarization-subversion) concentrated in the texts) suggests a condition in which the middle-range of communicative competence has been violently elided: it is "for loss" of such a band of possibility that the hypertrophied scientific jargon of the Bell Laboratories stands in unmediated, indeed irreconcilable, relation to the "sufficient / bewildered / humility" of the text bodies (56). As Smith says in "Simon," one of the *Boy Poems*: "these alternatives can not be harmonized." But their dissonance is, as his practice consistently shows, itself ample ground for a compelling and disclosing poetics.

LEE ANN BROWN

At the close of *Crush* (1993), her early and influential Steinian anthem to irreducible erotic and poetic plurality, Lee Ann Brown writes: "I say these things not because they happen but because many things happen" (*Polyverse* 187). The remark makes a fitting caption to *Polyverse*, Brown's vast and various debut volume of nearly two hundred pages, more anthology in fact than monograph, where tightly economized anagrams for the Muses, nimble exercises in style, twice-heard hymns, giddy collaborations, cultivated verse gardens, long distance sentences (five pages from capital to period), and every sensually shaped stanza known to lyric form, are enlisted to break down the poetry-impatient modern reader's resistance and open them to the pleasures of the art:

"After Sappho"

So many people
advised me against you.
How glad I am
we could not resist. (24)

Just consider the polyverted word-set of Brown's "Sestina Aylene," part of the section "Occasionally Named" in "Her Hearsay Hymnbook":

Beginning to pen a verse
I think of you —
what you must love
to do and do with ease:
Present a fruit or number
As from an empty

drawer. What's as empty
as the way we begin? Averse
to all Eve's droppers who number
our ways? Fact is, you
do much to ease
the why of Miss P. Love

or Funk: letter out. Love
letters love to be read as empty
poems or flowers named [heart's] ease,
the way a verse
faces to or on or in you,
for you can only then begin to number,

never delimiting that number
of ways in which you love
to make a poem. You
can tell a story of empty
necessity, a ring averse
to being filled too easily, to ease

simple closure. Easy
readings are possible but soon outnumber
even each other. A verse
demands a second love,
a torn page. Empty
breath slows through it, you

are surprised, you
read it slowly over, ease
into its second skin. Empty
fruits multiply and renumber
spaces to fill out love,
for ways to make a verse

not averse to being held a little longer. You
love to run and ease
into numbers of empty stays or stars. (74)

The direct address of one woman poet to another, the conversion of formal constraint to occasion for autotelic pleasure, the Zukofskian thinking-through of limited lexical sets are all typical of Brown's poetry, as is the thematic insistence on love, the incorporation of popular culture references, and the retention of ludic childhood practices (here, using the rebus image for "heart" in the text) as resources that nourish more sophisticated codes.

Brown's eclectic measures are often turned to descriptive purposes, from the ekphrasis of four flowers in "Cultivate" through the whole gritty, broke, overworked, pending condition of Manhattan bohemia in "Comfit" and "Daybook," to the book's many incidents of recollected or enacted eros (the opening line of "Demi-Queer Notion" for instance, "As I pinch my nipples & think of you"; or all of "Thang"; or a delicious translation of Paulus Silentarius that begins "Let's take off all our clothes, / Honey, and lie down / with our skins touching in every place possible"). Despite the premium on *sensed* as contrasted to merely *sensible* language, a referential element nearly always lends her poems traction, the "little resistance" it takes, as she says in "Resistance Play," to make her "come / to terms" (135). One can say of Brown's "polyversal" word, as Zukofsky said of his "revolutionary" one, that "if it must revolve cannot escape having a reference. It is not infinite. Even the infinite is a term" ("An Objective" 16).

One of Brown's favorite wordplays involves swapping the Latin etymology of "sist" (from *sistere*, to set) for the Old Norse one from which we derive the word sister (*systir*) in words like "resistance" or "transistor." As Elaine Equi recently pointed out in the *Boston Review of Books*, Brown's poetic genealogy acknowledges "enthusiasm [as] the mother ("We are the daughters of enthusiasm"), excitement the sister ("Where are my excitement sisters") (27). And while she devotes a lovely work in quatrains, "Sill Songs," to her biological sister Beth, more often Brown has in mind sisters by elective affinity, poets and musicians above all, with whom she collaborates in every meaning, and degree of action, implied by that word (letter sensitive as always, she long ago identified her initials in the second syllable of the word: col*lab*oration). If Stein (after whom Brown named her press Tender Buttons and under whose spell "Crush" was clearly written) is the mother of us all, and Bernadette Mayer the mother desirous "to please others in letters," even Frank O'Hara can get in, if ambivalently, on the engendering action:

> What's with these people
> boys or girls who tamp down
> the lyric impulse, the heart
> waiting in line, barefoot &
> illegal. Old-fashioned emotion
> is relegated to a loud radio
> void sometimes, but Frank O'Hara
> has faith in you & me even
> though or because we're girls.
>   ("To Jennifer M." 67)

JENNIFER MOXLEY

The first decade of Jennifer Moxley's poetry can be seen as an arc of successive formal integrations. Starting at zero-degree syntax with the pointillist lexical fields of *The First Division of Labour* (written 1989; published 1995), Moxley moved to syntactic ring-structures relying heavily on inversion and enjambment in *Enlightenment Evidence* (1996) before developing a disambiguated approach to poetic line in *Imagination Verses* (1996) that gathers a wild velocity and semantic volume in the ten poems of *Wrong Life* (1999). The subjective stances of these works differ as well. At the start of her oeuvre stand the words "how given chorus / a she complete" (*First* 1): the subjectivity is collective, inexorably gendered,[*] and censored by existing historiographic practices ("the annotated vanishing"). If *First Division* is a reflection *on* history (and as such indebted to the work of Susan Howe), *Enlightenment Evidence* is a reflection *in* history, where Rosa Luxemburg's life — subject to numerous relative arrests before the absolute one of her assassination in 1919 — is placed in a continuum shattering dialectic with the present-day of Gulf War America. There are naturally enough elements of dialog here and epistolary conventions of address deriving from Luxemburg's correspondence abound, but the more startling device involves a trans-historical doubling or fusion that effectively renders the first person pronoun choral/plural. The weave of pronominal person and number in the following section is typical, as is the interrogation of what underground living — political, poetic — does to those whose untimely ideals drive them to it:

> you are proud in your underground
> anxious of audience
> rumor by rumor you live
> like a shifting star
> no one could ever accuse out of mystery,
> you are living through me like a storefront
> who heart on my sleeve receives
> the blows directly, holy
> I am not nor wanted and yet
> truth drips down some days
> and people rise up, not holy

---

[*] The epigraph to *The First Division of Labour* is from Marx: ". . . there develops a division of labour, which was originally nothing but the division of labour in the sexual act."

this lifeless body but hollowed
and in the field of foreign ground
from the murderous public river it shall
rise up (21)

Choral and dialectical modes of address develop next into what Moxley, in her preface to *Imagination Verses*, refers to as an engagement with the "universal lyric 'I'" (x). As with the flagrant *literaturnost* of the book's design, the calculated anachronism of the generic "Verses" in the title, and the demonstrative embrace of that galaxy of emotive-linguistic excesses known in 20th-century American poetry by the name of Hart Crane in the epigraph "What blame to us if the heart live on," Moxley puts the words "universal lyric 'I'" out there like a dare to the doxological avant-gardist who learned in the 1970s to sneer at it as an "ideological constuction." But that neither this facile rejection, nor any equally facile return to some prior state of supposed self-transparency is the point can be seen in the first line of "Home World," the ode that opens *Imagination Verses*: "I will say what the register calls forth . . ." (3). The "I" conspicuously leads, but what it "will say" originates in "what the register calls forth," and that register is not only a utopically wide-horizoned experiential spectrum but also the unavoidable terminus of so many social relations in capitalism, the cash register, itself as much a concrete universal as the lyric I ever was.

Moxley, both in the early manifesto "Invective Verse" (1993) and the preface to *Imagination Verses*, envisions poetry as the negation or frustration of the limits society imposes on the expressive potential of subjects whether individual or collective. This negation is sometimes figured as explosive popular fury, as in "Ode to Protest," or as singular poetic task, as in "The Easter Lesson" of *Wrong Life*, which concludes in a ballade-like envoi where the conventional "prince" has become a poet:

Poet, at the mid-point of our life's journey the vault will set a block to entry,
young in thought the world, despite these apparitions of grace, shall abandon you
to its discrepancies. Can you manage the small acts of sacrifice
though they bleed the matter from your life? Can you doubt what you are risking
when, as the linchpin of four thousand years, you choose to provide the limits? (21)

Dante is the audible model for the lines, but a remark of Hegel's echoes here also: "Humans who want to be actual must be there, and to this end they must limit themselves. Those who are too fastidious toward the finite achieve nothing real at all, but remain in the realm of the abstract and peter out."* With this notion of the "limit" we come full circle to Kevin Davies's work, like Moxley's positioned at the limit, straining for transformation, and to the "simple poetic undertaking" Oppen proposed and each of the six poets I've discussed accept and distinctively interpret: "to see if life is livable, to make life livable. Without lying" (190).

—Providence and Paris, 1996-99

WORKS CITED

Adorno, Theodor W. *Negative Dialectics*. Trans. E.B. Ashton. New York: Continuum, 1990.

-------. "Cultural Criticism and Society." *Prisms*. 1967. Trans. Samuel and Shierry Weber. Cambridge: MIT P, 1981.

Bernstein, Basil. "Language and Socialization." *Linguistics at Large*. Ed. Noel Minnis. St. Albans, UK: Paladin, 1973. 225-42.

Brown, Lee Ann. *Crush*. Buffalo: Leave, 1993.

-------. *Polyverse*. Los Angeles: Sun & Moon, 1999.

Barber, Benjamin R. "Culture McWorld contre democratie: Vers une societe universelle de consommateurs." *Le Monde Diplomatique* 533 (1998): 14-15.

Burger, Peter. *Theory of the Avant-Garde*. 1974; 1980. Trans. Michael Shaw. Minneapolis: U of Minnesta P, 1984.

Bourdieu, Pierre. *The Rules of Art: Genesis and Structure of the Literary Field*. 1992. Trans. Susan Emanuel. Stanford: Stanford UP, 1995.

Dark Ages Clasp the Daisy Root. Ed. Andrew Schelling and Benjamin Friedlander in Oakland, California, 1989-1993.

Darragh, Tina. *adv. fans - the 1968 series*. (Buffalo: Leave, 1995).

Davies, Kevin. *Karnal Bunt* [tentative title]. Washington, DC: Aerial / Edge, forthcoming.

-------. *Thunk*. New York: Situations, 1995.

-------. *Pause Button*. Vancouver: Tsunami, 1992.

-------. "From *Overkill / a protocol*." *Raddle Moon* 17 (1998): 80-89.

-------. "From *Overkill / a protocol*." *Lingo* 8 (1998): 46-52.

-------. "From *Throb (Claymation Kakistocracy, or)*." *Boo* 6 (1996)

-------. "From *Duckwalkingaperimeter*." *Exact Change Yearbook* 1 (1995) 108-111.

-------. "From *Meanstreak*." *Raddle Moon* 14 (1995): 57-63.

-------. "From *Throb (Claymation Kakistocracy, or)*." *Impercipient* 7 (1995): 61-67.

-------. "From *Ephemerratatagalongonetceteradiosologoff*." *Impercipient* 5 (1994): 41-47.

Eribon, Didier. *Michel Foucault*. 1989. Trans. Betsy Wing. Cambridge: Harvard UP, 1991.

Evans, Steve. "The Dynamics of Literary Change." *Impercipient Lecture Series* 1 (February 1997): 1-54.

Encyclopedia Logic 92.148

———. Introduction to *Writing from the New Coast: Technique*. Ed. Juliana Spahr and Peter Gizzi. Providence: O•blek, 1993. 4-11.

Frank, Tom. "Titanic et la lutte des classes: La guerre sociale racontee aux enfants." *Le Monde Diplomatique* 533 (1998): 21.

Golding, Alan. *From Outlaw to Classic: Canons in American Poetry*. Madison: U of Wisconsin P, 1995.

Hegel, G.W.F. *The Phenomenology of Spirit*. Trans. A.V. Miller. Oxford: Oxford UP, 1977.

———. *The Encyclopedia Logic*. Trans. T.F. Geraets, W.A. Suchting, and H.S. Harris. Indianapolis: Hackett, 1991.

Hesiod. *Works and Days*. Trans. Hugh G. Evelyn-White. Loeb Classical Library 57: Hesiod, Homeric Hymns, Epic Cycle, Homerica. Cambridge, MA: Harvard UP, 1936. 3-65.

Hobsbawm, Eric. *The Age of Extremes: A History of the World, 1914-1991*. 1994. New York: Vintage, 1996.

Jakobson, Roman. *Language in Literature*. Edited Krystyna Pomorska and Stephen Rudy. Cambridge, MA and London: Belknap-Harvard UP, 1987.

———. "On a Generation That Squandered Its Poets." *Language in Literature*. 41-46.

———. "The Dominant." *Language in Literature*. 41-46.

Jarnot, Lisa. *Sea Lyrics*. New York: Situations, 1996.

———. *Some Other Kind of Mission*. Providence: Burning Deck, 1996

Jarnot, Lisa, Leonard Schwartz, and Chris Stroffolino, eds. *An Anthology of New (American) Poets*. Jersey City, NJ: Talisman House, Publishers, 1998.

Luoma, Bill. *Works & Days*. West Stockbridge and Great Barrington, MA: Hard Press / The Figures, 1998.

———. *Western Love*. New York: Situations, 1996.

———. *Swoon Rocket*. Great Barrington: The Figures, 1996.

———. *My Trip to New York City*. Great Barrington: The Figures, 1994.

———. "Poem (Face the arguments . . .)." *Impercipient* 7 (1995): 48-52.

Mayer, Bernadette. *Poetry*. New York: Kulchur, 1976.

Moxley, Jennifer. *Wrong Life*. Cambridge, UK: Equipage, 1999.

———. *Enlightenment Evidence*. Cambridge, UK: rem*press, 1996.

———. *Imagination Verses*. New York: Tender Buttons, 1996.

———. *The First Division of Labour*. Boston: Rosetta Chapbook, 1995.

———. "Invective Verse." *Writing From the New Coast: Technique*. Ed. Peter Gizzi and Juliana Spahr. Providence: O•blek, 1993. 182-83.

Nancy, Jean-Luc. "Finite History." 1990. *The Birth to Presence*. Trans. Brian Holmes et al. Stanford: Stanford UP, 1993. 143-66.

Nelson, Cary. *Repression and Recovery: Modern American Poetry and the Politics of Cultural Memory, 1910-1945*. Madison: U of Wisconsin P, 1989.

O'Hara, Frank. *Poems Retrieved*. Ed. Donald Allen. Bolinas, CA: Grey Fox, 1977.

Oppen, George. "'Meaning Is To Be Here': A Selection from the Daybook." *Conjunctions* 10 (1987): 186-208.

Ostashevsky, Eugene. "Dmitry Golynko-Volfson and New Petersburg Poetry." *Shark* 1 (1998): 74-84.

Silliman, Ron. "Canons and Institutions: New Hope for the Disappeared." *The Politics of Poetic Form*. Ed. Charles Bernstein. New York: Roof, 1990. 149-74.

———. "The Marginalization of Poetry by Bob Perelman." *Impercipient Lecture Series* 4 (May 1997): 1-12.

Smith, Rod. *Protective Immediacy (The Fire Works)*. Elmwood, CT: Potes & Poets, 1997.

———. *In Memory of My Theories*. Oakland: O Books, 1996.

———. *The Boy Poems*. Washington DC.: Buck Downs, 1994.

———. "John Cage." *Dictionary of Literary Biography*. Vol. 193: *American Poets Since World War II, Sixth Series*. Ed. Joseph Conte. Detroit: Gale, 1998. 33-45.

Spahr, Juliana. *Spiderwasp or Literary Criticism*. New York: Spectacular, 1998.

Stein, Gertrude. "Composition as Explanation." 1926. *Selected Writings*. Ed. and introd. Carl van Vechten. New York: Vintage, 1990.

Stroffolino, Chris. "The Inescapable Injustice of the Imagination: On the Recent Work of Jennifer Moxley." *Chicago Review* 43.2 (1997): 94-104.

Wallace, Mark. "A Reading of Against: Juliana Spahr as Poet, Editor, and Critic." *Tripwire* 1 (1998): 110-121.

Williams, Raymond. *Marxism and Culture*. Oxford: Oxford UP, 1977.

———. *The Sociology of Culture*. 1981. Chicago: U of Chicago P, 1995.

———. "The Politics of the Avant-Garde." *The Politics of Modernism: Against the New Conformists*. London: Verso, 1989. 49-63.

Zukofsky, Louis. "An Objective." *Prepositions: The Collected Critical Essays*. Expanded edition. Berkeley: U of California P, 1981.

Loss Pequeño Glazier

POETS | DIGITAL | POETICS

> A system / Itself / Both on the roots /
> Praxis / Where it is / Is between /
> Puzzles / Vivid forms
> — Bruce Andrews (50)

A GENEALOGY OF CONTEMPORARY POETRY IN THE LAST THIRD OF THE TWENTIETH CENTURY could not be complete without a consideration of major advances in new media. Though the connection between traditional print and digital media poetry can at times seem less than direct, a strong argument must be made for such a connection. An even greater possibility lies in the potential for digital media poetry *to make literal* specific defining innovative practices of the past century. To whatever degree one accepts the thesis of this direct connection, it is clear that the ramifications of digital media for innovative poetries are immense.

At the outset, the evolution of the Web over the past decade has decisively changed the economies that factor the production and circulation of innovative poetries. A print magazine or print press, for example, can no longer maximize their publishing efforts without a Web presence. To do without would be to unnecessarily exclude readers. They would also miss the chance to present supplementary materials that can draw potential readers to the work. Such materials include not only book descriptions and order information but also tables of contents, online appendices, excerpts — even the complete texts of books.* The impact of the Web on print publishing cannot be denied. It has even changed the meaning of "out of print" since the idea of inventory now extends to every copy of a book in an unimaginably large universe of bookseller locations. As an instance of this change, after a two-year wait I was notified yesterday by an online service that a copy of *The*

---

*Indeed, the idea of "the book" itself has been re-cast through this process, suggesting that the tangibles in these economies have forever shifted. Coach House Books (http://www.chbooks.com, 18 June 2002) regularly supplies full text online versions of books and Roof Books has recently embarked on a project to see how making available online versions, for free versus for a fee, of a book affect sales of that book. (See http://epc.buffalo.edu/presses/roof, 18 June 2002 and http://www.roofbooks.com, 18 June 2002.)

Policeman's Beard Is Half Constructed (1984) was just located for me. It would have taken a lifetime, given the vagaries of luck and circumstance, to acquire this title by random browsing in used bookstores. Given the rise of corporate bookstore chains and the ever-shrinking number of bookstores that will stock small press, there is no small magazine nor small press who really wants to reach readers that can now do without the prospects the Web brings to their door.

The online book marketplace presents a dynamic that was unimaginable in previous decades, a force that opens up possibilities pioneered by independent presses from the earliest movements to the present. Indeed, the relation between poetry and its production cannot be separated from the fact of the poetry itself. It is no small coincidence that poetry that reinscribes the status quo (with exceptions of course) has the whole apparatus of the ruling ideological machine standing at its side, the Pulitzer Prizes, the major presses, the public television specials about poetry. (In a sense such poetry can *claim* to stand outside of production since it remains in its center, the corporate conglomerate structure of the production of culture.) But what about production that seeks to instantiate a cultural alternative? You can find numerous instances of the relationship between these efforts and the fact of literary production. From Robert Creeley's Divers Press through the crucial output of the Mimeo Revolution (New York's *The World* and the publications of d.a. Levy for example) to the desktop publishing revolution of the 1980s, it has been a fact of literary history that *how* poetry is published is in direct relation to *what* it is. These engagements are intertwined and neither can stand alone.

It would follow then that the digital medium, especially when engaged for the purpose of circulating innovative poetries, cannot be isolated from its mode of production. What is to be made of this? Certainly, presses which focus on print can continue to use the digital medium solely for the circulation of print wares; obviously, the medium is so plural that there can be no lack of room for that activity. (Indeed, more power to any effort to circulate innovative poetry!) But is it not a fact of the human creative spirit that once a new tool comes to hand, the artist wonders what *else* can be made with it? More compellingly, for innovative poets, how can it not be possible that the medium — and its process of literary production — does not become part of poetry itself?

PRINT'S BLEEDING EDGE

TO FIND A MODEL FOR THE MERGING OF LITERARY PRODUCTION WITH TECHNOLOGY one needs go no further than one's local small press. Small press, in its many different manifestations, has fueled independent, dissident, and alternative forms of literary expression, at times pioneering new locations for writing. Whether seizing upon discarded mimeo machines, capitalizing on an available xerox, or taking advantage of a page layout program, small press can serve as the site where several production paradigms converge. What often happens is that, in small press, the production of literature and literature itself become intertwined. Since small press has historically engaged such issues, the border between small press and digital technology is especially interesting. Of particular note are two presses representing, in different ways, the heart of small press, Burning Press and Xexoxial Endarchy, operations which have been conscious of literary production. Each has used the Web both as a means of promotion and for its inherent qualities.

Luigi-Bob Drake's Burning Press is the publisher of the tabloid format *Taproot Reviews*, a crucial collection of reviews of small press publications. (The tabloid format is, within the world of small press, itself a literary production strategy.) For those interested in small press, *Taproot Reviews* provided essential material but had become increasingly difficult to find by the early nineties. Drake's vision of *Taproot* makes its resources most effective existing across several technologies. Accessible from *Taproot*'s Web page (http://www.burningpress.org/tree/abouttrr.html, 19 June 2002) are: (1) *Taproot Reviews* (TRR), the original paper version; (2) "*Taproot Reviews* Electronic Edition (TRee)," the e-mail version (also archived at the Electronic Poetry Center, http://epc.buffalo.edu/ezines/tree, 19 June 2002); (3) the "WWW version of *Taproot*" a cumulative, indexed, and searchable version at the Electronic Poetry Center (http://epc.buffalo.edu/ezines/treehome/treeHome.html, 19 June 2002), and; (4) "TReeWWW," reviews of and links to Web magazines (http://www.burningpress.org/tree/treeweb.html, 19 June 2002). The Web versions of *Taproot* have made hundreds of crucially important reviews widely accessible. Further, the Web actually expanded the possibilities of the print version of the journal, with the print version now moving on to focus more on news while "the Web archives focused on using the search and cumulative index as a historical document" (Drake n.p.). As this analysis shows, Burning Press has spread itself across technologies of dissemination with vision, foresight, and intelligence, functioning with alacrity within ever-shifting means of literary production. Burning press, Drake explains, is what he calls "a micropress publisher." This is an effort "consciously situating itself below the horizon of small press. We are advocates of modes of poetic production outside the canon" (n.p.). Once TRee had made its appearance on the Web, a number of extraordinary sister projects came into being. "The Web allows us to do some different kinds of things — the aggregation of the CybpherAnthology project, for instance — but most of our Web-based projects focus on Web-specific capabilities" (n.p.). A visit to the Burning Press site (http://www.burningpress.org, 18 June 2002), "an in-process attempt to locate community(s) among various online writing projects" (Burning, n.p.), features the "CybpherAnthology Project," "Wr-eye-tings Scratchpad" (an online laboratory and showcase for WWWeb-based intermedia), "Machine Made of Words" (a virtual gallery of online hypertext/vizlit and audioart), "InYrEar: Performance and Sound poetries" (sound files), "Textworx Toolshed" (downloadable programs for aleatoric text manipulation, manglement, etc.), as well as *Taproot Reviews*, (reviews and documentation of literary small presses providing a snapshot of the alternative poetry scene in the mid 1990's).

Another project that made a similar transition from innovation in its analog form to digital experimentation is Xexoxial Endarchy, a project started by Miekal And, Lyx Ish (then Elizabeth Was), and others. Significant works of experimental literature appeared in print and audio format under the aegis of this press. Like many small presses, Xexoxial was quite conscious of its means of production. The press was one of the first to publish on demand, stocking its titles as master copies that could be printed and bound when requested. Publisher Miekal And notes: "In some ways the concepts of archive & publisher have become very interchangeable for us" (And n.p.). How can production be related to the literature it produces? Miekal And suggests one way this might happen.

> When we first began we were most interested in publishing work which had no other venues for publication, or in particular not a large enough audience to warrant being picked up by offset publishers who needed to sell x amount of copies in order to meet the expense of the release. (n.p.)

This recognition of the means of literary production also allowed the press to focus on an international range of authors, with a particular emphasis on visual-verbal literature, producing an author list distinct from other types of publishers.

Xexoxial began incorporating digital technology into its production around 1985, first incorporating digital typography as a component of cut-and-paste and other handmade processes. The press has also concentrated on more digitally-specific projects, especially the *Internalational Dictionary of Neologisms* (http://cla.umn.edu/joglars/neologisms/dictionary.html, 19 June 2002), an online dictionary of neologisms begun in 1985. Xexoxial's website (http://www.cla.umn.edu/joglars/xe, 19 June 2002) contains links to press projects "Xexoxial Editions," "Xerolage," and "Audio Muzixa Qet." Through its focus on production, Xexoxial's approaches to the circulation of writing anticipated the Web paradigm, "years before the Internet became a household appliance" (n.p.). Because of this, the press underwent a rather seamless transition to the emergent environment and its new communities. Of the digital medium as a publishing environment and its relation to literary production, Miekal And notes:

> More options are presented in that in the old days I would have had to include an audio cassette to have sound accompany a book, or I would have had to approximate animation with the use of gesture & design in my books. In many ways works have become much more fully realized, more fleshed out. Perhaps because the options have become so vast with what you can do with online culture, it has groomed our vision to a more specific output, but the vision of global visual-verbal literature existing within an active community of like works is really starting to materialize on the Web with the same kind of force & virtue that one saw via the postal system in the 80s. (n.p.)

Miekal And himself has used a computer since about 1984 and he has also written a book called *Polynoise* which, he notes is, "Essentially ... about what I called then Noise Culture ... which anticipates a polyintermedia digital culture" (n.p.). The implications of the digital environment were great for And as an individual artist. In 1985 he began working with Hypercard, a programming environment which allowed him to create computerized hypermedia pieces combining text, animation, sound, and interactivity, works distributed through university BBS's and through the mail on diskette. In the digital medium, Miekal And's work is widely known as he continues to forge new paths for the press and as an individual artist. Available at And's new "Joglars Crossmedia Beliefware" site (http://cla.umn.edu/joglars, 19 June 2002) are a number of projects, those listed here as well as many more ground-breaking digital works including "Samsara Congeries," "Pataphysical Sobriety Test," "The Plagiarist Codex," "After Emmett," "Mesostics for Dick Higgins," "Seedsigns," and "Text_Tower."

Such presses are interesting because of their strategic navigation of literary production across print and digital media. A potential next step in thinking about literary production in the digital environment would be an examination of e-zines and purely digital publications such as *Jacket, Arras, Dichtung Digital,* the *Electronic Book Review,* Alienated.net, and other projects that, evincing the small press spirit, are also involved in an interrogation of the materiality and production issues of their medium. Most pressing, however, is to delineate how materiality relates to practice.

AN ABSTRACT OF DIGITAL PRACTICE

THE LINK WITH PRODUCTION has demonstrated that the small press spirit is a useful lens through which to view innovative practice in emergent media. However, small press is by nature a print-based phenomenon, and it is important to emphasize that the e-medium offers more than static letters on the screen. If we look at broader interactions between innovative literature and digital media in the late twentieth and early twenty-first centuries, notable ranges of activity become apparent. It must be stressed that this sketch of the field will appear markedly different than most maps of digital practice since the focus here is on *innovative* digital literary practice.

Such a sketch would span: (1) Poets who worked with computers before the Web, including such luminaries as John Cage and Jackson Mac Low; (2) Pioneers of e-poetry before and during the transition to the Web who made connections with innovative poetry, including programmer-poets such as John Cayley, Philippe Bootz, Jim Rosenberg, other Hypercard authors, and early Web developers; (3) younger New Media designers of specific medium-defining works, including Brian Kim Stefans ("The Dreamlife of Letters" http://www.rhizome.org/object.rhiz?2088, 20 June 2002), and Judd Morrissey and Lori Talley ("My Name Is Captain, Captain," Eastgate Systems, 2002), interface-based authors as well as programmers.

Not included here are hypertext writers who practice conservative or conventional poetics and artists who might be termed "pseudocode practitioners." This last area is a difficult one to define, relying on a subtle aesthetic distinction. Works in this category, though measures of mastery in the medium, could be said to focus on language issues more related to cybercultural theory than to innovative poetics. Though these are compelling aesthetic works, they fall outside of some of the material issues that an innovative poetics would pursue. Finally, mention must be made of major twentieth century innovators, poets who have defined the possibilities of innovative poetry in previous contexts. Bruce Andrews, Charles Bernstein, and Barrett Watten, poets mostly in their fifties and unarguably leaders in their fields, have come to new media poetries with particular and special insights and are thus of critically important interest. Bernstein has written a number of works that address writing and digital technology, including "Electronic Pies in the Poetry Skies" a hypertext essay that has been performed in a number of venues. (This work is newly available via the "Writings" section of Coach House's "Articles & Reports" page (http://www.chbooks.com/articles/index.html#writings, 18 June 2002). Andrews has published a penetrating analysis of new media poetics in his essay, "The Poetics of L=A=N=G=U=A=G=E" (http://www.ubu.com/papers/andrews.html, 18 June 2002) and has been an engaged and perceptive interrogator of the possibilities for digitally driven innovative writing processes. Watten's interest in "information poetics," the production of poetry from language sources including listservs, is evidenced by a number of his recent postings, presentations, and papers.

For an historical overview that includes many more specific examples, including discussions of works from Emmett Williams, Oulipo, and Mac Low and works circulated on magnetic media and the Web, the reader should see "E-poetries: A Lab Book of Digital Practice, 1970-2001." Published in *Digital Poetics* (Glazier 126-152). This detailed history was originally written for *The World in Time and Space* but then superseded by the present essay. "A Lab Book" provides an essential kernel for *Digital Poetics* as it attempts to chart half a century of digital practice and its relation to innovative poetry, from hypertext through kinetic/visual text to works in programmable media. Despite the various arguments it raises and its suggestion that this last area may ultimately prove the most interesting, *Digital Poetics* itself might be seen as a frame through which to engage the digital medium, the frame of contemporary poetics. Poets have been dealing with many of the same textual issues that are critical to digital media. Despite this fact, the literature of digital media rarely includes references to innovative poetry. The goal of *Digital Poetics* is to map some preliminary points of intersection between these conversations, the digital and that of innovative poetics, to try to find paths leading to an awareness of digital media *as writing*.

Suggested above is an abstracted list of practitioners, presented in order to define compass points on the map of the field of new media poetry. This outline of practice is admittedly broad in concept and limited in specifics; but this sketch is intentionally brief since what we want to identify are the salient forms that illuminate innovative digital practice as an extension of innovative poetries. Thus, the economy of this sketch is an effort to draw an axis of practice for new media poetries.

A NEW MEDIA POETICS

CONSIDERING DIGITAL WRITING AS LITERARY PRODUCTION and focusing on the potentials of its materiality we arrive at a threshold where innovative print practice seems to naturally extend into the digital medium. We can see the trajectories of late twentieth century innovative practice and we can identify the sites where these practices resonate in the new medium. Strikingly, however, this threshold also seems to function as a barrier. There are ways that innovative practices of the late twentieth century do *not* seem to effortlessly extend into new media. Here we must take stock of two major issues.

1. Not all digital projects are innovative. Being on the screen doesn't make it "new media." This confusion arises for several reasons: because the field of new media writing is new, because it tends to be more visual than print, and because it tends to be more cross-disciplinary and multimedia-based. Finally, there is the fact that when you see something for the first time, as they say to advertise summer sitcom reruns, it is new to you. Nonetheless, we are now at a more advanced stage in the evolution of our e-textual sensibilities. Thanks in part to the deluge of animated banners and the multitudes of unsolicited web sites proffered to us on a regular basis, we can now say that just because something is on screen does not mean it is innovative. But even when it comes to new media works self-described as literature, the distinctions are not always clear, especially when the technical aspects are sophisticated, clever, and skillfully crafted (as in the "pseudocode practitioners" mentioned above and some multimedia hypertext works). Of e-poems themselves, how do you separate the grain from the chaff? Finding digital literature that would be relevant to innovative poetics requires a good deal of discretion. Events such as E-Poetry 2001, which occurred in Buffalo last year, designed specifically as a poetry *festival*, are helpful in defining areas of interesting activity. (See the link from http:// epc.buffalo.edu/e-poetry, 20 June 2002.) Also useful are curated collections of innovative digital poetries such as the EPC's E-Poetry page (http://epc.buffalo.edu/e-poetry, 20 June 2002), the "Contemporary" section of Kenneth Goldsmith's UbuWeb (http://www.ubu. com, 20 June 2002), and the *Arras* "Gallery of Digital Poetry" (http://www.arras.net/ gallery.htm, 20 June 2002). Most important, however, is to *read* digital literature with as much discrimination as you would read print writing. Engaging in reading without, metaphorically speaking, being blinded by the glare from the screen is presently the most pressing task for writers and critics of new media writing.

2. There is a large core of innovative poets who continue their practice solely in the print medium. Especially striking is the number of younger innovative poets, whether calling

themselves new New American poets or practicing in other innovative poetry circles, who clearly work the edge of the possibilities of writing yet seem to cling to print as definitive. These are often poets who publish within the production means of small presses and who read in galleries and avant-garde art spaces: their seeming acceptance of the authority of print is baffling. Especially when one considers the art and music world, cross-genre and multimedia works have long been within our collective cultural conversation. Even within writing itself, a codexcentric position seems against historic developments in exploring alternatives to the hegemony of print authority — Olson's sense of breath, Antin's performances, the inspired trans-lineations of Weiner, the visual arts of the Concrete poets, the analog voicings of the sound poets, the methods of Language practitioners — as if the momentum to leap from the confines of the page paradoxically leaves one frozen midstep on the rooftop ledge. Further, despite a body of critical theory that has expanded definitions of the materials of cultural practice, the startlingly conservative assumption seems to remain that print is more serious, that there is more rigor in having words in print. But is it the rigor or the rigor mortis of print that marks that final threshold that cannot be crossed? It is the sense of authority of print that should be questioned. This is where the trajectory of innovative practice comes in. Clearly, critics should be aware of the dynamics of such authority — but most important are the poets. Those whose immediate concern is the working of words are sorely missed on the front lines where it is indeed language colliding in these new literary engagements. If print cannot be considered dead, at least we could agree it is inert. The features of new media writing — mark-up, scripting, and the dynamic subtleties of programming — offer rich, alternative locations for writing. In a sense this would be a call to get with the program and explore language that embodies action.

A new media poetics would argue that the most interesting fact is not simply crossing the digital line. It is no virgin terrain: there are plenty of people already there. Some truly interesting artists occupy this field — but there are also legions of conventional writers, re-representing poetry's dullest clichés with static rollovers, colored fonts, and swarms of predictable links. Yet, it could not be truer that the prime terrain of this medium is yet to be staked out. The most compelling subtleties of this threshold by no means have been fully explored — the threshold of what language is as material in the medium. What is needed is the poet's exploration of the pliant contours of digital media as language, language that is action in itself, language in its plural possibilities on the other side of the screen.

WORKS CITED

And, Miekal. "Re: Xexoxial Endarchy, A Few Details." E-mail to Loss Pequeño Glazier (2002): 18 June 2002.
Andrews, Bruce. *Wobbling*. New York: Roof, 1981.
"Burning Press." Web Site, http://www.burningpress.org: 18 June 2002.
Drake, Luigi-Bob. "Re: Some Questions." E-mail to Loss Pequeño Glazier (2002): 15 June 2002"
Glazier, Loss Pequeño. *Digital Poetics: The Making of E-Poetries*. Tuscaloosca: U of Alabama P, 2002.
"Xeoxial Endarchy." Web Site, http://www.cla.umn.edu/joglars/xe: 18 June 2002.

Alan Golding

NEW, NEWER, AND NEWEST AMERICAN POETRIES*

"KOALA — To survive you have to be willing to do anything. Anthologies! That's where the money really is, or might be. At least so I imagine from my fuzzy animal distance. Reprint the material! Dominate the gene pool! Rise like Godzilla and make them read you for fucking ever!" —Bob Perelman, "*The Manchurian Candidate*: a remake"

The AVANT-GARDE, WE'RE TOLD, IS, AT LEAST IN THEORY, DEAD. Meanwhile, the poetic "mainstream" is commonly argued to have become so diverse and democratically inclusive as to be unlocatable, unrecognizable as a mainstream. This same historical moment, however, with its purported all-inclusiveness that would render the notion of an avant-garde meaningless, has brought the publication of five self-consciously avant-garde anthologies of American poetry within a few years of each other: Eliot Weinberger's *American Poetry Since 1950: Innovators and Outsiders* (1993); Douglas Messerli's *From the Other Side of the Century: A New American Poetry, 1960-1990*; Paul Hoover's *Postmodern American Poetry: A Norton Anthology*; Dennis Barone and Peter Ganick's *The Art of Practice: 45 Contemporary Poets* (all 1994); and Leonard Schwartz, Joseph Donahue and Edward Foster's *Primary Trouble: An Anthology of Contemporary American Poetry* (1996).† What especially interests me in our current situation, and in these texts specifically, is the apparent re-emergence of a version of the late 1950s and early 1960s anthology wars, as anthology editors are once again unapologetically using terms like "avant-garde," "center," "mainstream," and so on.

---

*"New, Newer, and Newest American Poetries" first appeared in *Chicago Review* 43.4 (1997): 7-21.

†I have chosen these anthologies because they claim to represent a range of experimental practice (and it's worth noting how claims to cover the field of recent experimental writing continue to come from the time-honored editorial position of the white male). These ambitions stand in contrast to the more specific concerns of such recent gatherings as Maggie O'Sullivan's *Out of Everywhere* or Walter Lew's *Premonitions*, with their emphasis on linguistically innovative work by North American and UK women and Asian North Americans respectively. Historically situated "outside the outside" in Eliot Weinberger's phrase (xii), women and minorities have a different relation to the "mainstream vs. margin" rhetoric of recent experimentalist anthologies from that of white male writers with whom they may have much in common aesthetically.

Does the return of anthology wars rhetoric that I'll discuss here represent merely the flogging of a dead socioaesthetic horse? Jed Rasula, for one, argues that it does. He finds Weinberger and J. D. McClatchy, editor of *The Vintage Book of Contemporary American Poetry*, for instance, "waging a massively retrospective combat" — a combat centered on "nostalgic invocations of the 1960 anthology wars, with the editors cavorting about in period dress like history buffs reenacting the battle of Gettysburg" (449).* Rasula has a point here; it's no longer 1960. But if this debate is so outdated, why has its rhetoric returned to anthologies of innovative poetry in the mid-1990s? What function does that rhetoric serve now? Aside from maintaining a good deal of historically descriptive power, it is being used by contemporary editors to further the development or construction of a *New American Poetry* tradition derived from Donald Allen's influential 1960 anthology of that name — a text that these editors both explicitly and implicitly invoke. In turn, connection to *The New American Poetry* becomes a way for editors to situate historically and even help authorize contemporary avant-garde writing. The construction of this New American tradition via recent anthologies — especially in the rhetoric or self-presentation of these texts, rather than their structure, contents, and so forth — is my subject in this essay.†

Rasula is right to point out the limitations of what I would call the center-margin model that shapes both my chosen anthologies, in their different ways, and to some extent my analysis of them. One such limitation is the risk of a too-easy and falsely stable binarism. Weinberger and Hoover, for instance, both tend to assume that mainstream poetic practice and ideology is monolithic and that "we" know it when we see it. As Hank Lazer suggests, however, that this reduction of poetic variety to an allegedly monolithic mainstream is itself a "rhetorical straw man of the (similarly multiple) avant-garde" (136). Nevertheless, if we think of "center," "mainstream," and "margin" as cultural locations that are in process rather than fixed, these misleadingly topographical metaphors can retain some analytic usefulness. If I seem both to suggest the inadequacy of a center-margin model and also depend on it for understanding patterns in recent anthologies, my point is that this model is growing more complex rather than collapsing completely. Further, in defense of these

---

*Meanwhile, neither anthology represents exactly what it seems to. *American Poetry Since 1950*, self-consciously an anthology of historically marginalized work, programmatically excludes one major grouping within its own tradition of "innovators and outsiders," the Language poets. Conversely, McClatchy's *Vintage Book*, in one way the quintessential mainstream anthology of recent years in its choice of Bishop and Lowell as founding figures, excludes almost all examples of the scenic lyric that for many readers constitutes the contemporary U.S. mainstream.

†For further discussion of Weinberger's and Hoover's anthologies specifically, and for further detail on how other later editors variously modelled their anthologies on *The New American Poetry*, see my *From Outlaw to Classic* 30-35 and 179-81.

texts, a *cluster* of alternative anthologies, demanding more attention than isolated collections, can more effectively counter an otherwise pervasive anthological inattention to innovative work. The discrepancy between the level of scholarly attention to Language writing and anthologists' bypassing of it, for example, has meant that commentary on that writing has often been more widely available than the writing itself.[*] But with experimental poetries now anthologized in such bulk, not only such inattention but also aesthetic tokenism — the mainstream inclusion of some aesthetically challenging work as a marker for that which can be ignored literally as long as it is represented symbolically — should also become much harder to defend.

Among the editors of these recent anthologies, Weinberger and Hoover especially apply a center-margin model in their representations of post-World-War II American poetry, in a way that openly derives from Allen's *New American Poetry*. Weinberger begins his preface: "For decades American poetry has been divided into two camps." He rightly describes the relationship between these "ruling and opposition parties" as "full of defections, unaligned members, splinter parties, internecine disputes and ideas stolen across the aisle" (xi). Nonetheless, his governing metaphor explicitly invites a replay of the old anthology wars. Thus Weinberger's concluding historical essay on the post-World-War-II period consistently pits the avant-garde against the Establishment, upper-case E and all. He distinguishes "middlebrow" producers of "Official Verse Culture" from "anti-establishment" "bands of rebels" (397). Again echoing Allen, he also pits the avant-garde against the academy, although this move later becomes problematic when he wants to make "avant-garde" and "academic" synonymous for the purpose of critiquing Language poetry (406).[†]

A similar rhetoric of avant-gardism pervades Paul Hoover's introduction to his *Postmodern American Poetry* — a rhetoric that itself can be seen as one defining feature of the particular anthological tradition deriving from *The New American Poetry*. Hoover explicitly makes the "postmodern" of his title synonymous with "avant-garde": "Postmodernist poetry is the avant-garde poetry of our time" (xxv) — a debatable equation, perhaps, but I am less

---

[*] Rasula observes that although Language poetry "has been repeatedly and favorably singled out in prestigious scholarly journals" and "routinely discussed in monographs," "there are *no* language poets to be found in over five thousand pages" of nine of the most visible and widely used poetry anthologies published since 1984 (458-59).

[†] The self-conscious oppositionality on which Weinberger's anthology rests also seems directed at Helen Vendler's *Harvard Book of Contemporary American Poetry*, if we read as a polemical gesture his starting with Pound and Williams and ignoring Stevens just as Vendler does the reverse. This contrast serves as yet another reminder of how larger debates within literary culture — in this case, the thoroughly fruitless and oversimplified argument over modernism as the Pound or Stevens "era" — get played out in anthologies, often in unacknowledged ways.

concerned here with the equation's accuracy, and more with the fact that Hoover makes it.* He frames his introduction with assertions of the continued relevance and vitality, aesthetic and political, of avant-garde practice: "This anthology shows that avant-garde poetry endures in its resistance to mainstream ideology" (xxv), he notes early on, and ends by dismissing those critics who argue "*unpersuasively* that 'innovation no longer seems possible, or even desirable'" (xxxix; my emphasis). In fact, Hoover operates on a thoroughly progressive model of avant-garde writing, a model that seems driven by a certain anxiety: "The poetry now being produced is as strong as, and arguably stronger than, that produced by earlier vanguards" (xxxix).

As a Norton publication aspiring to avant-garde status, Hoover's *Postmodern American Poetry* complicates any debate over center and margin even as it occupies a particular position within that debate. But Hoover barely touches on the institutionalization of the avant-garde that his anthology could be seen to represent. Nor, although he mentions it, does he respond to Fredric Jameson's implication that the "postmodern" is synonymous with "mainstream," or at least can be seen as a symptom, rather than a critique, of mainstream ideology — the opposite position from Hoover's own. For Hoover, as I've said, postmodernism is "an ongoing process of resistance to mainstream ideology," employing "a wide variety of oppositional strategies" (xxvi-xxvii). Thus he organizes his introduction around familiar contrasts: on the one hand, terms such as "postmodern," "avant-garde," "oppositional," "transgressive," "resistance," "revolt," and on the other, "centrist," "mainstream," "bourgeois self" — terms that mirror Weinberger's sense of "camps," his "opposition," "outsiders," and "ruling party." Not surprisingly, given this terminology, the mini-history of post-World-War-II American poetry that Hoover provides has a familiar founding moment: "In analyzing American poetry after 1945, it is traditional to point to the so-called battle of the anthologies," Hoover argues, and even goes on to contrast the "model poet" of each side in that battle.†

---

* In a further canonizing move, the anthology's jacket blurb — not necessarily authored by Hoover himself, I realize — makes "postmodern" and "avant-garde" synonymous with the category of "major poetry." The blurb describes the text as "the first anthology since Donald Allen's groundbreaking collection to fully represent the movements of American avant-garde poetry." This claim is followed by the far more generalizing and less tenable one that the anthology "offers a deep and wide selection . . . *of the major poets and movements of the late twentieth century*" (my emphasis).

† The alleged characteristics of these opposed "model poets" are familiar enough that they do not need reiteration here. On a related issue, however, the "battle of the anthologies" is usually taken to refer to the differences between Allen's *New American Poetry* (1960) and Donald Hall, Robert Pack, and Louis Simpson's *New Poets of England and America* (1957), with Hall and Pack's 1962 second edition a follow-up entry in the debates. In framing the "battle" as one over Allen's collection and the 1962 edition of *New Poets*, Hoover grants *The New American Poetry* a chronological primacy that it did not in fact enjoy.

Continuing this familiar set of oppositions, *Primary Trouble* gathers, in the words of Leonard Schwartz's introduction, "writers associated with the 'avant-garde' or 'anti-academic' segment or 'experimental wing' of American poetry" — though Schwartz admits these as "labels that most in the end will find inconclusive" (1). The text "seeks to elevate a certain poetics into view against the mainstream poetics that might obscure it" (3). In the words of the book's jacket, and in an echo of Donald Allen's well-known preface, we have here "poetry outside academic and conservative traditions," including work from "younger generations of poets influenced but unnostalgic about the work represented in Donald Allen's seminal anthology *The New American Poetry*" (1). (The editors also follow Allen in concluding with a section of statements on poetics.)

The relationship to New American traditions in *Primary Trouble* turns out, not surprisingly, to be a complex and ambivalent one, however. More specifically, for Schwartz as for some other editors, Language writing — itself a movement traceable in many ways to New American sources — becomes the site where an editor seeks to work through these complexities, to test the connection between *The New American Poetry* and contemporary claims to avant-garde status. Schwartz suggests three main, and often overlapping, areas of practice on which *Primary Trouble* draws. The first includes those poets just mentioned, working in a processual poetics traceable to *The New American Poetry* and earlier. A second group includes poets associated with or influenced by the New York School. And a third includes "poets who share some of the formal concerns of, and even may be affiliated in part with, the L=A=N=G=U=A=G=E project" (2). As we shall see later with Ganick and Barone's *The Art of Practice*, *Primary Trouble* manifests an ambivalent desire (at least as expressed in the editorial introduction) simultaneously to affiliate with and dissociate from Language writing, especially in representing younger avant-garde writers. Schwartz acknowledges that some of the *Primary Trouble* poets share certain interests with Language writing, "without on the other hand sharing in that school's agenda for poetic hegemony" (2). Repeating this accusation elsewhere, Schwartz refers to "the hegemonic mode of experimental formalism known as language poetry" (3), stressing also the absence of pleasure in that work just as Weinberger (399) alleges its humorlessness. As with Weinberger, then, we again find the editor of an avant-garde anthology accusing one avant-garde group of a desire for "poetic hegemony." (Meanwhile, within the text, Robert Kelly gently echoes Schwartz's skepticism in his exposition of a meditative, self-questioning poetics "similar to, and . . . perhaps more efficacious than, the project of de-referencing language" [451] theorized by Steve McCaffery and Bruce Andrews.) Thus the old argument that the margin merely wants to become the center gets played out within the alleged margin's own circles, as part of the contemporary avant-garde's attempt at anthological self-definition.

What sense of the "margin" and of New American anthological tradition operates in Douglas Messerli's *From the Other Side of the Century*? His volume had been brewing, Messerli notes, since 1984, and in this sense it is the project that his 1987 *"Language" Poetries* interrupted and wanted to be. As his anthology's Other, Messerli puts forward "the academized bastion of the *Norton Anthology of Modern Poetry*" (31) — interestingly, at a point in time when Norton is publishing one of the two texts, Hoover's, that compete with Messerli for a similar textbook market. He too begins his editorial introduction, then, by implicitly invoking the anthology wars between Allen and Hall, Pack, and Simpson's "academized" *New Poets of England and America*. Though Messerli leaves largely unanswered his own question as to "the role of anthologies in general," he does claim that "no major volume has served our own generation" (31) as *The New American Poetry* served Allen's, and presumably presents his own text to perform that service.

Messerli is not alone among this group of editors in perhaps trying too hard to replicate the impact of *The New American Poetry* under different historical circumstances that make it impossible to do so. Marjorie Perloff has argued that recent anthologies of innovative poetics are characterized by two recurrent features: belatedness and buttressing. They suffer from a kind of anxiety of lateness in relation to *The New American Poetry*, that is; and they serve to buttress an already established tradition rather than exploring new avenues.[*] This view helps put any claims to newness in perspective. At the same time, however, it provides only a partial description of these anthologies' projects. For Weinberger, Hoover, and Messerli, unlike Allen, are engaged not just in presenting new work but in *historicizing* its precedents. Thus buttressing involves far more than the mere repetition that Perloff seems to imply; it involves maintenance and preservation, yes, but also rearticulation, addition, and critique. Taken as a group, and allowing for differences in editorial emphasis, these collections go beyond a buttressing of *The New American Poetry* in numerous ways: in their revival and representation of the Objectivists (in Weinberger and Messerli); in their use of generically hybrid texts and what Stephen Fredman calls "poet's prose"; in their use of visual texts; and in their representation of an experimental women's writing, especially in *The Art of Practice*, the only one of the group that is fully gender-equitable (a representation furthered specifically in O'Sullivan's *Out of Everywhere* and Mary Margaret Sloan's *Moving Borders*).[†]

---

[*] For a thoughtfully skeptical reading of the belatedness in Weinberger, Hoover, and Messerli, see also Rasula 461-65, who argues that they anachronistically "perpetuate the sectarianism that was manifest" in *The New American Poetry*'s oppositionality and display "a nostalgia predicated on a 'recuperation' of New American poetic dissidents, but the logic is flawed because they've come too late to get in on the fruits of first acclaim" (461).

[†] It is also the case, however, as some commentators have pointed out, that none of the collections radically reconceives the genre of the anthology itself. See, for instance, Lazer 160 n 5. Richard Kostelanetz criticizes

The construction of this New American anthological tradition is furthered and complicated by Dennis Barone and Peter Ganick's *The Art of Practice*, which both extends New American poetic practice and critiques its predecessor anthologies. This is one sense in which it can be seen as an anthology, in Daniel Barbiero's term, of "post-Language" poetries.* While *Practice*'s forty-five poets is close in number to Allen's forty-four, the earlier text does not seem to be a model. Rather, in the editors' words, "the impetus for this anthology was two [other] previous ones," Silliman's *In the American Tree* and Messerli's *Language Poetries*. There are deliberately no overlaps with either of these collections. At the same time, Barone and Ganick share with Allen, Silliman, Hoover, and Messerli a sense of resistance to the institutionalized poetics of their own historical moment: they construct an anthology "opposed to the so-called natural free verse poem," on the assumption that "poetry is not the place for expression of common or authentic voice" (xiv, xiii). (The fact that *The New American Poetry* helped promulgate a poetics that, in the debased form of the notorious workshop lyric, became a later version of the "academic" — that the collection generated both its own tradition and that tradition's antithesis — is the subject for another essay.)†

While Barone and Ganick describe their organization as "somewhat democratic (not chaotic or autocratic)" (xv), it's hard to tell exactly what these terms mean in context (the volume's admirable gender equity being an issue of distribution rather than organization of space). Beyond local appropriate juxtapositions, such as placing the work of co-editors Jessica Grim and Melanie Neilson side by side, the principle of organization remains largely

---

Hoover's *Postmodern American Poetry* for excluding what he considers a whole range of avant-garde work that might also have forced rethinking of the anthology's nature: "It completely omits sound poetry, visual poetry, neologistic poems, minimal poems, site-specific poems, video poetry, poetry holograms, computer poetry, and comparable experimental forms" (17).

*Barbiero's review of *The Art of Practice* is much occupied with issues of lineage and with what is to follow Language writing. It begins: "The 45 poets included in this collection can all be seen as extending an open-form tradition that runs, roughly, from Pound and Williams through Language poetry via Surrealism, Objectivist & Projectivist verse, and points between and beyond." Thus, "although much of the work can legitimately be thought of as post-'language' poetry," it is also "very much part of a tradition" (7, 13). While the term "post-Language" does not appear in *The Art of Practice* itself, publicity materials for the volume described it as containing "over 400 pages of poetry generally considered 'avant-garde' or 'post-Language.'" For collections that also articulate various forms of a post-Language poetics, see the double issue of o•blek, #12 (spring/fall 1993),"Writing from the New Coast"; and Spahr et al, *A Poetics of Criticism*.

†Compare Silliman's historicizing of Language writing as involving a "complex call for a projective verse that could, in the same moment, 'proclaim an abhorrence of "speech"' — *a break within tradition in the name of its own higher values*" (*American Tree* xv; my emphasis)

submerged.* A "democratic" organization does show up, however, in the refusal to elevate any one poet or group of poets to accrediting or originary status. Indeed, *Practice* begins and ends with anti-authoritarian tropes. In an implied critique of the Allen-Weinberger-Hoover privileging of the notoriously phallocentric Olson and of U.S. writing, this anthology of North American writing begins with a Canadian woman poet and editor, Susan Clark, and ends with a barely published younger Canadian poet and editor, Louis Cabri. The editors appear as the second and penultimate selections: close to (but, importantly, not actually) framing the collection, but still not pretending disingenuously to merge or hide.

In one sense, however, Ron Silliman becomes an accrediting figure in the text, by having the last word — an afterword — and historicizing the collection. Reversing the anthology's title in his afterword, "The Practice of Art," Silliman places *Practice* in the New American Poetry tradition without precisely connecting it to Allen's anthology. He describes the collection as "a survey of the broader horizon of the progressive tradition in North American poetry," and on this basis differentiates it from his own and Messerli's first anthology, which did not "set out to represent the big picture of what we might think of as Post-New American Poetry" (372). Silliman stresses that "it's essential to recognize what this book is not: *In the American Tree: The Out-takes* or *Language Poetries: The Next Generation*" (371). If "margin and center have shifted over the past decade," that shift has occurred partly within the margin itself, in the form of "a critique by example of a narrowly configured (and macho) language poetry" (372). Thus a "critical response to language poetry becomes an unspoken unifying principle of *Practice*" (375), as it does to some extent in *Primary Trouble*. This critique is precisely what I think the notion of buttressing cannot accommodate. At the same time, in this consciously historicizing and canonizing afterword (one half of a framing context that also consists of the editors' more aesthetically oriented introduction), Silliman devotes much of his argument to constructing a New American Poetic lineage. He argues that "*Practice*'s passionate relationship to the New American Poetry of the 1950s and '60s may be more visible than that of the *Tree* only because of the lower level of militancy in editorial focus" — more visible, note, but not more genuine. Then he turns to a specific example from *Practice* to reinforce this construction of a lineage: "[Norman] Fischer's work offers the quintessential evidence for the argument that language poetry (so-called) embodies a direct

---

*Barone and Ganick describe their editorial procedure as follows: "We asked each poet to choose his or her work for the anthology, but we asked for more pages than we planned to use. We then made a selection from each author's work. We hope that our anthology has some collaborative trace to its presence" (xv). One appeal of this approach is that it allows the poets significant input into the anthology's contents. But it remains unclear how one would locate the "collaborative trace" — how a reader could tell in what ways, or even if, a selection was shaped by dialogue between editors and contributor.

extension of the New Americans, albeit an extension that transforms and problematizes its own understanding of what came before" (374).

Repeating his gesture from *In the American Tree*, where his list of exclusions is longer than his list of inclusions, Silliman goes on to name ninety-three writers who could have been included in *The Art of Practice*. He concludes, collating inclusions and exclusions across both texts, "that more than 160 North American poets are actively and usefully involved in the avant-garde tradition of writing is in itself a stunning thought" (377). Stunning indeed, though not in an entirely benign sense. This statistic has various possible implications. From one point of view, such numbers make the avant-garde robustly unassimilable simply because of its size. From another, they intensify, even necessitate, the tendency to reify the avant-garde in the work of a selected handful of writers. There is by now a substantial history to the critical trope that invokes "so-called" Language writing (it's always "so-called") and then "explains" the label by trotting out a list of paradigmatic names: "the so-called Language poets, such as. . . ." From yet another perspective, the idea of an avant-garde becomes meaningless once it refers to at least 160 writers in a single historical moment (and remember, Silliman is collating actual and potential inclusions only for two texts). That avant-garde is close to the size of its mainstream Other.

If we are to see recent anthologies of innovative writing as engaged in the ongoing construction or buttressing of a New American Poetry tradition, what kind of consensus on that tradition do they achieve? Despite the different purposes, criteria, and to some extent periods covered by Hoover, Weinberger, and Messerli (to turn to the more historically inclusive collections), sixteen poets appear in all three texts. Of 287 selections from these sixteen writers, however, not a single selection appears in all three anthologies. Further, out of that 287, only nine poems overlap between even two of the anthologies. The closest these texts come to consensus is that they each reprint sections (though different ones) from Clark Coolidge's *At Egypt*. (Also, regarding the writers they agree on, there's only one minority, Amiri Baraka, and one woman, Susan Howe.) Is this fruitful difference? Is it tradition as heterology? Is it sensible marketing strategy, with each anthology seeking to differentiate itself as it covers somewhat similar ground? Or is it incoherence? Given such differences, what might the notion of a New American tradition mean?

These are questions beyond the scope of this essay, but it seems crucial at least to raise them, and to relate them to others. How will we continue to negotiate aesthetic and sociocultural definitions of the "marginal" that are frequently at odds with each other?[*] To what

---

[*] For thoughtful recent discussions of these issues that successfully problematize the aesthetic-vs.-sociocultural or avant-garde-vs.-identity-politics binary, see Lazer, Mackey and Nielsen. For anthologies that do so, see Lew and Phillips.

extent *do* such terms as "margin," "avant-garde," "mainstream" remain critically viable, especially when none of them can be monolithically defined? For contemporary anthology editors, they play a significant role in constructing genealogies for particular areas of American poetry. At the very least, their recurrence suggests how hard it is to avoid heavily overdetermined language in discussing the complex web of poetic and social relations that is the contemporary American scene.

In a recent interview, Lyn Hejinian acknowledges how the anthologies that I have discussed complicate relations between "mainstream" and "margin":

> My career's ended up so much better than anything I would have dreamed could possibly happen, that I could never complain about being excluded. So much good has happened. I don't have any justification for being pissed off. As we're looking at the end of this century and these huge anthologies that are coming out, this correspondence [among poets] with complaints about being marginalized is going to look pretty ludicrous. The language poets, for instance, are being taught all over the place. It's not maybe the mainstreaming of the work, but it's not by any stretch marginal. (21)

From one point of view, "these huge anthologies" do render complaints about marginality a little silly. After all, the intensive anthologizing of experimental writing is one of the most visible developments in American poetry in this decade. But these texts may also represent less a mainstreaming, as Hejinian says, than the latest resting point in an ongoing upstream swim against the dominant current — the current represented in a comment from Bob Dole, front-page news on the day that I travelled to deliver the talk from which this essay derives: "The mainstreaming of deviancy has to be stopped."

WORKS CITED

Barbiero, Daniel. "States of the Art." *Witz* 3. 2 (spring 1995): 7-8, 13.
Barone, Dennis, and Peter Ganick, eds. *The Art of Practice:: 45 Contemporary Poets*. Elmwood, CT: Potes & Poets, 1994.
Fredman, Stephen. *Poet's Prose: The Crisis in American Verse*. New York: Cambridge UP, 1983.
Golding, Alan. *From Outlaw to Classic: Canons in American Poetry*. Madison: U of Wisconsin P, 1995.
Hejinian, Lyn. "The Eternal Repository." By Dodie Bellamy. *Chain* 2 (spring 1995): 19-25.
Hoover, Paul, ed. *Postmodern American Poetry: A Norton Anthology*. New York: W. W. Norton, 1994.
Kelly, Robert. "Spirit / Vanguard Art." Schwartz, Foster, and Donahue. 450-51.

Kostelanetz, Richard. "Slight of Foot."*American Book Review* 16. 6 (March-May 1995.): 17.

Lazer, Hank. *Opposing Poetries*. Vol. 1, *Issues and Institutions*. Evanston: Northwestern UP, 1996.

Lew, Walter K., ed. *Premonitions: The Kaya Anthology of New Asian North American Poetry*. New York: Kaya, 1995.

Mackey, Nathaniel. *Discrepant Engagement: Dissonance, Cross-Culturality, and Experimental Writing*. New York: Cambridge UP, 1993

Messerli, Douglas, ed. *From the Other Side of the Century: A New American Poetry 1960-1990* Los Angeles: Sun & Moon. 1994.

Nielsen, Aldon Lynn. *Black Chant: Languages of African-American Postmodernism*. New York: Cambridge UP, 1997.

O'Sullivan, Maggie, ed. *Out of Everywhere: Linguistically Innovative Poetry by Women in North America & the UK*. London: Reality Street, 1996.

Perloff, Marjorie."Whose New American Poetry? Anthologizing in the Nineties."*Diacritics* 26.3-4 (fall-winter 1996): 104-23.

Phillips, J. J., Ishmael Reed, Gundars Strads, and Shawn Wong, eds. *The Before Columbus Foundation Poetry Anthology: Selections from the American Book Awards, 1980-1990*. New York: W. W. Norton, 1992.

Rasula, Jed. *The American Poetry Wax Museum: Reality Effects, 1940-1990*. Urbana, IL: National Council of Teachers of English, 1996.

Schwartz, Leonard, Joseph Donahue, and Edward Foster, eds. *Primamry Trouble: An Anthology of Contemporary American Poetry*. Jersey City, NJ: Talisman House, 1996.

Silliman, Ron, ed. *In the American Tree: Language, Realism, Poetry*. Orono, ME: National Poetry Foundation, 1986.

-------. "The Practice of Art." Barone and Ganick 371-79.

Sloan, Mary Margaret, ed. *Moving Borders: Three Decades of Innovative Writing by Women*. Jersey City, NJ: Talisman House, 1998.

Spahr, Juliana, Mark Wallace, Kristin Prevallet and Pam Rehm, eds. *A Poetics of Criticism*. Buffalo: Leave, 1994.

Weinberger, Eliot, ed. *American Poetry Since 1950: Innovators and Outsiders*. New York: Marsilio, 1993.

APPENDICES

APPENDIX A. PRELIMINARY CHECKLIST OF THE PUBLICATIONS OF FRONTIER PRESS, 1965-1972

compiled by Michael Boughn

1. Dorn, Edward. *Rites of Passage*.

a. First edition, 1965.

THE RITES OF PASSAGE | a brief history | EDWARD DORN

Perfect binding; pp. [i-vi] 1-155 [156]. 15 x 21.5 cm.

On copyright page: "Cover by Raymond Obermayr".

b. Second edition [retitled], 1971.

By the Sound | [line drawing of a house by the sea] | Edward Dorn | Frontier Press | Mount Vernon, | Washington | 1971

[1-13]⁴; pp. [i-vii] 1-199 [200]. 13.8 x 21 cm. Paper wrappers.

On copyright page: "Drawings by Flavia Zortea | Design by Ron Caplan".

Note: Ron Caplan writes: "The cover—an odd green, like a slash of light downward—that's not mine. . . . They tore off the 'old' ones and pasted the new ones on. Of course, the rest of the book was as I designed it."

2. Adams, Brooks. *The New Empire*.

Second edition, 1967 [1902].

[device] | BROOKS ADAMS | THE NEW EMPIRE | Frontier Press | Cleveland, Ohio [dot] 1967 | [to the left of the previous two lines] [publisher's logo]

[1-6]¹⁶ [7]⁸ [8-9]¹⁶; pp. [i-vi] vii-ix [x-xii] xiii-xxxvii [xxxviii-xl] 1-197 [198] 199-228 [229-232]. 13.7 x 20.8 cm.

On p. [iv]: a poem by Charles Olson. On copyright page [vi]: "The book was composed and printed by the Crimson Printing Company, Cambridge, and bound by Stanhope Bindery, Boston."

3. Sanders, Edward. *Peace eye.*

Second (enlarged) edition, 1967.

PEACE EYE | Ed Sanders | [device] | [publisher's logo] | FRONTIER PRESS | Cleveland, Ohio

Loose sheets triple-stapled through the spine and glued into paper wrappers; pp. [1-84]. 20.8 x 26.6 cm.

On p. [5]: introductory poem by Charles Olson. A 6.3 cm. wide strip of very red (C11) paper is folded around the cover, and on it [in black]: "2nd ENLARGED EDITION".

4. Woodward, W.E. *Years of Madness: A Reappraisal of the Civil War.*

First edition, second impression [photo offset], 1967 [1951].

[device] | years of madness | [device] | w.e. woodward | [publisher's logo] | frontier press, inc. | cleveland, ohio | 1967

Perfect binding; pp. i-vi [1-2] 3-311 [312-314] 14.5 x 23 cm.

On copyright page: "Copyright Helen Woodward 1951 | Copyright Frontier Press 1967"

5. *The Decline & the Fall of the "Spectacular" Commodity-Economy.*

First edition, 1967.

THE DECLINE & THE FALL | of the | "SPECTACULAR" | COMMODITY-ECONOMY | [publisher's logo] | FRONTIER PAMPHLET NUMBER ONE | FRONTIER PRESS

[1]¹⁰; pp. [i-vi] [1] 2-10 [11-14]. A single triple-stapled gathering. 15 x 22.7 cm.

On verso of title page: "This essay, 'The Decline and the Fall of the 'Spectacular' Commodity-Economy', originally appeared in the Situationist International, December, 1965." At foot of back cover flap: "design: ron caplan".

6. Hulbert, Archer Butler. *Paths of the Mound-Building Indians and Great Game Animals.*

First edition, second impression (photo offset), 1967 [1902].

HISTORIC HIGHWAYS OF AMERICA | VOLUME 1 | [rule] | Paths of the Mound-Building Indians | and Great Game Animals | ARCHER BUTLER HULBERT | With Maps and Illustrations | [publisher's logo] | FRONTIER PRESS, Inc. | CLEVELAND, OHIO | 1967

[1-9]⁸; pp. [i-ii] [1-11] 12-13 [14-17] 18-34 [35-37] 38-42 [43] 44-46 [47-48] 49-50 [51-53] 54 [55-56] 57-67 [68] 69-76 [77-78] 79-93 [94] 95-98 [99-101] 102 [103] 104-109 [110] 111-127 [128] 129-140. 13.2 x 18.8 cm.

8. Long, Haniel. *If He Can Make Her So.*

First edition, 1968

[first four lines in yellow green (C120)] IF | HE CAN | MAKE HER | SO | [black] Haniel Long | Selection and introduction by | Ron Caplan with a painting | from the work of John Kane | [green] [device] | [publisher's logo] | FRONTIER PRESS | PITTSBURGH, PA | U S A

[1-5]⁸ [6]⁶ [7]⁸; pp [i-viii] ix [x-xx] 1-3 [4] 5-16 [17-18] 19-23 [24] 25-27 [28] 29 [30] 31 [32] 33-35 [36] 37-42 [43-44] 45-49 [50] 51 [52-54] 55-79 [80] 81-83 [84] 85 [86-88]. 16 x 25 cm.

Contents: Introduction, "Haniel Long", by Ronald Caplan, Pittsburgh Memoranda (section title for the following 5 pieces) "Prologue," "Homestead 1892," "Mrs. Soffel 1902," "Henry George 1913," "Two Memoranda 1914," Notes for a New Mythology (section title for the following piece) "How Pittsburgh Returned to the Jungle," A Pittsburgher En Route (section title for the following piece) "New Mexico," Piñon Country (section title for the following piece) "The Bandits," The Grist Mill (section title for the following piece) "If He Can Make Her So," Malinche (Doña Marina) (section title for the following piece) "She who speaks to you ....," Atlantides (section title for the following piece) "The Simplest Way," Bibliography (section title for the following piece) "Selected Books of Haniel Long".

9. Dorn, Edward. *Twenty-Four Love Songs.*

First edition, 1969.

Twenty-four | Love songs by | Edward Dorn | frontier press | 1969 [slightly red C12] [device]

[1]¹⁶; pp. [1-32]. A single double-stapled gathering. Trim size 13.7 x 19.4 cm. Cream laid paper with vertical chain lines watermarked "LINWEAVE TAROTEXT". Cover size ± 15.2 x 22.6 cm., light olive (C106) stock with deckled fore edge.

On page 31: [slightly red] "Designed & printed in San Francisco by Graham Mackintosh".

Contains 24 numbered poems. The number at the head of each poem is printed in slightly red.

10. Long, Haniel. *Interlinear to Cabeza de Vaca.*

Second edition, 1969 [1936].

INTERLINEAR TO | [deep red (C14)] Cabeza | deVaca | [black] *His Relation of the Journey* | *Florida to the Pacific* | *1528-1536* | [deep red] [cross] | HANIEL LONG | FRONTIER PRESS

[1-2]^8 [3]^4 [4]^8; pp. [i-vii] ix-xii [xiv-xvi] 1-34 [35-40]. 10.6 x 17.6 cm.

Colophon p. [37]: "INTERLINEAR TO | CABEZA DE VACA | was originally published in 1936 by Writers' Editions, 'a cooperative group of writers | living in the Southwest, who believe that | regional publication will foster growth | of american literature,' and is here pub- | lished by Frontier Press in an edition of 4000 | copies in monotype Bembo and handset | Perpetua on Mohawk Vellum. | Design: Ron Caplan. 1969."

11. [White, Bouck]. *The Book of Daniel Drew.*

Second [?] edition, second impression [photo offset], 1969 [1910, 1911, 1930, 1937, 1965].

THE BOOK OF | [photo of Daniel Drew] | DANIEL DREW | NEW YORK CITY | FRONTIER PRESS

[1-5]^{16} [6-7]^{14} [8-14]^{16}; pp. [i-vi] vii-xii [1-2] 3-423 [424-428] .13.7 x19.7 cm.

Contents include "Introduction" by Edward Dorn.

At the foot of the inside flap of the dust jacket: "COVER DESIGN : RON CAPLAN".

12. McClure, Michael. *The Surge.*

First edition, 1969.

Cover title: on a folio of deep orange (C51) wove paper folded quarto, ± 16.2 x 23.8 cm., with deckled fore-edge, [medium olive (C107), upside down from right to left] "THE | SURGE". Inside front cover [medium olive] "MICHAEL | McCLURE | frontier | press | 1969

[1]^6; pp. [1-12]. A single double-stapled gathering. 15.5 x 23.3 cm.

On p. [11]: "*The Surge* was first published in *Foot*, (1962)". On p. [12]: "DESIGNED & PRINTED BY GRAHAM MACKINTOSH".

13. Berkman, Alexander. *Prison Memoirs of an Ananrchist.*

Second edition, 1970 [1912].

PRISON MEMOIRS | of an | ANARCHIST | ALEXANDER BERKMAN | [publisher's logo] | FRONTIER PRESS | PITTSBURGH

[1-16]¹⁶ [17]⁸ [18]¹⁶; pp. [i-xx] [1-2] 3-98 [99-100] 101-488 [489-490] 491-498 [499-500] 501-533 [534] 535-538 [539-540]. 13.6 x 20.8 cm.

At foot of dust jacket front flap: "COVER DESIGN : RON CAPLAN".

Contents include "Introduction: Alexander Berkman" by Kenneth Rexroth.

14. Büchner, Georg. *Lenz.* Translated by Michael Hamburger.

Second English edition, 1969 [1947].

LENZ | Georg Büchner | TRANSLATION BY MICHAEL HAMBURGER | FRONTIER PRESS | 1969

[1-2]¹⁶; pp. [1-6] 7-52 i-v [vi-vii]. 10.5 x 17.7 cm. Paper wrappers.

On p. [6]: "DESIGN BY RON CAPLAN"; pp. i-iv, "Introduction," by Michael Hamburger; p. v, "Principle dates in the life of Georg Büchner".

The first of a series that includes items number 16 and 19, all with identical binding.

15. Dorn, Edward. *Songs Set Two—A Short Count.*

First edition, 1970.

[slightly red (C12)] SONGS | [medium brown (C58)] SET TWO | [black] A Short Count | [medium brown] This volume | is to honor | the Scald | [slightly red] EDWARD | DORN | [medium brown] frontier press 1970

Perfect binding; pp. [1-32]. 11.3 x 15 cm.

On p. [32]: "designed & printed by Graham Mackintosh"

Contains 19 numbered poems. 13 is blank.

16. Williams, William Carlos. *Spring and All.*

Second edition, 1970 [1923].

Spring | & All | William | Carlos Williams | FRONTIER PRESS | 1970

[1-7]⁸; pp. [i-viii] 1-98 [99-104]. 10.6 x 17.7 cm. Paper wrappers.

On p. [vi]: "SPRING AND ALL WAS FIRST PUBLISHED IN 1923 | BY THE CONTACT PUBLISHING COMPANY"

17. Brakhage, Stan. *A Moving Picture Giving and Taking Book.*

First edition, 1971.

A | MOVING | PICTURE | GIVING | AND | TAKING | BOOK | STAN BRAKHAGE | FRONTIER PRESS | West Newbury Mass 1971

[1-3]⁸ [4]⁶ [5]⁸; pp. [i-viii] 1-65 [66-68]. 10.7 x 15.2 cm. Bound in leather covers with gilt stamped title.

On p. [67]: "DESIGN BY PHILIP TRUSSELL | 1971".

18. Dorn, Edward. *The Cycle.*
First edition, 1971.

The Cycle | by | Edward Dorn | Frontier Press | West Newbury Mass | 1971

[1]¹⁶; pp. [1-32]. A single double-stapled gathering. 24.2 x 32 cm. Paper wrappers.

19. Dorn, Edward. *Some Business Recently Transacted in the White World.*

First edition, 1971.

SOME BUSINESS | RECENTLY | TRANSACTED IN | THE WHITE WORLD | FRONTIER PRESS 1971

[1-6]⁴; pp. [i-x] 1-83 [84-86]. 10.5 x 17.5 cm. Paper wrappers.

Contents: "A Narrative with Scattered Nouns," "A Epic," "Of Eastern Newfoundland, Its Inns & Outs," "C. B. & Q.," "The Terrific Refinery in Biafra," "Driving Across the Prairie," "The Garden of Birth," "The Sheriff of McTooth County, Kansas," "Greene Arrives on the Set," "Some Business Recently Transacted in the White World."

20. Glover, Albert. *Trio in G.*

First edition, 1971.

A TRIO IN G | Al Glover | Frontier Press | West Newbury | Massachusetts | 1971

[1-4]⁸ [5]⁶ [6]⁸; pp. [1-92]. 15 x 20.8 cm. Paper wrappers.

On p. [6]: "Drawings and design by Philip Trussell".

21. H.D. *Hermetic Definitions.*

First edition, 1971.

[within an ornamental oval frame of roses in deep red (C13) and gray green (C122)] Hermetic Definitions | HD | [below] 1971

[1]⁴ [2-5]⁸; pp. [1-72]. 22.6 x 15 cm. Covers of heavy white stock glued at spine.

Contents: "Red Rose & A Beggar," "Grove of Academe," "Star of Day."

No imprint, no colophon, no copyright. This edition was printed from an autograph transcription of a manuscirpt version at the Beinecke Library. The title, "Hermetic Definitions," is printed as it appears on the manuscript. Inserted in the copy at Yale is a note by Norman Holmes Pearson: "Illegally published by Harvey Brown Frontier Press West Newbury, Mass. 1971, in what Brown asserts was an edition of 1600 copies 'none for sale'. If so, most were hidden for later profit. Note that the title is Hermetic Definitions rather than Definition and that the text differs from the New Directions edition. Text from an earlier version surreptitiously obtained by Brown." Brown continued to distribute to book free until he died in 1990. Hundreds of copies mildewed in his mother's basement.

22. Kelly, Robert. *Cities.*

First edition, 1971.

[two large dots over the "i"s] CITIES | ROBERT KELLY | FRONTIER PRESS | 1971

[1-5]⁴; pp. [i-vii] 1-65 [66-72]. 10.7 x 17.6 cm. Paper wrappers.

On copyright page: "AN EARLIER VERSION OF THIS ACCOUNT APPEARED IN THE IOWA REVIEW." "DESIGN BY RON CAPLAN".

23. Kelly, Robert. *In Time.*

First edition, 1971.

Robert Kelly | IN TIME | FRONTIER PRESS | WEST NEWBURY, MASS 1971

[1-6]⁸; pp. [i-viii] 1-11 [11a] 12 [12a] 13-33 [33a] 34-46 [46a-46c] 47 [47a] 48 [48a] 49 [49a] 50 [50a] 51 [51a] 52 [52a] 53 [53a] 54 [54a] 55 [55a] 56 [56a] 57 [57a] 58 [58a] 59 [59a] 60 [60a] 61[62-66]. 17 x 21.5 cm. Paper wrappers.

On p. [vi]: "DESIGN BY RON CAPLAN".

24. Anderson, Sherwood. *Mid-American Chants.*

Second edition, 1972 [1918].

Sherwood Anderson | Mid-American | Chants | FRONTIER PRESS | 1972

[1-9]⁴; pp. [i-viii] 1-62 [63-64]. 21.5 x 26 cm. Paper wrappers.

On p. [iv]: "Book Design by Ron Caplan"

25. Dorn, Edward. *Gunslinger: Book III.*

First edition, 1972.

Gunslinger | by | Edward Dorn | Frontier Press | West Newbury Mass | 1972

[1]²⁰; pp. [1-40]. A single double-stapled gathering. 19.8 x 30.4 cm. Paper wrappers.

On p. [5]: "BOOK III | THE WINTERBOOK | prologue to the great | Book IIII Kornerstone".

B. CHECKLIST OF THE PUBLICATIONS OF THE INSTITUTE OF FURTHER STUDIES, 1969-1997

compiled by Michael Boughn

1. Olson, Charles. ["That there was a woman"]. 1968.

1 p., 15.5 x 20.2 cm.

Dated, "March, 1968".

Folded once in an envelope, 16 x 10.5 cm., with the printed return address, "THE INSTITUTE OF FURTHER STUDIES | [device] [to the right of device] Box 25 [dot] Kensington Station "Buffalo, New York [dot] 14215".

Reprinted as Maximus III.189 (Butterick 583).

2. Olson, Charles. ["Added to making a Republic in gloom on Watchhouse Point"]. 1968.

1 p., 15.5 x 20.2 cm.

Dated, "March, 1968".

Folded once in an envelope, 16 x 10.5 cm., with the printed return address, "THE INSTITUTE OF FURTHER STUDIES | [device] [to the right of device] Box 25 [dot] Kensington Station "Buffalo, New York [dot] 14215".

Reprinted as Maximus III.190 (Butterick 584).

3. Olson, Charles. ["Wholly absorbed"]. 1968

1 p., 15.5 x 20.2 cm.

Dated, "'LX VIII".

Folded once in an envelope, 16 x 10.5 cm., with the printed return address, "THE INSTITUTE OF FURTHER STUDIES | [device] [to the right of device] Box 25 [dot] Kensington Station "Buffalo, New York [dot] 14215".

Reprinted as Maximus III.191 (Butterick 585).

4. Olson, Charles. ["I like something in the American which does honor a Hotspur of itself"]

Postcard, 17.7 x 12.7 cm. Recto, a photograph of Jacqueline Kennedy Onassis and Alice Roosevelt Longworth. Verso, eight hand written lines in blue signed, "Charles Olson": "I like something in the American which does honor a Hotspur of itself, | and even defines it as in fact close to the | condition of valor. What does, though, always ultimately | show up though, in their skin, or the health of it, some sickness | through seen almost to have the right | color or from the edge of known and admitted | danger—is some poverty (actually they have saved | themselves from the glories of god ism" | Charles Olson"

At top left of verso, "SOME OF THE SUBTLEST OF ALL POSSIBLE TRAIL-BACK, Mrs. Aristotle | Onassis, left, attending the christening of Rory Catherine Elizabeth | Kennedy, 11th child of the late Sen. Robert Kennedy, at St. Luke's | Church, McLean, Va., Sunday, Jan. 12, 1969, chats with Mrs. Alice | Roosevelt Longworth."

5. Olson, Charles. "Clear Shining Water." 1968.

Postcard. 41.7 x 19 cm. The card is double folded to 14.2 x 19 cm. On the front of the folded card is a drawing of "The Judgement of Paris" from a Greek vase, reproduced from Jane Ellen Harrison's *Prolegomena to the Study of Greek Religion*, p. 295. On the back is the printed return address, "THE INSTITUTE OF FURTHER STUDIES | [device] [to the right of device] Box 25 [dot] Kensington Station "Buffalo, New York [dot] 14215." Printed across the inside of the unfolded three panels, "CLEAR, SHINING WATER", De Vries says, *Altgermanische*". At foot of third panel, "CHARLES OLSON, | Institute of Further Studies, July 1st, | 1968".

Reprinted in *Additional Prose*. Ed. George Butterick (Bolinas, Four Seasons Foundation, 1974). 71.

6. Blake, William. Milton, pl 25 [*1968*].

1 p., 18.5 x 26.2 cm.

Double folded in an envelope, 19 x 10 cm., with the printed return address, "THE INSTITUTE OF FURTHER STUDIES | [device] [to the right of device] Box 25 [dot] Kensington Station "Buffalo, New York [dot] 14215".

7. Pound Ezra. "The Child's Guide to Knowledge" [1970?].

2 pp., 18.5 x 26.2 cm.

12 line epigraph by William Blake. Double folded in an envelope, 19 x 10 cm., with the return address, "The Institute of Further Studies | BOX 482 | CANTON, NEW YORK 13617".

8. The Magazine of Further Studies. Buffalo, NY. 1965-1969.

Appendices

705

Nos. [1]-6 [nos.1-3 undated]. All issues 22 x 28 cm. loose sheets wrapped in corrugated paper covers and triple stapled through the spine. The cover of each issue has a different art work.

a. No. 1: "Lament for the Makaris", by William Dunbar; "Berkeley," by Robert Hogg; "Seven," by John Clarke; "from Don Cherry," by Harvey Brown; "Four poems," by Albert Glover; "Mythology / Poetry, Bibliography 1" and "III Pleistocene Mythology, A Bibliographic Beginning," by John Clarke; "Five poems," by George Butterick; "Two poems," by Stephen Rodefer; "Jazz Clarke Poem," by Charles Doria; "You've lost that lovin' feeling," by David Cull; "from Mountain," by Fred Wah; "Three poems," by John Weiners; "Placemats," by John Clarke.

b. No. 2: "crow feather," by Ruth Fox; "Pleistocene Mythology," by John Clarke; "The Blue Garden," by Charles Doria; "I'd call you sweet but," by Colette Butterick; "For Andrew Crozier—wherever he goes, the same way, always," by John Temple; "Notes on the Possibility of a Phenomenological Poetics—The Body's World," by Charles Sherry; "Two Poems," by Charles Sherry; "ISHMAEL:8:X:sixtyfive," by Daniel John Zimmerman; "Plus X," by Patricia Jamieson; "Notes from Class," by George Butterick; "Nothing Done," by Jim Braemer; "Three poems," by John Weiners; "2 songs for children," by John Temple; "The Canoe, Too," by Fred Wah; "Notes (for I. Massey 9/28/65 on C. Olson)," by Albert Glover; "Poem for Planters," by Albert Glover; "It's no fun anymore," by Jack Clarke; "As to the Exomorphic," by J. Clarke; "The Lamo," by Charles Olson; "traitor poem," by Dave Cull; "Beasts of Burden," by Mac Hammond.

c. No. 3: "Al, | Imagine: simply to be an animal," by Charles Olson; "Furs," by Fred Wah; "Five poems," by John Weiners; "As I walked home last night," by John Temple; "Letter A," by Lewis MacAdams; "The Mountain, the creek, all ends in the lake," by Fred Wah; "from Black Creek," by Ruth Fox; "Sections from Subway," by George Butterick; "Two poems," by Duncan McNaughton; "Poem," by Robert Hogg; "The Lesbian is dead," by Duncan McNaughton; "Enough animus so it all has will," by John Clarke; "I see a whale in the Southsea, drinking my soul away," [review of Sailing after Knowledge, by George Dekker, and The Savage Mind, by Claude Levi-Strauss] by Albert Glover; [review of Human Universe and Other Essays, by Charles Olson] by John Clarke.

d. No. 4: "Hell and Heaven: Psychemimeisis to beyond the rainbow bridge," by David Tirrell; "The qanat spurts the geyser," by Ed Sanders; "By fixes only move," by John Clarke; "3 songs," by Robert Hogg; "for my friend," by Charles Olson; "Fingers of the Sun," by Ed Sanders; "Poem for Turning," by Fred Wah; "that otherwise than how the story goes," by Ron Caplan; "Proem," by George Butterick; "Drugs and the Unconscious" by John Weiners; "the mute," by Ed Billowitz; "by honor," by Ed Sanders; "Blake letter November 4 1967," by John Clarke; "Dear Royal Members my west view in this," by David Tirrell; "Letter, October 18, 1967," by Fred Wah; "Moon morning 6 Nov '67" by John Clarke; "A letter and a drawing for John Clarke 11/7/67," by Albert Glover.

e. No. 5: "Second tale: return," by Robin Blaser; "it is a dark cold hard tin forest," by Ron Caplan; "Letter, May 15, 1968," by Fred Wah; "La Barranca del Cobre," by Drummond Hadley; "Insulted," by John Weiners; "Where the daughter goes the mother must follow," by John Clarke; "The quality of goods, the explicitness," by George

Butterick; "[review of Megalithic Sites in Britain, by A. Thom], by Peter Riley; "from Art and Artist" by Otto Rank; "Prophetic hieroglyphs: world forecasts," by Albert Glover; "Magic rite," by Ed Sanders; "A plan for a curriculum of the soul," by Charles Olson.

f. No. 6: ["letter to John Clarke"], by Charles Olson; "I am very glad and all alone in the world," by Mary Leary; "He said, that when he would step out into the street," by George Butterick; "I point to my own absolute (?) experience of," by Fred Wah; "it was all tainted with myself, I knew it all to start with," by John Clarke; "Three poems," by John Temple; "Thinking along the lines that," by John Clarke; "A lifetime," by Robert Hogg; "I shall never forget the maniacal horror of it all in the end," by Robert Creeley; "Lockd in a fiery Tree," by Duncan McNaughton; "the black dog is third dog," by Albert Glover; "'. . .we found marginal," by Buri; "But what's wrong with mortality?" by Albert Glover; "SO," by Fred Wah; "Thirty-six years after my birth was the time," by John Clarke; "At this point I would distinguish the following kinds of form," by Robert Duncan; "Dear Diana—Buga Nov. 4, 1968," by Ed Billowitz; "so I put my hand out further, a little further," by Buri; "Dear Jack & Mary," by David [Tirrell]; "Ah no, I cannot tell you what it is," by John Temple; ""Out of the well-heads of the new world," by Fred Wah; " . . . so much as there is a steady flow of breath," by Fred Wah; "So like play," by Charles Olson.

9. The Curriculum of the Soul.

0 Pleistocene Man . . . . . Charles Olson
21 Vision . . . . . Drummond Hadley
22 Messages . . . . . James Koller
3 Woman . . . . . John Weiners
18 Ismaeli Muslimism . . . . . Michael Bylebyl
19 Alchemy . . . . . David Tirrell
16 Dance . . . . . Lewis McAdams
13 The Arabs . . . . . Edward Kissam
27 Sensation . . . . . Anselm Hollo
1 The Mushroom . . . . . Albert Glover
14 American Indians . . . . . Edgar Billowitz
11 Novalis' Subjects . . . . . Robert Dalke
2 Dream . . . . . Duncan McNaughton
7 Blake . . . . . Jack Clarke
12 The Norse . . . . . George Butterick
17 Egyptian Hieroglyphs . . . . . Edward Sanders
6 Earth . . . . . Fred Wah
24 Organism . . . . . Michael McClure
20 Perspective . . . . . Daniel Zimmerman
8 Dante . . . . . Robert Duncan
25 Matter . . . . . John Thorpe

15 Jazz Playing . . . . . Harvey Brown
28 Attention . . . . . Robert Grenier
23 Analytic Psychology . . . . . Gerrit Lansing
26 Phenomenological . . . . . Joanne Kyger
9 Homer's Art . . . . . Alice Notley
10 Bach's Belief . . . . . Robin Blaser
4 One's Own Mind . . . . . Michael Boughn
5 One's Own Language . . . . . Lisa Jarnot

C. WOMEN-EDITED (AND CO-EDITED) LITTLE MAGAZINES AND PRESSES (1953-1999)

Compiled by Linda Russo

I. POETRY

Folder (1953-56), ed. Daisy Aldan & Richard Miller
The Floating Bear (1961-69), ed. Diane di Prima (& LeRoi Jones [Imamu Amiri Baraka])
El Corno Emplumado (1962-69), ed. Margaret Randall, Mexico
Burning Deck (serial, 1963-65; press, 1966+), ed. Rosmarie & Keith Waldrop
Poets Press (1963-69), ed. Diane di Prima
Angel Hair (1966-69), ed. Anne Waldman & Lewis Warsh
Angel Hair Books (1965-78), ed. Anne Waldman & Lewis Warsh
The World (1967-76), ed. Anne Waldman
Stooge (1967-75), ed. Geoffrey Young & Laura Chester
0 to 9 (serial & press, 1967-69), ed. Bernadette Mayer & Vito Hannibal Acconci
Fire Exit (1968), ed. Fanny Howe, Ruth Whitman, William Corbett & Ben E. Watkins
Telephone (1970-83), ed. Maureen Owen
Vehicle Editions (1971-86), ed. Annabel Lee
OINK! (1971-85, *New American Writing*, 1987+), ed. Maxine Chernoff & Paul Hoover
Telephone Books (1972-84), ed. Maureen Owen
Chicago (1972-73), ed. Alice Notley
Unnatural Acts (1972-73), ed. Bernadette Mayer & Ed Friedman
Big Deal, (1973-77), ed. Barbara Baracks
Matchbook (1973-?), ed. Joyce Holland
Kelsey St. Press. (1974+), ed. Patricia Dienstfrey & Rena Rosenwasser. Founding members also included Karen Brodine, Kit Duane, Marina la Palma & Laura Moriarty
Five Trees (1974-79), ed. Eileen Callahan, Cameron Folson, Cheryl Miller, Jaime Robles & Kathy Walkup
Yellow Press (1975-82), ed. Richard Friedman, Peter Kostakis, & Darlene Pearlstein (& *The Milk Quarterly*, 1972-82)
Annex (1975-82), ed. Brita Bergland & Tod Kabza
Full Court Press (1975-82), ed. Anne Waldman, Ron Padgett, & Joan Simon
The Coldspring Journal (1975-76), ed. Charles Plymell, Pamela Beach Plymell & Joshua Norton
Tuumba (1976-84), ed. Lyn Hejinian
Effie's Press (1976-79), ed. Bonnie Carpenter
Frontward Books (1976-79), ed. Bob Rosenthal & Rochelle Kraut
Room: A Women's Literary Journal (1976-79), ed. Kathy Barr, Gail Newman, Teddy Ramsden & Barbara L. Starkey).
Gnome Baker (1976/8?-81), ed. Madeleine Burnside & Andrew Kelly
Station Hill Press (1977-86), ed. George & Susan Quasha
United Artists (1977-82) & United Artists Books, ed. Bernadette Mayer & Lewish Warsh
KOFF/KOFF Magazine Press (1977-78), ed. Maggie Dubris, Elinor Nauen, & Rachel Walling
Dodgems (1977), ed. Eileen Myles
Slug-on Books (1977), ed. Anon. (Eileen Myles, Susie Timmons, & Rochelle Kraut)

Caveman (1977), ed. Barbara Barg, Rochelle Kraut, Elinor Nauen, Alice Notley, Eileen Myles, & Susie Timmons

Lost Roads (1978+), ed. CD Wright & Forrest Gander

Remember I Did This For You/A Power Mad Book (1978-81), ed. Barbara Barg & Steve Levine

Vital Statistics (1978-80), ed. Sandra Braman & Douglas Woolf

Rocky Ledge/Rocky Ledge Cottage Editions (1979-81), ed. Anne Waldman & Reed Bye

Awede Press (1980+), ed. Brita Bergland

Qu (1980-83), ed. Carla Harryman

Xexoxial Endarchy (1980-82), ed. Elizabeth Was & Miekal And

Post-Apollo Press (1982+), ed. Simone Fattal

Raddle Moon (1983+), ed. Susan Clark

How(ever) (1983-92), ed. Kathleen Fraser, Assoc. eds. include Frances Jaffer, Beverly Dahlen, & Susan Gevirtz, Contributing eds. include Rachel Blau DuPlessis, Carolyn Burke, Chris Tysh, Diane Glancy, Adalaide Morris, Myung Mi Kim & Meredith Stricker

Giants play well in the drizzle (1983-92), ed. Martha King

Primary Writing (1983-85), ed. Phyliss Rosenzweig

Mirage (1984+), ed. Kevin Killian & Dodie Bellamy

O Books (1986+), ed. Leslie Scalapino

New American Writing (1987+; was *OINK!*), ed. Maxine Chernoff & Paul Hoover

No Trees (1987-89; 1997), ed. Lisa Jarnot

Avec (1988+), ed. Cydney Chadwick

Scarlet (1988-91), ed. Alice Notley & Douglas Oliver

Big Allis (1989+), ed. Jessica Grim & Melanie Nielson

Tender Buttons (1989+), ed. Lee Ann Brown

American Letters & Commentary (1989-91; 1993+), ed. Virginia Hooper, Peter Terres & Laban Carrick Hill (1989-91); ed. Jeannie Beaumont & Anna Rabinowitz (1993+)

Tight (1989-99), ed. Ann Erickson

Re*map (1990+), ed. Todd Baron & Carolyn Kemp

Troubled Surfer (1990-92), ed. Lisa Jarnot

6ix (1991+), ed. Alicia Askenase, Julia Blumenreich, Valerie Fox, Rina Terry, Heather Thomas & Phyllis Wat

Em Press (1991+), ed. Dale Going

Texture (1991-95), ed. Susan Smith Nash

Leave Books (1991-95), eds. (probably) included (but were not necessarily limited to) Elizabeth Burns, Jefferson Hanson, Charlotte Pressler, Kristin Prevallet, Pam Rehm, Juliana Spahr, Brigham Taylor, Bill Tuttle, Mark Wallace & Marta Werner.

Long news : in the short century (1991-94), ed. Barbara Henning

Texture press (1992+) & *Texture miniatures* (1992-94), ed. Susan Smith Nash

Avec Books (1992+), ed. Cydney Chadwick

indefinite space (1992+) ed. Marcia Arrieta

No Roses Review (1992-98), ed. Carolyn Coo

The Impercipient (1992-95), ed. Jennifer Moxley

Black Bread (1992-94), ed. Sianne Ngai & Jessica Lowenthal

Object (1992-94), ed. Robert Fitterman & Kim Rosenfeld

Cathay (1992), ed. Patrick Comiskey, Gale Nelson, Susan Smith Nash, & Elizabeth Robinson

First Intensity (1993+), ed. Lee Chapman

Volt (1993+), ed. Gillian Conoley

Chain (1994+), ed. Juliana Spahr & Jena Osman

Torque (1994+) ed. Elizabeth Fodaski

Proliferation (1994-?), ed. Mary Burger, Jay Schwartz & Chris Vitiello

apex of the M (1994-98), ed. Kristin Prevallet, Pam Rehm, Lew Daly & Alan Gilbert

Compound eye (1994-96), ed. Ange Mlinko

Re:ference Press (1995-96), ed. Beth Anderson

Tinfish (1995+, Tinfish Network, 1997+), ed. Susan Schultz
First Intensity Press (1996+), ed. Lee Chapman
etcetera (1996+), ed. Mindi Englart
Primitive Publications (1996+), ed. Mary Hilton
Explosive Magazine (1997+), ed. Katy Lederer
Gare du Nord (1997+), ed. Alice Notely & Douglas Oliver
Double Lucy Books (1998+), ed. Elizabeth Treadwell & Sarah Ann Cox
The Lights are Out (1998+), ed. Rachel Daley & Joshua May
Spectacular Books (1998+), ed. Katy Lederer
Atelos (1998+), ed. Lyn Hejinian & Travis Ortiz
Skanky Possum (1998+), ed. Hoa Nguyen & Dale Smith
Outlet (1998-2002), ed. Elizabeth Treadwell & Sarah Ann Cox
Second Story Books (1999+), ed. Mary Burger
Handwritten Press (1999+), ed. Kristin Gallagher
LEROY (1999+), ed. Renee Gladman

name (1999+), ed. Jessica Smith, Matt Chambers, Chris Fritton, & Rebecca Stigge

tripwire: a journal of poetics (1998+), ed. Yedda Morrison & David Buuck
Shark (1998+), ed. Lytle Shaw & Emilie Clark
verdure (1999+), ed. Christopher W. Alexander & Linda Russo

III. ASSOCIATED WEBSITES

Electronic Poetry Center, SUNY Buffalo, epc.buffalo.edu
non (1998+), ed. Laura Moriarty, socrates.berkeley.edu/~moriarty/
HOW2 (1999+), ed. Kathleen Fraser www.departments.bucknell.edu/stadler_center/how2
idiom press, www.idiomart.com
The Segue Foundation, www.segue.org
Small Press Distribution, www.spdbooks.org
Subpress Collective, www.angelfire.com/poetry/subpress/newbooks.htm

II. POETICS

Poetics Journal (1982-91, 1998), ed. Lyn Hejinian & Barret Watten
Poetic briefs (1991-98), ed. Elizabeth Burns & Jefferson Hansen
Prosodia: a new college of california poetics journal (1993[?]+), co-editors vary annually & have included Evelyn Slowik, Hoa Nguyen, Kathryn Retzer, Leslie Davis, Renee Gladman, Stephanie Baker, Elizabeth Burke & Trisha Roush
Chloroform : an aesthetics of critical writing (1997), ed. Nick Lawrence & Alisa Messer

CONTRIBUTORS

BRUCE ANDREWS is the author of over two dozen books of poetry and performance scores, most recently *Lip Service* (a recasting of Dante's *Paradiso*) from Coach House Press. His essays are collected in *Paradise & Method* and in the *Aerial* anthology devoted to his work. He is the Music Director of Sally Silvers & Dancers. His author page is http://epc.buffalo.edu/authors/andrews.

DANIEL BARBIERO is an archivist and writer living in Silver Spring, Maryland. His recent work has appeared in *Wittgenstein Studies*, *Philosophy Today*, and *Issues in Science and Technology*.

CHRISTOPHER BEACH teaches English and American literature at the Universdity of California, Irvine, and the Claremont Graduate University. He has published two books on American poetry and poetics, *ABC of Influence: Ezra Pound and the Remaking of American Poetic Tradition* (U of California P, 1992), *The Politics of Distinction: Whitman and the Discourses of Nineteenth-Century America* (U of Georgia P, 1996), and *Poetic Culture: Contemporary American Culture Between Community and Institution* (Northwestern UP, 1999). He is also the editor of *Artifice & Indeterminacy: An Anthology of New Poetics* (U of Alabama P, 1998) and the author of a book on American film, *Class, Language, and American Film Comedy* (Cambridge UP, 2002).

MICHAEL BOUGHN'S works include *H.D., A Bibliography 1905-1990* and *One's Own Mind*. The editor of shuffaloff press, his poetry books include *A little post-apocalyptic suite for RC with thanks for the rhino* and *Iterations of the Diagonal*.

PETER BUSHYEAGER'S reviews and articles have appeared in *Talisman*, *The Poetry Project Newsletter*, *New Art Examiner*, *Rain Taxi*, and other publications. His poems have appeared in *The World*, *Pagan Place*, *Chez Chez*, and *Oink*, among other magazines. His work appears in the anthology *Help Yourself* (Autonomedia, 2002) and a collection of poems is forthcoming from Ten Pell Books.

DAVID CLIPPINGER is an assistant professor of English at Penn State University and has published a range of articles on contemporary poetry that have been published or are forthcoming in *Pre/text*, *Sagetrieb*, *Chicago Review*, *Talisman*, *Harvard Review*, and other journals. His books include *The Body of This Life: Reading William Bronk*. His book on Bronk's poetry, *The Mind's Landscpae: William Bronk and Twentieth Century American Poetry* and *Accumulating Position: The Selected Letters of William Bronk* are forthcoming.

MICHEL DELVILLE teaches twentieth-century British and American literature at the University of Liège, Belgium. His published works include a study of J. G. Ballard (Northcote House, 1998) and articles on contemporary poetry and fiction. His book, *The American Prose Poem : Poetic Form and the Law of Genre* (UP of Florida, 1998), won the 1998 SAMLA Studies Award for an outstanding work of scholarship in the field of literary criticism, theory, or history.

JOSEPH DONAHUE was born in Dallas, Texas and grew up in Kerouac's hometown, Lowell, Massachusetts. He is the author of several books, including *Before Creation, Monitions of the Approach, World Well Broken,* and *Terra Lucida*. A member of the *Talisman* editorial staff, he co-edited *Primary Trouble: An Anthology of Contemporary American Poetry* with Leonard Schwartz and Edward Foster. A former faculty of the faculty at the Stevens Institute of Technology and the University of Puget Sound, he lives in Durham, North Carolina, and teaches at Duke University.

BRENT HAYES EDWARDS is an assistant professor in the Department of English at Rutgers University. Some of his publications have appeared in *Callaloo, Critical Inquiry, The New York Times, Representations,* and *Transition*. He is co-editor of *Social Text*. His book, *The Practice of Diaspora: Translating Black Internationalism in Harlem and Paris*, will be published next winter by Harvard University Press.

DAN FEATHERSTON'S poetry, essays, and reviews have appeared in various journals, including *Cross-Cultural Poetics, House Organ, Mandorla* (Mexico), *New American Writing, Poetic Briefs, Sulfur, Talisman, TINFISH,* and *Witz*, and in the anthology *POG ONE* (1999). His books and chapbooks include *Rooms* (Paper Brain Press, 1998), *Anatomies* (Potes & Poets Press, 1998), and *26 Islands* (Primitive Publications, 1999).

STEVE EVANS teaches poetry and critical theory at the University of Maine, where he is also the co-editor of *Sagetrieb: Poetry and Poetics after Modernism*. He recently edited *After Patriarchal Poetry: Feminism and the Contemporary Avant-Garde*, a special issue of the journal *differences* 12.2 (2001). His work has also appeared in *Qui Parle* and in the collection *Telling It Slant: Avant-Garde Poetics of the 1990s*. His "Notes to Poetry" are archived on the *arras* website at www.arras.net.

THOMAS FINK, a professor of English at CUNY-LaGuardia, is the author of the critical studies *The Poetry of David Shapiro* (Fairleigh Dickinson UP, 1993) and *A Different Sense of Power* (Fairleigh Dickinson UP, 2001) and two book s of poetry, *Surprise Visit* (Domestic, 1993) and *Gossip* (Marsh Hawk Press, 2002). His criticism has appeared in the journals *Contemporary Literature, American Poetry Review, Confrontation,* and *Twentieth Century Literature*, and his poetry has been published in *Poetry New York, Sycamore Review, Phoebe,* and elsewhere. His paintings hang in vrious private collections.

Contributors

NORMAN FINKELSTEIN is a poet and critic who has written extensively on modern poetry over the last quarter-century. He recently published a book on Jewish-American poetry, The first volume of his serial poem *Track* was published in 1999, and a second volume is to be published shortly, He is a professor of English and department chair at Xavier University in Cincinnati, Ohio,

EDWARD FOSTER is a professor of English and American literature and director of the Humanities Division at the Stevens Institute of Technology. He was the poetry editor of *Multi-Cultural Review* and is the founding editor of the journal *Talisman*, Talisman House, and Jensen/Daniels, Publishers. His books of criticism include, among others, *The Civilized Wilderness*, *Richard Brautigan*, *William Saroyan*, *Jack Spicer*, *William Saroyan: A Study of The Short Fiction*, *The Beats*, *The Black Mountain Poets*, and *Answerable to None: Berrigan, Bronk, and the American Real*. Among books he has edited are *Primary Trouble* (with Leonard Schwartz and Joseph Donahue); *Postmodern Poetry*; *Poetry and Poetics in a New Millennium*; *Decadents, Symbolists, and Aesthetes in America*; and the selected works of Stuart Merrill. His poetry has been collected in *The Space Between Her Bed and Clock*, *The Understanding*, *All Acts Are Simply Acts*, *Adrian as Song*, *Boy in the Key of E*, and *The Angelus Bell*, and *Mahrem: Things Men Should Do for Men*.

LOSS PEQUEÑO GLAZIER is a professor of Media Study, a Poetics Program Core Faculty member, and Director of the Electronic Poetry Center (http://epc.buffalo.edu) at the State University of New York, Buffalo. He is author of the award winning *Digital Poetics: The Making of E-Poetries* (Univ. of Alabama Press, 2002) and was the organizer of E-Poetry 2001, the first digital poetry festival ever held (Buffalo, 2001). He is the author of several books of poetry and numerous digital poetry projects. His work has been shown at the Guggenheim Museum, New York, and he has lectured and performed throughout the U.S. and in London, Paris, Berlin, Norway, Spain, Mexico, Cuba, Canada, and other countries. Selected digital projects and other material are available on his EPC author page (http://epc.buffalo.edu/authors/glazier).

ALAN GOLDING is Professor of English and Director of Undergraduate Studies at the University of Louisville, where he teaches American literature and twentieth-century poetry and poetics. He is the author of *From Outlaw to Classics: Canons in American Poetry* (U of Wisconsin P, 1995), which won a 1996 CHOICE Outstanding Book Award, and of numerous essays on writing in the Objectivist-Black Mountain-Language poetry line. Current projects include a selection of these essays, and a book on exploratory poetics and pedagogy. He also co-edits the Contemporary North American Poetry Deries for the University of Wisconsin.

JEANNE HEUVING has published several critical articles on twentieth-century American poets and poetics and a critical book, *Omissions Are Not Accidents: Gender in the Art of Marianne Moore*. She is presently working on a book *Restive Eros: Possession and Dispossession in the Twentieth Century*. that invesdtigates the writing of love and sexuality in twentieth-century women's poetry. Writing a hybrid fiction and poetry, she has published a chapbook Offering (bcc press) and recent work in *Talisman*, *How2*, *Bird-Dog*, and *Common Knowledge*. She is on the faculty of the University of Washington, Bothell, and the University of Washington Graduate School. The recipient of research grants from the NEH and Fulbright Foundation, she is a member of the Subtext Collective, a group dedicated to hosting innovative poetry readings in Seattle and is on the editorial advisory board of *How2*.

W. SCOTT HOWARD teaches at The University of Denver where he is an assistant professor of English. His forthcoming publications concern: theories of poetry and history (Plato to Susan Howe); the Vietnam Veterans Memorial, the AIDS quilt, and postmodern Arcadia; An Collins and the politics of mourning; and Milton's apposite imagination. Among his works-in-progress are *Anatolia*, a book of poems about memory, history, and culture; *Fantastic Surmise*, a study of early modern English elegies and historical discourses; and *John Milton's Divorce Tracts*, an edition of Milton's complete writings on divorce.

ANDREW JORON, who frequently drives while under the influence of surrealism, is the author of the following books of poems: *Force Fields* (1987), *Science Fiction* (1992), and *The Removes* (1999). He has also translated the *Literary Essays* of the German utopian philosopher Ernst Bloch (Stanford UP, 1998).

KATHRYNE V. LINDBERG is a professor in the Department of English at Wayne State University and is the author of *Reading Pound Reading: Modernism after Nietzsche*. and the co-editor of *America's Modernisms: Revaluing the Canon: Essays in Honor of Joseph N. Riddel*.

BURT KIMMELMAN is an associate professor of English at New Jersey Institute of Technology. He is the author of two book-length literary studies: *The "Winter Mind": William Bronk and American Letters* (1998); and, *The Poetics of Authorship in the Later Middle Ages: The Emergence of the Modern Literary Persona* (1996, paperback 1999). He is also the author of three collections of poetry, *The Pond at Cape May Point* (2002), *First Life* (1999) and *Musaics* (1992). He is currently developing a book on modern science and the mid-twentieth-century American artistic avant-garde, and editing *A Companion to Twentieth-Century American Poetry* (forthcoming).

DAVID LANDREY spent thirty-eight years teaching literature, thirty-five of them at Buffalo State Collage, where he was afforded the freedom to develop courses in American postmodern poets and thus to educate himself about what has been most interesting in letters in our time. He studied briefly with Charles Olson at SUNY Buffalo and feels blessed to have met and worked with so many exciting poets, known and unknown. The co-editor of *Drawing from Life: A Selection of Joel Oppenheimer's Work from the Village Voice* and of Oppenheimer's *Poetry: The Ecology of the*

Soul, he is the author of *Intermezzi to Divorce Poems and Dinner Table Scenes*. He believes intensely what he told his late son, who wanted to be an architect: "Terrific; poets and architects may save the world."

STEPHEN PAUL MILLER is an associate professor of English at St. John's University. His books include *The Seventies Now*, *That Man Who Ground Moths into Film*, and *Art is Boring for the Same Reason We Stayed Out of Vietnam*. He is also the co-editor of *The Scene of My Selves: New Work on the New York School Poets*.

STEPHEN-PAUL MARTIN, former editor of *Central Park* magazine, has published twnty books of visual writing, fiction, poetry, and non-fiction, including *The Flood, Not Quite Fiction, Instead of Confusion*, and *Open Form & the Feminine Imagination*.

ALDON L. NIELSEN is a professor of English in the College of the Liberal Sarts at The Pennsylvania State University. He is the author of *Reading Race: White American Poets and the Racial Discourse in the Twentieth Century* (1990), *Writing Between the Lines : Race and Intertextuality* (1994), and *C.L.R. James : A Critical Introduction* (1997). He is also the editor of *Reading Race in American Poetry : An Area of Act* (2000).

ALICE NOTLEY is among the most celebrated American poets of her generation. Her books include, among many others, *How Spring Comes* (1981), *Margaret and Dusty* (1985), *At Night the States* (1988), *The Scarlet Cabinet* (with Douglas Oliver, 1992), *Selected Poems* (1993), *Close to me & Closer . . . (The Language of Heaven) and Désamère* (1995), *The Descent of Alette* (1996), *Mysteries of Small Houses* (1998), *and Disobedience* (2001). She is also a visual artist. She was married to Ted Berrigan until his death in 1983 and then Douglas Oliver. With Oliver she edited the magazine *Gare du Nord*. She is the mother of the poets Anselm Berrigan and Edmund Berrigan. She lives in Paris.

PETER O'LEARY books include a collection of poetry, *Watchfulness* (Spuyten Duyvil), and a book of criticism, *Gnostic Contagion: Robert Duncan and the Poetry of Illness* (Wesleyan), as well as two Ronald Johnson volumes that he edited, *To Do As Adam Did: Selected Poems* (Talisman) and *The Shrubberies* (Flood Editions). He lives in Chicago, where he edits *LUNG*.

JOHN OLSON is the author of *Echo Regime*, a full collection of poetry from Black Square Editions. *Jurassic Chandelier*, a collection of short prose narratives, is to be published by Black Square Editions in spring, 2003. His literary criticism has appeared in the *American Book Review, Rain Taxi, Sulfur* and *First Intensity*. He lives in Seattle.

MARJORIE PERLOFF'S most recent books are *Wittgenstein's Ladder: Poetic Language and the Strangeness of the Ordinary* (Chicago, 1996, paper 1999), and *Poetry On & Off the Page: Essays for Emergent Occasions* (Northwester UP, 1998), and *21st Century Modernism* (Blackwell, 2002). She is Sadie Dernham Patek Professor of Humanities Emerita at Stanford UNiversity.

LINDA RUSSO is the author of *o going out* (Potes & Poets Press, 1999), *Don't Tell Me I Have a Silly Desire* (nominative press, 1998), *The 'WORLD'* (des Allerwirklichste Miniatures Press, 1998), Secret Silent Plan (Curricle Patterns, 2000). She is currently working on her Ph.D. in Buffalo, New York.

JULIE SCHMID received her Ph.D. from the University of Iowa. She currently works for the faculty union at Portland State University, where she is also an adjunct in the English Department. She has published a number of articles on performance poetry and on academic unionism. *Cogs in the Classroom Factory: The Changing Identity of Academic Labor*, collection of essays that she coedited with Deborah Herman, is forthcoming from Greenwood Press.

STANDARD SCHAEFER, the founding editor of *Rhizome,* is the author of *Nova* and *Waltzing the Map*. He is a co-editor of *Ribot Music* and the editor of Paul Vangelisti's *Embarrassment of Survival.* He teaches at the Otis College of Art and Design.

SUSAN M. SCHULTZ has lived in Hawai'i for a dozen years; she teaches English and directs the writing program at the University of Hawai'i-Manoa. Her poetry book *Aleatory Allegories* was issued by Salt Publishing in 2000, and *Memory Cards and Adoption Papers* is from Potes and Poets (2002). She edits *Tinfish*, a journal of experimental poetry from the Pacific as well as a chapbook series. She is also a literary critic, edited *The Tribe of John: Ashbery and Contemporary Poetry* (U of Alabama P), and has published essays and reviews widely.

LEONARD SCHWARTZ has received grants from the National Endowment for the Arts and ArtsLink. His work has appeared in such journals as *First Intensity, Agni, Denver Quarterly,Talisman,Conjunctions, Harper's, Partisan Review,* and *Exquisite Corpse*. His books of poetry include *Words Before the Articulate* (1997), *Gnostic Blessing* (1992), *Exiles: Ends* (1990), and *Objects of Thought, Attempts at Speech* (1990); his essays are collected in *A Flicker at the Edge of Things* (1998). He is also a coeditor of *An Anthology of New American Poets* (1998) and *Primary Trouble* (1996).

MARK SCROGGINS is an associate professor of English at Florida Atlantic University. He is the editor of *Upper Limit Music: The Writing of Louis Zukofsky* and *Prepositions+ : The Collected Critical Essays*. He is the author of *Louis Zukofsky and the Poetry of Knowledge.*

Contributors

MARY MARGARET SLOAN is the editor of *Moving Borders: Three Decades of Innovative Writing by Women* and the author of *Infiltration* and *The Said Lands, Islands, and Premises*.

GUSTAF SOBIN is among the foremost poets and novelists of his generation. A native of Boston and a graduate of Brown University, he has lived in France for the past forty years. His many books of poetry, including *Voyaging Portraits* (New Directions, 1988) and *By The Bias Of Sound* (Talisman, 1995), are among the most celebrated of our time. His fiction, notably *The Fly-Truffler* (1999), has been internationally acclaimed and widely translated.

BRIAN KIM STEFANS is the editor of *Arras: New Media Poetry and Poetics*, located at www.arras.net. Books include *Free Space Comix* (Roof, 1998), *Gulf* (Object, 1998) and *Angry Penguins* (Harry Tankoos, 2000); forthcoming from Atelos Books is a collection of essays and poems titled *Fashionable Noise: On Digital Poetics*. On-line works include "The Dreamlife of Letters," a Flash movie, and "The Truth Interview," an interactive interview/collaboration with the poet Kim Rosenfield, both of which can be found at Arras. He lives in Williamsburg, Brooklyn.

SUSAN VANDERBORG is the author of *Paratextual Communities: American Avant-Garde Poetry Since 1950* (Southern Illinois UP, 2001). An assistant professor at the University of South Carlolina, Columbia, she has published articles on Jack Spicer, Charles Olson, and Louis Zukofsky.

This and the following page constitute an extension of the copyright page.

author; the excerpt from John Clarke is reprinted by permission of the estate of John Clarke; the excerpt from D. Alexander's "Poem" in *Tottel's II* is reprinted by permission of Clayton Eshleman; the excerpt from Bruce Andrews' "No Tumble" is reprinted by permission of the author; the excepts from editorials in *Paper Air* are reprinted by permission of Gil Ott; the passage from Rosmarie Waldrop's "mother/tongue" is reprinted by permission of the author; the passage from Maureen Owen's poem in *o.blēk* is reprinted by permission of the author; passages from Ron Silliman's work in *Tottel's* 10 is reprinted by permission of Ron Silliman and Opal L. Nations; passages from Jerome Rothenberg's Bantu translations in *Tottel's* 1 are reprinted by permission of the translator; the lines from Steve Benson's "Echo" are reprinted by permission of the author; passages from Susan Howe in *The Difficulties* 1 are reprinted by permission of the author; the passage from Fiona Templeton in *Writing* is reprinted by permission of the author; the passage from Rachel Blau DuPlessis's "Draft 2: She" is reprinted by permission of the author; passages from *Avec* II and III are reprinted by permission of Cydney Chadwick; Aram Saroyan's poem from *This* II is reprinted by permission of the author; lines from Robert David Cohen's "Bee" are reprinted by permission of the author; the lines by Ralph La Charity are reprinted by permission of the author; the passage by Kit Robinson is reprinted by permission of the author; the passage by David Bromige is reprinted by permission of the author; the passage by Ray DiPalma is reprinted by permission of the author; Robert Kelly's "If This Were the Place To Begin" is reprinted by permission of the author; Excerpts from *QU* are reprinted by permission of Carla Harryman; passages by Ron Silliman are reprinted by permission of the author; passages by Charles Bernstein are reprinted by permission of the author; passages by James Sherry are reprinted by permission of the author; passages by Bob Perelman are reprinted by permission of the author. • Richard Kostelanetz's "Nymphomania" is reprinted by permission of the author. • Passages from David Antin: *What It Means To Be Avant Garde*. Copyright © 1993 by David Antin. Reprinted by permission of New Directions Pub. Corp. • Sun Ra. *Extensions Out: The Immeasurable Equation Vol. 2*. Chicago: Ihnfinity Inc./Saturn Research, 1972. Reprinted by permission of Thomas Jenkins, president, Sun Ra, Inc. • Sun Ra. *The Immeasurable Equation*. Chicago: Ihnfinity Inc./Saturn Research, 1972. Reprinted by permission of Thomas Jenkins, president, Sun Ra, Inc. • Material published in Robert Creeley, *Collected Poems of Robert Creeley, 1945-1975*, copyright © 1983 by the Regents of the University of California, is reprinted by permission of the University of California Press. • George Oppen: COLLECTED POEMS, Copyright © 1974 by George Oppen. Reprinted by permission of New Directions Publishing Corp. • Passages from John Taggart, *Standing Wave* (Lost Roads), copyright © 1993 by John Taggart, reprinted by permission of the author. • Passages from John Taggart, *Loop* (Sun & Moon), copyright © 1991 by John Taggart, reprinted by permission of Sun & Moon Press. • Passages from Lyn Hejinian, *The Cell* (Sun & Moon), copyright © 1992 by Lyn Hejinian, reprinted by permission of Sun & Moon Press. • Passages from Frank Samperi, *Lumen Gloriae* (Grossman), copyright © 1973 by Frank Samperi, reprinted by permission of Claudia Samperi Warren; Passages from Frank Samperi, *The Prefiguration* (Grossman), copyright © 1971 by Frank Samperi, reprinted by permission of Claudia Samperi Warren; Passages from Frank Samperi, *Quadrifarium* (Grossman), copyright © 1973 by Frank Samperi, reprinted by permission of Claudia Samperi Warren. • Loris Essary's "Poem at Pt. Reyes" is reprinted by permission of the author. • "Be Grave Woman" from *The Poems of Laura Riding* by Laura (Riding) Jackson. Copyright © 1938, 1980. Reprinted by permission of Carcanet Press, Manchester, Persea Books, New York, and the author's Board of Literary Management. In conformity with the late author's wish, her Board of Literary Management asks us to record that, in 1941, Laura (Riding) Jackson renounced, on grounds of linguistic principle, the writing of poetry: she had come to hold that "poetry obstructs general attainment to something better in our linguistic way-of-life than we have." • Paul Zelevansky's visual text image from Shadow Architecture at the Crossroads (CNC Press, 1988) is reprinted by permission of the author. • passages from "A Bibliography of the King's Book or Eikon Basilike" by Susan Howe, from THE NONCONFORMIST'S MEMORIAL. Copyright © 1993 by Susan Howe. Reprinted by permission of New Directions Publishing Corp. • John Stickney's "We Are Your Occupied Spaces" is reprinted by permission of the author. • Harry Polkinhorn's visual text from page 29 of his book Summary Dissolution (The Runaway Spoon Press), copyright © 1988 by Harry Polkinhorn, is reprinted by permission of the author. • All other materials quoted in the essays collected here are believed to fall into the category of "fair use" for book reviews and scholarly essays in journals. Any errors or omissions are inadvertent and will be corrected, with proper acknowledgments, in future printings.

INDEX

prepared by Andrew Joron

A

Abbott, Steve, 512
Abrahams, William, 232
Abulafia, Abraham, 627, 628
Acconci, Vito Hannibal, 269
Acconi, Vito, 520
Acker, Kathy, 187, 191–93, 307, 309, 314, 507, 512
Adam, Helen, 251, 499
Adams, Brooks, 39
Addison, Lloyd, 541
Adnan, Etel, 514, 516, 523
Adorno, Theodor W., 185, 248, 310, 334, 351–53, 481, 647n
Agamben, Giorgio, 352
Akhmatova, Anna, 514
Albiach, Anne-Marie, 342
Aldan, Daisy, 246, 250n, 252, 263
Aldington, Richard, 167
Alexander, Charles, 524
Alexander, D., 303
Alexander, Will, 293–95, 400–402, 524, 536
Algarín, Miguel, 642
Ali, Muhammad, 609
Allen, Donald, xiii, 34, 41, 66, 153, 244, 250, 333, 334, 498, 526, 537, 578, 685, 686, 687n, 688–91
Althusser, Louis, 310, 336
Altieri, Charles, 311, 321, 370
Ammons, A. R., 357, 358
And, Miekal, 677–78
Anderson, Beth, 654
Anderson, Jack, 459
Anderson, Laurie, 352
Anderson, Margaret, 246
Anderson, T. J., 536, 545

Andrews, Bruce, vii, 1–17, 138, 153, 300, 306, 307, 309–10, 312, 316, 324, 328, 335–37, 341, 346, 515, 518, 524, 606, 674, 679, 680, 688
Angeline, Mary, 524
Angelou, Maya, 232
Anthony, Earl, 548
Antin, David, 220, 307, 314, 338n, 367–73, 377–78, 416, 682
Aptheker, Bettina, 549n
Aquinas, Saint Thomas, 522
Arakawa, 458, 482
Arbus, Diane, 512
Archimedes, 518, 609
Argento, Dario, 512
Argüelles, Ivan, 393–96, 399
Arin, Jennifer, 524
Armantrout, Rae, 257n, 266, 271n, 315, 340, 341n, 342, 506, 521
Armstrong, Neil, 609
Arrieta, Marcia, 297
Artaud, Antonin, 291, 415, 422n
Ashbery, John, 70, 98–106, 201–3, 208, 217, 218, 224, 226–29, 298, 309, 315, 323, 330, 380, 393, 403, 456, 499, 507, 537, 592n, 597, 647n
Ashley, Mary, 201, 217, 218, 257n
Asimov, Isaac, 609
Atkins, Russelkl, 540
Atkins, Russell, 539
Attar, Farid Ud-Din, 127
Atwood, Margaret, 459, 462
Auden, W. H., 132, 149, 529
Augustine, Saint, 141, 507, 519
Austen, Jane, 507, 522
Auster, Paul, 50, 109, 110n

Index

Ayler, Albert, 618
Ayler, Don, 618

B
Bach, Johann Sebastian, 156
Bachelard, Gaston, 101, 102
Bacon, Francis, 426
Bakerroshi, Richard, 559
Bakhtin, Mikhail, 337, 338, 426n
Baldwin, James, 611
Ballentine, Lee, 399
Ballerini, Luigi, 296
Balzac, Honoré de, 507
Banks, Ernie, 638
Baracks, Barbara, 257n, 262–64, 307, 337, 340
Baraka, Amiri, 38, 291, 293, 542–45, 594, 616, 618–20
Barba, Sharon, 502, 503
Barbie, Klaus, 316
Barbiero, Daniel, 126n, 690
Barg, Barbara, 206, 213, 260n
Barnes, Djuna, 32, 262
Barnett, Anthony, 342
Baron, Todd, 293, 297, 509, 524
Barone, Dennis, 500n, 524, 684, 688, 690–91
Barrigan, Barbara, 524
Barth, John, 461, 466
Barthelme, Donald, 462
Barthes, Roland, 99, 291, 334, 336, 338–40, 455, 516, 650
Bartlett, Lee, 311n
Bataille, Georges, 334, 512
Baudelaire, Charles, 66, 217, 410, 456, 514
Baudrillard, Jean, 479–80, 603
Baum, L. Frank, 157
Beach, Christopher, 233–34, 267-78
Beauvoir, Simone de, 507
Beckett, Samuel, 84, 138, 292, 315, 481, 507, 516, 518
Beckett, Tom, 312–14
Bell, Alexander Graham, 609

Bellamy, Dodie, 273–75, 500n, 507, 509, 510, 512, 520, 653
Bellen, Martine, 524
Benedikt, Michael, 459, 461, 462
Benjamin, Walter, 291, 334, 339, 390, 481, 656
Bennett, Guy, 297
Bennett, Helena, 649n, 661
Benson, Steve, 305, 312n, 316, 324, 507, 511
Bentley, Scott, 653
Berg, Steven, 340
Bergé, Carol, 253, 257n
Berger, John, 232
Bergvall, Caroline, 352–53, 512
Berkman, Alexander, 40
Berkson, Bill, 206, 524
Bernheimer, Alan, 521
Bernstein, Basil, 661
Bernstein, Charles, 124, 125n, 153, 154, 204, 209, 225, 226, 266, 275, 296, 298, 300, 306, 309, 310, 312–14, 316, 321, 323, 324, 326–29, 331, 335, 336, 338, 341, 452, 455, 456, 463, 508, 509, 515, 598n, 602n, 650n, 655n, 679–80
Bernstein, Michael André, 89
Berrigan, Anselm, 260, 524
Berrigan, Edmund, 524
Berrigan, Ted, 202, 204, 206–11, 213, 216, 217–23, 260, 288, 315, 520, 530, 540, 664n
Berry, Jake, 475
Berryman, John, 244, 298n
Berssenbrugge, Mei-mei, 227, 272, 342, 508, 577, 578, 580–82, 587, 602, 606
Bertholf, Robert J., 58–59, 285
Bibbs, Hart Leroi, 618
Biggs, Mary, 233, 255
Bishop, Elizabeth, 122, 124, 127, 129–32, 137, 139, 142, 244, 685n
Blackburn, Paul, 149, 167, 526
Black Elk, 415
Blake, William, 24, 41, 44, 46, 66, 313, 398, 409, 412, 429, 433, 443, 446, 591n, 595, 597

Blanchot, Maurice, 334, 341, 461
Blaser, Robin, 69, 84, 95
Blavatsky, Helena Petrovna, 622
Bloom, Harold, 80, 96, 149, 326, 486
Blount, Sonny, 609–33
Blumenreich, Julia, 524
Bly, Robert, 57, 298n
Bodmer, Frederick, 622
Boehme, Jakob, 450
Boer, Charles, 38
Boggs, Grace Lee, 550n
Boggs, James, 561n
Bohr, Niels, 518
Bök, Christian, 595
Bolden, Buddy, 619
Bonaventure, Saint, 447, 449
Bond, Horace Julian, 551–52
Bontemps, Arna, 540
Boone, Bruce, 512
Bootz, Philippe, 679
Borges, Jorge Luis, 309, 392, 461, 462
Borkhuis, Charles, 402–4, 524
Bory, Jean-Claude, 497n
Bottoms, David, 339
Boughn, Michael, 34-48, 703-07
Bourdieu, Pierre, 244n, 647n
Bowles, Jane, 507
Boyle, Kay, 123n
Brainard, Joe, 206, 511
Braithwaite, Lawrence, 513
Brakhage, Stan, 40
Branch, Taylor, 524
Brannen, Jonathan, 496
Brashear, Jim, 521
Brathwaite, Edward Kamau, 630–32
Braune, Bev, 524
Brautigan, Richard, 207
Braverman, Kate, 295
Braxton, Anthony, 616
Brecht, Bertoly, 325

Bremser, Ray, 38
Brennan, Sherry, 521
Breton, André, 380–84, 386, 387, 389, 393, 402, 426, 427, 462, 507
Brodine, Karen, 257n, 262n
Brodsky, Joseph, 127
Bromige, David, 300, 304, 311n, 313, 458, 521
Broner, Sari, 511
Bronk, William, vii, xi, xiii, xiv, xv, 107–21, 124, 129, 132–40, 167, 171, 238, 286, 287, 434
Brooks, Cleanth, 499
Brooks, Gwendolyn, 123n, 509, 540
Brossard, Nicole, 315, 507, 511, 516, 597
Brown, Clifford, 38
Brown, Elaine, 551, 561, 566n, 567n
Brown, H. Rap, 547
Brown, Harvey, 37–38, 40, 41
Brown, James, 545, 621
Brown, Lee Anne, 218, 238, 261, 276, 277, 520, 654, 655n, 656, 666–68
Brown, Marion, 619
Brown, Michael, 638, 640n, 643, 644n
Brown, Norman O., 418n, 427
Brown, Rebecca, 257n
Brown, Rita May, 521
Brown, Sterling, 540
Browne, Colin, 317
Browne, Laynie, xvi, 524
Bruce, Debra, 257n
Bruno, Franklin, 297
Bruno, Giordano, 397, 415
Brunt, H. L., 232
Bryan, Sharon, 339
Bryant, William Cullen, 20
Buber, Martin, 29
Buchan, John, 458
Buchanan, Pat, 220
Buck, Paul, 342
Bukowski, Charles, 289, 290, 293, 295
Bunting, Basil, 147, 167

Bürger, Peter, 647n
Burgess, Anthony, 399
Burke, Carolyn, 273
Burke, Edmund, 334
Burns, Avery, 516, 653
Burns, Gerald, 316
Burnside, Madeline, 263, 280
Burroughs, Margaret G., 127
Burroughs, William S., 251, 306, 316, 526, 644n
Burton, Richard, 515
Buscani, Lisa, 639, 644n
Bush, George, Sr., 322, 328, 377
Bushyeager, Peter, 201-16
Butterick, George, 42, 195
Butts, Mary, 272
Buuck, David, 500n, 524, 655n
Bye, Reed, 260
Byrd, Donald, 48
Byrd, Richard E., 515
Byrum, John, 497n, 521

C
Cabri, Louis, 524, 655n, 691
Cadden, Wendy, 254
Cage, John, 307, 353, 511, 518, 519, 526, 537, 652, 664, 679
Calbi, Evan, 297
Callahan, Eileen, 262n, 511, 523
Calvino, Italo, 461
Cameron, James, 649n
Camus, Albert, 515
Cannon, Steve, 616
Caplan, Jeremy, 524
Caplan, Ron, 38–40
Caples, Garrett, 400, 401, 404
Capone, Al, 638
Capote, Truman, 609
Cariaga, Catalina, 516
Carll, Steve, 524
Carmichael, Stokely, 547, 565n

Carpenter, Bonnie, 262
Carroll, Jim, 260
Carroll, Noel, 356
Carroll, Paul, 251
Carter, Bunchy Alprentice, 547, 548n, 558–59
Carter, Jimmy, 232
Caruso, Jim, 295
Cavell, Stanley, 309, 336
Cayley, John, 679
Ceravolo, Joseph, 511
Cervantes, Miguel de, 507
Césaire, Aimé, 388, 389, 400, 422n
Cha, Theresa Hak Kyung, 187, 193, 198–200, 315, 507, 509, 515, 516, 518, 576, 578, 583–89, 591n, 594, 595, 602, 604
Chadwick, Cydney, 316, 524, 653n
Challender, Rena, 243
Champion, Miles, 654n
Chandler, Raymond, 289, 293
Char, René, 25, 30, 32–33
Charles, Ray, 565
Charles I (king of England), 195
Chatterton, Thomas, 94
Chaucer, Geoffrey, 128
Cheek, Chris, 314
Cherkovski, Neeli, 388
Chernoff, Maxine, 206, 459–60, 524, 640n, 653n
Cherry, Don, 38, 440
Chester, Laura, 502, 503
Cheval, Ferdinand, 446
Child, Abigail, 279n, 316, 317, 340–41, 507, 515, 516
Chin, Frank, 580
Chin, Marilyn, 587
Chock, Eric, 587
Chomsky, Noam, 509
Chopin, Frédéric-François, 101
Christian, Barbara, 611
Chung, Francis, 589
Cixous, Hélène, 273, 338, 352
Clark, Emilie, 655n

Clark, Hilary, 374, 375
Clark, Jeff, 404
Clark, Susan, 279, 317, 500n, 514, 691
Clark, Tom, 34, 45, 51, 203, 207, 541
Clarke, Cass, 47
Clarke, John, 34, 41–48, 314
Cleaver, Eldridge, 547, 548n, 554–55, 561, 563, 566, 568, 573
Cleaver, Kathleen, 556–57, 566n
Clifton, Lucille, 123n
Clinton, George, 614
Clinton, Michelle, 289
Clippinger, David, 107-21, 135, 231-42
Cocteau, Jean, 388
Codrescu, Andrei, 55
Cohen, Leonard, 42
Cohen, Robert David, 303
Cole, Norma, 271n, 274, 279n, 293, 342, 508, 511, 520, 523
Cole, Peter, 450, 514, 524
Coleman, Ornette, 38, 389, 614
Coleridge, Samuel Taylor, 46, 141, 604
Coltrane, John, 156
Columbus, Christopher, 609
Condee, Nancy, 201, 217, 218, 257n
Conoley, Gillian, 524
Conrad, Cynthia, 518
Conte, Joseph, 136–37
Cook, Al, 41, 42
Cook, James, 515
Coolidge, Clark, 203, 204, 209, 288, 292, 297, 300, 303, 307, 309, 316, 337, 338n, 520, 692
Cooper, Dennis, 289–91, 296, 512
Cooper, James Fenimore, 522
Cooper, Lisa, 524
Corbett, William, 520
Corbin, Henri, 425n, 442
Corder, Eileen, 507
Corman, Cid, 147, 150, 167, 171, 233, 308, 447, 499
Cornell, Joseph, 99, 100, 105

Cornford, Adam, 396–99, 524
Corso, Gregory, 60n, 527, 529
Cortázar, Julio, 461
Cortez, Jayne, 382, 388–89, 393, 400, 540
Cox, Sarah Ann, 524
Crane, Hart, 433, 523, 545, 647n, 670
Creeley, Robert, 24, 25, 35, 49–56, 65, 66, 85, 109, 118–19, 149, 152, 167, 170–71, 207, 240, 250, 286, 300, 456, 499, 508, 514, 515, 518, 526, 527, 597, 647n, 650, 657, 663, 675
Crosson, Robert, 291, 293, 295, 297
Crozier, Andrew, 38
Cruz, Juana Inès de la, 22
Culianu, Ioan Petru, 433
Culley, Peter, 654n
cummings, e. e., 513

D

Dahlberg, Edward, 149
Dahlen, Beverly, 253, 257n, 266, 270, 341n, 351–52, 378, 509, 511
Dalí, Salvador, 383
Daly, Lew, 524
Damon, Maria, 524, 639–40
Dante Alighieri, 32, 66, 150, 157, 393, 415, 419, 431, 446–49, 542, 670
Darragh, Tina, 256, 257–58, 314, 458, 511, 512, 518, 521, 651n
Davey, Frank, 312, 335n
Davidson, Dan, 521
Davidson, Michael, 95, 310, 311n, 313, 324, 330, 462, 511, 650n
Davies, Alan, 507, 515, 591n
Davies, Kevin, 606, 651, 653, 654, 656–59, 671
Davis, Angela, 547n, 553, 554n, 559, 564, 568–73
Davis, Dale, 287
Davis, Jordan, 520
Davis, Lydia, 461, 512
Davis, Mike, 295
Dawson, Fielding, 49, 51, 54

Day, Jean, 279n, 515
Debray, Regis, 549n
Degas, Edgar, 27
Deguy, Michel, 342
de Kooning, Willem, 426, 511
Deleuze, Gilles, 111, 310, 352, 601
DeLissovoy, Noah, 524
Delville, Michel, vii, 452-68
Dembo, L. S., 147
DeNoyelles, Bill, 520
Dent, Tom, 616
Deren, Maya, 587
Derksen, Jeff, 317, 352, 524, 605, 654n
Derrida, Jacques, 85, 127n, 134–35, 141, 185, 193, 299, 310, 334, 336, 338, 453, 454, 461, 518, 549n, 563, 658
Descartes, René, 141
Desnos, Robert, 381
Devlin, Paul, 644
Dewey, John, 518
Dib, Mohammed, 297
Dickinson, Emily, 53, 92, 96, 110, 123n, 195, 244, 245, 247, 269, 276, 281, 314, 329, 413, 431, 489, 511, 514, 518, 523
Dienstfrey, Patricia, 262n, 263, 264, 270, 271n, 272, 500n, 510, 514
DiPalma, Ray, 307, 335, 518
Di Prima, Diane, 38, 246, 251–53, 261, 502, 521, 529, 540, 542
Disney, Walt, 423
Dlugo, Tim, 213
Dobbelmann, Duncan, 524
Dodson, Owen, 540
Dogen, 508
Dole, Bob, 693
Dolphy, Eric, 156
Domingo, W. A., 572
Donahue, Joseph, xiii, xiv, 64, 75, 79–80, 228–29, 288, 514, 523, 684
Donnelly, Jean, 365n
Donnely, Dorothy, 201, 217, 218, 257n

Doris, Stacy, 513
Dorman, Sonya, 503
Dorn, Edward, 38–41, 542
Dostoyevsky, F. M., 489
Douglas, Emory, 554, 564–65
Douglas, William O., 609
Douglass, Frederick, 548n
Dove, Rita, 342
Dowell, Denzil, 552–53
Downs, Buck, 365n, 521
Drake, Luigi-Bob, 676
Dreyer, Carl Theodor, 586
Dreyer, Lynne, 341, 359–60, 518, 520
Drucker, Johanna, 263, 267, 271n, 278, 279, 305, 306, 341, 342, 352, 506, 517, 518, 521
Duane, Kit, 262n
Du Bois, W. E. B., 548n, 551, 555
Ducornet, Rikki, 382, 399–400
Dudley, Randall, 127, 569–72
Dull, Harold, 248
Dumas, Henry, 616, 618, 620, 622, 626
Dunbar, Paul Laurence, 606, 627
Duncan, Robert, vii, xiii, 22, 25, 28, 38, 42, 43, 46, 53n, 54n, 56, 64–81, 95, 149, 150, 237, 252, 253, 285, 306, 311–13, 315, 342, 407–9, 411–14, 416, 423, 424, 428, 431, 433, 436, 437, 441, 443–45, 448, 508, 523, 530, 647n
Dunn, Lloyd, 481, 482
DuPlessis, Rachel Blau, 139, 162, 174–78, 180, 181, 268–71, 314–15, 342, 507, 511, 518, 650n
Durand, Marcella, 524, 653
Duras, Marguerite, 516
Duvalier, François, 401

E

Eckhart, Meister, 22
Eco, Umberto, 340
Economou, George, 149
Edson, Russell, 459, 461
Edwards, Brent Hayes, 609-35

Eigner, Larry, 305, 307, 308–9, 590, 649n
Einzig, Barbara, 341, 524
Eliot, George, 522
Eliot, T. S., 32, 92, 129, 147, 149, 219, 244, 270, 322, 338, 433, 518, 537, 540, 598n
Elizabeth I (queen of England), 123n
Ellingham, Lewis, 216
Ellington, Duke, 610–11, 616
Ellis, Stephen, xvi, 524
Ellroy, James, 293
Elman, Richard, 110n
Elmslie, Kenward, 204, 210, 453
Eluard, Paul, 386
Emerson, Ralph Waldo, 28, 246, 330, 331, 413
Empedocles, 30
Engels, Friedrich, 458
Enslin, Theodore, xiii, 151, 167
Equi, Elaine, 514, 668
Erin, Christopher, 481
Ernest, John, 132, 135–36
Ernst, Max, 390, 404, 595
Eshleman, Clayton, 290, 291, 338n, 342, 416, 417, 422–27, 429, 653n
Essary, Loris, 317, 470–76, 484
Estep, Maggie, 644n
Estrin, Jerry, 524
Evans, Steve, vii, 646-75
Evers, Medgar, 567n

F

Fagin, Larry, 209
Fair, Ronald, 620
Falconetti, Marie, 586
Fallon, Ruth, 236
Fanon, Frantz, 521, 549n, 555, 566, 569, 571
Farrell, Dan, 654n
Fauchereau, Serge, 168
Faulkner, William, 293
Fawcett, Brian, 310
Featherston, Dan, 407-30, 518

Feelings, Tom, 618
Feld, Ross, 84, 95
Fenollosa, Ernest, 28
Ferguson, Deanna, 524, 606
Ferlinghetti, Lawrence, 609
Fink, Thomas, 217, 224-30
Finkelstein, Norman, 82–97, 162, 163, 165–67, 172, 174, 178, 180–82, 321
Finlay, Ian Hamilton, 341
Finley, Karen, 539
Fiofori, Tam, 613
Fischer, Norman, 508–9, 691
Fitterman, Robert, 509, 653, 654n
Fitzpatrick, Tony, 636–37
Fixel, Lawrence, 459, 461
Flaubert, Gustave, 657
Fodaski, Elizabeth, 513, 653
Folson, Cameron, 262n
Foote, Julia, 614
Forché, Carolyn, 127
Ford, Charles Henri, 380, 383, 390
Foss, Phillip, 312, 404, 436–37
Foster, Edward, vii, xiii-xvi, 18–33, 75, 95, 124, 285, 286, 287, 288, 514, 526–35, 653n, 684
Foucault, Michel, 193, 291, 338–40, 377, 385
Fourcade, Dominique, 153
Foust, Graham, 655n
Franco, Michael, xvi
Fraser, Kathleen, 225, 239, 247, 254–55, 257n, 270–74, 277n, 315, 341, 342, 498, 500n, 502, 510–12, 518, 521, 523
Frazier, Robert, 399
Fredman, Stephen, 311, 689
Freilicher, Jane, 511
Freud, Sigmund, 69, 186, 310, 314, 389, 392, 407n, 416n, 450, 461, 518, 548n
Friedlander, Benjamin, 313, 524, 649, 653, 655n
Friedman, Ed, 212, 305–6
Frost, Robert, 474
Fuller, Heather, 513

Index

Fuller, Margaret, 246
Fuller, William, 521
Fulton, Len, 243n, 250
Fyman, Cliff, 520

G

Gaines, Reg E., 539
Galbraith, John Kenneth, 609
Galilei, Galileo, 518
Gallup, Dick, 203
Gama, Vasco da, 609
Gander, Forrest, 524
Ganick, Peter, 314, 500n, 524, 684, 688, 690–91
García Lorca, Federico, 393
Gardner, Drew, 514
Garon, Paul, 382
Garvey, Marcus, 614
Gassner, John, 148
Gates, Henry Louis, 639–40
Gay, Michel, 312
Gburek, Jeff, 649n
Genet, Jean, 507, 554n
George, Stefan, 96
Gerstler, Amy, 295
Gery, Jihn, 228
Gevirtz, Susan, 509, 510, 516
Gibbon, Edward, 158
Gibbons, Reg, 640n
Gide, André, 291
Gilbert, Alan, 365n
Gilbert, Sandra, 245, 267
Gill, Eric, 46
Gillespie, Abraham Lincoln, 544
Gilmore, John, 622
Gilmore, Lyman, 57n
Gilonis, Harry, 127
Gins, Madeline, 453, 457–58, 482
Ginsberg, Allen, xiv, 66, 149, 150, 232, 251, 253, 260, 298n, 306, 340, 427, 499, 508, 518, 529, 540, 604, 644n, 652, 663

Giorno, John, 204
Giovanni, Nikki, 502
Giscombe, C. S., 510
Giulani, Alfredo, 296
Gizzi, Michael, 524
Gizzi, Peter, 315, 365n, 500n, 514, 518, 649n, 653, 654
Gladman, Renee, 510, 654
Glancy, Diane, 510
Glass, Philip, 156, 179–80
Glazier, Loss Pequeño, 243n, 655n, 674–83
Glazner, Gary, 637n, 638, 639, 643
Gleason, Madeline, 251, 499
Glover, Albert, 34, 35, 38, 40–45
Glück, Louise, 521
Glück, Robert, 507, 511, 512
Godfrey, John, 211, 463
Goethe, Johann Wolfgang von, 433
Gogh, Vincent van, 27, 426, 489
Going, Dale, 511, 521
Golding, Alan, 250, 323, 499, 650n, 684–94
Goldman, Judith, 524, 654
Goldsmith, Kenneth, 352, 353, 681
Good, Phil, 520
Gordon, Milton, 592
Göring, Hermann, 596
Gorky, Arshile, 380
Gough, Jenny, 518
Grahn, Judy, 254, 255, 503
Gramsci, Antonio, 377
Graves, Milford, 618, 619
Graves, Robert, 609
Green, Henry, 531
Greenblatt, Stephen, 523
Grenier, Robert, 153, 269, 300, 302, 328, 335n, 458, 508, 509, 649n
Grim, Jessica, 515, 521, 653, 690
Grosski, Peter, 288
Grosvenor, Verta Mae, 623
Grumman, Bob, 476, 493–96
Guattari, Félix, 111, 601

Gubar, Susan, 245, 267
Guest, Barbara, 201, 217, 218, 257n, 271n, 272, 342, 453, 499, 502, 506, 511, 514
Guthrie, Camille, 523

H
H. D., 40, 46, 167, 262, 272, 315, 410n, 411, 433, 502, 508, 511, 523, 647n
Habermas, Jürgen, 456
Hacker, Dean, 637n
Hagedorn, Jessica, 582
Hahn, Kimiko, 582n
Hall, Donald, 687n, 689
Halpern, David, 298n
Hamburger, Kate, 355–56, 358
Hamer, Fanny Lou, 551
Hamill, Janet, 257n
Hammer, Louis, 381
Hampton, Fred, 561n
Hankla, Susan, 257n
Hansen, Jefferson, 126n
Hardy, Thomas, 142
Harris, Claire, 510
Harris, Marie, 459
Harris, Wilson, 632–33
Harrison, Jane, 76, 89
Harryman, Carla, 226, 257n, 263, 305, 312n, 315n, 341, 342, 402, 464, 465, 505–8, 510–12, 520, 521
Hartley, George, 224, 311, 340n
Hartman, Yuki, 258, 578
Hartmann, Sadakichi, 578
Haselwood, Dave, 248
Haslam, Gerald, 236
Hatlen, Burton, 176
Hawthorne, Nathaniel, 519, 522
Hayden, Robert, 540
Hayles, N. Katherine, 353
Heap, Jane, 246
Heck, John, 481
Hegel, G. W. F., 648, 670

Heidegger, Martin, 29–30, 141, 352, 563
Heinowitz, Cole, 507
Hejinian, Lyn, 124, 125n, 142–43, 152, 163–67, 174–78, 180–82, 226, 244, 257n, 258, 262–65, 273n, 274, 275, 277–78, 287, 292, 296, 300, 305, 310, 312n, 313–15, 326, 328, 329, 335n, 341–43, 367–69, 372–78, 466, 467, 500n, 505, 508, 511, 514–16, 518, 520, 693
Helgeson, Jeff, 636
Heller, Michael, 137–38, 151, 162, 168–69, 172–74, 178, 180–82
Hemingway, Ernest, 31
Henderson, David, 616–18, 620
Henderson, Fletcher, 619
Henderson, Stephen, 541
Hentoff, Nat, 622
Heraclitus, 30, 35
Herbert, George, 141, 352, 446
Hernton, Calvin, 620
Herriman, George, 69
Hesiod, 66, 68, 661, 662
Heston, Charlton, 489
Heuving, Jeanne, xvi, 185–200, 524
Hickman, Lee, 291–93, 295, 314, 341–43
Higgins, Dick, 476, 518
Higgins, George V., 531
High, John, xvi, 288, 462, 524
Hill, Andrew, 618
Hill, Crag, 497n
Hill, Lindsay, 399
Hilliard, David, 566n
Hillman, Brenda, 524
Hillman, James, 426n
Hilton, Mary, 279
Hitchcock, George, 381, 389–91, 393, 396
Hitler, Adolf, 428
Hoefer, David, 399
Hofer, Jen, 524
Hogue, Cynthia, 524
Hölderlin, Friedrich, 30

Holiday, Billie, 594
Holland, Joyce, 263
Hollander, Benjamin, 316, 524
Hollo, Anselm, 518, 530
Hollowell, Andrea, 649n
Holman, Bob, 210, 212, 213, 217–19, 222–23, 638, 639, 641n, 642, 643n, 644
Holub, Miroslav, 292
Homer, 44, 66, 439
Honan, William H., 609
Hongo, Garrett, 582n, 595n
Hooker, Richard, 333
Hooper, Virginia, 524
Hoover, Paul, 206, 453, 524, 640n, 650n, 653n, 684–87, 689–92
Hope, Bob, 609
Horace, 127, 529
Hovey, Richard, xiv
Howard, Jean, 638, 644n
Howard, W. Scott, 122-46
Howe, Fanny, 257n, 271n, 292, 341n, 342, 343–44, 508, 513–14, 516, 518, 520
Howe, Susan, 91–93, 109, 110–12, 114–16, 120, 124, 125n, 138, 187, 193–97, 200, 225, 226, 236, 247, 257n, 258, 259, 266n, 269, 271n, 276–78, 281, 311, 313–16, 323, 328–29, 341–43, 352, 431, 434–35, 511, 515, 522–23, 590, 649n, 669, 692
Hoyem, Andrew, 248
Huggins, Ericka, 554, 559, 560, 562, 566, 568n
Huggins, John, 548n
Hughes, Langston, 515, 537, 540, 542, 552, 594, 617, 625, 629
Huidobro, Vicente, 395
Hulbert, Archer Butler, 40
Hulme, T. E., 167
Humphrey, Hubert Horatio, 609
Huncke, Herbert, 38
Hunt, Erica, 466, 506, 515, 536–37, 545, 546
Hunt, Laird, 524
Hunter, Emmy, 218

Hurston, Zora Neale, 514, 632
Hutchinson, Anne, 195
Hutton, Bobby, 570
Hyung Soon Huo, 516

I

Ibsen, Henrik Johan, 518
Ignatow, David, 298n, 459, 460
Inada, Lawson Fusao, 588n, 591, 594
Inman, P., 314, 518, 521
Ionesco, Eugène, 481, 518
Irby, Kenneth, 292, 314, 342
Irigaray, Luce, 273, 338, 523
Iser, Wolfgang, 486
Ismail, Jam, 576, 603–4, 606
Ives, Charles, 157

J

Jabès, Edmond, 341, 342
Jablonski, Joseph, 381
Jackson, George, 551, 559, 570
Jackson, Laura (Riding), 187–93, 270, 315
Jackson, Rebecca, 614
Jacob, Max, 461, 462
Jacques, Geoffrey, 545
Jaffer, Frances, 254, 270, 511
Jakobson, Roman, 46, 291, 337, 351, 650, 651
James, George G. M., 622
James, Henry, 601
James, William, xiv
James, Winston, 573n
Jameson, Fredric, 376, 585, 687
Jardine, Alice, 523
Jarman, Joseph, 616
Jarnot, Lisa, 462, 500n, 520, 652–54, 656, 659–60
Jarraway, David, 373
Jefferson, Blind Lemon, 349n
Jess, 285
Jesus Christ, 195, 198, 415n, 419, 432, 445
Jewel, 232

Joan of Arc, 199, 516, 586, 588
Johns, Jasper, 579n, 664
Johnson, Jack, 567n
Johnson, Peter, 459
Johnson, Robert, 614
Johnson, Ronald, 155, 156–59, 443, 445–48, 450
Johnson, W. R., 355
Jonas, Steve, 540
Jones, Bill T., 539
Jones, Charles E., 566n
Jones, Hettie, 250n, 540
Jones, LeRoi, 38, 251, 537, 540, 542, 620
Jong, Erica, 502
Jonson, Ben, 529
Jordan, Clifford, 38
Joris, Pierre, 414, 585
Joron, Andrew, 379-430, 399, 404, 523
Joselow, Beth Baruch, 521, 524
Joyce, James, 32, 158, 317, 516, 518, 604
Jung, Carl Gustav, 389, 416n

K
Kafka, Franz, 462, 489, 591n
Kalaidjian, Walter, 391
Kalleberg, Garrett, 524, 655n
Kandel, Lenore, 253
Karesh, David, 415
Katz-Levine, Judy, 257n
Kaufman, Bob, 386–88, 393, 540
Kaufman, Shirley, 503
Keats, John, 47, 429
Keckler, W. B., 404
Keller, Helen, 458
Kelley, Robin, 573n
Kellogg, David, 521
Kelly, Andrew, 263, 280
Kelly, Robert, 40, 41, 149, 152, 290, 301–2, 342, 389, 416–22, 429, 598n, 688
Kennedy, John F., 387
Kenner, Martin, 562

Kerman, Judith, 277
Kerouac, Jack, xiv, 488, 530, 560, 662, 663
Kgositsile, K., 620
Khaury, Herbert, 609
Khlebnikov, Velimir, 651
Kierkegaard, Søren, 518
Killian, Kevin, 216, 500n, 507, 509, 510, 512, 653
Killian, Sean, xvi
Kim, Elaine, 584
Kim, Myung Mi, 271n, 511, 516, 523, 577, 584, 589–91
Kim, Stephanie Hyungjung, 516
Kimball, Jack, xvi
Kimmelman, Burt, 161-84, 218
King, Stephen, 512
Kingston, Maxine Hong, 595n
Kinnell, Galway, 342
Kiyooka, Roy, 577, 591n, 595–97, 600, 601, 604
Klee, Paul, 387
Klein, Michael, 127
Kline, Franz, 60
Knott, Bill, 381
Koch, Edward, 609
Koch, Kenneth, 201–3, 208, 217, 218, 224, 225, 227, 341, 462
Koch, Peter, 396
Kostelanetz, Richard, 462, 476–77, 497n, 689–90n
Kosuth, Joseph, 458
Kovalski, Lisa, 524
Kraut, Shelley, 206, 210, 218, 260n
Kristeva, Julia, 273, 338, 339, 512, 518
Kröller, Eva-Marie, 595–97
Krukowski, Damon, 653n
Kuhn, Thomas, 507, 518, 613
Kumin, Maxine, 338n, 503
Kuszai, Joel, 653
Kyger, Joanne, 207, 251, 253, 256, 257n, 649n

L
LaBranche, Carol, 201, 217, 218, 257n
Lacan, Jacques, 273, 310, 336, 512, 518, 661

Index

La Charity, Ralph, 313
Lally, Michael, 219, 304, 500n, 521
Lam, Wifredo, 580
Lamantia, Philip, 379, 381–86, 388, 393, 394, 399
Landrey, David, 49-65, 285, 286, 287
Lang, Doug, 518
Lanier, Sidney, 629–30
Lansing, Gerrit, xiv, 514
Lao Tzu, 665
La Palma, Marina, 262n
Laughlin, James, 139, 147
Lauterbach, Ann, 226–27, 229, 351, 465n, 506, 515
Lautreamont, le comte de, 100, 382, 481, 507
Lavalle, Tomás Guido, 342
Lazer, Hank, 241, 311n, 326, 378, 524, 650n, 685
Lear, Edward, 85
Leary, Timothy, 609
Lease, Joseph, 217, 224, 229
Lee, Annabel, 249, 263
Lee, Bennett, 603
Lee, Christopher, 512
Lee, Don L., 539
Lenhart, Gary, 210–12
Lesniak, Rose, 206, 213
Leung, Ho Hon, 587
Levertov, Denise, 65, 66, 149, 167, 251–52, 262, 499, 503
Levine, Steve, 206, 210–12
Levis, Larry, 123, 125n
Lévi-Strauss, Claude, 509
Levi Strauss, David, 315
Levy, Andrew, 509
Levy, d. a., 675
Lew, Walter, 577, 584, 587–89, 591n, 684n
Lewis, Joel, 211, 212, 216, 524
Lewis, Wyndham, 598n
Lilley, Kate, 123n
Lima, Frank, 204
Lin, Tan, 518, 577, 578, 582–83, 589, 606
Lindberg, Kathryne V., 547-75

Liu, Timothy, xvi
Loftin, Elouise, 543–45
Loftis, N. J., 545
Logan, John, 251
Lombardo, Gian, xvi
London, Jack, 660
London, Rick, 509
Long, Haniel, 39, 40
Lookingbill, Colleen, 524
Lorde, Audre, 123n, 252n
Lovelace, Grace, 524
Lovell, Thoreau, 462, 524
Lovi, Steve, 248
Lowell, Amy, 537
Lowell, Robert, xiii, 131, 201, 244, 298n, 338n, 367, 431, 504, 529, 537, 685n
Lowenthal, Jessica, 653
Loy, Mina, 243, 245, 269, 270, 511
Lu, Pamela, 513, 515
Lubeski, Lori, xvi, 515
Lucas, Brian, 404
Lucretius, 446, 518
Luoma, Bill, 524, 649n, 653, 654, 655n, 656, 661–63
Luria, Isaac, 433
Lusk, Dorothy Trujillo, 524, 606
Luxemburg, Rosa, 669
Lyons, Kimberly, 524

M

Mac Cormack, Karen, 316, 513, 515
MacDonald, George, 69
MacDonald, Susan, 257n
Macintosh, Graham, 40
Mackey, Nathaniel, 64, 75–79, 88–91, 225, 287, 292, 311n, 315, 316, 344–45, 431, 436, 437, 440–42, 450, 510, 523, 536–37, 545, 630
MacLeod, Kathryn, 279n, 524
MacLeod, Scott, 521
Mac Low, Jackson, xiii, 308, 456, 518, 664, 679, 680
Magdalene, Mary, 195

Magee, Kevin, 518, 523
Magloire-Saint-Aude, Clément, 382
Maher, Miranda, 516, 521
Mahler, Gustav, 418
Mahrem, Murad, 285
Major, Clarence, 540, 601
Malcolm X, 556
Mallarmé, Stéphane, 19, 22, 317, 352, 410, 411, 516, 585, 587, 600
Mandel, Tom, 465, 514, 515
Mandelbrot, Benoit, 518
Mandelstam, Osip, 75
Mann, Paul, 95
Mansour, Joyce, 400
Mao Zedong, 558, 596
Marcoussis, Louis, 248n
Marcus, Morton, 459
Marcuse, Herbert, 481
Mariani, Paul, 410n
Marlatt, Daphne, 303
Marlis, Stefanie, 524
Marlowe, Christopher, 103
Marriott, D. S., 341n
Marsden, Dora, 46
Marsh, William, 521
Martin, Agnes, 581
Martin, Stephen-Paul, 469-97
Marwan, 426
Marx, Karl, 224, 226, 232n, 299, 308, 310, 336, 340, 376, 379, 381, 433, 481, 507, 555, 669n
Mason, Chris, 310
Massey, Irving, 42
Masteler, Richard, 238
Masters, Greg, 210, 211
Masuda, Barry, 602, 604, 606
Mather, Cotton, 522
Mathews, Jackson, 25
Matthews, J. H., 400
Maud, Ralph, 37
Mayakovsky, Vladimir, 644, 651

Mayer, Bernadette, 204, 205, 208–9, 211, 213, 214, 226, 238, 246, 253, 257n, 260, 261, 276, 300, 323, 341, 466, 500n, 507, 514, 519–20, 651, 652, 655n, 668
McAlmon, Robert, 46
McBride, John, 290
McCaffery, Steve, 309, 312, 316, 335–41, 343–44, 346, 348, 350, 352, 515, 585, 592n, 688
McClatchy, J. D., 685
McClure, Michael, 23–25, 40, 41, 56
McCorkle, James, 226n
McFarland, Ronald, 131
McGann, Jerome, 224, 311n, 324
McGovern, George, 609
McGrath, Connell, 315, 500n, 524
McKay, Claude, 549–50, 571–73
McKay, Nellie, 545
McLaughlin, Lissa, 257n
McLeer, Brigid, 517
McLuhan, Marshall, 609
McMorris, Mark, 536, 545, 654
Melnick, David, 153
Melville, Herman, 63, 92, 132, 200, 413, 489, 522
Merrill, James, 157, 298n
Merrill, Stuart, 578
Merwin, W. S., 124, 125, 143, 298n
Messerli, Douglas, 234, 292, 296, 299, 311, 322, 328, 333, 500n, 518, 524, 650n, 684, 689–92
Mezey, Robert, 340
Michaux, Henri, 461
Middleton, Peter, 338n, 342
Miki, Roy, 576, 577, 595–97, 600–601
Miller, Cheryl, 262n
Miller, E. A., 517
Miller, Richard, 246
Miller, Stephen Paul, 217-223, 227, 229
Millett, Kate, 523
Mills-Courts, Karen, 141
Milton, John, 122, 195
Mingus, Charles, 594, 616, 617
Minoru Yashioka, 342

Index

Miró, Joan, 383
Mittenthal, Robert, xvi
Mlinko, Ange, xvi, 520
Mobilio, Albert, 524
Mohr, Bill, 295
Monk, Thelonious, 156
Monroe, Harriet, 246
Montessori, Maria, 521
Moore, Marianne, 123n, 243, 245, 246, 270, 272, 502, 508, 511, 537
Moriarty, Laura, 262n, 271n, 279n, 506, 511, 513, 523, 655n
Morrison, Jim, 289
Morrison, Toni, 562
Morrison, Yedda, 500n, 510, 517, 655n
Morrissey, Judd, 679
Morrow, Brad, 653n
Morton, Jelly Roll, 618
Moschus, 123, 142
Motherwell, Robert, 380, 515
Mouré, Erin, 506, 518
Moxley, Jennifer, 279, 524, 649n, 653, 654, 656, 669–71
Muhammad, Elijah, 622
Mullen, Harryette, 345–50, 352, 464, 509, 512, 523, 536–37, 542, 545, 603, 630
Mullen, Laura, 518
Murphy, Michelle, 524
Murphy, Sheila E., 464, 514, 524
Murray, Aife, 511
Murray, Elizabeth, 222
Muske-Dukes, Carole, 290
Myles, Eileen, 210–14, 217–23, 259, 260n, 512, 520

N
Nabokov, Vladimir, 540, 609
Nagarjuna, 508
Nakayasu, Swako, 516
Nakel, Marty, 292
Nancy, Jean-Luc, 36, 652

Nash, Susan Smith, 240, 321, 322, 524
Nations, Opal L., 304
Nauen, Eleanor, 213, 260n
Naylor, Paul, 77
Neal, Larry, 618, 620, 621
Neff, Paul, 481
Neilson, Melanie, 509, 515, 521, 653, 654n, 690
Nelson, Cary, 647n
Nelson, Gale, 524
Nemet-Nejat, Murat, xvi
Neruda, Pablo, 389
Newman, Denise, 509, 511
Newton, Huey, 547–67, 573
Newton, Isaac, 455
Ney, Shiad, 509
Ngai, Sianne, 317, 500n, 524, 602, 605, 606, 653
Nguyen, Hoa, 603, 654
Niccolai, Giuliani, 291
Nichol, bp, 346, 600
Nicholls, Peter, 169
Niedecker, Lorine, 125n, 147, 151, 167, 270, 315, 502, 511, 537
Nielsen, Aldon, 347, 536–46, 617, 630
Nietzsche, Friedrich, 30, 134, 563, 566
Norse, Harold, 307
Northup, Harry, 295
Northup-Prado, Holly, 293
Norton, Thomas, 333
Notley, Alice, vii, 202, 206, 210–11, 213–15, 218, 243–44, 246, 247, 254, 257n, 260, 261, 274–76, 288, 436, 437–40, 442, 443, 511, 520, 526–35, 649n
Noto, John, 126n, 399, 524
Novalis, 46, 102
Nyland, Charles, 386

O
O'Brien, Geoffrey, 524
O'Connor, Flannery, 512

O'Hara, Frank, 201–6, 213, 217–19, 223–25, 227, 228, 244, 315, 346, 380, 393, 403, 499, 507, 511, 527, 529–31, 542, 597, 647n, 658n, 663, 664, 668
O'Keefe, Georgia, 581
O'Leary, Peter, vii, 431-51
Oliver, Douglas, xvi, 206, 529
Olson, Charles, 20, 34–39, 41–50, 53n, 55, 56, 59n, 63, 65, 66, 92, 123, 125n, 129, 157, 195, 244, 250, 252, 262, 300, 312, 342, 351, 410n, 411, 413, 415, 421, 424, 433, 436, 441, 446, 511, 515, 523, 530, 531, 537, 543, 597, 600, 658, 682, 691
Olson, John, xvi, 98-106, 404
Oppen, George, 21–22, 25, 123, 124, 133, 138–39, 147, 151, 167–75, 182, 499, 511, 515, 518, 537, 646, 651, 652
Oppenheim, Meret, 248n
Oppenheimer, Joel, 49–51, 55–63, 149
Oren, Michael, 617, 618
Orwell, George, 328
Osman, Jena, 237–38, 276, 279, 280, 500n, 515, 521, 523, 653
Ostashevsky, Eugene, 648n
Ostriker, Alicia Suskin, 269n
O'Sullivan, Maggie, 316, 333, 684n, 689
Ott, Gil, 308, 650n
Overstreet, Joe, 618
Ovid, 518
Owen, Maureen, 203, 209, 212, 213–14, 216, 248, 257–61, 271n, 307, 315, 500n, 511, 514, 515, 520, 523
Owens, Rochelle, 256, 257n, 342

P

Pack, Robert, 687n, 689
Padgett, Ron, 202, 203, 205, 206, 212, 213, 225, 287, 500n, 541, 595
Pagels, Elaine, 433
Paik, Nam June, 587
Palmer, Michael, 64, 69–73, 80, 86–88, 92, 109, 115–16, 120, 154, 307, 311, 316, 338n, 402, 511, 515, 582

Parker, Charlie, 620
Parks, Suzan-Lori, 352
Parshchikov, Alexei, 376, 377
Partch, Harry, 157
Pasolini, Pier Paolo, 291
Pastan, Linda, 503
Patrick, Pat, 622
Patterson, William L., 559
Patton, Julie, 510, 516, 518
Paul, Sherman, 369
Paulson, William, 337
Paz, Octavio, 291, 431
Pearcy, Kate, 348
Pearson, Hugh, 560–61n
Pearson, Norman Holmes, 40
Pearson, Ted, 649n
Pensak, Susan, 516
Perelman, Bob, 94–95, 299, 302n, 304, 305, 309, 311, 312n, 321–24, 335n, 340n, 341n, 452–54, 458, 463, 464, 465n, 467, 507, 650n, 684
Péret, Benjamin, 382
Perkoff, Stuart Z., 295
Perloff, Marjorie, 224, 311, 333-54, 355, 463, 466, 499, 522, 592n, 650n, 689
Perry, Lee "Scratch," 614
Perry, Milman, 44
Peters, Robert, 64
Pettet, Simon, xvi, 206, 288, 524
Philip, M. Nourbese, 510
Philips, Katherine, 123n
Phillips, Dennis, 290–96
Phillips, Frances, 257n
Phillips, Jayne Anne, 307
Phillips, Tom, 341, 477
Piaget, Jean, 472
Piercy, Marge, 502, 521
Pierre, José, 380
Pinney, Todd, 520
Pinter, Harold, 518
Piombino, Nick, 314, 462

Pitcher, Oliver, 617
Plath, Sylvia, 123n, 201, 367, 502, 504, 512, 527–29
Plato, 351, 409
Plautus, 147
Poe, Edgar Allan, 41, 244, 456, 629, 644n
Poggioli, Renato, 126
Polkinhorn, Harry, 476, 494–97
Pollock, Jackson, 60, 380
Pomare, Eleo, 620
Pommy-Vega, Janine, 257n
Popa, Vasko, 391, 461
Porta, Antonio, 291
Potts, Randall, 524
Pound, Ezra, 28, 32, 34, 38, 47, 65, 66, 148–50, 157, 158, 161, 167–70, 235, 243–45, 270, 300, 304, 313, 315, 321, 325, 333, 338, 411, 413, 423, 433, 446, 455, 499, 508, 514, 518, 537, 542, 573, 578, 585, 598n, 601, 647, 686n, 690n
Powell, Colin, 220
Prevallet, Kristin, 404, 520
Pritchard, N. H., 544, 545
Pritchard, Norman, 616, 617
Proust, Marcel, 515
Pruitt, Patricia, xvi

Q

Quartermain, Meredith, 511
Quartermain, Peter, 324, 326, 524
Quayle, Dan, 322
Quinn, Sally, 220

R

Rabelais, François, 507, 518
Ragan, James, 292
Rahman, Yusuf, 620
Rainer, Yvonne, 511
Rainey, Ma, 349n
Rakosi, Carl, 147, 151, 167
Ramazani, Jahan, 122, 123, 127, 130, 136, 143
Ram-el-zee, 614

Ramke, Bin, 124, 125n, 141
Ramsdell, Heather, 524
Randall, Dudley, 565
Randall, Margaret, 246, 253, 597
Rankine, Claudia, 524
Ransom, John Crowe, 502
Rappaport, Jill, 218
Rasula, Jed, 24In, 314, 324, 342, 419n, 420, 685, 686n, 689
Ratcliffe, Stephen, 372n, 508
Raworth, Tom, 524
Ray, Man, 247n
Raynor, Doane J., 349n
Reagan, Nancy, 489
Reagan, Ronald, 322, 328, 331, 377
Rechy, John, 290
Reed, Ishmael, 620
Reed, Pat, 649n
Rehm, Pam, 364–65, 450, 524, 649n
Reich, Steve, 156
Reich, Wilhelm, 424n
Reiner, Chris, 297
Reinfeld, Linda, 224, 311n
Retallack, Joan, 257, 269, 275, 352, 511, 514, 515, 517–18, 520, 523
Retsov, S., 288
Reverdy, Pierre, 72, 462
Rexroth, Kenneth, 147, 413n, 431, 578
Reznikoff, Charles, 147, 151, 167, 168
Rhee, Syngman, 586
Rich, Adrienne, 123n, 254, 255, 267, 342, 502, 529
Richardson, Dorothy, 269, 270, 272
Rigsbee, David, 127, 143
Rilke, Rainer Maria, 87, 445, 513, 523
Rimbaud, Arthur, 26, 333, 381, 382, 389, 410, 412n, 458, 596
Risset, Jacqueline, 342
Robbe-Grillet, Alain, 581
Roberson, Ed, 514, 544–45, 630
Robertson, Lisa, 512, 517, 518, 654n

Robinson, Charles, 234
Robinson, Elizabeth, 514
Robinson, Kit, 304, 305, 324, 330–31, 402, 524
Robles, Al, 588n
Robles, Jaime, 257n, 262n, 500n, 511
Rodefer, Stephen, 38, 465, 524, 649n
Rodia, Simon, 157, 446
Roditi, Edouard, 391–93
Rolfe, Lionel, 293
Rollins, Henry, 289
Rollins, Sonny, 545
Ronan, Stephen, 399
Ronk, Martha, 293–96, 342, 514
Roosevelt, Franklin D., 586
Rorty, Richard, 127n, 518
Rosemont, Franklin, 381, 382–83
Rosemont, Penelope, 381, 382–83
Rosenberg, David, 80
Rosenberg, Jim, 679
Rosenfield, Kim, 513
Rosenthal, Bob, 206, 210–13, 218
Rosenthal, Jane, 257n
Rosenthal, Jessica, 500n
Rosenthal, Laura, 55
Rosenwasser, Rena, 257n, 262, 263, 500n, 524
Rosenzweig, Phyllis, 518, 521
Rossetti, Christina, 123n
Rothenberg, Jerome, 149, 303, 338n, 342, 389, 414, 416, 585
Rothschild, Douglas, 653, 654
Roubaud, Jacques, 457
Roussel, Raymond, 382
Rowlandson, Mary, 194, 523
Roy, Camille, 507, 513
Ruddick, Lisa, 181
Ruskin, Kate, 524
Russo, Linda, 243-84, 708-10

S

Sacks, Peter, 122–24n, 127

Sade, Marquis de, 395, 507
Safire, William, 609
Saidenberg, Jocelyn, 520
Salach, Cin, 637n, 644n
Salerno, Mark, 297
Samperi, Frank, 150, 155, 156, 443, 447–49
Samuels, Lisa, 524
Sandbank, Shimon, 171
Sanders, Edward, 40, 41, 56, 250
Sandri, Giovanna, 297
Sappho, 349, 518
Saroyan, Aram, 204, 207, 302
Sarraute, Nathalie, 516
Sartarelli, Stephen, 524
Sartre, Jean-Paul, 515, 518
Saussure, Ferdinand de, 108
Savage, Tom, 299n, 306
Sawyer-Lauçanno, Christopher, xvi
Scalapino, Leslie, 226, 256, 274, 277, 311n, 316, 341, 342, 508, 514, 515
Schaefer, Standard, vii, 289-97, 524
Schelling, Andrew, 313, 524, 649, 653
Schenck, Celeste, 122, 123n, 127, 131
Schlegel, Friedrich von, 46
Schmid, Julie, 636-45
Scholes, Robert, 125
Scholnick, Michael, 210, 211
Schor, Mira, 524
Schulman, Sarah, 507
Schultz, Kathy Lou, 500n, 524, 655n
Schultz, Susan, 321-32, 510, 518
Schuyler, James, 201, 204, 206, 208, 211, 213, 217–19, 221, 224, 225, 227, 228, 526
Schwartz, Leonard, 64-81, 288, 500n, 514, 654, 684, 688
Schwerner, Armand, 167, 171, 342
Scott, Clive, 460
Scott, Gail, 507, 512
Scott, Jim, 507
Scott, Ridley, 649

Index 737

Scroggins, Mark, 147-60
Seale, Bobby, 547, 550n, 562, 565n, 566n
Searle, John, 358
Segal, Robert A., 432
Seidman, Hugh, 150–51
Selby, Spencer, 477–80, 484, 524
Senghor, Léopold Sédar, 388
Sexton, Anne, 123n, 201, 298n, 502, 504, 527, 528, 609
Seymour, Tony, 560, 561
Shakespeare, William, 23, 140, 149, 513, 523, 595
Shange, Ntozake, 509, 510
Shapiro, David, 202, 203, 205, 206, 217, 219, 224–27, 229, 500n
Shapiro, Karl, 233
Shaw, Lytle, 515, 655n
Shaw, Nancy, 654n
Shaw, W. David, 122, 123n, 127
Shelley, Mary Wollstonecraft, 200
Shelley, Percy Bysshe, 657
Shephard, Thomas, 195
Shepp, Archie, 291, 618
Sheppard, Robert, 333
Sher, Gail, 524
Sherman, Cindy, 602
Sherry, James, 299n, 306, 314, 316, 457–59, 467, 524
Shetley, Vernon, 321
Shikatani, Gerry, 577, 595, 600, 601-2
Shiraishi, Kazuko, 317
Shklovsky, Viktor, 313
Showalter, Elaine, 245, 267
Shurin, Aaron, 464, 509
Sia, Beau, 644n
Sidney, Philip, 195
Sikélianos, Eléni, 64, 73–75, 524, 654
Silliman, Ron, 95, 153, 154–55, 158, 161, 170, 225, 277, 300, 302n, 303, 305, 308, 311–13, 316, 321, 322–23, 325, 326, 328, 330, 335, 336, 340, 341, 343, 378, 457, 463, 464, 465n, 466, 500n, 508, 515, 591n, 650n, 690, 691–92
Simic, Charles, 389, 391, 453, 461–62

Simpson, Louis, 687n, 689
Sinclair, John, 618
singleton, giovanni, 510, 536
Sirowitz, Hal, 218
Sloan, Margy Margaret, vii, 288, 333, 334, 498-525, 533–34, 689
Slotkin, Richard, 522
Smith, Bessie, 349
Smith, Charlotte, 123n
Smith, Dave, 339
Smith, Marc, 636–39, 641, 643
Smith, Patricia, 637n, 638, 639, 640n, 642–43, 644n
Smith, Rod, 328, 521, 653, 656, 664–65
Smith, Stevie, 521
Smith, Weldon, 620
Smithson, Robert, 307
Snellings, Rolland, 616, 620
Snyder, Gary, 38, 530, 588
Sobin, Gustaf, vii, 18–33, 286, 292, 342, 514
Sokal, Alan, 455, 457
Solt, Mary Ellen, 497n
Sonbert, Warren, 507
Song, Cathy, 591n
Sontag, Susan, 488
Sorrentino, Gilbert, 110n, 291
Southwick, Marcia, 257n
Soutine, Chaim, 426
Spacey, Kevin, 103, 106
Spahr, Juliana, 237–38, 276, 279, 280, 349n, 500n, 507, 510, 518, 523, 585, 653, 654, 655n
Sparrow, 217– 223
Spatola, Adriano, 291
Spellman, A. B., 540, 618
Spenser, Edmund, 523
Spicer, Jack, xiii, xiv, 22, 69, 82–96, 216, 251–52, 261, 285, 291, 293, 380, 453, 462, 512, 530
Spiller, Hortense, 349n
Spivak, Gayatri Chakravorty, 338
Spriggs, Ed, 620
Sprinkle, Annie, 539

St. John, David, 290
Stafford, William, 338n
Stanley, George, 248
Stanley, Henry Morton, 609
Stearns, Ethie, 520
Stefanile, Felix, 132
Stefans, Brian Kim, vii, 576-609, 653–55n, 679
Stein, Gertrude, 32, 65, 66, 153, 167, 169–70, 181, 208, 244, 245, 247, 269, 272, 276, 298, 300, 304, 309, 311n, 315, 317, 324, 325, 343, 345, 346, 353, 374, 411, 502, 504, 507–9, 518, 519, 531, 537, 540, 591n, 598n, 647, 650, 655, 666, 668
Steinberg, Lois, 257n
Sterne, Laurence, 518
Stevens, Wallace, 116, 129, 132, 135, 225, 330, 508, 515, 518, 523, 595, 686n
Stewart, Jimmy, 232
Stickney, John, 482–84
Stockfleth, Craig, 394
Strang, Catriana, 524
Strauß, Botho, 456
Stroffolino, Chris, 365n, 500n, 524, 653, 654, 655n
Sundiata, Sekou, 644n
Sun Ra, 609–33
Suzuki Daisetsu, 515
Swedenborg, Emanuel, 458
Swensen, Cole, 316, 514, 521, 523
Swinburne, Algernon Charles, 122, 123n, 128, 142
Sze, Arthur, 580, 582n, 587
Szwed, John, 609, 611, 621–23

T
Tabios, Eileen, 582
Taggart, John, 135, 155–56, 162, 170, 177–81, 308, 309, 342, 450, 524
Talley, Lori, 679
Tanaka, Roy, 576–78, 584, 591–94, 601, 605
Tardos, Anne, 524
Tarn, Nathaniel, 435–36
Tashjian, Dickran, 380

Tate, James, 123, 125n
Taylor, Cecil, 616
Tejada, Roberto, 524
Temple, John, 38
Templeton, Fiona, 316, 507, 516
Thackrey, Susan, 514
Theocritus, 123
Theresa, Saint, 516
Thilleman, Todd, 524
Thomas, John, 291, 295
Thomas, Lorenzo, 310, 507, 509, 616–18, 623
Thoreau, Henry David, 20, 307, 331, 446, 522
Thorpe, John, 47
Tillman, Lynne, 512
Timmons, Susie, 260n
Todorov, Tzvetan, 338
Tolson, Melvin B., 540
Tolstoy, L. N., 351
Tomlinson, Charles, 167
Toomer, Jean, 540
Toop, David, 614
Torra, Joseph, xvi
Torregian, Sotère, 381, 388
Torres, Edwin, 516
Toscano, Rodrigo, 524
Towle, Tony, 211
Trachtenberg, Paul, 64
Traherne, Thomas, 22
Tranter, John, 655n
Treadwell, Elizabeth, 524
Tropp, Gloria, 539–40
Tropp, Steven, 539
Trotsky, Leon, 376
Truitt, Samuel R., 520
Trussell, Philip, 40
Tu, Hung Q., 516, 603
Tuma, Keith, 395
Turner, Nat, 614
Tyler, Parker, 383
Tysh, Chris, 279n, 524

Tyson, June, 623
Tzara, Tristan, 395

V
Valaoritis, Nanos, 391, 392–93, 396, 399
Valery, Juliette, 663n
Vallejo, César, 150, 290, 393, 422n
Vanderborg, Susan, 298-321
Vangelisti, Paul, 290–97
Van Peebles, Melvin, 565
Varèse, Edgard, 527
Vaughan, Thomas, 418
Veitch, Tom, 204
Vendler, Helen, 140, 686n
Verdicchio, Pasquale, 293, 524
Vertov, Dziga, 587
Vickery, Ann, 323
Vicuña, Cecilia, 516
Viereck, George Sylvester, xiv
Violi, Paul, 212
Virgil, 47, 66, 123, 395
Vygotsky, L. S., 472, 473

W
Wagner, Richard, 433
Wah, Fred, 38, 41, 42, 577, 595, 597–600, 604–6
Wakoski, Diane, 290, 416
Walcott, Derek, 342
Wald, Priscilla, 228
Waldman, Anne, xiii, 202, 205–6, 209, 211, 214, 246, 253, 257n, 259, 260–62, 500n, 502, 508, 513, 520
Waldner, Liz, 524
Waldrop, Keith, 109, 119–20, 253, 277, 500n
Waldrop, Rosmarie, 109, 110, 112–16, 246, 249, 253, 257n, 271n, 273, 275, 277, 292, 311n, 313, 315, 333, 341, 453, 454–59, 465, 467, 500n, 506, 516, 523
Walker, Margaret, 540
Walkup, Kathy, 262n, 263
Wallace, George, 567n
Wallace, Mark, 126n, 363–65, 655n

Wallace, Ricky, 567
Wallace, Robert, 98
Ward, Diane, 290, 341, 506, 515
Warhol, Andy, 205
Warsh, Lewis, 202, 205, 207–11, 213, 215–16, 253, 260, 520
Washington, Peter, 127
Watson, Craig, 178
Watten, Barrett, 265, 269, 300, 303, 305, 309, 311, 312n, 313, 321, 323, 328, 338n, 340n, 341, 343, 402, 465, 500n, 507, 508, 515, 650n, 658, 679, 680
Wayman, Tom, 316
Weatherly, Tom, 540–44
Webster, Ben, 594
Webster, John, 333
Weeks, Laurie, 512
Weigel, Tom, 211
Weil, Simone, 46, 514
Weinberger, Eliot, 423–24, 598n, 650n, 684–86, 688, 689, 691, 692
Weiner, Hannah, 261, 271n, 341, 360–61, 466, 509, 511, 518, 682
Weiners, John, 38
Welish, Marjorie, 511
Wells, Ida B., 569
Wesling, Donald, 460
West, Mae, 428
Wetzsteon, Ross, 56, 58
Whalen, Philip, 207, 244, 287, 508, 526, 530, 531
Wheatley, Phillis, 545
Whitman, Ruth, 503
Whitman, Walt, 26, 50, 51, 122, 244, 303, 413, 415, 429, 431, 450, 578, 595, 655, 658
Whorf, Benjamin Lee, 21
Wiebe, Dallas, 315
Wieners, John, 514
Wilbur, Richard, 225, 298n
Wilde, Oscar, 463, 579
Wildman, Eugene, 497n
Williams, Anne, 356, 357

Williams, Emmett, 497n, 680
Williams, Jonathan, 62n, 157
Williams, Oscar, 513
Williams, Raymond, 647n
Williams, Robert F., 559, 565n, 573
Williams, Roger, 112
Williams, William Carlos, 24, 25, 34, 40, 62, 65, 66, 147, 149, 150, 157, 167–71, 239, 243–44, 270, 298, 302n, 311n, 330, 338, 374, 411, 413n, 431, 446, 499, 518, 523, 531, 537, 542, 544, 600, 686n, 690n
Willis, Elizabeth, 514, 654
Wiloch, Thomas, 399
Winch, Terence, 518
Winet, John, 507
Winslow, Pete, 381, 386, 388
Winthrop, John, 38
Wittgenstein, Ludwig, 35, 127n, 154, 299, 309, 310, 336, 338, 352, 454, 455, 457, 507, 518, 650, 664
Wittig, Monique, 526
Wolfe, Alan, 641
Wolsak, Melissa, 524
Wong, Nellie, 257n, 587
Wong, Shelley Sun, 585
Wong-chu, Jim, 603
Woods, Gregory, 587
Woodward, W. E., 39
Woolf, Virginia, 267–70, 518, 522
Wordsworth, William, 141, 463
Wright, C. D., 266n
Wright, James, 298n
Wright, Jay, 450, 540, 610
Wright, Jeff, 210
Wright, Rebecca, 257n

X
Xu Bing, 516

Y
Yang, Naomi, 653n
Yates, Katie, 524
Yau, John, 217, 228, 315, 402–3, 460–61, 514, 576–80, 582n, 592, 598n, 606
Yeats, W. B., 270, 349, 410n, 652n
Yi Sang, 588
Young, Al, 542
Young, Geoff, 654
Young, Karl, 476
Young, LaMonte, 156
Yourcenar, Marguerite, 516
Yu Guan Soon, 516, 588
Yurkievich, Saul, 342

Z
Zanzotto, Andrea, 291
Zawadiwsky, Christina, 399
Zeiger, Melissa, 122, 123n, 127, 143
Zelevansky, Paul, 488–93, 497n
Zeller, Ludwig, 396
Ziolkowski, Thad, 649n
Zukofsky, Celia, 148, 153, 167
Zukofsky, Louis, 65, 147–59, 162–63, 167–69, 171, 174, 175, 179, 181, 300, 309, 311n, 411, 446, 447, 455, 499, 518, 537, 629, 647n, 650, 667, 668
Zukofsky, Morris, 148
Zweig, Janet, 521